THE HISTORY OF
THE WORKING CLASSES IN SCOTLAND

THE HISTORY OF
THE WORKING CLASSES
IN SCOTLAND

BY

The Rt. Hon. THOMAS JOHNSTON
P.C., M.P.

FORWARD PUBLISHING CO. LTD.
26 CIVIC STREET, PORT DUNDAS
GLASGOW, C. 4

THIRD EDITION

PREFATORY NOTE TO SECOND EDITION

First published in 1920, the collection of essays upon the history of the working classes in Scotland which comprise this volume have been out of print for several years. I had intended, as occasion and leisure were offered me, to amplify the later essays, especially those dealing with the last quarter of the XIX. century, and to add considerably to the sections on the history of the trade unions.

But, alas, the leisure for the necessary research work never came my way, and now a stream of new tasks and duties would so appear to preclude any hopeful prospect of my securing that leisure in the near future, that a second edition is issued, differing only from its predecessor to the extent of some minor typographical alterations.

I am, however, rather proud to be able to say that from the first edition there is nothing to withdraw, and in it there is nothing to amend, the historical pundits and apologists for the existing order of Society having failed, although some of them sought with diligence enough, to find anything upon which to base a charge of inaccuracy in fact or of error in interpretation.

The history of a country is the history of the masses of its people, not the history, legendary or otherwise, of a few selected stocks ; and if the indictment in the following pages be substantially accurate —if the slaveries, robberies, murders, class cruelties, and oppressions be proven, as I submit they are proven—then the greater part of the drum and trumpet history and ruling caste ancestor worship with which our children, generation after generation, are primed, would appear to be more than ever ridiculous and irrelevant.

It is an abiding and indisputable truth that a people which does not understand the past will never comprehend the present nor mould the future. And it is as a contribution towards such an understanding that these essays are republished.

THOMAS JOHNSTON

Monteviot, Kirkintilloch
October, 1929

CONTENTS

CHAPTER I.

THE SLAVERY PERIOD.

"We can trace the pedigree of princes, fill up the catalogue of towns besieged and provinces desolated, but we cannot recover the genuine history of mankind. It has passed away with slight and partial notice by contemporary writers, and our most patient industry can hardly at present put together enough of the fragments to suggest a tolerably clear representation of ancient manners and social."—*Hallam*.

> "Ah! freedom is a noble thing,
> Freedom makes men to have liking
> To man all solace, freedom gives;
> He lives at ease who freely lives.
> And he that aye has lived free
> May not well know the misery,
> The wrath, the hate, the spite, and all
> That's compassed in the name of thrall!"
>
> —*Archdeacon Barbour*.

THE original cause or causes of human slavery is not so much a question for the historian as for the philosopher, since, when discussing it, we are discussing not recorded "facts" but speculations and inferences. Primeval man, heedless of the curiosity of his posterity, has left us neither carved record nor oral tradition of his social relationships, but there is a fair presumption that slavery was unknown in the purely nomadic stages of society. When a tribe of men, bound together solely by the tie of kindred (belief in descent from a common ancestor), living by the fruits of the chase and having no settled habitation, captured a man of another tribe, it is highly improbable that they reduced him to slavery. He would be a source of weakness to them—another mouth to feed; and when M. Comte hails the introduction of slavery as the first great step in civilization, he means it was only when the victor conceived that he could make use of, and profit from, the vanquished that he spared his life. This conception of use and profit was only possible when the victor and his tribe had a fixed habitation and were practising agriculture, for then the captive could be set to do the laborious work of hoeing and reaping, and he could demand no freeman's share in the community goods, but must needs be content with a bare subsistence on such scraps as were thrown to him. In the so-called "free com-

B

munities " of early times, whilst it possibly was true that there was for the " free " man equality with all other " free " men, the vast mass was condemned to hopeless thraldom.* In Athens, for example, the lowest freeman was considered poor were he not possessed of six or seven slaves ; liberty and equality were the possessions of the privileged classes alone.

With the growth of pastoral and agricultural communities, therefore, slavery arose.

But not only did men lose their freedom through failure in war ; they lost it through famine. In early times, when rapid transit was impossible and the exchange of goods was limited to small areas, a failure of the crops in a district meant starvation to the bulk of the inhabitants ; and particularly in the ninth and eleventh centuries, when an enormous number of famines are recorded, the only method of escape open to the poor freeman was to sell himself and his family for bread. In an Anglo-Saxon MS. of about the time of the Norman Conquest we find a lady manumitting some slaves " whose heads she had taken for their meat in the evil days."† Later on it is probable that any and every pretext was used to compass the enslavement of the remaining freemen. An English ordinance, promulgated about 1554, declares that : " If any inhabitant refuses to assist the Bailiff in maintaining order, he shall lose his freedom."‡ And we know that in Scotland, in 1230, a landowner holding his lands by royal charter could challenge a small landowner possessing no charter, and the charter-possessor had the privilege of fighting the duel by substitute. By this cowardly means, in the succeeding century and a half, many " original owners " were dispossessed, and as after they were dispossessed they were given fifteen days in which to find a lord and master, it followed that they mostly became serfs upon what had once been their own freeholds.§ If they failed to find a master within the time specified, they, being guilty of serious misdemeanour, were fined in five cows by the king, and accepted as " King's Slaves " until a suitable owner could be found for them.

Yet whatever be the method by which slavery was instituted, there can be no doubt but that right from the earliest recorded times it was the common condition of the working class. Attached to each castle and abbey was a farm steading or grange, in which were kept the cattle, the farm implements, and the *nativi* or native men who

---

Historical Essays—E. W. Robertson.
†*Archæologia*—Wright, xxx., p. 233.
‡The term " freedom," however, may here only mean burgess-ship in a town.
§*Acta Parl. Scot.*, vi., pp. 9, 51, 70, 74, *et seq.*, and M'Intosh *Hist. Civilization in Scotland*, i., 224.

were reckoned as stock, and could be, and were, bought and sold, as the owner of the grange found necessity. It has been suggested that these *nativi* were the descendants of the native men who had occupied the land prior to the Saxon and Norman invasions, but Cosmo Innes* cannot distinguish between the *nativi* and the bondsmen. In early charters disposing of lands to monasteries or to individuals, we find the phrases : *Cum bondis et bondagis* (*i.e.*, with bondmen and their holdings and services) and *cum nativis* (*i.e.*, with natives or neyfs). The bondmen may have been like the *adscriptitti* who were not absolutely slaves, for their master could not sell them apart from the estate upon which they were born; and we have documentary evidence—abundance of it—that the neyfs could be sold like oxen or sheep without any such limitation as pertained to the bondmen. The bondmen may have been those who lost their freedom through famine or for any cause other than conquest ; but their slavery, like the slavery of the neyfs, was hereditary ; and the only apparent difference is that in the former case the slave was astricted to a particular glebe or estate, while in the latter the slavery was unconditional. The serf, down to the early part of the fourteenth century, had no rights, no privileges, and no family name ; he was rated equally with the cattle that browsed upon the meadow and the deer that bounded through the glen.† He wore a peculiar dress, and had his head shaven bare, as an ever-present reminder of his social inferiority ; his evidence was not accepted against a freeman in a Court of Justice.‡ Marriage could not be contracted among the servile classes, who were simply regarded as cattle or stock, and joined or separated, as it suited the interest and convenience of the masters. Indeed, for these unfortunate classes there was no law but their masters' will and caprice.§ Even among " dependent freemen," marriage could only be contracted " with the permission of their lord." The great estates, lay and clerical, kept stud books‖ recording the pedigrees of their human stock ; and when the poor unfortunates, goaded beyond endurance, sought safety in flight, as they very frequently did, they were hunted down by a legal recovery writ issued in name of the King, all the Sheriffs, Provosts, and " good men " being enjoined to search for the fugitives. The barons in particular seem to have

---

*Scotch Legal Antiquities, p. 50.

†*Kingcraft in Scotland* (Ross), p. 37.

‡Appendix to Robertson's *History of the Reign of Charles V.*, p. 357.

§Macintosh *Hist. Civ. Scot.*, i., p. 155. See also Potgiesserus *de Statu Servorum* (lib. ii. c. 2).

‖*Reg. de Dunfermline*, p. 220.

treated their serfs with savage cruelty, and Professor Cosmo Innes declares, speaking of the gallows hills : " I know some where the surrounding ground is full of the remains of the poor wretches who died by the baron's law."* Of the most odious custom of all, the *Jus Primæ Noctis*, by which the lord of the soil could claim possession of a woman serf for the first night after her marriage, we have some evidence in Scotland, though energetic attempts have been made by Dr. Frazer, Professor Vinogradoff, and others to prove that it never existed at all. But Professor Hector Boece, our earliest historian, asserts in his *History of Scotland* (1527) that King Evenus delivered a decree allowing the lords to deflower the daughters of their vassals. This King Evenus is supposed to have reigned in Scotland some time about the year 60 B.C., and his "law" permitting the daughters of a lord's tenantry to be outraged by the lord on their marriage eve, Boece declared, held force until the time of Malcolm Canmore in the latter half of the eleventh century.† And when Dr. Johnson visited the Island of Ulva on the west coast of Mull in 1773 he was assured by the clan chief, M'Quarrie, who boasted that his family had owned the island for 900 years, that " the *Mercheta Mulierum* mentioned in our old charters did really mean the privilege which a lord of the manor, or a baron, had, to have the first night of all his vassal's wives. . . M'Quarrie told us that still on the marriage of each of his tenants, a sheep is due to him, for which the composition is fixed at five shillings."‡ This marriage tax, this *mercheta mulierum* undoubtedly did exist all down the feudal period, and is supposed by some to have been the money compensation or surrender value granted to the lord for the relinquishment of his right to the " first-fruits " of the females on his estates, a right rigorously exacted from all other forms of property. Again, there are virile traditions of the exercise of this barbarous privilege in the Orkney Islands, and among some of the older peasantry there are traditions of women hacking and disfiguring their faces in order to escape the laird's "due," and that the indifference with which illegitimacy was generally regarded, despite two or three centuries of desperate Presbyterian effort to blot it out, can be traced back to a period when the only assured method by which a handsome working class bride could escape spending her marriage night at the castle, was to postpone her wedding until she had become a mother.

Scot. Leg. Antiq., p. 39.

†Boece's account of the *Jus Primæ Noctis*, or law of the first night, is followed by George Buchanan in his *Rerum Scoticarum Historia* and by Sir John Skene in his *De Verborum Significatione* (1797).

‡Boswell's *Journal of a Tour in the Hebrides.*

The only legal reference we can find to the sex relationships between the landowner and his female serfs is an enactment which runs thus : "If a master be proved by the visnet to have had connection with his serf's wife, the serf shall obtain his liberty, but shall receive no other enach."* Skene tells us† that a female bondslave was valued at an equivalent of three cows ; that if the wife of a carl was slain his lord got the slaughter fine (Kelchyn), though some small compensation evidently went to the widower ; and that in later times a " serf or mercantile " woman paid 3 cows to the land superior on the occasion of her marriage. In any case the *Jus Primæ Noctis* could hardly be a custom until marriages between serfs were recognised, and, as we have shown, such marriages were unknown in the early slave period.

In the *Quoniam Attachiamenta*, which forms part of the *Regiam Majestatem*, or collection of the ancient laws of Scotland, there is given the legal method by which a freeman may surrender his freedom and the legal process by which the lord may ensure that he never regain it. When any freeman desired protection of a lord he surrendered himself in the lord's court by pulling his forelock before the lord, and if he should afterwards repent or seek to escape, the lord might seize all his property excepting to the value of fourpence.‡

Several of the deeds of sale or gift preserved in the National MS., and in the ancient chartularies, throw much light on the absolute slavery of the working class of the period between David I. and the War of Independence. In the earliest "slavery" deed, preserved in the chartulary of Dunfermline, King David I. gives Kagewin and Gilliepatrick and Ulchil for ever to the Church of the Holy Trinity at Dunfermline, and all good men are enjoined to restore to the Church whatsoever *cumberlachs* (*i.e.* fugitive slaves) may have escaped and be presently in the possession of other lords.

The National MSS.§ contain a charter of Malcolm IV.'s time (1153-1165) granting the Prior of Coldingham power to recover runaway serfs without hindrance from the King's loyal subjects.‖ William the Lion grants to Bishop Jocelin of Glasgow and the Church of St. Kentigern there, "Gillemachoi of Conglud with his children, and all rights to them and theirs." Some of the neighbouring barons appear to have stolen serfs belonging to the Abbey of

---

Reg. Majestatem, 2 c. 9, Act. Parl., i., 608.
†*Celtic Scotland*, vol.iii.
‡*Reg. Majestatem*, cap. 5, 6, p. 122.
§Part i., No. 30.
‖See also " Serfdom in Scotland and its connection with the Early Church "— R. Small, *Scot. Evangelical Review*, July, 1878.

Scone, and King William enjoins the barons to return the stolen property *instanter*. Deeds of gift, executed during William the Lion's reign, are extant certifying transfers of the serfs, "Halden, William his brother, and their children and following" by the Earl of Dunbar to the Abbey of Kelso ; and Richard de Moreville, constable of Scotland, sells to Henry Saint Clair, "Edmund, son of Bonde, and Gillemichael his brother, their sons and daughters, and the whole progeny descended from them, and also their heirs, for three merks, which he will give to me." David, Earl of Huntingdon, grants the Earl of Mar "Gillechriste, son of Gillekuogal, the two Gillechristes, and Gillen and Gillemart." The prior of Coldingham buys from Adam of Lesser Riston "Turkil Hog and his sons and his daughters" for three merks of silver, "which in my [Adam's] great want they gave me of the money of the house of Coldingham ; " and for a similar sum he buys "Joseph, son of Elwold, and all his issue," from Henry of Prendergeste. This Henry appears to have been in financial straits, for he grants his neyf, "Reginald, the provost" and all his posterity, freedom from thraldom, on having been paid "twenty merks of sterling" by Patric, Burgess of Berwick. Provost (prepositus) in this case can hardly mean that the serf Reginald was a highly placed municipal official in Berwick, for Berwick, we know, was one of the Royal Burghs, touching on which we shall have something to say presently. But perhaps he was only a bailiff of some description on the Prendergeste estate and had acquired the nick-name of Provost. Still there is the significant intimation that the man who found the twenty merks to secure Reginald's freedom was a burgess of Berwick ! Prendergeste also sells to Coldingham priory Osulf the Red, and Walter his son, and their heirs to all posterity for 10 merks. Roger Fitzwalter is bought for two merks ; "William of Newbiggin, and Brunhild his wife, and Walter and Mabel, their children, and all the issue" are bought for fifteen shillings. The laird of Symetlaw, who prefaces his disponing charter with the salutation, "Health in the Lord," grants Alan, son of Toch, and his heirs to the house of the sacred Trinity of Loutru. In Alexander III.'s time Malise, Earl of Strathearn, "for the sake of charity and the weal of his soul," grants in pure and perpetual gift "to God and to the blessed John—Apostle and evangelist, and to the Abbey and Convent of Inchchaffray, John called Starnes, son of Thomas, son of Thor, with all his offspring." The same recipients get "Gilmory Gillendes, our slave, with all his followers." Lord Hailes remarks of this charter that the name Gilmory means servant of the Virgin Mary, and that the serf was probably so named in her honour. Gillendes means "Southern lad," and denotes that he was probably descended from an English prisoner. Other charters of similar purport might be cited, but sufficient evidence has been given to indicate the nature of the slavery which was the common condition of the overwhelming mass of the working class from the period of the earliest authentic records down to the later years of the thirteenth century. It did not disappear suddenly ; no great cataclysmic change swept it away ; it wore away gradually, silently, almost imperceptibly, because new economic and social conditions had come into being, and these conditions demanded that the old slavery should go. We should have liked to read that some great moral regeneration of the upper classes, or some great class conscious revolt of the lower, had with dramatic suddenness abolished the old and ushered in the new ; but, as we shall see, fundamental changes are impossible until the conditions are ripe, and the ripening is the tale of long and dreary years.

Professor Innes, who claims, rightly as we think, that slavery died out in Scotland long before anywhere else in Europe, declares its disappearance to be the work "of that grand emancipator, the Church " ; but, as Sheriff Scott Moncrieff has observed,* he nowhere gives "any facts " in support of his claim, while it seems certain that in the last recorded dispute over slaves, which occurred in 1364 in the Sheriff Court of Banffshire, the Bishop of Moray "obtained the verdict of an assize finding that Robert, Nevyn, and Donald were the natives and leigemen of the said Lord Bishop and the Church of Moray, and his property." Our own opinion is that this "early slavery " owed its destruction to a large number of causes. To begin with, the Central Authority, *i.e.*, the Crown, had from King David I.'s time felt the necessity of limiting so far as possible the power of the nobles, many of whom were really kings in their own territories. One of the methods adopted by the Crown for this purpose was the creation of Royal Burghs, inside the boundaries of which—and they were very wide, those of Rutherglen, for instance, running almost as far as Falkirk—the neighbouring Lord had neither power nor jurisdiction. The burgesses in the Royal Burghs dealt directly with the King : they were his tenants and freemen : they had wide privileges of trade and government, and the King in turn looked for their support when his own position was threatened. The Royal Burghs were oases in the desert ; and if a serf could escape from his owner and live for a year and a day on a burgage tenement inside a Royal Burgh without challenge he was

---

* "On Serfdom in Scotland."—Sheriff Scott Moncrieff. *Transactions of the Banffshire Field Club*, 16th February, 1882.

free for all time.*   It is true that the purchase of a burgage tenement by a propertyless runaway was an almost impossible feat, and it has been surmised by, among others, the late Sir James Marwick, that this first "Freedom" Act was designed to prevent the nobles from securing control in the burghs through their serf deputies ; but, be that as it may, the number of Burgh freemen grew rapidly, and the Crown did much to assist them by ordaining, among other things, that all serfs were to be inviolate from recovery during a Royal Burgh fair, and by increasing, as opportunity offered, the number of Royal Burghs.   Again, on the large Church estates it had gradually become the settled policy to give a tenant limited freedom and in return to demand from him a money rent and certain specified services ; and this practice was followed by the more far-seeing barons.   Indeed, "steelbow" tenancy, where the landlord stocked the farm and demanded a money and a service rent from the tenant, was quite recently, if it is not still, in existence in Scotland.   Freedom was thus slowly broadening down, due on the one hand to the necessities of the Crown and on the other to the development of agriculture, when it received a great leverage in the so-called War of Independence.   The bulk of the men who followed Wallace and Bruce had been serfs ; they had associated with townsmen who knew what freedom meant; they had, for the time being at least, escaped from the cruel domination of the Lord and his bullying bailiff; they had developed on the battlefield a consciousness that they were the equals, in the last resort, of the knights and men at arms they speared at ; many of them had run away to the wars, choosing possible speedy death to a certain lingering one ; at the wars they must have acquired a sentiment of nationality ; and it was unthinkable that when Bannockburn was fought and won they would go back to the old settled slavery.   So it is that immediately after 1314, as the charters and assize records betoken, there is everywhere a slackening of the bonds, and a disposition evinced by the serfs to demand rights and privileges ; and Professor Innes has extracted from the Register of Dunfermline a narrative, dated 1320, of great interest, giving as it does, evidence of a collective effort on the part of the serfs for more tolerable conditions :

"In 1320, on the feast of St. Peter, an inquest was held in the Chaple at Logy concerning the liberties which the Abbot of Dunfermline's men of Tweeddale claimed from the Abbot.   First, they sought to have a bailiff appointed by the Abbot of their own race, who should repledge them from more oppressive lay courts to the Abbot's court.   To that the assize of inquest made answer, that such bailiff should be given them, not of fee, but

---

Acta Parl. Scot., i., p. 23.

of usage. Their second demand was that if one of their race verge to poverty, or fall into helpless old age, he shall have support from the monastery. To this the jury replied, that the abbey was not bound to this as of right, but from affection because they were its men. The third article was, that if any of their race slay a man or commit any other crime for which he must seek the immunity, he shall be sustained as long as he stays there at the expense of the monastery. The jury declared that the abbey would do so to a stranger much more to a man of their own and of the race of the claimants. Lastly, they claimed that if any of their race commit homicide and incur a fine therefor, the Abbot and convent shall be bound to contribute twelve marks towards the payment of the fine. To which the jury made answer that they had never heard such a thing all the days of their lives."*

They thus obtained collective recognition, a shop steward of their own, a guarantee against poverty, an old age pension, and immunity. But they must pay their own fines, though what was the use of anybody fining a propertyless and wageless slave is not clear. By the end of the fourteenth century the old chattel slavery had died— and died without any legal enactment ; but it must not be supposed that the agricultural workers were now free men. It is true they were not bought and sold like so many sheep ; it is true they now paid rent (a sign of civilisation) either in money, in kind, or in personal services, or in all three ; but the personal services were so odious and so exacting as almost to amount to slavery, even using the term in its customary acceptance. The tenant was now "free," but he had to devote the best days of the harvest time to cutting his lord's corn, without recompense or wages, while his own corn rotted ; he was free—free to starve ; no "owner" was interested in seeing that he got fed or clothed ; his property, when he could gather any, was liable to irregular raids by the landowner ; he was tried in the baron's court by the baron's law, imprisoned in the landlord's pit, and hanged on the landlord's gallows ; he was free in name only, and not transferable with the soil ; in reality and in practice he was still a slave.

Among the Highland clans, the buying and selling of men seems never to have been a custom. In very early times the chiefs were elected, although always from the same stock, and every member of the clan claimed blood-brotherhood with his chief, who was really only the leader of the Army, the organiser of the fighting force, the defender of the territories and the honour of the tribe. The meanest member of the clan was jealous of his rights and privileges, and the sentiment of kinship with his chief (however fictitious it may have been), even when the chief had usurped the clan lands and assumed a feudal power and feudal rights over his clansmen, prevented the trafficing in human flesh which went on in the lowlands, where the baron was of alien blood and had conquered by alien force.

*Innes " *Sketches*," p. 143.

CHAPTER II

UNDER THE BARONS.

"I know some (gallows hills) where the surrounding ground is full of the remains of the poor wretches who died by the baron's law."—*Scotch Legal Antiquities*, p. 59 (Cosmo Innes).

"I may be comparit to the dull ass compellit to bayr ane importabil burden for I am dung (kicked) and proddit to gar me do and thole the thing that is above my pouer . . . I labour night and day to nourish lazy, idle, useless men, and my reward is hunger and the sword. How can I tak paciens, considerand that ther can na thing be eikkyt (added) to my parsecutione but cruel dede (death). My corn and my cattle are reft from me, I am exiled from my takkis and my steddying, the mails and fermes of the grond that I laubyr is hychtit to sic ane price that is fors (necessary) to me and my bairns to drink wattir. The tiends of my corn are not only raised above the fertility of the soil, but taken out of my hands by my tyrant brethir. If I gain money by trade or mechanic craft, I am compellit to lend it to them, and when I crave my dettis, I am cuffed and maltreated . . . Ther for I am constrenit to cry on God for vengeance on al violent usurpators, whilkis parpetrates sic cruel ini quities on the desolat pure pepil."—*The Complaynt of Scotlande* (1549).

GREAT historical epochs do not begin suddenly; they do not end abruptly; there are no harsh dividing lines in the picture of the past. Our customs are the result of long evolutionary processes, and although it may be true that at one given moment in time a certain form of social relationship was not, and that at a later given moment it was, no serious historian claims for it a sudden or a miraculous birth. Institutions are like the tones in a landscape : they fade and merge into one another, and "sudden birth" and "sudden death" are the perquisites of the dramatist, not the realities of the historian or the biologist.

So with feudalism. At the break-up of the Roman Empire and the irruption of barbarism in Europe, with the Frankish hordes sweeping down upon the fertile plains of Gaul, there was certainly slavery, certainly private property in land, and already (and this was the soul and the essence of feudalism) a distinct practice of holding land from a superior in return for certain military services and obligations. Co-existent with this slavery, private property, and feudalism, there throve here and there the old clan system with its common property ; and although feudalism was a necessary result of conquest, since without a feudal organisation among the conquerors the communistic tribes could not have been held in perpetual subjection, there is no precise period in Gaul, in Britain, or anywhere else from which we can date the inception of that feudal system. The method of inception and its motive may be understandable enough. A district would be subjugated, and the lordship of it donated to some powerful swashbuckler on condition he would acknowledge that he held his powers and his privileges from the King, to whom also, as occasion required, he would furnish a specified number of soldiers. The feudal lords were therefore in effect deputy kings, providing military support to their superior and in turn being supported by him when they were attacked by marauding barons of their own kidney or menaced by rebellions and insurrections of the despoiled and enslaved peasantry. The system was a mutual insurance. Instead of a thousand petty and independent individual owners or group owners, kept perpetually at internecine war in defence of their properties, there arose a structure of mutual dependence. The King, in theory, was sole proprietor ; he feued out his "rights" to henchmen who acknowledged his supremacy, guaranteed him support, and in turn were supported by him. The greater henchmen again, feued out in certain districts the lordships and plunder rights thus acquired to lesser henchmen, who acknowledged the greater henchmen as their superiors ; the lesser henchmen in turn had vassals who paid *them* tribute, every man in his rank paying tribute and giving service to an overlord—that was the stability of the feudal system. Feudalism spread and developed. By the end of the tenth century it could be said of France : "Nulle terre sans seigneur"* (no land without its superior), and there is no reason to doubt but that some rudimentary and incipient form of the system had appeared in England. Scotland, however, was still a land of independent clans owning a light, fitful, and voluntary allegiance to any central authority, and there must have been in the lowlands thousands of peasant proprietors, the descendants of the Roman legionaries, who, retiring from the Army at the age of 45, were given four acres of land in freehold.† On the eastern sea-board were the Saxon colonists — most unpromising material they for exploitation ; in the far north, the sons of the wild rovers from "Norroway, Norroway, ower the faem ; " on the west the Scots from Ireland ; and in Galloway the intractable Picts. Many a long day was to elapse ere all these would be welded together into one nation, acknowledging one king and suffering baronial tyrannies and plunderings !

History of the Reign of Charles the Fifth—Robertson, p. 354.
†*Glasgow Archæological Society Transactions*, 1864, vol. iv., p. 403.

Then in the middle of the eleventh century thirty thousand thieves landed at Hastings for the sack of England. Every known Norman robber had been invited to the banquet, and when the battle of Hastings had been fought, and William the Conqueror had divided up the various manors and lordships from Kent to Northumberland among his followers, each one according to his degree building castles, dungeons, and gallows trees, England had been feudalised.   William himself tore down 36 churches and burned out 36 parishes in Hampshire in order to secure a hunting waste ; he cut off the hands and feet from 32 men for a joke ; the land from the Tees to the Humber was laid waste and was for years untilled.   By the early part of the twelfth century there existed in England 67 forests, 30 chases, 781 parks for wild animals, and there was in constant appliance a barbarous code of penal laws to preserve the hunting rights for the barons, upon whom, we are told, "no oath was binding."*

To the King of Scots, who was king in name only, here was an object lesson in government ; here was a method of suppressing the independence of the clans ; here was a method of extending and strengthening the power of the Crown ! Invitations were extended to certain successful Anglo-Norman bullies to come north and take, if they could, the clan lands from the disagreeable chiefs ; and the invitation was cordially accepted by, among others, Robert de Brus (who set about reducing 200,000 acres in Annandale to "order " and "obedience "), Roger de Quincy, Robert de Balliol, and Robert de Comines (or Comyn), a son of the De Comines who had been given the lordship of the Carlisle district, but who, with 300 of his followers, had been murdered by the outraged populace of Durham.   These feudal adventurers encountered fierce and prolonged opposition.   For over two centuries, notably in Morayshire and Galloway, there raged a series of civil wars and rebellions ; indeed, Mr. John Hill Burton says that four centuries passed ere Scotland lay submissive to the full grip of the feudal force † ; but of the details of the struggle only meagre reports have come down through the landlord seive.   There was a four years rebellion in Moray, beginning in 1130 ; then a rebellion in Galloway ; another rebellion in Moray in 1161 ; another in Galloway in 1175.   In Galloway the tongues of the children were torn out so that the accursed clan legends of freedom should not be told to a fresh generation.   De Quincy was beleaguered in his castle, and after the battle of the Standard the enraged Gallowegian peasants massacred every Frenchman and every Englishman they could lay their hands upon.   "The Norman

---

*M'Intosh *Hist. Civ. Scot.*, i., 191-197.

†*History of Scot.*, vol. i., p. 351.

adventurers," drily observes Mr. Hill Burton, "were shy of Galloway as a suitable place of residence." Every legal artifice was utilised by the Crown in support of the feudal freebooters. The King in Council decreed that anyone offering resistance to a charter-holder was subject to the penalty for rebellion, which was death ; small freeholders were told that actual possession for four generations was not sufficient ; they must apply for and obtain a feu charter, or their lands were confiscate to the Crown ; possession for less than four generations was illegal possession, and the holders were summarily expropriated. In 1248 it was decreed that no non-charter-holder's oath was to be valid in any suit involving the life and limb of a charter-holder. In 1230 charter-holders were given the power and the privilege of fighting their duels by substitute, thereby facilitating the assassination of pertinacious freeholders and chieftains at the hands of professional champions, while the barons themselves ran no risk. The families of dispossessed freeholders were given 15 days in which to make submission to a lord ; if they failed to do so, they were fined 5 cows. The castle works, says the *Saxon Chronicle* referring to the English dungeons built by the barons, were filled with devils and evil men who dragged thither peasant men and women supposed to possess property, "and hanged them up by the feet, and smoked them with foul smoke They hanged them by the thumbs or by the head ; they put knotted strings about their heads, and writhed them so that it went to the brain." This was the feudal investiture of the poor.

Famines and starvations ensued ; none but serfs would cultivate the land, and they only with the whip over their heads; vast areas went out of cultivation, and distress so grew that in William the Lion's time a statute was passed calling upon the barons so to conduct themselves that they troubled not "Gods people with penury, poverty, and destruction." But the process of slow robbery went on steadily and effectively. The barons were given full powers of jurisdiction over their domains, and were "bound by no form of process or restrained by any law, statutory or common."* In their courts they tried every sort of case—even pleas of the Crown, murder, and treason. They had rights of *Fossa* and *Furca, i.e.*, pit and gallows. By the latter they could gibbet any vassal : by the former they could immure in pit or dungeon, or, as they usually did with women, drown. Torture they specialised in. We read of red hot tongs put between a young woman's shoulders and under her armpits until the tongs were cold † ; of another young woman who got the bones of her fingers broken by a "harrow bore" ; and

---

Social Life in Scotland—Rogers. Grampian Club Pubns., vol. ii., p. 41.
†Pitcairn's *Crim. Trials*, ii., 44-46. *Ibid.* iii., 491.

of others who were starved to death in the dungeons. At St. Andrews (a church prison, by the way) the pit had a diameter of 7 feet at the top and 27 feet at the bottom, while the depth was 30 feet. The baron's prisons were usually under the arches of bridges or within the damp vaults of the castle. By their Crown charters they had been given "the woods and plains, the pastures and meadows, mosses and marches, the running waters, ponds and fish tanks, the roads and paths, the brushwood, jungle heaths and peatries, the coalfields, quarries, stone and limestone, with the mills and the sucken, the smithies, the brew houses and the salt works, the fishings, hawkings and huntings."* They were exempt from tolls, but had the right to exact them from "lower classes" ; they possessed rights of *Theme*, that is, the power of declaring whom among the people on their estates were "free " and whom slaves. But they do not seem to have dared to impose the English forest laws upon Scotland†; perhaps the continual feuds and uprisings in Scotland prevented the development of sporting estates ; certainly no kept deer would have been safe in Morayshire, where gangs of dispossessed clansmen lived by open blackmail upon the feudal grantees, and, whenever opportunity offered, dispensed a wild retributive justice.

Around this earlier feudal period a web of ridiculous romance has been woven, and proud families, whose fortunes rest upon alleged national heroisms, sacrifices, and services rendered by an ancestor in the twelfth, the thirteenth, or the fourteenth centuries, and whose hired minstrels and lackey historians still provide school book lies, are not, we presume, over kindly disposed to the pitiless and searching analysis to which the modern investigator subjects the Norman struggle for the Scottish throne and its perquisites, which struggle, to this very day, is facetiously termed "The War of Independence." The feudal romancers—Fordoun, Wyntoun and Barbour—in Sir Herbert Maxwell's words, have "discreetly suppressed the record " of the De Brus rebellion to enforce his claim as heir male to the throne on the death of King Alexander III. Such a record—for the chroniclers wrote when the Bruce dynasty had commenced—would have been "to the discredit of the ruling house."‡ We are only told that there was "widespread suspicion of foul play " over the death of the little Maid of Norway. We never have it emphasised that King Edward of England did not interfere in Scots' affairs until he was invited to do so by the two noble claimants to the Scottish throne—De Brus (grandfather of King Robert de Brus) and De Balliol—who both acknowledged Edward as their feudal overlord. And of 1296, when the English King, to enforce

---

Celtic Mag., January, 1887.
†See Forest Laws in Appendix to vol. xi. of *Exchequer Rolls.*
‡*The Making of Scotland*, p. 36.

his overlordship, harried Scotland with fire and sword, even Fordun is constrained to make hint about "the innocent populace" who "lay mangled far and wide over the land, defenceless against the ravening of these wolves." We know, however, of the "Ragman's Roll," where nearly 2000 nobles, knights, and ecclesiastics swear fealty to the English King, and that among them is young Robert de Brus. But we know little of William Wallace's first rising in 1296, or of how, in the succeeding year, he was "chosen by the commons of Scotland as leader to raise war against the English."* Who were these "commons?" Were they the dispossessed clansmen, the ex-freeholders? Were the burgher classes unitedly behind Wallace then? What part did Wallace's "chief lieutenant," Alexander Pilche, the Inverness burgher, play in the struggle? If at bottom Wallace's revolt was not a last effort to cast off feudalism from Scotland, why did the Scoto-Norman nobles hate him so? It could scarcely have been that they esteemed themselves more "highly born" than he, for well they knew, most of them, that they were but one or two removes from nondescript barbarism. Yet, that they did hate him is undoubted, and even the two possibly genuine nationalists and English haters among them, Sir Wm. Douglas and Bishop Wishart of Glasgow, ran in haste to meet the English general, Warenne, with the assurance that "they were no parties to the rising of William Wallace." And when, after success had come failure, was Wallace not deserted "by all men who had property at stake"? Listen to Sir Herbert Maxwell, the most recent historian of the period. "Little that is definite is known of Wallace's movements after the defeat at Falkirk, but it may be readily believed that he had lost some of his ascendancy in consequence of that event. At all events, the meeting of barons above described may be assumed as hostile to his influence, or de Brus would not have been there." In truth, the "Good King Robert" of our school books played a most despicable, vacillating, and traitorous part in the by no means clearly-defined drama of the times. On August 28th, 1296, as Earl of Carrick, he does fealty to the English King; in 1297 he renews his oath of fealty and raids Lanarkshire with the English. Then he joins Wallace, then surrenders to the English King at Irvine, and receives pardon for his temporary treachery to his feudal overlord. In 1298 he is in Edward's service in Galloway. In 1299 he sees an opportunity of striking a blow for his own advancement, so he attacks Edward's castle of Lochmaben. In 1302 he is surreptitiously appealing for aid to the King of France, while still assuring Edward of his loyalty; and in October of that year attends the English Parliament. In 1303 he gets an advance of salary from Edward, and is appointed Sheriff of Lanark. In 1304 he attends

---

**The Scalacronica of Sir Thomas Gray.*

King Edward's Parliament at St. Andrews, and sends, at his own expense, engines of war to assist the English forces in the capture of Stirling Castle. In 1305 he gets the Umfraville lands in Carrick, attends the English Parliament; and in August "is probably a witness at the trial and execution of Wallace." Then in 1306, according to the *Scalacronica*, he sent his brothers, Thomas and Neil, to John Comyn "asking him to come to the church of the Minorite friars at Dumfries so that they might have a conversation. Now he had plotted with his two brothers aforesaid that they should kill the said John Comyn on the way"; but Comyn spake the two Brus' so fair that they could not find murder in their hearts. On arriving at Dumfries Comyn was thus addressed by Robert de Brus : "Take my estates and help me ; be king or give me your estates, and I'll help you." Comyn refused, and was promptly murdered.* Brus was now an outlaw hunted by the Comyns and their friends and by the English ; but he was not by any means the poor but chivalrous hero who (in the school histories) got inspiration from spiders on Rathlin Island.† He had many powerful friends ; he rallied to his support the churchmen who resented English interference in their affairs and who had seen their lands and buildings spoiled by Edward's soldiers. Galloway and Moray were ready, as in Wallace's time, to rise in any cause that savoured of opposition to feudalism. The south country people indeed had been rendered desperate. In Bain's *Calendar of State Papers* we read of how Sir Matthew de Redman, in Dumfries, "imprisoned William Jargon, and notwithstanding a fine of forty shillings given for his goodwill, impressed all the carts in the country, and carried off William's corn to the value of 10 marks." By decrees he (Redman) extorted fines from the people, "some the mark and others more or less, forgetting possession, he and his sergeants seek occasion to grieve and distress the poor people by tallages. . . . He also took all the beasts that came one market day, to the number of 100 oxen and cows, and afterwards took fines before delivering them, except 5 cows, which he sent to Stirling ; 2 of these being taken from a poor stranger, Thomas of Hardingstone by name, who had bought them for 16 shillings, and keeps them still, though his sergeant had 6 pence to deliver them up."

The crazy and sickening barbarities practised on the women and children at the sack of Berwick by the English were still fresh in men's minds, and the indications are that, so far as the commons of Scotland were concerned, the prevailing feeling was not pro-Brus

---

Scot. Hist. Review, 1905-6, p. 329.

†As a matter of fact he spent the winter of 1306-7 not in Rathlin but at the Norwegian Court. (See *Scot. Hist. Review*, 1908-9, p. 131, based, we expect, on the statements of Fabyan and other English writers of the period).

but anti-English. In the north Alexander Pilche, the "brave and capable leader," who had been a "chief lieutenant in 1297," and who, though only a burgher of Inverness, was "a man of great influence in Moray," again roused the people to arms ; and Inverness Castle "fell easily, although the Earl of Ross was still Edward's man." The Earl surrendered, and Brus, in order to attach him to his standard, re-granted him his lands, and added "the lands of Dingwall and Ferncrosky."* And that was the situation in a nutshell. The commons rose against the feudal castle, and Brus, after the victory of the commons, not only rehabilitated the feudal baron but added to his wealth and extended his power.

"The truth is (says Mr. Joseph Stevenson), and it must be confessed with shame and sorrow, that the Scottish nobility, as a body, were not true to Scotland. The source of this lamentable weakness is to be traced to the operation of the Feudal System. With few exceptions, these nobles held lands in England ; and their ardour was cooled and their efforts paralysed by the knowledge that their possessions in that kingdom would be forfeited to the Crown on the first moment that they exhibited any active sympathy with their countrymen in arms against Edward. . . . It is painful to be compelled to observe that throughout these transactions, whenever the name of Robert Bruce is mentioned, it is nearly always connected with some measure hostile to the independence of his country."†

Aye, and when all is said that can be said of the mail-clad free tenantry, the trained men of arms, the knights, the burgesses, who fought so stoutly that bright sun-lit Monday of June, on the field of Bannockburn, was it not the non-mailclad division who, after the first shock of the armoured forces, threw themselves on the English host, and smashed it to a chaotic rabble ? This light reserve division—15,000 to 20,000 strong—has been smeared off the battle-picture : not fighting men, only ghillies, only camp-followers ! An aristocrat lie ! They were the sma' folk, and the poueraille : the sma' folk being yeoman and the poueraille being, literally, poor folk. They were not mail-clad, but they had come to fight, and they were deliberately held in reserve until the first shock of the mail-clad men was over. They were the working class, and it was their charge on the field that won the battle of Bannockburn.‡ And, after Bannockburn had been fought and won, among the first acts of the new Anglo-Norman-Scottish noble who had climbed to the throne was the granting to his nephew, Thomas Randolph, of the Earldom of Moray and the burghs of Elgin, Forres, Nairn, the customs of Inverness and the burgh of Lochmaben, estates in Dum-

---

*Scot. Hist. Review, vol. vi., pp. 134-5.

†Documents Illustrative of the History of Scotland, 1286-1306, vol. i., p. lii.

‡E. M. Barron, in his Scottish War of Independence, effectively disproves the allegation that the reserve division was only a rabble of camp followers or "ghillies."

C

fries, Berwick and the Isle of Man.   To the Earl of Ross he gave the
town of Cromarty.   Though the burghers had been his staunchest
supporters, he assailed their liberties, superseded their charters,
and handed over their privileges and their properties to their enemies
—the barons.*   And if our interpretation of the character of the
"Good King Robert" and the real nature of his dynastic struggle
require farther proof, let it be had in the fact that in the year 1328
he entered into a disgraceful treaty with the English king, whereby
he agreed to pay (or rather, he agreed to make his people pay) the
sum of £20,000 for that worthy king's assistance in securing the
removal of the papal ban which had been placed upon him, and for
open recognition by the English Court that he was really king of
Scots.   Sir James Douglas (the "Good Sir James") was to recover
his lands in England, and Lord Henry Percy, Lord Wake, and Lord
Henry of Beaumont were to get back their lordships in Scotland.†
It was a pleasant family party again !

Twenty-eight years elapsed between the death of King Alexander
and the success of de Brus at Bannockburn—years of travail to the
poor, their houses fired and their crops destroyed—and three-
quarters of a century after Bannockburn, in the earliest extant piece
of Scots verse, old Andrew of Wyntoun looks back the Brucean years,
and sings :

> " Quhen Alysander oure Kyng wes dede
> That Scotland led in luv and le (law),
> Away wes sons (plenty) of ale and brede,
> Of wine and wax, of gamyn and gle."‡

And modern scholarship, in an analysis of the official documents of
the first quarter of the fourteenth century, hastens to absolve Wyntoun from any charge of poetic exaggeration, by declaring that at the
end of the reign of Robert de Brus "the happy and prosperous
Scotland of the days of the Alexanders" had gone.   The resources
of the people had been destroyed.§

So much, then, in somewhat discursive digression upon school-
book romance.   Let us go back to the ordinary everyday life of the
people in the earlier feudal period !

The serf, the chattel slave who could be bought and sold, we have
already discussed.   We have now to consider the vassal, the alleged
free man, the tenant-at-will who ploughed the soil, for which he paid
the baron rent in money, in kind and in services.   He had, it is true,
a certain measure of personal liberty : he could not be bought and
sold ; but he could be starved and robbed ; he could be taxed out

---

*M'Intosh *Hist. Civ. Scot.* i., p. 372.
†*Exchequer Rolls*, 1264-1359, vol. i., pp. ciii.-cv
‡*The Orygnale Cronykil of Andrew of Wyntoun.*
§*Exchequer Rolls*, Pref. vol. i., p. lxviii.

of existence. When the vassal died, his widow or his heir had to pay a heriot or death tax of the best horse or ox to the baron, firstly on the death of his predecessor, then on taking possession him (or her)-self. For the privilege of having his daughters married he must pay a merchet or maiden marriage tax. An annual rent in money or in produce must be paid ; a tenth part of his annual produce to the church dignitaries for their intercessions with Divine Providence on his behalf, and another ninth part to the baron, to whom, in addition, he must make four times every year an offer of poultry and cattle. The baron's bailie also exacted a tax for the privilege of gathering brushwood on the great man's preserves ; eight annual taxes in the shape of "duty fowl " for the benefit of the young laird from the time that gentleman came of age until he married : taxes for the outfit of the baron's daughters when they were wed ; taxes for the arming and equipping of the baron's sons when they took the field ; and taxes for their ransom if taken prisoners of war. In addition, two days' unpaid service per week had to be given on the baron's estate—one hundred days in the year to be given at such times and in such proportions as were demanded—and since the baron invariably demanded his free labour at seed-time and harvest, the vassal's own lands must be sown and reaped in the night time.* He must have his corn ground at the baron's mill on the baron's terms. He must assist the baron on his sporting expeditions ; he must fell his timber, fight his battles for him, labour at the building of his castle, take turn at night watch, find horses for the baron's carriage, lodge his soldiers. He must find free quarters and food for the baron should he chance to come his way ; he must walk backwards from the great man's presence, and kneel if they met on the roadway.† He got "justice " in the baron's court, casti-gation from the baron's bailiff or locksman ; was racked and torn in the baron's torture chamber, and was hanged on the baron's gallows tree. For the baron's debts, the vassal's goods were seized by creditors, and for the baron's misdeeds the vassal frequently was punished. The vassal was the victim of every castle caprice and whim. Physically, mentally, and morally, he was crushed.

In 1574 the vassals on the estate of West Ferry and Monifieth pled with the Privy Council to safeguard them from their laird, who is knocking down their houses and chasing them with whingers and swords.‡ In 1692 a boy is sentenced by a baron's bailie to be nailed by the ear to a post and so to stand for an hour without motion, and

---

*Mr Hume Brown, in his *Scotland Before* 1700, says they (the poor) also
    reaped their crops on Sundays, but, that there was no class war in Scotland !
†As late as 1732 the waiters who carried food to the Duchess of Buccleugh had
    to do so *on their knees*—Rogers' *Social Life in Scot.*, vol. i. p. 95.
‡*Reg. Privy Council*, First Series, i., 429.

then "to be allowed to break the griss nailed without drawing of the nail."* Of the last Lindsay of Dunrode (1693), who moved about among his miserable tenants attended by twelve soldiers mounted on milk white horses, we are told that "when playing on the ice he ordered a hole to be made in it, and one of his vassals, who had inadvertently disobliged him in some trifling circumstance, immediately to be drowned "† ; in 1607 Earl Marischall of Donottar Castle gets a burgess plumber from Aberdeen, Anderson by name, to come with his servants and lay lead pipes for a castle fountain, and when Anderson brings the lead—160 stones of it—" and completes the job at great expense," the Earl claps him in the dungeon until he will pledge to provide the Earl with £700 worth of lead and until he will give a "discharge" for the work already done.‡ In the Orkney and Shetland Islands the odal tenants clung desperately to their ancient freedoms, although generation after generation of feudal barons oppressed, ravished, and murdered them. Odal, the negation of feudal, comes from *Allode* or *Allodium,* a compound of the German article *an* and lot. Odal lands mean lands obtained by lot—evidently the method of division resorted to by the Norwegians when they conquered the northern islands—and odal tenure, somewhat akin to peasant proprietorship, was the tenure common in Orkney and Shetland when they were ceded to Scotland by the King of Norway in 1470. Wealthy and prosperous must have been the odallers when they could afford to pay an annual tribute to the feudal barons who were sent by the Scots Crown to rule and plunder them, of no less than 3000 head of cattle, 5000 bolls of grain, 6280 stones of butter, and 700 gallons of oil.§ But their prosperity was short-lived when the barons and the bishops got to business. In 1530, so severe and oppressive were the exactions of the Earl of Moray's bailiff, that the odallers rose in arms against him, and the Crown interfered on their behalf. In 1561 the then governor, Lord Robert Stewart, Queen Mary's "natural" brother, doubled the teinds and stole odal lands ; finally he was deposed for cruelty. In 1600 Earl Patrick Stewart out-heroded Herod. He ordered fresh and unheard of taxes such as "ox-money " to be imposed for his own behoof ; he burned the archives of the burgh of Kirkwall and suppressed its liberties. He abolished the Althing, or Council of the Free, a democratically-elected institution which combined the functions of Parliament with a Court of Justiciary. He razed

---

* *Book of Regality of Grant,* cited in Rogers' *Social Life in Scot.,* iii., 44.
† *History of Rutherglen and East Kilbride*—Ure, p. 152.
‡ *Reg. Privy Council,* 8th January, 1607.
§ *Maitland Club Pubns.,* vol. lxxv., p. 14.
‖ For account of oppression in the Islands see *Our Noble Families* (Johnston), pp. 31-34.

to the ground all the little odal mills, and decreed that all corn
must be ground at his mills, and the fee paid to his millers ; he
created heavy tolls and customs ; claimed sole possession of all
commonties, the sea-beach and the fishings ; haled odallers before
his courts and threatened them with death and torture if they
would not formally donate their lands to him ; prohibited assistance
to wrecks as an infringement of his pretended rights of wreckage ;*
evicted owners upon any frivolous pretext ; invented new offences
for which he could demand fines in his own courts ; forced second
payment of taxes ; added one-fourth to the standards of measure
and weight when the taxes were being paid ; had his castle at Birsa
built by the forced labour of the people "without meat, drink, or
wages ; " tortured prisoners prior to murdering them "by gibbet,
fire, or water " before the window of his hall. "Confiscation for
his benefit," says one writer, "was the object and the consequence
of every such conviction." Similar oppressions from 1614 to 1624
were the daily conduct of his two successors in the tacksmanship
of the islands ; and all three seem to have annexed large areas of
the Church lands which the bishops in pre-Reformation times had
acquired by the simple process of fining and mulcting "adulterers
and incests " of their possessions. Then from 1633 to 1635 a new
and ingenious device of suppressing the few remaining odallers was
resorted to. Letters of lawburrows had become so common that
sometimes a laird "would procure them against no fewer than a
hundred poor people. Unable to pay the expense of a journey to
Edinburgh to find the requisite caution, these persecuted persons
were forced to give up such means as they possessed, and were thus
reduced to destitution."† To these barbarities and robberies there
could be only one ending, and we have it graphically depicted by the
Bishop of Orkney in 1634 :

" The ground yeilds thame (the poor) no cornes and the sea affords no
fishes unto thame as formerlie it wount to doe. The picture of death is
seene on the faces of manie. Some devoure the sea ware ; some eat dogges;
some steale foules. Of nyne in a familie, seven at once died, the husband and
wife expyring at one tyme. Manie ar redacted to that extremitie that they
ar forced to steale and therafter ar execute ; and some have desperatelie
run in the sea and drowned themselffes."

Over the once happy, prosperous islands lay the pall of feudal-
fostered famine !

In the south country, during the later years of the fourteenth and
the first quarter of the fifteenth centuries, the barons carried matters

---

*He evicted 7 merks of land from Powl Nicholson in Cullswick, because Powl
　had dared to take some bolts from a piece of wreckage which had drifted
　ashore.—*Old Stat. Account of Scot.* Sandsting and Aithsting.

†*Reg. Privy Council*, vol. v., p. 41.

with a high hand.   They lived at free quarters on the husbandry "*;
that is, they sojourned or sorned (their own feudal phrase) wheresoever there was food and "entertainment."   Gradually, however,
as this perpetual robbery forced the tenants into hopeless destitution, the barons would turn their attention to the fat larders of the
Church.   The Abbot of Paisley was compelled to find free quarters
for two noble sorners called Angus and Lennox who, with 200 retainers, had come unbidden "to keep their Christmas at their libertye
and pleasur."†   There were no leases, all tenants being tenants-at-will
and liable to arbitrary eviction on a moment's notice.   True, in 1401
Parliament had decreed that good cause must be shewn before such
summary evictions could be justified, but little did the barons care
for Parliamentary declarations.   In 1449 another ineffective decree
was issued to the effect that no tenant who held a lease could be
dispossessed by the mere fact that his lord sold or transferred his
estate‡ ; and in 1491 an Act was passed limiting the periods of
eviction to Martinmas and Whitsuntide.   Creditors of the nobles
could seize the property of their debtors' tenantry ; and what
Hector Boece called the continual "exercitatioun of chivalry,"
destroyed the crops and made the people feel that it was useless to
till the soil at all.   The poor bore the brunt of every war and every
invasion.   King Henry VIII., in his orders to Hereford, the Commander of his troops in Scotland in 1544, commissioned him "to
put all to fire and sword, to burn Edinburgh town, to raze and
destroy when you have sacked and gotten what you can out of it.
. . . Sack Holyrood House and as many towns and villages about
Edinburgh as ye conveniently can.   Sack Leith and burn and
subvert it, and all the rest, putting man, woman, and child to fire
and sword without exception, where any resistance shall be made
against you."   In St. Andrews ("the Cardinal's town ") no creature
whatever was to be spared.   The extent to which these devilish
instructions were carried out may be guessed from the report sent to
Henry after the sack of Dunbar : "They looked for us to have burnt
the town of Dunbar which we deferred till the morning, when those
within it were newly gone to their beds ; and in their first sleeps,
closed in with fire, men, women and children were suffocated and
burnt."   "The atrocities of the invasion," says Macintosh, "really
fell on the poor labourers ; and there was no help for them in Scotland, except to pray to God that He would take vengeance upon their

---

*M'Intosh *Hist. Civ. Scot.*, i., 375.

†*Scotland Before* 1700—Hume Brown, p. 6.   This feudal practice of sorning
    was called Cuddiche (and latterly, Conveth) in the north.

‡The Hopetoun family was vainly endeavouring to overturn this principle in
    the Law Courts so late as 1773.—*Lord Cockburn's Letters to his Gardener,*
    Scot. Hist. Socy., vol. x. lv., 24.

oppressors."* The people of Scotland, said Pedro de Ayala, did not dare to build good houses nor plant trees ; they lived almost entirely on fish, and seemed to consider their position so hopeless that they made no effort to build permanent houses of any kind. Bower, who wrote in James II.'s time, declared that : "Confounded as we are with daily tyranny, oppressed with rapine, spoil and tribulation . . . . The groans of the humble and the miseries of the poor whom I myself, who write this, have seen this very day in my own neighbourhood—stripped of their garments and inhumanly despoiled of their domestic utensils." When a tenant was foolish enough to improve his holding the laird's men came in armed hundreds and turned him out to make room for a relative of the laird ; and down to 1549, if a tenant were turned out by a third party, he could not claim reparation direct, but must get his laird to institute a legal process. But hopeless apathy and fatalism among the poor could be carried too far—for the barons—so an edict was promptly forthcoming that every labouring man must either own half an ox in plough or dig 7 feet square daily. The peasant proprietors having disappeared, the barons adopted the Steelbow system of tenancy ; that is, they stocked the farms and charged rent not only for the land but for the stock as well ; epileptic men were gelded, leprous women and their children were buried alive ; there was always a tassel on Buccleugh's gibbet knob.† Feudalism had reached its zenith in Scotland.

But it must not be supposed that the peasantry, though scattered and disunited, suffered these barbarities without a murmur of retaliation and revolt. Away back in 1457 there are traces of "great convocations made in the realm . . . to resist the Lords of the ground."‡ Down on the borders remnants of the old clans, such as the Armstrongs, fought feudal dominance until well into the sixteenth century, and would only be ruled "after such manner as their fathers have used before them " ; they had a persuasion, said Bishop Leslie in 1565, that "all property is common by the law of nature and may be appropriated by them in their necessity . . . If possible they avoid shedding of blood. . . Their promise is held inviolable and no crime more heinous could be imputed than violated fidelity." The peasantry seem to have been specially hostile to Sheriff Officers, who were alleged to take bribes from the barons to so manipulate the King's Courts that a sufficient jury was always unobtainable when a poor man made complaint against a rich robber. Sometimes these Sheriff Officers were waylaid and beaten to death.

Long before the Church Reformation in the sixteenth century,

---

*Hist. Civ. Scot., ii. 325.
†Exchequer Rolls, vol. vi. 32.
‡A Discourse on the Removing of Tenants—Walter Ross, W.S. (1732), p. 13.

great writers and poets like Dunbar, Henryson and Lyndsay had
made the cause of the poor their own.   In the *Complaynt* we are
told that aristocrat blood is of "na better cullour nor the blude of
ane plebien or of an meckanic craftis man " :   that metals were
melted to make household utensils and not "to be gunnis and cannons
to sla doune the pepil" ;   and the sum and substance of the writers'
opinion of the impartiality of the law courts is that :   "As to juggis
justice that rengis presently in our country, God may send a better
when He pleases."   But the barons were beyond the reach of the
poet's shaft ;   in their own domains they defied the common law :
in point of fact, they made their own laws—they and their Heralds,
Pursuivants, Councils and Bailiffs.   When James I. interfered on
behalf of the people they murdered him * ;   they regularly employed
professional assassins ;   they refused to follow the king in the war
with England which terminated in the disaster at Solway Moss,
because by revoking all the grants of Crown land which had been
made during his minority he "had encroached upon the old rights of
their class "† ;   they defied the customs and robbed and imprisoned
the collectors—the Earl of Douglas, in particular, engaging in a
systematic attack upon the collectors for years ;   they carried on
private wars among themselves and they banded in leagues against
the Crown ;   some of them, like Argyll in Queen Mary's time, took
bribes from the English for keeping Scotland in a broil.‡   There is
no question of a possible mistake in inferences or estimates here.
The pre-Reformation feudal baron was an unmitigated scoundrel,
an adept in every villainous practice, skilled in every form of cruelty
and oppression and knavery ;   and it was he as well as his successors
that Thomas Carlyle limned in his commentary on Scott's *Tales of a
Grandfather :*   "It is noteworthy that the nobles of the country
(Scotland) have maintained a quite despicable behaviour since the
days of Wallace downwards—a selfish, ferocious, famishing, un-
principled set of hyenas, from whom at no time, and in no way, has
the country derived any benefit whatsoever."   Nor are the estimates
of the other semi-impartial historians any less emphatic.   Colville
refers to "those rats of oppression, the barons,"§ and M'Intosh
declares that "We have no example in ancient or modern times of
men so utterly unscrupulous."‖

Early Glasgow—Sir James Marwick, p. 33.

†M'Intosh *Hist. Civ. Scot.* ii., 61-2.

‡*Fragments Regarding the Ancient History of the Hebrides*—" Senex," p. 49.

§*Byways of History.*

‖*Hist. Civ. Scot.* ii.   It is rather curious that the chief, if not the only, instance
  of baronial iniquity which seems to have fixed itself in the popular mind,
  is the hanging of Cochrane (" the upstart mason ") over Lauder Bridge.
  But Cochrane apparently was murdered not for his democracy but for the
  advice he had given the King, whereby the coinage was suddenly debased.
  Exchequer Rolls, vol. ix. (1480-7), pp. lxi.-lxvi.

The Barons and the Reformation of the Church.

The great upheaval of the sixteenth century, usually referred to simply as The Reformation, has been the happy hunting-ground of the professional theologians for well nigh three and a half centuries, and the net effect of the clouds raised by their disputations and bickerings is that the real motive, meaning, and result of the destruction of the Roman Catholic power in Scotland has been almost wholly obscured. The sectaries of the Hope Trust and the Society of Jesus fight fiercely upon such texts as Indulgences, Mass, or the private life of John Knox; and between them they have not only succeeded in confusing the public mind over the real nature of the Reformation, but they have suffered the baronial thieves, whose covetousness and greed were its most notable feature, to escape the historical execration which is their due. In saying this we do not seek in any way to question the seriousness or the importance of several of the principles involved in Knox's campaign, nor are we blind to the immense social effect of the great popular exhortations nor to the fervent propagandist enthusiasm with which they were delivered. We do not under-rate the spiritual quickenings of the sixteenth century or the definitive hall-markings which Knox and the preachers gave to Scottish life and character; but though we are not concerned in these pages with theological issues, it is essential we should express the opinion that they did not play the major part in the drama of history which our church friends would have us believe. The Reformation was more of an economic movement than a religious revival, and the very fact that a few short years of attack sufficed to overthrow the great and powerful Romish hierarchy is evidence, if none other was available, that there were great social influences on the side of the reformers. As a matter of fact, the Reformation (to give the movement its customary appelation) can not be properly understood unless its feudal surroundings and setting are appreciated, and unless cognisance be taken of the social grievances and the economic motives which loamed the soil.

Observe, first, the Church itself! The Druids, the priests of the pagan Picts, had long disappeared before the Christian Culdees; and the Culdees in turn had been swallowed up and transmogrified in the Roman Catholic priesthood, who were organised on a feudal basis, lesser men holding minor offices from the great prelates.

By the beginning of the sixteenth century the Church had grown wealthy. During the ages of faith vicious nobles sought remission of their sins by donating to Mother Church part of the lands which they or their fathers had stolen ; the prelates, usually good business men, had added field to field as occasion offered, and never lost their grip on an acre which had entered their rental books ; moral delinquencies, as in the Orkneys, were punished by fines of land ; the goods and chattels of intestate persons were seized for the welfare of the souls of intestate ones ; and in the early years of the sixteenth century the Church, as is proved by the incidence of taxation, owned half the entire land revenues of the country.* Sir George Mackenzie's estimate was that the teind in pre-Reformation times equalled about one-fourth of all the land-rent of the country ; and as one-fourth of the soil was wholly Church property, the total Church revenues would be one-half of the entire national land revenue. The annual revenue of the See of St. Andrews alone was £45,000, a huge sum in those days ; and the Bishopric of Glasgow owned 18 baronies of land, embracing upwards of 240 parishes. But it was true then, as it is to-day, that wheresoever the carcase is, there will the eagles be gathered together, and the very wealth of the Church became its undoing. Kings and nobles intrigued their sons, legitimate and illegitimate, into the more remunerative offices, so that not only did a feudal spirit rule the Church, but in high places there were dissolute lives and open scandal which accorded ill with even the lax moral precepts of the age. Of Bishop Cameron of Glasgow, we read that "he ended his days more like an ancient Roman than a Christian prelate," so great was his love of splendour and good living. King Robert II. and Elizabeth Mure of Rowallan had, before their marriage (to use the language of the Pope's famous letter), "a multitude of each sex " of children, and their temporal welfare seems to have been carefully attended to. One of them, "James Steward," was given the canonry and prebendary of Stobo, in the Cathedral of Glasgow ; another, "Thomas Steward," rejoiced in the archdeaconry of St. Andrews, the deanery of Dunkeld and a canonry in Brechin. In 1416 "Allan Steward " (there appear to have been quite a host bearing the noble name !), an illegitimate son of the Earl of Atholl and Caithness, though only 12 years of age, was given the canonry and prebendary of Dunkeld. Two years later he also got Cruden and other benefices. In 1497 James Stewart, aged 21, a son of King James III., became primate of St. Andrews. A brother of the Earl of Glencairn, aged 26, was Bishop of Lismore,

---

**Scotland in the Time of Queen Mary*—Hume Brown, p. 187. See also Prof. Masson's Preface to *Reg. Privy Council*, vol. i., 2nd series, and Spottiswood's Account appended to Keith's *Catalogue of Scottish Bishops.*

and in his spare time officiated as Provost of Trinity College, Edinburgh. "Latterly," says Bishop Dowden, "most of the stewards and bailies of the greater ecclesiastics were great nobles, and frequently the office was hereditary."* Bishop Chisholm of Dunblane, who was sworn to celibacy, married one of his daughters in 1542, to Stirling of Keir, and not only presented the young bride with a dowry of £1000, but provided her and her husband with hospitality for five years.† And just before the Reformation "three of the natural sons of King James, half brothers of Queen Mary, held *in commendam* (*i.e.*, in trust) benefices in the old Church, and were going about in the year of the Reformation as nominally ecclesiastics in virtue of their benefices, though in reality laics, and with no intention of ever being anything else."‡ Lord James Stewart was prior of St. Andrews at the age of five ; Lord John had been prior of Coldingham "from childhood," and Lord Robert had fulfilled the duties of (and drawn the revenues from) the office of the Abbot of Holyrood "from infancy." Against this capture of the Church by the greater barons, and against the epicurean splendour of the life prelatic, the Lollards and certain of the friars protested in vain. Friar Erith, at Dundee, who had publicly urged a stricter walk and conversation on the feudal dignitaries who were rioting in the treasures of the Church, was buffeted by the armed followers of the Bishop of Brechin for his pains. The secular or parochial clergy who dwelt among the people were becoming less and less full parsons or rectors, drawing all the teinds, and more and more simply vicars or chaplains for the absentee titulars §; they were, indeed, farmers of the church revenues, driven from above to extort the last penny from the parishioners, and many of them leading lives which flagrantly violated their induction vows.|| But the attitude of the people to the regular or monastic clergy (the 'flocks of friars," as Knox called them) is more difficult to understand. "The convents," says Sheriff Mackay in his preface to the thirteenth volume of the *Exchequer Rolls*, "were to a great extent the poorshouses of this period. The medieval church, with all its corruptions, at least partially solved the problem which still perplexes modern civilisation." There were 30 hospitals or poorshouses from Turriff to the Lowlands, where poor travellers, or aged persons, or diseased or leprous individuals, might have free sustenance and

---

*The Medieval Church in Scotland, p. 286.

†M'Intosh Hist. Civ. Scot., ii., p. 41.

‡Reg. Privy Council, vol. i., p. cxv.

§Just before Reformation about 740 parish ministers were simply tacksmen for absentee ecclesiastics.—Reg. Privy Council, i., 2nd series, cxii.

||Dowden's Med. Church in Scot., 308-314, Lyndsay's Satire of the Three Estates.

shelter ; but the friars seem to have grown so considerably in number that the hospital revenues were all consumed in their maintenance, and nothing was left for the poor or the sick.   At least so we gather from the extraordinary Beggar's Warning which was surreptitiously affixed to the door of every religious house in Scotland on New Year's Day, 1559.   The document in question, headed, "The Beggar's Warning," bears the opening announcement that it is from :

> "The Blind, Crooked, Bedrels (bedfast), Widows,
> Orphans, and all other Poor, so visited by the hand of
> God as they may not work,
> To
> The Flocks of all Friars within this realm."

The demand was for "restitution of wrongs bypast, and reformation in time coming."   The friars were told that they were "hale of body, stark, sturdy, and able to work," but that "under pretence of poverty (and nevertheless possessing most easily all abundance)" they had most falsely stolen from the poor their benignity and alms.   They (the friars) were accused of having, by false doctrine ("learned of your father, Satan ") impressed the nation with the idea "that to feed, clothe, and nourish you, is the only acceptable alms allowed before God, and to give one penny or one piece of bread once in the week is enough for us."   All friars were therefore warned to remove themselves before the feast of Whitsunday next so that the poor might enter into possession and enjoy "the haill commodities of the kirk."*

The threat seems, in some cases, to have been literally carried out at the succeeding Whitsunday † ; some of the religious houses were destroyed and some abandoned and the revenues of the Crown from the burghs increased, because the local exchequers were relieved of their share in the maintenance of the friars.‡

But we must search deeper for the great motive forces of the Reformation.   Aggrieved beggars in themselves were powerless, and the moral laxities of the clergy would not cause great excitement in the sixteenth century.   What, then, so crippled and crumbled the old Church that it fell without a struggle, no single class in the community unsheathing a sword in its defence ?

Church dues or taxes were called tithes or teinds (really tenths) of all the products of all the tenantry on all estates.   The tithes were both predial and personal, *i.e.*, they were exacted equally on farm produce and on the profits of industry, trade, or skill.   Those who evaded the tax were called "sons of perdition," and were excom-

---

*Knox's *Works*, i., p. 320.
†Taylor Innes's *John Knox*, p. 84.
‡*Exchequer Rolls*, xix., p. lviii.

municated—a risk which was run with cheerful frequence in these "ages of faith" by men of all ranks.* The Church curse on such of her sons as refused to meet her assessments promptly was an artistic and effective piece of work :

> "Cursit be thai syttand, standand, rydand, gangand, slepand, waikand, etand, and drinkand ; in hows and out of hows. Cursit be thai fra the crowne of the hede to the soile fute. . . . Few be thar daies, other men bruke thar possessionis . . . thar duelling be with Dathan and Abroyne the quhilkis the erde swellyit for thar syn. And as this candil is castyn fra the sycht of men swa be thar saules castyn fra the sycht of God into the depast pot of hel ever to remane with cursit Nero, the wikkyt emperour, and his cursit falowschip."†

In addition to curses the withholder of tithe rendered himself liable to a fine of 12 kine to the king, besides being compelled *vi et armis* to satisfy his titheholder. The barons, of course, lent their aid, Duncan, lord of Carrick, making public intimation that if any of his vassals should receive excommunication, he, Duncan, 40 days thereafter, would confiscate all the goods belonging to such vassal.‡ A tenth of the young of sheep, goats, kine, horses, and a tenth of grain, garden and orchard produce, leeks, kail, eggs, milk, butter, cheese, fish, pigeons§ ; a tenth of the profits on milling and on trade. If a farmer bought sheep with lambs from another parish, he paid tithe to his priest, who settled with the priest in the exporting parish, the proportion of the tithe due to each being calculated from the date of conception of the animals to the date when the young ceased to suck their dams‖ ; nothing was overlooked, from the tenth egg of the cottar's hen to the tenth sheaf of the farmer's grain or the tenth bird in the baron's dovecot. Farmers were forbidden to garner their sheaves until the vicar's man had selected the tenth share he would be pleased to take, and sometimes he was so dilatory in calling for the tax that the entire crop was wasted. Farmers who scattered the selected tithe through the fields were called "sons of perdition," as were also those daring souls who instituted the boycotts against clergymen when they came to sell their tithed corn. Then there were the hateful and galling corpse presents or mortuary dues. "The most valuable animal of the deceased shall be paid to Mother Church for a mortuary."*a* When the widow had no animal to give, the

---

*Selden's *History of Tithes*, ch. vii.

†*The Missal of Arbuthnott*, p. lxxi.

‡When the people of Caithness rose in revolt and murdered their bishop, King Alexander II. ordered that 400 of the participating peasants should be gelded as a punishment.—Andrew Lang's *Sir George Mackenzie*, p. 172.

§*Statuta Ecclesiæ Scoticanæ*, vol. ii.

‖Dowden : *Medieval Church in Scotland* 169.

*a*Stat. Eccl. Scot., ii., 47.

largest and best cloth, called the "uppermost cloth" or blanket, was taken from the bed. There was also special church taxation at Easter, called the Easter penny, which, though at first a voluntary contribution, was latterly enforced as a due. There were Sunday pennies, Candlemas lights for the purification of the Virgin Mary, and offerings at marriages, baptisms and confessions. Sir David Lyndsay puts into the mouth of *Pauper* in his "Satire of the Three Estates" a pathetic story of the grinding hardships endured by the poor from these ecclesiastical burdens. *Pauper* says he will declare the "blak veritie;" he has been supporting his father and mother:

> " And with my labour I did thame baith susteine,
> We had ane meir, that caryit salt and coill,
> And everie ilk year scho brocht us hame ane foill;
> We had thrie ky that was baith fat and fair,
> Nane tydier into the toun of Air;
> My father was sa waik of blude and bane
> That he deit; quhairfore my mother maid great maine.
> Then scho deit within ane day or two,
> And then began my povertie and wo.
> Our gude gray meir was baittand on the field,
> And our landslaird tuik hir for his hyreild.*
>
> The Vikar tuik the best cow be the heid
> Incontinent, quhen my father was deid,
> And quhen the Vikar hard tel how that my mother
> Was dead, fra-hand he tuke to him ane uther.
> Then Meg, my wife, did murne, both even and morow,
> Till at last scho deit for verie sorow.
> And when the Vikar hard tel my wyfe was dead
> The thrid cow he clekit be the head.
> The umest clayis† that was of the rapploch gray,
> The Vikar gart his clark bear them away
> Quhen all was gaine, I micht mak na debeat
> But with my bairns past for till beg my meat,
> Now have I tald you the blak veritie
> How I am brocht into this miserie."‡

"The worst wolves," says Henryson, "are lords that have lands as a loan from God and set them to mailliaris or rentallers; they vex the tenant ere half the term be gone with pykit querills for to make him flit or pay the gersum§ new agane." In addition to his legal levies on other people's cattle, the parish priest had rights of common

---

*Heriot or death tax taken by the landlord.
†Uppermost bed-cloth, already explained.
‡Lyndsay's *Works*, p. 450.
§The feudal fine leved on the renewal of a lease.   Still obtains in Scotland as a *Casualty.*

pasture for his own cattle. He was one village tyrant ; the barons'
bailie was the other.

But the Church could have withstood the hostility of the poor
farmers of the ground and the gangrel bodies of the highway ; alone
their antipathies to the Church do not explain the Reformation. We
must turn also to the little hives of industry and commerce—the
burghs. Here the merchant class grumbled loud against the forty-
five saints' days per annum upon which the Church demanded a
complete cessation of work* ; these holidays, besides the Sundays,
interfered with profits, and, so far as the merchants could see, served
no useful purpose. Commerce, then, stood for the Reformation,
and saw to it that "the majority of these holidays were proscribed
both on the ground of religion and political economy, but it was
long before the mass of the people were persuaded to abandon their
observance."† As a matter of fact, the abolition of the holidays
after the Reformation created such a set of troubles that the ministers
were forced to demand a return to the *status quo ante ;* and an Act
was hurriedly passed in 1598 decreeing that Monday of each week be
a weekly holiday on which it was unlawful for servants to cut the
lord's "corns" or do household work, the reason given for the Act
being that the people were turning Sunday into a day for hunting
and games and pastimes, "pretending that na day in the oulk [week]
wes granted to thame for thair releif fra thair lawbour except the
said Sabboth."‡

We read also that "the enterprising merchant likewise" in the
Reformation times, "looked askance at a body of men [the priests]
who, while ceasing to be active producers of wealth, were yet its
principal consumers"§ ; and immediately the controlling hand of
the prelates was withdrawn from the ecclesiastical burghs (such as
was Glasgow) the merchants promptly seized the exclusive management of the municipal machine.‖ The crafts, too, though doubtless
unaware of the designs harboured by the merchants, joined in the
general clamour. The Church was subjecting them to all sorts of
irritating taxation ; in Edinburgh, the master cordwainers had
to pay a penny weekly to the Altar of St. Crispin and to take turn
about in finding "a priest's meat," while the apprentices were at
entry mulcted in six shillings and eight pence for the altar, and the
journeymen on initiation had to find 4 merks for the same object.
Again, at great cost and trouble, the crafts were compelled to get up

---

The Medieval Church in Scotland.—Dowden, p. 246. Mr Hume Brown says
   the saints' days numbered " about fifty."
†*Scotland in the Time of Queen Mary*—Hume Brown, p. 162.
‡*Acta Parl. Scot.*, iv., 160.
§*Scotland in the Time of Queen Mary*—Hume Brown, p. 187.
‖*Sketch of the Incorporation of Masons*—Cruickshank, p. 198.

annual "plays" and processions in honour of their several patron saints, practices these which they were only too glad to discover to be idolatrous ! Now to the social and economic grievances of the beggars, farmers, merchants and craftsmen, add the open and unadulterated greed of the barons and the eloquence and personal magnetism of Knox, and you have all the conditions which brought about the downfall of the Roman Catholic hierarchy. Not all the eloquence of Knox, though he did on one occasion move "three thowsand persons to shed teares," nor all the manifest sorrows of the working class, could have caused the collapse of Roman ecclesiasticism in the sixteenth century, had not our old nobility allied itself to the Reformers, and allied itself with the fervour and enthusiasm generated by vision of immediate gain. The Church absorbed half the annual land revenue of Scotland : the nobles coveted that revenue. There is the secret of the Reformation !

True, the coveteousness was not of mushroom growth : it was of old standing. As early as the year 1208, Patrick, Earl of Dunbar, had stolen pasture lands from the monks of Melrose ; and from 1425 right down to the eve of the Reformation Parliament is continually ordering some nobleman or other to withdraw from ecclesiastical property he has wrongfully appropriated. One method of theft in vogue was for some powerful baron to offer his services to a bishop. The baron would "protect" the bishop ; he would collect the bishop's rents and dues for him, and so relieve him of the "Corpse present" and "Uppermost Cloth" odium. In return he would accept the heritable bailieship of the bishop's domains and recoup himself for his trouble by heavy fining of prisoners and by other customary baronial devices. On pretexts of this nature the Lennox family had ensconsed themselves on the Bishopric of Glasgow and the Huntly family on the Bishopric of Aberdeen. The other method of quietly commandeering Church property, that of simply securing the appointment of a baron's* younger or illegitimate son to abbacies, priories, bishoprics, etc., we have already described. The Church, attacked from without and ravished from within, fell. In her hour of trial she had no helpers. Here and there where a baronial family held sincerely by the old faith or surreptitiously held Church property and feared investigation and a demand for restitution should the Reformers be successful, there remained a peasantry which did not (and do not to this day) accept the new doctrines ; but, speaking generally, the great feudal church disappeared almost in a night. Her wealth had been her undoing.

That our estimate of the social forces which made the Reformation possible is the correct one we can support by citations from the

---

*Throughout this chapter we have used the term baron to include all grades of " noblemen."

writings of many modern historians of acknowledged repute. Mr. Law Mathieson says that "The Reformation was not wholly, or even mainly, a religious force." . . . . It was "headed by the nobles who were chiefly interested in engrossing the monastic estates ; but the Protestantism which the nobles accepted, and the peasantry conformed to as a mere form, was received with enthusiasm by many of the gentry and superior townsmen " . . . The Reformation "tended both to create and to organise a middle class."* Says Dr. Rogers : "The nobles paid an external respect to ordinances, but they were really unconcerned about any description of religious belief. They carried arms and used them against each other on the slightest provocation. They accepted bribes in dispensing justice. . . . They brought their followers to court and overawed the jury. They changed from Popery to Presbytery, and then to Prelacy as their interests prompted."† Mr. Galloway, in his lecture to the Glasgow Archæological Society in 1864, was even more emphatic. He said :

" Instead of patiently seeking to increase their rentals by improved culti- vation of their own lands, they began to covet the better-managed posses- sions of the Church. Under the pretext of removing from the clergy the odium of collecting the tiends, they got themselves appointed lay titulars, and did not always deal fairly by the priests. The advancing tide of reforma- tion in religious doctrine on the continent and in England showed them how they might acquire Church lands as well as tiends. Conscientious scruples soon yielded to covetousness, and such of the great landlords as saw a pros- pect of ultimate success, became early and zealous, though, for a time, generally secret, reformers. Without the aid of a majority of the tenantry and the servile classes, success in such a struggle was, of course, impossible. A baron might hang a dependant for refusing to be a reformer, but if he ventured to do much in that line he must expect assassination ; he therefore preferred to convince and to enforce conviction by promising a share in the plunder. Fully half a century passed before a majority of the peasantry could be persuaded to resolve on a revolution in order to expel the Catholic clergy and let the barons peaceably seize the Church lands."‡

We are afraid this last assertion of Mr. Galloway's, about the half century effort to convert the peasantry, will not stand analysis. The peasantry, as we have shewn, had serious grievances of their own against the Church, or rather against the administrators of Church property and the collectors of Church assessments and dues ; and it would not require fifty years' urging to rouse them to support a movement for relief. If they could have swept away the

---

The Awakening of Scotland, p. 5.   See Colville's *Byways of History*, p. 98, for an almost similarly expressed opinion.

†*Scotland : Social and Domestic*—Chas. Rogers, LL.D., p. 33.

‡Lecture on Ancient Agriculture—Glasgow Arch. Socy. *Trans.*, 1864, p. 417.

D

tiends by themselves, doubtless they would have done so long before
the middle of the sixteenth century ; and they knew too much of the
barons to trust them in any agitation whatsoever. Likely enough
the barons encouraged and fomented the popular detestation of the
Church dues, but that is a vastly different thing from saying that the
barons forced the campaign for the abolition of these dues upon an
unwilling people. Again, if there had been a serious fifty years'
movement against the Church, and if the success of that movement
depended upon the amount of popular support it received, would not
the Church have been busy making concessions to the harassed
tenantry ? Would it not have been shewing itself as the friend of the
poor and contrasting itself in a favourable way with the barons ?
Yet it is only in 1559 that the Church declared officially that the
mortuary dues(the kirk cow and the best bed blanket) were not to be
taken from the very poor. The reforms authorised by the Pro-
vincial Council in the Church, says Bishop Dowden, "came too late."*
    Mr. Macintosh, too, coincides with the other historians we have
quoted. "Many of the nobles," he says, "from motives of self-
interest, professed a willingness to embrace the reformed opinions,
and gradually ranked themselves on the side of the Reformers ; as
time passed and the prospects of the division of the Church lands
approached, they became more and more ardent in their adherence
to the principles of the Reformation.†" And Mr Hume Brown
simply declares that : "We know with what covetous eyes the needy
(sic) Scotch nobles regarded the vast revenues of the Church "‡
The Reformation successful, the nobles speedily showed their hand ;
they stipulated that two-thirds of the lands of the old Church should
be left to the "auld possessors" for their lifetimes, and then they
promptly set about securing resignation and alienations from the
various Church dignitaries. They quarrelled and scrambled and
stole while the amazed and shocked preachers protested in vain.
Of the remaining third which had been annexed to the Crown, the
"auld possessors" (*i e*, the nobles) secured a third, the Crown a
third, and the Church a third ; and well might Knox savagely declare : " two parts are freely given to the Devil, and the third part
must be fairly divided between God and the Devil. Well, be witness
to me that this day I say it, or it be long the devil shall have three-
parts of the third." He had learned something. His proposals
embodied in his *Book of Discipline* were that the tiends of all land
should be taken by the Reformed Church and used for three definite
purposes : (1) for the upkeep of the Kirk ; (2) for the support of the
disabled and the aged poor and the provision of work for the une-

Medieval Church in Scot., pp. 183-190.
†*Hist. Civ. Scot.*, ii., 39.
‡*Scotland in the Time of Queen Mary*, p. 187.

ployed, and (3) for a public elementary education for every child ; but he was promptly assured by the nobles that he was suffering from "a fond imagination," one Protestant aristocrat brusquely admonishing him with the words : "Stand content, that Buke will not be obteaned !"* Nor was it obtained in the form and to the extent Knox desired. As Mr Hill Burton puts it : "The Protestant clergy, sagacious as they were in most things, seem to have made the mistake of supposing that the active energy with which their lay brethren helped them to pull down Popery was actually the fruit of religious zeal and to have expected that they took from the one Church merely to give to the other. The landowners on their part thought such an expectation so utterly preposterous that they did not condescend to reason with it ; but without hypocritical attempt to varnish their selfishness, called the expectations of the ministers ' a fond imagination ' "† At first Knox did not fully comprehend the character of the barons. Of Wishart of Pitarrow, who had got himself installed as Comptroller, Knox, remembering Wishart's protestations of allegiance to, and enthusiasm for, the new Kirk, said : "The good Laird of Pitarrow is an earnest professor of Christ, but the muckle devil receive the comptroller, for he and his collectors are become greedy factors "‡ ; and when he hears that the teinds are being more than ever ruthlessly demanded (albeit they are now privately pocketed) he writes : "with the grief of our hearts we hear that some gentlemen are now as cruel as ever over their tenants as ever were the Papists, requiring of them whatever before they paid to the Church, so that the Papistical tyranny shall only be changed into the tyranny of the lord or of the laird." The longer he lived the better he knew the barons, and on his deathbed he was denouncing the "nobilitie" who "had greadilie gripped to the possessions of the kirk "§

We must not be understood as offering the opinion that economic motives alone inspired the Reformation. Nor are we insensible to the very marked effect upon the *morale* of the people which flowed naturally and inevitably from the appeals to the Old Testament

*Knox's *Works*—Laing's edition, ii., 29.

†*History of Scotland*, iv., p. 49.

‡Knox's *Works*—Laing's Edition, ii., 299.

§See also Pont's *Sermons Against Sacrilege* and Spottiswood's *History*, i., pp. 331-373. Fairly full accounts of the robbery of the Church Lands at the Reformation are given in Prof. Masson's Preface to *Reg. Privy Council*, 2nd series, vol. i., pp. cxvii-cxlv. ; Keith's *Historical Catalogue of the Scottish Bishops* (Russell's Edition, 1824), and Jamieson's *Bell the Cat* (Stirling, 1902). Later on the nobles encroached upon and appropriated ministers' glebes ; but details are difficult to procure. See, however, "Diary of Rev. John Mill of Dunrossness (1740-1803)," *Scot. Hist. Socy.*, vol. v., p. 147.

writings made by the preachers. Indeed, the reason why we have
entered at some length upon a consideration of the Reformation in
these pages at all is because we are deeply impressed with the disintegration and undermining of feudalism which resulted from the
efforts of Presbytery to popularise the old Hebraic prophets. John
Knox had appealed to the mob from his study window; there had
been mass meetings and popular lectures; kings and barons might
still oppress and bully, but now it was known that there was a King
of kings and a Lord of lords: men heard of One greater than Caesar,
to whom the meanest cottar had direct appeal; there arose a sense
of individual worth, a conviction of spiritual independence, a notion
of equality before God, and it grew and developed till it shook the
fear of the barons from the breasts of common people and shattered
the social superstititions which kept the Poor numb and spell-bound
while Privilege picked their pockets. Post-Reformation Scotland
was a new Scotland; the dim glimmerings of democracy arose with
the Kirk Sessions, and although, as we shall see later, newer
savageries and newer shackles came to depress and crush the peasantry, there were now men of lowly birth who, buoyed up and
inspired with great spiritual ideas, could, and did, offer stern resistance to oppression and threaten kings on their thrones And
not only a sense of spiritual equality had come to the people, but
the invention of printing and the spread of education. Gunpowder,
too, tended to put combatants on a more equal footing. One generation had been dumb and servile of soul; its successor was out on the
moorlands and the moss hags singing the old hundred and twenty-
fourth psalm, that psalm whose plaintive, appealing, haunting tune
and fierce determined wording still stirs our pulse and hardens our
fibre in this the twentieth century Baronial feudalism was in
danger whenever the cottars learned to chant :

> " If that the Lord
>   Had not our right sustained
> When cruel men
>   Against us furiously
> Rose up in wrath
>   To make of us their prey.
>
> Then certainly
>   They had devoured us all,
> And swallowed quick
>   For ought that we could deem ;
> Such was their rage,
>   As we might well esteem.
> And as fierce floods
>   Before them all things drown,
> So had they brought
>   Our soul to death quite down.

> But bless'd be God
>   Who doth us safely keep,
> And hath not giv'n
>   Us for a living prey
> Unto their teeth
>   And bloody cruelty.
>
> Even as a bird
>   Out of the fowler's snare
> Escapes away,
>   So is our soul set free :
> Broke are their nets
>   And thus escapéd we."

Yet whatever it may have meant ultimately in social spirit, the Reformation brought immediate economic disaster to the working class. Mr Hume Brown says that the misery was not "materially increased "; but we do not require even the testimony of contemporary writers to characterise such a statement as absurd. James Melville, writing to the Earl of Angus in 1584, complains that the rents, lands, and livings of hospitals and alms houses are taken by "gentilmen burgesses for right nocht," and that the buildings are everywhere decayed and their monetary foundations lost and abolished. We have already seen how the forty-five holidays were wiped out, and we require to possess but a very elementary knowledge of economic processes to appreciate the effect this would have upon unemployment. Since men now worked practically a day extra every week, fewer "hands " would be required, and such workers as were discharged would have no hospitable monastery doors at which to present their aumous dishes. The barons, more cruel than the ecclesiastics they had displaced, still levied the tiends ; and forced labour (which we have already discussed in a previous chapter) became the guiding principle in the legislation designed to bolster up the rising manufactures. Well might a sixteenth century poet, Maitland of Lethington, sing :

> " It is a grit petie for to se
>   How the comouns of this cun tré
>   For thift and reif and plane oppressioun
>   Can nathing keip in thair possession.
>   Sum comouns that hes been weill stakit
>   Under Kirkmen ar now all wrakit
>   Sen that the teynd and the kirk landis
>   Came in grit temporale mennis handis."*

For the little that we know of the life lived by the peasant for the two centuries that succeeded the Reformation, we are for the most

---

Aganis Oppressioun of the Commouns—Pinkerton's *Ancient Scottish Poems,* ii., 321.

part indebted to such records of the Baron Courts as are extant and
have been published. Not that these baronial court records can be
trusted to present to us the grosser infamies and the more outrageous
tyrannies ; but such as these records are—and bearing in mind the
fact that they deal only with petty cases that to-day would be tried
by a magistrate or by a police judge, and considering who their
editors have been, and the probability that ere the documents were
allowed to leave a baronial charter chest they would be carefully
purged of anything likely to tarnish the name and fame of the present
laird's ancestors—they present us with the most reliable data we
possess, of the every-day distresses of the poor labourers of the ground
The feudal law courts, of course, were a pertinent of the baronial
family. Each noble had his own law court wherein he, or his bailie,
"tried " cases, and announced new estate laws. He clung jealously
to his right of pit and gallows when he possessed it, and he saw to it
that there was no legal process but his own whim or caprice. Of
course there were juries—servile juries of his own appointment—
who simply existed to register the behests of the prosecution. In
very early times these juries or courts of birlaymen may have carried
on the traditions and the practices of the old Neighbour courts of
pre-feudal periods ; but by the year 1475 a jury which found a
verdict for the defendant against baronial wishes was liable itself
to be tried before a special jury of twenty-five landlord proprietors
for "wilful error," and if found guilty (the twenty-five proprietors
would take good care of that part of the programme !) were given
one year's imprisonment and lost their personal effects.* There
was henceforth a marked reluctance to act as "juror," and as the
form was kept up, the selected and impanelled unfortunates could
not be blamed if their decisions were remarkably free from anti-
landlord bias. Sometimes, indeed, even this pretence of real jury
trial was openly scorned, as, for instance, when the baron hanged
his culprit first and called together his jury afterwards.† These
rights of heritable jurisdiction, as they were called, once given by
the Crown could not be recalled, though the barons claimed and
exercised the power to dispose of them by sale or gift, and when in
the middle of the eighteenth century, after the second Stuart rebellion, the British Government, in limiting the territorial powers
of the barons, sought to abolish these legal jurisdictions, the barons,
with one united voice, shrieked "confiscation," and demanded heavy
monetary compensation. Altogether the Scots nobles claimed for
£602,127, and were probably deeply aggrieved that the Treasury
could only find them £152,000. The Duke of Hamilton, true to his
family traditions, made a bold bid for £38,000 ; but a landlord

---

Kingcraft in Scotland—Ross, pp. 56-7.
†*Social Life in Scotland in Eighteenth Century*—Graham, 229.

parliament awarded him only £3000. The Earl of Galloway claimed £6000, but got only £321, and the Earl of Selkirk asked £33,000, but got nothing, thus being the only bandit among them whose goods were accurately valued.*

Torture, of course, which was not forbidden in Scotland till 1708; was a regular practice in baronial "law." In England it was always illegal, but in Scotland it flourished in various forms—breaking on the wheel, burning at the stake, branding on the brow or on the right hand,† mutilation, tearing with pincers, disembowelling, chains, the pillory, the stocks, flogging, the treadmill, ducking of witches to discover the "devil's spot," the rack, the thumbscrew, the pilnie-winkis, the boot, the caschielawis, the long irons, the "waking" (keeping the prisoner from sleep), the "turkas," piercing with needles, scourging, strangulation, dismemberment, flaying of the skin, "thrawing the heid with raipes," and so on. Mackenzie, in his *Criminal Law* (1678) tells us that even in Edinburgh certain crimes were usually tried at night privately, and the malefactors immediately hurried off to the Nor' Loch, whose waters closed over them, without even a record being made in the Journal book of their unhappy fate. Naturally as we get nearer the nineteenth century there is discoverable a disposition on the part of the people to resist by force of arms the more savage decrees of the baron's court. At Inverurie, the people rose and drowned an extraordinarily vicious bailie in the river Spey‡ ; and the traveller, Hall, relates an anecdote which, while it has its hopeful side, yet illustrates the extreme subservience to the laird which was customary with the vast mass of the populace. At Ballindalloch, on the Spey, a poor man had been sentenced to death, and the gallows not being ready he was put in the baron's pit while the scaffold was being erected. At length everything was in order, and the baron's men called upon the prisoner to come up ; but instead of coming up the doomed man drew a sword and threatened to slay the first individual who came down for him. Persuasion and threat were equally unavailing, until at last, the victim's wife appeared and cried : "Come up quietly and be hangit, Donal', and dinna anger the laird."§

In the early Baronial Court a suitor once he had lodged his plea did not dare withdraw it, for that would have deprived the baron of the perquisites he exacted upon passing sentence. In cases where the

---

*For a list of the various heritable jurisdictions in 1747 see the late Sir James Marwick's "Municipal Institutions of Scotland."—*Scot. Hist. Review*, vol. i., pp. 284-6.

†In Dunfermline Regality Court the letters burned on the unfortunate victim were *Dun* and *Reg* (Dunfermline Regality).

‡Graham's *Social Life in Scot. in Eighteenth Century*, ii., p. 230.

§Hall's *Travels in Scotland*, ii., 404.

baron was himself prosecutor and judge, and the accused some poor wretch who had transgressed an estate regulation, the fine imposed by the judge went into the judge's pocket.   The courts at first were frequently held on hills and elevated places (hence the number of hills still known as the "law") and afterwards in the castle, and here the tenantry repaired at stated intervals in fear and trembling. The peasants of the fourteenth century in England had gone on strike against the death and marriage taxes to which they were subjected : had indeed, says Professor Oman, "confederated themselves into conventicles and taken an oath to resist lord and bailiff, and to refuse their due custom and service."*   The peasants of Swabia, in Germany, in 1526, after massacring every person of "noble birth" whom they could lay hands upon, and after burning the baronial castles had formulated a working-class Magna Charta† ; but in Scotland the convocations of the labourers of the ground appear to have been small affairs, and, possibly due to the isolation of the hamlets and villages, easily crushed.   Until the fifteenth century in Scotland, money rent plus military and manual services were the terms of occupancy of a holding : then the law of landlord's hypothec (which remained on the statute books until the beginning of the twentieth century) came into operation.   When the great privilege of a lease was given, though usually it was only for three years, a *grassum* or entry fine of an extra year's rent must be paid, plus a sum known as "introitus ;" sub-letting was prohibited, and women forfeited leases if they married without the baron's permission and approval‡ ; arbitrary fines of all kinds were levied with impunity ; at Cupar, for instance, the tenants were fined for allowing marigold to grow on their holdings—a fine of a sheep for every single marigold plant discovered.§   In the sixteenth century vassals who refused or failed to assemble at the summons of the baron suffered, in the one case, death, in the other house burning ; rival claimants to the barony, sometimes three or four in number, "would severally plunder" the families of deceased tenants "under the plea of exacting caupe or herezeld " ‖ (heriot or death tax).   This heriot robbery, though prohibited by an Act of Parliament in 1617,a went on merrily and

---

*Quoting Réville in *The Great Revolt of* 1381.

†They demanded liberty to choose their own pastors ; no tithes except on corn ; abolition of bondage ; huntings, fishings, and forests to be common property ; no farther encroachments by nobles on the meadows and commons.—*History of the Reign of Charles the Fifth*, Robertson, p. 269.

‡*Exchequer Rolls*, vol. ix., p. xxxiv.

§*Social Life in Scot.*—Rogers, i., p. 198.

‖*Ibid*, p. 204.

aActa Parl. Scot., iv., 548.   The Merchet or Marriage Tax in full operation in 1600, persisted in a modified form to 1748.

without interruption until 1703, when the barons allowed it to be commuted in each case for a payment of 20 merks ; at Lossiemouth, sheep stealers are drowned* ; at Forfar, Fenton of Ogill is given power to hold courts and try cases of theft and apply the fines to his own uses† ; the tenants of Cupar Abbey are ordered to provide and maintain one or two armed and mounted soldiers ; the lairds are the guardians of tenants declared insane and heirs under the legal age, and not only enjoy the property and possessions of the wards during minority or non-age, but have the marriages of female heirs in their gift, and naturally wed their own sons into ownership.‡ In the seventeenth century Cromwell shears the nobles of part of their powers by abolishing the military services which tenants had been called upon to render to their feudal superiors, but money rents rise in consequence ! From the Island of Tiree in 1662 the chief of the Clan Maclean extracts the following annual tribute : Money rent, £3200 ; mill rent, £40 ; every 6 merklands pays also 40 bolls of victual, a total value of £4266 13s. 4d. ; also from every six merklands a Martinmas cow, a Whitsunday cow and calf, 12 stones of cheese at 2 merks per stone, 12 quarts of butter at 2 merks per quart, 16 wedders at £16, four dozen of poultry with eggs at £8, six bolls of horse corn straw and groom's meat free, value £12 ; also from the whole island peats to the value of £32, and a sail and hair-tackle for a galley. Weavers paid 1 merk for permission to weave, and Maclean's falconers were to have "free quarters and lambs, etc., for the hawks." Last, but not least, the poor islanders were to find free quarters and food for the great Maclean himself, and for his tail of one hundred "gentlemen men " during all the winter months.§ What an honour it must have been to support and serve the hundred and one idle gentlemen-men for six months out of every twelve !

In 1700 the taxes paid to the Keiths of Dunotter from the tenants of Dunottar, Fetteresso and Garrock, in addition to the money rents, were 49 firlots of bear, 816 bolls of meal, 33 bolls of corn and fodder, nearly 1000 hens, four two-third marts, 10 stones of butter, 261 capons, 1200 eggs, 9 swine, also leits of peat from Cowie moss and coals from "Stanhive " (Stonehaven).∥

Probably the most grievous and irritating feudal robbery was that known as the multure. Every baron erected a mill on his estate—

---

*Extracts from the Register of the Regality Court of Spynie—Spalding Club Miscellany, ii., Chap. ix., p. 130-4 and 146.

†Exchequer Rolls, xv., p. lxxvii.

‡Ibid, xiii., p. cviii.

§Rental of Tiree in 1662 from the Argyll Charter Chest.—Scot. Hist. Review, April, 1912, p. 344. The money, of course, is Scots money.

∥Article, " Dunottar and its Barons."—Scot. Hist. Review, 1904-5, p. 401. A mart was a cow or ox fattened, killed, and salted.

at least he got his vassals and tenants to erect it for him—and this mill, when erected, was rouped out by the baron at as high a rent as possible to some budding capitalist miller. The tenantry of course were compelled to have their corn ground at the feudal mill; they were, in feudal phraseology, "astricted" or "thirled," and with this monopoly milling there were, of course, monopoly charges. The multure or fee charged by the miller might be anything—there was no limit to the imposition—but it usually ranged from one-thirtieth to one-twelfth of all the grain which passed through his hands. In addition, the miller's servant, who usually did the work, imposed duties or fees for himself, and which under the designation of "knaveships" or "sequels" usually amounted to a bannock, a lock and gowpen from every sack. There appears also to have been a tax known as "Drymulture," which was laid on every acre of corn whether it was ground or not; and woe betide the peasant or the farmer who sought surreptitiously to have his corn ground elsewhere than at the baronial mill. Down swooped the defrauded miller, and the horse and grain were forfeit! And not only was every tenant robbed by monopoly multures: he was compelled to give personal services in maintaining the mill, bringing home the mill stones (a laborious business where there were no roads, and the great grindstones had to be rolled along the uneven ground by means of tree axles running through a hole in the centre of the stones); the dam dykes had to be repaired; and all sorts of little vexatious odd and end jobs had to be undertaken in rotation.* We are told that there were also multure dues to the baron, though he already had his mill rent from the miller, "and so great was the profit from these multures to the baron and to the miller that Act after Act had to be passed ordaining the tenants to confine all their grinding to the mill of the barony. The handmill of the cottar against the watermill of the landlord strove for centuries back, before even the monks of St. Albans sallied forth and captured the handmills of their vassals and paved the floor of their refectory with them."† Continuous complaints came from the farmers against being kept a long time in waiting at the mill; continuous disputes about "whose turn next"; continuous charges that the miller was guilty of stealing more than the Baron Court had allowed him. At Stitchill, in Roxburghshire, there was frequent legislation against peasants who dared to buy bread for penny bridals in Kelso market, and who did not get their bridal wheat milled at the Stitchill mill. The fine for these enormities at first was £10, and later "the laird (Pringle of Stitchill)

Mills and Multures—Nenian Elliot. Hawick Archæological Society Pubns., 1882.

†*Records of the Baron Court of Stitchill.* 1655-1807.—Scot. Hist. Socy., vol. 50, pp. xv.-xvi.

further decreed that no bride dwelling within this barony shall make her bridal outside this parish wheresoever the bridegroom shall happen to dwell, for the benefit of the mill duties on the malt and wheat, under a fine of £20." Every bride had to be robbed in her own parish and not in the parish of any other laird.

It was not until the year 1799 that these multures could be commuted for a money payment to the laird; and some tenants in Midlothian, as late as 1853, were astricted to mills on the water of Leith, paying on every 18 bolls of malt one firlot for multure, one peck for knaveship, a quarter peck for the mill boy, and a firlot and a peck and 12s. to "the horseman who carried the grain to and fro." No baron ever allowed a "right," however iniquitous or shadowy its origin, go from him without getting an equivalent cash return. The nobles of Scotland were the pioneers in the compensation for injury business. Well might they call themselves "sorners" and "suckeners."*

In our search for the realities of peasant life under feudalism, let us make farther search in the Baron Court Records. Here at Corshill, near Stewarton, Ayrshire, between the years 1666 and 1719, we find the laird, Cunninghame of Corshill, fining his tenants for evading the multures; exacting £5 fines for fruit stealing in his gardens, or tree-breaking, or broom-cutting in his parks; £10 fines for trespass, or for picking stones from the laird's dykes; and convicted parties to lie in the stocks until fines were paid. The tenants, so the baron-bailie decrees, must maintain the laird's dykes or pay in default a fine of £4, and the court officer is to poind goods to that extent†; in disputes between tenants, one charging another with loss of crops through strayed cattle, the laird pockets not only the court "expenses," but the awarded damages as well. Rebels against landlord made law were not uncommon, and they make fleeting passages through the case lists. In 1672, Edward Smith is fined £40 for striking the "laird's man" on the head with a stick; and John Lachlane, the tenant in Mossyde, not only refuses to give his feudal services, but roughly handles the laird's officer; for this he is to sit in the stocks during the laird's pleasure and pay a fine of £20. Whether he evaded his corporal punishment or no, we cannot tell, but four years later, in 1676, he is being dunned for the £20 fine which he has so far refused to pay. The tenants of the town of "Hareschaw" are ordered to build and repair the "commone kilne" at their own charges; those who refused to be mulcted in a fine of £4 to the laird,

---

*The Suckener was he who possessed the astricted lands; the term Sorner has already been explained.

†The rigorous nature of these fines may be appreciated from the fact that the annual wages of a servant girl of the period was 40s., a pair of shoes, an apron, and "a new shirt."

and the town is charged 6s. for the trouble given the laird in issuing the decree. Tenants are to provide horses to drag the millstones on their edges, so as not to damage the grinding surface ; no one in Stewarton is to keep hens during seed-time and harvest, and later, this regulation is so extended that no one may keep poultry from 1st April till 1st October ; only the laird and his bailie may go before another judge or into any other law court than the laird's court at Corsehill fortalice—this to preserve the court dues and fines for Laird Cunninghame—and there is a fine of £5 on straying litigants ; nobody is to have horse or kye, unless he first feus grass land— a fine of 10 merks on defaulters here—poultry keepers during the forbidden period to have fowls confiscated besides being taxed 14s. for each fowl ; in 1709 the fine is raised to £4, evidence perhaps that dire necessity had compelled the cottars and peasants to supple- ment their meagre fare with eggs.* From the records of the Baron Court at Stitchill in Roxburghshire, we learn something of the imposts of taxation for special objects, which in addition to the dues and services already described, formed the fiscal policy of the feudal baron.† There were, of course, no leases ; tenure was from crop to crop, and tenants were removable at will. The baron fixed the parish burdens for education ; for the maintenance of the beddall, the village tyrant who even in winter time rang the bell at 4 a.m. and 8 p.m. ordering the commencement and the cessation of work ; for the "outreiking ane soldier for the parish," and for, if necessary, compensation for his wounds, and pension for his age ; there was also a half-penny rate for the expenses of the Baron Court, and every tenant had to find a worker day about for cleaning the kirkyard of rubbish (penalty for omission, £5 Scots), for repairing the Church buildings and so on, and riddles, barrows, etc., had to be supplied free. Widows had to pay share of expenses incurred in rolling home the mill stones (one woman is called upon to pay £3) ; everybody is levied in unpaid labour for making ditches, building dykes, enclos- ing, planting trees for the laird, and "casting the mill lade for the common enemy, the miller." The penalty for cutting a laird's tree was at least £10 ; but if we are to accept literally the old peasant rhyme, it might mean even death.

> " Oak, ash, and elm tree,
>   The laird may hang for a' the three ;
>   But for saugh and bitterweed,
>   The laird may flyte, but mak naething be 't."‡

For behoof of the village blacksmith, a parish tax called "sharping

*Corsehill Baron Court Book Records, 1666, 1719.—Pubns. of Ayrshire and Galloway Archæological Socy., vol. iv., sect. ix., pp. 70-239.

†*Scot. Hist. Socy.*, vol. 50, pp. xiii., *et seq.*

‡Rogers' *Social Life in Scotland*, ii., p. 46.

corn " was levied ; and in return he had to keep ploughshares and reaping hooks in order. Of the cottars who laboured to the tenant farmers, we can discover very little of moment. Their houses were single apartment mouse-holes of mud,* and their common, everyday food was oatmeal moistened with hot water and seasoned with salt ; their women-folk were the pack-horses of the period, carrying everything—grain, hay, and manure—on creels on their backs ; and by suitable arrangement of their petticoats they carried travellers and passengers across the fords. One cottar in partial rent is bound to bring 10 loads of coal from England for the laird, and 4 loads for the Lady Dowager. For the pasture of every horse on the hill, one extra load of coals must be carried. The cottars, between them, must drain "the east loch." They laboured for their own sustenance in the waste places of the meadows, and they were given permits to gather fuel in the woodlands and the peat mosses ; and in the large ranges of common and forest land their pigs and geese might rove and their cows might feed, herded by the small boys of the village.

From the Court Book of the Barony of Leys † we get farther illustration of feudal glamour and romance, this time, as it must have enveloped the Aberdeenshire peasant. The laird appoints the blacksmith to whom all tenants must go for "iron-work," and to whom all must pay an annual "smydie boll." One, Jon Cambell, is given the office of "pundlar " for keeping the woods in the barony, and is empowered to poind "for ewere man, womane, hors, or nolt that is apprehendit within the said dykes, 3 shillings and 4 pence." For every sheep which strays into the laird's preserves the owner must pay 8d. If Jon Cambell is the pundlar, Jon M'Ky is the "officer" entrusted with the duties of poinding, and he appears to have been unpopular. He seizes and poinds James Patersoune's horse, but James deforces him and takes back his horse, for which proceeding he, James, is ordered by the baron court to pay the laird £40 in money compensation, to sit in the stocks for 24 hours and "his haill guids and gear to be escheit to the laird, conforme to the act of parliament." In 1623 the peasants are solemnly warned against burning green or dry sticks taken from the laird's plantations. In 1625 one man is convicted of wounding another, and the laird takes the £40 fine which he imposes; there is also "five li [pounds] of sythment to the pertie " who suffered the wound. In 1628 it is ordained that if tenants have not their "pultrie and capones " ready for the laird's collector, "everie ane in thair awin seasone," they will

---

*At Stewarton, in 1658, the houses of the working-class were " built so low that their eaves hang dangling to touch the earth." At Inverness bottomless baskets sufficed for chimneys.

†Spalding Club *Miscellany*, vol. v., pp. 221-229.

be compelled to pay double dues. Delays in furnishing the larder at the "big hoose" were dangerous.

In 1628 no one is to brew malt for sale unless he first pay the laird one stone of tallow by way of purchasing the right to trade. In 1634 any brewster selling ale to a domestic servant of the laird is to pay the laird a fine of "tene punds, *toties quoties*." This does not mean that the laird, Burnet of Leys, had conceived any hatred of intoxicants, but merely that he had entered the brewing business on his own account. In 1637 no tenant is to presume to have slates at his own house, but is to bring them all to the laird, or be fined £10 for disobedience. And any man who "disobeys to go to the slatehill and dig slates when asked, will be fined £10 for each refusal." In 1643 it is announced in court that servants leaving the laird's service must pay him 40s. for each day on which they deprive him of their labour, and husbandmen servants are to pay 20s. per day, 10s. per half day, and 5s. per quarter day on which they abstract themselves from work. This was the right to toil, with a vengeance! In 1646 it is decreed that the laird's peats must be led first from the moss, and no peats are to be taken until his stacks are completed, otherwise a fine of £10 on husbandmen, £5 on cottars, and 40s. on all other delinquents! In 1649 the laird's officer complains that the wicked and perverse tenantry, instead of giving him their fowls, go "to burgh and sell them, so that the laird's house is altogether misserved." Shame upon such wickedness, and as a curb to it in future he who refuses to hand over his fowls at the time and place stipulated by the officer will be fined 12s. for every capon, 6s. for every hen, 3s. for every "chilkin"; and if such fines are not paid within 24 hours the offender's goods are to be poinded.

At Urie, in Kincardineshire, though the lairds, the Barclays, were Quakers, a similar perpetual petty robbery went on, and Mr. Barron, who edits the Baronial Court Records from 1604 to 1707, sums up thus:

> "Against him (the proprietor) one and all made common cause, while the fines exacted by the Baron Court must, in many instances, have been utterly inadequate to meet his losses. It would appear to have been esteemed no felony to pilfer from the laird, no moral evil to destroy his property. . . . They stole his peats, they trespassed on his hainings, they leapt his garden dykes to puirloin, we presume, his lettuces and gooseberries, and generally they made it to be felt that however earnestly they were prepared on all occasions to defend their private rights, his were not such as were entitled, in their opinion, to be regarded."*

This, somewhat verbosely, is the lie direct to Mr. Hume Brown's assertion that there never was class war in Scotland. Originally— probably as late as 1385—"the Neighbour's Court" or Court of

The Court Book of the Barony of Urie in Kincardineshire.—Scot. Hist. Society.

Burlaw, a popularly elected tribunal, which met at the Moot Hill or Mound to settle little civil disputes, had rights of jurisdiction quite independent of the baron court; but at Urie, as elsewhere in the seventeenth century, these rights had gone and the birlaymen were now simply subservient jurors in the baron court; they were, says Mr. Barron, "essentially the creatures of the proprietor," allowing him to absorb the fines and the forfeitures, allowing him to seize the lands and the revenues of the royal burgh of Cowie, allowing him to farm out the teinds at a profit, and allowing his officers to exact little irritating fines and perquisites on their own behalf. In the Court "everything is so adjusted as to serve the interest of the strong against the weak, the lord against his helpless vassal and dependant," and yet the tenants must give "suit and presence" to the judicial farce; they must attend the court three times yearly or be fined for absenting themselves, just as the baron himself was fined for non-attendance at Parliament. At Urie, the court fixed the price of bread and ale, but orders the baker and the brewster to supply their commodities at cost price to the laird's house. During harvest-time everybody—even mere squatters like the grassmen and herdsmen, who had no land rights of any kind, and of whom, for the first time, we catch a fleeting glance—must do "service" on the laird's farm. A tax on every ploughgate of land is imposed for the schoolmaster, and there are the usual fiercely resisted services due to the miller, the bringing of water to the mill in time of storm, the freeing of the mill race from weeds, and so on— services and charges more bitterly resented when, as at Urie, the miller was an absentee, who merely farmed the mill from the laird and employed a "pecaman" or servant who undertook the work on condition that he was allowed to abstract a gowpen of meal from every sack.* At Urie, feudalism is not concerned solely with the land; its exactions extend also to the sea. The laird has a fishing boat, and there is a crew of fishermen who can be compelled to go to sea in fair weather. These fishermen pay an annual rent for the use of the boat; they keep it in repair; they lay past the proceeds of part of every catch as a sinking fund from which to provide a new boat, and they pay a yearly custom of "one hundred haddocks or three large cod" to the laird's lady, "together with a pint of oil from every fishermen." This was bad enough, but over on the western coasts it was beaten by the Duke of Argyll. That gentle-man had in 1663 secured a tack (*i.e.*, a lease) of the dues on all the herring caught on the Western seaboard, "including the isles thereof, great and small loches and creiches from Pentland Firth to the Moule of Galloway or any part thereof, and where the sea flowes within the watter of Clwyd." It seems, however, that the M'Leans

---

*A " gowpen " was a double handful—both hands together.

of Lochbuie and Dowart, and M'Leod of Dunvegan, considered this
an encroachment upon their particular preserves, and they compelled their fishermen to deliver up to them the whole "take" every
Saturday morning. The fishermen being thus robbed already,
could not again be robbed by Argyll, who accordingly sets up a
characteristic whine, declaring the action of the chiefs of M'Lean
and M'Leod to be "unlawful and most unjust oppression. Not
only are the poor fishermen rendered unable to satisfie their dewes,
discouraged in their vertue and industry, but," and so on, and so on.*
A Campbell of Argyll denouncing oppression of the poor was a sight
for the gods !

At Urie, as on every other barony, the tenants were required to
build and maintain their own farm steadings, the stone only being
supplied by the laird. Out-going tenants (and they were frequent
enough) took every part of their houses with them except the four
bare walls, even unroofing to get their beams and rafters. The
in-going tenant started *de novo*, and on as rude a scale as possible ;
ornamentation or evidence of surplus wealth of any kind being a
sure incitement to farther baronial theft. When one laird fell out
with another, it was the pleasant fashion of the times for the victor
to distrain on the loser's tenantry. In 1642, for example, we find
Graham of Blaatwood complaining that Archibald Douglas, brother
to the Earl of Queensberry, had managed to get him lodged in prison,
and that during his temporary incarceration Douglas "tooke from
the compleaner's tennents 44 ky and oxen, 15 horses and meares,
and five score ewes and wedders . . . . and have left his lands
waist, and can gett none of his rents to pay his debts or interteane
himselfe."† There was no solicitude, you will observe, for the lack
of "interteanement" endured by the poor "tennents" who had
had their goods and chattels reft from them. If a laird's tenants
should take their trade and custom to some fair or market outwith
his jurisdiction, he promptly conceived the idea of setting up markets
and fairs on his own account, compelled his tenantry to patronise
them, and collected for himself the custums duties.‡

Under such conditions as these, is it any wonder the agriculture
was "barbarous," and the land in consequence rack-rented even at
1s. per acre ? And yet landlords had "inconvenient superabun-

---

Reg. Privy Council, 3rd series, vol. ii., xxxiv-xxxv.

†*Reg. Privy Council*, vol. vii. (1638-43), pp. 347-8.

‡Lord Maxwell set up such a fair at Mylentown of Urr and forced the tenants
    of the Stewartry to go there. The Dumfries Town Council took the matter
    before the Privy Council and won their case in 1672, but five years later
    we find them paying him 1000 merks Scots to withdraw his precious market
    altogether.—*Some Incidents in Troqueer Parish*, G. W. Shirley, Dumfries
    and Galloway Arch. Socy. Pubns., p. 139.

dantcy " ; Stewart of Appin had in rent an ox for every week, a goat or a sheep every day, and fowls, eggs and cheese, "past all reckoning " ;* and the people who provided these things at such cost to themselves and their children were despised for their pains. The Earl of Strathmore described his workers as "these kind of cattell " ;† and indeed it is difficult to harbour feelings other than of repugnance towards a peasantry so slavish and so cowardly that it worked for 14 hours per day for six days each week, supplying these rude aristocrat pirates and their ladies with a superabundance of the good things of life, while they themselves sold their children to the plantations for food,‡ abode in "misery, hunger, and the shadow of death," regarded hogs' feet and ears as a delicacy,§ and lived in chimney-less hovels where they had been smoke-wizened from infancy, and where they slept on the floor beside their cattle.|| The servile labour, the bonnach, or bonnage days on the laird's farm without wages were given without a murmer ;a after the wet harvest of 1757 a laird could refuse an instalment of rent and turn "15 families of cottars out of doors in a severe storm of snow,"b and nobody thought of shooting him ; in the succeeding year a poor woman is publicly whipped through the streets of Edinburgh before being banished for the horrible crime of hen-stealing ; and almost at the dawn of the nineteenth century, as the minister of the parish of Dunnet in Caithness tells us, the people were ploughing the laird's land for him, carrying the manure on their backs, reaping, threshing, "manufacturing" his crop and carrying it to market, giving him "part of their sheep, cattle, swine, geese, hens, and eggs, and a small victual and money rent." They were, he concludes, "next thing to slaves."c Over at Wick, besides a heavy money and victual rent, there were "an infinite variety of minute services to the landlord."d The poor tenants had each to supply a plough in Spring and plough half an acre of the laird's home farm ; find a man between them to sow his seed ; send harrows and harrow the ground ; supply two persons to carry the manure ; lay the manure on his fields ; in summer, mow his "natural grass," make it into hay, cart it, carry it

*Graham's *Social Life in Scot. in* 18th *Century,* p. 163.

†*Diary of First Earl of Strathmore of Glamis,* p. xxxvii.

‡Graham's *Social Life in Scot. in* 18th *Century,* p. 147.

§*Ochtertyre House Book,* p. 140.

||*Scotland : Social and Domestic*—Rogers, p. 248.

aStat. Acc. Scot., vi., 146.

bA *Discourse upon the Removing of Tenants*—Walter Ross, W.S. (1782), p. 105.

cNew Stat. Acc. Scotland, vol. Caithness-shire, p. 40.

dIbid, p. 147. It should also be remembered that roads, ferries, and bridges were made and repaired by " Statute Labour," tenants, servants, and cottars being compelled to give so many days free labour per annum for this purpose.

E

to the yard, stack it ; weed his corn ; cast 400 feal for building, and 300 divots for roofing his houses ; in harvest-time, cut his corn, carry it, and stack it ; furnish the winlins for thatching his stacks, draw straw to thatch his houses and straw ropes to bind down thatch ; each to thresh so much corn in his barn, dry it in the kiln, carry it to the mill ; then carry the meal to the girnel and ship it for exportation abroad ; carry one letter each in rotation to any person in Caithness as desired by the laird ; give so many peats, dress so much flint, winter so many of his cattle, and pay him one fat lamb, two geese, so many hens, chickens, eggs, etc.

In their spare time they raised sons for enlistment against Napoleon who was popularly credited with a desire to invade this country for the purpose of suppressing the liberties of the people !

Meantime the hereditary jurisdictions having been abolished, the administration of "justice" in the rural districts had been trans- ferred to the Justices of the Peace (who were mostly the old barons under a new name), and the dispossessed tenants, now working as hired labourers to the large capitalist farmers who had begun to supplant them, were having their wages "fixed" and their hours of labour "regulated." These statutes of labourers, as we have already seen, were in thriving operation in the burghs ; and both sets of statutes—burghal and county—were designed to secure cheap, starvation-rated labour from the husbandmen and cottars who had been uprooted from the soil and now formed a more or less vagrant and pauperised class. Of course there were other methods current for extracting profit from the unemployed, the needy, and the im- poverished peasantry. At Aberdeen, for example, a regular slave market existed from 1740 to 1746, a company of enterprising capi- talists, which included a bailie of the city and the town clerk depute engaging themselves actively in kidnapping people in the rural districts and selling them to slavery in the American plantations : no fewer than 600 men and women being thus shipped in six brief years from the Aberdeen slave market.* But the most approved feudal-capitalist method of dealing with the working-class after the hereditary jurisdictions had gone, was the method of strict wages' regulation. One instance will suffice to illustrate the general rule. At the Dumfries Quarter Sessions on 5th March, 1751,

"The Justices of Peace, considering that notwithstanding of the former regulations and acts made anent servants' fees, and the time and manner of hiring servants, the said acts are broken and disregarded to the great hurt and prejudice of the tenants and land-labourers occasioned by the extra- vagant humour of servants by reason of the present plenty. For remedy whereof, the said justices, to the effect that there may be due order and regulation anent the premises in time coming, do ordain and enact that the

---

Scotland : Social and Domestic—Rogers, i., p. 68.

fees of servants within this shire from and after the term of Whitsunday next, 1751, until it shall be thought expedient to make new regulations concerning the same, shall be as follows, viz. :—

That a domestick servant man who can plow, thatch, mow hay, bind, cart, car, and harrow and work all husband work, and is an ax-man for all husband utensils, shall have any fee agreed upon betwixt his master and him, not exceeding two pounds ten shillings sterling yearly, or two pounds five shillings and two pairs of shoes.

Item, that a barn man who can thresh in the winter season, herd a sufficient hirsel in summer, and can lay on loads and drive carriages and is capable to serve at kiln and miln, shall have any fee agreed on as said is, not exceeding £1 16s. 8d. or £1 11s. 8d. sterling and two pairs of shoes.

Item, a young man or lad who can lead or drive the plough in winter or herd calves or stirks in summer, shall have any fee agreed on as said is, not exceeding 18s. 4d. sterling yearly, or 13s. 4d. sterling and two pairs of shoes.

Item, a strong, sufficient servant woman for barn, byres, shearing, brewing, baking, washing, and other necessaries within and about the house shall have any fee agreed on as said is, not exceeding 30s. sterling yearly or 25s and two pairs of shoes.

Item, a lass or young maid who can spin or card in the winter season and herd in summer shall have any fee agreed on, not exceeding 16s. 8d. sterling yearly or 13s. 4d. and two pairs of shoes.

Which respective fees above-mentioned are hereby declared to be in full satisfaction to men and women servants of all that can be asked or craved or shall be given to them for their year's fees as above mentioned. Declaring that where the master gives or the servant receives any greater fees than those above expressed, such feeing is hereby declared not only void and null, but also both masters and servants who shall presume to contravene the premises shall be liable in ten pounds Scots each, to be paid to the procurator-fiscal, upon their being convicted thereof before the Justices of the Peace, either by their own oaths or by witnesses, and that *toties quoties*, which fines shall be applied by the said justices as they shall think proper, and declaring that where any surplus or bounty such as grazing or wintering or nolt or sheep, shoes, shirt, linen apron, or any other additional bounty whatsoever, shall be given and received by any master and servant more than what is particularly above appointed, the same shall be accounted a transgression of this Act, and the parties, transgressors fined and punished, conform thereto as above ; and because there may be several private pactions and underhand dealings between masters and servants which may be so privately transacted that neither the Justices of the Peace or constables can have any knowledge thereof, therefore for redressing such abuse, it is hereby declared and ordained that whatever person or persons shall dilate any master or servant who have contravened the premises by giving or receiving greater fees than those mentioned, and shall prove or make out the same by witnesses on oath of party, the informer shall have one-half of the fine incurred for any such transgression, with his expenses off the other half of the fine to be modified by the justices. And whereas great inconveniences happens by servants feeing at any time they please and by their feeing for less than one full year . . . therefore servants must fee at Whitsunday or Martinmas or be fined a half-year's fee and given such other punishment as the justices may decide.   If the master desires he may keep his servant for twelve months, and in no case for less than six months from the date of feeing.

"And whereas there is a great penury of good servants, and that many of them are frequently much inclined to idleness, and both men and women often leave their service and keep themselves idle without any visible lawful employment, for preventing all which inconveniences for the future the said justices hereby enact and ordain that no persons who have been in the use of hiring themselves as domestic servants to husbandmen or labourers of the ground† shall betake themselves to any other employment without a license from two Justices of the Peace under pain of twenty shillings sterling besides being liable to be obliged to serve as a domestic servant for the space of a year to any person who shall apply to a Justice of the Peace for that purpose, and if any person want a labouring servant, either man or woman, and can discover any person fit for service not engaged, who is not following some lawful business, or who has been formerly a domestic servant and has not got a license to employ him or herself otherways, upon a complaint thereof to any one Justice of the Peace, any such servant shall be obliged to enter home to such master claiming him or her."

Then follows intimation that a servant desirous of leaving his master at the expiry of the time originally contracted for, must give three clear months' notice of his intention in the presence of two witnesses, or serve another year.   Masters are to make "timeous and punctual payment "of the fees.   This is "for the encouragement of servants " who in all likelihood had not been paid regularly in the past.

"And further, the said justices enact and ordain that all persons who have been ordinary servants or are in any capacity or ability to serve, both men and women, older and younger, and are not presently in service, that they immediately apply themselves thereto and fee themselves to such persons as have occasion for them, not exceeding the said fees and wages above-mentioned, otherwise to be reputed and holden as vagabonds and punished as such, and that the justices in their several districts cause apprehend all such idly-disposed persons as shall after the term of Whitsunday next be found within the same, and incarcerate them until they are willing to serve."*

The mesh could scarce have been drawn more tightly.   The small baronial tenants now about to be swept out of economic existence by the clearances necessary to large scale capitalist farming had crystallized their grievances in the couplet :

> " Ane to saw, ane to gnaw,
> Ane to pey the laird witha'."

And additional imposts were being laid upon them thick and fast. Roads were wanted in the development of the estates ; very well, the tenants must make them ; and so in 1719 an additional week's unpaid labour is taken from all able-bodied males for the creation and preservation of the highways.   Six days per annum for statute

---

†Husbandmen and labourers of the ground here mean tenant farmers.

*Dumfries and Galloway Antiquarian Society Proc., 1864-5, p. 37.

labour and the people to find their own horses, shovels, picks and flint stones, was the original order ; and it was only after many long years of grudging toil on the part of the peasantry that the statute labour services were commuted for an annual money payment. But here already, in the Dumfrieshire Statute we have quoted, we find regulations for the scientific exploitation of the labouring cottar class—so soon, alas, to be swollen in numbers—on a basis of wage-slavery. Feudal theft had discouraged agricultural advance, and the transition to large capitalist farming told with additional weight against the poor. Famines became frequent—one in 1783, one in 1796, one in 1799 and one in 1800—during which, declared Dr. Somerville of Jedburgh, "thousands perished of starvation." Ague, asthma, consumption, rheumatism (or *pains* as the people called it then) caused by low ceilings, damp houses, poor diet, labouring in the peat mosses, and so on, were rampant diseases. The houses were but heather-covered hovels, and even in the year 1811, their low roofs were constructed of tree branches and sods, rotten straw or ferns.* Topham, the traveller, refers to the "extreme ugliness of the lower orders," and writes that "temperance and labour are in the extreme, yet instead of ruddy cheeks, sprightly faces, and graceful figures, we find haggard looks, meagre complexions, and bodies weakened by fatigue, and worn down by the inclemency of the season" ; and the letters of Robert Burns are full of vehement protests against the cruel conditions endured by the working class —"nerves," he said, "sinews, health, strength, wisdom, experience, genius, nay, a good part of their very thought, sold for months and years, not only to the necessities, the conveniences, but the caprices of the important few."† Everywhere around him Burns saw terrible oppression, feudal dues still being exacted down in Nithsdale, the laird exacting his multures though there were no baronial mills at which to grind the corn ; everywhere the poor, like Burns' own father, forced to "thole the factor's snash," while the "laird gets in his rackit rents, his coal, his kain and a' his stents." Our great democratic singer had no illusions about landlordism. He and his "toiled with the ceaseless toil of galley slaves," and lived amid "nakedness and hunger and poverty and want," that parasitical lairds should be not only well fed and well clad, but should have a plenitude of counters for their midnight gamblings with" the devil's pictured beuks."

But by the beginning of the nineteenth century the old uncurbed

---

Principal Macfarlane's General View of Agriculture in Dumbartonshire (1811). So shameful were the housing conditions in the Hebrides that one-third of the children born died ere reaching the age of twelve.—*Scotland : Social and Domestic*, Rogers, i., 52

†Letter to Mrs. Dunlop

untrammelled power of the barons had gone, and each generation of men had seen fresh economic forces making onslaughts at its remaining citadels, and wider social ideals sapping and undermining its foundations. Printing had spread knowledge and made for democracy : gunpowder had equalised chances in warfare and had rendered pregnable every feudal keep and stronghold ; the reformation had sent rumbling through every hamlet the stern challenges of the old Hebrew prophets ; the struggles for the Covenant had popularised the psalms and smashed the divine right of kings ; trade, commerce, a nascent capitalism, and the necessities of centralised government had, between them, gradually eased off one baronial due, commuted another for cash, and absorbed, transformed, or adapted a third ; franchise campaigns, agitations for repeal of the Corn Laws, railway developments, postal service, a cheap press—each and all of them have contributed to the transformation and to the partial crippling of the baron's power. Even in its decline what a wonderful all-embracing sweep it possessed ! How it penetrated everywhere, kneading itself so thoroughly into our social habits that still to this day none of us may live without its reckoning. As late as 1884 the Crofters' Commission discovered men and women in Skye who were giving an annual ten days' free labour to the laird, buying hooks from him to cut his corn, liable to instantaneous eviction, having their rents doubled between terms ; and to this very day the new superior on his entry to the estate may, and sometimes does, claim one year's rent not only of the land, but of the property built on the land. The late Lady Howard de Walden called up no less a sum than £40,000 from Kilmarnock at one sweep, a proceeding characterised by the then Town Clerk as "an exorbitant levy of blackmail " ; and the Town Clerk of Dumfries, in his evidence before the Select Committee of the House of Commons on Feus and Leases (Scotland), 1893, declared that the factor for Lord Herries "said or did nothing till buildings were up and then made a pounce for the value of the buildings as well as the value of the land."* In the year 1910 the Earl of Galloway imposed a similar exaction on the feuars on his estates. Casualties of Superiority, duplicands of feu duty every 19 years, and a whole mesh and net work of feudal exaction, still surround us, an ever-present reminder that the baronial old man of the sea is yet astraddle our backs. Every cottage owner pays direct his feu (feudal) duty ; every tenement dweller pays it through his rent ; every bag of coals, every ship's plate, every house rafter, every stone on a wall, every tumbler of water still pays baronial tax. Nothing escapes—neither the sunshine in the alley, nor the boots on our feet, nor the food we eat ; every-

---

*Select Committee on Feus and Leases (Scotland), 1893. Evidence and Report, pp. 1-17.

where the all-encircling arm of the feudal baron! It is still on statute that the holder of a barony may pursue at his own court for feu-duties and rents, and have jurisdiction in civil actions up to 40s.* Even yet the House of Lords may paralyse legislation for two years.

In parish kirk and in public ceremonial, in his assessments and his taxes, in his privileges and his monopolies, the feudal baron still offers himself as an insult and a challenge to Democracy.

---

*The Court Book of the Barony of Urie—Barron, xvii.

CHAPTER III.

EARLY LABOUR LEGISLATION.

"The social legislation of the Puritan period in Scotland reveals in that legislation all through a noteworthy and unexpected indifference to individual liberty, and the circumstance is the more curious because it is almost as much out of accord with the social legislation of the corresponding period in England as it is with the spirit of our own time . . . in Scotland restraints on the migration of work-people only began to come into being for the first time after the Reformation.—*The Edinburgh Review*, January, 1899.

THE immediate result of the Reformation was economic disaster for the working-class. The barons had seized practically supreme power in the State, absorbed the Church lands and Church wealth, which was reckoned to be one-third or one-half of the total wealth of Scotland : sneered at the Protestant clergy's demands that a portion of the estate of the old Church should be devoted to the poor and to the expenses of education, and had turned the old Church pensioners and employees adrift as "masterless men." Beggars, vagrants, and vagabonds of all descriptions swarmed in bands up and down the country : the rags of misery flapped everywhere. To meet this situation, John Knox and the Reformers proposed that the idle poor should be set to work, under disciplinary conditions, a proposal that the barons, who were becoming increasingly interested in industrial enterprises, regarded with great favour, since it provided them with a pretext for the forcible acquisition of cheap labour. Every kirk session was poor, the stout and sturdy beggars were a perpetual source of worry and trouble, and no legislation likely to remove vagrancy would be received with anything but gratitude. So we find in the years immediately succeeding the Reformation a series of enactments preventing labourers from bettering their position by migrating to other districts, the entire population of gypsies, sorners, vagrants, and genuine unemployed cast into prolonged or perpetual slavery to such private employers as should choose to take them ; wages' rates limited by statute ; workers in mines and in salt pans, with their wives and children, reduced to a slavery not unlike that endured by the medieval serf ; and social and religious reformers, unemployed, "disagreeable persons" of all sorts, sold to colonists in the plantations beyond the seas as "Christian servants."

In July, 1606, an Act was passed forbidding salters, colliers and coal-bearers to leave their employment without their master's permission ; "no person within the realm hereafter shall fee, hire, or conduce any saltaris, coalyearis, or coal-beararis without a sufficient testimonial" from their previous employer ; employers are given permission to apprehend "all vagabonds" and "sturdy beggars to be put to labour" ; any employer who takes a collier or salter without a testimonial is held liable to a fine of £1000 Scots, whilst the workman, if he has taken "forewages and fees" from his new employer, is to be esteemed a thief and punished in his body. In September, 1607, the Act was extended to metal mines,* and it is interesting to observe that the King's Advocate, one of the leading members of the Privy Council, had a month previously taken a lease of the Hillderstane silver mines.† In 1641 commissioners were appointed to look after the new manufacturing monopolies which were being granted, and we find that one of the first edicts in industrial legislation is that no one is to hire, receive, or entertain any of the "servants of the said works without the consent of the masters thereof." In 1644 a statute ordains that "all hired servants" are to serve their masters from "this present upon the same conditions as they have done formerly and not to remove nor leave their masters" without consent in writing, under a penalty of £50 Scots. Here we have the Scots equivalent of the English statute of labourers ; not only was the worker tied to his master, but he was forbidden by the law of the land to seek or receive increased wages or more favourable conditions of employment. During the Cromwellian "Commonwealth," although no fresh industrial slavery regulations appear to have been issued, 2000 Scots were sent to the plantations in America and the West Indies.‡ For the twenty years about 1673 "notorious vagabonds" were shipped off in big numbers, and entire "cargoes" of "Christian servants" were sent to the Barbadoes. Between 1648 and 1651, says Professor Firth, "at least 40,000 of her (Scotland's) hardiest sons had been either slain or swept into captivity" ; in two years alone, 10,000 Scots were emigrated to Ireland, though there were many "Yrish beggars" still on our highways ;§ in September, 1685, 100 captives were shipped for New Jersey, but fever breaking out on board ship, only 40 survived the voyage, a tragedy little to be marvelled at since "much of the flesh which the captain of the ship had provided for the prisoners began to stink before they sailed out of Leith Road, and in a few days it was not eatable . . . . And so Pitlochrie (the grantee) enjoyed nothing of

---

*Register of Privy Council, vii., 434.

†Edinburgh Review, January, 1899.

‡"Scottish Trade with the Plantations before 1707."—Scot. Hist. Review, vol. 6.

§Scot. Hist. Review, vol. 4.

the produce of near an hundred prisoners gifted him by the Council "*
In 1661, immediately after the "Commonwealth," the disabilities
already imposed upon colliers and salters were extended to "water-
men who laves and drawes water on the coalheugheid and gatesmen
who work the wayes and ports and windsmen," and the reason
given for this extension is stated frankly : because these workers are
"as necessar to the owners and masters of the said coalheughs as the
coal-hewers." In the same year it is again declared illegal to
"intyse, resset, or intertaine," the servants or the apprentices of the
manufacturers without written permission. The manufacturers,
besides the privilege of cheap labour and a monopoly of trade, were
declared exempt from taxation. Everybody who had "influence"
got a monopoly—soap at Leith, cloth at Haddington, sugar refining
at Greenock ; and even the Greenland fishing was restricted to a
"patentee " ; the industrial system had begun.

In 1621 the agricultural labourers had been specifically swept
into the net. The poor labourers of the ground (*i.e.*, the farmers)
suffer greatly by "the fraud and malice of servants," who either
refuse to be hired "without great and extraordinary wages," or hire
themselves only from Martinmas to Whitsunday, after which they
immediately set off for "their gain and advantage " to take high-
priced seasonable jobs at mowing, reaping, or turf-cutting. This
naturally did not suit the farmers, so it was declared illegal for a
farm servant to leave at Whitsunday, unless he could prove to the
satisfaction of a local Justice that he had already secured permanent
employment elsewhere. If he could not prove this he must continue
working in the summer at the winter rate of wages.

But if the condition of the employed was bad, that of the unemployed was infinitely worse. Everywhere landowners were finding
it profitable to raise sheep for export and to supply the wool market
market at home ; and this change to sheep-farming "makes its
appearance just, as in England, in the growth of enclosures, with the
same effect of dislocation of labour."† The landowner, too, was
thinning out his retinue and cutting down unnecessary expenses in
every direction, for there was no longer profit in a large private
bodyguard or army, and every possible penny of capital was required
for investment either in some infant industry yielding large profits
at home or in some Darien scheme abroad. And so, faster than the
manufacturers could seize them, grew the numbers of the unemployed
Thirty years after the Reformation, it is estimated they amounted
to one-tenth of the total population ; and, to accentuate the misery,
famines were frequent. Chambers, in his "Domestic Annals,"
gives 1586 as a "famine and death year " ; 1595, as a famine year ;

---

*Woodrow : *History of the Sufferings of the Church of Scotland,* ii., 566.
†*Labour in Scotland in the Seventeenth Century*—E. A. Horne, St. Andrews, 1905.

1598, a year of starvation; 1600, starvation, and the King himself forced to beg for supplies of food for a royal baptismal function; 1612, a year of scarcity; 1623 a year of great famine, with deaths from hunger; and Calderwood, in his "History of the Kirk of Scotland," describes the year 1624 as one of dearth and famine, "and money poor anes are dying and starving at dykes and under stairs for cauld and hunger."

As far back as 1424 there had been vagrancy laws* defining what persons should be given tokens permitting them to beg, and ordaining the retribution which should fall on the sorners who, being able-bodied, refused to work. Beggars were licensed between the ages of 14 and 70, and those caught begging without a license were ordered "to pass to crafts for winning of their living, under pain of burning on the cheek and being banished the country." In 1449, we read, "sornars, overlyars and masterful beggars" are to be imprisoned "as long as they have any goods of their own to live upon," after the which, "their ears are to be nailed to the trone or to any other tree and then cut off, and themselves banished the country," and "gif hereafter they be found again, that they be hangit." In 1457, "bards and feigned fools, and sic like runners about" are added to the list of itinerant oppressors decerned against; and in 1503 it was ordered that none be given a beggars' token or permission to solicit alms except "crukit folk, blind folk, impotent folk and waik folk"; and in 1535 this privilege of begging was limited to the birth parish of the token-holder. There was no provision whatever in Scots law for the relief of the able-bodied poor, though previous to the Reformation at least the care of the "poor indeed," the crooked, blind, impotent, and weak folk was theoretically one of the liens on the revenue of the Church,† and it is not improbable that many of the able-bodied when in desperate straits presented their aumous dishes at the Church doors and were not turned empty away. In 1574 strong beggars after conviction were to be scourged and burned through the gristle of the right ear with a hot iron about an inch in compass; for the second offence they were to suffer death as thieves.‡

The first real Scots Poor Law, in 1579, caught up and consolidated all the legislation of the previous 150 years, and ordained that a convicted vagrant might have his usual sentence of stripes or ear-burning commuted to a year's service to any private employer who would take him; his children, between the ages of five and fourteen, might be seized by anyone and "held at work" without wages— the boys until they were twenty-four and the girls until they were

---

* "History of the Scots Poor Laws prior to 1845."—Memorandum by late Prof. Smart to Poor Law Commission Report, 1909, pp. 289-314.

† Prof. Smart, *Ibid*, p. 292.

‡ *Acta Parl. Scot.*, iii., 87a, 140a.

eighteen. In 1597 the administration of this Act was handed over
to the kirk sessions, and in the towns to the magistrates, and the
servitute of the convicted tramp and his children was increased to
their entire life-times. The kirk sessions, to their credit be it said,
seem to have been unwilling to undertake the disagreeable task—
perhaps in some districts they were unable to find employers seeking
slave labour—and they seem generally to have contented themselves
with appointing a "Bedill" whose duty it was to push the vagrant
poor outside the parish boundary. This policy, of course, did not
improve matters any ; and Parliament, in 1600,* complains that
strong and idle beggars "ar sufferit to vaig and wander throuchout
the haill cuntrey," and calls upon the presbyteries to compel the
kirk sessions to fulfil the letter of the law. Still the kirk sessions
were obdurate, and latterly, in June, 1605, the employers of labour
themselves were empowered to pick their own employees from the
swarms on the highway. "All maisterfull and strong beggaris,"
says the statute, "may be tane by any man, ard being broght to
any sheref, bailyie of regalitie or burgh; and gettend thame declarit
maisterfull beggaris, may set his burning irne upon thame and reteane
thame as slaves, and gif ony of thame thairefter escaipe the awner
may have repetition of thame as of uther gudes."† Thirteen protestant prelates, it may be said, were privy to this Act‡ In the
succeeding year (1606) coalmasters and salt-pan owners are given
powers to lift what labourers they choose from the highway, without
even the necessity of haling them before a magistrate. In 1607 the
owners or lessees of metal works are given similar powers, and special
Acts are passed occasionally granting specified individuals—*e.g.*,
Sir James Hope, in 1649 and 1661, for his mines in the Leadhills—
powers which vary little, if at all, from those granted generally in
the Acts of 1605 and 1606. In 1617 the children of the indigent,
that is, the poor,were legislated for, after the same manner (though,
with considerably more sympathy) as in the enactments already in
force for dealing with the children of tramps. If the indigent child
were under fourteen years of age and the parent or guardian consented
or if over fourteen with his or her own consent, the kirk session in
landward parishes and the magistrates in burghs could bind him or
her over to any individual who would accept the charge until the age
of 30 was reached. Until that age the child was the master's property, working for him, subject to his discipline, barring torture and
death. The practice of contracting out poor children lasted down
to our own day. In the early years of the nineteenth century the
pauper children of Edinburgh were being dispatched to David

---

*Act 1600, c. 28.

†*Reg. Privy Council,* vii., 56.

‡*Edinburgh Review,* January, 1899.

Dale's cotton mills in Lanarkshire, where they slaved from 6 a.m. to 6 p.m.,* and all over Scotland the master handloom weavers were indebted to the Poor Law authorities for a supply of cheap child labour. In 1843 the Governors of the Town's Hospital of Glasgow were indenturing out their poor girls for 5 years, to, as the indenture form says, "serve and obey." For each day absent or unable to work the child became indebted to the master in the sum of one shilling and if, as always, unable to pay this fine, two days were added to the duration of "apprenticeship." These "absent days shall be liquidated and proved by the master's word or oath if required, in place of all other proof." For the first four years no wages were given, but on the fifth year 10 per cent. of the "earnings" were allowed, and on the expiry of the servitude "a new suit of clothes" was provided.

To the Act of 1617 can probably be traced the custom by which the colliers and the workers at the salt pans "arled" or bound their children for life to the slavery in which they themselves existed.† By the law of Scotland, every child was born free, but under the 1617 Act the indigent collier could bind over his child at the baptismal ceremony to his master, by accepting "arles" or earnest money. Legally, of course, the child was only bound until he was 30 years of age, but as when he was 30 he was held to have served a year and a day, and had thus automatically bound himself, the slavery in the pits had become practically hereditary. It was still, of course, in the option of the collier to refuse to bind his child, but the pressure of his employer, his own degraded environment and upbringing, and the fact that servitude to some employer was the common lot of the working-class, probably accounts for no recorded instance of parental refusal to "arle" away the freedom of a child.

In 1621 an Act was passed, extending the privilege, already granted to mineowners, to apprehend labour wherever they chose, to all other employers, and power was given "the justices and constables" to "force and compel all loose men and women to serve for competent hire and wages." Again, in 1641, we find Parliament‡ ordaining that "maisterless men" must labour at "reasonable rates," and commissioners are appointed to fix the money meaning of the term "reasonable." By the law of 1649 (c 161) any British subject could capture Scottish vagrants and could "dispose of thame to be employed be others in wark for their meat and cloth allanerly

---

*Graham's *Social Life in Scotland*, p. 268.

†Children's Employment Commission, 1842, Appendix to Report, i., 386.

‡Act of 1641, c. 100. No coalmaster was allowed to pay his collier more than £1 2s. 6d. sterling yearly, and the men must work 6 days a week or be fined 20s., and be subject to corporal punishment at the coalowner's pleasure. The thumbscrews or pilliwinks was one form of punishment.

(only)." This seems perilously near chattel-slavery again. After
the failure of Montrose's rebellion, in 1650, eighteen of his followers
were "reserved" for slavery, six being given to General Leslie,
probably in recognition of his military prowess ; six to the great
"Protestant martyr," the Duke of Argyll ; and six, being "lusty
fellows," to Sir James Hope for his lead mines. Leslie and Argyll
were at this period both coal, and consequently slave, owners. During the Thirty Years' War, "thousands" of vagrants were sent by
Privy Council warrant to shed their beggar blood for the King of
Denmark or Gustavus Adolphus, and under the Commonwealth, as
we have already stated, the export of "Christian servants" to the
plantations was a regular practice—a practice systematically
pursued by the Restoration Parliament.* The Restoration Parliament indeed went a step farther in aid of its "friends" ; not only
did it permit the wholesale enslavement of the unemployed, but it
actually decreed that the slave-owners were to be paid a gratuity for
enslaving them. On December 23rd, 1662, for example, the Privy
Council passed an Act granting the Earl of Eglinton, who was
alleged to have suffered much under the Puritan *regime* for his
Royalist principles, the exclusive privilege of arresting the vagrants
and the temporarlily unemployed in the counties of Galloway, Ayr
and Renfrew, and setting them to work in his wool factory, which
he had established in the old citadel of Ayr, obligingly granted to
him as part recognition of his valuable services to the king. The
vagrants he was to have for fifteen years, and the "persons out of
service and masterless for the time," and those who, "albeit they
beg not," who "have no trade, stock, or visible lawful way to maintain themselves," he was to have for five years. They are to work
for their meat and clothing only, and the Earl is to receive from the
heritors of the parishes in which his slaves were born a certain
specified monthly sum towards his expenses. In the succeeding
year other shires were thrown open on similar terms to other manufacturers, but a magistrate's concurrence must be secured and the
heritors have to pay for four years only—two shillings Scots† per
day for the first year‡ and one shilling Scots per day for the succeeding three years. The term of slavery is made eleven years for
vagrant and unemployed alike. Whatever befell these organised
slave-labour factories we do not know, but Lord Eglinton's effort
does not seem to have been a financial success, for the citadel was
sold in 1687 to a brewery syndicate, and the Archbishop of Glasgow
had previously been compelled to request his lordship to do something

---

*Chambers' *Dom. Annals*, ii., 211-2 ; iii., 304 ; also Fountainhall's *Decisions*
 (Bannatyne Club), pp. 495-6, 586.
†One Shilling Scots was equivalent to one penny sterling.
‡See *The Muniments of the Royal Burgh of Irvine*, ii., 92.

with "the many very loose and dissolute persons employed in your lordship's manufactory whose conversation is very scandalous."

In 1672, correction houses, following the English workhouse model, are called by Parliament for every county town, but the expense was too considerable and the demand (and others which followed it) went unheeded. Glasgow and Edinburgh, however, had already "correction houses" packed with "vagabonds, idle beggars, whores, thieves, and masterless persons," and when the surplusage grew overwhelming, gangs were despatched to the open arms of the colonial governors.

In 1698, after the "Glorious Revolution of King William," the manufacturers were empowered to retain their child captives not for eleven years only, as allowed by the Act of 1663, but until the age of 30 was reached. The only difference then between the factory slave child and the mining slave child was that the one could get free at the age of 30 and the other could not, but remained perpetually bound. Still the vagrants and the unemployed swarmed everywhere, and in 1698 Fletcher of Saltoun estimated their number at 200,000 (in a total population of a million and a half), and, in despair, saw no other remedy but compulsory slave owning by every family in the country, the number of slaves to increase with the family income—a sort of early form of graduated income accession—and a sale of the remainder "to the gallies or West Indies."*

Occasionally, too, the criminal escaped hanging, when there was a neighbouring employer of labour in need of another slave "hand." On the 5th of December, 1701, for example, the Commissioners of Justiciary for securing the peace of the Highlands handed over convicted thieves as perpetual and unrestricted slaves—one to the Earl of Tullibardine, and one to Sir John Erskine of Alva—and ordered brass, iron, or copper collars to be rivetted round their necks. The collar of Sir John Erskine's slave bearing the inscription, "Alexander Steuart, found guilty of death for theft at Perth, the 5th of December, 1701, and gifted as a perpetual servant to Sir John Areskin of Alva," was dragged up in a fishing net many years afterwards in the Firth of Forth, and now lies in the Scottish Antiquarian Museum. Mr. Chambers offers the speculation that the poor fellow may have drowned himself to escape the tortures and the misery of his servitude.† Again, in his "Memorials of Alloa" (p. 99), Mr. Crawford mentions a local tradition concerning two criminals who, about the beginning of the eighteenth century, were sentenced to a similar servitude, one of them said to have been fixed in the Duke of Atholl's colliery at Blairingow and the other in a colliery belonging to the Earl of Mar. Towards the end of the seventeenth

---

Second Discourse.

†*Dom. Ann.*, iii., 246.

century an attempt seems to have been made by the fishing masters to secure their men in perpetual slavery, but the proposal, as we learn briefly from Fountainhall,* was condemned as contrary to Christian practice and the mildness of our Government !—a strange observation, surely, when one considers the practice of the Christian employers and the mildness of the Government in other trades and industries.

That all these assaults on the fundamental principles of human liberty should have taken place in an age dominated by an ethic which expressed itself in the phrase that "all men are equal in the sight of God," appears at first sight inexplicable ; but if reference is made to our remarks upon the Reformation it will be seen that from the beginning of the seventeenth century the barons had usurped practically supreme power in the State, without having been infected in any way with the democratic or semi-democratic notions of the popular preachers ; and in the infant industries and factories which were everywhere springing up it was not likely that they would leave unused any possible legislative weapon by which they could control an unlimited supply of cheap labour. On the other hand, the doctrines of the preachers and their disciplinary tendencies played into the hands of the barons. *The First Book of Discipline,* a scheme of ecclesiastical government and social guidance drawn up by John Knox and other ministers, and intended as a necessary corollary to the Confession of Faith, was, says Knox's biographer, Mr. Taylor Innes, even, on the Church side, somewhat too despotic ; it transplanted from Geneva certain rigid ideas of discipline and regulation, and it endeavoured to fix and define the everyday details of individual life with bureaucratic rigidity and harshness. Doubtless the intention of the Divines was laudable enough ; all men were to be swept into the bosom of the universal kirk, and their place therein apportioned ; those not able to work, "the poor indeed," were to be supported, and the idle and vicious were to be compelled to work ; but these very desirable principles were seized upon by the commercial barons and utilised as pretexts for the acquisition of that semi-servile and wholly unpaid labour we have just described.

---

*Diary, 16th February, 1698.

CHAPTER IV.

THE FORCED LABOURERS.

"The experience of all ages and nations, I believe, demonstrates that the work done by slaves, though it appears to cost only their maintenance, is, in the end, the dearest of any."—*Adam Smith* : "*The Wealth of Nations*," iii., 2.

"When I was a lad in charge of my uncle, the Priest of Dunipace, one proverb more precious than all the riches of the world, he taught me, which has ever lived in my memory :—

> *Dico tibi verum ; Libertas optima rerum.*
> *Nunquam servili sub nexu, vivito fili !* "
>> My son, I tell thee soothfastlie
>> No gift is like to liberty.
>> Then never live in slaverie !
>>> —*John of Fordun.*
>>> (Words attributed to Sir William Wallace.)

WE have seen how the legislation of the seventeenth century compassed the enslavement of large masses of the working-class, in the interest, as the early baronial capitalists hoped, of low wages, or indeed of no wages at all, and as the preachers hoped, to the end that the parasitic predatory swarms of vagabonds who infested the highways would be converted into disciplined, God-fearing, respectable producers of wealth. We shall now endeavour to pick up such traces as we can of the life these poor forced labourers were compelled to live, and see how the fond hopes of both barons and preachers were destroyed, inasmuch as the slavery resulted on the one hand in the raising of wages to such an exorbitant figure as compelled the masters themselves to demand the freedom of their slaves, and on the other hand created an outcast and degraded class, more hopeless and more degenerate, if that were possible, than the old road vagrants had been.

Fletcher of Saltoun, in his *Second Discourse* (1698), writing after a national experience of three-quarters of a century of slavery legislation, sees, despite that legislation, the unemployed still increasing, and can only suggest that the slavery net be farther spread and the meshes narrowed to prevent escape; he tells us that "so long as the one half of our country, in extent of ground, is possessed by a people who are all gentlemen only because they will not work, and who, in everything, are more contemptible than the vilest slaves, except that they always carry arms, because for the most part they live upon robbery," permanent betterment of social conditions is impossible. Yet some-

F

thing must speedily be done ; in ordinary times, declared Fletcher, we have 100,000 outcasts ; to-day, as a result of the extraordinary distress caused by "the seven ill years," 1693-1699 (when, through cold Springs and wet Autumns, food prices rose to an enormous figure, and entire parishes in Aberdeenshire were depopulated),* there are two hundred thousand people "begging from door to door." half of them living

> without any regard or subjection, either to the laws of the land or even those of God and Nature ; fathers incestuously accompanying with their own daughters, the son with the mother, and the brother with the sister. No magistrate could ever discover or be informed which way one in a hundred of these wretches died, or that ever they were baptised. Many murders have been discovered among them ; and they are not only a most unspeakable oppression to poor tenants (who, if they give not bread or some kind of provision to perhaps forty such villains in one day, are sure to be insulted by them), but they rob many people who live in houses distant from any neighbourhood."

Fletcher's remedy for this sad state of affairs, caused partly, be it noted, by the economic consequences which flowed from the policy pursued by the barons after the Reformation of the old Church, was that vagabond children should be taken by every man of estate so that he may "have a little manufacture at home" which might "bring great profit to the master." Yet so amazingly proud were these vagabonds and so desperately hostile to "that which they will be sure to call slavery, that unless prevented by the utmost industry and diligence, upon the first publication of any orders necessary for putting in execution such a design, they will rather die with hunger in caves and dens, and murder their young children, than appear abroad to have them and themselves taken into such a kind of service." So "for example and terror three or four hundred of the most notorious of these villains, which we call jockies, might be presented by the Government to the State of Venice, to serve in their gallies against the common enemy of Christendom." These proposals were made a century after the Reformation, and made withal by a man who was a Radical reformer and who in his way was a humane and far-seeing patriot, and who grudged "himself every delicate morsel he put in his mouth when he considered that so many were dead and so many more struggling at that minute with death" ; he suggested strict conditions against the ill-treatment of the slaves ; they were to be provided with clothes, diet and lodging, taught the principles of morality and religion, forbidden to work on Sunday, taught to read, and allowed to go to Church, provided with hospitals for their old age ; but his were proposals for the farther enslavement of the people and the farther enrichment of "men of estate," and it requires no extraordinary stretch of the imagination to reconstruct the contemptuous attitude adopted

---

Stat. Acc. of Scot.—Aberdeenshire.

towards the safeguarding conditions by the "men of estate," whenever the Laird of Saltoun's slavery extension proposals received the
sanction of law. From the year 1579, as we have already shewn,
ordinances imposing servile labour on the people had been of frequent occurrence; but we have here quoted Fletcher's *Discourse*
to shew that the mass of the people, after an hundred years of it,
regarded such labour with abhorrence, and indeed would "rather
die with hunger" than submit to its degrading shackles. Modern
apologists for the ruling castes in post-Reformation and neo-capitalist
times may descant as they will upon the re-birth of learning, and
upon the industrial and commercial developments of the seventeenth
century; but it is impossible to disguise the fact that the period
was one of extreme misery and degradation for the working-class—
a misery and a degradation so severe and so humiliating that the
working-class refused to be a working-class, preferring the greater
part of it, a life of vagrancy and theft.

Yet not only were the early Scots capitalists thus legally supplied
with an unlimited area of servile labour, their infant industries
were safeguarded by high tariffs; in the home market their monopoly was legally protected, and in some instances the old Craft
Guilds were abolished in their favour. The grantees of the linen
monopoly, for example, secured the legal destruction of the Weavers'
Craft Guild; they had arbitrary powers over their employees, made
their own laws, and fixed bodily punishments for insubordinate
or rebellious workmen. In 1686 they secured the passage of an Act
of Parliament which decreed that all Scots corpses must be buried in
Scots linen, and this Act was only rescinded in 1707, when the wool
interest convinced the legislature that it was more fitting that Scots
corpses should be clad in woollen garments.* At the Newmills
monopoly in Haddingtonshire a prison was erected inside the
factory, and chronic insubordinates were dismissed from the neighbourhood lest they should "debouch" others;† petty thieves were
kept in prison "till the mercat day, and thar to stand in time of the
mercat, two hours, with a paper mentioning their fault in great
letters"; workers who ran away (some appear to have run to the
manufactory at Hamilton, possibly because of better conditions
there!) were brought forcibly back. Desertions seem to have been
common, and the Newmills directors are continually recording
their anxiety to secure men "that we need not fear the running
away"; they offered wages—women and boys 1s. 10d. sterling per
week and men about 4s. sterling per week—but the wages appear
to have been insufficient to provide more than the bare necessaries

---

Acta Parl. Scot., c. 94, 1707.
†*Records of a Scots Cloth Manufactory at New Mills, Haddingtonshire*—W. R.
  Scott, vol. xlvi. of Publications of Scot. Hist. Socy.

of life, for we find in the same records that the factory master was allowed 2s. sterling per week for the boarding of each apprentice. In 1686 the directors fixed a minimum rate of wages, evidently reducing the previous rates. This particular factory seems to have employed about 700 workmen, some skilled foreign mechanics, a few of whom, we read, "would not obey orders but incited the others to quarrels, and it became necessary to ask the co-operation of the Provost of Haddington to have two discharged men removed from the district." The company enjoyed a rigid monopoly, any person in Scotland found in possession of English-made cloth being compelled to hand it over to the hangman to be publicly burned; it was exempt from taxation and from import and export duties, and it secured the contract for providing the military with uniforms—a contract designed, as the Act of the Privy Council rather naively puts it, "to distinguish sogers from other skulking and vagrant persons."* Little wonder, is it, that the shareholders received dividends upon their capital amounting to 67 per cent. in 7 years ?

In most of the other monopolies, conditions were similar, and the monopolists were as similarly driven to gradually change the basis of their worker's remuneration from "meat and clothing only" to fixed money wages. The harsher the conditions of toil and the smaller the money wages, the greater was the difficulty experienced by the capitalists in retaining their slave workmen. Major Lun, who had secured the monopoly for the manufacture of needles, complains, in 1661, that his apprentice boys run away no matter howsoever he may pun sh them. The white paper monopolists who engaged themselves in a bitter struggle with the candlemakers for the country's rags, and who signalled their success by reducing "the wages of the rag pickers,"† were forced ultimately to raise again the wages of their employees. Soap monopolists (against whose exactions there was loud public clamour from 1619 to 1623‡), gunpowder monopolists, Greenland fishing monopolists, ropework monopolists, wool factory monopolists (William Black, advocate, got powers to tax Aberdeenshire £1000 for each of 5 years "for support of apprentices to learn the trade at his factory "), "worsett " monopolists—all sought cheap pauper labour, and all were forced, despite the repeated activities of Parliament on their behalf, to pay continually increasing money wages. In 1632, a Scottish fishing monopoly was created,§ among the chief purposes of the creation being, as the preamble assures us, to accustom "lazie and ydle people to work "; and the governors were given power to ordain

*Chambers' *Dom. Ann.*, ii., 419.
†*Scot. Hist. Review*, v. 3, p. 75.
‡M'Intosh : *Hist. Civ. Scot.*, v. 3, p. 314.
§*Acta Parl. Scot.*, vol. 5, p. 239.

"statuts, lawes and ordinances whatsomever concerning thair
attendants, servants, fishers, mariners, maisters of shippes, thair
factors and others attending the fisher trade." The "four or more"
permanent judges whom the governors were empowered to appoint
for the administration of "justice" to insubordinate workmen,
could "make, establishe and promulgate temporarie lawes," and
could order the infliction of "panes als weill pecuniarie as of imprisonment." From the decisions of these judges there was no appeal to
the ordinary tolbooths or courts; and the administration of the
law at sea, or rather the holding of "pleyes" between the fishermen
and the monopolists, was placed in the hands of judges-depute who
were selected during the voyage by "the maisters and merchants
themselffes or their prin[ll] factors." In other words, the entire
control of the lives and liberties of the fishermen of Scotland, with
the exception of a few fishermen who worked in certain specified
waters, was placed in the hands of the directors of the Fishing Company. The monopoly appears to have been extinguished in 1690,
but not because, as Fountainhall would have it, that our free institutions abhorred slavery. The Fishing Company came directly into
conflict with many of the Highland proprietors, and disputes regarding
vassals and local landowning privileges were of common occurrence;
and at the earliest possible moment the riparian proprietors would
seek the abrogation of a monopoly charter which allowed alien
capitalists to plunder their waters. Again, as in other industries, it
was discovered that servile labour was costly labour, so in fishing it
was seen that more willing work and better results could be secured
by giving the fishermen at least a nominal freedom. And the freedom they received was in truth but nominal, for after 1690 they were
plundered right and left, and the net result of their freedom was
probably that they were worse off than they had been under the
monopoly. On the east coast the fishermen were subject to an
impost, called size duty, which was the money equivalent of an ancient
privilege of the Crown, whereby a certain proportion of the herring
taken by every boat had to be set aside "for the service of the king's
kitchen"; and on the west coast, in addition to this size duty,
which is said to have amounted to 16s. 8d. per boat, whether the
fishing was a failure or not,* the landlords exacted as a feudal due
"one night's fishing in the week." A note was kept of the results of
each night's catch, and at the end of the week the landlord seized
"the produce of the night that yielded the largest quantity."

In all the industries demanding a certain skill and willing application from the workers, forced labour was of short duration. The
vagabonds from the roads could not be disciplined; their "conversation was very scandalous"; bodily punishments failed to make

---

*Bremner's *Industries of Scotland*, p. 516.

them mechanics; they mutinied, rioted and ran away; and the employers quickly discovered that the erection and up-keep of tolbooths and prisons inside their works, where dozens of their mutinous and insubordinate employees were "punished" by being kept in idleness, was a costly drag upon their infant industries. Bribes, in the shape of wages, had therefore to be offered; and repeated pressure from a Parliament intent on solving the unemployment question by forcing the vagabonds to work without wages for the monopolist manufacturers was carefully disregarded by the manufacturers themselves. But in two industries, requiring a large supply of unskilled labour, the form of slavery we have been considering took root and flourished for well nigh two hundred years. In early times, landowners had worked their mines with their own estate labourers; but with the development of manufactures and with the increased demand for coal, there arose a large demand for outside labour, and fees and bounty-money were freely offered to induce fresh labour to the coalheughs. But by the year 1592 the coalowners seem to have resorted to conscriptory methods of securing labour, for an Act of Parliament of that date refers to the "ungodly persons" who, for "revenge and spite" were setting fire to the coal-heughs;* and we have a record† of the trial and execution of one, John Henry of Little Fawside, who had set alight the heugh belonging to Mungo M'Call. John had been a common working miner, who had lost his "liberty and commandment" and had conceived "ane deidly rancour and evill will" therefor against his master. And by an Act of 1606, whatever of slavery had crept into mining, was definitely crystallised and legalised. Colliers and salters were declared to be "necessary servants," who, without any paction, and merely by coming and taking work in any coal-heugh or at any salt-pan, were declared serfs for life, while their children were bound to the same servitude on the parents accepting arles or earnest-money on their behalf. This acceptance of arles usually took place at the baptism of the child, but later on it seems that the child was bound for life, even if not arled, by the mere fact of assisting its father at his work. No miner was to be employed without production of a permit from his last employer; runaways could be reclaimed within a year and a day; coalowners and their agents were to be fined for "intromitting with" colliers bound by another master; and the owners of coal mines and salt-pans were given the usual powers to apprehend vagabonds and set them to work. The servitude so legalised was perpetual, the collier being bound for life. And another Act in 1614 granted the owners additional powers. They could fine and punish their workers at

---

Acta Parl. Scot., iii., p. 575 (1592).

†Pitcairn—*Criminal Trials*, iii., p. 361.

will ; they could withhold wages, sequestrate goods, suspend from employment, and punish "in their personis, by scourging, laying in the stockis, or lang imprisonment."* Still it is evident that the coalowners, like the other employers, early discovered the heavy costs of servile labour, for when the Privy Council in 1621 fixed the price of coal at 7s. Scots per load—a price which seems to have been a considerable reduction on the prices previously obtaining—the owners were mightily offended, declaring that their working costs were increasing owing to the demands of the "base fellows" whom they employed. The Privy Council hearkened to the owners' plea, and obligingly raised the price to 7s. 8d. per load. From an Act of 1641† we learn that the colliers had been in the habit of taking holidays at "Pasche, Yoole, and Witsonday," a practice which the Act condemned as "to the great offence of God and prejudice of their maisteris." Holidays were therefore abolished and a compulsory six-days' working week instituted, with a penalty for non-observance of "twentie shillings for everie day" misused as a holiday. The customary "punishment for thaire bodies" was added as an additional deterrent ; and the Act extended serfdom to all workers employed "about" coal heughs or salt-pans.

It must not be supposed, however, that all this repressive legislation was accepted without protest from the coalminers. In 1661 Sir Ludovic Stewart of Minto was forced to petition the Privy Council that the magistrates of the Royal Burgh of Rutherglen be "authorised to compel the colliers of the coal-heugh to work and prevent them from diverting themselves from his service,"‡ a petition which seems to indicate that the more enlightened public opinion of the time refused to assist the coalowners in their efforts at an unrestricted slavery.

In 1656, when Tucker, Cromwell's commissioner, wrote his report, there were evidently 20,000 people dependent for their livelihood on the coal-heughs and salt-pans, and Tucker seems to have been specially struck with the terrible condition of the salt-pan serfs. He refers to their "vilenesse" and "unworthinesse," and declares that "besides their infinite povertye and miserableness, they are to be esteemed rather brutes than rationals." The poor unfortunates condemned to this servitude in the mines and salt works became as a race apart ; they were buried in unconsecrated ground ; some of them wore metal collars round their necks ; they were bought and sold and gifted like cattle ; unless in certain extraordinary instances, like the lead miners at the Leadhills in Lanarkshire,§ they were

---

Records of Mining in Scotland—Cochrane Patrick.
†*Acta Parl. Scot.*, v., 419.
‡*Acta Parl. Scot.*, vii., App. 30a.
§Ramsay of Ochtertyre's *Scotland and Scotsmen*, ii., p. 323.

wholly unlettered ; they developed a jargon of their own, and were regarded with superstitious fear and terror by the majority of their fellow-countrymen ; they lived in colonies ; and in every old mining district in Scotland local tradition still tells of how the "brown yins" or the "black folk" allowed no stranger near their habitations. Their alleged "privileges" consisted in exemption from taxation and from military service and in the legal obligation which rested with the owner to provide for them in sickness and in old age, and to supply a coffin for their burial.* Lord Cockburn, the Whig jurist, who wrote shortly after the serfs were freed, declared that while the collier and salter slaves could not legally be "killed or directly tortured by their masters," in every other respect they were held to be "cattle," possessing no human rights†

The testimonies given to Mr. R. H. Franks, the commissioner appointed to report in 1840 upon the employment of children in the Scots mines, shewed that, under the slave system, insubordinate miners were punished by having their necks placed in iron collars or "juggs," which were "fastened to the wall"; and an old slave miner, James M'Neill of Tranent, who died in 1844, at the age of 72 years, declared that in his day refactory miners, with their necks encased in these iron collars, were "nailed to the stoopside or to a prop at the pit bottom for a whole day at least," and that at other times the insubordinate miner was punished by "tying his hands in front of the gin horse and compelling him to run round the gin gang, back fore-most before the horse, when winding the coal up the pithead," and a variation was secured by forcing the prisoner to push the gin round, while the horse was "lowsed" and looked on.‡ Hugh Miller§ has given us a striking description of a slave village in the immediate vicinity of Niddrie Mill, near Edinburgh. The houses were a "wretched assemblage of dingy, low-roofed, tile-covered hovels." The collier women, "poor, over-toiled creatures," carried all the coal up a long turnpike stair inserted in one of the shafts, and it was calculated that each day's labour was equivalent to carrying a hundred weight from the sea-level to the top of Ben Lomond. No wonder "they cried like children under their load," no wonder a "peculiar type of mouth . . . wide, open, thick-lipped, projecting equally above and below . . . like savages," was developed The legal subjection, then, in which the miner had been placed had not raised his moral status, as the Reformed Church hoped, or professed to hope that it would. It had instead, by earning for him the contempt of other classes of society and by alienating him from the

---

*Graham's *Soc. Life in Scot.*, p. 266.

†*Memorials of his Time*, by Henry (Lord) Cockburn, p. 77.

‡*History of Tranent*—P. M'Neill, p. 22.

§*Schools and Schoolmasters*, p. 303.

movements and forces which raised or tended to raise the conditions of labourers in other industries, produced in him, as an anonymous writer well acquainted with slave mining conditions put it, "savage and brutal manners, destitute of all principles of religion and morality, perfectly indifferent to the opinion of the world."*

The orthodox historian, though he has not considered the subject worthy of mention at all, would in all probability, if he were questioned, placidly attribute the freeing of the coal slaves to the development of humanitarian sentiment towards the end of the eighteenth century. But that is demonstrably not the case. There were mining serfs in Scotland long after Granville Sharp's statute protecting the negro slave who had escaped to a British port. There were mining serfs in Scotland in the days of Chatham and Cowper and Burke and Fox. The humanitarian sentiment of the time was doubtless hostile to slavery abroad, but no parliamentary tears were shed over the slave labour in the Scots mines ; and liberationist declamations were strictly reserved for the benefit of those from whose servile toil the liberationists and their friends derived no profit. The miner slave in Scotland was freed in the same holy cause in which he was enslaved—the cause of low wages. The ever-increasing demand for coal, due to the vigorous development of industry in Scotland, necessitated an ever-increasing number of colliers, and as this increased number could only be secured by drawing upon outside and non-servile labour, money and other bribes had to be freely offered by the coalmasters. Tennant speaks of "strangers" who took work in the mines near Kirkcaldy, evading the cruel custom of serfdom by "previously stipulating to the contrary" ; and a Mr. Gibson of Durie, advertising for colliers in the *Edinburgh Courant* in 1743, offered, besides good wages, a written undertaking to allow his workers to leave him upon a week's notice being given. In the same year, Sir John Baird of Newblyth, the owner of the Gilmerton collieries, and the Marquis of Lothian, were forced to advertise for the capture and return of runaway colliers.†The coal owners, towards the last quarter of the eighteenth century, found it impossible to supply the huge demand for coal which the new iron works of Carron and Clyde were placing upon the market, and some of them, finding that their only method of securing a sufficient supply of colliers at cheap rates and of rendering coal mining popular, or at anyrate less unpopular than it was under the slave regulations then obtaining, engaged themselves to bring about the gradual emancipation of their workers,‡ in the hope that when slavery was abolished,

---

Considerations on the Present Scarcity and High Price of Coals in Scotland— Edin., 1793, p. 23.

†Chambers' *Dom. Ann.*, iii., 248.

‡Hoare's *Memories of Granville Sharp*, i., 228, 389.

coal-mining would offer greater attractions to the working-class : there would be a huge influx of fresh labour and wages would fall. They recognised at last that slavery had been a sad economic mistake ; they saw that slavery engendered a scarcity of labour ; that it frightened competition away, and that it left the slave in the position of a monopolist and consequently enabled him to secure high monopoly wages. In every other industry wages were lower in Scotland than in England ; but in coal-mining the wages in Scotland vastly exceeded the wages in England ; and Professor Millar was assured* that a Scots collier working 8 hours earned 2s. (or 12s. per week), while a Newcastle collier for a week's work could only earn 9s. In addition to this superiority in wages, the Scots serf collier enjoyed a free house and coal, free candles for his pit work and free maintenance in his old age. Adam Smith, lecturing in 1763, declared that : "The wages of a day labourer (in Scotand) is between 6d. and 8d., that of a collier is 2s. 6d. If they were free their wages would fall. At Newcastle, the wages exceed not 10d. or 1s. ; yet colliers often leave our coal works, where they have 2s. 6d. and run there, though they have less wages."† Although Scots colliers, coal-bearers, and salters were expressly excluded from the benefits and provisions of the Scots Habeas Corpus Act of 1701, and although, when heritable jurisdictions were abolished in 1747, as a consequence of the second Stuart rebellion, the workers in and about coal mines and salt-pans were still left to the arbitrary justice and still more arbitrary punishment of their hereditary owners, the mineowners, as a body, were being driven by economic circumstances to agitate for the freedom by their slaves ; but when Professor Miller wrote in 1771 there were still some who "with a timidity natural to those who have a great pecuniary interest at stake," are "averse from altering the former practice until such alteration shall be rendered universal by Act of Parliament." So anxious were the coalmasters to secure cheap labour by the expedient of rendering coal-mining popular through freeing the slaves and making the collier a free contract labourer, that they did not seek compensation from the State for loss of "property." They appreciated their own interests and the real facts of the case too clearly even to pretend either humanitarian zeal or self-sacrifice, and the Bill which, at the instigation of the Earl of Abercorn and other coalowners, was introduced into the House of Commons in March, 1775, for the freeing of the slaves, was carried rapidly through both Houses of Parliament without opposition, and became law on the 1st day of July in the same year. The preamble of the Bill indicates with commendable honesty the purpose of its promoters ; it was to prevent the loss

---

On Ranks, pp. 307-308.

†*Lectures*—Adam Smith, 1763, p. 99.

suffered by coalowners and the general public through persons being discouraged from learning the art or business of colliers or coal-bearers and salters by their becoming bound to the collieries and saltworks for life, where they shall work for the space of one year, "by means whereof there are not a sufficient number of colliers, coal-bearers and salters in Scotland for working the quantities of coal and salt necessarily wanted; and many new-discovered coals remain unwrought and many are not sufficiently wrought, nor are there a sufficient number of salters for the salt works, to the great loss of the owners and disadvantage of the publick."* No sooner was the Act passed than the poor mining slaves (not knowing the safeguard-ing provisions which Parliament had imposed) broke out into frantic ebullitions of joy. The first day of July was to be kept memorable for all time and its annual recurrence dedicated to festival and holiday-making ; some of the Earl of Abercorn's slaves, accompanied by 2000 spectators, marched with flying banners and musical accom-paniments from the Duddingston colliery to the Earl's castle to thank their benefactor, and while there were "hospitably enter-tained " ; it was felt that the last shackles of servitude had been removed. But all was not yet well with the collier. An examina-tion of the Act itself shews that while all new workmen entering coal pits after July 1st were to be regarded as free labourers (although masters could take apprentices, indentured and contracted) the old hands were only toobtain their freedom after certain stipulated periods of time, those who were under 21 years of age had to serve as slaves seven years longer ; those between 21 and 35 years of age had to serve as slaves ten years longer ; those between 35 and 45 years of age had to serve as slaves seven years longer ; and each and all of them were required to train an apprentice in the meantime, under a penalty of having three additional years added to the defaulters' servitude. Colliers over 45 years of age were only required to serve three years from 1775, and wives and children were to be freed at the same time as their husbands and fathers. But if any collier was guilty of taking part in an "unlawful combination " for the raising of wages, before the day of his emancipation arrived, he was to serve two additional years as a punishment ; and if, as the Act seems to indicate, such an additional two years could be added for each and every effort made by a collier to form or join a Trade Union, the liberation of a discontented serf might be postponed indefinitely. Again, no slave could be freed unless he instituted legal proceedings in the Sheriff Court, and incurred all the cost, delay, and trouble of a law suit ; and as any coalowner who was hostile to the new Act could always ensure that his serfs were finan-cially in his debt and unable to find the money necessary to establish

*Cap. xxviii., Geo. iii. Act, 15th year.

their freedom in the courts, it followed, as a general rule, that the slave was only liberated by death. The result of all these restrictions was that coal-mining remained unpopular and the mine-owners in Scotland were still forced to pay higher wages for labour than were their English confreres. And so the liberating Act of 1799, which finally abolished slavery in the coal mines and saltpans of Scotland, was urged upon Parliament by the more far-seeing coalowners themselves. There was no public excitement, no public agitation, and Lord Cockburn tells us* the matter was not "even mentioned in the *Scots Magazine;* people cared nothing about colliers on their own account, and the taste for improving the lower orders had not then begun." There appears, however, to have been an anxiety on the part of the miners to ensure that the new Act would not be burdened by vicious and restrictive clauses, for some 500 of them in Lanarkshire banded together, subscribed two shillings per head, invited the co-operation of all other colliers in Scotland, and sent a Glasgow lawyer to "lobby" the House of Commons during the passage of the Bill. The treasurer of the miners thus associating was Hugh Dunbar of Westmuir, and the clauses particularly objected to were those fixing wages by Justices of the Peace, compulsion of miners to work six days a week, and illegality of combinations.

The miners were now free—freed in the cause of low wages—but the immediate effect was not, as the coalmasters hoped, a rush of labour to the now-dignified calling of winning coal, and a consequent lowering of wages : it was a rush from the mines, a rush away from the old servile associations, away from the old miseries and the old degradations. Robert Bald, writing in 1808,† declares : "Many of the colliers have of late, particularly within these eight years past, betaken themselves to the work of common labourers at half their original wages"; and farther, that men of other trades would do all kinds of dangerous work connected with a mine, but if they were asked to do the work of a collier "they would spurn the idea, even with double wages." Dr. Robert Chambers relates an anecdote which vividly presents to us the slavery we have just been considering and its comparative proximity to our own times : In the year 1820 Mr. Robert Bald, visiting the Clyde iron-works, came across an old servant there, called "Moss Nook." The then proprietor of the Clyde iron-works was Mr. Colin Dunlop, whose father had taken a fancy to "Moss Nook," who had been the property of a coalowner, Mr. M'Nair of the Green. Mr. M'Nair swopped or "niffered" his slave "Moss Nook" for a donkey owned by Mr. Dunlop senior !‡

Works, ii., p. 6.
†*General View of the Coal Trade in Scotland*, p. 76.
‡*Dom. Annals*, iii., p. 250.

CHAPTER V.

THE DEMOCRATIC THEOCRACY.

> " The Solemn League and Covenant
>   Whiles brings a sigh and whiles a tear ;
>   But Sacred Freedom, too, was there,
>   If thou'rt a slave, indulge thy sneer."
>
> *—Burns.*

> " But, Robin, your mither was auld and puir,
>   And the seasons cauld and keen,
>   The white, white snaw was on her hair,
>   The frost film ower her een.
>
> She leeved on a handfu' o' barley meal,
>   A drink frae the spring sae cauld—
>   O Robin, Robin, a heart o' steel
>   Might bleed for the weak and auld !
>
> O Robin, Robin, I kenna hoo
>   The lee was faither'd first,
>   But (whisper again, lest they ken, lest they ken !)
>   They thought the puir body accurst !
>   They thought the spell had been wrought in Hell,
>   To kill and curse and blight ;
>   They thought she flew, when naebody knew,
>   To a Sabbath of fiends, ilk night.
>   Then ane whose corn had wither'd ae morn
>   And ane whose kye sicken'd doon,
>   Crept, scared and pale, wi' the leein' tale
>   To the meenisters, up the toon.
>
> They bade her tell she had wrought the spell
>   That made the tempest blaw,
>   They strippit her bare as a naked bairn
>   They tried her wi' pincers and heated airn
>   Till she shriek'd and swoon'd awa' !
>
> O. Robin, Robin, . . . they doomed her to *burn*,
>   Doon yonner upon the quay . . .
>   This night was the night . . see the light ! see the light !
>   How it burns by the side o' the sea !
>
> *—Robert Buchanan.*

WHILST it is no part of the proper business of this volume to discuss the theological divisions, controversies and troubles which play so large a part in our national records, it is vitally necessary for the student of working class history, to understand and to appreciate in its proper relationship the real meaning and significance of the Covenanting struggles which convulsed Scotland from the downfall of Roman Catholicism in the sixteenth century, to the triumph of a modified and somewhat chastened Presbytery in 1688, at least in so far as these struggles impinged upon the lives of the common people. True, no period of our national history has been more frequently or more copiously written : a babel of warring partisan voices still canvasses vehemently the virtues of the covenanting hill-folk ; and laborious volumes expound the aims and objects of Recusants, Remonstrants, Solemn Leaguers, Protestors, and Malignants ; but the whole period is still to us something of a bottomless blank : something of an inscrutable mystery. Be that, however, as it may, the Kirk of the seventeenth century is ever with us, in our language, our habits, our traditions, our lives ; it penetrates everywhere, prescribing for us the decorum in which we must perforce spend one-seventh part of our days, enveloping us at baptism, at marriage, at death, and playing no mean or unimportant part in the education of our children and the making of our laws.

The present day popular notion that the Scottish Reformation was a vast democratic upheaval, is, as we have already proved, a mere travesty of the facts. Hatred towards the financial exactions of the old Church was undoubtedly strong among the commons ; but the real motive force behind the Reformation was the aristocracy, which had cast covetous eyes on the Church estates. The fomenters of the religious revolution in Scotland, says Dr. King Hewison, were not "the illiterate cobblers, tanners and abject persons : " the evangelical party were "mostly nobles, owners of small estates, persons of means, and men of patriotic spirit "* ; but when, the Reformation over, and the Church estates added to the rent rolls of these worthy evangelicals, Knox and his friends suffered speedy disillusionment. There was to be nothing for the kirk ; those who had expected otherwise being haughtily informed that they suffered from "ane fond imagination " ; there was to be nothing for the poor and nothing for education out of the revenues of the Church estates ; so far as the nobles were concerned the Reformation had gone far enough. The ministers were in dire straits for lack of stipends ; the Rev. David Fergusson of Dunfermline "had to borrow money to feed his family " ; some ministers "eked out a precarious livelihood from the voluntary offerings of their poor flocks, or from the scanty produce of a few acres of Church land, which no one had been sacrilegious enough to seize ; some kept inns, others served as tapsters of wine and ale ; still others speculated in grain, lent out money to usury, or became servitors to the nobility and gentry." In 1590 the Rev. Mr. Bell of Cadder had no manse, and lived in his

---

*"The Covenanters."—J. King Hewison (1908), vol. i., pp. 4, 10, 162. See also Robertson's " Hist. of Scot.," iii., p. 116, *A Diurnal of Occurrents*, p. 269, and Calderwood's *History of the Kirk of Scotland*, ii., p. 42.

steeple. Beath "had no church, and the indwellers having forgotten there was a Sabbath, used that day for work and sports." Many ministers did not obtain glebes until 73 years after the Reformation, and the acquisition was not obtained without local vexation, strife, and even bloodshed. The clergy carried arms for self-defence against the rich "evangelical" heritors,* and some of them were imprisoned for their pulpit strictures upon the robbers. At Edinburgh, in front of Lord Lennox's lodging, a mob "with bear heads and laud voices sang to the praise of God and the testifeing of grait joy and consola- tion, the 124th psalm, ' Now Israel may say, and that trewlie' etc., till heavin and erthe resondit."† The old slavish subservience to the nobility was being undermined by the preachers, who dared even to inform the king that he was after all but "God's sillie vassal"; and the Presbyterian form of Church Government, with its semi- democratic organisation and its perpetual insistence that Christ was its head and not King James, was daily sapping the foundations of feudalism.‡ This fact both king and nobles recognised. King James VI. advanced his claims to "divine right," and demanded an episcopal government in the Church which would, by giving him power to select the bishops, keep the whole Church organisation under his control. No bishop, he thought, would ultimately mean no king. But the nobles had not the faintest desire to see the bishops firmly established again ; *that* might involve the return of the stolen Church lands ; and rather than suffer such a calamity they would tolerate within certain limits the unbridled tongues of the ministers and the galling discipline of the presbyteries and the kirk sessions. And galling indeed to them must that discipline have been. Knox and his friends might not be able to secure for the Reformed Church the patrimony that was expected ; but they could at least subject the morals of professing Protestants to a disciplinary rigour and a public examination that sent many an aristocratic delinquent half mad with rage and vexation. Thus in 1563 Knox forced Lord Lauderdale to do public penance before the congregation at Largo, for an illicit amour, and in 1567 the Countess of Argyll had to appear in sackcloth during worship at Stirling§. Well might Froude say that "something of the storm about to break over Scotland may be traced to an absence of wordly wisdom in the new born Church."||

---

*"The Covenanters," pp. 155-159. The Regent indeed said there would be no peace in Scotland until some of the ministers were hanged.

†*The Psalms in Human Life*—Prothero, p. 240.

‡In 1584, Melville rebuked the Privy Council for presuming to "judge the doctrine and control the ambassadors and messengers of a King and Coun- cill greater nor they and far above them."

§*Politics and Religion in Scotland*—W. Law Mathieson, i., 104.

||*History*, viii., p. 303.

On the one hand, then, we have the king struggling for fuedal episcopacy as a barrier to the democratic, anarchical, republican notions
which Presbytery fostered ; on the other hand we have the ministers
sternly insisting that they would have no spiritual master but Christ,
and claiming for themselves and their sessions large disciplinary
powers over the moral conduct of peer and peasant ; and between
the two we have the nobles, fearful of episcopacy lest it should result
in their being compelled to return stolen Church lands, but hating
furiously the new-born impertinences of the merchant folk and the
ministers, who, sitting in kirk session, presumed to hector and lecture
them without so much as "by your leave ! " Naturally the tension
on the ties which bound the ministers to the Crown grew with every
fresh episcopal inroad made by the Crown into the "Reformation
principles," as these were understood by the anti-Erastian clergy ;
but when, in October, 1626, King Charles I. revoked the land grants
made to the Scottish nobles by his father after the Reformation, the
aristocracy began to swallow its hatred of Presbytery, and in 1638,
in order to preserve itself from farther royal encroachments, not
only joined the ministers, but actually led them in the signing of the
famous National League and Covenant, whereby the signatories
banded themselves to resist popery and prelacy to the death. This,
then, was the real meaning of the Covenant of 1638, signed first,
by the way, not in Greyfriars Churchyard, but in Greyfriars Church,
by the Earl of Sutherland—a desire to safeguard the landed properties of the nobles. "His (Charles I.'s) contumelious and impolitic
treatment of the aristocracy," says Dodds, "was the groundwork of
all the mischief that followed after, both to the king's government and
family."* Had Charles I. stuck simply to his Act of Revocation
it is likely enough that the ministers would have supported him,
and the nobles would have been forced to disgorge ; but his continual harping on his "divine right," and his scornful declaration
that the Presbyterian was not a religion for a gentleman, and his
impolitic action in attempting to force his Liturgy upon the Scottish
Kirk, drove the ministers into the arms of the aristocrats, and finally
cost him his crown and his head.

Opinions may vary as to the share even the ministers had in the
struggles, the anti-monarchial, anti-prelatic struggles of the period,
but it is morally certain that the labouring classes took little or no
active interest in what was for them but a game in high politics.
The Covenant of 1638 was a nobles' movement, and the editor of
"The Diary of Sir Thomas Hope (Lord Advocate) "† points out

---

*Dodds' *The Scottish Covenanters*, p. 27, quoting Balfour's *Annals*, ii., 128.
　　See also *Politics and Religion in Scotland*, Mathieson, vol. i., p. 383, and
　　Macintosh : *Hist. Civil. Scot.*, vol. iii., pp. 43-4.
†Mr. James Colville. See *Scot. Hist. Review*, 1905-6, p. 427.

that "the clergy, even the leaders, get no prominence in the Diary, strengthening the general impression one must form that the momentous rising of 1638 was essentially a movement of the barons, deeply roused by the king's threatened resumption of the Crown teinds in the hands of the lay patrons." Wherever the clergy were unwilling to sign the Covenant, the local nobles "overcame their scruples;" at General Assemblies the barons turned up with their armed retainers; Sir William Dick, the great banker, financed the movement, and a farther step in open rebellion was taken when the Solemn League and Covenant was signed in joint agreement with the English Parliament for the extirpation of Popery, Prelacy and whatsoever should be found contrary to sound doctrine and the power of godliness! The Covenanters had triumphed; but the Montroses, Leslies, Moncks and Cromwells drenched Scotland red with blood in the few succeeding years which elapsed, ere again a Stuart king sat on the throne and episcopacy was by law established.

Nor can it be said that the Covenanting leaders and armies were more humane, more generously disposed, or more civilized than the leaders and armies of the Stuart kings. After the battle of Alford in 1645, when the Duke of Montrose gave the Covenanting army the slip, "the baffled Covenanters," we are told on high covenanting authority :*

> "had a miserable revenge in murdering in cold blood the female camp-followers—women and babes—left behind in this precipitate movement, an illustration of inhumanity equalled by the model army under Fairfax and Cromwell, who, at Naseby, butchered the Irish in terms of the Ordinance of 24th October, 1644, and imitated by Leslie† more than once, notably at Philiphaugh, when he dispatched the women and captives, and at Dunaverty, where he extinguished the garrison after its surrender on quarter given."

This Philiphaugh butchery was done with the connivance and concurrence of the Covenanting nobles, Argyll and Buccleugh. On another occasion Leslie had 80 women and children drowned at Linlithgow without sentence or the least formality of law, an action which probably met with the hearty approval of the ministers who were clamouring for the blood of Royalist captives and assuring the uninitiated that "the Lord was angry at the law's delay."‡ It is well that we should have no illusions about these Covenanting clergy; brave undaunted fellows, many of them, as became men who were firmly convinced that they were the specially favoured and anointed deputies of the Most High, and who had in their veins proud aristocrat blood, but they were narrow, bigoted, cruel, stupid

*The Covenanters—J. King Hewison, i., 423.
†General Leslie, the little crooked-back soldier, was the leader of the Covenanting Army.
‡Hewison—Ibid, p. 430.

G

and barbarously bloodthirsty ; and as we shall see in a moment, they carried on, each in his own parish, a species of white terror which has left its mark on the labouring classes to this very day.

The Covenanting leaders, being who they were, "barons or gentlemen of good note," says Baillie, were instinctively Royalist ; they submitted to and supported a Presbyterian form of church government, because a national reversion to Popery or Episcopacy meant a return of the Church lands which they had secured after the Reformation ; but they stood nevertheless for a monarchial form of State government, since their own feudal rights and privileges were bound up with monarchy. Their ideal was a Covenanted king—a king who would covenant himself to the support of the new Church arrangements, but who in other matters of State would preserve the feudal *status quo.* This naturally did not suit Cromwell and the English republicans, and Cromwell came north at the head of an army to crush any latent or active support which the Stuart kings hoped to secure from the Scottish barons. At Dunbar, in 1650, his (Cromwell's) soldiers report that the Scots were picking "our horses' beans, eating our soldiers' leavings ; they are much enslaved to their Lords " ;* and again, "the meaner sort . . . under their own great Lords . . . work for living no better than the peasants of France."† The attention paid to the economic condition of the working classes by the Cromwellian officers does not, however, seem to have been relished by the parties most concerned, for, we read, the whole country went aflame after the Cromwellian General, Monck, had sold 500 Scots prisoners captured at Dunbar to servitude in the Barbadoes at so much per head ;‡ and it is not likely that, when Cromwell made what he called "a sweet beginning " by killing a great many Covenanters at Musselburgh, he would endear himself to the class which would suffer the bloodshed.§ But he certainly did his best in other directions to weaken the power of the Covenanting barons ; he abolished Church patronage, to the great disgust of the Lord Buccleugh, who protested against this curtailment of the "just rights " of the nobility and gentry :|| he tore from the Church walls the machines and engines of ecclesiastical punishment : he prohibited religious persecution, to the great rage of the ministers who, in the Assembly of 1648, had declared against a " wicked toleration " of creeds, and he razed baronial fortresses to the ground.

In the hey-day of the Covenanters none but themselves were allowed to hold public office, and the Church Assemblies were care-

---

Cromwell's Letters and Speeches—Carlyle, ii., 189.

†*Ibid*, ii., pp. 638-9.

‡*Scotland and the Protectorate*—Firth (Scot. Hist. Socy.), pp. 82, xxx.

§*Kingcraft in Scotland*—Ross, p. 84.

||*Annals of Scot.*, iii., p. 391.

fully packed by the ruling class. At the Glasgow Assembly in 1638, for example, there were present as elders no fewer than 17 peers, 9 knights and 25 landed proprietors with titles from their lands. But pack the Assemblies and the public offices as they might, they could not suppress altogether the detestable Presbyterian clergy, one of whom, Naysmyth, at the Assembly of 1649, went so far as to propose that all teinds should be given up to the Church. Argyll, Cassilis, and other "evangelical" brethren hotly repudiated this "confiscatory" doctrine, and declared tiends to be only *jure humano* "It is not good to awalkin sleeping dogs," quoth the sapient Duke of Argyll.* Then came the death of Cromwell and the restoration of the Monarchy in the person of Charles II., whom the nobility of Scotland hastened to palm off upon the Presbyterian clergy as a real Covenanted king. The aristocrats simply tumbled over one another in their haste to do homage to the new monarch "They had never," says Macintosh, "been scrupulous about the means of attaining their ends . . . In past struggles many of them had joined with the people" (*i.e.*, the clergy) "against the Crown and the Government, but recently that line of action had been a losing and ruinous one, and there was no prospect of any personal advantage to be gained by it . . . Sentiments and convictions were thrown to the winds with scorn and contempt, religious convictions, covenants, equity and justice might all go to the wall."† To the uninitiated outsider it was a marvellous swing of the pendulum, and the Turkish Emperor said "that if he were to change his religion he would do it for the king of Britain's God, who had done such wonderful things for him."‡

But scarcely had Charles II. become firmly seated upon the throne, than he, by an Act Recissory, abrogated all the legislation of the Covenanting period ; he re-introduced Episcopacy, made proposals for the sustenance of the Bishops, restored patronage, and declared private worship to be a nursery of sedition ; ministers who preached without licence from a bishop, and parishioners who absented themselves from Church on Sundays, were declared guilty of sedition and liable to heavy fines and imprisonments ; non-attending burgesses were to lose one-fourth of their goods and their burgess-ship, and in addition to suffer corporal punishment. Lairds were to be responsible for their tenantry, and informers were to get half of the fines. Parliament was carefully closed for 6 years against any possible suspicion of democracy by decrees which ordered the bishops to elect 8 nobles, the nobles to elect 8 bishops, and the 16 so elected to

---

*Balfour's *Annals*, iii., 418.

†*Hist. Civ. Scot.*, iii., 120.

‡*Chronological Notes of Scottish Affairs from* 1680 *till* 1701—Lord Fountainhall, p. 46.

elect 8 county members, and these 24 in turn to select 8 commissioners from the burghs.   These 32 individuals were to be Lords of the Articles and to govern Scotland under the king's commissioner, Lauderdale, who had never forgotten or forgiven the affront to which Presbytery had subjected him in Largo Kirk.   But the tyranny bred spirited resistance.   Four hundred ministers left their charges and their manses, many of them taking to preaching in the fields.   Soldiers drafted to the west and south-west of Scotland only embittered the peasantry and led to armed conventicles ; and the perpetual and persistent fining and robbery of the people and the remaining Presbyterian lairds was, as Woodrow shews clearly, the sole motive which led the aristocrats to support episcopacy and the sole cause of these desperate struggles at Drumclog, Pentland, and Bothwell Brig.   In one year (1666) £50,000 in fines were raised in the South-west of Scotland.*   If a landlord did not attend Church, his tenantry were compelled to pay his fine, even if the tenants themselves were regular worshippers.   Coats and women's plaids were taken in fines, soldiers were quartered upon the poor ; "religious prisoners " were handed over to Mr. George Hutcheson, merchant, Edinburgh, for sale to the slave plantations at Barbadoes ; and so robbed were the commons of Galloway that when the soldiers met a beggar by the wayside they would ask him in jest "if he were fined." And yet, so great was the theological intolerance of the period, that Woodrow finds time amidst all his chronicle of suffering to assure us that "about this time the Council came to some good resolutions against Quakers and Papists," the adjective "good " meaning, of course, exceptionally severe.

Spies and informers on conventicles or field preachings were to get the fines levied on everyone under the rank of landed proprietor, fines from whom were reserved for the aristocrats.   In a few brief years the fines in the County of Renfrew alone totalled £90,000 in money sterling.   The Marquis of Atholl, who had the gift of certain fines from Duke Lauderdale, made £5000 in one year.   Tenant conventiclers forfeited all their property to their lairds.   Death was decreed as the fate of the field-preachers.   The Bishop's Court of High Commission was kept busy fining, branding, imprisoning, exiling, and was aptly compared to the lion's den, into which led many tracks, but from which none returned.

This rapacity and tyranny could have but one ending—rebellion ; and rebellion there was.   Suddenly, in 1666, from the bleak bogs of Galloway, guant, desperate peasants and preachers seized muskets, disarmed the soldiers of General Turner, whom the peasants called "bloody-byte-the-sheep," and marched, 2000 strong, through

---

History of the Sufferings of the Church of Scotland—Rev. Robt. Woodrow (1721), vol. i., p. 237.   See also Hewison : *The Covenanters*, ii., p. 73.

Ayrshire and Lanarkshire on Edinburgh ; but they had no organisation, and were easily routed on the Pentland Hills by the king's troops under General Dalziel. Those who survived the slaughter suffered torture from the boot and the thumbscrew ; some were hanged at the insistent instigation of the bishops, despite the fact that they had been given quarter by the soldiers on the battlefield. The peasantry of the east country shewed no mercy to any stray fugitive whom they happened to come across ; bitter memories of the cruelties and absurdities of Covenanting rule, the "jougs," the branks, the stools of public repentance, perhaps accounting for the popular antagonism to the preacher fugitives, just as it probably accounted for the Edinburgh mob which met the Bothwell Brig prisoners some years later at Corstorphine with the mocking cry : "Where's your God ? Where's your God ? " After this affair on the Pentlands, additional facilities were offered for the enrichment of the nobles at the expense of the poor, under the plea of "pacifying the disturbed districts." An army was quartered upon the people of Galloway ; conventiclers were to be hanged and their goods confiscated—half of the fine going to the miserable informer ; cottars were fined £20 for failing to get their children properly (that is, episcopally) baptised ; servants, for a similar omission, were mulcted in half a year's fee ; fines and transportations to slave plantations were the order of the day. "It was better," said Lord Lauderdale, "that the West bore nothing but windlestraws and laverocks than that it should bear rebels to the King," and accordingly in 1678, an Army 10,000 strong (6000 of them Highland clansmen) were sent south to annihilate the conventiclers and spoil such part of their gear as had escaped previous plunderings. Clean, clean was that harvest, and when the clansmen retu ned spoil laden to their mountains, they left behind them burgesses. cottars, and small bonnet lairds, ruined and homeless, lurking about in the caves and the moss-hags with a shabble in one hand and a Bible in the other, ready for any enterprise which promised revenge upon their enemies. The events of 1679 are familiar to every Scotsman : Archbishop Sharpe stabbed to death in face of his daughter ; Drumclog, with Captain Claverhouse defeated ; Louden Hill ; Hamilton Moor ; the thousand prisoners tied two by two in Greyfriars kirkyaird, and kept there in the open for several weeks ; the hangings ; the sellings into slavery in the plantations at Barbadoes ; fines and forfeitures galore ; Sir John Dalrymple, the old Protestant rebel, prosecuting people for "resetting" (*i.e.*, harbouring and even speaking to) fugitive Bothwell Brig-ers, a crime not seldom punished by death ; the Earl of Atholl turning wild Highlanders on to the massacre of conventiclers, whereby "some were killed, some plundered, others barbarously stripted naked, and weemen forced and many taken prisoners ; so that where the Sanctuary was thought strongest, the assault was most fierce, toward the town of St. Johnston."* But the Duke of Argyll was the "star turn" of the period. His father, a cowardly old ruffian, had gone to the block under circumstances which have enabled a certain school of romancers to pass him off as a "Martyr for the Covenant" ; but the son objected to be called a Presbyterian ; he suggested tortures for the ministers implicated in the rebellion. Ever with a keen eye to the main chance, he bought up the Earl of Huntly's debts and mortgages and juggled the other creditors out of their share ; he was a notorious oppressor of his tenantry ; and in 1680, having secured the Island of Mull from the Chiefs of the Clan M'Lean, who had been ejected for non-payment of an alleged debt, he was engaged in a vigorous rack-renting of the tenantry. This Mull-debt business was his undoing. It seems that he had originally lent £10,000 to the M'Leans, but by decreets and forfeitures and interest-mongering decisions, given in his own Courts against the M'Leans, this sum rapidly rose to £200,000, and the M'Leans being unable to pay, he got a commission of fire and sword against them. On being ejected, the M'Leans sought revenge ; they organised Huntly's creditors with Cameron of Lochiel and others, who were afraid Argyll meant to attack them next, and on a quibble about a religious test they forced him to flee the country, thereby earning for him in the story-books an imperishable name as a Protestant martyr, though he cared as much or as little for Protestantism as did Sir John Dalrymple who, in the South country, was suborning false witnesses against Lord Bargany's theological integrity with a view to securing his estates.† Indeed, a vast amount of the persecution of conventiclers under Episcopacy was only superficially theological : at bottom it was estate-grabbing. In 1683 the Government emptied its gaols of sodomists, adulterers, murderers and thieves in order to accommodate those against whom theological charges could be made, likely to result in heavy fines. From 26 heritors in Roxburghshire no less a sum than £274,737 (Scots) was taken as penalty for non-churchgoing, though by the Cess Act of 1681, heritors were to be relieved by their tenants, tradesmen, cottars and servants.‡ The Sheriff-depute of Renfrewshire was indicted for "oppressive acts" done in order to get money to himself,§ as also were Pringle of Rig, Sheriff-depute of the Merse,

---

*St. Johnston, ancient name of Perth city. Matthew M'Kail's description in *State Papers. Dom. Chas. ii.*, 407.

†Sir John, by the way, afterwards became a zealous adherent of King William and his "glorious Revolution," when Presbytery again triumphed in 1688.

‡Four years later, in 1685, the heritors were still farther relieved by the "Poll Money Act."—*Acta Parl. Scot.*, viii., 483.

§Fountainhall's *Chronological Notes*, pp. 79, 88, 107.

and others ; and the numerous sentences of transportation to Caro-
lina and other slave ports can safely be ascribed to the inducements
held out to the judges by Robert Barclay, Robert Malloch, and other
prosperous slave-shipping agents.* These oppressions naturally
fanned the fanaticism of what Lord Rothes called "the sects of the
dunghill " ; and "the Society People"—Cargill, Cameron, Renwick,
and the other preachers in the moss-hags, declared open war on the
Government ; they disowned the tyrant Charles II. ; they denounced Episcopacy and all its works ; they refused to pay taxes ;
they issued proclamations declaring that while detesting and ab-
horring "that hellish principle of killing all who differ in judgment
and in persuasion from us " yet those "informers who raise the hue
and cry against us and the soldiers and judges " would be dealt with
"as ye deal with us." But for them it was the killing-times : one
by one they were picked off, each meeting death unflinchingly as
became men who had fought the good fight.   Round the Wild Whigs,
Wanderers, Faithful Remnants, Hillmen, Cameronians, and Mac-
millanties, tradition has woven a story which one would not willingly
let die. James Rumbold, the maltster, admitting in court that "his
rooted opinion was for a Republick against Monarchie, to pull down
which he thought was a duty and no sin ; and on the scaffold began
to pray for that party, but was interrupted, and said, if every hair
on his head were a man, he would venture them all in that quarrell"
—no miserable, half-hearted opinion trimming there !   And what a
despicable revenge the judges had upon him ; he was partially
hanged, his breast ripped up, his heart pulled out and thrown into a
fire, his head struck off, and parts of his body sent as a warning
message to the market crosses of Glasgow, Dumfries, New Galloway
and Jedburgh.   Some were so tortured by the rack, the boot, and
the thumbscrews in the Courts, that even the Duke of Hamilton
protested that any sort of crime could be proven by such despicable
methods ; some—"the common prisoners"—were despatched at a
profit to the slave plantations ; some had "a piece of their lugg cutt
off " ; some women were drowned, some burned on the shoulders
with red hot irons ; some men had their ears torn out by the roots,
their fingers wrenched asunder, and the bones of their legs shattered ;
some women, stripped almost naked, were whipped publicly through
the streets ; † uniformed aristocrats stole openly from poor travelling
packmen, justices fleeced the defenceless, officials tampered with
and corrupted the coinage, soldiers were defrauded of their wages
by their officers ‡ ; and despite an ever-simmering pot of rebellion,
we are told that "the reign of Charles II. closed on the 6th of Febru-

---

*Fountainhall's *Chronological Notes*, pp. 96, 115, 140.
†*The Rise and Influence of Rationalism in Europe*—Lecky, ii., p. 41.
‡Hewison's *The Covenanters*, ii., 123.

ary, 1685, amidst a scene of oppression, suffering, and corruption
unmatched in the worst times of the nation's history.*

But the Episcopalian and Aristocratic tyranny had over-shot
itself ; its excesses and extravagancies had driven the merchant
class and the financiers *holus-bolus* into a determined party intent
upon driving out the Stewart kings and their bishops, once and for
all.   Not, of course, that the merchants had the slightest sympathy
with the Cargillites and the Cameronians, who had rejected all mon-
archies and hereditary principles, but, simply, they wanted sober,
settled, steady and responsible government.   Upon William Prince
of Orange they fixed their choice, and at his landing as Protestant
king the reigning Stewart fled and the glorious Revolution of 1688
was *un fait accompli*, the Scottish nobles, as one would expect,
being heavily bribed to acquiesce in the intrigues of the period†
and receiving liberal compensation for such patronage and other
rights as they were induced to surrender.

It was now the turn of the other side to exhibit a tyrannical
intolerance—an intolerance perhaps scarcely to be wondered at
when one thinks of the men from the hidie holes, the men with one
ear, the women with the branded cheek and the seared shoulder,
soldiers whose tongues had been bored with red-hot irons for "blas-
pheming their officers," and the survivors from the malarial fever
colonies, re-entering society.   The curates of the old *regime* were
ruthlessly chased out with their wives and families to beggary.   The
Rev. Wm. Law, the first Presbyterian minister after the Revolution,
at Crimond, was deposed by the Presbytery of Aberdeen for daring
to assert in a sermon "that virtue was more natural to the human
mind than vice."‡   In Galloway the Presbytery refused to allow
"Papists" to marry, refused even to allow a male Protestant to
marry a "Papist" woman, refused to baptise the children of "Papist" parents unless the parents gave a pledge that the child would
be educated in the Protestant faith and produced a Protestant
sponsor ;   Catholic servants were not allowed to have Catholic
masters nor Catholic masters Catholic servants ;   Catholic widows
had their children taken from them and aliment for their upkeep
extracted forcibly from the mother's estate ;   in business matters
and in court cases, the oath of a Catholic was outside the law and
had no weight ;   although Catholic marriages were refused, if two
Catholics dared to live together they were liable to excommunication—a fearful sentence, involving complete social ostracism, no
one being allowed to sell the excommunicated persons food or to let
them a house ;   and although Parliament, in 1690, had abolished the

*M'Intosh—*Hist. Civ. Scot.*, iii., 163.
†*Leven and Melville Papers*, 417.
‡*Law's Memorialls.*—Ed. by C. K. Sharpe (1818), p. x.

civil penalties of excommunication, the Presbyteries clamoured for their re-imposition.* Nor did the bounds of religious freedom widen without such bitter opposition from the sectaries that one is justified in coming to the conclusion that theological toleration is a contradiction in terms. In 1778 all the Synods, except that of Aberdeen, protested against the repeal of penal laws against Catholics, and Principal Robertson of Glasgow, who had advocated repeal, was denounced as a "pensioner of the Pope." In 1780 a Catholic Chapel was burned by an Edinburgh mob ; in 1833 the General Assembly of the Church of Scotland was passing resolutions against the education, at State expense, of Catholic children ; in 1837 the Assembly indicted Dr. Cleland, the famous statist, for declaring in his contribution to the Statistical Account of Scotland that a certain Catholic sermon he had heard was "powerful," one member of the Assembly characterising the statement as so "disgraceful" that he "could not restrain his indignation." The publisher of the Statistical Account (Blackwood) was forced to apologise, and to declare that he "would sooner have put his hand in the fire than sanction anything of the kind" (i.e., the printing of Dr. Cleland's laudation of a Catholic sermon). In 1839 we find the Synod of Glasgow and Ayr pleading, with only two dissentients, for the repeal of the Catholic Emancipation Act. When the great secession from the Established Church took place and the Free Church was formed—450 ministers and 200 probationers voluntarily leaving manses, emoluments, and social status for conscience sake—some lairds who adhered to the old kirk refused the new congregations ground for holding meetings, forbade them even to obstruct the highways, and forced them to worship on the seashore betwixt high and low tide-marks. The great Guthrie himself preached in the open at Canonbie with blue-bonneted elders clearing away the snow from the collection plates. Kirk Sessions and Heritors refused adherents of the Free Church a place on the poor's roll, deposed dissenting schoolmasters, dismissed dissenting servants, and ejected dissenting tenants. But the Free Church, in turn, was not one whit more tolerant than its great antagonist. In 1845 the "Frees" demanded the abolition of University tests so far as they themselves were concerned, but they desired them strictly enforced against such "atheist" cattle as Jews and Unitarians. Catholic Professors, they said, should be dismissed. Priestley, the Unitarian, should be forbidden to teach chemistry : Herschell, the Jew, should be forbidden to teach astronomy. Orating at Symington Green, one of the seceders thus prayed for and referred to the soul of the parish minister, John Wilson : "Thou knowest that the silly, snivelling body is not worthy even to keep a

*"Some Incidents in Troqueer Parish."—Shirley. *Dumfries and Galloway Arch. Socy. Proc.*, 1910. pp. 156-161.

door in Thy house. Cut him down as a cumberer of the ground ;
tear him up—root and branch, and cast the wild rotten stump out
of Thy vineyard. Thresh him, O Lord, and dinna spare ! O thresh
him lightly with the flail of Thy wrath, and make a strae wisp of
him to stap the mouth of hell !"* Well might Lord Cockburn
lament that, "the Quakers alone excepted, no sect has the remotest
idea of what toleration means."†

So far, then, a brief outline of the Theological struggles in post-
Reformation times ; but ere we consider the relationship which the
various Theocracies—democratic and otherwise—bore to the working-class, it is essential to dispel the current illusion that the Covenanting leaders, even the leaders of the hillmen and the hunted
heroes of the moss-hags, were poor men. They were not. Prophet
Peden was a bonnet laird ; Johnston of Warriston, Erskine of Dun,
and Bruce of Kinnaird were aristocrats ; "no fewer than eighty
per cent. of the ministers during the whole Covenanting period were
graduates of universities ‡ "; John Welsh was a grandson of John
Knox and son of a minister ; Donald Cargill, who had been called to
the Barony Parish of Glasgow, was the son of a lawyer ; Richard
Cameron's father was a merchant ; John Balfour ("Burly") was a
portioner in Kinloch ; Richard Hackston was laird of Rathillet :
he had bought some confiscated land from Primate Sharp for £1000,
and the bargain not being implemented, Sharp threw Hackston into
gaol. On his release Hackston swore : "God damn him if ever he
went to church so long as there was a bishop in Scotland ! "   James
Renwick, alone of all the martyr leaders, seems to have had a working-
class origin, he being the son of a Nithsdale weaver. Gibb, the
Bo'ness sailor, who founded the sect of Gibbites or Sweet Singers,
and who seems to have possessed something of a magnetic power in
drawing women away from their husbands,§ may have been
"working-class," as also may Moon-clothed Mother Buchan, who led
her vagabond flock into the far wilds of Galloway in search of the
Mount of Ascension ; but the revolutionary theological tradition
and the evangelistic fervour which has come down to us is distinctly
of mercantile and bourgeois origin. Towards the end of the "killing
times " Cargill's followers may have been thinned out of all but
labourers and mechanics, who carried knives with the inscription :
"*This is to cut the throat of tyrants* " ; but none of the religious up-

---

*Fasti Ecclesiæ Scoticanæ, i., 231.

†Cockburn's *Journal*, i., 45, 83, 226. ; vol. ii., 32, 48, 113, 115. The Quakers
   in Scotland have always been roughly treated, and more particularly so
   in the seventeenth century, when the least they could look forward to was
   imprisonment and exile.

‡*The Covenanters*—Hewison, i., 162, 273.

§Gibb, by the way, was transported to America, and seems to have gained some
   notoriety among the Red Indians.

heavals were of peasant origin ; and for long after the Presbyterian triumph in 1688, it was the custom for the minister to bow from the pulpit to the principal heritors according to their right of precedence, and sometimes there were violent disputes among the gentry as to who was entitled to the first bow.* And not only from the Reformation in the sixteenth century downwards have the ministers been middle-class in origin and in social sympathy, but the kirk sessions and the presbyteries have been carefully manned by representatives of the landed gentry, the tradesmen, the merchants, and the large farmers, to the exclusion of the poor. This fact must be borne in mind when we are considering the disciplinary rigour with which the moral codes and the parish social legislations were weighted against the peasant, whether under the curates of Episcopacy or under the ministers of Presbytery. Beneath the dramatic struggle of the systems and the sects, under the rule of each and of both, the poor were branked, and stocked, and gouged, and imprisoned, and publicly admonished with a harshness and a cruelty which has left its mark in the cringing submissive spirit in which the Scots rural peasant regards, even to-day, his be-collared "betters."

The kirk sessions regarded themselves "as watchemen ower Christ's flok " —watchmen with special instructions against sparing the rod. They put down the old system of hand-fast marriages whereby men and women contracted themselves on trial to each other for a year and a day before going to the priest for official ratification of the marriage ; † they undertook the reconciliation of quarrelsome couples ; they gave or withheld Church lines or testimonials without possessing which a servant might have his wages arrested ; ‡ they specialised in sexual inquisitions, ferreting out with great ingenuity and punishing with a savage ferocity every little lapse and side slip from the narrow way. Life under these theocratic zealots was a dreary round of fastings and toil. The village bell awakened the workers at 4 a.m , even in winter, and it did not ring cessation from toil until 8 p.m.,§ and marriage feasts being the happy blinks in the grey lives of the people, it behoved the sessions to decree that none but four persons beyond the blood relations of the bride and bridegroom should be present. At Ashkirk, in 1638, Adam Moffat, piper, for his offence, clearly proved, of piping at bridals, was ordered to stand at the kirk door every Sunday during the pleasure of the session "barefoot and barelegged." Pro-

---

*" Clerical Customs in the Olden Time."—Rev. D. Hogg, Kirkmahoe, in *Dumfries and Galloway Antiq. Socy. Proc.*, 1863-4, p. 50.

†See Scott's *Monastery*, chap. xxv.

‡This, too, as late as 1710. See Dr. Cramond's *The Records of Elgin* (New Spalding Club), ii., 328.

§*Records of the Baron Court of Stitchill*, p. xxxiii.

miscuous dancing was banned by the Assemblies. At Perth, after the Reformation, ante-nuptial intercourse rendered the participants liable in a fine of £40 Scots, or imprisonment for 8 days, before being taken to the market place and forced to sit for two hours in the stocks. A repetition of the offence was punished by the parties having their heads shaved.* As the ministers refused to marry people ignorant of the Lord's Prayer, the Creed, and the Commandments, illicit "carnal dealings" increased with alarming rapidity, and, as at St. Andrews, kept the spiritual policemen busy.† There first offenders, after undergoing searching cross-examination by the session, were imprisoned in the kirk steeple, and ordered to sit on the penitent stool and wear a sackcloth gown in front of the congregation at the Sabbath services ; ‡ when the minister proceeded to administer public reproof the penitents stood up bareheaded amidst a congregation which sat wearing hats and bonnets. At the expiry of the imprisonment in the steeple, offenders had to pay the kirk beadle two shillings ere being released. In 1567 the penalty for a first offence was a fine of £40, imprisonment for 8 days on "breid and small drink," and exposure, bareheaded, and fastened to the market cross for two hours ; for a second offence, the fine was 100 merks, the imprisonment doubled, and "baith the heides of the man and the woman to be schavin " ; for the third "fault," the fine was increased to £100, the imprisonment tripled, and the parties taken to "the deepest and foulest pule, or watter of the towne or parochin, thair to be thryse dowkit and thairefter baneist the said towne . . . for ever."§ At St. Andrews some kind-hearted relatives who had sheltered a young woman who had a "misfortune," were fined 40s., and ordered to make public humiliation for not giving information to the session. Single women were regarded as ticket-of-leave criminals, and had to undergo regular examination and cross-questioning as to behaviour. Female delinquents in the Canongate parish of Edinburgh were compelled to wear, for six hours at the cross, an iron mask with prongs for entering the mouth, called the branks ; afterwards the women were to be houseless, since no one was to let a convicted fornicatrix a house under the penalty of 40s.

---

*At Perth such offences must have been of frequent occurrence, for the Session appointed a barber for the purpose.—*Perth Kirk Session Records*, p. 230.

†*St. Andrews Kirk Session Register*—Ed. by Dr. Hay Fleming. The labels "Adultereris" and "Fornicatoris" mark the vast majority of the "sins.'' People were refused marriage for inability to recite the Lord's Prayer, the Creed, and the Commandments, and were also fined 40s. for their ignorance.

‡The Penitent or Repentence Stool is still exhibited to visitors at Holy Trinity Church, St. Andrews.

§*Acta Parl. Scot.*, iii., p. 25, 26.

At Elgin, in 1656, John Anderson and Agnes Gillanders were whipped out of the town on suspicion of fornication in the kirk steeple.   Corporal punishment, of course, was solely at the discretion of the civil magistracy, but since the magistrates' bench and the kirk session were frequently composed of the same individuals, the recommendations of the ecclesiastical court to the civil court seldom, if ever, went unheeded.   In 1559 the authorities at Dundee decided that fornicators convicted of a second offence should "stand 3 hours in the gyves (fetters) and be thrice doukit in the sea."   In 1562 the sin had grown so common, it was decided that "baith the man and the woman be skurgeit at the cairt ers and baneist the town."   In 1564 impure women were taken to the market cross and had their hair cut off.*   These brutal punishments naturally were reserved for the poor ; nor does it appear that the moral police went to the bedside of any of the wealthier delinquents "and in her extremity examine her anent the father of her child."†   The rich might be called upon to suffer public humiliation on the Stools of Repentance, but the delinquents were so many that the ordeal, probably by reason of its very familiarity, ceased to be anything more than a slight discomfort.   Adultery was punished more severely, sometimes indeed the dread sentence of death being meted out ; ‡ sometimes the offender was carted through the town on market day and ere being "dowkit ower the heid " in some foul pool, was peppered by the school children and others with "rotten eggs, filth and glar " ; he then had to stand, Sunday after Sunday, till the session was satisfied, bare-headed and barefooted, and finally he was banished.§ At Aberdeen, in 1568, adulterers stood in sack-cloth, bareheaded and barefooted, with the particulars of the offence written on a paper fastened round their heads, while the minister lectured them before the whole congr gation.|| In 1596 the Kirk Session of Glasgow had a pulley attached to Gla gow Bridge for the public ducking of breakers of the Seventh Commandment.   As late as 1792 fines were still being levied on immorality in a parish at the gates of Aberdeen,a and in the year 1809 public penance had not been abolished at Mauchline in Ayrshire.b

Something might have been said for the continuance of these ferocities and savageries had experience shewn the theologians that

*History of Old Dundee—Alex. Maxwell (1884).

†Dumfries and Galloway Arch. Socy. Pubns., 1910, p. 154 .

‡Scotland : Social and Domestic—Rogers, ii., 241.

§St. Andrews Register, ii., p. 793.

||Ecc. Records of Aberdeen (Spalding Club).   In Dumfriesshire poor offenders
   had their heads " torkit " or punctured at the Cross on market day.—
   Dumfries Antiq. Socy. Trans., 1900-5, p. 96.

aStat. Eccl. Scot., ii., 286.

bOld Church Life in Scotland—Edgar, i., 301.

their penal regulations wrought some good amendment in the habits of their parishioners, but when experience had shewn the severities to be not only useless, but actually productive of grosser " sins " than the ones they were intended to crush, it is difficult to imagine why, generation after generation, the kirk sessions acted as they did. The savage punishment of illicit motherhood became a fruitful cause of infanticide ; and yet, despite it all, at Perth, in the year 1580, out of 211 baptisms, no fewer than 85 were of children born out of wedlock ; and in 1574, no fewer than 27 per cent. of the births in Aberdeen were illegitimate. The frequency of the public humiliations killed modesty, and the Duke of York was probably accurate enough when he said that they " rather made scandals than buried them." The crime of Sodomy was unknown before the Reformation, but it grew to large proportions afterwards.*

Woman being, according to the clergy, the channel through which sin had entered the world, was subject to exceptional "discipline." In Roman Catholic times female users of profane language were "weighed and considered according to their blood, and estate of the parties that they are coupled with," but under the Democratic Theocracy woman was not so much a slave chattel as a temptation to sin. The Kirk Session of Perth would not allow an unmarried woman to live alone, or two sisters to keep house, together, " for fear of scandal." The Kirk Session of Canongate ordered one, Marjore Brison, whose crime had such extenuating circumstances attached to it that the magistrates had pardoned her, to appear in Church for three successive Sundays "bairfit and bairlegit," and wearing a colourless petticoat. In 1606 the Kirk Session of Ayr made Janet Hunter " stand in her lynnings at the cross on market days and at the Kirk door seven days, and in the public place of repentance," for scolding her husband. In 1643 the Kirk Session of Monifieth provided their officer, Robert Scott, "with ane pynt of tar to put upon the women that held plaids about their heads " in church. In 1671, for the alleged crime of "drinking the good health of the devil," Marion M'Call of Mauchline was taken to Edinburgh and "scourgit " from the cross to Netherbow, then had her tongue bored and her cheek burned, and warned not to return to Ayrshire under pain of death.† In the St. Andrews records, a case is recorded where a woman for "mis-saying and disobedient to her husband is bound over in £10 and to sit in the joiggis xxiii. howris," and a man who mis-called his wife was forced to go on his knees before the congregation and, holding his tongue by his fingers, shout "Fals tung, thou leid ." As late as 1790 the magistrates of Stirling were actually taking counsel's opinion as to whether they should publicly

---

Politics and Religion in Scotland—W. Law Mathieson, i., 187.
†*Old Church Life in Scotland*—Edgar, i., 261.

whip a woman who had returned from banishment in a state of
pregnancy.*

Under the zealots there was great expansion of the Decalogue ;
and the calendar of "sins" and "scandals" for which poor offenders
must "stand the session" and make public humiliation and repentance, grew to such a length that it covered almost every human
activity except praying, fasting, and toiling for the lairds and the
merchants. Absence from Kirk was a sin ; playing golf on fast
days ; running through the town "under silence of nycht ; " drinking ; drinking during times of sermon ; all varieties of Sabbath
breaking, from carrying a load to the laying-out of skins to dry ;
"flyting" ; ungodly speaking ; "extraordinar drinking" ; "drinking
ontymouslie" ; suspicious company keeping ; mis-spending gear ;
"dancing" ; tulzeing, and ongodlie behaviour" ; wrestling ; kissing
a maid "on the causeway" ; giving trouble to neighbours ; playing
cards and dice ;† watering kail and "playing bogill about the stacks"
on the Sabbath ; taking snuff in Church ; sleeping in Church ;‡
being a "naughty person" (banishment for this enormity !) §;
describing one of the elders as "a mansworn slaverie loon"||; mocking
at piety ; being "sensibly drunk" ; teaching children to say papa
and mama instead of father and mother was one of the causes of
God's wrath.*a* Sabbath-breaking came under the heading of "vice
and enormities," and the elders who had each command of a certain
district, made regular domiciliary visits on the search for non-
church goers. During such visits they were accompanied by church
officers armed with halberts, and they had summary powers of
fining all " swearers" who committed a lapsus in their hearing,
in the sum of eightpence. At St. Andrews two cadgers are haled
before the session for travelling on the Sunday, and although their
excuse, that they had stayed too long in Dundee on Saturday owing
to "storme of wether," is accepted, they are bound over not to
commit the like enormity again. The Kirk protested not only
against Sunday markets, but against Monday markets, because the
thoughts of tradesmen strayed on Sundays to the mercantile possibilities of the morrow, and matters commercial must have got somewhat complicated during fast weeks, when, as in 1653, the Wednesday was given over to eight hours' preaching, the Saturday to two

Social Life in Scot.—Rogers, ii., 36.

†*Records of the Kirk Session of St. Andrews*, i., lxx.-lxxii.

‡*Politics and Religion in Scotland*—Mathieson, ii., 217.

§*The Records of Elgin*—Cramond, ii., 343.

||*Old Church Life in Scotland*—Edgar, i., 238. In 1650 a man was fined for not
taking off his cap to a Linlithgow bailie.—*Scot. : Social and Domestic.*,
Rogers, i., 66.

*a*Walker's *Biographia Presbyteriana*, i., p. 140.

or three sermons, and the Sunday to twelve hours' attendance in Kirk, and four thanksgiving sermons were delivered on the Monday. The preacher who could hold out for a five hours' exhortation was reckoned of great power.* The Kirk protested against trade with Spain and Portugal, for these were papist countries, and contamination was dreaded ; merchants were compelled to close their booths two forenoons each week for the preachings ; in 1653 a man was summoned before the Kirk Session of Stow for daring to visit his sick mother on the Sabbath ; in 1732 the Kirk Session of Elgin issues frequent fulminations against those who draw water from the wells on the Lord's Day, and sends offenders before the magistrates for ci vil punishment ; before the same session in 1762, "Elizabeth Frigg, servatrix, Barnhill," is "dismissed with a sessional rebuke for carrying home some things in her lap on Sabbath night which her master had bought at the market on Saturday. She came not home till the Sabbath night, for which her master was angry with her." In Lumphunan parish, in 1785, a man was solemnly excommunicated "for going to see his mother on a Sabbath day and taking a stone of meal to her " ; at St. Andrews children found romping on the streets on Sabbath day were flogged, and the theological fanatics of that same city surely reached the limits of absurdity when they proposed that "No husband shall kiss his wife, and no mother shall kiss her child on the Sabbath day ;"† on the Moray coast it was a sin to rescue drowning fishermen on Sunday.‡ At Dunfermline, in 1685, apprentices were whipped before the Session for Sabbath-breaking ; everywhere the vocations of "minstrel " and "piper " were proscribed ; poetry was a profane and unprofitable offence ; merrymaking was condemned.§ Anyone convicted of a third breach of Sabbath day regulations forfeited all his goods and estate. At Elgin, in 1659, the Rev. Murdo M'Kenzie scoured the town at Christmas-time to prevent the popish observance of eating geese ;|| indeed, Christmas itself was abolished by Act of Parliament and was not re-legalised until after the Union of the Legislatures a ; at Dunfermline, in 1641, a man was fined for putting a roast to his fire on the Sunday the Kirk Session of Glasgow had an elaborate set of branks and juggs for the public punishment of "flyting women"; sometimes absentees from the Sunday preachings were condemned

---

*Buckle's *History of Civilisation in England*, iii., 204-206.

†Rev. Mr. Lyon's *History of St. Andrews*, i., p. 458, quoted in Buckle's *Hist Civilisation in England*, iii., 253.

‡*Letters from a Gentleman in the North of Scotland,* i., p. 173.

§*Scotland : Social and Domestic*—Rogers, p. 28.

||Scott—*Fasti*, v., 151. In the late 18th century shaving on Sunday was considered by the Seceders to be a serious profanation of the Lord's Day.

aBy the Act of 1712.

to sit on the Gowk's stool during so many sermons; usually, however, the master of a family had to pay a fine of 3s. 4d. sterling for every member of his family who, being in good health on the Saturday night, did not put in an appearance at Sunday worship;* married men and women were subjected to the most outrageous cross-examination on intimate sexual affairs;† to the Kirk Session of Saltoun, in October, 1640, the parish bailie reported that, pursuant to their decree, he had poinded from refractory and contumacious people, viz. :—"from Jeane Reid, ane pan; from Margaret Fluker, ane coat; from Agnes Litster, ane yron pot; from Helen Allen, ane coat," etc.‡ Honest doubters of scriptural dogma were sharply sentenced to public humiliations in sackcloth, as Dougald Roddan of Troqueer parish discovered after he had avowed his belief that "there were but bitts of the Bible the word of God" and that "women had no souls"; the poor the aged and the infirm were relieved out of church collections, the richer heritors escaping poor's tax, so long as they could dodge attendance at kirk, but the alms could scarcely have been regarded as unadulterated blessings by the recipients, for it was accompanied by a necessary attendance at kirk and a regular catechising and theological examination; unlicensed beggars were put in the thieves' hole or the kirk vault; at Aberdeen, in 1608, the swarm of able-bodied beggars who thronged the kirkyaird during sermon and refused to come in to the hearing of the word, were threatened with imprisonment; by Act of Parliament in 1581, swearers convicted of a third offence were either to be imprisoned for a year and a day, or banished, but in the south country the sessions improved upon this by barring from the Communion table "all those who used any kind of minced oaths such as heth, teth, fegs, losh, gosh or lovenanty;" at Gask, in 1679, we find the session appointing a man to instruct a poor orphan boy how to beg and "quhair to goe" as his boarding-out was over-great a financial burden upon the kirk funds, which perhaps is not altogether to be marvelled at when we read, on December 18th, 1732, that the Kirk plate had collected from the canny country-folk no less than "fifteen pounds of ill hapenyes"§—an excellent illustration this of the truth of Gresham's Law that, bad money drives good money out of circulation; among the recipients of session alms at Gask we find, in 1772, one "Solomon, an Arabian Christian, recommended by the Patriarch of Jerusalem"; the enterprising Solomon got six shillings, every coin of it, doubtless, in "ill hapenyes."

---

*Dumfries-shire and Galloway Ant. Socy. Proc., 1863-4, p. 61; Ecc. Records of Aberdeen (Spalding Club), p. xxx.

†Ibid (Aberdeen Records), p. 59.

‡Dumfries and Galloway Arch. Socy. Proc., 1910, p. 158.

§Scot. Hist. Review, 1904-5, p. 32.

H

It is difficult to understand why the Scots people should have "cowered with such a willing submission" under all this white terrorism ; true, here and there, as at St. Andrews, there were rebelliously-inclined individuals who kicked against the pricks ; the "ill hapenyes " just referred to do not indicate an overwhelming reverence for the sessions.   When General Monck shipped away the ecclesiastical leaders of Dundee to English prisons, the people, we are told, thought "the loons were weel away " and refused to pay a reek tax to secure their liberty ; * but the real reason, we expect, for the tame submission to the tyranny lies partly in the fact that the common people were still semi-serfs with the slave blood sluggish in their veins, and partly in the terrible consequences which followed the dread sentence of excommunication.   The form of ex-communication ran thus :

> " Havyng God only befoir owr ees [so and so] be excommunicat, seperated, and cuttit of from the congregacion and misticall body of Christ Jesus, and all benefittis of his trew kyrk (the hearyng of Goddis word only except) ; delivering hym oneto Sathan for the distruccion of the flesche, that the spirit may be saved in the daye of the Lord ; and at nane of the faythfull fearyng God, fra this hour furth, accumpany wyth hym in commonyng, talkyng, bying, selling, eating, drynkn, or other way quhatsoever, except thai be appoynted of the kyrk for his amendment."

A similar social ostracism was placed upon any individual discovered disobeying the edict by having converse or dealing with the denounced one ;   and Parliament assisted the Kirk by declaring that such excommunicated persons as failed to reconcile themselves to the Kirk within 40 days were to be outlawed as rebels and their goods and chattels forfeited.†   And not only Parliament, but each feudal baron in his domain and each burgh magistrate on his bench assisted the Church in, and used the Church for, this "discipline " of the poor.   At Stitchill the Baron Court assisted in the ecclesiastical punishments, and delinquents chained in the stocks or the jougs at the Kirk door suffered during the pleasure of the laird.   At Lasswade the Baron Court prohibited farmers from employing servants who had not their testimonials *vised* by the kirk session, and in the same barony, in 1696, all "tenants' wives, colliers, servants, and children were ordered to go to the grieve's house on Sabbath days and march with him to the parish church " ; also, it was ordained that "all children who shall meett togither in clusters on the Lord's day to play togither (as ordinarily they do) their parents be advertised thereof and commanded to belt them privately for the first and second fault," but for the third offence they are

---

*Hewison's *The Covenanters*, ii., p. 39.   See also *Perth Kirk Session Records*, p. 231.

†*Acta Parl. Scot.*, iii., 76.

"to be belted publicly on the coale-hill by there parents . . . on Munday morning thereafter." Absentees from kirk service were ordered to stay indoors all Sabbath under a penalty of, for a man and wife, 2s. Scots, for a servant, 1s. Scots, and for every child over 6 years of age 6d. Scots.* In Aberdeen the penalties imposed by the magistrates for non-attendance at Sunday sermon were for a burgess and his wife, 13s. 4d., and for a craftsman 6s. 8d ; for non-attendance at week-day sermon the burgess was mulcted in 2s. and the craftsman in 1s ; and the clergy were diligent in spreading horrible stories of the evil things that befell rebellious people who did not reverence and obey their spiritual advisers. Men who put out their tongues at ministers had the misfortune to have their tongues stick out for ever ; and traders who refused to finance kirk projects had their progeny turned imbecile for three generations.

But the records of these little village popes of Presbytery are not all black with class tyranny and cruelty and superstitious folly, as the struggles to create and preserve a system of compulsory education bear witness. True, long before the Reformation there were grammar schools for the teaching of Latin, and lecture schools for teaching in the vernacular tongue ; † teachers were licensed, if not greatly encouraged, by the old church ; and the sons of barons and free-holders were compelled to attend until at least they "had perfect Latin " ; but John Knox and the Reformation enthusiasts gave to the Reformed Kirk a wider, a more complete, and a vastly more effective educational system. On paper the new system was splendid : it provided for the compulsory education of all children, if necessary right up to the Universities, but it did not provide the cash, and the heritors and wealthy parishioners generally saw no reason why they should pay for the education of the progeny of the "rascal multitude." From 1560 to 1633 literally nothing was done beyond the creation of spasmodic and half-starved curricula of reading and writing which the kirk sessions offered the children of such parishioners as were able to contribute to the cost ; though in some places the children of the poor were taught *gratis*. But the Knoxian tradition still persisted, and in 1633 the bishops were given powers by Parliament to tax the heritors and the parishioners for education, if they could secure a local majority in favour.‡ In 1646 such a tax or stent was made compulsory, local majority or no ; and fifty years later the heritors were ordered by Parliament to provide commodious schoolhouses and find a yearly salary of from 100 merks (£5 11s. 1d. sterling) to 200 merks (£11 2s. 2d. sterling)

---

* "The Barony of Lasswade."—James Steuart in *Chambers' Journal*, August, 1912.

† M'Crie's *Life of Melville*, p. 361.

‡ *Education : Scotland.*—First Report of Commissioners (1865), xxvii.

for every schoolmaster, having relief from the tenants for half the cost. But, alas for the importunities of the Kirk and the good intent of Parliament, in many districts the heritors stubbornly refused to yield the funds, and as late as 1706 there was no school at Girvan ; by 1711 neither school nor schoolmaster at Dailly ; * by 1715, in Fife, only one man in three and one woman in twelve could write ; by 1720 few, if any, of the common people of Galloway could read, and the schoolmaster, who could not eke out an existence from the birds slain at the cockfighting contests on Fastern's eve, the occasional basket of eggs, bundles of peat divots and so on brought him by his scholars, ran every chance of dying from sheer hunger ; he was simply tolerated by the rich class as a sort of ornamental parasite, and if he had the hardihood to beg that his nominal salary—less, considerably less, than the wages paid to the artisan—should not be nominal, but real, he was informed that his pupils would be withdrawn from his school.† In 1735 the parishioners of Dalgain, Riccarton, Kirkoswald, Craigie, New Cumnock, Dailly, Bar, Muirkirk, Auchinleck, Symington, Stair, and Monkton were induced, probably by their ministers, to take legal action against the heritors for non-provision of schools and teachers' salaries. In 1752 there was neither school nor schoolmaster at Auchinleck, and in 1758 a similar state of things existed at New Cumnock. Even in the schoolmasters' charter of 1802, Parliament fixed the maximum annual salary at £22 4s. 6d. In the larger burghs, where the Kirk influence was more potent, matters were not so bad.‡ As early as 1675, for example, Rutherglen had a common school for the compulsory instruction of all young per ons between the ages of 6 and 12, and ome consistent effort was made by the Sessions right down to 1873, when the State took control of education out of Church hands altogether to guarantee the masses a knowledge of the three R's. Not that the poor children were always carefully enrolled—far from it ; did not Dr. Guthrie estimate, in 1863, that there were some 2000 ragged children in Edinburgh who were outside the educational polities of the city ? Still the Church must be given credit for having insisted, despite three centuries of discouragement, upon the inalienable right of every child born in the realm to a full and a free drilling in the rudiments of reading, writing, and arithmetic.§

But no proper or adequate conception of the theological tyranny of the times we are considering can be formed unless due prominence

---

Old Church Life in Scotland—Edgar, ii., 74.
†Graham's *Social Life in Scotland in the Eighteenth Century*, ii., 161.
‡See *History of the Burgh and Parish Schools of Scotland*—Grant.
§It is also worthy of passing note that in May, 1847, the United Presbyterian resolved " in favour of secular, without religious, education by the State."
—Lord Cockburn's *Journal*, ii., p. 179.

is given to the revolting tortures and murders of thousands upon thousands of poor old Scotswomen which took place as a result of the great witchcraft superstition.   At every mercat cross and on every gallows hill, throughout the length and breadth of the land, the innocent victims of clerical delusion and magisterial greed were burned to the death ; professional witchfinders over-ran the country ; ignorant clergymen and still more ignorant kirk officials sought diligently for women who might be on terms of intimacy with the devil, and woe be to them upon whom the least breath of the malevolent suspicion fell ! Interrogation before the Session, upon "evidence" elicited from poor distracted and hysterical victims by savage tortures unknown even in the hellish annals of African heathendom, verdicts of guilty, and sentences of roasting alive were pronounced ; and for a century and a half every burgh and parish in Scotland seems to have offered to Heaven its regular incense of a stench of burning flesh—human flesh, the flesh of the mothers and grandmothers of the labouring poor. We shall never perhaps know the number of the victims, but we can at least here adduce evidence, shocking though it be and gruesome, to prove that such polite historians as have merely in a depreciatory and minimising way deigned to notice the subject at all, equally with the historians who write for class hire and deliberately obliterate everything calculated to enlighten the working people on the real and vital happenings of the past, are merely useless fictionists and class servers, their alleged history but a conglomeration of half truths and whole lies. Professor Hume Brown cautiously estimates the number of witches burned in Scotland at four thousand ; * the writer of the preface to the published records of the Baron Court of Stitchill puts the number at eight thousand,†—an enormous number in the vastly smaller populations of the sixteenth, seventeenth, and eighteenth centuries.

The witchcraft delusion, of course, was not peculiar to Scotland ; there were witch-burnings in England, and as early as the year 1515, we read, 500 witches were executed at Geneva during three months, and during twelve months at Como no fewer than 1000 convicted women were destroyed ; but in Scotland the mania grew to dimensions and raged with a ferocity elsewhere unequalled. Here, in this country, from 1563 on to 1722, did a cow sicken, or a harvest fail, or a storm menace shipping, or a rich man or a clergyman die suddenly, then nothing so certain as that there was a coven or gang of witches at work ! The minister, accompanied by two of his elders, made "a subtle and privy inquisition " of the parishioners.‡   Boxes were put up in Church where anonymous accusations could be

---

Scotland Before 1700, p. 207.
†*Scot. Hist. Socy.*, vol. 50, p. xxxvii.
‡Dalyell's *Darker Superstitions of Scotland*, p. 624.

dropped. Did some poor old dame meander in her talk, did her clashy old tongue annoy an elder with gossip, then the minister named her publicly from the pulpit and the startled congregation was enjoined to supply evidence against her. Meanwhile she was completely ostracised. Suspicions accumulated. Finally she was haled before the Session for examination, an examination conducted, says Lecky, "eagerly, passionately, with a thirst for blood that knew no mercy, with a zeal that never tired.*" Did she deny her intimacy with the devil, then a professional witchfinder might be employed, or torture might be immediately resorted to. If the specialist were employed, he commenced his researches by first blindfolding the suspected woman, stripping her naked, binding her to a chair, and making a keen scrutiny of her body for any devil's mark. If a brown mole-ish mark was anywhere discoverable, particularly among hair roots, the witch-finder rammed a witch-finding needle three inches long into the flesh at the marked spot. The woman was then asked to point to the exact spot at which the needle had entered her flesh, and if she failed (as she usually did)† she was, of course, guilty,‡ for it was indisputable that whatever part of one's body the devil might mark, would thereafter be insensible to touch. Guilt having been thus proved, the victim was cross-questioned as to her accomplices, since the devil usually kept his followers in each parish organised in separate covens or gangs of thirteen members. If the poor woman was "obdurate," and refused to invent the names of other twelve women as devil's servants, she was put to the torture. A witch's bridle was put over her head,§ four prongs being inserted in her mouth, one each to the tongue and the palate and one to each cheek; she was then chained to a ring in a cell and kept without sleep by skilful "wakers," who took turn about at the vigil.‖ Food and drink were refused her; at intervals she was hung up by her thumbs, which were tied together behind her back; she was whipped; lighted candles were applied to the soles of her feet, between her toes, and into her mouth. If she still refused to invent the names of her accomplices she might be clad in a hair-shirt soaked in vinegar to draw off her skin. From these tortures four out of six accused women at one trial are said to have died.*a* Sometimes

---

Rise and Influence of Rationalism in Europe, i., 128.

†The spots may sometimes have really been anæsthetics.

‡Pitcairn's *Ancient Criminal Trials in Scotland*, vol. iii., p. 601.

§Minutely described by Pitcairn in *Crim. Trials* (Bannatyne Edn.), vol. i., part ii., p 50.

‖In Dunfermline every citizen had to take his turn as "waker of witches." One woman complained to the Privy Council that she had been kept awake for 20 days, and naked, but for a sackcloth over her.—Mathieson's *Politics and Religion in Scotland*, ii., 160.

*a*Byways of History—Colville, p. 240. Chambers' *Dom. Ann. of Scot.*, ii., 61, 154, 219.

their legs were crushed with wedges in the "boot," their heads "thrawn" with a rope, their fingers twisted in the thumbscrews, and their nails turn off with pincers.   Once we come across the case of a poor woman in Kirkwall, one Alison Balfour, who, after bearing her own torture without flinching, finally swore everything her tormentors put into her mouth, through seeing her husband, her son and her daughter (a child of seven years) tortured before her eyes ; and ere she was burned at the stake she made a recantation of her bogus "confession " and asked the pardon of God for even yielding to the making of it, but pled with a pathos that no words can describe how, though she had suffered her own bodily pains unflinchingly, she had yielded when she heard the cries of her little daughter in the agony of the thumbscrews, for she was "sair vexed "*

When a woman ceased to be obdurate, and yielded up the names of her "associates," each "associate " was, of course, arrested, and a similar course of examination and torture arranged, the parish ministers having thus little difficulty in keeping themselves busily employed against the army of Satan. If, by any mischance, a scarcity of victims should occur in a district, the Presbytery might appoint a solemn fast for "the discoverie of the gryt empyre of the deivill in this countrey be witchecraft " ; in some districts the fast was supplemented by the employment of a pardoned witch as a sort of witch detective.   At Glasgow, in 1597, for example, one, Margaret Aitken, had her life spared on condition that she would make a general discovery of witches whom she professed to be able to recognise by a certain secret mark on the eye ; through her activities "divers innocent women . . . were condemned and put to death."

Perhaps we could best convey to the reader an impression of the real nature of some of these gloomy barbarities by abbreviating and bowdlerising (for there is great plenitude of sexual grossness) one of the trials recorded by Pitcairn.† In the year 1590, one, David Seaton, a baron's depute-bailie in Tranent, had a maid-servant, Geillis Duncan, whom he suspected of being in league with the devil for some nefarious purpose or other. He therefore privately "examined " her by means of thumbscrews and by thrawing her head with a rope. Yet would she confess nothing. Latterly he discovered the devil's mark upon her throat, whereupon she, in terror, confessed that she was a devil's servant [she may have spoken truer than she knew], and implicated "innumerable " others, including, Dr. Fian, a schoolmaster. As a result, many of the

---

Ancient Crim. Trails, vol. i., part ii., pp. 215-222.

†Pitcairn's *Ancient Crim. Trials*, i., part ii., 376-7.   Thomas Palpla, another Kirkwall victim, was in the thumbscrews for 11 days and 11 nights, then put in the boots, " he being naiket in the meane tyme and skairgeit with towis in sic sort that thay left nather flesch nor hyde upon him."

"innumerable" host were executed, all of them except two being "reputed for as civill, honest women as anie that dwelled within the cittie of Edenbrough before they were apprehended." King James, who professed himself to be an authority on Demonology, examined one of the implicated women, Agnes Simpson, himself, but she stoutly denied any acquaintance with the devil, and was therefore ordered to prison for torture and examination for the devil's mark which "he puts upon his own with his tongue in some privie part of their bodie, usually under hair for the sake of concealment." The poor woman had her head thrawn with ropes, "according to the custome . . . being a payne most grevous," and had all the hair upon her body shaven off, whereupon the devil's mark was discovered. She then confessed that she had sailed away in the air in a riddle with other 200 witches, and that she had met the devil in North Berwick Kirk at dead of night, where he had compelled the observance of certain indecent rites. The King, incredulous, said she was an "extreame lyar," but Agnes whispered to him certain secret conversations he had had with his Queen, and he then no longer doubted the mad nonsense which she confessed about cats which could raise tempests, about the curative powers of toads' venom, and about carnal dealings with the devil (vividly described). Dr Fian was then put to the torture, and "confessed" the most outrageous sexual nonsense, evidently with a view to escaping farther mangling in the "boots." He escaped from prison, was re-captured, had his finger nails torn off with smith's pincers, and through his fingers were thrust needles "up to the heads" : still he denied he was a warlock ; then his legs were smashed in the "boots," being "crushit and beaten together as small as might bee, and the bones and flesh so brused that the bloud and marrow spouted forth in great abundance" ; finally, still denying guilt and recanting his original "confession," he was burned on the Castle Hill of Edinburgh in January, 1591.

Once an accusation was made there was small chance of escape. For some little time after the Reformation the civil magistrates refused to carry out the witchcraft sentences, but this roused the General Assembly of the Kirk, which in 1597 complained that the magistrates set convicted witches at liberty, and declared its intention of excommunicating any magistrate who, in time to come, would not apply the death penalty after conviction.* Farther, the magistrates were encouraged to assist the Kirk by being granted the property belonging to executed witches ; † and when the great chirurgeon (surgeon) craft found its trade attacked in every parish

---

Proc. Soc. Ant. (Scot.), 1887-8, p. 245.
†*Memorialls* (1638-1684)—Rev. Robt. Law (Sharpe's Edn.), lxix.

by one or more female folk herbalists,* there was added another
economic interest to the anti-witch campaigns ; certainly the mere
charming away of warts and toothaches by incantations and herb
brews was not legally punishable by death, but the medical profession did its utmost to stamp out the blackleg competition, and
encouraged the clergy in their cruel and nefarious work.† One
case is on record where the Presbytery of Lanark, finding that a poor
old woman had been adjudged by the Commissary of Lanark to be
guilty of charming only, "continued to labour more earnestly, until
on 5th November (1640) they consider they have sufficient materials
for bringing her to trial, quherupon the Pre. byt ry thinks themselves
bound not to suffer a witch to live."‡ It has been said that final
acquittal on a charge of witchcraft was so rare that only three instances of it have been recorded in the judicial records, and in one
of the three cases (that of Agnes Simpson, in 1591, referred to *ante*)
the majority of the jury, who acquitted, were proceeded against for
"wil ul error." § When the cases, after coming before the sessions
and the presbyteries, were referred for sentence not to the judicial
authorities of the towns but to the assize courts in the country dis-
t icts, acquittal does not appear to have been much more common,
Sir George Mackenzie observing that "scarce ever any " escaped.
And when the sessions failed, even after diligent search, to gather
evidence, however flimsy it might be, against a woman, they salved
what hey called their consciences by ordering her to "make sackcloth repentence for being suspected of witchcraft."‖ The ministers
nd their sessions based the justification for their hatred of witchcraft upon such Biblical texts as the last verse of the 20th Chapter of
Leviticus, the 18th verse of the 22nd chapter of Exodus, and on the
18th chapter of Deuteronomy, and their delusions assumed sometimes fearful proportions. The Rev. Robert Kirk of A erfoyle, in
his *Secret Commonwealth*, thus describes the w tches' mark : "a spot
that I have seen, as a small mole, horny and brown coloured throw
which when a large brass pin was thrust . . . till it bowed and
became crooked, the witches, both men and women, nather felt pain
nor did bleed, nor knew the precise time when this was doing to them,
their eyes only being covered." King James VI., another pecialist,
in his *Daemonologie*, explains that the reason why women are more

---

Perth Kirk Session Records, p. 232.

†Some landowners, like Chisholm of Comer, in 1662, got rid of undesirable
    or wealthy tenants through accusing them of witchcraft.—Lang's *Sir
    George Mackenzie*, p. 41.

‡"The Confessions of the Forfar Witches."—Joseph Anderson, LL.D., in
    Proc. Soc. Ant (Scot.), 1887-8, p. 243.

§*Scot. Hist. Review*, 1904-5, p. 244.

‖Dalyell's *Darker Superstitions of Scotland*, p. 665.

addicted to witchcraft than are men is because "that sex is frailer than man is, so it is easier to be entrapped in these grosse snares of the divell, as was over-well proved to be trew, by the serpent's deceiving of Eve at the beginning which makes him the homelier with that sex sensine." Captain Burt relates how a minister told him seriously that "one man succeeded in cutting off the leg of a cat who attacked him, that the leg immediately turned into that of an old woman and that four ministers signed a certificate attesting the fact " * ; and one of the "counts" upon which the Rev. Donald Cargill excommunicated "Bluidy Mackenzie," the Lord Advocate, was that he (Mackenzie) had interfered in favour of a tortured "witch."† Even the pious Woodrow is constrained to report that the ministers were "indiscreet in their zeal," and when finally in 1735 Parliament repealed the statutes against witchcraft, and made the convicted witch a mere cheat and condemned her not to the stake but to the pillory, the only protests came from the clergy.‡

It is difficult for a later age to reconstruct the psychology of these clerical witch-finders. That they believed they were doing vigorous battle with the devil, we may agree ; that they were impelled and assisted in their savageries by powerful economic interests, the medical profession, the magistrates' bench, and the lairds, we have seen ; but it is not clear why men and women, who merely consulted the witches for herb cures, should be put to death, nor is it clear why the tortures should have been so fiendishly savage, nor why, so often, the victims should have been burned alive. Mr. Andrew Lang says that what went on in the name of witchcraft was a web of fraud, folk medicine, fairy tale, hysteria, and hypnotic suggestion, including physical and psychological phenomena still unclassified.§ But that does not cover the whole ground. Why, for example, should Satan, when he came to Scotland, so frequently devote his energies to women, and why should all, or nearly all, of the witchcraft trials retail gross and realistic evidence bearing upon sexual relationships alleged to have been between the accused women and his Satanic Majesty ? Mr. Burns Begg, ingeniously hazards the guess that there were a large number of discharged soldiers on tramp who to credulous women represented themselves as the devil, and by so doing gained an extraordinary ascendency over their minds. This may have been the case where the "witches" confessed later on before the Session that the devil originally appeared to them as a

---

*One of the most credulous of the witchcraft experts in his day was Professor Sinclair, who held the Chair of Moral Philosophy at Glasgow University, and who was the author of "Satan's Invisible World Discovered."

†*Sir George Mackenzie : His Life and Times.*—Andrew Lang, p. 46.

‡*Scotland : Social and Domestic*—Rogers, p. 30.

§*Hist. of Scot.*, ii., p. 432.

strong able-bodied man ; but what are we to make of the mental
condition of the poor unfortunates who alleged that the Devil came
to them in the guise of a bee or as a pretty boy in green clothes ?
And what are we to make of the witches' song which the devil asked
his victims to sing :

> " Commer goe ye before, commer goe ye,
>   Gif ye will not goe before, commer let me ? "

Certainly the accused women seem always to have been of the
labouring class. Once, indeed, a professional witch-pricker called
John Kincaid, whose reputation among the clergy seems to have
been chiefly based upon the fact that he operated with six and eight
inch needles—being some three to five inches longer than those used
by his competitors—made the mistake of accusing "a noble lady "
of witchcraft. But this was more democracy than his Age could
stand, and John was despatched as a common felon to the prison at
Kinross. In the rural districts lairds who might be in trouble with
Presbytery upon their own accounts might seek to appease their
spiritual advisers, as did the Marquis of Douglas in 1649, when he
arrested 11 women on a charge of sorcery, and sent them to Presbytery for examination, with just such an *insouciance* as he might have
displayed if he had appeased the owner of a menagerie by sending
him a catch of rabbits.* The juries were composed of "landowners
and other responsible residenters."† and that the common people
were quite alive to the class nature of the iniquisitions is evident from
the fact that the executioner or other official in charge of the witch-
burnings was sometimes pelted with stones.‡   Little need we wonder.
Sometimes the poor victims were "wirreit at ane staik " (*i.e.*,
strangled) before being "brint in assis," but usually the sentence
simply reads "*convicta et combusta* " (*i.e.*, convicted and burned),
and the Earl of Mar told the Privy Council, in 1608, how, with a
piercing yell, some women once broke, half-burnt, rom the slow fire
that consumed them, struggled for a few moments with despairing
energy among the spe tators, but soon, with shrieks of blasphemy

---

**Scot. : Soc. and Domestic*—Rogers, ii., 188.
†Trials for Witchcraft at Crook of Devon, Kinross-shire (1662)—*Proc. Soc. Ant.*
    1887-8, p. 215.   In 1598 the Laird of Lathocker took a suspected witch,
    Geillis Gray, from the minister at Crail, and so tortured her that she was
    unable thereafter to work for her living.—*St. Andrew's Register*, f. n., p.
    882.
‡Dumfriesshire *Antiq. Socy. Trans.* (1900-5), p. 103.

and wild protestations of innocence, sank writhing in agony among the flames.*

Now let us endeavour to form some idea of the extent of these witchcraft persecutions. Pitcairn says the first case in Scotland occurred in 1563, when Agnes Mullikane of Dunfermline was "banist and exilt." In 1569 William Stewart and a Frenchman called Paris were burned at St. Andrews for "witchcraft, ingromancye and utheris crymes," and in 1572, at the same place, a woman was burned, John Knox himself being the officiating prosecutor.† In 1575 a woman was summoned for sorcery before the Session of St. Andrews, but fled with her husband, who declared that "his wyffe feared and thairfoir they durst not byde."‡ In 1579, thirty persons, in Ross and Ardmanach, we are informed, came under the spiritual shadow which attended the Reformation of religion, and were "delated" for sorcery and incantation.§ In 1588, Alison Pearson, of Byre-hills, Fifeshire, was, after most extravagant confessions, convicted of sorcery.‖ Between 1544 and 1660 the witchcraft cases coming before the Privy Council are so numerous that the index in the published register fills three columns.a In the year 1590, a woman called Bessie Roy is thus charged; "Thou are indicted for a common away-taker of women's milk in the whole country, and detaining the same at thy pleasure, as the whole country will testify"; in the same year 200 witches and warlocks were "bagged" at North Berwick. Seven years later "many wer execute" at St. Andrews, including a detachment forwarded by the minister of Pittenweem; at Aberdeen "a sweet beginning" was made with 23 women who were burned living.b Between 1619 and 1622 no fewer than 7 commissions to try witchcraft in Inverkeithing were issued by the Privy Council, and as each trial usually involved a large number of women and as the evidence given in one trial was held as evidence even against women who were not themselves upon trial, blanks being left in the charge sheets for such fresh names as

---

*Sum wemen wer tane in Broichtoun (Broughton, now part of Edinburgh) as witches, and being put to ane Assize and convict, albeit they perseverit constant in their denyell to the end, yet thay wer Burnit Quick efter sic ane crewell maner, that sum of thame deit in despair, renunceand (renouncing their baptism), and blasphemeand; and utheris half brunt, brak out of the fyre and wes cast in quick in it agane, quhill thay wer brunt to the deid."—*Haddington MSS.*, Advocates Lib. Edin., 422.

†*St. Andrews Kirk Session Register*, part i., p. 7.   See also *A Historie of James the Sext.*

‡*St. Andrews Kirk Session Register*, p. 7.

§*Exchequer Rolls*, vol. xx., Pref. lxiv.

‖*Border Minstrelsy*, ii., p. 213.

aReg. *Privy Council*, vol. 8, 2nd and 3rd series.

bProc. *Soc. Ant. in Scot.*, 1887-8, p. 245.

might be discovered during the trial, each commission meant a
holocaust of victims.* During the years 1622 to 1625 some fifty
guilty persons were delated for sentence to the Privy Council, and
nearly half of them were from Inverkeithing and Culross ; † women
were burned in Corstorphine, Eastwood, Auchterarder, Niddrie,
Eyemouth, Anstruther, Dysart, St. Andrews, Edinburgh, Fossoquhy,
Leith, and other places. One woman at Carmunnock, Margaret
Wallace by name, was accused by the minister, the Rev Archibald
Glen, of "killing Robert Muir, his good-brother, by witchcraft."
The charge failed, and some six years afterwards the Rev. Archibald
died, whereupon the Session and the Presbytery promptly accused
the woman of encompassing his death in revenge. She was charged
with laying upon him "ane uncouth sickness, whereof the said Mr.
Archibald, sweating, died." In vain did the poor accused woman
plead that "in truth the said Mr. Archibald died of a consumption
of his lights." She was burned.‡ In 1623 Thomas Grieve, at
Edinburgh, was executed after a process instigated by the Surgeon's
Guild for curing of Wm. Cousine's wife by causing her husband to
heat the coulter of his plough, cooling the said coulter in water from
the holy well, and then giving her the water to drink. In 1626-7
nine search commissions were issued for Dysart, nine for other
towns in Fife, and thirty-two for the County of Aberdeen. § The
details of the cases dealt with between 1629 and 1631 by the Privy
Council would fill volumes. Isobel Young, spouse to an Eastbarns
portioner, is first strangled and then burned on the Castle Hill of
Edinburgh, and a similar fate befalls Agnes Finnie of the "Poteraw
of Edinburgh ; " "several " are burned in Orkney ; Kate Oswald,
spouse to Robert Achison in Niddrey, charged with being habit and
repute a witch, having carnal dealings with the devil, and bewitching
John Nisbet's cow so that it gave blood instead of milk is worried
at a stake ere being burned ; Alexander Hamilton, a beggar who
was refused an alms by Lady Ormestoune, called upon his friend the
devil to assist him in revenge ; so the Lady died, and Alexander
was burnt as a reparation ; Alison Nisbet in Hilltoun is burned ;
and Eliza Pae, the maltman's wife in Eyemouth, just secures ac-

---

*Hume *On Punishment for Crimes*, ii., 559. King James latterly saw that
  many of these commissions of justiciary were being used and abused
  against innocent persons (Chambers' *Dom. Ann. Scot.*, i., 292), though he
  himself had sold many of them to barons and burgh magistrates. Commissions entitled their holders to search for, torture, and execute witches.
  —Macintosh—*Hist. Civ. Scot.*, ii., 274.

†Mathieson—*Politics and Religion in Scotland*, ii., 157.

‡*Memorialls on The Memorable Things that fell out within this Island of Britain
  from 1638 to 1684*—Rev. Robt. Law (Sharpe's Edn.), Preface lvi.

§*Reg. Privy Council*, 2nd series, vol. i., pp. xii, xiii.

quittal on a charge of sinking ships and conversing with Satan.*
In 1637 Isabel Malcolm is convicted by the Presbytery of Strath-
bogie of "charming," but her case is continued "in the hope that
she should be found yet more guilty " ; and another poor creature
admits that she had received 6d. from the devil, who had informed
her "that God bade him give her that and ask her how the minister
was and other questions."†

The General Assembly of the Kirk which met in 1640 required
ministers all over the country, "carefully to take notice of charmers,
witches, and all such abusers of the people, and to urge the Acts for
Parliament to be execute against them," as if every clergyman of
the previous three-quarters of a century had not been zealous
and diligent in purging the land of Satan's accomplices ! Three
years later there is another outbreak of savagery ; in Fifeshire alone
during a few brief weeks over 30 women are burned ; Janet Barker
and Margaret Lauder, two Edinburgh servant women, are "detected"
by one James Scobie. The women are burned, and Scobie leaps
into fame and is in great demand. The Church Assembly asks Parliament for a standing Commission to try cases. In July, 1646, the
Kirk Session of Auchterhouse appoints a public fast "because of the
scandal of witches and charmers in the district," and also because the
neighbouring congregations "have long been starved by dry-breasted
ministers." In 1649 there is a savage epidemic of women-burning
all over Fife, Perth, Stirling, Linlithgow, Edinburgh, Haddington,
Berwick, Peebles and Lanark, and in a single afternoon Sir
James Balfour witnessed the issuing of no fewer than twenty-seven
commissions;‡ in one little village 14 or 16 women are said to have
been burned,§ at Torryburn, a village four miles from Dunfermline,
one out of every three old women was prosecuted for witchcraft.‖
In England, however, by this time, so far from encouraging tor-
turings and inquisitions, the authorities were actively stamping
them out ; in the *Mercurius Politicus* for October 23rd, 1652, there
is a case reported where the English judges ordered the minister,
sheriff, and tormentors to be found out and to have an account taken
of the ground of their cruelty ; but in Scotland, let the Government
be as it may—Covenanting, Episcopalian or Cromwellian—the
tortures and the burnings went on steadily. In 1656 John M'William
Sclater was burned for being the devil's cloak-bearer ; in 1658
Margaret Anderson of Haddington confessed herself guilty of witchcraft, but afterwards retracted, saying she was "distracted " when

---

Spottiswoode Socy. Miscellany, part ii., 47-72.

†Macintosh—*Hist. Civ. Scot.*, iii., 261-3.

‡*Annals*, iii., 436-7.

§Mathieson—*Politics and Religion in Scot.*, ii., 160.

‖*Dunfermline Kirk Session Records*, 14, note.

she made the confession ; the minister, however, was not thus to be baulked of his prey, and signed a deposition that his victim "was quite sound in her mind when she made the confession." She was burned along with a warlock called John Carse. In 1658 Margaret Taylor, Janet Black, Katherine Rany, and Bessie Paton were burned; in 1659 five women, called the Stentoun witches, were burned ; in 1659 eight women and one man were burned at Tranent after some extraordinary confessions of *coitus cum diabolo ;* in the same year nine victims were roasted at Dumfries. Of the Alloa witches dealt with by the Presbytery of Stirling on 11th May, 1658, three were burned and one died in prison, one of the victims in this case admitting that she had been in the devil's service for 20 years ; she had first met the devil "in Isabell Jamesone's little house where she dwelt herself all alone, and who came in to me in the said house in the likeness of a man with broune cloathes and ane little blak hatt, who asked her, what aileth you ? She ansorit, I am ane poor bodie and cannot gett wheron to live. He said, Ye sall not want if you will doe my bidding, and he gave me five shilling and bade me goe buy ane peck of meill with it, and I went to the tron and bought ane peck of piess meill with it, and it wes gude money " ; he then sent her for "ane Chopine of aill " and they ate and drank together ; he spent the night with her ; she said she would be his servant, to which he replied "Ye must quyte God and your baptisme," which she did, "and he gave me his mark on my eyebrie by ane kiss "; she was to call him, she said, "by name Johne and I sall nevir leave you, but do anything to you that ye bid me. Thereafter in the groof of the morning I convoyed him doune the bowrig, where he vanished from me." That is certainly the kind of story explained by Mr. Begg's theory of the tramp soldier, and it is fairly typical of the sad muck which, by the gloomy superstitions of an ignorant clergy, was construed into demoniacal revelation.

In 1660, under the reign of the Merry Monarch, a regular epidemic of women-burning swept the Church* As one writer puts it : "Whatever satisfaction the return of King Charles the Second might afford to the younger females in his domains, it certainly brought nothing, save torture and destruction, to the unfortunate old women or witches of Scotland." Innumerable warrants were issued, and "for some years the Castlehill of Edinburgh and the heights in the vicinity blazed with the dry carcases of the miserable victims." In the North country ignorant justices and foolish clergymen condemned almost every old woman upon whom their malevolent suspicions fell to the torture and the stake.† In 1661 commissions were issued galore ; three justice-deputes were kept busy once a week

---

*See *Acta Parl. Scot.*, vii., App. 31 ; *Records of the Justiciary Court*, vol. i:
†Sharpe's Pref. to Law's *Memorialls, cit. op.*, lxviii.

at Dalkeith and Musselburgh in trying witches; in August of that year, John Rae, the traveller, asserts 120 women were burned; Janet Watson, at her trial, admitted that the devil came to her "in the likeness of ane prettie boy in green clothes, gave her his mark, and left in the likeness of ane blak doug"; when next he re-appeared he came as "a great bee and stung her shoulder" and called her "Weill Dancing Jenot." † Poor Isabel Gowdie, at Auldearn, was bullied into declaring: "I deserve to be reivin upon iron harrows and worse if it culd be devysit." One woman at Nairn implicated 37 others. At Margaret Hutchison's trial in Edinburgh, "the young laird of Duddingstone, deponed that a witch who had lately suffered for sorcery had mentioned that Hutchinson was as great a witch as herself and had attended several of the devil's select parties. Upon this she was found guilty, strangled, and burnt." No conception of the sifting of evidence, no mercy, no sense, only a dull, blind, and cruel fanaticism! Strangled and burned! In 1662, commissions are still being poured forth, but the authorities in Edinburgh forbid the ministers to use torture.* And one infamous wretch is whipped through the streets of Edinburgh for making false accusations against women. But the new humanism is a long way from the hearts of the clergy, and the tortures and the inquisitions proceed apace! At the Crook of Devon, twelve women and one man are tried; all are poor, the man cannot buy "himself a pair of shoon"; one woman, Margaret Hoggan, is 79 years of age and "may have died from excitement and terror in the course of her trial"; of the 13 accused only one, Margaret Pittendreich, escapes, and that temporarily because of her pregnancy—she is to come up for sentence afterwards; two married women, whose names had been used during the trial, were seized, strangled, and burned.‡ Dalzell gives 150 as the number of victims in 1662.§ In 1664 nine women were burned together at Leith; in 1673, Janet M'Nicol, condemned by the Earl of Argyll, Sir Colin Campbell, and Ninian Bannatyne, was strangled at the Gallows Craig; in 1697, Thomas Aitkenhead was hanged for attributing a post-exilian date to the pentateuch;|| in the same year, two men and four women (the Renfrewshire witches, as they were called) were burned on the Gallows Green at Paisley, one poor warlock escaping the torture by committing suicide on the previous evening. In Renfrewshire under the curates of Episcopacy there had been no burnings, and even with Presbytery in the ascendant,

---

†Pitcairn's *Ancient Crim. Trials*, îii., 601.
*Chambers' *Dom. Ann. Scot.*, ii., 220, 277, 278, 285.
†*Spottiswoode Socy. Miscellany*, ii., 71.
‡*Proceedings Socy. Antiq. Scot.*, 1887-8, pp. 212-218
§*Darker Superstitions of Scot.*, 669.
||Story told in Lang's *History of Scotland.*

the Commissioners at first refused to act; but the clergy were eager and ferocious for blood, and during the great trial in 1697 a minister, Henderson, preached a savage sermon to the Commissioners from the text, "Thou shalt not suffer a witch to live."* At Kirkcudbright, in 1698, a poor old woman from Dalry, called Elspeth M'Ewan, was burned; and from the Burgh Treasurer's accounts we can gather some idea of the ceremony. Her burning cost £5 (Scots of course) for peats, sixteen shillings for coals, four shillings for ropes wherewith to bind her securely as she was being roasted; the tar barrel cost £5 4s., the carter's account was 6s., and two shillings was allowed the executioner for "ane pint of aill qn she was burning" (it would be thirsty work!), eight shillings to the drummer who officiated, and £5 5s. drink-money to the executioner, the drink being specifically stated as being consumed "at several times."

Silently, the nightmare rose from Scotland; by the year 1702 we can only find one witch being hanged in Edinburgh †; and the last burning seems to have taken place at Dornoch, in 1722, where, on a bitterly cold day, a poor old grandmother was brought out to the faggots; the arrangements were scarcely complete, and, as a special favour, the poor old body was allowed to sit beside the fire which was to consume her while the other instruments of her death were being prepared.‡ In 1734 the Presbytery of Elgin dismissed a charge against a "reputed charmer" on her promise not "to do the like again," and although there were inhuman monsters still at large in the pulpits—men like the Rev. Thomas Boston of Ettrick, who likened unbaptised infants to "toads and serpents which men kill at first sight, before they have done any hurt"—and although, even as late as 1743, the Synod of the Secession Church was protesting against the repeal of the laws against witchcraft, the days of the women-burning were over. The Church had great internal struggles at her hand to keep her busy. Science was slowly bringing men a wider outlook and a more reasonable explanation of the phenomena of life.

---

*Metcalfe's *History of Renfrewshire*. References given to the "witch-findings" at Greenock, Inverkip, Paisley, Kilmacolm, etc.

†*Scot. : Social and Domestic*—Rogers, i. p. 29.

‡*Justiciary Records* (Scot. Hist. Socy), Preface by Sheriff Scott Moncrieff, xxvii.

I

CHAPTER VI.

THE STRUGGLE IN THE TOWNS.

" The desire for gain or self-advantage which, from the outset, was the *raison d'etre* of the Gild Merchant and many other gilds degenerated at times into the most reprehensible forms of selfishness. The gildsman may have been kind and loving towards those of his own fraternity, but he was too often harsh and oppressive toward non-gildsmen."—*Gross, " The Gild Merchant,"* p. 36.

" Craftsmen dominated in turn over the unfree worker, and waged a constant war against the invasion of their own trade monopolies from without. It was in truth, as has been observed, . . . ' a hard age for the dependent classes, wherever they were, and the bondmen in burgh may at times have cast many a wistful glance towards the blue hills in the distance.' "—*Edinburgh Guilds and Crafts*, Marwick, p. 38.

" In the homely burghs of Scotland we may find the first spring of that public spirit, the voice of the people, which in the worst of times, when the Crown and the law were powerless and the feudal aristocracy altogether selfish in its views, supported the patriot leaders, Wallace and Bruce, in their desperate struggle, and sent down that tide of native feeling which animated Burns and Scott, and which is not yet dead. . . . Whatever of thought, of enterprise, of public feeling, appears in our poor history took rise in our burghs and among the burgess class.—*Ancient Laws and Customs of the Burghs of Scotland*, Burgh Records Society, Preface, p. xlix.

DURING the cruel and stormy period wh n the feudal system was being imposed upon Scotland, commerce was carried on under great disadvantages. The travelling pedl r, with his caravan or his horse, was liable to have his goods raided by the marauding barons and their retainers ; no stores or land depots were secure from pillage : the shippers on the seas were a prey to the sea-rovers. For defensive and commercial purposes the merchants formed great associations called Guilds or Gilds ; and they, in turn, were federated into Hanses, which corresponded somewhat to our modern Chambers of Commerce, but these Hanses did not survive the Brucean or "Independence" wars. As the Guilds became wealthy, they demanded from the Crown special protection and privileges in return for the taxation they were called upon to bear ; and although it was not always possible for the kings to fulfil their guarantees of protection, charters promising protection and special privileges were freely granted. These charters created Royal Burghs, within the confines of which no lord or baron had authority ; the "*probi homines*," the good men, that is, the free-men, were to choose their own bailies and Council ; they were to make local regulations ; they were given power to hold fairs and markets ; their merchants might travel all over the land and be free of all customs and tolls ; none but they could import or export certain classes of merchandise ; their representatives (indeed, at first, every free-man), were entitled to be present and vote in Parliament.

The burgess was simply a king's tenant, paying his maill or rent to the king's bailie, and recognising no overlord but the king himself. He must be a free man and the possessor of a toft or tenement of land inside the burgh ; he must attend three courts yearly ; he must ake his turn at watching and warding. If in addition to being a burgess, he was a member of the Gild, he must pay his share of the common civic burdens, *i.e., scot* and *lot* ; none but he could sell wool, hides, or other merchandise to foreign merchants ; only he could buy wool to dye ; only he could cut cloth, possess a baker's oven, keep hand-mills for grinding, or make lard for sale. If charged with an offence, the burgess could demand trial by his peers in a burgh court ; and he could purge himself of the charge by the oaths of twelve leal burgesses. He could demand duel of an abbot or a friar or an earl or a baron, but they could not require him to fight ; he was free from all fines consequent upon the effusion of blood during a quarrel ; it was unlawful to strike him with a baton or a stick ; he was not required to pay the merchet tax upon the marriage of his daughter ; he was free from the Herezeld or death tax ; the king's bailie himself could only take a legal "loan" from him of a sum not exceeding 40d., and that for forty days, and if the money was not refunded in time the burgess was to " lend " no more money unless of his own free will.*

It is difficult to distinguish in these early times the local Burgh Council and its magistrates who were elected at open meetings by the "haill community "† of free burgesses (women included, though they themselves seem never to have been chosen as administrators), from the Merchant Guild and its officers. Indeed, in the earliest times the Guild sometimes overshadowed, sometimes even appears to have absorbed the municipal government.‡ That the Guild did not include *all* the burgesses is evident from the early Guild statutes, and the distinction between the wealthy merchant class and the merely prosperous craftsmen-burgess class, became more marked as time went on ; but in the reigns of Alexander I. and David I., every burgess, merchant or no, was a favoured citizen, and the very neces-

---

Leges Quator Burgorum, lv.

†*Statuta Gilde*, p. 38. In 1508 men and women, married and single, were entitled to vote for the parish clerk.—*Legal Practice in Ayrshire*, Murray, p. 59.

‡*Edinburgh Guilds and Crafts*, Marwick, p. 24.

sities of the Crown in its struggle with the nobles was rapidly increasing the number of the burghal communities. Every Royal Burgh established meant not only greater prosperity for the wealthy class, meant not only that the ecclesiastics, barons and courtiers could be assured a supply of wines, silks, and swords from abroad, meant not only an assured taxation to the Royal Exchequer, but meant an additional outpost of the central authority against the rude, lawless feudal nobles, some of whom had grown so powerful as to threaten the supremacy, if not the very existence, of that central authority.

Not to be outdone in the struggle, the more powerful ecclesiastics began the founding of ecclesiastical burghs on their own domains ; earls and lords followed suit with burghs of regality, and the barons created burghs of barony ; but in church burgh, burgh of regality, and burgh of barony, the lord, ecclesiastical or lay, retained the superiority, appointed the magistrates, or at least vetoed the appointment of such of them as might not be subservient to his wishes at all times ; and plundered the public exchequer as often as his own purse became light. In the Royal Burghs alone were the middle-classes reasonably secure and possessed of any estimable degree of civic liberty ; there they were not precarious tenants liable to summary ejection ; their rents were fixed and definite and paid to the Royal Exchequer in a lump sum by the magistrates ; vast areas of common land were donated to them ; they had full rights of jurisdiction inside the burgh boundaries ; in short, they bore the same relation to the Crown as did the feudal lords themselves ; burghal communities had been incorporated into the feudal system with a baronial *status*. In William the Lion's time the merchants of Perth had trading monopolies over all Perthshire, the merchants of Aberdeen over all Aberdeenshire, the merchants of Inverness over all Inverness-shire ; and although repeated attempts were made by episcopal authorities and by lay-lords to invade these privileges, the merchant burgesses, in all but rare instances, successfully resisted outside interference, and in no case did a chartered burgh ever formally surrender its independence. They demanded representation with their taxation ; and in 1326, when they granted the king an extra tenth of a penny on all the rents to meet his war expenses, they stipulated for the abolition of "certain old odious exactions." They became one of the estates of the realm ; insisted, as in 1295, on their right to be one of the consenting parties to the ratification of foreign treaties ; and as early as the beginning of the twelfth century had taken part in the choosing and enthronement of King Alexander I.[*]

The four earliest Burghs to receive royal sanction—Edinburgh,

Scots. Legal Antiq.—Cosmo Innes, p. 99.

Roxburgh, Berwick and Stirling—had a well-defined code of burghal laws, dating at least from 1124-1153, called The Leges (Quator) Burgorum, and these four burghs, at their annual convocations, settled all inter-burghal disputes, and in course of time fathered the annual meeting known to-day as the Convention of Burghs. By the Leges Burgorum it was decided that no alderman, bailie, nor "beddell" was to be permitted to bake or brew for sale in his own house during his term of office; the staffing of bake-houses was to be limited to a master, 2 servants and a "knayfe"; and the "lord of the oven" was to have for each use of his oven ½d.;* burgh grieves were to be elected at the first "mute" or public assembly after the feast of St. Michael; false witnesses were never again to be heard; bondmen who had fled to a burgh could not be retaken by their owners during the progress of a fair; indeed, durings fairs and festivals the ordinary civil and criminal jurisdiction was in abeyance, and a special Court, called "The Court of Dusty Feet"† was created to decide disputes; Gildsmen who worked with their own hands were to lose their freedom; they must employ servants for manual labour; and husbands were only to be responsible for their wives' debts settled by "dome of courte" to the extent of 4d., but the offending wife was to be chastised as a bairn. Magistrates were elected for one year only and must on election swear to keep the customs of the town, and that they shall not hold law on any man or woman for wrath, or hatred, or dread, or love; nor for rudeness, nor love, nor hatred, nor loss of their silver, "they sal nocht spare to do richt till all men." They must hold at least four open courts per annum, and extra courts on the supplication of twelve good men.‡

So closely intertwined were the functions of the Merchant Gild and the Burgh Magistracy at the inception of Burghs Royal, that the Statutes of the Gild frequently throw light upon burghal customs. No bargainer, we read,§ was to have a knife with a point; none except sons and daughters of gildsmen were to be received to the fraternity of the Gild, unless on a payment of 40s.; merchants or pedlars who brought in herring, salt, corn, beans, or pease must sell at cost price as much as sustain the purchaser's household; pleaders from without (i.e., imported lawyers) were to be prohibited from attending the courts. Burgesses' sons were of age when they could number and tell silver, or measure cloth with an ell-wand, or "do other their father's business and affairs.||" No king's bailie or servant was to keep a tavern or bake or sell bread in the burgh; and

---

*Leges Burgorum, lvi.

†"Municipal Institutions of Scotland."—Scot. Hist. Review, vol. i., p. 274

‡Fuller's Berwick, p. 241-243.

§Statuta Gilde, 8.

||Regiam Maiestatem, Lib. ii., cix.

none outside the burgh was permitted to have a brew-house unless he be a baron, earl or landholder having the right of pit and gallows.* Brethren in poverty were to be collected for to the extent of 20s. ; rebels were to be expelled, and their houses demolished ; the children of each burgess were to have equal inheritance of the father's goods.†

A brief experience of merchant class control of the burghs, however, evidently convinced the Crown that the magistrates might be none the worse of periodical supervision, and a sort of itinerant court of justice was instituted, called "The Chalmerlan Air," and the King's Chamberlain was directed to make regular and systematic visits to the burghs with the object of preventing abuses against the poor and of seeing that the royal statutes and regulations were enforced. Among other offices he must undertake, the Chamberlain was instructed to inquire if the bailies do justice equally to the poor and the rich, if they take gifts for doing justice: about bakers' weights and fleshers' unsound meat ; "also anent them who violentlie intruse themselves into other menis lands and occupie the samin unjustlie "; about cooks who sell re-heated food, to the manifest deception of the people ; about king's bondmen in hiding ; if taxation was conformable to the means of rich and poor ; about the common good funds ; "gif widowes are compellit to watch " ; about excessive tolls any harsh usage of stranger merchants ; about those who draw their neighbours before the ecclesiastical courts instead of the burgh courts; also " of those who spare the ritch and cause summons the puir to be on the assize " ; if there are any slanderers, rebels, or walkers on the night-time ; of any outside lords forcing the burghs to pay rent ; if landmarks and bounds are strictly adhered to ; if there be and "confederacioun or band by which the nychtburhede is wrangwisely greffyt or pur men oppressyt " ; or if any lands have been given to "religiouse men " without leave of the king.‡

How necessary must have been some controlling influence upon the merchant class is clearly evident when we consider how consistently they struggled to acquire and conserve the burghal privileges for a small coterie of rich traders, and how they sought to regulate and control the handicraft burgesses. Mr. Kemble says of the inception of these Gilds : "They were sworn brotherhoods between man and man, established and fortified upon oath and pledge ; and in them we completely recognise the germ of those sworn communes, which in the times of the densest seignorial darkness offered a noble resistance to episcopal and baronial tyranny, and formed the nursing

---

*Constitutiones Noue Pro Burgensibus.

†Fragmenta Collecta, ii., iii., xvi.

‡" Inquiries of the Chalmerlan Air—Ancient Laws and Customs of the Burghs of Scot., vol. i., pp. 114-153.

cradles of popular liberty.* Opposition to seignorial tyranny they undoubtedly offered; but at a very early period in Scots history they had shed their democratic elements, they refused to permit fleshers, fullers, dyers, weavers, shoemakers, and fishermen who worked at their trade to become members of the Gild; their servants were given arbitrary powers to seize and apprehend anyone alleged to be infringing the Gildsman's rights; † they not only excluded craftsmen but they assumed the right to regulate the crafts and fix their profits; their assemblies were held in secret; they refused to allow the craftsmen burgesses to participate in the burghal administration; they secured an Act of Parliament stipulating that shipmasters must have at least three "serplaris of their awne gudes" or at least that amount committed to them by a Gild brother; ‡ they stood aloof from the crafts, says Mr. Cosmo Innes, as the nobles of later times did from the *roturier.* § The early Gild statutes amply demonstrate the character of the Merchant Gild. It was a benefit society of merchants which ran with, and sometimes absorbed, the burgh. In the laws of King Alfred (891-901) it is enacted that the Gild must pay half of its member's fine if he should be convicted of murder; for the other half, say the laws, "let him flee."‖ The Berwick statutes, the oldest in Scotland, declared that the brother who, in his old age, falls "crukyt or pure or in ane uncurable seyknes and in poverty," is to be relieved; there was to be no deceit between Gild brother and Gild brother, but any brother who negligently falls out of Gild membership is to be boycotted in word and deed, succour being refused him even if in peril of his life.*a* There are to be dowries for daughters, attendance at funerals, assistance in Court; and when a Gild brother buys herrings, all other brethren present are to be entitled to share at his purchase price. Fraternity there was, though in scope and operation it was limited to a mere handful of wealthy burghers; but outside the Gild Hall were the Master Craftsmen, who, as early as the thirteenth century, seeing themselves despised and scorned, prepared for what proved to be a long and bitter struggle, in which they were to be aided by the journeymen who "worked for meit, and drinke, and fee," and by the apprentices who hoped one day to be journeymen, and, if luck favoured them, perhaps even Master Craftsmen.

The stone-masons claim that theirs was the first Craft fraternity

---

*The Saxons in England, vol. ii., p. 310.

†*Assise Willelmi Regis.* §39.

‡*Acta Parl. Scot.*, 1457, c. 10, vii., p. 49.

§*Ancient Laws and Customs*, Preface, p. vii.

‖"Observations on Early Guilds of Merchants and Craftsmen."—Sir James
    D. Marwick, *Proc. Phil. Socy.*, Glasgow, 1886.

*a*Statuta Gilde, §16.

in Scotland, and their antiquity is proved by the masons craft-marks on the old round tower of Brechin, built about the year 1020.* Probably many of the early skilled masons were foreigners imported by the ecclesiastical authorities for Church building, and they probably travelled about in communities to the Church renovations and erections. But by the middle of the fourteenth century almost every craft had its Union organised in active hostility to the un-freemen on the one hand and to the Merchant Gild on the other. No man was allowed to join a Craft Gild unless he had served his apprenticeship and a certain number of years as a journeyman, and had secured a burgess ticket, and was prepared to pay the heavy initiation fees demanded by the Craft officers. Usually, however, exceptions were made in favour of the applicant who had married a Craftsman's daughter. The Craft Gilds were modelled somewhat on the Merchant Gild—they sought a rigid monopoly in their own particular trade, powers to prevent un-freemen (that is, non-burgesses and non-craftsmen) from competing with them, powers to control the hours of labour, the quality of work, and to punish recalcitrant members. These powers were secured by charters of Incorporation or "Seals of Cause," sometimes granted by the Crown and sometimes by the local magistracy; but they had not been granted, and they were not retained, without a struggle, and although the local magis-trate merchants may sometimes have granted the Seal of Cause in the hope that regulation of the trade would result in better work-manship, there seems little doubt but that the chief source of the Craftsmen's privileges was the desire of the Crown to bind to itself in the contests of the time a powerful and a growing interest.

In 1424, James I. ordered every craft in every town in Scotland, with the consent of the magistrates, to choose a wise man to act as Deacon, and to "assay and govern all werkis that beis made be the workmen of his craft."† But the results of this Act were de-clared to have been "scenes of turbulence" (probably due to inter-ference with the un-freemen, who, as like as not, would be supported by the magistrates), and in 1426 the office of Deacon, characterised as dangerous to the public safety, was abolished and Craft meetings forbidden on the ground that they were but "assemblies of conspir-ators." But the Craftsmen organised their forces all over the country and brought such pressure to bear on the Crown, that in 1457 the goldsmiths of Edinburgh had their privileges and their Deacon restored to them : and six years later the office of Deacon was general in all trades. In 1469 an Act was passed destroying the last shred of popular election of the magistracy and council. In future the old council was itself to select the new council. This Act was

---

*Sketch of the Incorporation of Masons.—James Cruickshank, p. v.
†Acta Parl. Scot., vii., p. 11.

believed by the Craftsmen to have been forced from the king by the merchants who had loaned him considerable sums of money, and a very pretty story comes down to us regarding one of the tricks resorted to before the Act of 1469, securing full hereditary control of the Magistracy, had been forced from Parliament by the merchants. The merchants, says Pennecuick in his " Historical Account of the Blue Blanket "—the Blue Blanket was the name given to the banner of the Edinburgh Craftsmen—"murmered for want of payment . . . the magistrates and merchants in concert raised a mob and gave directions to the ringleaders what and how far to act, to insult the King as he was passing the streets to the Parliament House, who, after a scuffle with his guards, violently seized upon his Sacred Majesty and thrust him within the walls of their common gaol." The Trades were instantly convened and agreed to raise the lieges for a rescue. This was done, and the King was conveyed in triumph to Holyrood Palace. The magistrates, "knowing the weak side of Cuthbert, the Deacon-convener who headed the Trades, brib'd him by a lusty purse of gold to betray his trust. The King next morning sent for Cuthbert (whom he call'd his faithful general) and told him, He had a grateful Remembrance of the Loyalty and Valour of his faithful subjects, the Trades of Edinburgh, and was resolved to confer some remarkable token of favour upon them." Cuthbert, well instructed by the Magistracy and Merchant Council how to behave, answered : "May it please your Excellent Majesty, We, your obliged and devoted Servants, the Trades of Edinburgh, did nothing but what was our bounden Duty. But since your Majesty is graciously pleased not only to remember but reward our dutiful Behaviour, I presume, in name of my Brethren, to beseech your Sacred Majesty to make your most faithful and loyal Servants, the Trades of Edinburgh, in all Time coming free of that toilsome affair of being Magistrates of the Burgh and let the disloyal merchants be henceforth loaded with the office." The King, surprised with the supplication, gave a smile and said, "Cuthbert, It shall be done." The man's treachery was soon blown about, to the amazement of the Incorporations. These latter applied to the Courtiers to represent to the King how grossly they had been betrayed. The King asked for the story in writing, and when he got it, re-granted their old-time privileges of taking part in the election of the magistracy. The Convener, Cuthbert, was murdered at the North Loch near a well "yet known by the name of Cuthbert's well."

The Act of 1469 was designed, according to its preamble, to obviate the yearly trouble and contention at election times "through multitude and clamour of common simple personis," and the remedy for the clamour of the simple persons was to forbid them to vote at all. In future the old Council would choose the new, and both together would choose the magistrates; but each craft was to have one representative at the choosing of the magistrates. In 1474 it was decreed that four of the old Council were to retain office in the new Council. In 1503 "none but merchants were to exercise jurisdiction," and, as they were not necessarily resident merchants, the common property disappeared rapidly during their tenure of office. In 1535 it was stipulated that the Merchant Magistrates must be "indwellers," but that Act was not enforced. In 1487 an Act had been passed declaring that the "using of deyknnis of men of craft in burrowis is rycht dangerous," and may, as they use it, cause a "convocatioun and rysing of the Kingis liegis"; they had farther made regulations contrary to the "commoun proffet, "by prohibiting their members from finishing jobs which another member had left unfinished for one reason or another, and deserved therefor "great punytioun." Masons, wrights and other craftsmen had been demanding "thair fees als weill on the haly dais as for wark dais, or els they sall nocht labour nor wirk"; also they had demanded that none may complete another man's work. It was therefore declared that deacons were to cease for a year doing anything but inspecting the fineness of craft work; those who asked fees for holidays were to be indicted as common oppressors, and *all* craftsmen were to be punished who refused to complete a job. In 1493 the deacons are again "rycht dangerous" and abolished. In 1535 Commissioners were appointed to fix prices for shoemakers, smiths, bakers, and brewers, and to punish breakers of their ordinances. Among the experiments in compromise was one by which the magistrates were allowed to select the Deacons, but the Crafts would have none of it, and it fell into desuetude. In 1540 another Act against combinations was passed, and unfreemen were to be employed. In 1543 the magistrates selected by the old Council of Edinburgh were almost exclusively of the merchant class, and the incensed Crafts raised a mob, who invaded the Council chamber, while the Deacons drew their swords. In 1551 disturbances broke out in all the burghs, when, in pursuance of an Act of Parliament, "reasonable prices" were affixed to the Craftsmen's work by the magistrates. Again in 1555 the unlawful office of Deacon is denounced as the frequent cause of civic commotion and unlawful combinations between the Crafts of various burghs. In 1556 Queen Mary regranted the Crafts the legal right to choose their deacons and to assist in the choosing of magistrates; but the Town Councils refused to allow the Act to operate, and broils and commotions ensued. Finally, the King (James VI.) was invited to arbitrate between the parties, and he decided that neither side was to hold conventions, and that the Crafts were to be subject to the Town Councils. In 1607 the extortionate prices charged by craftsmen were denounced by Parliament, and permission was given the lieges to employ un-freemen. In 1661 Companies for making linen, cloth, etc., were empowered to attract foreign artisans who should pay nothing for their "freedom," and who should be free from all taxes and burdens, thus effectively smashing up the Linen Makers' Craft Union.

In the 16th and 17th centuries, however anxious the Crown might be to conciliate the Crafts, it was evident that Parliament was still heavily weighted on the side of the merchants, and King James VI., who was doubtless heartily tired of the incessant commercial struggle, in a letter to his son, Henry, denounced both sides with a refreshing wealth of invective. The merchants, he says, "think the whole common weale ordained for making them up, and accounting it their lawful gaine and trade to enrich themselves upon the loss of all the rest of the people. . . . They buy for us the worst wares and sell them at the dearest prices ; and albeit the victuals fall or rise of their prices, according to the aboundance or skantenesse thereof, yet the prices of their wares ever rise but never fall, being as constant in that their evil custom as if it were a settled law for them " ; and the craftsmen, says the king, think "we should be content with their wark, how bad and deare so ever it be, and if they in anything be controlled, up goeth the blew blanket."*

Such strictures on both the merchant and the manufacturing classes (if we may roughly so describe them) were certainly not groundless, and for over 300 years there are perpetual complaints on behalf of the consumers against one or both of these privileged sections. Forestalling the market, regrating, adulteration, artificial scarcities, exhorbitant prices, were continually being denounced and legislated against. In William the Lion's time baker's prices were fixed, and any baker discovered withholding his bread from sale in order to create a scarcity was punished by having his bread confiscated "to be delt to the pure folk " ; the makers of "evil ale " were fined 8s., or, if they preferred the alternative, put in the Kirk-stool ; the ale was forfeit and divided between the poor and the brethren in hospital ; forestallers, that is, those who purchased before the authorised times of market (9 a.m. in winter and midmorn in summer) were severely punished ; dealers in meat and drink were bound to sell their entire stock on demand, barring goods to the value of 4d., which they might retain for their own household use.†
In 1496 we find demands for the confiscation of goods cornered against the market, and an Act was passed authorising confiscation for the "second fault " ; a similar Act was passed in 1535 ; and in 1551 prices are so "doublet and triblit " that "the poor are at the point of perishing," and magistrates in burghs and sheriffs in the

*King James' *Works*, pp. 163-164.
†*Transactions*, Glasgow Arch. Socy., vol. 4, p. 341.

"landward" were authorised to see that the various Craft Deacons fix fair and equitable prices immediately; "hoarders-up" and those who demanded larger prices than the magistrates and the sheriffs agreed to, were to be punished both in body and in goods "with all rigour *" In 1566, when Queen Mary and her Court visited Jedburgh, the prices of commodities were so raised by the burgesses that the Queen was forced to call upon the local Council to demand wholesale reductions. The Estates of Parliament doubtless did their best to keep the exploitation of the public by the trading classes within reasonable limits—they forbade the export of grain during times of famine; they limited the rate of interest on money and grain to 10 per cent., and they denounced the Trustifiers and the extortionate Craftsmen with all the maledictory fervour of which the old Scots language was capable—but the nature of a private monopoly is to set its own interests against the common weal; and as monopoly was in the Middle Ages the only conceivable means and method of commerce, "fair" prices were impossible. In 1639 the Privy Council issued a proclamation declaring that :

"... There is numbers of people within the merches of this kingdome, who preferring thair awne filthie lucre and gayne to the commoun weale, ar now bussie in gaddering togidder the whole victuall that they can find ather to be bought or exchanged, and this victuall they keepe and hold up to a dearth and will nowayes vent nor sell the same but at suche untolerable and unreasonable prices as the poore people dow not beare, so that if the infection sall spread anie where ellis, it is verie likelie that the poore sall not get victuall but at unreasonable appetite and pleasure of thir regraters and hoorders of victuall."†

The Privy Council frequently fixed maximum prices for twelve months in advance; but their decrees were futile against "the avaricious persons who pretend scarcity"; and down as late as March, 1787, we find the Procurator Fiscal in Edinburgh raising an action against the Incorporation of Fleshers and against its members individually for forstalling the meat market and "selling at advance prices whereby double profit was taken on the commodity."‡ Of course the trading class then, as now, had its misadventures and its losses—given sometimes in the records with an emphasis on detail which conveys to a later age a certain whimsical humour. In, for example, a report on the state of the Burghs Royal presented to the Convention of Burghs on 9th July, 1691, we read :

"In Anno 1681 the inhabitants (of Perth) for ther farder encouradgement of trade having again caused build ane other new ship at Leith called the Eagle of Perth, and after two or three voyadges made yr with, the owners

---

Ancient Laws and Customs of the Burghs of Scotland, vol. ii., p. 73.
†*Records of the Privy Council*, 1635-1637, vol. vi., p. 439.
‡*Scots. Magazine*, 1787, p. 152.

therof haveing loadening her to Holland, George Fergussone ther skipper therof runne away with her and her loadening, and never returned from Virginia again, to the value of at least 10,000 lib."

And again :

" (Kirkcaldy) George Tod, Jully, 1690, went over to Ostend and bought ane big ship about 300 tuns ; after he had bought her he died ther, August, 1691, and his brother bringing her home was lost, he and all his companie, with a quantity of brandie."

For over three centuries the struggle lasted between the Merchant and the Craft Guilds. Time and again, with the varying fortunes of the contestants, the Act of 1424, giving the crafts power to choose their own deacons,was repealed and re-enacted.* Sometimes, as in Glasgow and Edinburgh, the dispute was temporarily patched up by a Decreet Arbitral—the judgment of a sort of compulsory arbitration tribunal—but these decreets sided regularly with the merchants, and not only left the crafts in a permanent minority in the local Councils, but stipulated that only merchants could act as Provost, Treasurer, Dean of Guild or Bailie. By the Act of 1469, direct popular representation on the Councils had disappeared, and for almost two centuries the crafts seemed to have concentrated on maintaining their right to participate in the election of the burgh officials. But in the 16th century they appear also to have demanded Council representation and the right to deal in manufactures relating to their own special wares. In 1552 the Convention of Royal Burghs decided that each Burgh Council should contain 2 craftsmen and 10 merchants. In 1582 electoral disturbances took place in Glasgow, the "multitude" answering the Bailies "with tumultuous wordis, mening as apperit, to seditioun," and, breaking in the Council house door, "invading and persewing the said baillies and counsaille with contumelious and dispytful wordis."

In 1672 the trend to Free Trade began, the trade of weaving being thrown open to all comers, the export of all native commodities to be free, and any citizen might import certain commodities ; but right up to the passing of that Act the merchants had insisted upon their trading privileges, and through the instrumentality of one, David Wemyss, a Dundee merchant, were securing £20 fines from a number of weavers in Glasgow and Gorbals who had been engaged surreptitiously in exporting linen.† In the eighteenth century the self-elected Councils still had two merchants to each craftsman. In 1775, at Stirling, we come across a story which illumines, clear

---

*_Acta Parl. Scot._, 1424, c. 17 ; 1427, c. 4 ; 1491, c. 19 ; 1493, c. 14 ; 1555, c. 26 ; see also Bain's _History of Aberdeen Guilds_, 79, 329 ; _Records of Convention of Burghs_, ii., 469-479.

†_Reg. Privy Council_, ii., 3rd series, xxxiv.

as day, the mercantile method and the mercantile mind. Certain Magistrates and Town Councillors, notably Henry Jaffray, James Alexander, and James Burd, had secretly signed an agreement "to secure to ourselves the total management of the burgh, to support each other at all times," to appoint a Town Clerk who would share his fees with the signatories, and "in order to render ourselves popular in the burgh and that our management may be acceptable to the whole inhabitants, we engage that when a vacancy happens in the charge of any of the town's ministers, we shall procure the same to be filled up by an evangelical minister or preacher such as shall be most agreeable to the bulk of the people."* When that secret agreement came to light the evangelical working classes must have suffered a shock—not assuredly a lasting shock, for they failed to impress their progeny with the obvious moral (witness the composition of Stirling Town Council to-day !), but still a shock of some kind ! In 1793 the crafts secured the privilege of importing their own raw materials, but not manufactured goods—a privilege still reserved for the merchants ; in 1823 they were allowed to import English manufactured goods without restriction, a legal decision having been secured that England was not now a foreign country. But it was not until after the Reform Act of 1832 that the great public agitation against both merchants and crafts—against their rapacities and their obstructions to developments in trade—produced a Parliamentary Commission of Enquiry, whose findings finally secured an Act abolishing the privileges and monopolies of both classes.† The Commissioners reported that in many towns the privileges had been voluntarily given up, and that public opinion was manifestly hostile to the others. Professor Brentano, in his "History and Development of Gilds," says that the craft guilds died at the hands of large capital, and there is, of course, a very considerable measure of truth in this. The discovery of steam power, for example, meant the factory system, and the factory system meant the smashing of the craft guilds. But there was another and even more potent factor in guild disintegration. For over two centuries ex-army and ex-navy men, on being discharged from the Services, were given powers by Act of Parliament to engage as "King's Freemen" in whatever trade or calling they chose. The conclusion of the Napoleonic wars added vastly to the numbers of these "King's Freemen," and between the rising of capitalism on the one hand, and the swarm of King's Freemen on the other, perpetual and costly lawsuits to enforce their monopolies, and a public opinion which was developing into a forcible antagonism, the Craft Guilds died and were buried without a tear. They had been called into

---

Scotland : Social and Domestic—Rogers, i. p. 43.
†*Municipal Corporations (Scot.) Report*, 1833, vol. i., p. 85.

being to fight monopolies; they remained to perpetuate them. Their very existence was a menace to the working class, and right down to the end they strove, might and main, against the common people. They opposed the Income Tax and Catholic Emancipation,* and their ideas of Parliamentary and Municipal reform certainly did not include working-class franchises or representation. On the pretence that their craft guild monopolies guaranteed skilled workmanship, they extorted famine prices from the community, and they raised their entrance fees against journeymen so that only a select coterie might manufacture and trade. James Watt, the discoverer of steam-power, had opened a shop in Glasgow in 1757, but the guildsmen declared he had infringed their trading rights, and they forced him to abandon the sale of mathematical instruments and to shut up his shop. In Aberdeen, in addition to his burgess fees, a journeyman must pay, if he desired to join the Hammermen's Guild, £85; if the Shoemaker's Guild, £90; if the Guild of Wrights, £90-£100. The Guild of Fleshers in Stirling numbered only 8 persons, two of whom only were resident in the burgh, and two, their sons, were not actually engaged in the fleshing business; the entry money had been successively raised from £25 to £100, and at the beginning of last century no new applicants were admitted except sons of existing members, and they at a special rate of £8. The sons of bakers in Glasgow were admitted members of the Baker's Guild on payment of £3, while "strangers" were forced to pay £100. The sons of Perth Glovers were admitted for £1, "strangers" for £100. Nobody in Edinburgh was allowed to make *aqua vitae* for sale except members of the Surgeon's and Barber's Guild.† The Edinburgh Goldsmiths could seize the working tools of all "un-freemen" in Edinburgh and its suburbs; the bakers could seize the "flour baiks" of outsiders from the landward, which were not in their opinion of the right "stuffe and weicht," and they secured a local council regulation decreeing that loaves sold by "un-freemen" must weigh 4 ounces more than the craft loaf.‡ Un-free shoemakers who bought leather before the freemen were stocked were fined and imprisoned, and young men under thirty years of age were prohibited from opening cobbler's booths in order that "the freemen may have their servants to serve thame." The Edinburgh tailors, in 1584, were protected by Council regulations declaring that un-free tailors who "levis

---

*The Incorporation of Wrights in Glasgow—Reid, p. 32.

†The Surgeons in the sixteenth century became a superior race and disjoined from the Barbers. The stripes on the Barber's pole still indicate bleeding and bandaging-up. In 1589 one, Mark Libertoun, was admitted to the Edinburgh Guild " to cow, clip, schaife, and wesche," but not to practise " chirurgie."

‡Incorporated Trades of Edinburgh—Colston, p. 48.

licentiouslie" and worked in private houses and lofts are either to be subject to a free master or imprisoned.   Under the free masters they had to work from 5 a.m. "without leiff quhill nyne hours at evin" for 12d. and their meat.   Those who refused to work for the free masters were to have their goods poinded, and only released on a fine of 40s. being paid to the Tailor's Deacon.   At Irvine Fair, in 1617, two un-freemen from Kilmarnock were arrested and imprisoned without trial for hawking their wares.*   In 1618 the Edinburgh bakers, anticipating the syndicalists, refused municipal authority, and decided to refer all disputes to their deacon.   In the same year the "boyis and paigeis" formed an unauthorised guild, and demanded from each new page "some certane peeceis of gold" to be spent in "drinking riot and excess for receiving of him in their society or brotherhaid"; "black-legs" were "shamefully and unhonestlie misused," even when behind "thair maisteris bakis, sua that ofttymes some jarris and miscontentment."   That guild was promptly broken up.

In the fifteenth century the Edinburgh Hatmakers' Guild fixed the term of apprenticeship at seven years, but sons of craft members were to be let off with three years ; strict injunctions were laid down against sewing, renewing, or mending old hats.   Shoemakers' apprentices must serve five years, and three years thereafter as journeyman "or ellis marie ane Burgess Dochtor."   Non-guildsmen and boys engaged in the fleshing trade were expelled from the town unless they agreed to become hired servants or apprentices of a member of the craft ; and Acts were secured to punish workmen who took exorbitant prices.   In 1577 un-free bonnet-makers were ordered to stand by themselves on the "unfree" portion of the street, during market day ; in 1578 it was decided that free-men should not be required to pay customs duties which were still to be levied on un-freemen ; in 1584 all taverns kept by non-guildsmen were summarily closed ; in the beginning of the seventeenth century there are loud complaints that too many trade competitors have been admitted to "freedom," and the entry monies were raised as a barrier to fresh entrants.   This naturally led to a rapid increase among the un-free craftismen, of whom it was complained that they "eatt the meatt out of friemenis mouths."†   About this time the apprentices appear to have been running off to the suburbs and setting themselves up in business, competing with their erstwhile masters ; for an Act was securd confiscating their works to the common good funds.   In 1669 it was proposed to admit anyone to freedom of trade on payment of a certain fixed fee ; but the Craft Guilds strained every effort against the proposal, and finally succeeded in defeating it.   Even

---

Register Privy Council, O.S., vol. xi., 1616-1619, p. 124.
†*Edinburgh Council Records*, vol. xx., fol. 71.

the modern method of limitation of output as a preliminary to the raising of prices was not unknown to the medieval manufacturers; in 1541 the shoemakers of Aberdeen were convicted by a jury of deliberately making " insufficient shoes " and selling them above the legal price. The adjective "insufficient," it is true, might here refer to the quality and not to the quantity of the footwear; but it is difficult to see how a lowering of quality could command increased prices, particularly when in the landward districts there would be the usual number of un-free shoemakers ready and willing at all times to dump their cheaper wares into Aberdeen. Search in what Municipal or Craft Guild records we choose, the manifest straining after a rigid and exclusive monopoly is evident. In Brechin, a master weaver called Grim, who had purchased large quantities of hard fish and candles for his workers, "as they could not afford to pay dear prices for small quantities," and who had recouped himself by stopping the costs out of his men's wages, was ordered to desist by the local guildry (association of crafts), as the practice interfered with the fishmonger and the dry-goods guildsmen's profits. In Aberdeen the craftsmen had to pay higher shore dues than the merchant guildsmen, and the craftsmen in turn persecuted "un-free" traders—no fewer than 80 prosecutions taking place in one year In Cupar the Hammermen mulcted "strangers" in £30 before the strangers were licensed to commence business, while the fee for craftsmen's sons was only £1 1s. In Rutherglen, strangers stabling their horses during a fair were forbidden to bring their own corn, but must purchase from local dealers.* Even as late as 1736 poor women shop-keepers in Edinburgh had their goods confiscated by order of the Town Council because they interfered with the guild monopolists. The pretext given for the raid was surely surprising enough to the dispossessed : "There are a great many women servants and others who, turning wearie of their services, have, out of a principle of avarice and habit of laziness, taken up little shops ! " Avarice, indeed !

The crafts, however, performed some useful public functions; they fought the large private trader monopolists and they kept a watchful eye on the knaveries of the self-elected councils and the all but self-elected magistrates. In the palmy days of the sixteenth and seventeenth centuries, when, as we shew in another chapter, the common lands were in process of spoliation, when the seven common mills on the water of Leith were "let " by the Edinburgh Council to Nicolas Udart, capitalist, "for his services to the town "; when the salt-pans and the fishings were being leased and gifted away, the Craft Guilds acted as a drag on thieves and resetters alike. In 1661, when the linen cloth monopolists were importing operatives

---

History of Rutherglen and E. Kilbride—Ure, p. 73.

K

from abroad and offering them freedom from taxes and public
burdens, the crafts—though their motives may have been selfish—
entered emphatic and successful protests ; and a few years before,
they had organised what was evidently a rude form of national
strike against Lord Erskine and his Tanning monopoly. That
gentleman, who was son and heir of the Earl of Mar, the Lord High
Treasurer, had secured from the Privy Council the sole right of
tanning hides in Scotland. For each hide stamped by his agents
(and all unstamped hides were illicit and liable to confiscation) he
was empowered to charge 4s.   To fight this monopolist, the shoemakers raised a national agitation. In 1619 they were charged before
the Privy Council with "steiring the people up" by raising the price
of boots and shoes, and although their defence was that they must
needs do so when Lord Erskine was charging them 4s. for stamping
each and every tanned hide, the Privy Council ordered them to
continue selling their wares at the old prices, and threatened recalcitrants with £40 fines and severe bodily punishments. But the
agitation was maintained by the craft of shoemakers, and in March,
1621, we find nearly 150 of them indicted at Edinburgh for refusing
the "instructions" of Erskine's agents. In the succeeding year
72 of the strikers again appear in answer to a summons and are
denounced as rebels, a fate which also befel some 69 shoemakers all
over the country who, though summoned, failed to put in an appearance.* The persistent hostility of the shoemakers finally rendered
the monopoly useless.

The wholesale corruption of the Town Councils in the sixteenth
and seventeenth centuries, though it culminated towards the beginning of the eighteenth century, in an all but general insolvency
of the burghal finances,† was doubtless mitigated somewhat by the
Craft Guilds. The magistrates had powers to fix craftsmen's fees‡
and holidays, and the consequent perpetual strife and clash of
interests gave the Craft Guilds adequate reason for keeping an

---

*Among the 69 sentenced in absence were about a dozen from the Strathblane
and Strathendrick valleys, whose family names are still known in the old
hamlets, thus illustrating the permanence of stocks in the rural districts—
"John Edmenis in Bofrone, Wm. M'Cadde at the Kirke of Killearne.
Henry Auld and John Millar at the Kirke of Fintry, Wm. Cowane and Wm.
Bauchop in Fintry, Andrew Buchanan at Duntreath, Gilbert Craig at
Strathblane, Walter Williamson at Ballagane."—*Reg. Privy Council,*
vol. xx., p. xii.

†*Scot. Hist. Review,* vol. i., p. 280.

‡"Shop profits" also were regulated. In Aberdeen, for example, the profit
on fish was limited to one penny on every twelve pence. Previous to
1471 every Saturday was a holiday ; but in that year an Act was passed
forcing the Crafts to work to 4 p.m. on Saturdays. If they refused they
were to be fined their whole week's wage.

interested eye on the doings of their "betters." The net result was perhaps that there always existed in the burghs a group of outside critics acting as a deterrent on magisterial peculation. And, in truth, much need was there for a deterrent. Provost Drummond of Edinburgh, in 1685, was openly accused of pilfering three to four thousand merks from the Common Good fund of the City.* In Rutherglen, we are told, it was the practice of the Provost and bailies to :

> "Nominat and elect a counsell by and to themselles whairby some leiding and factious men have brought in on the Counsell all there friends, alleyes, relationes, and adherents. And so have practized and endevored to inhawnce and perpetual the Magistracie to themselles for a long tyme ; and to make use of and dispose upon the commone goodis, revenewes and caswalities of the burgh as they thought fitt without controlement, to the great prejudice and rivine of the publict interest."

From 1671 to 1710 the Crafts secured representation, and limited the tenure of office by the Provost and the Bailies to one year ; but in the latter year monopoly again triumphed with a Council decision that only ex-Bailies could become Provost and only ex-Treasurers could become Bailie, and only Burgesses holding "threttine pundland " could be either. All plotters against this regulation were to lose their freedom and pay a fine of £100 Scots.† The Town Council of Dundee, in a dispute with the Town Council of Perth, had, in 1581, claimed precedence over the latter body because its constitution was "purer," i.e., it had excluded craftsmen from all municipal office whatsoever.‡ At St. Andrews, Sir Patrick Leirmonth of Darsy had "sinisterlie made certain statutes electing himself to the office of Provost for life " and his son and heir provost in his absence, "meaning thairby to obtene the said office to himself and his aires heritablie to the perpetuall thrall and tyrannie of the said citie." He had filled the town's offices with his adherents, had stolen the Burgh charter, had voted himself the "great customs," the "escheats of the town," and the common lands ; had broken up the Guilds, admits freemen daily, and pockets the entrance fees ; had given his third son the corn market customs, and generally had plundered everything he could lay his hands upon. Among the complainants to the Privy Council on the subject were representatives of all the crafts, including one gentleman who advertises himself as a "Tymmerman " and one who is not ashamed to report himself as a "cadgear."§ The Privy Council granted a commission of enquiry, but, as the Council records shew, the trouble lasted for several years, and

---

*Chronological Notes—Lord Fountainhall's *Diary*, p. 143.
†*History of Rutherglen*—Ure, p. 61.
‡*Edinburgh Guilds and Crafts*—Marwick, p. 118.
§*Privy Council Records*, iv., p. 42, 1585-1586.

it required incessant vigilance on the part of the citizens to defend their patrimony and their privileges. About the same period, Bailie Jackson of Renfrew—the "alleged baillie," say the craftsmen protestors—made "his private gayne and commoditie of the commoun gude of the burgh, quhairupoun he hes bene sustenit thir divers yeiris bigane." In Aberdeen the race of Menzies had usurped the Provostry and all other offices, pocketing and dilapidating everything. The burgesses demanded popular election, and that the town's books be kept in a safe place and (curiously enough) in "indifferent hands."[*] Occasionally, it is true, the magistrates, where their economic interests were not involved, shewed some disposition of sympathy towards the poor and the oppressed, as when, for example, in 1597, they were incurring Presbyterial censures for freeing the poor wretches whom the Church courts had "convicted" of witchcraft;[†] but even their stand against the cruel superstitions of the Reformed Kirk was halting and infrequent, and the purblind theological foolishness of the age was often carried into the Council Chambers. One instance will suffice. A Roman Catholic of Aberdeen, called Gibb, had named one of his terriers Luther and another Calvin; whereat the Magistrates "publicly reproved him and sagaciously ordered the two dogs to be hanged at the Market Cross."[‡]

Though the free handicraftsmen of the Craft Guilds had been absorbed into the hierarchy of feudalism and themselves repressed and regulated the lives of the classes below just as class consciously as they in turn were dominated and beset by the merchant monopolists, still their very status in society and the very nature of their struggles forced them occasionally into battling for popular rights. When, in 1581, the Privy Council established a rigid press censorship by forbidding printers to print anything that had not been previously "sene, vewit and examinit be wise and discreit persons," deputed for the purpose, the printers had craft support in an agitation for unrestricted publication. Sometimes the craftsmen, as in Glasgow, rose in arms against the magistrates,[§] sometimes they are found assisting the magistrates in defending the burghal interest against the neighbouring barons; occasionally they were forced to fight both baron and magistrate. When Lord Herries was terrorising Dumfries;[||] when Clapen of Carslogy was seeking "a licht motioun" (a slight quarrel) to ruin the inhabitants of Cupar and annex its conmmon lands;[a] when Young of Seton was striving to intrude on the burgh

---

[*]*Privy Council Records* iv., 1585-6, p. 533.
[†]Macintosh—*History of Civilisation in Scotland*, ii., 276.
[‡]*Scot. Hist. Review*, v., p. 180.
[§]M'Ure—*Hist. of Glasgow*, p. 133.
[||]*Reg. Privy Council*, O.S., iii., pp. 12-14.
[a]Ibid, pp. 515-516.

lands of Forfar ; * when Walter Scott and Touris of Inverlayth had to be ejected from the commons of Selkirk ;† when Currour of Inchdrour had secured letters of caution against "puir meane men (of Banff), all fisheris and puir craftsmen, and not worth £40," and sought to stir up some of his friends in the town "to mak a contentioun" so that he could find pretext for ruining the "cautioned" ones ; when Sibbald of Rankeillour's attempt to appropriate Cupar Muir was met by a burghal boycott—no man labouring to him and no one tenanting his farms ; or when, at Hawick, in the early eighteenth century, the people rose in rebellion against Buccleughs' chamberlain and his pretensions of riding their fair, and fixing and taking their customs, and after killing several of his guard, chased the chamberlain home for his life.‡—were not the Crafts foremost in the struggle ? And when the magistrates of Glasgow were endowing Lord Boyd with the common lands and finding him frequent tuns of wine from the public funds, or the magistrates of Rutherglen rouping away the common green, the Craft deacons were prompt in protest.§ and they sided powerfully with the Glasgow magistrates in hostility to Sir George Elphinston, who had a market (on the stolen ground of St. Ninian's croft at the Bridgend) in opposition to the burgh market ;‖ they probably supported the merchants in their strife with the syndicate composed of the "twelve leading capitalists of the time," who, in the beginning of the seventeenth century, had secured a "tack" of the customs duties, on payment to the Crown of 115,000 merks ; and the resultant public exposure produced at least some mitigation of the swindle, for, on the expiry of the "tack" in 1616, Archibald Primrose, the leading capitalist of the group, could only secure renewal at a public auction and by a purchase price of 210,000 merks !

It is a matter of great difficulty, the reconstruction of the conditions of life in a medieval Scots burgh. The burghs themselves would appear to modern eyes as mere hamlets, though, of course, large areas of land owned and controlled by the burgh authorities, surrounded the houses of the "in-dwellers." There were common pasturings, common herdsmen, common rabbit-warrens. Usually there existed regulations—at Paisley, for example,—limiting the

---

*Reg. Privy Council, O.S., vol. 7, p. 408.

†Ibid, 355-405.

‡*Feudal Practice of Riding Fairs and Levying Customs.*"—Murray Hawick Arch. Pubns., 1876. p. 8.   Down to 1862 Buccleugh levied customs on every article brought to market, for every 3lbs. of butter ½d., every web of cloth 1d., every load of meal 4d., every puppet show 2d., and so on. On that date he sold his rights to the Magistrates for a money payment.

Marwick's *Early Glasgow*, pp. 130-179.

By-ways of History—Colville, p. 162.

parcels of land annually allotted to each burgess to five roods, but the regulations were frequently broken. Cultivation was carried on under the Runrig System. The poorer class houses were low-roofed and thatched with straw or heather and divots : and the better class houses were covered with red tiles ; the floors were earthen and the windows narrow and dingy ; the streets, narrow mud ruts at the best, were frequently "abusit be middingis" among which browsed or picked a swarm of dogs and pigs and fowls. There was no street-lighting, and the lieges mostly went to bed at sundown to do battle with innumerable fleas. The burgesses took turns in rotation as night watchmen, and seem chiefly to have engaged themselves in marking down for arrest "walkeris on the night" discovered near their neighbours' gardens. In 1576 the General Assembly of the Kirk had granted ministers and Bible-readers permission to "tap aile, beer or wine, and to keep an open tavern," but grave complaints were made against the excessive drinking of the artisans, and in 1617 the Privy Council ordered all taverns to close nightly at 10 p.m.* Strangers were lodged for one night only, without rigorous enquiry as to their antecedents and the purpose of their visit. The leper folk were segregated at one end of the town and profligate women, who wore a distinctive dress, at another. Men lost their "freedom" for slight misdemeanours, and in the graver offences justice, rough and ready, was tempered by a great reverence for omens and signs. In one instance of a criminal convicted of theft and sentenced to be hanged on his own door step, the rope broke, and the mischance was accepted as the will of God ; the criminal was accordingly "duly banist and nocht hangit becaus the raip broke," and because (so the justices had now discovered) he was "ane pure man with small bairnis and for pete of him, the prouest, baillies and counsall bannasis him for all the dais of his lyf."† When broils and tumults broke out, the burgesses, both merchants and craftsmen, were summoned by the common bellman to come with their weapons ; those who failed to appear promptly forfeited for ever their "freedom." In 1530 the Provost of Edinburgh convened a citizen's meeting to consider the steps necessary to the ending of the oppression done them by "gentlemen," and the resolution come to was that every person should arm himself until a more suitable remedy was found of ridding the good town of the common oppressors. In the

---

*The black list of habitual drunkards is not a modern institution. As far back as 1668 the Rutherglen Magistrates, seeing that J—— P—— is "frequentlie" drunk, warn all brewers and ale-sellers against supplying him with liquor "except what they sell to his wyfe and bairnes for the use of the house and familie." Intimation of this warning was made in the usual way—by towk of drum through the town.

†*Scotland Before* 1700—Hume Brown, p. 200.

Edinburgh Council Records, under date October, 1529, we read that 19 persons were banished, among them being one, William Calder, for the crime of buying wild fowls contrary to statute; "Janet Brown, for her general demerits"; and "an Irishman that sung with a lass and would not work." In 1554-5, the Edinburgh Accounts note the expenditure of two shillings "for cords to . . . bind a woman when she was burned on the cheek." When the Councils interfered in moral questions they were almost as cruel and heartless as the ecclesiastical authorities, as, for example, at Aberdeen, in 1538, when female delinquents clad only in a shift went before the Sunday procession to beseech the magistrates and good men for forgiveness; for subsequent offences these women had their "crag put in the jougs." "Horrid cursing and swearing" (a common offence) gossiping and tale-bearing, were punished with the branks; petty thieves were put in the stocks and whipped. In 1560 Edinburgh harlots were carted through the town for a first conviction; for a second they were burned on the cheek and banished; if they returned to the town they suffered death. In Edinburgh, Leith, and the large towns there were daily scourgings, hangings, nailing of lugs, and boring of tongues; female thieves, for a first offence, had their noses "pinched"; and as late as 1830 "notour" thieves were hanged; in 1538 the magistrates of Haddington sentenced a man "to be bund at the erss of ane cart," and to be whipped through the streets before being banished; in 1700 the magistrates of Stirling paid 20s. for "scourging two, lugging two, and burning two thieves." Every tavern was a brothel; and in 1562 a special hole was reserved in the North Loch for the dipping of fornicators, who were afterwards scourged at the cart's end, their heads shaven, and banished. Shopkeepers were compelled to close early on Tuesdays and Thursdays. In 1567 it was decreed by the Estates of Parliament that no women should adorn herself with dress above the rank in burghal society held by her male relatives—unless, of course, she was a harlot, and for her class special costumes were designed. Fairs and markets were the great burghal "special occasions," the authorities rigidly extorting taxes from all articles and commodities exposed for sale. Everything was regulated: how goods were to be manufactured and used; the prices at which they must be sold; who might traffic in them; the area of such traffic; the strength of ale was fixed; tallow candles even could only be made on fixed conditions—the wick to be measured and the candle weighed. Nothing was too great and nothing too small to escape a code of regulations.

Attendance at the religious festivals and processionings in pre-Reformation times was compulsory, and each craft must march in its appointed order, its members bearing or carrying the tokens and banners of their craft. All processionists must wear "green cottis";

and elaborate provision was made for the subsequent banqueting and junketing. Great attention was paid to the spectacular and dramatic entertainments on the festival days ; but the Reformed Church frowned on the "heathen idolatries " ; and the plays wherein strutted the Robin Hoods and the Little Johns, and "women sing about summer trees" were legally condemned.* Burgh justice was frankly and flagrantly class justice. Apprentices, beggars, and the poor generally were the victims of regular magisterial "attention," and even the organised free craftsmen had learned by bitter experience to distrust the impartial decisions of the merchant justices, and they frequently made demonstrations in force with the object of terrorising the bench when a fellow-craftsman was on trial.† Though the craft organisations may have varied somewhat in form in the different burghs, they generally followed pretty much the same pattern. Craft Guilds and Merchant Guilds were alike benefit societies or associations ; both sought charters of incorporation or seals of cause empowering them to make petty regulations for the welfare and profit of their members, and both sought to prevent outside competition. In William the Lion's time (1165-1214) they approximated in some respects at least to modern conceptions of the Joint Stock Companies. If a "foreign" trader arrived with a load of merchandise, the Dean of the Merchant Guild and the Deacon of the Craft Guild were entitled to make him the first offer for his goods, and no one, if the offer was refused, was allowed to purchase at a lower price. If the Dean bought the goods the profits went to the Town treasury ; if the Deacon bought, the profits went to the Craft funds.‡ In later times, when the craft organisation became more rigid and monopolistic, there does not appear to have been any joint purchasing. The members of the Craft met regularly to discuss prices, conditions of labour, new methods of production, or new regulations and impositions laid upon them by the Town Council of merchants. They elected a Deacon, in whose august presence no member must curse or swear under liability to expulsion§ and whose duty it is to preside at their meetings, to represent them on public occasions, to inspect the quality of the members' work, to lead them in processions, and to meet with the Deacons of the other crafts in the Deacon Convener's Court for the joint discussion of craft grievances and joint resistance to the magistrates on the one hand and the unfreemen on the other ‖ Each craft, too, founds

*Ancient Laws and Customs of the Burghs of Scot., vol. ii., p. 81.
†Scotland in the Time of Queen Mary—P. Hume Brown, p. 154.
‡The Guild Merchant—Gross, p. 208.
§Excerpts from the Ancient Records of Weavers' Society of Anderston.
‖By 1763 the Crafts had certainly begun to fight each other—the weavers joining with certain other trades to " bear down, if possible, the dearth of grain so industriously promoted and held up by our meal-mongers, notwithstanding of the great plenty in the land."

or endows (in pre-Reformation times) a chapel or an altar in the neighbouring church ; it takes part in the great Church ceremonials, processions and masqueradings ; it provides mutual help, assistance in distress, provision for the burial of its dead, and to widows and orphans of its members ; maintains the customs of the craft, and arranges entrance fees, holidays and so forth ; it decides the number of apprentices a freeman may have ; it forbids freemen to entice away the apprentices of other freemen, or to "roup, sell, or interchange "their apprentices."* Not only were the free craftsmen themselves obliged to finance by fines and levies the upkeep of the Church altars, but the apprentices and journeymen, for the privilege of labouring to these free craftsmen, were called upon for contributions. In Edinburgh, for example, the apprentice masons were taxed one-half merk at entry for the altar of St. John in St. Giles Church ; and in 1475, while every master weaver had to "give the priest his meat," the hired servants were called upon for 4d per annum for altar charges. Usually no one was admitted to Craft membership unless he had first served his apprenticeship and then (unless he were a craftsman's son or had married a craftsman's daughter) worked as a journeyman for a stipulated number of years ; but sometimes the deacons and the crafts, on payment of the Craft entrance fee, did not insist upon production of the burgess ticket. This relaxation naturally was resented by the magistrates, who declared it to be an attempt to deplete the burgh funds and to enhance the power of the crafts ; and at Aberdeen, in the sixteenth century, the magistrates spiked the craft guns for a time, by decreeing that two-thirds of the Craft entrance fees should be paid over to the Common Good of the town. Perhaps the enforcement of this decision was one of the contributory causes to the riots of 1638, when the crafts " convened with swords, pistollis and lang wapynnis."

In few of the Burghs of Barony and Regality did the Superior tolerate even a pretence of popular election of the magistrates. They were his magistrates, and the Craft Guilds seem to have made no effort to demand a voice in their election. The Baron Superior could appropriate the municipal revenues ; † and although in the seventeenth century these "private" burghs obtained trading rights upon condition that they made themselves liable to the same taxations as were the Royal Burghs, they were always more or less of an irritating weapon which the barons could use against the Crown and the larger manufacturers and merchants ; and successive attempts were made, as the central authority grew stronger, to extinguish their privileges. Some towns, such as Greenock, Port

---

*Sketch of the Incorporation of Masons and The Lodge of Glasgow St. John—
    Cruickshank, p. 63.

†Report of Municipal Commissioners, 1835, p. 20.

Glasgow and Falkirk, had neither burgesses nor Craft Incorporations, but these towns were in great minority, and the general conditions we have sketched held sway all over Scotland.   Before 1846, when the privileges of the Incorporations were abolished and an elective Municipal Council established, some towns, such as Johnstone, Beith, Barrhead, Keith and Lochwinnoch, had no constitution at all ; some, like Stonehaven, Stornoway and Girvan, had a burgess right of magistrate election subject to approval by the Superior ; the others were either Royal Burghs or simply pocket burghs belonging to the neighbouring land magnate.   By the Burgh Reform Act only Edinburgh and Glasgow Town Councils were compelled to admit to membership both the Deacon Convener of the Crafts and the Dean of Guild.   Everywhere else the Deacon of the Crafts lost his municipal *status*, and only in three other towns, Aberdeen, Dundee and Perth, were the newly-elected councillors to receive among them the Dean of Guild.   He whose function it once was to admit people to the freedom of the town, to make regulations for the buying and selling of goods, he who decided boundary disputes and fixed the march stones, indentured apprentices, supervised public works, and whose decisions were subject to no revising authority but the Court of Session—he is now an anachronism, his very municipal existence tolerated, not for any sentimental affection towards an historical continuity but simply because no one considers his abolition worth an agitation.

And the servants, the journeymen, the labourers, the orra men in the burghs, the real town working-class who lived below the Craft Guilds and toiled on century after century for meat and fee—what of them ?   Alas! the burghs were so small and intercommunication so difficult and so dangerous that it was not with us as with the English.   No huge working-class organisations came into being to mitigate the sufferings and improve the conditions of the labouring man.   True, we catch a fleeting glimpse of a ploughman's guild in the Lothians ; but we have no servant's revolt such as Mrs. Green and Professor Oman report as occurring in England.*   Nor, we believe, is it possible to estimate from a consideration of wages and prices, the rise and fall of the standard of working-class comfort, as Professor Thorold Rogers estimated it for England.†   Scotland was not a nation ; it was a loose aggregation of small but practically self-supporting communities, and scanty supplies and high prices at Aberdeen may quite well have been coincident with plenty and comparatively low prices in Dundee or Glasgow.   Famines, mostly due to

---

Town Life in the Fifteenth Century and *The Great Revolt of* 1381.

†Even Professor Rogers' panegyric on the " Golden Age " is being challenged. Abram, in his " Social England in the Fifteenth Century," points to the great number of unemployed workmen.

baronial feuds, were frequent, but they were not national famines ; and prices and wages must have exhibited marked variations not only at different times in the same district, but in different districts at the same time. In very early periods, of course, as we have already shewn, the servant was a chattel slave ; he was stock. In William the Lion's time, if the servant in burgh were wounded on the face by his master and permanently disfigured, he was entitled to receive a fourth part of his value and also "the price of the bloodshed " ; * and a burghal regulation (much quoted to prove the anti-slavery tendencies of the burgesses) to the effect that any slave residing in a burgh for a year and a day and possessing a burgage tenement became *ipso facto* free, was really not a piece of early anti-slavery legislation, but a far-seeing attempt on the part of the burghal authorities to prevent outside barons from effecting a lodgement inside the burgh and securing share of its trading privileges through a bondman deputy.†

Before the sixteenth century we have really few definite indications of the economic or social condition of the hired men. Un-freemen had their goods searched by the privileged crafts, thus causing "disquiet," and the seal of cause granted to the Masons of Glasgow in 1551 decreed that "no master shall give or pay his fellows but as he may deserve, so that he may not be deceived by false workmen "; and in 1593, after the heat and fervour of the Reformation, though the letter of chattel slavery had gone, its spirit was very much alive in the Act of Parliament which held a master answerable for the theological opinions of his servants. In 1598 the Privy Council fixed prices for twelve months ahead ; servants' wages were to be 4s., while a pint of ale was 12d., eight ounces of wheaten bread 8d., a hen 6s. 8d., a dozen laverocks and other "bus burdis " 2s., two "dowis " (pigeons) 2s. 6d., a peck of oats 5s., and a servant's bed for the night 12d.‡ The four-shilling wages here are quite evidently in addition to board and lodging. In 1606 the "ignorant multitude " of Glasgow had evidently been giving the Magistrates some trouble, for these officials put upon record their belief that the people ought to live "under the obedience of thair magistrattis, quhilk becometh the memberis of ane commonweale " . . . and "the ignorant and commoun multitude ar easeilie to be induceit to factionis and alterationis, and that subtile, craftie, and politicque bodyis mycht draw thame ignorantlie upon vane pretenssis and schawis of libertie, to follow thair factious and seditious humouris, to renounce thair obedience to thair magistrattis and to schaik at the cair of thair awne

---

Frag. Coll., c. 10. See *Acta Parl. Scot.*, i., 738.
†*Edin. Crafts and Guilds*—Marwick, p. 5.
‡*Reg. Privy Council*, vol. v., O.S., p. 507.

commounweale.*" Before the Reformation, we know, there were, besides Sundays, about 47 Saints days on which it was unlawful to work, but the master class seized the opportunity afforded by the Reformation to abolish most of these holidays as popish observances —a proceeding, says Professor Hume Brown, in which the mass of the people only after a long time, and with great reluctance, acquiesced.† Even in 1641 an Act had to be secured by the coalmasters to force the colliers to work six days per week, under a penalty, and a fine to the coalmaster of 20s., for every idle day taken by a collier. "It was," says Hume Brown, "with genuine feudal class feeling that the privileged burgess regarded his less favoured fellow townsmen (non-burgess and unfreeman) who could not follow any handicraft, nor engage in any form of trade and merchandise, nor partnership with freeman, nor be employed by him in any business capacity either at home or abroad. Shops and stalls were closed against him : in market he could only buy in prescribed hours : in Edinburgh market place on market days he must take up his position on the opposite side of the street from the freemen.‡ . . . the relations between the two sections of the community suggest a certain parallel to the relations which existed between the plebians and the patricians in ancient Rome."§

Men might be equal in the sight of God, but there was to be no nonsense about equality before the Parson, and the seating of the Churches in Edinburgh was carefully approximated to the different orders of society. The nobility, the provost, the bailies, council, elders and deacons were to be seated first, honest merchants and craftsmen in vacancies, "providing always that nowhere the apprentices or servants of the merchants or craftsmen, or other common people take up the places and seats of the said merchants and craftsmen "|| Free trade in servants and apprentices was discouraged, and no master was to "lift, hous, herbery nor ressaue " any other master's workers.*a* Savage and indeed murderous legislation against unlicensed beggars was rendered of no avail through "the preposterous pitie of the country people," whose stomachs doubtless turned at the spectacle of poor, helpless, unemployed men and women being first publicly scourged, then burned through the gristle of the right ear with a hot iron about an inch in compass, and (for a second "offence ") suffering shameful death.*b* The magistrates of Ruther-

---

Reg. Privy Council, vol. vii., O.S., p. 240.

†*Scotland in the Time of Queen Mary,* p. 162.

‡And he had in the fifteenth century to pay a special penny tax for the privilege. —*Ancient Laws and Customs,* vol. ii., p. 50.

§*Scotland in the Time of Queen Mary,* p. 138.

||Macintosh—*Hist. Civ. Scot.,* vol. ii., p. 247.

*a*Edinburgh Cordwainers' Seal of Cause (1509).

*b*Acta Parl. Scot., 1574, iii., 87a, 140a.

glen were forced to act as slave-catchers for Sir Ludovic Stewart of
M nto, when the poor coal serfs belonging to that gentleman made a
dash for Rutherglen and l berty * In Edinburgh in the sixteenth
century the servants of the Tailor Craft worked from 5 a.m. till
9 p.m., "without leiff," for 12d. and their meat. Lest strangers
might mistake the servant for the master (an unlikely event) various
Acts of Parliament were passed to fix the colour of clothing which
servants must wear. On week days they were to be clad in grey
and white, and on holidays in light blue, green or red ; their wives
must wear the husband's colours and sport only curches of their own
making, and the price of the cloth must not exceed 40d. an ell. A
few years later a concession was made : the common people might
go clad in cloth, coloured black, white or green—provided it was
purchased from a Scots manufacturer ! But artistry in dress was to
remain a manufacturer's dream; for over two hundred years afterwards the women of the working-class went barefoot and considered
themselves Fortune's favourites if their shoulders were encased in
a plaid.

In 1574 the owners of the salt pans are found complaining about
the recent rise in servant's wages, and one hundred years later the
coalmasters of Glasgow are tormented with the same grievance ;
their hewers had "exhorbitant wages," and had the intolerable
impudence to refuse to work more than four days in every six ; they
also exacted full wages at seed time and harvest and spent their
idle days in drinking.† Strong temperance advocates, these coalowners ! In the sixteenth and seventeenth centuries three Acts
are passed permitting servants to wear the cast off clothing of their
masters—a blow this at the linen manufacturers. Drink money or
Capie cogie was provided on all jobs.‡ In the early seventeenth
century Saturday afternoon became regarded as a workers' half-
holiday in every trade except agriculture, which to this day retains
its medieval semi-serf six day working week. In 1617§ we have our
Statutes of Labourers (which contrary to common opinion were not
confined to England), Statutes of Labourers naked and unashamed.
Justices at the February and August quarter sessions were authorised
to fix the wages of workmen, labourers and servants, and to imprison
and farther punish at sweet will those recalcitrants who refused to
work at the terms so fixed. As the Justices were themselves the
employers, we can understand the indignation and angry remon-
strance with which the Act was received by the labouring classes,
and we can understand how the select coterie of callous ruffians who

---

Acta Parl. Scot., 1661, App. 30a.
†*Reg. Privy Council*, i., 3rd series, xliv.
‡The Mason's " Foundin' pint " is not yet extinct.
§Act of 1617, sect. xiv.

called themselves the Estates of Parliament and who themselves stood to benefit by this shameful statute, should have felt it necessary to coat the pill by ostentatiously inserting a clause commanding employers to pay the wages fixed by the Justices. The insertion of this clause, said the draftsmen of the Act, is necessary "to induce the servants to submit." The politicians of the present day have not bettered much the tricks of their seventeeth century progenitors ! How the Justices used their powers in the rural districts, we shall see later on, but that they were not allowed to die of inanition, we may guess at once from the fact that the Act of 1617 was repeated both in 1655 and in 1661. In the Royal Burghs, of course, the Magistrates already had arbitrary powers in the fixing of servant's wages' and these powers were used to the uttermost. Meantime a perfect hurricane of wages bills came from Parliament. In 1617 the shearers had their maximum fixed ; in 1630 the wages of the herring fishers were limited to £4 12s. 6d. (Scots) per week for 16 men ; in 1641 the colliers maximum "fee" was fixed at 20 merks ; in 1644 no hired servant was to leave his master without that master's written consent; and in 1656, "if a servant under fourteen years of age offend aga nst the Act for the observance of the Lord's Day, the Master" (so said Parliament) "shall pay one shilling or punish the servant at the sight of the public officer." In 1661 an Act declared that heavy pena t es wou d attach to anyone who enticed or resetted any other man's apprentices ; and n 1672 provision was made for "disobedient servants" in the correction houses, where they were forced to work and were "corrected according to their demerits."

From the records of the Royal Burgh of Rutherglen we get a pretty complete picture of the burghal statutes fix ng the wages, hours and labour conditions of the working class. The Rutherglen statute is of date 1660, and is self described as

"a remedye . . . for excessive pryces of fies and waidges, introduced of late in tymes of plentie by the covetousnes, idlenes, and other corrupt practices of some evill affected servands and workmen." The Town Council and Magistrates now decree that "during the scarsnes of money and cheapnes of victwall NO persone . . . give nor take more fie or waidges nor is heir efter exprest. To witt :—

"A commone able man servand, for all sorts of husbandrie, £10 Scots, a pair of double solled shooes, and a paire of hoise, and no more.

"A man servand of younger zeires or halfang 10 merks termly, a pair of shooes and no more.

"An able woman servand for all necesserie worke, 10 merks termly, a pair of shooes, an ell of lining in winter, and an ell of playding in summer.

"A lass or young made, fowr punds Scotts, with a pair of shooes termly and no more.

"The harvest fee of an able man sheirer, 8 punds and a peck of meill, with meit and drink ; if hired by the day, ½ a merk and two meals. An able woman, 6 punds, a peck of meal, and meat and drink or 5s., and two meals a day.

" A woman or lass for day's work in weeding of lint, cloveing, spinning, cardeing, yarne-winning, or any such worke, 12d. Scots and 3 meals and no more.

" A thrasher, 4s. Scots, 2 meals and no more.

" Masons and Wrights not to exceed a merke without, and ½ merke with, meit and drink.

" Barrowmen not to exceed ½ merke without and 40d. with, meit and drink.

" Theiker of howses is to have 10s. without and 5s. with, meit and drink.

" Tailors are not to exceed 40d. and their dyet.*

" Commone workeman or labourer to get the same as the barrowman.

" If any workman, woman, or labourer within this burgh shall refuse to work and serve upon the pryces respective above wryttin, they shall be imprisoned and further punished as the Magistrates shall think fit. And if any workman or servant man or woman shall require and exact greater fees and wages than these before expressed, they are to be fined according to the discretion of the Magistrates.

" Ordered also, that no man servant or woman servant unmarried, upon any pretence shall take up house and work at their own hand without a warrant from the Magistrates.

" Ordered likewise, that no inhabitant or servant, man or woman . . presume to fee themselves in harvest-time to any person or persons dwelling without this burgh without a special license from the Magistrates had ther unto, under the pain of 5 pounds money."

There is no mistaking the nefarious intent of that statute : wages were fixed ; no one might refuse to work at these wages without rendering himself liable to imprisonment and punishment at the discretion of the magistrates : no one was to set up house and start business without warrant from the tradesmen and merchants with whom he sought to complete, and no one was to be allowed to take another job outside the burgh. The slavery was complete. The price of foodstuffs might rise, but the wages were stationary. The teind boll of oatmeal in Rutherglen might rise as it did from £6 6s. 8d. in 1660 to £8 6s. 8d in 1663, or to £9 12s. in 1674, or to £10 in 1699 ; but the wages of the working class were fixed and immovable ; at any rate, that was the undisguised intention of the framers of the statute.

A careful search of burghal records would shew that local regulations of this nature were common everywhere in the early seventeenth century. In Peebles, for example, in 1610, the magistrates warned servants that they must be prepared to do any sort of work ordered by their masters under a penalty fine of 6s. 8d. to be deducted from wages for each refusal ; and in 1640 no servant was to be permitted

---

*All these wages are in Scots money, *i.e.*, 12d. Scots = 1d. sterling. A merk equalled about 6s. 8d. sterling.

to fee himself outside the burgh ; a census of all the "coillaris and mean housholders " was to be taken, and each one warned personally that if he accepted service outside the town he would be fined £20, and banished for life ; if he returned he was to be "brunt and markit with the tounes merk.*" In 1628 seven poor shoemakers of Cupar were imprisoned by the magistrates because they had refused to produce boots and shoes at the prices fixed by the local Council. They declared that the price of boots and shoes depended upon the price of hides, bark, lyme, etc., and they, in an appeal to the Privy Council against the sentence they were suffering, demanded that such fair prices should be fixed as would give an "allowance to the compleaners of that whilk the law of God and nature gives to thame for the fruiet of thair labours and interteanement of thair families " and although the Privy Council heard this appeal and were told that the complainers were but "honest simple men who live by their work and labour " they had no hesitation whatever in upholding the magistrates and sending the Cupar shoemakers back to jail.†
"Corbies do not pick out corbies een ! "

All these municipal regulations curtailing wages naturally evoked bitter resentment among the labouring classes, and the jails were not built which could accommodate the strikers. Everywhere there seems to have arisen, as if by magic, a strange spirit of independence. Here, a desperate rebel defies the magistrates ; there another smote his master on the face. In Aberdeen one William Walker, a fisher, calls his master "a thief's son," pushes him into the water and "hits him with a stone on the breast "; and William Duncan, a shoemaker's servant, goes at night into the house of a master shoemaker named James Hall, draws a sword and threatens his life "because he would not allow his servant to go out of the shop with him to eat a lamb's leg, as desired.‡ But a hard, hard age for Reformers was the seventeenth century, and daring spirits who challenged iniquity and tyranny were assured of martyrdom, each ruling class standing firm and four square, prepared to stick at nothing in defence of its privileges and powers. The first apostle of financial purity in administration discovered that. George Nicol, the son of an Edinburgh tailor, who by sheer ability had become clerk to the Secretary of State for Scotland, had the temerity, in 1634, to inform King Charles that the Lord Chancellor (Viscount Duplin), the Earls of Morton and Strathearn, Lord Traquair and the Lord Advocate, Sir Thomas Hope, were jointly engaged in robbing the public purse. The indignant King summoned the accused nobles and lawyers to meet Nicol and face his charges before the throne ; but ere the trial was due they had, courtier like

---

Gleanings from the Records of the Royal Burgh of Peebles—Renwick, p. 178.
†*Reg. Privy Council*, vol. ii., p. 178.
‡M'Intosh—*Hist. Civ. Scot.*, vol. iii., p. 247.

got the King's ear, and poor Nicol found himself in the dock instead of the witness box, charged with the crime of impugning the honour of his Majesty's faithful servants. At first the King had authorised Nicol's trial to be undertaken by the Justice General; but this did not suit the high positioned thieves, who succeeded in cancelling the order to the Justice General and in securing an order that they, the men whom Nicol had accused, should themselves be his judges. Meanwhile the tailor's son lay in prison, his documentary evidence stolen from him, refused pen and ink, and finally, without trial of any kind, he was sentenced by the corrupt rascals who had become his judges to get "sax whippes upon his naiked backe," to undergo a term in the public pillory, as a lesson to all would-be reformers, and lastly to be banished for life.* It was small consolation to him as he stood in the pillory with his lacerated back to know that he was pitied and mourned over by crowds of poor people "who generally believed he suffered wrongfully."

The wages regulations of the seventeenth century which we have referred to, undoubtedly called into being associations and agreements of some kind among the workers, and these associations as they increased and developed became, as Mr. and Mrs. Sidney Webb have shewn,† the first trades unions. The Trade Union did not evolve from the Craft Guild : it was brought into existence to fight the Craft Guild, and whether we can, or can not, properly designate the working class associations of the early eighteenth century as Trade Unions, pure and simple, is a question for pedants. The fact remains that at the end of the seventeenth and at the beginning of the eighteenth centuries, the commercial processes in Scotland had undergone a change, and that change—the crushing out of the small "master" with his single servant and his single apprentice and the substitution of the "large master" with his several servants and his several apprentices—combined with the frantic use of municipal machinery to crush and still farther degrade the working man, compelled the wage-earners to form themselves into anti-craft Guild Associations, and these we shall discuss in another section.

Reg. Privy Council, vol. v., xlvi.
†*History of Trades Unionism.* Preface.

L

CHAPTER VII.

THE REIVING OF THE COMMON LANDS.

"The wrong committed is now irrevocable."—*Crofters' Commission Report* (1884).

"It must be declared that . . . every particle of their [landlords] alleged landed possessions and rights which they cannot *prove* to have been acquired legally and equitably, shall at once be reclaimed as public property."—*Dr. Alfred Russell Wallace.*

AFTER many years of historical disputation there seems to be no reasonable doubt but that the earliest and universal form of land ownership was tribal or communal. The land was common property, and the conception of unrestricted private possession in the soil would probably be as alien to our pre-historic forefathers as the conception of private ownership of the atmosphere is to us to-day. In Saxon times there was, first folc (folk) land or people's land—the land held by the village community as a community ; and second, the boc-land or book land —land granted to individuals by charter ;* and folc-land, long anterior to boc-land,† was certainly the original form of soil ownership in Scotland. Even when the land became boc-land, the old folk-land system was not entirely suppressed, and in grants and charters tracts of land were withheld from private ownership and reserved for the use of the community. Lord Eversley doubts whether the Saxon or manorial system ever obtained a foothold in Scotland,‡ but Mr. Chambers § declares that the Saxon settlers in the south-east of Scotland undoubtedly lived under the land regulations which form such an interesting study in English history, and he has abstracted from the Chartulary of Melrose records of early grants of commonty which seem to justify that opinion. "The pastures," he says, "the woodlands, the peataries or mosses, were enjoyed in common by the manorial tenants, each person having a right of common in proportion to what he tilled of the manor." But before the Saxon system, there was the Celtic system, of which, fortunately, we have considerable traces, not only in the ancient Irish law tracts but in the not yet dead agrestic customs of the outer Hebrides. It is impossible, of course, to say how far the land regula-

---

Landholding in England—Mary A. M. Marks, p. 12.
†Preface to *Ancient Laws and Customs of the Burghs of Scotland* (Burgh Records Society), p. xxxvii.
‡*Commons, Forests, and Footpaths*, pp. 4-5.
§*Caledonia*, vol. 3, p. 134.

tions and the clan ownerships of the Irish law books* were practised
in Scotland by the Irish emigrants who settled upon our Western
coasts. Was it here with us, as in Ireland till the Danish invasion ?
Was the chief but the military commander elected by the adult
males—those who had passed the stage of "the encircling of the
beard ? " Was he but the administrator of the common property
with his rights and his privileges and his duties clearly defined ?
Did we have in Scotland descent through females—the sons belonging
to the tribe of the mothers—a relic of the matriarchal age ? Was
the land tribal land, and tribal land only ? To these questions the
Celtic historians have given affirmative answers, though with varying degrees of emphasis, according to whether they are dealing with
early or late Celtic periods. Mr. Innes, in his *Origines Parochiales
Scotiae*,† writes of the "system of the Celts, where the chief led the
clan indeed, and administered the common property for the benefit
of all, as the patriarch of the great family, not as the lord of the soil."
Mr. Skene says :‡ "Private property in land did not exist at first,
but emerged from the right of common property vested in the community . . . The oldest tenure by which land was held was by the
tribe in common . . . the Ri, or King, had no seperate possession
of land, but in this respect was on an equality with the freer members
of the tribe and entitled only to the same right of pasturage for his
cattle on the pasture land and to his share of the arable land annually
alloted to him." Chiefs guilty of gross violation of the conventional
duties of their position were deposed § Tacitus says the Pictish state
was "chiefly democratical." Again : "Each clan continued after
the *ceann-cath* was changed into the king, to be the owners of their
respective districts in common and to elect their own local or district
governments of chief, tanister, and cheftains, and to support them
by a voluntary tribute denominated *calpa* (the brawn of the leg)·
The clan tribute in Ireland was called *tuarasdal*, literally, wages."||
But the strongest proof of the early land communism of the Celtic
tribes lies in the agricultural customs which, despite the ravages of
feudalism, despite the thunder of hostile Parliaments, and despite
the antipathy of laird and factor, has persisted down to our own
day in the outer Hebrides.*a* In the year 1847 there were still in the

---

*Particularly the " Senchus Mor " in the *Early Irish Laws,* vol. 2, xlvii., 3, p·
    53.
†Vol. ii., part i., p. xix. See also Pref. *Acta Parl. Scot.*, vol. i.
‡*Celtic Scotland*, vol. 3, p. 138, 139, 142.
§Report to Directors of Royal Patriotic and Industrial Society of Scotland
    (1852), by their Secretary, Chas. Bond.
||*The Poetry and Traditions of the Highland Clans*—Stirling Lib. Pamphlets
    (Glasgow), vol. 99, p. 7.
*a*Appendix to Evidence and Report of Crofters' and Cottars' Commission, 1884,
    vol. v., p. 451, *et seq.* ; S ene's *Celtic Scotland*, vol. 3, p. 382 *circa.*

Highlands 37,305 acres of common pasture land, and in the outer islands a sort of co-operative share-and-share alike farming of the soil called run-rig, which is probably the only remaining institution linking us directly to our Aryan ancestors. Run-rig is a corruption of *Roinn Ruith*-division run or division common, and was the usual mode of agriculture all over the North until little more than a century ago. Each township elects its own constable, who, upon accepting office, "takes off his shoes and stockings. Uncovering his head, he bows reverently low, and promises, in presence of heaven and earth, in presence of God and man—Am fianuis uir agus adhair am fianus De agus daoine—that he will be faithful to his trust." In some places the elected Constable takes up a handful of earth instead of uncovering his feet. The object is the same—to emphasise by bodily contact with the earth, that he is conscious of being made of earth, to which he returns. After the harvest is gathered in he summons the people together for "Nabac" (neighbourliness). The meetings are held at night, and are "orderly" and "interesting," and at these meetings all the business of the township is decided by majority vote. What proportion of land will be put under green crop next year ? That is settled. Then the constable divides the arable land into rigs or divisions ; lots are cast, what a man draws he holds and tills for 3 years (one-third of the soil being thus re-alloted every year) ; part of the soil is set apart for the relief of the poor, for "the kindness of the poor to the poor throughout these islands is wonderful." A man must not allow his land to go to waste, since that would hurt the community ; they have a Common Good fund, into which go all fines, and this is used by the constable, after due resolution moved and carried at the Nabac, for the purchase of fresh stock, bulls, tups, etc. ; they reclaim much moorland—"not infrequently, however, these land reclamations are wrested without acknowledgement from those who made them." Should a crofter or his family fall sick, his fellow crofters help on his work ; if a man's horse dies "his neighbours bring on his work concurrently with their own," and if necessary help him to buy another horse. Unfortunately, the local laird or his factor, though they exact "four times the rent" from the run rig communities that they can exact from the large farms, are ever on the look-out for opportunities of smashing up the run-rig system by individual tenancies. This "the more intelligent people regret," for the houses of "tenants of the run-rig system are warm, good, and comfortable. These tenants carry on their farming operations simultaneously, and not without friendly and wholesome rivalry, the enterprise of the one stimulating the zeal of the other. . . . Compassion for the poor, consideration towards the distressed, and respect for the dead are the characteristic traits of these people. This is indicated in their sayings, ' Succour to the poor and to the dead (in burying) and the sympathy with the distressed are three things which a wise man never regretted,"' and "The division of the land is made with care and justice. This is the interest of all." Such tenants, we are told, as have least departed from run-rig husbandry are the most comfortable in North Uist. The Constable engages the Town Herd, apportions him ground for potatoes and bere, and collects and pays his wages. In some parts the tilling, sowing and reaping is done in common, and the produce divided equally at harvest time ; but whatever variations there be, the agrestic custom is always based fundamentally upon the idea of common ownership—common land. The clergymen, too, both Roman Catholic and Protestant, it is pleasing to record, stand united in defence of the ancient customs and the ancient ways ; but the laird slowly usurps ; he cannot tolerate free and independent communities, and the writer of the appendix to the Crofter and Cottars' Commission Report, already referred to, winds up (strange to find such language in a Blue Book !) with a beautifully poetic wail over the passing of the Nabac townships and their run-rigs. Probably, he says, they are the only remaining examples in Scotland, if not in the British Isles :

> " of this once prevalent system of holding the land and tilling the ground. And perhaps it is in the fitting order of things that these, the last lingering footsteps of this far travelled pilgrim from the eye of day, should here sink down on the bosom of endless night, where the last rays of the setting sun sink and disappear in the mysterious fading horizon beyond. . . Yet I cannot help heaving a sigh of regret on seeing a system once and for ages the land system of millions of the human race, now disused, discarded, and disowned, disappearing, and for ever, on the shores of these eerie Western Isles, washed by the Atlantic tide, whose waves pour their dirge-like strains over the dying, while the wail of Celtic Sorrow wails on the lonely ear of Night :
>
> > ' Cha till, cha till, cha till mi tuille.
> > ' I return, I return, I return, nevermore ! ' "

So deeply rooted in the instincts and usages of the people was this communal ownership and working of the soil, that when feudalism from the twelfth century onwards, became the theory and practice of our governors, it was found impossible, even in charter grants flowing from the Crown and vesting in the grantee practically unlimited power over life and limb on his estates, to altogether disregard the old customs. The King might declare himself supreme power, and in feudal theory all land rights were vested in the Sovereign ; the barons who held from the Crown, and the Church which held from the barons, may have had rights of pit and gallows over the unhappy tillers of the soil, but King, Barons, and Church all regarded as inevitable the continuance of the old Celtic system in so far as it allowed even the poorest of the poor the free and unrestricted use of commonty lands for his geese, or his swine, or his hens. "During," says Chambers, "the good old times of David I. and his grandsons we have seen that every hamlet had its common, without which the cottagers could scarcely have existed."* So that, under feudal tenures, Saxon tenures and Celtic tenures alike, in every district, every village, there were certain lands clearly recognised as common lands, lands to which every man, rich and poor, noble and serf, had indefeasible rights of use ; and, if the folklorists are to be believed, and if below all the pomp and pageantry of conquest the agricultural populations toiled on generation after generation, little disturbed by the race changes among their rulers,† then it is possible, and indeed probable, that the common lands and tillage in common, stretch back away to the pre-Aryan, stone-circle totem-fearing people who inhabited our land before History began.

"Looking over our country," says Mr. Cosmo Innes,‡

> " the land held in common was of vast extent. In truth, the arable—the cultivated land of Scotland, the land early appropriated and held by charter —is a narrow strip on the river bank or beside the sea. The inland, the upland, the moor, the mountain, were really not occupied at all for agricultural purposes, or served only to keep the poor and their cattle from starving. They were not thought of when charters were made and lands feudalised. Now as cultivation increased, the tendency in the agricultural mind was to occupy these wide commons, and our lawyers lent themselves to appropriate the poor man's grazing ground to the neighbouring baron. They pointed to his charter with its clause of parts and pertinents, with its general clause of mosses and moors—clauses taken from the style book, not with any reference to the territory conveyed in that charter ; and although the charter was hundreds of years old, and the lord had never possessed any of the common, when it came to be divided, the lord got the whole that was allocated to the estate, and the poor cottar none. The poor had no lawyers."

Now, in endeavouring to trace the methods by which the people were robbed of their heritage in the soil, we must remember that the records have mostly either been accidentally lost or deliberately destroyed; we must be careful not to confuse Crown lands with common lands or commonties ; and we must eschew consideration meantime of the clearances—Highland and Gallowegian—though, of course, in the compulsory "removing" of the early nineteenth century, vast areas of common land were absorbed by our old nobility. The Crown lands varied greatly in extent at different periods : swollen by forfeitures after unsuccessful rebellions, and diminished by lavish grants to King's progeny, legitimate and otherwise, and to successful beggars and sycophants at Court. In the time of Alexander III. the Crown

---

Caledonia, vol. 3, p. 144.
†*Folklore as a Historical Science*—Gomme, p. 342.
‡*Scotch Legal Antiq.*, p. 154.

lands were very extensive.* Before 1350 they were dilapidated ;†
by 1486 their gross yearly revenue was only £10,600.‡ But the
common lands proper disappeared into the omnivorous maw of
private landlordism, down three main avenues, and these three
main avenues it is now our business to examine.

Firstly, there was the enclosuring legislation dealing with the
common lands in the parishes outside the Highland-Celtic area and
not belonging either to the Royal Burghs or to the Crown. As early
as the fifteenth century there were evidently "brekaris of the King's
Commone," and an Act of 1600 (c.13) declares that "persons who have
cultivated or enclosed the King's common, muir, or other commonties," are "to be tried by way of molestation and to restore the
same within a year and a day ; if they fail they shall be deemed to
have committed purprision." Tucker, Cromwell's Commissioner,
reported that the gentry of Fife have "wholly driven out all but their
tenants and peasants even to the shore-side."§ In 1647

> " The Estates of Parliament Taking to their consideration the complaintis
> of severall heritors of eist Lothian, mid Lothian, Lithgowshire, Lanerk-
> shire, Air,
>
> " Alledging themselves to be heavilie wronged in the commounties and
> muirs they have richt to By some of their neighbours that Lyes narrest to
> these commounties and maks their awne particular benefit of them. And
> in that respect will not suffer them to be divided " . . . so that "these
> commounties that now ar most barroune may be reduced to gude corne land.'
> The Estates remit to the Lords of Session "to be decided and determined be
> them according to justice and equitie . . . with power to them to find out
> and prescryve the justest and most equitable way of dividing such comoun-
> ties."∥

This (with an occasional modernisation of the spelling) is the first
legal blow at the commons in the counties referred to. The poor are
not consulted, their wishes nor their necessities ever considered ;
but the consent of the superior of the soil must be secured, and the
majority of the adjacent heritors must agree before a division can
take place ; but the commons of Royal Burghs and those in which
the Duke of Hamilton, the Earls of Loudoun, Haddington, Dalhousie,
Roxburgh, and Maxwell of Ninesweall, and Mr. James Sydserf of
Ruchlaw are interested, are excepted from the provisions of the Act.
Then, in 1695, the procedure is simplified, and the area of appro-

---

*Macintosh—*Hist. Civ. Scot.*, i., 251.

†Cochrane Patrick—*Medieval Scotland*, p. 85.

‡*Exchequer Rolls*, vol. 9, p. lxix. The Rolls give the revenue as £106,000, but
 there is an obvious error in the addition of the constituent sums.

§Tucker's Report in *Miscellany* of Scottish Burgh Record Socy. (1881). See
 also *Scotland in the Time of Queen Mary*—Hume Brown, p. 26.

∥*Acta Parl. Scot.*, 1647, c. 430.

priation extended, by an Act* providing for the division of commonties or common muirs (commonties belonging to the King or to
Royal Burghs excepted), mosses that cannot conveniently be divided
to remain common.   This Act was passed on a petition of 4th July,
1695, that "all the commonties or common muirs within the kingdom
shall be divided " by any three justices of the Peace whenever a
division is claimed by any single heritor having an interest in the
common, "notwithstanding of any opposition that may be made
by the plurality of the heritors having interest in the commontie."
Writing of Roxburghshire, Chambers says :† "Smailholm parish
had the honour to begin the dividing of commons and approximating
the parts, and such has been the effect of this example that there are
now no commons in Roxburghshire, which once had commons everywhere, as we have seen."   So far, then, the reiving of the commons
belonging to the villages in the "settled " districts ; but away in
far Orkney and Shetland this Act for the division of commons was
to have ruinous effects for the common people and enrichment for the
lairds not even contemplated by its framers.   The Court of Session
has decided that Orkney and Shetland must be regarded as within
the scope of the Act of 1695, though the lands there were held not by
feudal but by udal tenure (*i.e.*, freehold ownership), each tenant being
unrestricted owner of his soil.   "Under the provisions of this Act,"
say the Crofter Commissioners of 1884, "the partition of commonty
has proceeded mainly during the last fifty years. . . . The wrong
committed is now irrevocable."   The privileges of udal tenure have
been arbitrarily destroyed, and the common pasturages called
scathalds have been privately enclosed by the larger lairds.   As the
law now stands, all commonties over £1000 in capital value or over
£50 in annual rental can be divided on petition by a single heritor
through the Court of Session, or if under these sums in value, by the
local Sheriff Court, and these decisions can not be appealed against.

Let us now turn to the methods of landlord and aristocrat attack
upon the runrig tenants and their sparse privileges which had
hitherto escaped the robber barons.   What run-rig was we have seen,
and it was common all over Scotland in the seventeenth century.
In the western coasts and in the north the lands were still run-rig
and common : the chiefs had not, as a rule, received charters from
the King, neither had the tribesmen ; the lands were still really held
under Celtic tenure.   Tradition says that Malcolm Canmore got the
chiefs to acknowledge him as the fount of their rights, and that they
each delivered to him at Scone a handful of the soil of their various
tribal territories as an indication of their submission to feudalism.‡

Acta Parl. Scot., vol. ix., p. 462, c. 96, 1695.

†*Caledonia*, vol. 3, p. 144.

‡Scott's *Tales of a Grandfather.*

Hence, it is said, arose the Moot Hill of Scone, the *Omnis Terra*, all lands being represented there ; but, be it observed, the chiefs themselves only enjoyed their tribal rights by tanistry, *i.e.*, life tenure, and they could not bind posterity. Farther, no Act was ever passed in Scotland confiscating all land property to the Crown, so that no king had any legal right whatsoever to donate the soil. In England, William the Conqueror was careful to legally confiscate property before he began to grant it away ; but such procedure was never taken in Scotland, and all Crown grants were really *ultra vires*. The Gaels never recognised the feudal grantees. Moray—feudalised Moray, where the native chiefs had been hunted out—was the one district in Gaelic eyes "where all pretty men had a right to take their prey " ; in other words, the feudal owner was a usurper and a thief, and towards him the ordinary codes of honour could not be extended. "Even the charters did not convey rights to property in the soil ; they merely gave to the grantees military and judicial superiority, and the right to take fixed rents."* For long centuries the common people clung doggedly to the old free institutions of their forefathers, recognising quite clearly that the acceptance of feudalism meant for them slavery and degradation. In 1597 an Act was passed demanding from the chiefs production of their title to the soil. They had none, but they secured lawyers who manufactured for them what Skene calls "spurious pedigrees " and "titles to the land which did not exist." As far back as the twelfth century, the King, in Council, had decreed that actual possession for four generations was no valid title ; holders must secure feudal charters,† and the struggle and the turmoil between the twelfth and the eighteenth centuries was at bottom a struggle between the patriarchal tribe and the feudal baron, between the non-chartered, semi-communist Gaels and the ruthless, remorseless, grasping descendents of the pirates who had followed William the Conqueror to the plunder of England. But a time came "when lawyers discovered that the lands of the tribe could not be held or vindicated, or perhaps could not have money raised upon them without writ, and then came the feudal investiture. The Crown charter was taken, of course, to the chief, who got the whole land of the tribe in barony. And in the charters of the lands of a great clan the Crown charter bestowed upon the chief all the rights of jurisdiction, civil and criminal, with pit and gallows, instead of his old patriarchal authority. It was an immense advantage, commercially speaking, to the lord." He could now raise money upon his lands and sell them. "But it was not so advantageous for the poor clansmen, who had never thought of writings to bind their

---

*See *Poetry and Traditions of the Highland Clans*, already referred to.
†"The Highland Land Question Historically Considered."—John Macintosh in *Celtic Mag.*, January, 1887.

patriarchal head, and who now found themselves with no title to property, often without any written leases or rentals. They became altogether dependent upon the will of the laird, and fell a long way below the position which they had held before the lands were feudalised. That, I think, was the most flagrant injustice inflicted by lawyers."* Still, the old tribal spirit never died. "Senex," the Glasgow family historian, tells us that about 1759 the people on the Riddel estate at Ardnamurchan were "so barbarous" that they refused to pay rent to anyone who was not their chief by blood, and soldiers had to be sent up to teach them to pay.† And the Earl of Malmesbury, in his *Memoirs*, reports of the year 1833 that a stranger could fish and shoot over almost any part of the Highlands without interruption.‡

The Act abolishing run-rig and enclosing run-rig lands passed, like the appropriation of the Commonty Act, in 1695 was not likely to be of much immediate use to the Highland lairds (notice, too, how near we are to the rebellion of 1715 !), but it was certainly of great immediate benefit to the Feudal-Georgian lairds in the non-tribal districts. The Act itself, entitled, "Act anent lands lying Run-rig," proceeds thus :§ "Our Sovereign Lord and the Estates of Parliament" considering "the great Disadvantage arising to the whole Subjects from lands lying run-rig" and such run-rig lands being prejudicial to planting and inclosing, ordained that "wherever Lands of different Heritors ly run-rig, it shall be leisum (lawful) for" any Heritor to apply to the Sheriff, to the Steward or Lord of Regality or to the Justices of the Peace "to the effect that these lands may be divided according to their respective interests . . . after due and lawful citation of all parties concerned." But the said judges, "in making the forsaid Division, shall be and are hereby restricted, so as special regaird may be had to the Mansion houses of the respective Heretors, and that there may be allowed and adjudged to them the respective parts of the Division, as shall be most commodious to their respective Mansion houses and policy, and which shall not be applicable to the other adjacent Heretors." Special regard to the mansion houses of the rich ; no consideration whatever given to the poor ! It is a fitting epitaph on the second of the great methods by which our common heritage was stolen. Not only were the hearthstones of the poor broken for enclosure dykes but the common pasturings and muirs over which these run-rig tenants had rights of usage were silently added to the laird's acres, and the poor were set adrift, to vagrom and to wander. It was the beginning of that

---

Scotch Legal Antiq.—Innes, p. 157.
†*Fragments Regarding the Ancient History of the Hebrides*, p. 7.
‡*The Northern Highlands in the Nineteenth Century*—James Barron, p. xxxvii.
§*Acta Parl. Scot.*, vol. ix., 1695, c. 36, p. 421.

great rural upheaval which a later age has dubbed the Clearances ;
it produced rebellion in Galloway ; and even a Duke of Argyle,
whose family revenues rested largely on these run-rig clearances,
and to whose class-biassed historical eye the laird could do no wrong,
is constrained to admit that " the abolition of the run-rig system was
always most unpopular in Scotland. In Tyree, as elsewhere, it was
abolished and could only be abolished by the authority of ownership."*
In other words, the Highland proprietors, like the south country
proprietors, cleared off the old system, with its "flavour of communism" and to which "the people clung with a dull and blind
tenacity," by a hired soldiery and by armed estate officers. Individual tenancy was not a natural evolution from common tenancy ;
it was a super-imposed system, and its primary purposes were an
enlargement of rents and the acquisition by the heritors of thousands
of acres of what was to all intents and purposes common land. The
run-rig system, says the writer of the Appendix to the Crofters'
Commission Report already quoted, was not devised by fools ; it
was the land system of a "shrewd and intelligent people," and it
was the deliberate opinion of the Deer Forest Commission (1892)
that the Highlands ought to revert to "a large extension of the
club farm system. Under it crofters have no individual hill stocks
but only a joint ownership in the stock. . . . When this system is
carried on honestly and properly, not only is the very most made of
the ground, but the individual crofter is more certain of his or her
return than otherwise."

But there was a third great channel down which our common
lands disappeared ; magisterial peculation in the corrupt years
prior to 1833, when our magistracy was self-elected, was confined to
the commercial and land-owning classes, and was subject to no
popular supervision in any shape or form. Previous to the year
1469 the provosts and bailies of the Royal Burghs were popularly
elected, but in that year, owing to some alleged great clamour of
"simpil personis" against magistrates who held office for longer
than one year, Parliament chose to silence the "sinful personis " by
carefully enacting that the old councils had themselves to elect their
successors ; and both old and new councils, sitting together, were
to choose the officials for the ensuing year. Each craft in the burgh,
it was true, was entitled to send one representative to the meeting
which chose the officials, but no extraordinary stretch of the imagination is required to grasp the elusory nature of that concession to
democracy. By this Act of 1469 popular election had been suppressed ; and from that year until the Burgh Reform Act of 1833,
the landowners and the commercial *bourgeois* class controlled all
burghal administration of the common lands, and controlled it in

Scotland As It Was and As It Is—Duke of Argyll (1887), pp. 272, 384, 386, 431.

such a way that vast areas of common lands were quietly appropriated, trust funds wholly disappeared, and to such a length did the
plunder and the corruption develop, that some ancient burghs with
valuable patrimonies went bankrupt, some disappeared altogether
from the map of Scotland, some had their charters confiscated, and
those which survived to the middle of the nineteenth century were
left mere miserable starved caricatures of their former greatness,
their Common Good funds gone, their lands fenced in private ownership, and their treasurers faced often with crushing debts.

In another chapter we attempt a rough outline of the story of the
rise and fall of the Burghs of Scotland ; here we must confine ourselves briefly to the burghal common lands, relying, unless where
other reference is given, upon the House of Commons Committee
Reports of 1793, 1819, 1820 and 1821, and upon the bulky, badly
arranged, indexless volumes which bear the reports of the Commissioners appointed to enquire into the state of Municipal Corporations in Scotland in 1832.

The chief, if not the only, reason for the creation of Royal or King's
Burghs, being to provide the Crown with a convenient breakwater
here and there against the surgings of a feudal aristocracy which
threatened to assume supreme power in the State, it was necessary
that the King's burgesses should have absolute freedom from the
jurisdiction of the neighbouring baron and should have an adequate
patrimony. The Kings, therefore, granted wide privileges and vast
territorial estates— estates "which were truly in the nature of trust
estates and strictly inalienable "—for the common good use of their
chartered burghs. In early times, so vast were these Royal Burgh
territories, that their boundaries often met ! Even in 1617 the
jurisdiction of the Magistrates of Rutherglen extended from Pol-
madie on the south side of the river Clyde to Carron ; * the entire
parish of Ayr at one time belonged to the Burgh of Ayr ; Aberdeen
"once possessed lands which extended many miles in circuit round
Aberdeen, granted by the Kings of Scotland, for the use of the
town."† Even the towns which did not hold their charters from the
Crown, but from the neighbouring baron, possessed wide territories
of commonty ; and, adding together the common lands of the
Royal Burghs, the common lands of the Burghs which held their
foundation rights from private individuals, the extensive commons
of the villages and the hamlets, the common pasturages and grazings,
and the commons attaching to run-rig tenancies, we shall be rather
under than over estimating the common acreage in the latter part of
the sixteenth century, at fully one-half of the entire area of Scotland.

In King Malcolm's time extensive grants of forest land were given

---

*History of Rutherglen and East Kilbride (1793)—Ure, p. 13.
†" Report of Select Committee on the Royal Burghs of Scotland, 1819," p. 31.

to Edinburgh ; but the charters were "lost," and with the charters
the land. Prior to the end of the fifteenth century the Common Good
lands were being let out on short leases ; but in the year 1508 power
was given the Town Council to alienate in perpetuity. At the
Reformation the Council received many religious endowments, and
in 1603 the superiority of the town ran from "Edge Buklingbray"
to "Almond Watter, to the mid watter of Forth." Property was
also held in Leith and Newhaven. In 1630 the magistrates "voluntarily" renounced much of their powers, and after James IV.'s
time the alienation of common land to favoured individuals proceeded apace. When, in 1638, Captain Thomas Hamilton, an
Edinburgh merchant, instituted a process before the Privy Council
to force Sir James Fleming and Sir James Dick, two late Provosts,
to produce the town's books, he was acting within both the letter
and the spirit of an Act of 1535, which allowed inspection of documents relating to Common Good funds. But the Council refused
his request ; "it looking too popular and democratick."* Between
1807 and 1818, £28,000 worth of land was alienated, and between
1818 and 1833 land to the value of £7609 was sold ; in 1832 the Council betrayed its legacy trusts by investing them for other purposes ;
and in 1833 Edinburgh, once so wealthy a burghal community,
became insolvent, and handed over its assets to trustees. The
superiority of the ecclesiastical burgh of the Canongate was secured
at the Reformation by Lord Justice Clerk Bellenden, who also made
an attempt to secure its other property, but was frustrated by the
King who declared he had "nae right to it "; he (Bellenden), however,
at the same time possessed himself of the lands of Falkirk, afterwards
passing them on to the Livingstones of Callender. In 1783 the
estate of Falkirk was obtained by Forbes of Callendar, who straight-
way applied to the Court of Session for a division of the Falkirk
Muir, and secured it all with the exception of 31 acres.

Elgin, a Royal Burgh of the time of William the Lion, had been
handed over, free tenants included, to Thomas Ranulph, by King
Robert Bruce, in the fourteenth century. Falkland (Fife), which
in 1459 had "common pasturage on the Lomonds of Falkland,"
had alienated £2300 worth of heritable property between 1790 and
1833. Forfar (an honourable exception) had not alienated land for
over a century ; instead, its Council had bought off Lord Strathmore
and his tolls and customs, and in 1833 owned property almost to
the value of £19,000. Forres, an ancient Royal Burgh, had its
charters destroyed and was handed over, like Elgin, to his favourite
Ranulph, by Robert Bruce. It had "alienated at an early period,
and for trifling feu duties, property in lands and fishings which have
of late (1833) become of very great value." It still owned the Cluny

---

*Fountainhall's *Decisions*, vol. i., p. 231.

hills, planted with valuable trees and drew £388 yearly in land rent, besides receiving £59 in feu duties. That there was still some public spirit extant was evidenced by the fact that the tree-planting had been done by the Town Council, and the Commissioners reported "grumbling" about the closing of a public road through a neighbouring estate. Fortrose, the worst managed burgh in Scotland, had suffered gross mismanagement under its perpetual self-elected provost, one Roderick M'Farquhar, who had held office for 23 years. "He suffered no one to participate with him in power "; he misappropriated money ; went to law with the burgh funds on his own account ; could not produce vouchers for his expenditure ; and was obligingly assisted by his friend, the Innkeeper and Treasurer, who disappeared from the town during the Commissioners' visit. Under this M'Farquhar *regime* the town lost some valuable clay-pits, Platcock green and Craigburn, while some ground was simply taken possession of by a neighbouring laird.

The story of the reiving of the common lands of Glasgow has been elsewhere retailed,* the Boyds, the Crawfords, the Lennoxes, and the Campbells, after the Reformation, securing control of the magistracy and helping themselves and their friends both to the burgess and the ecclesiastical lands. In 1574 we find "William Maxwell, merchant, in name of the merchants, and six of the deacons of crafts, in name of all the crafts and of the community" dissent from " the granting of any part of the common muir to James Boyd, or others, further than had already been given."† In 1575 the Council, under Lord Boyd, decided "that if anyone of its members revealed anything spoken of or treated of at its meetings he should be removed from the Council and never admitted to it again, but should be held infamous and be deprived of his freedom."‡ In 1588 parts of the Easter and Wester commons were sold by public roup. In 1600, we read, "In order to avoid requests of great men for giving off parts of their common lands, as well as on account of encroachments on these lands by neighbours, to the great loss of the town," the Town Council agreed that parts of these lands should be sold and "reiven furth "; but quarries, coal, limestone and mosses were reserved. A week later (3rd May) the deacons, on behalf of the crafts, promptly dissented from any common land being given off to any person ; and in or about the same year the crafts, for some reason or other, rose in arms against the magistrates. § In 1681 Parliament ratified an

*See the present writer's *Our Noble Families* and the late Sir James Marwick's *Early Glasgow.*

†*Glasgow Records*, i., pp. 9-10.

‡Marwick's *Early Glasgow*, p. 147.

§M'Ure's *History of Glasgow*, p. 133 ; *Glasgow Charters*, i., part i., pp. 211-9, 605-20.

Act of the Convention of Royal Burghs, empowering the Magistrates of Glasgow to sell part of their common muir.* From the ratification it appears that John Campbell of Woodside had got in 1676 all the "little Mailings" in the Wester Common for 10 merks Scots yearly; Bailie James Ffairie had feued "all and haill the lands of Cowlaires, Seggieholme, with the hill thereof and west part of that hill called the Sight hill" for 10 merks Scots yearly; and Ninian Anderson, merchant burgess, had got the "Lymehouse boig" for 10 merks. On 10th July, 1691, the provost asked power from the Convention of Royal Burghs to sell the lands of Provan, because the city was heavily in debt owing to past "magistrats . . . imploying the common store for their own sinistruous ends and uses, wherein, if the petitioner should be expres in the particular it wold exceedingly tend to the dishonour and disparagement of those whose dewty it was to have been patriots and supporters of the place." Powers were granted, and the lands in question, which would have been worth in 1833, £100,000 to £150,000, were sold at a very low price.

In 1833, Greenock owned no land, but had its own Town Hall and public offices,—gasworks, markets, cemetery, and schools. It also owned churches, manses and warehouses. Hamilton still owned a common muir, a public bleaching green, some 60 acres of land, and markets, but its rights of electing its magistrates had been lost to the Duke of Hamilton by prescription (*i.e.*, non-use for 40 years). Inverkeithing, whose public lands once stretched to the Crossgates, about 4 miles off, had feued away most of its patrimony. Inverness, in 1591, owned the "lands of Drakes and forest of the same : Markhinch, with common pasturage, called the Burgh haugh, Woodpark, Burnhills, Claypots, Milnfield, the Carse, Corn Lands, the Common Muir, the Water of Ness both sides from Clachnahagyag to the sea with fishings "; but most part of these soil rights had been alienated by methods which the Commissioners reported as "highly censurable." In 1617 we find the then Lord Lovat driving the townsmen of Inverness off their peat mosses and with a pretty taste in invective, describing the magistrates as "lownes, lowsie knaves, villanes and beboshed doggis."† Many of the lands were privately acquired by the magistrates; in 1783 and in 1785 the provost secured for himself some portions of the Town's common, and in 1797 one of the Councillors bought land which, with but slight improvement, returned him yearly almost the capital sum he had expended at purchase from the Council. Between the years 1794 and 1833, the Magistrates of Inverurie alienated burgh property to the value of £2449, which alienations are not to be wondered at when we read

---

* *Acta Parl. Scot.*, viii., p. 431, c. 157.
† *Scot. Hist. Review*, vol. 5, p. 424.

that between 1805 and 1817 "£600 17s. 6d. had been expended in paying tavern bills, for the entertainment of the Council, to an individual who then was, and still is, an innkeeper as well as resident chief magistrate, and in paying travelling expenses (not incurred on burgh business) and newspapers for the magistrates and council." This same chief magistrate had embarked upon a brick-making speculation, which, entailing a monetary loss of £180, was finally borne by the Burgh funds. The town still drew annually in feu-duties £73 6s. 8d., but the corruptions and alienations were so notorious that petition was made by the burgesses to the Court of Session for inspection of accounts. The judges refused the application.

Irvine still owned 422 acres arable and 100 acres moorland ; also mills, a quarry, farm-houses, feu duties of £197, town house, shops, markets, washing-houses, a loom-shop, gardens and "an extensive common," all of which is very surprising, for we read that the Earl of Eglinton held sway as a "Merchant Councillor, and he and his friends were superior to the law of rotation as they always took in two silly persons to shift."* Jedburgh owned "little land " ; Kilmarnock had re-sold to its Superior lands which it had purchased in 1700, and now was possessed only of half-an-acre and two washing-greens ; Kinghorn, reported in 1692 as deriving extensive revenues from "our comon grasse " and "the grass of the Rodding braes,"† is distinguished for extensive alienations conducted in a semi-secret manner ; Kintore had disposed of all its lands to the family of Keith (Lords Kintore), and held "now no property ; " Kirkcaldy, in 1644, had owned about 487 acres (the lands of E. and W. Muir-houses, the lands of Hunger-him-out, John Millers Pendicle, Middle Commonty and South Commonty), but it was all feued away in 1723 and 1750. Kirkwall, which by its charter of 1536 had received large areas of land, had made extensive alienations in 1793. Mr. Horne, W.S., for the Commissioners of Woods and Forests, handed away 10,000 acres common belonging to Kirkwall, Stromness and Shandwick,‡ and Kirkwall now only owned a few farms and crofts and some waste land, the cathedral, a school and a town hall ; Kirkcudbright still drew annual land rents to the value of over £900. The ancient Royal Burgh of Cowie (Kincardineshire), which got its original charter from King David I., was re-erected into a free burgh in 1541, and was at the beginning of the seventeenth century a "flourishing and wealthy town," had entirely disappeared ; "no vestige of the burgh now remains ; the burgh lands, together with Auchtorthies—at one time a portion of the lordship of Urie—form

---

*The Awakening of Scotland, 1747-1797—Wm. Law Mathieson, p. 104.

†Miscellany—Scot. Burgh Rec. Socy, p. 96.

‡Parliamentary Paper issued 25, 8, 52.

the modern estate of Cowie."* Of Lanark we read : "A considerable portion of the property has been alienated, but a large portion remains." In these Lanark transactions, not only the customary "neighbouring proprietor" but also the hereditary provost had benefited considerably, and during the Franchise Reform agitation of 1792 he (the Provost) was shot at and his orchard wrecked. The public property extant in 1832 consisted of lands, houses, a mill, feu-duties, a common of 500 acres, an extensive plantation, six shares (value £600) in the Clydesdale Inn, washing-house, hospital, green, grammar school, etc., estimated at £25,784. At Lauder, with a total burghal and parish population of 2063, there still remained over 1700 acres of common land, of which 895 acres were arable. Prior to 1814 its extent had been much greater, but in that year the magistrates enclosed part and feued it out to the highest bidder ; and the extent of the feuing may be gauged by the fact that the town was now (1832) receiving £100 annually from that source alone. Of old time the common belonged to the burgesses, and the arable lands were cropped in rotation and the proceeds "equally distributed by lot" among all the burgesses ; only resident burgesses were entitled to graze their cattle on the common. Tillage and pasture were still fixed by lot, but the privileges had been restricted to burgesses, and the burgesses had been by various pretexts cut down in number. First it was decided that no one should be admitted burgess who was not the owner of one of the small strips of land lying between the town and the common, called burgess acres. There was no legal authority for this stipulation. The burgess acres, once 315 in number, gradually fell into fewer and fewer hands, until when the Commissioners reported there were only 105, the purchase price of each being about £200, and the lot being in the hands of 25 resident and a few non-resident burgesses. Then the burgess entry fee was raised from £5 in 1796 to £30 in 1832, a proceeding as illegal as the restriction to owners of burgess acres, but even more effective in limiting the rights of common to a few favoured individuals. At Lochmaben, the large farm of Priesthead held by the town for " many ages," was sold privately in 1801 to the father-in-law of the provost, no mention of the transaction appearing in the minutes, and the town was reported as now "irretrievably bankrupt." Indeed the Court of Session, after the Priesthead sale, had been forced to sequestrate the Burgh—a proceeding rendered perhaps the more necessary by the fact that "Thomas Johnstone, the other baillie, cannot subscrive " (*i.e.*, write his name).

Montrose had escaped the general pillage rather by good luck than by the good intent of its middle class rulers. Between 1790 and 1817

The Court Book of the Barony of Urie, 1604-1747—Barron (Scot. Hist. Socy. Pubns.), p. xli.

M

portions of its heritage had been sold in lots at 1s. per square yard, but in 1817, by an oversight, the magistrates had not been elected in accordance with the set or constitution of the burgh, and the Government issued a warrant for an election by poll of all the burgesses.[*] The result was the deposition of the old corrupt magistracy and their friends, and the election of "advanced reformers." To this fortunate misobservation of the set of the burgh, the people of Montrose owed the fact that, in 1832, they had a common property of £54,986, comprised of lands, houses, a harbour, money invested in public works, and £1300 in the bank. Musselburgh at one time "possessed very extensive property . . . but a great part of it was sold or feued many years ago"; still, in 1832, it owned 5 mills, a brick and tile work, quarry, parks, haughs, links of Musselburgh and Fisherrow, commons, plantation, ground at Ravenshaugh, harbour, schools, town hall, assembly room, salmon fishings, steel-yard, and six shares in the race stand, a total value of £35,000. There had been many "private sales" during the preceding 50 years. Nairn, we are told, "formerly possessed a considerable extent of landed property, of which very little now remains"; but the reiving is difficult to trace, owing to the loss of part of the town's records and the imperfect and unsatisfactory state of the remainder. In 1823 a Court of Session action was raised against the magistrates by the burgesses; but the Court, as was its wont, upheld the thieves and dismissed the action on the ground that the Council records were not produced; "heavy costs" were given against the burgesses and "numerous other technical objections were in reserve," ready, if by any chance aberration of justice, the Court should order the defenders to produce the town records. Newburgh (Fife) in 1631 had owned over 400 acres, of which only 174 were left. New Galloway, once a Royal Burgh, now owned nothing : the provost lived in London, and the Town Clerk in Kirkcudbright—20 miles away.

Sir Hew Dalrymple Hamilton seems to have been the chief beneficiary in "the distribution" of the property of the citizens of North Berwick ; he paid £400 for the island of Craigleith, but only £100 of this sum reached the Town Treasurer, who was, by the way, refused access by the Town Clerk to the municipal ledgers ; in 1832 the town still possessed some land, a small croft, market stalls and a bake-house. The burgh of Paisley, granted in 1460 by the Abbot of Paisley to the provost, bailies and community, with a right to the burgesses to hew stone in the Abbey quarries, possessed, in 1832, property worth £53,914, including an inn, "buildings at the cross," houses, stables, sheds, markets, schools, coal-rees, a dye-work, a foundry, a quarry, bowling green and house, and common lands valued at £9,958 ; between 1790 and 1830 the magistrates had hived

[*] Lord Cockburn's *Memorialls*, p. 321.

off property valued at £25,963, including the estate of Ferguslie, sold for £12,000. From the town lands of Peebles, we are told, there were great alienations "long ago,"* though, in the 40 years before the Commissioners reported, property valued at £1491 had been disposed of ; it still owned lands and feu-duties, a corn, flour, and barley mill, a waulk-mill, with houses and machinery, schools, tenements, shares in the Tontine Inn and in the gas company, a farm, and a quarry.

Perth, in William the Lion's time, was granted privileges of trade and commerce all over Perthshire, and owned extensive areas of land. Between 1746 and 1830 there were "numerous and extensive" alienations ; between 1800 and 1828 the burgh muir was enclosed and feued away ; Gowrie house and gardens had been donated in an extravagant excess of loyalty to the Duke of Cumberland, and being sold by him, were re-purchased by the burgh ; the corruption of its magistracy was notorious even in an age when corruption was common—£3000, for example, being spent on re-building an arch of the bridge over the river Earn, while an entire bridge three miles farther up cost only £500 ; in 1832 it still retained ownership of lands at Meikle Yullylum and Uthank, Dawhaugh, Cow Causeway, Soutarland, North and South Inches (100-120 acres), Sand Island, Maggie's Park, etc., and mills, granaries, oil mill, sawmill, fishings, harbours, coal and wood yards and lime sheds.

In 1593 Peterhead had owned the moss, fisherlands, and certain commons and pasture rights ; the commons were divided in 1774. At the Reformation the burgh of Pittenweem became possessed of "all and haill that great house or lodging of the monastery of Pittenweem and lands between Anstruther Wester and St. Monace and Abercrombie," also the lands of Balcaskie and Grangemuir except "the commonties be east the march stones pertaining to Anstruther W. and Milntown." The town still owned lands, mills, slaughterhouse, byre, shipbuilding yard, and shares in a granary ; and although there was no mention made of recent alienations, and although it was drawing nearly £200 from its common "mures and braes," there was danger, for the noble family of Kellie resided in the immediate neighbourhood. At Port Glasgow, a "feuars town" dating from 1668, reliable information was difficult to obtain ; but the Council owned buildings, warehouses and ground valued at £15,300, a coal ree, flesh and fish markets, dry dock and engine, a school, gas work, fire engine, etc. Portobello about 1760 "was only a single cottage, surrounded by an extensive common " ; seventy years later

---

*At least one of these alienations is detailed in Renwick's *Gleanings from the Records of the Royal Burgh of Peebles*, 1604-1652. Chap. xiii. shews how by a combination of open theft and legal trickery " Hamilton Hill glided out of the Burgh's possession."

it was a town without a constitution, with no common land, indeed owning nothing whatsoever. Queensferry had sold its Ferrymuir lands to Dundas of Dundas ; but there was "no reason for selling and no satisfactory account of where the purchase money went " ; only the common called the Loanings was retained in 1832.

In his preface to the first volume of the Burgh Records Society, the Editor, Mr. Cosmo Innes, declares that "in some, but rare, instances the lords were so powerful or so artful as to establish a permanent influence within the burgh, but only by sufferance or by violence. I know of no instance where a chartered burgh formally surrendered its independence." If cavil can be offered this, it may perhaps best be done in the case of Renfrew, for when in 1429 the Campbells controlled the burgh they signed away its rights to the then Duke of Argyll ; in 1703 Queen Anne conveyed to the Council "much property in land and fishings," and in 1832, even despite a century of assiduous theft, rents and feu-duties brought to the public exchequer an annual sum of £2162. There were four recent sales of land to the provost ; in each case he was buyer and seller and sanctioner of the sale, and in one instance the minutes of the Council bear testimony to the fact that the only reason for the sale is that it would be "beneficial to the provost." He was also lessee of the canal, upon such terms that the canal was no benefit to the burgh, and the tone of the local administration may be judged by an item in the annual accounts : "Tavern expenses for magistrates, £153 9s."

In Rothesay the Factors of the Earl of Bute were practically hereditary provosts ;* but the Commissioners in 1833 reported that the town still owned the lands of Craigmore, an east and a west common, two washing greens, two small loanings, gardens and a part of the shore frontage.† Rutherglen, whose superiorities had once extended to Carron water, in 1833 only retained 32 acres of arable land called the green, property in Castle Wynd, house and garden in Farme Loan, town's mill, council hall and schoolhouse—a total value of £10,000. St. Andrews had feued away in 1797 the Pilmour Links and commonty, ostensibly for the purpose of wiping out debts on the Town Church ; but was still in possession of the North and South haughs, lands in Priory and Newmiln, East Bents, Grey Friars Gardens, coal yard, ridge at the harbour, public land known as "the Scores," part of Windmill brae, salmon fishings and mills. Sanquhar burgesses divided up the common muir among themselves in 1831, leaving to the town only 181 acres valued at £24.

In the year 1681 we find in the Acts of the Scots Parliament a long

---

The Awakening of Scotland—W. Law Mathieson, p. 104.

†*N.B. Daily Mail*, 26, 12, 61.   Reference to encroachments upon burgh land at Ardbeg road.

ratification of the arbitral decree between the Burgh of Selkirk and the Earl of Roxburgh and other lairds,* regarding the division of "the great and vast bounds of ground called the Common of Selkirk." The common, it appears, had "lain unprofitable these many ages," and has been the seed and ground of much trouble, contention, and debate," so Earl Roxburgh and his fellow heritors had nominated two arbiters and the Burgh of Selkirk two, and these arbiters "apportioned " the common ; in later times the Pringles of Clifton appear to have benefited by farther alienations ; and when, in 1748, the burgesses petitioned the Court of Session regarding the plundering of their Common Good, the demeanour of the judges was so hostile that they did not press for a judgment. In 1833 Selkirk still retained two commons, divided (except a small portion reserved for the burgesses' cattle) into 5 farms, Dunsdale haugh, 3 mills and mill lands, feu-duties, and a salmon fishing on the Ettrick, carrying a total annual rent of £1039.

Stirling, in the seventeenth century, possessed lands and property of "considerable " value ; but its magisterial corruption was carried to so great an extent that Lord Advocate Dundas confiscated its charter, and in 1705 the Convention of Royal Burghs authorised the sale of all its lands to pay its debts. In 1833 its sole assets were fishings in the Forth, 3 acres at the burgh mill, some ground called "the Valley," corn market and granaries, and some house property and churches. Stranraer, naturally, was in a "very embarrassed state," for its business had been conducted beyond the memory of living man by a non-resident provost, the Earl of Stair, by his two Edinburgh agents and by "his factor in the country." So late as 1829 this "Council " was selling the common muir. The story told by the records of the Burgh of Tain is the same sad story of the other northern burghs ; in 1587 it owned the lands lying between the four girth crosses, the lands of Innerraithie, Gorlinges, Clerk Island, and Priest Island ; in 1833 it owned but 50 acres. At one time Tain owned 3000 acres of moorland, but on "the conterminous proprietors making considerable encroachments," the magistrates concluded that in whatever encroachments there must be, they, the magistrates, should be the encroachers, and so they feued out the moor among themselves at 6d per acre. Whithorn, whose Council was manned carefully by dependents of the Earl of Galloway, owned nothing in 1833 but a croft and a windmill ; and the same noble family, by the same ignoble process, had secured for "trifling feu-duties " almost the entire 1200 acres which had constituted the ancient royalty of Wigton. For a feu-duty of £16 the Earl, who was "patron of the place," took over Wigton lands yielding an annual rent of £400 ; and it is a matter of some wonderment that the docile sycophants who constituted the magistracy did not also part with

*Acta Parl. Scot., vol. viii., p. 419. See also vol. x., 307b.

the lands of Gallowhill and Philiphall, the town hall, the ball rooms, and the schoolhouse.

Wick had lost in the law courts its limited right of commonty over the Hill of Wick, and owned no property ; Abernethy owned nothing, nor did Alloa. Bathgate was the proud possessor of the site of a fountain and a right of servitude over $4\frac{1}{2}$ acres of moorland. Beith had no local government of any kind ; Bo'ness owned nothing ; Castle-Douglas owned only a shop ; Coldstream was stripped bare, not even possessing "rights in its street dung" ; Crieff had two fields ; Dalkeith, nothing ; Dunkeld, nothing; and Dunoon, nothing. In 1785 the only remanent property of the Burgh of Dunse was an "extensive common" ; but in that year the common was divided between the neighbouring Superior and his feuars ; in 1833 all was gone except 10 acres of moor and a whinstone quarry. The property of Fraserburgh—parks, links, etc., was vested in the feuars. Eyemouth owned nothing, nor did Gatehouse-of-Fleet. Galashiels had not even a constitution. Galston owned nothing, and Girvan but a few houses. Hawick (in 1833 drawing annual rents of £345, and owning land and property valued at £6,317) seems to have put up a spirited fight against the Duke of Buccleugh's attempt, in 1770, to appropriate its common muir. The case came before the Court of Session, and "after having been defended in court for some time, was by reason of the deficiency of the burgh funds, referred to the arbitration of the Lord Chief Baron of Exchequer." The result was a foregone conclusion ; the Lord Chief Baron divided the common, donating a "large part" to the Duke of Buccleugh and other conterminous heritors. In 1833 the people are, say the municipal commissioners, "aggrieved, but the decreet arbitral, followed by possession for upwards of 50 years, bars all discussion as to the title of the proprietors. No blame can attach to the magistrates and council for the time, who appear to have done their duty in defending the rights of the burgh." Kilsyth, Johnstone (which had no constitution), Keith, Langholm, Largs, and Kirremuir owned nothing. Huntly had lost its charter giving privileges of common pasture, fuel, and quarries, and these rights had been withheld by the Duke of Gordon "for about 60 years." Kilmaurs' burgesses and feuars owned 5 roods of common land. Only the burgesses of Kirkintilloch had rights in the scanty commonties. Gardenstone drew £10 annually from "the estate of Johnstone." The heritors of Lerwick had already secured the common lands. Melrose owned nothing ; Newmilns, only a public green ; Portsoy, nothing ; and Pollokshaws only a washing green, some houses, and an inn. Maybole had lost its records prior to 1721, and now owned but a little house property, the ball green, and 4 falls of land, the commissioners significantly reporting that in the year 1516 the provost and prebendaries of the local church were given power to let out their lands, and that this power was given "with the advice of Gilbert, Earl of Cassilis." Rosehearty, in 1681, had possessed rights of pasture in certain lands, and the commonty of the Cairnhill of Pitsligo and certain mosses, including "the large moss called the Red Moss"; but these rights had been alienated in 1811. Stewarton owned nothing, and Stonehaven only "a right of common and pasturage of trifling extent, two small farms, a piece of ground at the Cross, and £384 in harbour shares." Stornoway owned its quay; Strathaven and Thurso owned nothing.

The old title deeds of the Royal Burgh of Arbroath were taken by force from the Abbey and destroyed by George, Bishop of Moray, but the new charter granted by James VI. in 1599 specifies as burghal property "the common muir and lands called Muirlands." These lands were feued out in the latter part of the eighteenth century for little over £1 per acre. In 1833 the town property, including the White Hart Inn, was valued at £35,874. Aberdeen, in 1459, owned, among other lands, those of Rubislaw, Counteswells, Haselhead, Forrester Hill, and Northfield Cruieffs, extending altogether about 14 miles in circumference; it also possessed very valuable salmon fishings on the Dee and the Don. But in 1551 the then magistrates procured from the Crown a new charter which permitted them to dispose of the common property by perpetual feus. Before this time even nineteen year leases of town property were forbidden by the Courts, but immediately upon receipt of the new charter all the fishings and most part of the lands were feued away in perpetuity for insignificant feu-duties to favoured individuals. Fishings worth, in 1819, a rental of £10,000 were bringing to the town in 1833 only £27 7s. 8d.; between 1793 and 1817 heritable property valued at £19,444 was disposed of, the Common Good was squandered recklessly, and in the latter year the city, in a state of "hopeless insolvency," surrendered the management of its estates and its revenues to its creditors. The Burgh of Annan, once in possession of extensive territories, had suffered alienations almost as extensive; its common muir was divided among the "town and country heritors" at the beginning of the nineteenth century, and in 1833 its remanent revenue was derived thus—£53 10s in land rent, £182 in feus, and £90 from fishings. One of the contributory causes to the necessity for these Annan alienations is probably unique in Scots burghal history. The Sheriff of the county had been imprisoned in Annan gaol for a debt of over £2000, and the magistrates very generously allowed him the run of all the building, and permitted him to hold his courts in the Town House within the gaol. This proceeding the Court of Session and the House of Peers declared to be a deliberate violation of the magistrates' duty and "subjected the magistrates in the debt," which debt, of course, was immediately paid from the Common Good funds of Annan. Another debtor, warded for a sum of £1200, had escaped from Annan gaol in the early years of the nineteenth century, and again the Common Good was mulcted.

Anstruther Easter, about 1700, had a law-suit with Sir John Anstruther over its right to the collecting of street dung, and was forced to sell its common land for £500 to liquidate the costs. The lands in question were sold a few years later for £5000. Anstruther Wester, in 1833, still owned its East Common, West Common, West Muir, two Milltown Muirs, the Burns, and the Billowness. Ayr still possessed an extensive common, though much land had been feued away. At Newton-on-Ayr the "Freeman's Daills" (Deals—drawn annually by lot) were feued away in 999 years' leases for an "elusory feu-duty." Banff, in 1581 a wealthy and prosperous community, has been "skinned" by the families of Fife, Banff, and Findlater, and the Municipal Commissioners give an illustration of the process from the records of 1738, when the then Provost is discovered purchasing 20 acres for thirty shillings !

Brechin at one time held extensive superiorities, certainly running to over 1760 Scots acres ; but most of it was feued prior to 1770 ; and away back in 1681 an Act of Parliament was passed ratifying the alienation of a great part of the common muir (made several years previously by the magistrates, with the consent of the "late Bishop of Brechin ") in favour of Carnegie of Balnamoon.* But in 1833 Brechin still held common land and kept a common shepherd. Burntisland, created a Royal Burgh in 1568, had its liberties assailed in 1625 by Sir Robert Melville, who brought an action against the town for reduction of charter ; but the action was withdrawn upon the town thirling itself to Sir Robert's mills. "There is," as the Commissioners significantly point out, "a blank in the town's records at this date " ; in 1835 the common land yielded a revenue of £253. Campbelltown owned no property, the Duke of Argyll refusing to give even a permanent title for the schoolhouse land. Crail had alienated most of its heritage, but still owned lands, quarries, houses, etc., in sufficient quantity to pay all the burgh annual expenditure. Cromarty, under what compulsion or by what trickery we know not, parted in 1670 with its wide territories to Sir John Urquhart for a mere song—5000 merks Scots, with an annual feu duty of 20 merks ; two years later the Council petitioned Parliament that they were "depauperat " and "dispeopled "; they were expunged from the list of Royal Burghs, and Urquhart stepped in, appointed a baron bailie, and the freedoms, the privileges and property of Cromarty were gone ! Of one time prosperous Cullen, on the Moray firth, the Commissioners declare : "The property of the burgh was in ancient

* *Acta Parl. Scot.*, vol. viii., p. 402, c. 144.

times considerable, but it was alienated to the family of Seafield ";
and again : "The town" (once a Royal Burgh) "is so unimportant
that some years ago the family of S afield removed it from the situation which it then occupied—being too near their residence—to its
present site." The treasurer's books shewed that the town's financial
assets had been "lent" to the same noble family. The lands of the
Burgh of Culross had passed into the hands of Sir James Gibson
Craig, who had planted 80 acres of the common muir ; to the hands
of the Dundonald family, who had received over 500 acres "now
covered with wood"; and Sir Robert Preston and Dundas of Blair,
are specially mentioned as "fortunate owners" of other ex-burghal
properties. Cupar, once in possession of 1000 acres, had feued most
part of them by 1735 at an outside feu-duty of 1s. per acre ; but there
had been no fewer than 42 alienations between 1790 and
1830, occasioned, we suppose, by the magisterial practice of borrow-
ing money from themselves at twelve per cent. interest. Dingwall's
"extensive property" had been feued or given away, all except 7 or
8 acres and some fishings ; the proprietors, we are told, refuse to
pay lighting charges, and "the town is not now lighted." Dornoch
had lost its all. Dumbarton, with at one time superiorities running
to Loch Lomond, was even in less prosperous times fair game to the
Dukes of Argyll, who during the latter half of the eighteenth century
controlled the Council by means of "Councillors elected from every
corner of the country ";* and during that halcyon time the provosts
and magistrates helped themselves and their friends to the finances
and the properties of the burgh with a shameless indifference to the
loud and angry protests which came periodically from the burgesses
and the common people. In February, 1787, for example, the
burgesses of Dumbarton brought an action before the Court of
Exchequer against the magistrates in order to force them to produce
their books in Court ; and the defence was, that the Act of 1535,
upon which the burgesses founded, was in desuetude, and that the
Convention of Royal Burghs was the only body entitled to supervise
the actions of the magistrates. Sir John Dalrymple, one of the
judges, referring to this plea, said that the Convention was the most
incompetent possible revising authority because the burghs comprising it "were all and each of them guilty of the same malversations
of which the magistrates of Dumbarton were at present accused."
The majority of the judges, however, decided against the burgesses.†
Dumfries, a Royal Burgh prior to 1214, with many lands and privileges, was granted in addition all the possessions and revenues held
by the Grey Friars in the neighbourhood during the fifteenth century ;
but gross swindling and theft had pared the estates away. The

---

*Awakening of Scotland—W. Law Mathieson, p. 104.
†Scots Magazine, February, 1787, p. 97.

councillors were usually tacksmen of the Common Good ; "the heirs of eleven provosts of Dumfries owned property which had once belonged to the burgh" ; and in 1833 the total land revenue remaining was £114 from feu-duties and £179 from land rents.   Maxwelltown possessed no property.   The Town Chamberlain of Dunbar alleged that his books had been burned in 1827, so that no details can be given of the alienations there ; in 1832, however, the common remaining was valued at £5000, and the publicly-owned lands, mills, houses, and quarries at £9,500.

Dundee, in Charles II.'s time, appears to have owned the lands of Logie, with mansion-house, gardens, and orchards, 16 acres of lands of Balgay, and other minor acreages.   In William and Mary's time it got such part of the forfeited estates of the Earl of Lauderdale and Sir Robert Milne as lay in the neighbourhood :—Dudhope, the Burgh of Rottenraw, the acres of East Ferry, the lands and almon fishings of Draffine, the lands of Duntoune of Baldovie, Kirkton, Oxengate of Ratecults, and Catermiln in Perthshire.   Previous to Lauderdale's disappearance we can understand the reason of the chronic penury of Dundee, and we can guess what lies behind that item reported to the Convention of Royal Burghs by the Treasurer of Dundee in 1692 : "At law with my Lord Lauderdail for 7 years—£20,000 00 00." Scots money, of course ; only £1666 13s. 4d. in present day coinage, but it is one of the methods by which the common lands of the people disappeared.*   Another similar item of expense is given thus : "For maintining the honour of the good town in waiting on noblemen and others in whom the burgh is concerned—£1200."   In the later part of the eighteenth century, particularly during the 40 years' *regime* of the notorious Provost Riddle, alienations were of common occurrence, and between 1792 and 1833 property worth £19,710 was disposed of.

In James VI.'s time the Burgh of Dunfermline owned the lands of Balyeoman, the east and west town greens, Kingseathill parks, and Daasdendanhill ; in 1833 it still owned several farms, "part of the muir with the coal which for some years has been worked on account of the burgh," 700 acres (150 of which are planted with trees), the Halliblade acres and some houses at the town colliery ; the grass from the common green and the common loan brought £39, and £121 came from the common land.   There had been several alienations in the early part of the nineteenth century, however, and although the alienations were made by public roup, it was discovered, at the enquiry of 1819, that one of the methods in vogue was for a bailie to bid against all-comers until he secured the property, and then at the next secret council meeting succeed in getting the Council to knock the price down to a fraction of what he had publicly offered.

Miscellany—Scot. Burgh Records Socy., p. 62.

Still it is to the credit of the Dunfermline councillors that they alone, of all the councillors in Scotland, supported the agitation for a wider municipal franchise and refused to be silenced by the complacent and self-interested declaration of the Convention of Royal Burghs that reform would "unhinge a constitution which had stood the test of ages." Dysart reported itself in 1692 ruined by "defending and maintaining of the town's propertie against the Lord Sinclair and Sir James Cockburne," the former gentleman having secured possession of the harbour of Dysart "by ane decreet got surreptiously before the lordis of Session "; all that was left was "the hand bell and the pettie customes." By 1833, however, the town possessed a farm, a quarry, the harbour, and gardens and houses. Earlsferry, in Fyfe, owned only one acre of land, some small feu-duties, a harbour and the "right to play golf on the links " ; Kelso (whose town records had disappeared) possessed a reservoir, a small field, and some shares in the Tweed bridge. The historian of East Kilbride tells us briefly that "The common . . . was once very extensive, but excepting a few acres is now enclosed " ;* and the historian of Tranent† declares that the common there was "of great extent," had been "free to all villagers from time immemorial," but had been "taken over " by the Superior and the feuars with the assistance of a special Act of the Privy Council.

An analysis of the various documents bearing upon the estates forfeited after the rebellion of 1745 shews, that despite the runrig and enclosuring Acts already considered, the commonties in the rural districts of Scotland were still of considerable extent. In 1790, after the bankruptcy of the York Buildings Company, the Seton estates, which they had purchased, fell to the agent for their creditors, thereafter being disposed of to the Earl of Wemyss. "After Mackenzie acquired the estate," we read,‡ "the active little village community of Seton was entirely broken up and dispersed, for when called upon to produce the title deeds of their properties, most of them, it was found, had no titles to show, their houses and lands having been handed down to father and son through many generations. Those who were unable to produce their titles were at once unconditionally turned out of their houses, while the few who sent off their parchments to Edinburgh beheld them no more, and had likewise shortly after to follow suit, leaving their ancient heritages behind them." On the Perth estate the commons, in 1747-1756, were still of great extent, as was evidenced by the Government survey.§ Omitting roods and falls, the common acreage, detailed by the surveyor, for the parish of Muthill alone, was

---

*History of Rutherglen and E. Kilbride—Ure, p. 203.

†History of Tranent—P. M'Neill, p. 222.

‡M'Neill's History of Tranent, p. 193.

§See Northern Chronicle, 15th June, 1910.

		acres.
Common Moor of Alichengrew, ...		33
,, ,, ,, Strageth,...		100
,, ,, ,, Drumquhar and Cult, ...		84
,, ,, ,, Cottary, ...		87
,, ,, ,, Milran and Drumnahard, ...		3
,, ,, ,, Lintibbert (with pasture), ...		123
,, ,, ,, Blairnroar, ...		3194
,, ,, ,, Megginch, ...		93
Oakwoods of Drummond and Broadmeadow, enclosures where tenants had pasturage rights		112
Moor of Strathill		131
Parkneedless enclosure, carrying rights of pasturage ... ... (This enclosure was to " enhance the beauty of the house.")		249
Moor of Craignech, ...		179
,, ,, Tomrechan, ...		558
,, ,, ,, (part), ...		9
,, ,, Middle Glenichorn, ...		450
Drummond Moor, ...		249
Orthal Commonty (part Moss), and Loan of Drummond Mill, ...		...1176

In the Barony of Balquhidder there were 1368 acres common ; in the Parish of Comrie 5058 acres common, in the Barony of Callender 2206 acres common, in the Barony of Milnab 83 acres common, in the Barony of Auchterarder 22 acres common, in the Barony of Stobhall 589 acres common, in the Barony of Kinbuck there had been 1528 acres of commonty in the Cambuschinny Moor ; and of Sheriffmuir (1226 acres) we read : "This Moor is commonty to lands of several neighbouring gentlemen, so that nothing useful can be expected until it is divided. Several parties carved out holdings after the troubles in 1745. Balhaldie has made considerable enervallment. He keeps a herd who on all occasions turns off the Kinbuck cattle greatly to the prejudice of the tenants."

At the beginning of the nineteenth century, one eleventh (13,800 acres) of the entire area of Renfrewshire was common ; * and Lord Cockburn, the Lord Advocate, writing in 1845† on the formation of the Edinburgh Society "for protecting the public against being robbed of its walks by private cunning and perseverence," says :

"When I was a boy, nearly the whole vicinity of Edinburgh was open Beyond the Causeway it was almost always Highland. Corstorphine Hill, Braid Hill, Craiglockhart Hill, the Pentland Hills, the sea-side from Leith to Queensferry, the river-side from Penicuik by Roslin and Hawthornden to

---

*Chalmers' *Caledonia*, vol. vi., p. 798.
†*Journal*, 1831-1854, vol. ii., p. 104.

Lasswade, the Valley of Habbie's How, and innumerable other places now closed or fast closing were all free." . . . Much of it by indulgence of owners, but "much more of it because the people had acquired prescriptive rights" in unenclosed country. . . . "Law (to prevent enclosure and theft) was dear," the gentry were in favour of private property, and "each Justice protected his brother, knowing that he would shortly require a job for himself. Thus everything was favourable to the way-thief, and the poor were laughed at. The public were gradually man-trapped off everything beyond the high road."

Sometimes determined resistance to encroachment succeeded in preserving for the public a remnant of their old-time property, as the women of Dunoon succeeded in saving the freedom of their Castle Hill from the Duke of Argyle.* Sometimes the peasants spent their money in vain, as the Braidwood folks did when they sought legal redress against the filching of their common and loch.† But law was dear and hostile, and fanatical burghers or peasants who would defend the common patrimony by force were generally bullied or starved out of the district as a preliminary process to the theft.

Glasgow Post, 8/8/35, 15/8/35, 10/9/35 ; *Courier*, 5/8/38.
†*Daily Mail*, 28, 3, 62. The Sheriff at Hamilton told the people they could produce "no written title."

THE CLEARANCES.

CHAPTER VIII.

" Come away ! far away ! from the hills of bonnie Scotland,
  Here no more may we linger in the mountain—in the glen—
Come away ! Why delay ? far away from bonnie Scotland,
  Land of grouse and not of heroes ! Land of sheep and not of men.
    Mighty hunters for their pastime
    Needing deserts in our shires
    Turn to waste our pleasant places,
    Quench the smoke of cottage fires.
Come away ! Why delay ? Let us seek a home denied us,
O'er the oceans that divide us from the country of our sires."
                                                    —*Charles M'Kay,*

TOWARDS the end of the seventeenth and in the early years of
the eighteenth century the landlords discovered that their
lands could be put to more profitable use than they were
under the old club-farming, run-rig system of agriculture still in
vogue. One large farmer would yield more to the laird than did the
swarm of disagreeably independent cottagers and ex-men-of-arms,
who carried on a semi-communal and meagre rent-yielding tillage,
dotted indiscriminately over the laird's estates. The raising of
sheep was becoming more profitable than the raising of corn, and
large sheep farms were impossible with the hill grazings and the
commonties unenclosed and open to the cattle and the geese of
the village communities, which communities, as often as not, harboured one or two of the dour intractable saints, who had learned
much about the rights of man out there in the moss hags in the days
of the Covenanting persecution. Rents could not be individually
increased to club-farming peasants ; and as the power of the
Crown and the power of the Law Courts had for ever crushed the
private wars of the feudal nobles, a tail of tenantry was no longer an
asset to the laird. In days gone bye he had gauged his prosperity
and his power by the number of men he could command in the field
and the foray ; now his peasantry was a source of weakness, preventing that free and unfettered development of his estates which the
commercial and social economy of the time demanded. Economic
value, in short, had shifted from the Retainer to the Rent !

A Society for the Encouragement of Agriculture had been formed
in 1733—twelve years before the second Stuart rebellion—and 300
landowners had taken membership ;* but some 13 years before that,

*Macintosh—*Hist. Civ. Scot.*, vol. iv., p. 337.

in Galloway, enclosures and clearances had taken place upon such a scale as to produce serious rioting on the part of the peasantry. The Rev. Robert Woodrow, writing on May, 1724, supplies us with interesting details.† "It's certain," he says,

"great depopulations have been made in the south, and multitudes of familys turned out of their tacks and sent a-wandering. The lairds of Murdoch, Herron, and others have turned much of their estates into grass. Some parishes, particularly that of Girtoun, are almost whole enclosed, and scarce six or seven familys left ; and these gentlemen take leases of other gentlemen's lands and inclose them. They say, one gentleman, either Murdoch or Herron, in Scotland and England, has in lease upwards of thirty thousand merks' worth of land in grass ; and has parks all the way the cattail go up to England. Thus multitudes of familys are cast loose. I hear that the gentlemen and they are in some kind of treaty. What the upshot shal be I cannot tell."

But again, on the same date, he says, he hears from "Galloway and Nidsdail and Dumfreice of a great gathering of people, to the number of 500 or 600, for demobilising of enclosures and gentlemen's parks." The gathering, it seems, had begun about Dumfries, and the people comprising it "have the name of Levellers and Dyk-brakers . . . They bear no armes, but of late, since the Justices and gentlemen began to oppose them ; and now they have armes." As is the way of our race, they began by memorialising the authorities, but no notice being taken of their appeals, they arrived in armed bands at Kirkcudbright, led by Basil Hamilton, one of the wealthier farmers who had sided with the peasantry. There, and at other market crosses, they publicly read their manifesto, expressing "much regard for the Government," but firmly declaring their resolve to abide on the lands of their fathers. In June, 1724, Woodrow hears from a Mr. David Warner, who had been in Galloway for some six weeks that "the common people there are very lazy " and "all very poor " and behind with their rents—some of them, six years in arrear. The "gentlemen" accordingly were forced to inclosure, through the "laziness and idleness of the tenantry" (which excuse seems to have been all down history, a favourite device of the plunderers of the poor !), but two of the wealthier farmers refused to assist in the landlord machinations and stood boldly forth at great personal sacrifice as leaders of the dispossessed. They were, declares Woodrow's informant, "pragmaticall" men, and "their manner was to appoint a meeting on Teusday, and continou together till Thursday, and then seperat." In bands—men, women and boys—led by the two pragmaticall Radicals, they scattered the dykes in the nighttime, and during the day they hatched schemes and plots for the better governance of the country. They declared "the government of the country was now in the hands of the tenantry . . . ordering

---

† *Analecta or Materials for a History of Remarkable Providences*, vol. 3, p. 153.

all that had any debates to come to them and they would determine."
At first the terrified lairds sought a compromise, but their offers were
contemptuously refused, and for weeks Galloway was ruled by the
pragmaticall communists.   Lord Creighton arrived at length with
two troops of horse, but so great had grown the popular insurrection
that the country gentry considered two troops insufficient, and each
Justice refused to "take the odium" of authorising reprisals until
a larger army was forthcoming.   The "Levellers" scoffed at the
soldiery, and commandeered 80 "cattell, worth about four pound
per piece."   In return the lairds plan the seizure of three clergymen
as instigators of the rebellion, but the seizure is fraught with
over-much danger, and the plan is abandoned.   Then come five
additional troops of horse under Major du Carry, who "is very
tender of the country people, and must unwilling to do anything
to irritate them.   The gentlemen push him to severity, but he is for
soft measures."   Still, somehow, the leaders are trapped—probably
under cover of an armistice—trapped some of them in bed ; and
"on Sabbath was eight days, May last, there was a new proclamation
sent through by their emissary to Sanchair (Sanquhar) and up and
down the country, ordining man, woman, and child to meet them at
three places on Teusday, June 2, with armes that they might stand
in their defence ; and complaining of the severity of the souldiers
on the woman."   The soldiers lie in wait at the "randevouse."   At
mid-day "about thirty rebels appear" on the other side of the watter,
gote some ale and drank the king's health, and confusion to the
inclosers."   These were attacked, and 16 prisoners taken.   "When
they wer carrying over the prisoners at the boat of Balmaclellan
some weemen appeared, which oblidged them to goe back till more
forces came ; and after that one of the weemen going to pull off one
of the souldiers was hurt and troad on by the horse."   As a descriptive writer, Woodrow's correspondent fails miserably, for he now
flies off from the scene of battle to tell us that the Levellers' biggest
meeting was 1100 persons :

> "They speak very loudly that they will burn the gentlmen's houses
> over thar heads in the night-time ; and indeed unless some way be found to
> imploy so many poor people and familys in the wool manufactorys or by
> fishing, which is entirely neglected on the coast of Galloway, where there are
> aboundance of excellent codd, its hard to say what the end of this broyl
> may be."

Later on we hear that they (the peasantry) "were soon dissipated
and repeated their representations, and a Commission was given to
the Lord Advocat to enquire into their grievances and to send them
up to Court, which certainly is the safest way."   Undoubtedly it
was the safest way —for the lairds ; and that the people gained
nothing from the meshes of legal and court trickery we may safely
conclude from the fact that in November rebellion is again open and

widespread. "Upwards of 1000 persons in the shire (Galloway) have their bread taken from them "; they are pulling down the enclosures ; they nail their manifesto to the door of Sorbie Church, and when the laird orders the Bedell to tear it down, they tear down the laird's dykes, and the soldiers are helpless. One of the Stewartry Levellers secures an audience of the king, who orders his Lord Justice Clerk to report to him on the truth of the Leveller's story.   Whether, concludes the parson of Eastwood, "this affair will come before Parliament, I know not ; but I wish it wer brought to a good issue." In May, 1725, the soldiers are "holding the people in," and in June "ther are many of them begging up and doun.   The souldiers have calmed them, and some proposalls they say of erecting manufactorys of wool at Wigtoun, Stranrauer, and Kirkcudbright, which lye very commodiously for trade ; and if the Earl of Stair's project hold, will employ the poor who are turned out by the inclosures.   However, this, with the malt tax and the disarming of the Highlands, do extremely sour people's spirits."

But the policy of enclosuring was "economic " ; it brought under cultivation large tracts of waste and common grazing land ; it produced a larger supply of food stuffs to meet the high-priced demand from an increasing population which, owing to the incessant warfare engaged in by our Governments, had its foreign supplies periodically cut off ; an increased area under cultivation produced more rent ; and as the rights and necessities of the poor were a secondary consideration, the ruthless clearances and ejectments of the peasantry, which began in Galloway, soon became a general feature in Lowland agricultural economies.

For the succeeding three-quarters of the century high prices ruled ; but with the cessation of the French wars after the capture of Napoleon Buonoparte, prices of food-stuffs fell, and the landlords and large farmers proceeded to farther and more drastic clearances of the peasantry in order to procure large unbroken tracts for sheep-grazing. By our fiscal system the importation of animal food was forbidden—in the interests, of course, of the landlords—and the most casual survey of the movements of population recorded by the parish ministers in the *New Statistical Account of Scotland* give us some rough indication of the extent to which the south country was swept of its peasantry at the beginning of the nineteenth century—swept for sheep !*

In the Liberton Parish of Lanarkshire there was a net decrease of population between 1821 and 1831, due to "the consolidation of

*Sporadic clearances, due to special local conditions, had taken place here and there in the Lowlands shortly after the Rebellion of 1745, and following one or two bad harvests, the landlords rouped the peasants' crops for rent, the peasants in question, " making their last farewell of the land which gave them birth."—See *A Candid Enquiry into the Causes of the Late and Intended Migrations from Scotland* (1771)—Anon.

N

farms," and in the latter mentioned year twenty people had emigrated to America. In Dolphinton parish, between 1755 and 1791, the population decreased by 100. In Dunsyre Parish there was a steady decrease every decade between the years 1783 and 1821, and the clerical recorder ascribes the depopulation "to the union of small farms and the dislike which the farmers entertain towards what are generally denominated cottars . . . There was once a considerable village at Weston. But now the remaining cottages are chiefly inhabited by the servants and families belonging to the farms of that name." In the Parish of Weston and Roberton the population fell from 1102 in the year 1755 to 740 in the year 1791, and the reason for the decrease is stated succinctly enough : "The system had come into vogue of throwing several small farms into one large farm, and, as a matter of course, driving the small tenants with their families out of the parish." The parish of Crawford, too, shews a decrease, of which the minister says : "The practice, which now so generally prevails in this country, of uniting many small farms into one is no doubt the chief cause . . . There is perhaps no parish where this practice has so generally prevailed as in this ; and indeed nearly half of this extensive parish is in the hands of non-resident tenants— the resident tenants occupying only two or three farms. In the memory even of the present generation, fifteen families lived where there is now scarcely the vestige of a ruin." The parish minister of Cadder, who in 40 years saw his population almost halved, reports in similar strain : "The love of money" ; he says, "and the desire to lay house to house and field to field have made many parts of this parish, once populous, now a wilderness. The few who yet linger here of former generations can tell of ten farm steadings in their remembrance now effaced from the map of the parish. . . . . The decent families have been reduced and scattered . . . Many passages in "The Deserted Village" apply strongly and appropriately to the parish of Cadder." The population of the Parish of Carmichael fell by one-eighth in 40 years ; that of Pettinain fell by 30 in 10 years ; that of Carstairs fell steadily for 20 years ; that of Wandell and Lammingtoune fell from 599 in the year 1755 to 331 in 1840, and the reason of the decrease is that "many farms once let separately are now possessed in lease by one and the same individual. . . . This is the great cause of the decrease in the population." Walston's population decreased by one-fourth, and Covington and Thankerton's by one-fifth in 56 years. Of East Kilbride we read : "The upper part of the parish was greatly depopulated by the accumulation of small farms into large ones."

Nor was rural Lanarkshire an exception. In every agricultural district of Scotland the same rooting-out process was in effective operation. Of Jedburgh, in Roxburghshire, the local parish minister

says : "Many farmhouses have disappeared ; and in more than one
instance the site of a village is occupied by a single farm-house
with its appendages. On the Jed are the ruins of four corn mills.
. . The monopoly of farms, though undoubtedly favourable to
agriculture, has yet deprived the community of many of its most
valuable members, by reducing them to the necessity of emigrating.
It has lowered the character of the peasantry and promoted the
increase of pauperism." The Riddell estate, in the same county,
was denuded of its peasants in the year 1819, most of them emigrating to Canada or to the United States of America. Of Melrose
Parish we read : "A small farm is nearly unknown. The displacing
of the old small tenants, distinguished as they were by a primitive
simplicity of manners, was at first viewed with deep regret ; that an
entire barony should be committed to one man was exclaimed against
as a public grievance." Roberton's population fell in the latter
half of the eighteenth century by one-sixth ; and the parishes of
Southdean, Maxton, Roxburgh and Smallholm all shew large de-
creases. The clergyman of Linton regrets that "there are now no
remains of the once considerable villages of Hoselaw and Linton. . . .
To these sources is to be traced that very general desire of emigration
to Canada which of late (1845) the class of hinds has manifested ;
and the children of those whom no worldly motive could have torn
from their native hills and valleys, now, without a tear, nay, with a
sort of exultation, leave the land of their fathers." The population
of the parish of Hounam fell from 632 in the year 1755 to 260 in the
year 1831. During the same period land rent rose from £2720 to
£5000, and "whole families, besides single individuals, have within
these last few years emigrated to America. The farmers, paying
more attention to their sheep walks than formerly, hardly allow a
single house to stand on any part of the farm, excepting such as are
necessary for their shepherd's accommodation ; and landlords themselves do not encourage the erection of more cottages than are
absolutely necessary." One non-resident tenant has no fewer than
five farms. In Hobkirk the decrease is one-seventh in 20 years ;
in Oxnam parish "every village is abolished " ; and in Bedrule the
parish minister explains the enormous decrease in his flock by the
" decay of cot-houses and the tendency of late to convert arable into
pasture lands, which require fewer hands." Incidentally he informs
us that in the year 1834 thousands of emigrants from Scotland fell
victims to a cholera epidemic in Canada. "This helped to stifle
emigration." In his *An Old Berwickshire Town*, Mr. Robert Gibson
says :*

" Bedshiel, which is now a single farm . . . consisted in former times of
five farms and a village, whose inhabitants held one of the farms " jointly

*p. 120.

and severally.'   These lands were called ' acre lands or south crofts.' . . . In
the village there was an officer, usually called the ' burleyman,' appointed
to keep order and settle any disputes that might arise amongst the acre-
holders."

In the County of Peebles the plight of the peasantry was as bad.
Traquair parish had been halved and entire villages erased from the
map. Tweedsmuir had fallen in population by one-third ; Drum-
melzier by one-third ; and Eddlestone, Kirkurd, Manner, and
Skirling parishes had all had their clearances.

In Selkirkshire the braes of Yarrow had "of late " seen a "considerable emigration to America."   In Dumfriesshire (Tinwald
and Trailflat parish) "the present cottars die out or remove " ; from
Kirkmahoe parish 40 persons have emigrated to America during
"the last ten years " ; in 20 years, "farm monopoly " in the par sh
of Applegarth and Sibbaldbie has eliminated a population of 200 ;
in St. Mungo parish the lairds are pulling down the cottages ; the
parishes of Cummertrees, Dornock, Durrisdeer, Glencairn (which is
reduced by almost 400 people), Eskdalemuir, Tynron, and Langholm (300 of a decrease in ten years) all are being cleared for sheep,
and, be it noted, as the villages are cleared the common lands of the
villages and the common grazings are quietly absorbed by the lairds.
In Buteshire (Kilmore parish, Arran), four hamlets are razed to the
ground and included in a great sheep walk, the erstwhile inhabitants
of the hamlets driven either to swell the pauperism of the Ayrshire
towns or to the prairies of North America ; and the 68,350 acres
(Scots) of common in which they had acquired at least prescriptive
rights are appropriated by the then Duke of Hamilton.*   Every
or almost every, rural community in Scotland was subjected to the
same weeding out process—from Orkney and Shetland in the north
to Galloway in the south, cottagers, cottars, run-rig crofters, and
small farmers were swept ruthlessly from the soil, factors scorning
their tears and courts of law their rights.   From the Lowland hamlets came to the industrial towns a steady stream of destitutes,
owning no capital but their muscles, knowing no trade but that of
tilling the soil and herding cattle—destined, if fortunate, they and
their children to the miserable, half starved drudgery from which
an unregulated capitalism wrung fabulous profits ; if unfortunate
to a nameless pauper's grave.   To join them came the Iri h immigrants driven from *their* native land, and together they formed the
lowest trata of labourers, whose descendant, weakened, wiz ned and
under-sized, is still with us, a problem *sui generis*, a menace to our
civilisation and a standing testimony to the terrible debt which
private landlordism owes the working-class.

New Stat. Account of Scotland, vol., Buteshire,   . 57-6 .

North of the River Forth the eviction of human beings for sheep was carried on with so great a barbarity and on so colossal a scale as to arouse the anger and disgust of the whole civilised world. The numbers evicted will never be properly estimated—thousands of people being silently "cleared" from lonely glens far from the ken of the few city pamphleteers who interested themselves in the fate of the "puir wild heilandmen"; and the pamphleteers, even when writing of clearances within their own cognisance, were always far more concerned to expatiate upon the savagery of the eviction methods and upon the piety and peacefulness of the evicted than upon the actual numbers of people swept from the soil, or upon the brave, determined resistance which thousands of them undoubtedly offered the destruction of their homes. To appeal successfully for public sympathy a hundred years ago, it was deemed necessary to minimise in every way the turbulent, rebellious occurrences which scared the northern sheriffs and sent many a policeman and estate officer home with a broken head. But this bowdlerisation of the records by the contemporary friends of the crofters, added to the inaccessibility (to the press) of many of the cleared districts, and so the general disposition of the time to regard the Highlanders as a wild, hungry, thievish race, whose extermination would be a national gain, prevents us to-day from making anything beyond an approximate arithmetical estimate of the scattering of the Celtic people by the landlords of the north. The following tabulated list of Highland clearances is therefore not complete; here and there the same clearance may be included in two different "evictions," though, so far as possible, this has been guarded against; and in any case, as no allowances have been made for natural increases when reckoning the county population figures, it is permissible to assume that the evictions in the counties were much in excess of those indicated in a mere decrease between the census figures at different decades :—

District.	Number Evicted.	Landlord.	Date of Eviction.	Reference.
Skye.	"Greate many people."	M'Donald of Sleat.	1739	M'Kenzie's Highland Clearances, p. 249.
Perthshire.	"Clearances."	Drummond.	1762	Innes—Scot. Leg. Antiq., p. 265.
Glengarry.	"Small voluntary emigration." 500.	Glengarry.	After 1745.	M'Kenzie's Highland Clearances, p. 266.
Strathglass.		Macdonell.	1788	„ „ p. 285.
Perthshire.	Rural population decreased by 21,348.	Various, Breadalbane alone evicting 2500 between 1793 and 1853.	1831-1881	„ „ pp. 349 and 520
Glengarry.	The disbanded soldiers of the old 76th regiment with relations and 2 Gaelic ministers.	Macdonald.	1802	„ „ p. 266.
Inverness-shire.	3000.	?	1801	Telford—Caledonian Canal Report.
Strathglass, Aird, and Glen Urquhart.	5390.	Macdonell.	1801-3	M'Kenzie's Highland Clearances, p. 285.
W. Highlands and Islands.	10,000 (includes last two tabulated evictions).	—	1800-6	Sheriff Brown's "Strictures and Remarks on the Earl of Selkirk's 'Observations on the Present State of the Highlands of Scotland'" (1806).
Glen Tilt.	800.	Atholl.	Early 19th century.	Crofters' and Cottars' Commission Report, vol. iv., p. 3346.

District.	Number Evicted.	Landlord.	Date of Eviction.	Reference.
Sutherlandshire.	15,000.	Sutherland.	1811-1820	Hugh Miller's "Sutherland as it was and is, or, How a Country can be Ruined."
Rum.	400.	Clanranald.	1826	New Stat. Acc., vol., "Inverness," p. 152.
Muck.	"Similarly cleared."	Clanranald.	1826	,, ,, p. 152.
N. Uist.	600.	Macdonald.	1828	,, ,, p. 171.
S. Uist.	"Frequent emigrations."	,,	After 1772.	,, ,, p. 171.
Sleat (Skye).	"Cleared."	,,	1811	M'Kenzie's Isle of Skye, p. xvii.
Kilbride.	"Cleared."	,,	1811	,, ,, ,,
Lovat Territory.	"Hundreds evicted."	Fraser.	Before 1830.	M'Kenzie's Highland Clearances, p. 291.
Glendessaray and Locharkaig.	"Great numbers."	Lochiel.	1830-1840	,, ,, p. 293.
Kintail.	"A great many."	Seaforth.	Beginning 19th century.	,, ,, p. 307.
Letterfearn.	50 families.	Innes.	,,	,, ,, p. 307.
Letter of Lochalsh.	"Cleared."	Various.	1801-1881	,, ,, p. 307.
Fortingall.	2185.	Various.	1801-1881	,, ,, p. 346.
Lochawe (Argyll).	45 families.	Campbell.	?	,, ,, p. 349.
Luing (Argyll).	44 families.	,,	?	,, ,, p. 349.
Mull (Argyll).	4171 families.	,,	1821-71	Report of the Highland Relief Board (1849).
Morvern (Argyll).	1027 families.	,,	1801-71	,, ,, ,,
Tiree (Argyll).	"Considerable emigrations."	,,	1849	,, ,, ,,

District.	Number Evicted.	Landlord.	Date of Eviction.	Reference.
Argyllshire.	39,892. (One-half of the rural population of the county. Nearly all the figures in the previously mentioned Argyllshire evictions are included in this Argyllshire total.)	Various.	1831-1881	M'Kenzie's Highland Clearances, p. 362.
Cromarty.	280.	?	1838	Barron's Northern Highlands, p. xxix.
The Black Isle.	50 families.	Various.	1840-6	M'Kenzie's Highland Clearances, p. 310.
The Lews.	2460.	Matheson.	1841-1863	" " p. 312.
Ross-shire.	3341 (decrease in rural popn.).	Various.	1871-1881	" " p. 520.
Knoydart.	"Savage and brutal evictions."	Glengarry.	1853	" " pp. 267 284.
Guisachan.	200.	Marjoribanks.	1855-1873	" " p. 292.
Glenelg.	500.	Baillie.	1849	" " p. 293.
Kincardine (Ross).	"Some hundreds."	Ross.	1843	London Times' Correspondent, writing 15/5/1845.
Kindeace.	90.	Robertson.	1845	"
Newmore.		"	1845	"
Strathconan.	400-500.	Balfour.	1840-5	M'Kenzie's Highland Clearances, p. 520.
Inverness-shire.	18,000.	Various.	1841-81	" " p. 520.
Caithness-shire.	Decrease in rural pop., 1454.	"	1871-81	" " p. 520.
Sutherlandshire.	Decrease in rural pop., 3000.	Sutherland.	1851-81	" " p. 520.

District.	Number Evicted.	Landlord.	Date of Eviction.	Reference.
Kilbride (Arran).	360.	Hamilton.	1793-1801	*New. Stat. Acc.*, Buteshire, p. 25.
Kilbride (Arran).	300.	,,	1821-1835	,, p. 25.
Kilmore (Arran).	576.	,,	1801-1811	,, p. 25.
Kingarth (Arran).	144.	,,	1821-1831	,, p. 77.
Sutherlandshire.	90 families.	Sutherland.	1807	M'Leod's *Gloomy Memories*, Letter iii.
Sutherlandshire.	" Several hundred families."	,,	1809	,, ,, ,,
Reay (Caithness).	" Many of the poor people."	?	1831-1845	*New Stat. Acc.*, "Caithness," p. 18.
Canisbay (Caithness).	50.	?	1801-1811	,, ,, ,, p. 27.
Dunnet (Caithness).	50.	?	1809-1811	,, ,, ,, p. 40.
Watten (Caithness).	2000.	?	1745-1845	,, ,, ,, p. 53.
Burness (Orkney).	80.	?	1832	,, ,, " Orkney," p. 105.
Evie and Rendall (Caithness).	230.	?	1789-1821	,, ,, ,, p. 202.
Holme and Paplay (Caithness).	25.	?	1821-1831	,, ,, ,, p. 204.
Sutherlandshire.	900.	Sutherland.	1830	Barron's *Northern Highlands*, p. xxvii.
Skye.	2000.	MacLeod.	1830-1880	M'Kenzie's *Isle of Skye*, p. xliii.

At the very least, then, the bare figures tabulated above shew clearances of over 125,000 people in the Highland counties, and as there must be thousands of individuals covered by the phrases, "a great many," "frequent emigrations," etc., and as there are indications, as we shall see in a moment, of other extensive expatriations not included in our table, we are justified in estimating the total number of people cleared from the Highland counties at not less than two hundred thousand !

As early as 1739 there had been ships "gon from thiss country with a greate many people designed for America," but the wife of Sir Alexander M'Donald of Sleat, who was reported as responsible, wrote the Lord Advocate of the day, denying that her husband had "concurred in forcing these people away," though it was admitted that some of his estate agents had "organised" the exodus. Mr. Cosmo Innes, however, puts the first great Highland Clearance as occurring on the Drummond Estates in the year 1762; while Mr. Barron asserts it to have taken place on the Glengarry Estates in 1782,* where the land rent rose from £700 to £5000 in thirty-two years. There was, says the latter writer, "a large emigration from Knoydart in 1786, and another even larger in 1802." This second emigration was of "hundreds of Highlanders," and required three vessels to transport them to America. The famines of 1782 and 1783 in Ross-shire among the crofters naturally deprived the landlords of their rents, and "the Gentlemen Landholders and Gentlemen Clergy" met to discuss matters. Among other things they resolved that as the county "has been for these two hundred years back over-rented," and as the people were presently in destitution, they (the lairds) would not drive "the tenantry into despondency" by forcing payment of arrears meantime. They would take their balances by degrees. But they emphatically denounced such tenants as had sold quantities of victual clandestinely "which ought to have been delivered to their masters";† and it was made evident that a non-rent paying peasantry, which actually had the hardihood to demand that its own maintenance should come before the landlord's rent, would receive short shrift where sheep farming was properly understood. In 1792 clearances in Ross-shire and Sutherlandshire produced "serious riots, the people attempting to drive the sheep away," and a Committee of Crofters are recorded by the *Scots Magazine* to have collected money and purchased therewith £16 worth of powder for defensive purposes. M'Kenzie thus describes one of the Ross-shire riots.‡ At Coigeach, he says, there was a "stout resist-

---

The Northern Highlands in the Nineteenth Century—James Barron, vol. i., p. xxvi.

†Crofters' and Cottars' Commission Report, Appendix, p. 422.

‡*Highland Clearances*—Alex. M'Kenzie, F.S.A., Scot., p. 307.

ance, the women disarming about 20 policemen and sheriff officers, burning the summonses in a heap, throwing their batons into the sea, and ducking the representatives of the law in a neighbouring pool. The men formed the second line of defence in case the women should receive any ill-treatment. They, however, never put a finger on the officers of the law, all of whom returned home without serving a single summons or evicting a single crofter . . . . The result is that the Coigeach tenants are still where they were, and are to-day among the most comfortable crofters in the North of Scotland." Again, in Ross-shire, in 1820, there was a fierce and determined resistance offered to the military at the entrance to Glencalvie. Sheriff M'Leod, in charge of the expedition of evictors—police, soldiers, and factors' bodyguard—without formally calling for the Riot Act to be read, indignantly ordered the soldiers to shoot down the crofters who were barring the way. One young girl called Mathieson was killed, and many were wounded, but the infuriated crofters, with weapons in their hands, rushed on the troops, who, after a momentary stand, fled ignominiously, "only two of them escaping with whole heads." The sheriff's coach was smashed to atoms, and as a result of the struggle "the people kept possession of the glen." Similar resistance was offered at Culrain on the braes of Downie, and for years afterwards no stranger's life was safe, even gaugers being stripped naked and hunted from the district ; and an organised system of signalling was devised whereby crofters could be summoned whenever danger threatened.

In the county of Sutherland the peasantry, unfortunately, did not resort to the same methods of effective resistance. "Active resistance there was none," says Hugh Miller, despite the fact that in the eleven years between 1811 and 1820 no fewer than 15,000 people were forcibly ejected "from their snug inland farms, by means for which we would in vain seek a precedent, except perchance in the history of Irish massacre." This strange phenomenon of slavish quiescence while their houses were being burned, their crops destroyed, and they and their children sent awandering on the face of the earth, can be explained only, we think, as Donald Macleod explained it in his "Gloomy Memories of the Highlands," by the extraordinary success which had attended the theological ministrations of the landlords' nominees in the parish pulpits. The clergy (with one noble and outstanding exception—the Parish Minister of Farr) taught insistently that these evictions were ordained by God as punishment for sin, and that opposition to a "divine" decree was unpardonable sacrilege ; and an impartial observer of similar ejection atrocities, writing a generation later, offers testimony of a like nature to Macleod's. "It is owing," says the *London Times* Special Commissioner in 1845, "to the influence of religion alone that they refrain from breaking into open and turbulent resistance of the law."

Elsewhere we have told the story of these Sutherlandshire evictions,* of how entire parishes were swept bare :

"Crops were standing uncut in many cases ; the houses had all been built by the tenants or their ancestors ; and they, the tenants, had nowhere else to go.   It is true, many of the crofters were offered "allotments" on the barren seashore ; it is true they were given the privilege of gathering whelks for food, and of fishing in the rough seas of the outer main if they could lay their hands on sufficient money to purchase a boat.   Still, they had no money for boat purchasings ; they had no desire to leave their ripe crops at a landlord's whim, and betake themselves away from the family croft on the ancestral strath to make corn grow on sea-shingle!   They thought their homes were their own, and that, having improved it, they had some rights in the soil and in the growing crops.   Alas ! down swept the Apaches from Dunrobin Castle ; whole parishes were "cleared," roof trees pulled down, and the little crofts, and frequently the miserable furniture, committed to the flames, with the women and children weeping by the roadside.   In one or two cases the pillagers did not even trouble to remove sick persons before setting fire to the thatch ; women almost in child-birth were thrown on the roadside; ruin—red, hopeless ruin—everywhere, cruelties and savageries almost unmentionable and unbelievable, clouds of smoke filling the valleys, and the peasantry that had been a country's pride, hunted, ragged and homeless, to a barren coast."

Sometimes the contents of the crofter's girnal was thrown over the neighbouring precipice, and—when the evictors were intoxicated—dogs, hens, and cats roasted alive.   One old woman, aged 80, Isabella Graham by name, in the Parish of Lairg, who had been a tenant on Toroboll for fifty years, was forced to sleep in the open fields for 15 weeks.†   James Macdonald, aged 81, a retired revenue officer, in giving evidence before the Crofters' Commission in 1884, declared that the expelled Sutherlanders were refused shelter in the houses even of relatives whose houses had not been destroyed, a notice on the church door intimating that those who gave shelter would in turn be evicted.   Even the graveyards were not sacred. One man, Angus Campbell of Rogart, who attempted to erect a temporary shelter "on the grave of his father," was "moved on." The authorities, preparing for even more extensive clearances, designed a bogus rebellion and called frantically for military assistance.   A sheep farm manager named Reid declared "he had been threatened by the natives, whereupon troops were rushed into Sutherlandshire, some few wondering peasants were clapped into gaol for the sake of realism, and the rebellion was over " !

Our Noble Families, p. 54.
†MacLeod's *Gloomy Memories*, p. 117.

To the Crofters' Commission, a witness representing the crofters of Leadnagullen, declared that after the Strathnavar evictions they were given unreclaimed land at a rent of £2 10s. After they had reclaimed it, the rent was suddenly raised to £20.* Driven to the rock clefts by the shore, such of the poor people as did not emigrate were hunted and harassed at every opportunity by the factors. Seventeen water bailiffs were appointed to see that none of the streams were fished ; two mussel bailiffs were appointed to see that the starving crofters were prevented from gathering mussels for fishing bait. Marriages were forbidden, and this, says MacLeod, has "already been the cause of a great amount of prostitution, and has augmented illegitimate connections and issues fifty per cent. above what such were a few years ago—before this unnatural, ungodly law was put in force." Everything short of actual instantaneous murder was done in Sutherlandshire at the beginning of last century to exterminate the working-class. And not only in Sutherland ; everywhere in the crofting counties, in the furtherance of a great wool and mutton speculation, the little farm "toons" were razed to the ground and the people banished beyond the seas. From Inverness-shire, in the year 1801, three thousand persons were evicted, and by the year 1808 the grazing lands bore 50,000 sheep. In 1807 an emigrant ship from Caithness was lost on the shores of Newfoundland, and 130 lives lost.† In 1816 there was a large emigration from Thurso, "partly for Lord Selkirk's property on the Red River " and partly "engaged to Mr. Logan's property " ‡ in North America. In 1828 six hundred people sailed from Lochmaddy ; in 1829 several packed vessels left Skye for Cape Breton ; in 1830 nine hundred people left Sutherlandshire ; in 1831, we are told,§ the remanent peasantry's "best food consists of shell-fish and a kind of broth made of seaweed, nettles and other wild plants, into which is infused a small sprinkling of oatmeal " ; in 1836-1838 there were extensive emigrations from Lochaber, in 1838 two hundred and eighty people sailed from Cromarty in a vessel leaky and insufficiently provisioned ; in the same year the evictions in Harris "excited much comment" ; in 1841 clearances at Durness in Sutherlandshire provoked rioting, the people evidently by this time questioning the divine origin of their oppressions ; in 1840 an additional 463 are recorded as sailing from the "North Coast," 500 from Uig and Tobermory ; and the parish minister of Croick, in Ross-shire, went with his banished flock to Nova Scotia ; in 1841 one hundred and ninety people were driven from Reay in Caithness, and in the same year an Inverness-

---

Evidence, vol. ii., p. 1611.

†*Inverness Journal*—13/11/1807.

‡*Inverness Courier*—28/6/1816.

§Barron—*Northern Highlands in Nineteenth Century*, p. xxvii.

shire landlord and member of Parliament for the county, Mr. Baillie, desirous of receiving State assistance in emigrating the hunger-smitten *miserables* who now cringed on every Highland coast, got a Parliamentary Committee of Inquiry to report that on the Western coasts of Argyll, Inverness, and Ross, and in the outer Islands, there was "an *excess* of population of 45,000 to 80,000 souls." These famine-swept products of the clearance policy terrified the landlords themselves. The prospect of paying poor law rates for every additional pauper's brat had never been calculated upon in the factor's offices at the inauguration of the clearances which had produced the paupers ; and now that the pauper problem had arisen it never occurred to the landlords to end the horrors of famine by repatriating the people on the soil. The only remedy they saw was continued emigration ; and as the people were too poor and the landlords too unwilling to find the passage-money, the coffers of the State were called upon for the funds necessary to a policy of "assisted emigration."

In the years 1782, 1807, 1817, 1836 and 1837 there was a scarcity of foodstuffs, which almost amounted to famine ; but in 1846-7 the continual scarcity, due to the ever-lessening area of soil under cereal cultivation, was aggravated by a potato blight, and there ensued a destitution and a starvation from the effects of which our northern peasantry has never rallied. In Brocodale, and in Barra, people died of actual hunger ;* one-third of the population of South Uist were in actual starvation. In Islay, the parish minister of Kilmeny reported : Oatmeal was poor in quality, and the best of the barley was ordered off to the distilleries for the landlord's rent, while "5000 souls" wasted away in hunger. In Ulva (Mull) the peasantry were "miserable beyond description," and there will be "many deaths here soon unless something be done immediately." In Iona "most of the tenants have consumed the only cow." In Tobermory the parish minister pled for assistance to the "emaciated forms" of men and women—some of whom had not tasted food of any kind for 24 hours ; he feared "some will perish," and so dire was the distress around him that theological differences were forgotten, and he had fed "two of the Frees who had no particle of food for their families." In Assynt, says the parish minister, the people are eating the seed-corn, and "hundreds of my poor parishioners will, ere two months elapse, be in eternity." In Eddiston the "paupers are barely kept alive."

The distress, particularly in the Hebrides, was aggravated enormously by the extravagant and extortionate rents charged by the landlords. In the halcyon days of the kelp industry, before the heavy import duties on Spanish barilla were abolished, the lairds

---

* "Report on the Outer Hebrides," by the Glasgow Relief Board, August, 1849

on the coast doubled and trebled their rents; but when the kelp industry was ruined by the free importation of barilla, the rents were not reduced. Donald Macleod, referring to Barra, says: "When kelp was in great demand the former proprietor started a kelp manufactory, at which the services of all the spare hands in the island were required. He always preferred labour to money, and when he found that the crofters could pay their rent in three months, he increased his claims gradually until each crofter required to keep a labourer there all the year round. After the manufacturing of kelp stopped, the rents continued at the same figure. This is the whole secret of the Barra destitution."* And this testimony receives ample confirmation from Colonel John Gordon, the owner of the islands, who, in an exculpatory memorandum to the Secretary of the Highland Destitution Committee,† admitted that his predecessor, in 1830-1833, erected alkali works in Barra; that to get the necessary money for the erection of these works he halved all the crofts on his estates, and charged each half croft at the former whole croft rental; that five hundred crofters refused to pay this hundred per cent. increase and emigrated to America; that 700 crofters from other cleared estates were brought in to take their places; that the alkali scheme was not a success, and the proprietor failed; that the estates for the succeeding three years were in the hands of creditors who swept "mercilessly off, for arrears of rent, almost the whole stock of cattle which these crofters possessed, and the property thus fell into my hands burdened with a population of 2300 inhabitants without property or employment"; that the people were now demoralised; and that the only remedy he could see for the existing state of affairs was to send "one-half of them" out of the country "by emigration or otherwise."

What an instructive sidelight upon the ravages of landlordism!

Subscriptions raised in the south to alleviate the distress were utilised by the landlords—relief only being given in return for labour, and this labour, of course, was employed in the improvement of the estates, the making of roads, and so on. But still, the children, say the reporters to the Glasgow Relief Board, were "looking half-starved and prematurely old"; 55 per cent. of one island population were unable to read; in Scalpa and in Mingulay there were no schools of any kind; in Lewis "the females seemed no better than slaves," and did the work of "lower animals." Fresh evictions at Solas, Dunskellar, Middlequarter, and Malagate on the Macdonald Estates produced fierce and desperate resistance; Colonel Gordon complained to the Government that the people had stolen from him nearly 3000 sheep (a "very exaggerated" statement, says the

---

Gloomy Memories, p. 136.

†Stirling Lib. Pamphlet Collection, vol. ii. p. 47.

Relief Board Report, there having been only 1132 sheep "stolen". In Barra the peasants were living in miserable hovels, without chimneys or windows, and sometimes without stool, bed or bed-clothes. The poor fishermen were swindled right and left by mer-chants, who gave them inferior meal in exchange for their fish—inferior meal which wou d not amount to in money value twenty shillings, and that for a whole year's catch of fish. On Mingulay the people were for 10 days without an ounce of meal of any kind ; they lived on a few fish caught in a bay and on *sealbhag* (sorrel) ; and they "saw no one of a higher class than the ground officer." But he would doubtless be sufficient, and we need not suppose that their grief would have been excessive had this sole remaining repre-sentative of the higher class taken himself and his exactions for ever from their ken.

Meanwhile, in Argyllshire, the clearances were proceeding apace—Lochawe, the Island of Luing, Mull, Morvern, and Tiree being swept of their crofting populations. The Rev. Doctors Macleod "had seen their parish almost emptied of its people. Glen after glen had been turned into sheep walks . . . the torn walls and gables left standing like mourners beside the grave. . . . At one stroke of the pen two hundred of the people were ordered off . . . and finer men and women never left the Highlands."[*] Many of the emigrants from the Duke of Argyll's Mull estates died of cholera on the high seas.[†] Of 400 emigrants on one of these coffin ships only 15 reached the other side of the Atlantic alive ; and Mr. Labouchere, in the House of Commons on the 11th February, 1848, speaking on a single year's emigrant death-roll, declared that : "Out of 106,000 emigrants from Ireland and Scotland, 6100 perished on the voyage, 4100 on their arrival, 5200 in the hospitals and 1900 in the towns to which they repaired."

At Solas, North Uist, in 1849 the people were brutally evicted from their homes and growing crops, and though the Sheriff refused to execute his warrants upon four old crofters who were lying upon sick beds, his escort was stoned by an outraged populace, who had been forced—men, women, and children—to sleep shelterless, foodless, and hopeless on the bare wet beach. For the rioting, four men were sentenced at Inverness to four months' imprisonment each, Lord Cockburn, the Whig Jurist, observing that "the slightness of the punishment will probably abate the public fury."[‡] Three years later, on the same estate (Macdonald's), began the Suisinish and

---

[*]See " Reminiscences of a Highland Parish," in *Good Words* Mag. for 1863 ; also, same Mag, August, 1882.

[†]Highland Relief Board Report, p. 19. See also *The Old and New Highlands and Hebrides*—Cameron, pp. 14, 22, 25.

[‡]*Journal*, vol. ii., p. 248.

Boreaig evictions.* Thirty-two families were suddenly swept down upon while the husbands and fathers were away from their homes ; among the evicted was an old woman of 96 years of age, who was forced to seek shelter in a sheep's cot ; and it was only after the local Inspector of Poor was threatened with prosecution for dereliction of duty that he consented to allow the old woman and her grand-daughter the monthly sum of 1s. 3d. each for maintenance. At Knoydart, in late October of 1853, the evictions were even more savage, aged widows being left to face the winter by the dyke-sides or in caves ; the aged, the sick, the suffering—all were burned out like vermin. In 1851 the Gordon estates were cleared, fifteen hun-dred to two thousand people being forcibly transported to America.† Every pennyworth of property the poor people possessed was con-fiscated ; some individuals who resisted were handcuffed ; families were sent by different ships—some mothers never to see their children again ; dozens died on the voyage, and the survivors prowled about in Canada without property, without even the English language, with no trade or handicraft but that of agriculture, and no means or opportunity of exercising it. Beggars in an alien land they certainly were ; and probably, like other propertyless emigrants,‡ many were forced to contract themselves away as slaves.

In the forties a fresh series of evictions had begun in Ross-shire. Highly-rented and prosperous tenants (some of them paying almost £4 per acre in rent) were warned off by Robertson of Kindeace in 1843 ; but a posse of police which attempted to execute the writs was roughly handled at Glencalvie, being seized and bound by an army of women who burned their papers. At Greenyards, near Bonar Bridge, 200 women armed with stones formed the vanguard of the peasants' defence in a regular battle. Sheriff Taylor, who led the attacking forces (well supplied with firearms and liberally saturated with alcoholic liquor), struck the first woman who barred his way. This was the signal for a rush towards the police, the women in front shouting imprecations and throwing stones, and a fierce melee ensued "till the bravest of the women got their arms broken." Even after victory was theirs, the police "continued clubbing the protectless creatures until every one of them was stretched on the field, weltering in their blood, or with broken arms, ribs, and bruised limbs. In this woeful condition many of them were handcuffed together, others tied with coarse ropes, huddled into carts, and carried prisoners

---

*Real Scottish Grievances—Donald Ross.

†Our Noble Families, pp. 2-4.

‡M'Kenzie's Highland Clearances, p. 394. Also, Cameron's Old and New High lands and Hebrides, where it is recorded that the Highland slave emigrants taught their fellow negro slaves the Gaelic language.

O

to Tain." Next day "patches or scalps of the skin with the long hair adhering to them " were picked up on the battleground.

In the volumes of the *New Statistical Account of Scotland* for the crofting counties, the parish ministers, though by no means so outspoken in their strictures on landlord oppression as their brethren in the south, are yet moved here and there to utter a timid protest. In the parish of Rosskeen report we read : "the depopulation of the country is an acute evil . . . . There is no longer an independent peasantry. . . . Their spirits are embittered by oppression "; in the parish of Dores the population fell in 10 years from 3100 to 1300 ; in the parish of Laggan, "where about 80 years ago there was a dense population, there are to be found now only a few scattered shepherd's huts "; in Glenorchy, Lord Breadalbane had reduced the population in 10 years from 1860 to 831 ; the minister of Glenmoriston tells us, in surprise, that his congregation's "attachment to their landlords is still very great "; in Glenelg we are told "the ancient population must have been very considerable, probably double at least of what it is now "; and the clerical reporter for Snizort (Skye) declares that "want drives many to seek in the wilds of America for the comforts denied them in their native land." Distress in Reay (Caithness) is "great in the extreme. The most of the parish has been converted into sheep farms, and consequently the poor people have been ejected from their houses and lands, many of them reduced to indigence and misery, and others necessitated to emigrate to a foreign land ; " in Canisbay "the money brought into the parish by the fisheries is all required to answer the demands of the landlords." These clearances must in no wise be confounded with the later clearances for Deer Forests. These were clearances for sheep, not for sport. Indeed, the Earl of Malmesbury, in his *Memoirs*, writing of the year 1833, says that "a stranger could fish and shoot over almost any part of the Highlands without interruption, the letting value of the *ferae naturae* being unknown to their possessors." Here and there, it is true, grouse shootings were already rented, but as a general rule the clearances effected before the middle of last century were designed for the rent increase which sheep farming entailed. During 40 years of the sheep boom Highland land rents rose by 600 to 800 per cent.; between 1862 and 1882 the rental of the Sutherland estates rose from £35,000 to £73,000 ;* landlords of every economic school and every political party acted with the same purposeful private greed, with the same defiance of humanitarian sentiment, and with the same indifference to national welfare. The Munros of Novar who cleared Kiltearn, the Ramsays of Kildalton who swept the Oa of Islay, the Gowers of Sutherlandshire were "Liberal " in politics : the Balfours of Strathconan and

---

*Cottars' and Crofters' Commission Evidence, vol. 3, p. 2528.

the Gordons of Barra were Tories of the bluest breed ; and no one of them had the slightest intention of allowing his little private idiosyncracies in the more or less mimic warfare of party politics to interfere in the slightest degree with his class advantage. The real landlord point of view was frankly expressed by that eminent Liberal politician, the late Lord Aberdeen, when, on the 27th December, 1852, he said : "I declare that in my opinion no Government in the country is now possible except a Conservative Government—and to that I add another declaration that no Government in this country is now possible except a Liberal Government. The truth is that these terms have no definite meaning. These terms it may be convenient to keep up for the sake of party elections."

The evictions of the Clan M'Lennan from Strathconan by the Balfour trustees were carried out in a most barbarous manner, and to this day the spot is shewn where the dispossessed men and women crouched together, praying rather for a merciful death than that they should be driven farther from the strath of their birth. When the father of the late leader* of the Conservative party fell heir to the estates "the gallows had succeeded the fever," for he directed prompt eviction of other twenty-seven families, and to-day a parish, which in 1831 had a population of 2023, carries only 445 people, mostly ghillies and their dependants on a London brewer's hundred square-mile deer forest.

The barren aspect of the Highland counties by the middle of last century can best be gauged from an eloquent descriptive report issued in 1849 by one of the still too few crofters' champions who were lifting their pens on behalf of the distressed peasants. Says Dr. Maclauchlan ;†

"Many of our readers have passed along Loch Lochy, and they have likely had the mansion of Auchnacarry pointed out to them, and they have been told of the dark mile, surpassing, as some say, the Trossachs in romantic beauty ; but perhaps they were not aware that beyond lies the wide expanse of Loch Arkaig, whose banks have been the scene of a most extensive clearing. There was a day when 300 able, active men could have been collected from the shores of this extensive inland loch, but eviction has long ago rooted them out, and nothing is now to be seen but the ruins of their huts, with the occasional bothy of a shepherd, while their lands are held by one or two farmers from the borders. Crossing to the south of the great glen, we may begin with Glencoe. How much of its romantic interest does this glen owe to its desolation ? Let us remember, however, that the desolation in a large part of it is the result of the extrusion of the inhabitants. Travel eastward, and the footprints of the destroyer cannot be lost sight of. Large tracks along the Spean and its tributaries are a wide waste. The southern bank of

*Balfour.

†*The Depopulation System of the Highlands*—Rev. Dr. Maclauchlan (Edin.), 1849.

Loch Lochy is almost without inhabitants, though the symptoms of former occupancy are frequent. When we enter the country of the Frasers, the same spectacle presents itself—a desolate land. With the exception of the miserable village of Fort Augustus the native poulation is almost extinguished, while those who do remain are left as if, by their squalid misery, to make darkness the more visible. Across the hills, in Stratherrick, the property of Lord Lovat, with the exception of a few sheep farmers, and a very few tenants, is one wide waste. To the north of Loch Ness, the territory of the Grants, both Glenmoriston and the Earl of Seafield, presents a pleasing feature amidst a sea of desolation. But beyond this again, let us trace the large rivers of the east coast to their sources. Trace the Beauly through all its upper reaches, and how many thousands upon thousands of acres, once peopled, are, as respects human beings, a wide wilderness! The lands of the Chisholms have been stripped of their population down to a mere fragment; the possessors of those of Lovat have not been behind with their share of the same sad doings. Let us cross to the Conon and its branches, and we will find that the chieftains of the MacKenzies have not been less active in extermination. Breadalbane and Rannoch, in Perthshire, have a similar tale to tell, vast masses of the population having been forcibly expelled. The upper regions of Athole have also suffered, while many of the valleys along the Spey and its tributaries are without an inhabitant, if we except a few shepherds. Sutherland, with all its atrocities, affords but a fraction that have been perpetrated in following out the ejectment system of the Highlands. In truth, of the habitable portion of the whole country, but a small part is now really inhabited. We are unwilling to weary our readers by carrying them along the west coast from the Linnhe Loch northwards; but if they enquire, they will find that the same system has been, in the case of most of the estates, relentlessly pursued."

Still the evictions proceeded. At the very hour, says M'Kenzie in his *Highland Clearances*, that Nana Sahib was being crushed and Cawnpore taken by the 78th Regiment, the fathers, mothers and children of the 78th were being evicted within a few miles of Dunrobin Castle.

Guisachan was "humanely" cleared by Sir Dudley Marjoribanks between 1855 and 1873; about 1845 Cameron of Lochiel was transplanting his peasants for deer; by 1848 the club farms of Strathconan had been obliterated by laird Balfour; between 1851 and 1863 Sir James Matheson of the Lews paid "the passage money to Canada of 2231 souls from his estates"; in 1880 Mr. A. C. Pirie of Aberdeen, who had acquired Leckmelm in the parish of Lochbroom, took from his tenantry all their arable and pasture lands, and though he allowed them to remain in their cottages forbade them access to employment and stipulated that they should not keep even a hen. This, naturally, made rent-paying impossible, and in January, 1882, a cottager, Murdo Munro, with his wife and young family, were turned out homeless in the snow. The agitation raised by the local parish minister, the Rev. John MacMillan, over this signal atrocity, added to the public opinion which had been created by John Murdoch in the *Highlander* newspaper, was the real beginning of the clamour which finally resulted in the State concession of fixity of tenure in the crofting counties. In the same year fuel was supplied to the flame by two evictions on the Lochcarron estate ; here the laird had taken umbrage at certain families because one young man connected with them had the temerity to sue the ground officer for libel in the Sheriff Court. The suit was successful, and damages of £22 13s. 8d. secured ; but scarcely had the case closed ere the young man's relatives were ejected from their homes, one of the relatives being an old man of 81 years, now paralytic and bedridden, and another being a man who had paid rent for 40 years. On the morning of the evictions a huge crowd gathered from the neighbouring parishes, and no sooner had the Sheriff got the furniture dragged out than he and his police were roughly hustled away, and the furniture returned, the more ardent spirits declaring that "they would not see their brothers treated thus, even if they hanged for it." Meantime, over in the Lews the people were being driven and harassed into open revolt. Rents were arbitrarily raised between terms ; if a crofter's sheep strayed beyond the limits of his holding, it was seized and returned to the owner *minus* its ears unless the distressed crofter paid half a crown in ransom ; crofters made roads, but their wages therefor were impounded ; the church at Glen Inch had now no worshippers, and the manse had been converted into a shepherd's hut ; at Talisker the crofter's corn was thrown into the river to make room for a distillery ; estate workers were removed ten miles from the scenes of their daily toil ; at Struan Mor, marriages were forbidden ; hospitality to strangers, or agitators as the factors called them, was a sure prelude to eviction ; crofter's dogs were shot at sight ; children ran naked ; the women were forced to give so many days free labour at the laird's harvest ; the hill pasturings were taken away, and the rents not reduced—often, indeed, they were raised ; churchyards were closed and the poor forced to bury their dead "in the sea or in the peat moss." The *North British Daily Mail*, which had energetically taken the side of the poor harassed crofters, reported that thirty men had been imprisoned for crying out "Baa ! " after an unpopular tacksman ; Sheriff Ivory raided every house in the township of Herbista at midnight, and without legal warrant ; the Rev. Donald M'Callum of Lochs was summarily arrested for "inciting the lieges to class hatred " ; in the township of Peinness, a few miles from Portree, a poor woman, Mrs. M'Rae, actually had her two months' old baby poinded for rent—the baby being valued at sixpence, and a collie puppy, poinded at the same time, was valued at one shilling ! The story of Donald Nicolson of Totescore, as given by Mr. Dugald Maclachlan, banker, Portree, to the Crofters' Commission in 1882, will serve as an illustration of what the people were suffering in the western islands. Donald, who was over 70 years of age, had his rent suddenly doubled by the tacksman ; he reluctantly agreed to pay the extortion, and then just as suddenly another £1 was added ; this he could not pay, and was evicted ; the neighbours were ordered to refuse the old man, his son's wife, and her two children shelter, under pain of eviction, and they were accordingly compelled to sleep in a cart shed, afterwards securing an old stable for a habitation. He was then sued for breach of interdict, and fined 10s., with the alternative of five days' imprisonment. The expenses of the interdict were £8. Then there was a year's rent due, and in addition to that he was charged with "violent profits," which means the doubling of the rent for remaining in possession after the term. The whole came to £35 odds. Incoming tenants were charged with the arrears alleged to be due by outgoing tenants ; the factors themselves became "general dealers" and charged ruinous prices for foodstuffs and equipment, while they effectively silenced all competition by raising the rents of those who shewed a disposition to engage in trade. But the climax was reached in oppression when the Laird of Glendale affixed to the Post Office doors, the following intimation :—

> " *All beasts bought from the crofters will be seized, whenever found, unless the purchase price be paid to me.*"

These shameful tyrannies, although practised in lone straths, and where protest meant instant forfeiture of all means of earning even a bare and meagre living, were yet sometimes desperately resisted. The crofters were crushed, but here and there individuals and communities defied the tyrant. At Bernera, in the Lews, in 1874, the Sheriff Officer and his assistants, on a nefarious eviction expedition, had been chased for their lives ; one witness before the Crofters' Commission made the open threat that "if we don't get justice, we will go to prison ourselves, or else we will sell our lives as dear as possible " ; another witness intimated that the people "were hearing such good news from Ireland that they were inclined to turn rebels in order to secure the same good results." On the Braes of Portree in 1882 a Sheriff Officer was forced by a crowd of 200 persons to burn the summonses he was sent to serve, and his assistant was covered with the contents of "certain domestic utensils, fully charged." It was decided to arrest the ringleaders, and a huge force of police, some of them specially imported from Glasgow and accompanied by press correspondents, attended Sheriff Ivory on his expedition. Here took place the celebrated "Battle of the Braes," in which over a dozen policemen were wounded.* Skye was aflame, and the

---

*See *Dundee Advertiser* Report, reprinted in M'Kenzie's *Isle of Skye*, p. 27-34.

authorities refused such prisoners as had been captured the usual jury trial, despite protests in Parliament and in the London press. A determined attempt was made to rescue a few prisoners who had been lodged in Portree Gaol, and from all the outlying districts came "irregulars" to join the rebels. Masts of shipping in the harbour were taken for battering rams, and although police with rifles were posted in the houses surrounding the gaol the building would have been rushed had not some of the crofters' leaders interfered. In the autumn of the same year Lord Macdonald determined to assert his authority over the Braes crofters, and issued summonses ordering them to remove their sheep from the slopes of Benlee. Now, Benlee, as Macleod of Macleod, another landlord, injudiciously admitted in the press at a later stage, "was a common, and, as is well-known, what is common to all is of little value to any"; but it was evidently of some use to the crofters, who indignantly refused to accept the summonses, and the women hunted the messengers back to Portree. The crofters prepared for a fresh attack, and posted their children as sentries. The situation became serious for the Highland landlords, and great pressure was brought to bear upon Lord Macdonald at the Argyllshire County Ball and elsewhere to settle the dispute peaceably "in the interests of his own class"; but that gentleman was adamant; he appealed for the assistance of two Companies of soldiers, but Sir William Harcourt, the Home Secretary, acting, it is said, upon urgent appeals from military headquarters in the Highlands, refused the request. Highland troops could not be "trusted" for such work; and a *posse* of police had to return with the summonses again undelivered. Then the County Council of Inverness—landlord almost to a man—besought police assistance from the other counties and the burghs of Scotland, but the burghs point blank refused aid, and the County response was so meagre that no farther proceedings were attempted, and Lord Macdonald had finally to ask the crofters to "let him down easy," and "save his face" by paying him a nominal rent for the grazings of Benlee. This impudent and cunning request was unfortunately agreed to by the crofters, thereby admitting his right to Benlee, handing away a precious heritage, and yielding up to the enemy the advantages their successful resistance had secured for the distressed crofters all over the Highlands. In the same year a gunboat, the *Jackal*, had to be requisitioned to overawe the people of Glendale and to induce certain crofters summoned for contempt of Court to proceed to Edinburgh for sentence. In November, 1887, took place the famous deer drive in the Lews, in which over 1000 crofters, after months of preparation, and after gathering together every old musket and spear they could lay their hands upon and led in orderly fashion by the patriarchs of each little community, set

themselves to drive the deer into the sea.   During the drive, which
lasted several days, two hundred head of deer were slaughtered ;
a great camp was erected, the patriarchs drew parallels between their
escapade and the wanderings of the children of Israel, and the people
were worked up to such a pitch of rebellious excitement that when the
raid was over the authorities dared only to prosecute a handful of
the raiders, and this handful were adjudged not guilty by an Edinburgh jury and carried in triumph down the High Street by a populace which shouted "Down with the Tyrants ! "   In 1888 cattle-
driving on a large scale began at Aignish and Galston ; and Riot
Act readings, prosecutions, and imprisonments were the order of the
day.   At Assynt the crofters took violent possession of land, from
which the Duke of Sutherland had previously driven them, and here
again assistance of the gunboats was requisitioned ; all the crofters
were arrested except Hugh Kerr ("The Modern Rob Roy "), who
evaded the authorities for over two months.   At the Hills of Muie,
desperate "squatting" was met with wholesale arrests ; but
public attention had been aroused, a Parliamentary Commission of
Enquiry was secured, and the result was the Crofters' Act, which
reduced rents (in some instances by 60 per cent. and 70 per cent),
cancelled most of the arrears, and guaranteed fixity of tenure and
fair rent in all the crofting counties, except Argyllshire, where the
out-voters managed to return a Tory member whose appearance
in Parliament added to his own assurances that the county he represented was hostile to any interference with the landlords, was sufficient to debar the crofters there from the protection—meagre as
that protection was—given the crofters in the other Highland
counties.

But by the time the Crofters' Act was passed a whirlwind of
economic retribution was being reaped by the landlords.   Land,
to retain its fertility, must undergo perpetual labouring, and the
devastated Highlands gradually lost their nutritious grasses, which
gave place to rushes, heather and bracken.   Year after year less and
ever less stock could be carried on the sheep runs, and the new Free
Trade policy had opened our ports to the competition of Australian
wool.   Prices fell, the sheep farmers could not pay the rents
demanded of them, and thousands of acres were thrown upon the
hands of the landlords, who by the terms of the leases were forced
to take over the sheep at a valuation.   But if there was "no money "
in sheep, there was money in sport.   Plutocrats from America, like
Mr. Winans ; brewers from England, like Lords Burton and Tweed-
mouth ; successful gamblers fresh from a scoop in the Kaffir
Market ; cotton capitalists ; satiated aristocrats ; mighty Nim-
rods from the Piccadilly Clubs ; nay, even the Gaekwar of Baroda,
hired the Highlands for a solitude, swept away the shepherds, and

at certain stipulated periods of the year came with French cooks and in tartan kilts to slaughter deer and grouse and rabbits. There had always been a considerable number of wild deer in the Highlands ; but the depreciation in rent value of the sheep-runs and the increasing number of idle rich people in the towns, who were satiated with the tamer pleasures and yearned for the "noble blood sports," were the causes of that extraordinary increase in the acreages devoted to sport, of those farther clearances of the rural working-class and of that persistent drainage through emigration of our best blood and brawn, which for a time, leaving behind few but the dull, the unadventurous and the servile-blooded stocks, the poorest of the poor, the aged, and the helpless, seriously imperilled our persistance as a race and threatened our physique and our *morale* with irresistible degeneration. Between 1883 and 1908 the acreage under Deer increased in the crofting counties thus :*

Year.	Year.	Year.	Year.
1883	1898	1904	1908
Acreage.	Acreage.	Acreage.	Acreage.
1,709,892	2,510,625	2,920,097	2,958,490

In the twenty-five years there had thus been an increase in five counties† alone of one and a quarter million acres. But the desolation of sporting land is not the curse of the crofting counties only. By the year 1908 there were about 195,000 acres in Aberdeenshire‡ under grouse, deer and rabbits ; in Ayrshire, 850 acres ; in Banffshire, 75,000 ; in Buteshire, 5000 ; in Dumbartonshire, 2300 ; in Fifeshire, 1100 ; in Forfarshire, 60,000 ; in Kincardineshire, 5600 ; in Kirkcudbrightshire, 9100 ; in Nairnshire, 6,800 ; in Perthshire 199,000 (of which the Duke of Atholl owned 91,700 acres, and his son, the Marquis of Tullibardine, 14,500), all of them acres exclusively devoted to sport. In addition there are large areas of deer forest land not included in these figures, because, a few sheep being allowed to graze on the "forests," they are officially reckoned as agricultural land. Bearing these facts and figures in mind, the steady decline in the numbers of our rural peasantry during the last decade is understandable. In the northern portion of Scotland between 1891 and 1901 the population decreased by over 6000 ; in the north-western portion by 2300 ; in the southern portion by 10,300 ;§ and the total net decrease in the rural districts was 42,704, or 4.60 per cent.‖ Notwithstanding the fact, said Dr. Clark in a lecture at Edinburgh,a

---

*Parliamentary Paper, 220, 1908.

†There are six Crofting Counties, but Orkney and Shetland has no Deer Forests.

‡Parliamentary Paper, 344, 1908.

§Sutherland—*Call of the Land*, Appendix A.

‖Census, 1901, vol. i., p. xxiv.

aScottish Land League Tract—" Private Property in Land," 1911.

that Argyllshire contains towns such as Dunoon, which, taking some of Glasgow's overflow, has doubled itself in 50 years, its total population is 31,912 less than in 1831. "The growth of the deer forests is the principal cause of the depopulation of Argyll. In 1883 there were 216,698 acres under deer in the county; in 1904 there were 409,748. . . . Inverness is the capital of the Highlands, yet its landward parish, which receives the overflow of the town, had a population of 5801 in 1901, but in 1911 it had only 3736. Nearly one half of the county of Inverness has been turned into deer forests." Lord Eversley has analysed the economies of eleven purely agricultural parishes in East Aberdeenshire,* and has shewn that between 1860 and 1908 (a period of general agricultural depressions) land rent rose on an average by 36 per cent.; the population declined by 1747 persons, and no fewer than 363 crofts disappeared from the valuation roll, the parish of Old Deer alone shewing a decrease of 200 small holdings. Landlord apologists are wont to declare that the deer forests are unsuitable for agriculture, and doubtless it is true that in the higher altitudes tillage would be non-economic; but the fact remains that the Royal Commission (Highlands and Islands, 1892), scheduled 1,782,785 acres of land then devoted to sport or sheep grazing as suitable for the creation of new small holdings or the extension of holdings already in existence;† and what the landlord apologists really mean is that deer pay better than men. Land run to waste, land misused, land devoted to anti-social practices, yields more rent to private owners than land tilled by peasants. And so, say the lairds, the peasant must go. The deer may eat the peasant's corn (unless he sit up all night guarding it); grazing land for his cow is refused, as on the Chisholm estate at Strathglass, because the factor declares the arable land "is absolutely indispensable to the deer forester."‡ Robbed of his grazings, bled white by his factor, harassed at every turn, the peasant hopes against hope for that long delayed reform in the Land Laws and the Game Laws which generations of politicians have promised him, and he sees his children book their assisted passages for the other side of the world, or drift to casual labour and the unemployed processions of the large towns

---

Journal of Royal Stat. Socy., vol. lxx., part 2.
†Cd., 7681, 1895, p. xxii.
‡Evidence before Deer Forest Commission.

CHAPTER IX.

THE POLITICAL DEMOCRACY.

"That demon of mischief, that pest of Scotland."—*The Lord Advocate on Thomas Muir—Daly's "Radical Pioneers of the Eighteenth Century,"* p. 193.

"So long as property upon which our whole system has long been founded, shall continue to return the House of Commons, I shall not despair, but if the elective qualification shall ever be reduced so low that the property element is made merely nominal and a greatly increased proportion of that House shall be returned by mere population, I fear that our boasted constitution must soon sink into that democracy which seems to be the natural result of every government where the people have become politically free. I wish I could believe that any people who have obtained the means of engrossing supreme power can be induced by education to refrain from grasping it. . . . It was the glory of the first Reform Bill that it not only avoided a revolutionary triumph of just discontent, but by giving its due influence to property, steadied the whole political system."—*Lord Cockburn, Whig Leader—"Journal, 1831-1854," ii.,* pp. 272-3.

"Don't be deceived by the middle classes again! You helped them to get the Reform Bill, and where are the fine promises they made you? Don't listen to their humbug any more. Stick to your charter. Without your votes, you are veritable slaves."—*Chartist Orator in 1841—M'Carthy's "History of Our Own Times," i.,* 89.

IT has been the fashion with some publicists, intent upon propagating the idea of Scottish Home Rule, to refer to the Auld Scots Parliament as a benign national institution, and to its absorption in the English Parliament as a national calamity. Nothing could well be farther from the truth. It was not a national Parliament : it was a feudal oligarchy—venal, corrupt, and despicable, servile to the Crown, and tyrannical to the people. In early times, when the Exchequer or a foreign foe threatened the dynasty, the King summoned a great Council of the *Episcopi*, the *Abbates*, the *Barones*, and the *probi homines* (these latter being the "good men" or small vassals who held land directly from the Crown) for advice—and financial assistance.

By 1427 this Parliamentary privilege had grown so costly that the freeholders were compelled to adopt the principle of representation, whereby each county could be represented by a minimum number of two delegates, but with the reservation that any freeholder could attend Parliament if he so wished. In 1681 Parliamentary privileges in the shires were limited to freeholders who held land of £400 Scots valued rent, the peers, of course, not being limited by any such regulation, but sitting by right of rank. As the burghs grew in financial power it became necessary to rope them in, and so great was the demand for their presence that the Burgh Commissioners were fined for non-attendance. These Burgh Commissioners, of course, were selected by the self-elected Town Councils, and represented only the large trading and burgh landowning interests.

Before the Reformation, Parliament was really composed of peers, bishops and archbishops, unwilling burghal representatives, and still more unwilling "small barons" from the shires—indeed, in some of James IV.'s Parliaments no shire freeholders put in an appearance at all—and not until the Parliament of 1560, when some 160 freeholders turned up to abolish the old religion, was there any attempt on the part of the barons and the merchants to use Parliament for their own ends. After the Reformation, Parliament fell into the hands of an executive elected at the opening of the session, and this election over, the members of Parliament were free to return home. The executive, called the Lords of the Articles, were chosen thus : the nobles chose eight bishops, who in turn chose eight nobles, and the sixteen thus chosen selected eight barons and eight burgesses ; and this state of affairs obtained until the year 1610, when the number of Parliamentary "representatives" was limited to thirty-three nominated by the King. One hundred years later this nominated caucus was bribed out of existence by King William's commissioner, Lord Melville* in, as Dr. Ross has aptly said, "as dirty a cloud of fraud, corruption, and scoundrelism as the history of the world can find parallel." And that is the real story of the "auld sang" national Parliament.

Now, in endeavouring to understand clearly why this nominated caucus of aristocrats was swallowed up in the Parliament at Westminster, it is not enough to say, and to say truly, that the caucus itself was bribed out of separate existence by the "secret money" of the English Government ; but we must grasp the consequences of two great events which at first sight have no connection whatever with the existence or otherwise of an Edinburgh Parliament. Firstly, we must remember that though the "glorious Revolution" of 1688 had seated King William on the throne and sent the Stuarts abegging round Europe, there was still a powerful Jacobite sentiment in Scotland, ready to rally to a Stuart flag should a foreign army with a Stuart at its head descend upon Scottish shores. Nor was this a remote contingency, as King William and his advisers well knew ;

---

*For the history of the Old Scots Parliament see Wight's *Inquiry into the Rise and Progress of Parliament*, pp. 20-361 ; Professor Sanford Terry's "Scotch Parliament," *Scot. Hist. Review*, vol. iv., pp. 49-61 ; Dr. Ross's "Kingcraft in Scotland," *Blackwood's Magazine*, November, 1834, etc.

and as one way of meeting it, William sought to abolish the Scots
Parliament and bring all the legislators to London, where he could
have them under his effective control. William knew the men he
had to deal with, and his method was not coercion and threat, but
cash down. In 1690 he wrote assuring his Commissioner in Scotland that he would make good "what employment or other gratifications you think fit to promise"; he so excited the cupidity of the
Duke of Argyll that that gentleman busied himself in preparing "a
schedule of places and pensions by means of which 30 members of
Parliament might be detached from the opposition"; while Queensberry, who had already spent £500 in bribery, and was asking £1000
for extensions, wrote: "If money could be had I would not doubt
of success in the King's business here."* Lord Melville, the King's
Commissioner, was active with Royal money among the Scots nobles†;
Lord Breadalbane was given £20,000 with which to bribe the Highland cheiftains who, if they so preferred, might each have instead of
£2000 a dignity under the rank of an earldom. The apportion-
ment of these bribes is somewhat of a mystery. Why, for instance,
should Lord Banff be content with £11 while the Earl of Marchmont
got 1100 guineas? But there is no mystery about the bribery,
whatever there may be about the division of the bribes. It was
open and unashamed, and quite in accordance with the canons of
morality of the governing class—a governing class whose judges
habitually took "budds" or bribes and whose king's advocates did
not scorn humble £2 tips, or, as they called them "gratifications."
But the mere greasing of a few selected aristocratic palms did not
quite engender the public opinion necessary ere the Scots Parliament
could be safely abolished, and as the rising capitalist and money-
lending class was at that particular time in a state of great irritation,
William and his advisers found themselves compelled to extend the
area of corruption. Every school-boy has read something of the
Darien Scheme; but the history primers used by our School Boards
do not give the whole truth; they tell of the great boom in Darien
shares, and of how money-lending Scotland enthusiastically subscribed the capital which was to develop a rival to the East India
Company and shower storms of gold, far beyond the dreams of
avarice, into the coffers of the bailies and the barons, the magistrates
and the merchants who were fortunate enough to secure shares.
But the school primers do not tell how the charter was got by
fraud and the bribing of "several great men" who were to get two
per cent. of the profits for their good services in securing Royal
assent to the monopoly; nor how the Scots Parliament hastily
passed an Act authorising administrators of trust funds and burgh

---

*The Union of 1707—W. Law Mathieson, p. 251.
†Leven and Melville Papers, 417.

funds to invest in the Darien Golconda ; nor how, when the King understood how he had been deceived into granting a charter likely to affect detrimentally the monopoly hitherto enjoyed by his English capitalist friends in the East India Company, he turned adrift his two Secretaries for Scotland ; nor how the English colonial governors got orders to boycott the Scottish settlement at Darien, and interpreted their orders so literally that at Jamaica starving refugees were refused provisions and Scottish crews flying distress signals at sea were refused assistance ; nor how the blame for the financial smash and the dissipation of the golden dreams was laid at the door of the English King by a swarm of ruined speculators whose national patriotism rose as rapidly as their capital had declined.*
The Darien shareholders had dreamed of themselves as Nabobs : now they were paupers ; they had secured by the methods afore-mentioned a charter freeing their Company from taxes for twenty-one years, and guaranteeing that "if any of the persons or effects of the Company should be seized or damaged," such damage was to be made good "at the public charge " ; and now, behold, their charter was waste paper and their money was gone, and the cursed greed of the thrice accursed English was responsible for the disaster ! William's course with the distressed Scots capitalists was simple ; he bribed them to his will ; he offered what he called an "Equiva-lent " for the loss of the Scots Parliament ; he offered £398,085 10s., to be used in refunding the speculators their capital "with interest " and in discharging arrears of Government pay, in return for a Union of Parliaments. Capitalist Scotland rejoiced, swore eternal loyalty to William, suffered the Scots Parliament to snuff itself out, and awaited the "Equivalent," which ultimately came guarded by Dragoons who were stoned on the streets of Edinburgh by a non-investing working-class mob, roused to anger by this flaunting of the cash nexus.† By the Treaty of Union, "all heritable offices, superiorities, heritable jurisdiction, offices for life and jurisdictions for life " were reserved to the owners thereof ; Scotland was to be represented in the British Parliament by 45 commoners and 16 peers, the forty-five commoners to come, fifteen from the burghs and thirty from the counties ; and for the first Parliament members were to be selected not by their constituents, but by the existing Scots Parliament.

And that was the origin, the history, and the end of the auld sang !

At the first election after the Union, the Government, says Bishop Burnet, "laid it down for a maxim not to be departed from, to

---

*See *The Early History of the Scots Darien Company*—Hiram Bingham, and
  The Union of 1707—W. Law Mathieson, p. 253, *et seq.*
†" The Union of Parliaments "—P. Hume Brown in *Scot. Hist. Review*, 1906-7,
  pp. 127-131. Working-class riots also took place at Glasgow and Dumfries.

look carefully to the elections in Scotland, that the members returned from there might be in entire dependence on them and be either Whigs or Tories as they should shift sides " ;* and right down to the Reform Bill of 1832 this policy was pursued with a venality and a corruption scarcely conceivable. In the Scots counties only land-owners had votes. Buteshire had only 12 electors, and the average county electors' roll bore no more than 80 names, of whom about half were bogus parchment barons—fictitious voters created by some great landlord to give him the dominating voice in the selection of the county member. As if the landed interest were not sufficiently safeguarded, the old Scots Act of 1661, which allowed the county members £5 Scots per day for expenses during attendance at Parliament, had been abrogated at the Union ; and in 1710 an Act was passed at Westminster requiring every member of Parliament to possess an annual income of £300 from freehold land, and right down to the year 1858 no man unable to prove himself as the owner of an "assured income " was allowed to represent a constituency.† In the burghs there were, all told, 1303 electors—self-elected magistrates and councillors—but they again were mostly dominated or bribed by some neighbouring lord, and the net result of the electoral system prior to 1832 was that the forty alleged representatives of Scotland represented nobody but "the great lord, the drunken laird, and the drunkener bailie."‡ From such a political system the common people could hope for nothing. Bribery, corruption, nepotism, and class piracy at the public purse were things done in the light of day—open, shameless, and wholesale. The Scots M.P.'s sold their votes, and so servile and so docile were they to their Government paymasters, that Lord Liverpool was moved in gratitude to declare that "Scotland was the best conditioned country in the world."§ At the end of the eighteenth century, says Lecky, Scotland "was habitually looked upon as the most servile and corrupt portion in the British Empire."‖ Many of the Scots M.P.'s took weekly from Walpole's cashier ten guineas for services rendered, and Ferguson of Pitfour, looking back upon his Parliamentary career, declared : "I have heard many arguments which convinced my judgment, but never one which influenced my vote." It was the political Indian summer of the Scots landed gentry. M.P.'s, by thrift and frugality, might retire after having "served their country " for five years at Westminster, and no "leading voter " in Scotland experienced the

History of His Times (Edition 1833), v., p. 400.

†*The Unreformed House of Commons*—By A. and E. G. Porritt, vol. i., p. 151 ;
　　Jeremy Bentham's *Plan of Parliamentary Reform* (1818), p. 61.

‡*Scotland and the French Revolution*—Meikle, p. xviii.

§Porritt (see *ante.*), v. 2, pp. 3 and 4.

‖*England in the Eighteenth Century*, iii., pp. 578-9.

slightest difficulty in procuring well-renumerated State employment for his sons. Not only that, but instances are upon record of Government loans being floated upon terms so favourable to the lenders (who were always "friends" of the ministry in power) that the shares could be sold at a profit of ten per cent.; and in the first quarter of the nineteenth century, public attention was called to the pickings enjoyed by the grim, iron hero—Duke of Wellington (*vide* the school history books!), who had got himself ensconced at the chief seat in the Treasury, as Prime Minister of Britain; the Duke had held many well-renumerated military posts; he had been the lavishly-paid ambassador at Paris and at Vienna; after Salamanca he had been voted a grant of £100,000; after Toulouse, £400,000; and after Waterloo, £200,000. He had got a service of plate from Portugal worth £400,000; he had his salary as Field-Marshal, his salary as Commander-in-Chief of the British Army in Europe, and a salary from the Allied Powers as Commander-in-Chief of the Army of Occupation; he drew a salary as Colonel of the Royal Horse Guards; he had large emoluments from the contractors who clothed and fed his regiment; Spain had granted him an estate worth £10,000 per annum, and he drew incomes from an estate donated to him in Portugal, and from a Dutch estate granted him as Prince of Waterloo.* Politics was simply the high road to plunder for the landed interest, and every man who owned a franchise— even a bogus one†—owned a valuable financial asset. There was no conception of Democracy among the politicians; and when a church membership under Crown patronage dared to petition that the second minister should be given the place of the first minister (who had died) a member of the Cabinet replied with hauteur "that the single fact of the people having interfered so far as to express a wish, was conclusive against what they desired";‡ and another appointment was instantly made.

But during the last half of the eighteenth century strange foreign-bred ideas had found a lodgment here and there among the middle classes: and the peasants expropriated from the soil and forced to sell their labour for miserable weekly wages tending machinery in the newly-built factories, imbibed a spirit of class unionism and lost that personal human touch with the laird which was of the essence of feudalism. The middle-class saw the legislature controlled by a

---

*Bentham's *Plan of Parliamentary Reform*, p. 154.

†In 1832 the bogus freeholders made a vigorous effort to secure money compensation for loss of their electoral privileges, but, though supported by Lords Haddington and Aberdeen, the claim was more than the nation could stand, and their petition simply lay on the table of the House of Lords!

‡Lord Cockburn's *Memorials of His Time*, p. 90.

select coterie of corrupt aristocrats ; they had heard of how easily
the American colonists had shaken off the English governors during
the War of Independence ; and the working-class, as well as the
capitalists, heard of how the Bastille fell in France, and as food prices
rose, and the struggle in the early factory hells for a bare living grew
more intense, the ground racked and cracked below the political
edifice built in 1707, and only the blind denied that a reform was
imminent.

The middle-classes, known as Whigs, were the first to move.
They had no thought of enfranchising shopkeepers, tradesmen and
the lower orders generally ; but their capital had developed iron-
works at Falkirk, and factories in Fifeshire, Forfarshire, Renfrewshire, and Glasgow ; and they paid taxes which they saw being
squandered by individuals who despised them and who arrogantly
exercised hateful patronage privileges in the Church and still more
hateful legislative privileges in the selection of the subjects for taxation. The remedy, thought the early Whigs, was shorter Parliaments and the inclusion of the middle class in the parliamentary
system ; and it was to farther these objects that Thomas Hardy, a
native of Falkirk, founded the London Corresponding Society in
1791. Other Societies were founded about the same time, notable
among them being the "Society for Constitutional Information "
and "The Friends of the People," the latter having a membership
subscription of two and a half guineas, and announcing that one of
its objects was to " counteract the more radical tendencies " of the
other societies. In 1789 the Whig Club of Dundee had congratulated the National Assembly of Republican France, and hoped
"that the flame you have kindled will consume the remains of
despotism and bigotry in Europe " ; Lord Lauderdale had been in
Paris during the upheaval there, and although he boasted (or
perhaps because he boasted) "a studied contempt of general
opinion " had harangued the mob *pour la liberte ;* Lord Sempill offered
the French Soldiers of Liberty 6000 pairs of shoes ; Lords Buchan
and Daer were swirled into the new enthusiasm ; and the fall of the
Bastille had been celebrated by public dinners at Edinburgh, Dundee and Glasgow. But the excesses of the French revolutionists
scared off the aristocratic Whigs, and the Reform movement in
Scotland fell into the hands of the younger lawyers and the mercantile class. For a time the sun shone upon their campaign. The
Corn Law of 1791, by giving bounties to exporters of corn and imposing duties upon imports, the proclamation against seditious writings,
the Government's opposition to democratic change in municipal
administration, the repeal of the Test Act, the abolition of the slave
trade, all combined to fan the flame of revolt. Riots broke out all
over the country ; in Edinburgh the mob was uncontrollable for

P

three days, hissed and stoned the Dragoons, threw dead cats at the City Guard, and smashed the Lord Advocate's windows, and a hastily summoned force of marines and soldiery could only secure order by firing upon the rioters ;* from Portsoy in the north, where the people celebrated the anniversary of the French Revolution by the firing of cannon, to Langholm and Duns in the south, where the Toll Bars were smashed ; from Lanark where the hereditary provost was shot at and his orchard wrecked, to Aberdeen, where a tree of liberty was planted amid great rejoicing—everywhere there was tumult, disturbance, and a shaking of the chains.   The scared spies of Lord Dundas, who at that time was "managing" Scotland, reported doleful things to their master ; in Dundee the general disposition of the people was "very bad," and the lower classes were violent for reform ; Perth was "a dangerous place " ; Montrose was "very violent," and in many villages the discontent found vent in effigy-burning of the great Dundas himself.   Thomas Paine's pamphlet, "The Rights of Man," though officially suppressed as seditious, was openly hawked in the cities, and, since advertised by suppression, had been translated into Gaelic, and was spreading rapidly through the Highlands.   Men read how, in France, manhood suffrage followed the payment of two sous in taxes, how nobility and tithes were abolished, how game laws were not harsh, and how chartered towns and monopoly commerce had disappeared ; and when in addition to all the ferment thus caused, the harvest of 1792 failed, and a famine swept the industrial districts, we can imagine the set of circumstances in which the Friends of the People Societies were formed in Scotland.†

The great organiser of the agitation was a young Edinburgh advocate, Thomas Muir, who five years before had been expelled from Glasgow University for siding with a professor who was being victimised for his advanced opinions.   Muir had written squibs against some of the reactionary members of the University Senate, and they, in turn, made things so hot for him that he was compelled

---

Scots Magazine, 1792, pp. 256, 307.

†For accounts of these societies and the Botany Bay tragedies, which closed the careers of the early political martyrs, see *Scotland and the French Revolution*—Henry W. Meikle (1912) ; *The Awakening of Scotland*, 1747-1797—W. L. Mathieson (1910) ; the volumes of the *State Trials* for the period ; Lord Cockburn's *Examination of the Trials for Sedition in Scotland* ; the *Forward* newspaper from December, 1911, to March, 1912 ; *Fighters for Freedom*—W. Stewart ; *Radical Pioneers of the Eighteenth Century*—J. Bowles Daly ; " Report of the Committee of Secrecy of the House of Commons," presented by Mr. Secretary Dundas, 15th March, 1799 (Stirling Lib. Pamphlets, vols. 57 and 84) ; Lord Cockburn's *Memorials of His Time* (113-117) ; *The Martyrs of Reform in Scotland*—A. H. Millar.

to abandon his studies for the kirk, and betake himself to Edinburgh to study law. Muir was a born rebel, and gathered about him everyone who had sympathies with the French Revolution, as a magnet attracts iron filings. He rose rapidly in his profession; his rooms were the reform centre in Edinburgh; and during his frequent visits to his father's home at Huntershill, near Glasgow, and in the performance of his duties as an elder of Cadder Parish Church, he did not fail to propagate his faith in democracy, and to organise associations and clubs for the overthrow of the existing political tyranny. It was he who organised a meeting of the middle classes in the Star Hotel, Glasgow, on the 30th day of October, 1792, for the purpose of forming a Friends of the People Society in the city which should co-operate with the London Society in demanding "equal political representation and shorter parliaments"; it was he who conceived and organised the Convention of the Reform Societies for the December following in Edinburgh; it was he who framed the Convention's standing orders; it was he who denounced leaders, and congratulated the Convention upon paying little attention to leaders; it was he who insisted, despite the frantic pleadings of the milder conventionists, upon reading the treasonable address from the revolutionary society of United Irishmen; it was he who toured the weaving districts and addressed the mobs at Kirkintilloch, Kilmarnock, Paisley, Lennoxtown, and innumerable other places; it was he who, though declaring himself meantime no Republican and setting his face steadily against riot and insurrection as being "more likely than not to harm the people's cause," inspired the three hundred delegates at the Edinburgh Convention to conclude the proceedings by standing, and holding up each his right hand, take a solemn oath to live free or die. Suddenly the Government swooped down upon the agitators. Dr. James Anderson, Editor of the Edinburgh *Bee*, was haled before the Sheriff for his sympathies with the French revolutionists. James Tytler, an Edinburgh chemist, who had written a pamphlet urging the non-payment of taxes till Parliament granted manhood suffrage, and who declared that "all unrepresented classes were robbed and enslaved," was cited for sedition in January, 1793, and, disappearing in time to America, was outlawed, the Canongate Society of the Friends of the People promptly undertaking the maintenance of his wife and family.* Three Edinburgh printers—Morton, Anderson, and Craig—for drinking in a canteen a toast to "George the Third and last, and damnation to all crowned heads," and for advising the soldiers present to join the Friends of the People, as thereby they would get bigger wages, were given nine months' hard labour and ordered to find security

---

*Tytler had edited "The Historical Register," and had founded no fewer than five periodicals.—*Scot. Hist. Review*, 1904, p. 147.

for three years. An Edinburgh writer, Callender, fled in time, but his bookseller got three, and his printer six, months' hard labour. Callender is said to have reached the United States and to have been the founder there of the Yellow Press. A Mr. Muir received by mistake a letter from Kirkintilloch intended for Thomas Muir regarding the distribution of pamphlets, some of which described Parliament as "a mere out-work of the Court, a phalanx of mercenaries," and others referred to the House of Commons as "a vile junta of aristocrats"; the clue was followed up, and Thomas Muir was arrested. He was granted bail, and left for France to plead with the Revolutionaries there not to commit regicide, as the guillotining of Louis XVI. would damage greatly the cause of reform in other lands. Muir intended to be back in time for his trial, but the outbreak of hostilities between England and France delayed him, and on his landing at Stranraer he was arrested as a fugitive from justice, and, loaded with chains, was taken to Edinburgh to face Lord Braxfield and a picked and packed jury. Thomas Muir knew that his fate was sealed; the aristocrats glared at him from the jury box; brutal Braxfield whispered to a juryman: "Come awa', Maister Horner, come awa', and help us to hang ane o' thae damned scoondrels!" the Lord Advocate triumphantly declared, as he pointed to Muir, "This is the man . . . whom I most wished to get hold of." Yet, Muir, though aware of his doom, spoke bravely in his defence for three long hours, paying less attention to the Government touts and mean, despicable pension-hunters like the Reverend Thomas Lapslie of Lennoxtown, who tried to swear his life away, or to the poor servant lassie from his father's house who was bribed against him, or even to douce, honest David Dale and his other friends whose convenient forgetfulness and shortness of memory in the witness box nearly drove the Lord Advocate frantic with rage—he paid less heed to the trial or to its incidents than he did to the great cause of human liberty for which that day he was spokesman. A brilliant, eloquent address! For years afterwards it was the favourite piece of declamation in the schoolrooms of the United States of America; and even to-day the printed record of it shines out from the musty volumes of the State Trials, a beacon on the dark hilltops of the distance. "As for me" he concluded:

> "I am careless and indifferent to my fate. I can look danger and I can look death in the face, for I am shielded by the consciousness of my own rectitude. I may be condemned to languish in the recesses of a dungeon, I may be doomed to ascend the scaffold; nothing can deprive me of the recollection of the past—nothing can destroy my inward peace of mind arising from the remembrance of having discharged my duty."

But Braxfield had no bowels of compassion, no dim glimmering notion that the eloquent man in the dock before him was the greatest

Scotsman of his day, and that he, Braxfield, would pass into history with Pilate for the deed he was about to do. Braxfie'd was was but the representative of the landowning class, whose monopoly grip upon the State had been challenged and disturbed ; and here, before him, was the challenger, in his power. In the summing up from the Bench Landlordism spoke :

"Is the panel guilty of sedition or is he not ? Now, before this question can be answered, two things must be attended to that require no proof. First, that the British Constitution is the best that ever was since the creation of the world, and it is not possible to make it better. For is not every man secure ? Does not every man reap the fruit of his own industry and sit safely under his own fig tree ? . . . Then Mr. Muir had gone among ignorant country people making them forget their own work, and told them that a reform was absolutely necessary for preserving their liberty, which, if it had not been for him, they would never have thought was in danger. I do not doubt that this will appear to the jury, as it does to me, to be sedition. The next thing to be attended to is the outlawry. Running away from justice— that was a mark of guilt. And what could he be doing in France at that period ? . . . and he pretends to have had influence with these wretches, the leading men there. And what kind of folks were they ? I never liked the French all the days of my life, and now I hate them. . . Multitudes of ignorant weavers. . . . Mr Muir might have known that no attention could be paid to such a rabble. What right had they to representation ? I could have told them that Parliament would never listen to their petition. How could they think of it ? A Government in every country should be just like a corporation, and in this country it is made up of the landed interest which alone has a right to be represented. As for the rabble who have nothing but personal property, what hold has the nation of them ? What security for the payment of their taxes ? They may pack up all their property on their backs, and leave the country in the twinkling of an eye, but landed property cannot be removed."

So runs the official report of the summing up, but it has been Angli-cised, for we know that Braxfield habitually spoke in braid Scots. And it was followed by a verdict of guilty and a sentence of 14 years' transportation to Botany Bay, and an expression of high judicila opinion that a public whipping ought to be added. Even the jury of landowners were astounded and were contemplating a petition for mitigation of sentence, when an alleged threat of assassination from some of Muir's followers fired their class hauteur, and the proposal was dropped. The brutality of the treatment given Muir was the subject of debate in Parliament, but only two Scots members could be found to vote for a re-trial, and it was in vain that Fox shouted "God help the people who have such judges ! " So Thomas Muir, the first political prisoner from Scotland for the penal settle-ments, went first to the hulks and then to Botany Bay, the man-o'-war sent by the French Directory to rescue the prisoner *en route* failing in its object. Muir's subsequent history reads like a page from fiction. Rescued from Botany Bay and its horrors by a ship fitted out for the purpose by President George Washington o the United States ; wrecked on the western coasts of North America ; taken by a Spanish schooner to Vera Cruz, thence to Havannah, and finally, as prisoner of war sent to Spain ; when near Cadiz, the Spanish ship encountered a British frigate, and Muir, who fought desperately for the Spaniards, lost an eye and a cheek-bone ;* then imprisoned in Spain, and later, by special request of Napoleon Buonoparte, liberated as a French subject ; feted at Bordeaux, and his portrait, "Le célébre Thomas Muir," everywhere on sale ; enters Paris like a conquering hero ; is subsidised with French Government money, and begins the concoction of schemes for the invasion of Britain ; but his frame had been wrecked and he died in January, 1799, and was buried at Chantilly. He had given his life for political democracy in the land of his birth ; perhaps had he known that the Scots people would value their franchises so lightly that they would hand them over regularly at election times to Braxfield's class—had he forseen that, perhaps he had spared himself his sacrifice !

Meanwhile the judicial outrage upon Muir had not only infused a new determination in the breasts of the reformers but had roused thousands of the working class to a virulent pitch of class hatred. Braxfield was kept busy. John Elder, bookseller, Edinburgh, and Wm. Stewart, merchant, Leith, were indicted for publishing a translation of the French Declaration of the Rights of Man, "which," they said, "is agreeable to sound reason and common sense," and for issuing medals bearing treasonable inscriptions, inasmuch as they declared that "the nation is essentially the source of all sovereignty." Stewart disappeared before the day fixed for his trial, and the case against Elder was dropped. Robert Burns, down in Dumfries, was plainly told by his superiors in the Excise that the Government regarded him as a disaffected person and had taken careful note of the fact that he had sent carronades to the French revolutionaries, and that he had publicly given the toast : "Here's the last verse of the last chapter of the last Book of Kings." Not only so, but it was officially known that the poet had taken some part in a theatre riot in Dumfries when the loyal strains of "God Save the King" were drowned with cries of the French *Ca Ira ;* and he had sent two poems and a somewhat injudicious letter to Captain Johnstone who had launched out in his *Edinburgh Gazetteer* on the side of the reformers. This letter almost resulted in Botany Bay for Scotland's greatest singer, and, in truth, good men did go there for less.

" Go on, sir. Lay bare with undaunted heart and steady hand that horrid mass of corruption, called Politics and Statecraft. Dare to draw in their

---

*P. Mackenzie's *Life of Thomas Muir*, p. 39, *et seq.*, and *Reminiscences*, part. i.

native colours those ' calm thinking villains whom no faith can fix ' whatever be the shibboleths of their pretended party."

The letter being arrested in the post, Burns was warned, and, as he said, "having a wife and little ones," he decided to lie quiet ; but not for long, evidently, as in April, 1793, we find him writing to Erskine of Mar that he has three sons :

"with souls ill-qualified to inhabit the bodies of *slaves*. Can I look tamely on and see any machination to wrest from them the birthright of my boys— the little independent Britons, in whose veins runs my own blood ? No, I will not ! should my heart's blood stream around my attempt to defend it."*

Meanwhile the legal machinery was busy. James Smith and John Mennons of Partick were indicted for holding a public meeting there and demanding manhood suffrage. Smith disappeared, and was outlawed, and the case against Mennons was dropped. Captain William Johnstone, the owner and editor, and Simon Drummond, the printer of the first independent Scots newspaper, were arrested for making a laughing-stock of Lord Braxfield by faithfully reporting him, an offence which even Lord Cockburn, the Whig historian of a later day, could not forgive. The *Edinburgh Gazetteer*, says Cockburn, was a "vulgar, intemperate, popular organ," and that description summates and crystalizes the real attitude of Whiggery to the radical wing of the reformers. "Vulgar and intemperate " because it was "popular," "vulgar and intemperate " because it asked not only the rights of citizenship for merchants and traders but for all men, poor as well as rich. And what was the offence of the *Gazetter ?* Faithful, accurate reporting of Braxfield, if you please. Here it is, the libel, rescued from the silence of a century and a quarter :

"The Reformers talk of liberty and equality ; this they hae in everything consistent wi' their happiness ; and equality also. However low born a man may be, his abilities may raise him to the highest honours of the State. He may rise to be Lord Chancellor, head o' the law ; or he may rise to be Archbishop of Canterbury, the head o' the kirk ; and tak precedence o' a' ranks but the bluid-royal. What mair equality wad they ha'e ? If they hae ability, low birth is not against them. But that they hae a richt to representation in Parliament I deny. The landed interest alone should be represented in Parliament, for they only hae an interest in the country. In God's name, let them gang. I wish them not to stay ; but I deny they hae a richt to representation in Parliament. I only mainteen that the landed interest pay all the taxes. The shoon, I alloo, are dearer by almost a half than I remember them, owing to the additional taxes on leather which the exigencies of the State require ; but it is not the mechanics and labourers who pay that tax, but the proprietors o' the land ; for I remember when I could pay a labourer with half the sum I can do now. I am therefore of the opinion that the present constitution is the best that ever existed."

*See *Life and Works of Burns*—Dr. Robert Chambers : Wallace's Edn., vol. 3, pp. 379-386, 413-5.

Johnstone indeed proved that he had not seen the "copy," being under medical treatment for an eye trouble at the time, and had nothing whatever to do with the particular issue complained of ; but he was convicted of general Reform wickedness, was sentenced to three months' hard labour, and bound over in a security of £500 —a security which the Crown lawyers unsuccessfully attempted to impound at a later date when Johnstone again mixed himself up with the second Convention of the Friends of the People.   Drummond, the printer, was also given three months' hard labour, and ordered to find £100 security for his future "good behaviour."

During all this turmoil the "lower orders" seem to have been imbibing "dangerous" notions about an equality of property, and this appears to have added to the venom with which the political reformers were assailed by the Government and its judicial tools. Everywhere landowners, parish ministers (with a few honourable exceptions, like the Rev. Mr. Dunn of Kirkintilloch), sinecure possessors and hunters, and sycophants of all kinds, rushed into associations for "preserving Liberty and Property against Republicans and Levellers," and passed frantic resolutions in support of the Government.   The Rev. Thomas Somerville of Jedburgh sought to convince his parishioners that the landlord's lot was not a happy one, and that Society was ordered wholly for the welfare of the poor, by declaring (probably with his tongue in his cheek) that :

"families of the lowest fortune are not debarred like the Indian cast from ascending and mixing with the higher orders of Society. On the contrary, while the rich and the noble languish under the stagnation of a stationary and determinate pre-eminence, a peculiar source of hope and animation is open to men of humble station in the higher gradations of rank and fortune, to which they may aspire by cultivation of genius, exertions of industry, and success in adventure."*

The Leith merchants, in public meeting assembled, declared that our constitution, civil and religious, was "the happiest that the course of human affairs ever produced among men," and that it was "the subject of admiration among surrounding nations "; the people should avoid the agitators, who were but designing, disappointed, and discontented men.   The "Heritors and Inhabitants of Culross," for whom the Earl of Dundonald signed, pledged their lives by resolution "against all Republicans and Levellers, and that we will defend our properties against all plunderers who may attempt to rob us upon principles of equity."   The "respectable inhabitants " of "Campsy" met to declare that reformers were "infidel and senseless " (the hand of the Reverend Lapslie is there !).   At Kirk-Newton, East Calder, and Paisley the respectable inhabitants simi-

Observations on the Constitution and Present State of Britain.

larly met and similarly resolved. The Glasgow Tories issued a pamphlet proving that the existing Government was progressive since it had just removed the tax upon families which kept female servants, and since it now named its judges for life and so made them more independent.* Great reforms were thus coming gradually and without rebellion, declared the heritors and minister of the parish of Crawford Douglas. The Rev. James Hall of Lesmahagow spoke strongly from his pulpit against the "seditious murmurers" of his congregation, and Principal Hill of St. Andrews University, the Rev. Stevenson M'Gill of Eastwood, the Rev. Porteous of Glasgow, Divinity Professor Hunter of Glasgow University, and other prominent "divines" preached manfully and regularly from the text : "Meddle not with them that are given to change ! "

But the aristocrats and their lackeys meddled anxiously and earnestly, and well indeed they might, for Dundee had taken to open processions led by men with flaming barrels on their heads ; the sailors at Aberdeen and Leith indulged in a prolonged strike which, to the shame and disgust of the ruling caucus, was only settled after a Provost had humbled himself by acting as arbiter and granting concessions ; the colliers, "influenced by some new notions," refused to work ; the farmers were "wild for reform ; " conventions of delegates from political societies met in Edinburgh, and, led by able men threatened the whole fabric of aristocracy ; Scotland was on the verge of Revolution, and Braxfield and his band of legal assassins in Edinburgh, being aware of that fact, assigned themselves the task of extirpating with despatch every reform leader. Muir lay awaiting the hulks in August 1793 ; a month later he was joined by Thomas Fyshe Palmer, a Unitarian minister whose offences were numerous, having not only issued treasonable literature and been in close association with dissatisfied weavers in Dundee, but had stirred up Corn Law riots, demanded universal suffrage, and openly announced his opinion that the House of Commons had joined the coalition against the people, and that "our little liberty is fast setting, we fear, in the darkness of despotism and tyranny." The next victim for transportation was William Skirving of Strathruddy, a dour, determined, able and energetic man, upon whom, after Muir, had fallen the secretaryship of the Friends of the People Conventions; he had invited delegates from England and Ireland for the formation of a British Convention, pledged through a secret Emergency Committee to take joint immediate action should the Government pass a measure suppressing public meetings and free speech, or suspend the Habeas Corpus Act. That British Convention was held, many delegates attending, Messrs. Gerald, Margarot, and Sinclair, representing London, a Mr. Brown representing Sheffield, Hamilton

---

Publications of the Glasgow Constitutional Association, 1793.

Rowan, Butler and Dr. Drennan representing the United Irishmen ; and on 5th December, 1793, it was dispersed by a strong force of police led by the Lord Provost of Edinburgh. But Skirving re-summoned the delegates for the succeeding night. They met in a joiner's shop in "Lady Lawson's Yaird," where Rankeillor Street now stands ; Gerald was in the chair, and as the Sheriff-Substitute surrounded them with policemen carrying lighted torches, he (Gerald) rose dramatically and cried, "Behold, the funeral torches of Liberty!" Next night Skirving was in the open street making a formal protest to the citizens against the illegal dispersion of the Convention, and announced his intention of re-summoning another Convention at an early date. Alas ! no more conventions would William Skirving, the bonnet laird of Strathruddy, call together, for Braxfield sentenced him to 14 years' transportation to Botany Bay, and he was so brutally treated *en voyage* by the convict-ship master that he died shortly after landing. Gerald, the most eloquent prisoner ever brought to the Bar in Scotland, and whose oration in defence was widely published in pamphlet form,* was also transported for 14 years ; and a similar fate awaited Margarot who had advised armed associations. Margarot, by the way, was the only one of the transported reformers who lived to serve his sentence and return again to Britain ; years afterwards we come across traces of him interesting himself in a weavers' strike at Glasgow, a fact which goes far to disprove Lord Cockburn's story that he died a Tory. Scott, the Editor of the *Edinburgh Gazetteer*, who had advocated the assassination of tyrants, had to flee the country ; and Sinclair, the English delegate to the Convention, saved himself by turning Government spy. Fletcher, the advocate, who had the temerity to champion the reformers in Court, fell under dire suspicion and his wife was "credited with guilloting hens in her backyard in order to prepare for higher game " if the reformers should succeed in gaining the upper hand.

The savage sentences already noted, though they succeeded in destroying the effectiveness of the Friends of the People Society, fanned the insurrectionary flame all over the country ; pamphlets poured forth in hundreds, one of them, bearing Margarot's indictment, having an edition of 100,000 ; Shelley, the poet, begged the exiled patriots to accept "one Briton's grateful song"; Burns' *Tree of Liberty*, and Wilson the Paisley weaver poet's *Address to the Synod of Glasgow and Ayr* became immensely popular ; riots broke out in the manufacturing centres ; loyal plays in Edinburgh theatres were disturbed by shouts of "God save the people " and "The sow's tail to Geordie ! " Pikes were forged everywhere ; many hundreds of weavers in Paisley had purchased arms ; barracks had been erected

---

*A pamphlet entitled " Gerald : a Fragment," formed the chief propaganda asset of the Society of United Scotsmen several years afterwards.

for the sole purpose of segregating the soldiers from the "disloyal people," but vigorous attempts were made to "educate" the soldiery in "Reform principles ; " a New Convention was summoned for England, and "delegates of humble rank" were selected at Perth, Strathaven, and elsewhere ; and the discovery of an insurrection organised by the secret executive of the Reformers was reported to the House of Commons on 6th June, 1794. Thousands of working-men were assured that political reform was but a preliminary to a more equitable distribution of property, and this fact, with the French Revolution stories still fresh, and gaunt, hungry, working-class orators holding forth that "a king ought to be sacrificed to the people once in every hundred years," kept the middle classes in a state of nervous excitement and caused the "loyalists" to form companies of volunteers and stigmatise all who refused to join them as "Black Nebs." And that these middle class fears were not wholly imaginary is apparent from the dying confession of Robert Watt, who was hanged at Edinburgh for high treason in 1794.* Watt, who with Samuel Downie, an Edinburgh silversmith, the latter afterwards pardoned, was condemned to be hanged, drawn and quartered for treason, had originally been a Government spy, but becoming convinced that the Reformers had truth and justice and reason on their side threw himself enthusiastically into the more revolutionary side of the struggle and himself organised and planned a great rebellious upheaval. He was on the Committee of Ways and Means of the Friends of the People Society, and employed a staff of agitators and organisers, among whom were Archibald Wright, an Edinburgh weaver ; John Craig, in Perth ; and one John Fairley, to tour the country and get everything in readiness for a replica of the French Revolution. The Government got wind of the preparations (as well they might when there was scarcely a blacksmith's shop in the country not busily engaged in the forging of pikes), and Watt was arrested, and hanged on the 15th day of October, 1794, the efforts to lay hands upon his staff of touring organisers, though kept up for a considerable time, proving fruitless, in consequence of the dogged refusal of the members of the political societies all over the country to remember anything when questioned. Watt's dying confession gives us a clear idea of the organising ability which had lain behind the projected revolution :

" The first movement was intended to be made in Edinburgh, London, and Dublin ; while every town throughout the Kingdoms was in readiness to act according to the plan, on the very first notice, which was to be given by

---

The Declaration and Confession of Robert Watt Attested by Rev. Dr. Baird, Principal of Edinburgh University, and Rev. T. S. Jones of Lady Glenorchie's Chapel—Bell & Bradfute, Parliament Close, 1794 ; also *State Trials,* vols. 33 and 34.

couriers despatched by express.   The nature of the plan was this :—A body of men to the number of four or five thousand were to be assembled in a place to be fixed on.   These were to be armed with pikes, guns, grenades—to be properly divided with proper leaders.   In regard to Edinburgh, these were to be placed at the Gaelic Chapel, head of the West Bow, Tolbooth ; or head of the High Street—that when the soldiers came out they might be sur rounded.   In order to prevent bloodshed, means were to be used to gain as many of the soldiers as possible over to the other side.   The regiment was to be enticed out by companies.   But previous to this the Magistrates, Lords of Justiciary, Commander-in-Chief, and many others in town to be selected, were to be apprehended, but to be treated in every respect becoming their station in life and detained until the mind of the ensuing Convention or, rather, Parliament was known.   There was no intention whatever to put any to death ; but if found guilty of oppression and injustice to the patriots, to share a similar fate with them, viz., transportation.

" The manner in which the soldiers were to be induced to leave the Castle was by means of a letter either signed by the Lord Provost or Commander-in-Chief, previously in custody, ordering the Commandant to send a company without any ammunition (?) to a fire that was to be kindled in St. Andrew's Square, under the pretence of its being a house on fire ; and the said company to be secured and disarmed in the meantime.   The most of the remainder to be drawn out in the same manner by means of fires kindled in succession in the other quarters of the city.

" But in case they either could not be drawn out of the Castle, or had obtained information of what was a-doing, they were to be compelled to surrender, by being deprived of victuals—the incarceration of the Commander-in-Chief and the influence of party among themselves favouring the the plan.

" The Public Houses and the Banks were to be secured, by placing proper persons as centinels (?) over them till the proprietors and managers appeared next morning.   The same were to be consulted with by qualified persons to be previously chosen.   The property of such persons either residing in town or country deceived (?) inimical to liberty, in the hands of the Bankers was to be sealed up, but what was necessary for their maintenance till their fate was known.

" The Post Office was to be taken possession of, as thereby all intercourse would be cut off between such as were hostile to the patriots, while the channel of information was left open for them. . . . All this was to be accomplished about 6 or 7 in the morning, then couriers despatched, troops marched and proclamations previously prepared were to be issued to the landholders and officers under Government as did not cordially unite with the patriots in their views and designs, not to go above three miles beyond their dwelling-places under pain of death—to farmers not to conceal any export of grain ; to shipmasters not to carry any person coastways without giving intimation of the same . . . to the nearest Justice of the Peace that the same might be called to an examination under a similar penalty—to such persons as were authorised to levy men to deliver up their commissions and men to persons to be nominated, under the same penalty."

When all this had been accomplished, a long catalogue of legislative and administrative abuses, already carefully considered and drawn up, had to be presented to the King along with a demand that he should dismiss his advisers and dissolve Parliament, "the same to be replaced by men in whom the people could confide."

It is difficult to guess the motives which impelled Watt to emit such a declaration. Perhaps he thought the mere publication of the plan would inspire fresh public thought in a similar direction ; perhaps he had it bribed out of him by promises of a remission of his sentence ; it may be that he was anxious finally to clear his character before men from the taint of his early career as a Government spy. But whatever his motive, the immediate result was a fresh frenzy among the aristocrats, a fresh turning of the screw upon all persons suspected of reform opinions, and the total disappearance of the Friends of the People Societies. Yet scarcely had the Government got the ablest of the middle class reformers transported or hanged and their sympathisers cowed and silent, than the agitation broke out in a stratum lower down and in a more dangerous and virulent form. The Friends of the People had concentrated upon Manhood Suffrage and Shorter Parliaments ; now new secret societies, called United Scotsmen, composed mostly of working-men, were demanding universal suffrage, voting by ballot, payment of Members of Parliament, annual elections, and breathing fire and slaughter upon the Corn Acts, the Game Laws, Spies and Informers, the Mutiny Act, and the Impress Service. A succession of bad harvests manured the ground for them ; corn, which in 1792 was 43s. per quarter, in 1796 was 75s. per quarter, and in March of the year 1795, as Lord Cockburn tells us, the people of Edinburgh were reduced to so great a state of famine that one-eighth of the entire population had to be kept alive by "charity." As was to be expected, sporadic riotings took place, corn mills were raided and so on, but a definite organised political movement was lacking, and the sinecurists carried matters with a high hand. We read, for example, of how six baker boys of good character, simply for creating a noise, were arrested on the streets of Edinburgh by one of the clerks to the Town Council, and of how they were transported without trial, or charge, or conviction.* The poor had neither liberty nor guarantees of life. Every expression of desire for change, every aspiration towards democracy, had been crushed ; and even the dissatisfied middle-class feared to assist in opening the flood gates of political reform when the news came of the later excesses in France. True, there had been a Society of United Scotsmen formed publicly in Glasgow in 1793,† but it was a mild, loyal, ineffective sort of literary society ; and in 1796 one Alexander Leslie, an Edinburgh bookseller, had been engaged in the surreptitious dissemination of seditious literature ;

---

*Cockburn's *Memorials*, p. 98.

†*Glasgow Advertiser*, November 11-15.

but it was not until the Militia Ballot Act was enforced, compelling all men between the ages of 19 and 23 (except married men with more than two children and those who were already Volunteers) to submit to a ballot as "candidates" for the Army, that the blaze broke out again and the secret and dangerous United Scotsmen Societies were formed.

The Army was hated by the working-class. Was it not the brutal engine used by the vile aristocrats to crush aspiring democracy both at home and abroad ? ; and the Volunteers who were at that time paid and deliberately organised "to wean the popular mind from French politics" were boycotted and shunned. Yet the Government needed more troops for its continental wars, and the offer of bounties to recruits not bringing the required number of enlistments, the fiat went forth that 6000 men were to be forcibly commandeered through a militia ballot. Upon the parish school-masters who kept the registers of birth and upon whom devolved the duty of drawing up lists of the men eligible for the ballot, fell the chief odium. At Carstairs the mob burned the schoolhouse and secreted the parish registers. In the Prestonpans and Tranent district the colliers' wives and children, led by a woman called Joan Crookston, sacked the village schools and drove the schoolmasters into hiding. Indeed, the discontent at Tranent finally developed into a formidable riot, when the County authorities, supported by troops of cavalry, appeared to "draw" the victims. At Tranent a resolution had been publicly and unanimously passed by the people and presented to the Ballot Officers, declaring that :

"Although we may be overpowered . . . and dragged from our parents, friends, and employment, to be made soldiers of, you can infer from this what trust can be reposed in us, if ever we are called upon to disperse our fellow-countrymen or to oppose a foreign foe."

But the resolution was unheeded ; the Riot Act was read, and on the 28th of August, 1797, the Cinque Ports Cavalry, well plied with drink, enjoyed a massacre of men and women, shooting, spearing, slashing and riding down a populace armed only with stones ; the troops attacked innocent non-rioters travelling quietly on the high-way, and killed men among the cornfields as if they had been part-ridges. In all, eleven persons were officially listed as "slain," but the bodies of others were afterwards discovered at the reaping of the harvest ; many were wounded. For its comments upon this butchery the *Scots Chronicle*, then supposed to be under the editorship of an able Whig advocate, Morthland, who figures frequently in the Reform agitations of the period, was haled before the courts by Mr. Cadell, the deputy Lord Lieutenant, but the evidence of fact was so strong and so clear, that though the servile scoundrels on the Court of Session found Mr. Cadell entitled to damages, the House of Lords, on appeal, reversed the decision, and ordered Mr. Cadell to pay expenses.*

Riots against the Militia Ballot similarly broke out at Kirkintilloch, Freuchie, Strathaven, Galston, Dalry, and in several parts of Aberdeenshire. For participating in a riot at Eccles, in Berwickshire, Braxfield sent four men to Botany Bay. But up in Perthshire it seemed as if the Revolution had veritably come at last, for 16,000 men and women had risen at the call of Angus Cameron, a wright in the Parish of Weem, and were marching and countermarching, surrounding Castle Menzies, and forcing Sir John of that ilk to repudiate the Militia Ballot, compelling even His Grace the Duke of Atholl to swear he would not operate the Act until the "general sentiments of the country were made known," and despatching a regiment of rebels to Taymouth Castle to clean out the armoury there. Cameron, who is said to have been a great orator, rode on horseback at the head of his forces, and the organising genius of the rising, one James Menzies, junior, a merchant in Weem, appears to have made strenuous efforts to find equipment for a squadron of cavalry. But the people were without arms, and when the Government rushed sufficient troops to Perthshire, Cameron's army melted away, and he and Menzies were captured without much difficulty.† Latterly they were indicted for sedition, but on being granted bail, Cameron disappeared and the case against Menzies dropped.

Beginning in the Spring of 1797, the Society of United Scotsmen spread rapidly. New members were charged sixpence on entry, and the monthly subscription thereafter was threepence, and these sums were spent on travelling propagandists who went everywhere, even into small villages where only three or four members could be secured. No branch was permitted to enrol more than 16 members, and when that number was reached and new applicants for membership were discovered, another branch was formed. Each branch met regularly and secretly, and when two or more branches in one parish met it was usually for the purpose of selecting a delegate by ballot for the county meeting, which was held every six weeks. Every possible precaution against spies was taken. Whom had been selected by ballot as the delegate to the county meeting no one knew but the branch secretary and the delegate himself ; at the county meetings delegates to the National Conventions were selected by ballot, but the place at which the Convention was to be held was not disclosed even to the delegate fortunate in the ballot ; all he got was a slip of paper from the County secretary, bearing the name

---

History of Tranent—P. M'Neill, Chap. xi.

†*State Trials*, vol. 26, pp. 1166-1170, and Meikle's *Scotland and the French Revolution*, pp. 181-192.

of a man, called the "Intermediary," who would in due time call
for him and conduct him to the National Convention. The National
Convention met every seven weeks, usually, it has been suspected,
in Glasgow or its neighbourhood; and these frequent meetings
were considered necessary, for the United Scotsmen believed that
"the emancipation of the country was at no great distance, when
they should rally round the standard of liberty," and with schoolhouses ablaze and Cameron sending a rebel call through the Gaelic
speaking districts, and desperate misery and hunger everywhere and
with law scorning Irish immigrants coming into the towns, there
seemed some basis for the belief. Yet these United Scotsmen did
not underrate the dangers which beset them. They remembered
the fate of Muir and Gerald and the other Friends of the People;
indeed, among them were men like George Mealmaker, the Dundee
weaver, who had narrowly escaped Braxfield's net when the Rev.
Thomas Palmer had been arrested and transported, and men like
James Kennedy, who had been assistant secretary to Skirving, and
who had spent the past five years as a Reform Organiser with the
noose never far from his neck. So it behoved them to be careful.
Even in the National Convention itself there was a secret committee
of seven, and every member of the organisation was required solemnly
to take the "Oath of Secrecy."

> "In the awful presence of God, I —— —— do declare that neither hopes,
> fears, rewards, nor punishments shall ever induce me, directly or indirectly,
> to inform or give evidence against any member or members of this or similar
> societies for any act or expression of theirs done or made collectively or
> individually in or out of this society in pursuance of the spirit of this obliga-
> tion. So help me, God."

Members were also bound by oath to endeavour "to form a brother-
hood of affection among Britons of every description," to strive for
equal political franchises for "all the people in Great Britain"
(Query: Had they already conceptions of womanhood suffrage?)
and to support afflicted and unfortunate fellow members. In some
districts—Dundee, for example—the entrance fee was only one penny,
but everywhere the subscriptions seem to have been sufficient to
pay the local delegate 1s. 6d. per day, plus travelling expenses, when
away from his work and on the Society's business. The most
elaborate precautions were taken to ensure secrecy. The secret
salutation was: "I love light," to which the Faithful replied: "I
hate light," and thereafter a sign was made by joining the two hands
together, mixing the fingers and turning the hands with palms out;
the answer to this was made by placing one hand on the back of
another and mixing the fingers. A rising was being carefully planned,
with the burning of the houses of the rich as a first step, but the
organisation was suddenly exposed by spies whom the Government

had wormed into one or two of the Societies, and such leaders as did not fly in time were arrested. Of course the policy of keeping the branches segregated and secret preserved the identity of thousands of members from the ken of the police, and no amount of browbeating or bribery could possibly induce extensive discoveries. In Dundee, George Mealmaker, a weaver and a leading agitator in the East of Scotland since the days of the Friends of the People, for administering illegal oaths and for hawking about seditious literature, was transported for 14 years by a jury composed entirely of the people whose houses had been marked down for burning. During his trial his poor fellow members, though harassed and savagely bullied, lied desperately, declaring that they did not know him ; and one witness, David Douglas, a wright in Cupar, went himself to prison rather than give incriminating answers to questions designed to injure Mealmaker.*

In the same year (1798) Robert Jaffray of Stirling, for proposing in a public house the toast : "The old dog's head cut off, the bitch hanged, and all the whelps drowned," meaning thereby, as the Crown Prosecutor declared, "death and destruction to the king, queen and royal family," got 3 months' imprisonment, and was bound over for one year. David Black, a weaver in Dunfermline was outlawed, and James Paterson, another weaver from the same town, was transported for 5 years by a jury carefully picked to contain eleven " landed gentlemen." Both had corrupted soldiers from their allegiance to the king, administered United Scotsmen oaths in Nicol's tavern and rejoiced publicly at the Irish rebellion.

No farther prosecutions for sedition are given in the records until June 1800, when William Maxwell, a sergeant in the Militia, was sentenced to seven years' imprisonment for distributing among the soldiers a pamphlet entitled " A Catch." In 1802 Thomas Wilson, a Perth weaver, was given two years banishment for spreading sedition among the farm labourers, but from 1799, the date of the inception of the combination laws, down to 1824, when these laws were repealed working class struggles seem to have been chiefly industrial. It was a period of savage, untrammelled commercialism, with, especially in the textile trades, machinery displacing hand labour, and a steady decline in weavers' wages. Political agitations there must have been, as, for instance, when Major Cartwright, a brave and honest English aristocrat, toured Scotland agitating for universal suffrage; he got great audiences, but no newspaper dared take an advertisement or give a report of his meetings; and at every extraordinary wages or employment crisis the clamour was not only economic

---

*According to the Report of the House of Commons Committee of Secrecy, other two United Scotsmen were charged—Dyer and Archd. Gray. The latter escaped to Hamburg. There is no farther trace of Dyer.

Q

but was clearly suffused w th aspirations towards democracy in government, and the belief is apparent that political inequalities were regarded as the prime cause of economic disaster . Still the immediate struggles were for bare bread, and universal suffrage and annual parliaments would require to wait until hunger was satisfied. Another powerful factor in allaying the political discontent was doubtless the boom given to certain iron and other trades by the huge demand for war munitions and stores created by the campaigns against Napoleon ; and we observe that after the suppression of the United Scotsmen there are no arrests for sedition until 1817, when the French peace had been signed and the commercial boom had been shattered by the cessation of the Army demands. To this slump in production, with its inevitable unemployment of thousands of artisans, and the return to civil life of a large number of soldiers, there were added two frightfully bad harvest seasons and rumours of open rebellion in Ireland. Suddenly and spontaneously great open-air demonstrations were held and excited mobs hearkened again to perfervid orations upon the necessity of capturing the administration of the country. There had been meal riots all over Scotland in the black winter 1800-1801 ; but the shameful Corn Law Act of March 1815, which prohibited the importation of foreign corn so long as the home price was not greater than 80s. per quarter, produced a desperate frenzy in the manufacturing districts. Wages had been steadily falling, now there was a widespread unemployment, and here was the Government deliberately raising the price of cereals in the interests of the landlord class ! So the workers turned again to politics for relief. If only they could force themselves on to the voters' rolls, all would be well, for henceforth they would make the laws to suit the working folk !

At Glasgow, Perth and Dundee there were riots. Major Cartwright, from the English Hampden Club, came again and harangued hungry multitudes at Greenock, Ayr, Renfrew, Paisley, Stirling, Alloa, Dunfermline, Newburgh, Perth, Cupar Angus, Forfar, Brechin, Crail, St. Andrews, all along the eastern coast to Aberdeen and back again to Glasgow via Fifeshire. Everywhere societies and committees for the furtherance of universal suffrage were formed, and by the end of the year 1816 there was scarcely a village in Scotland where there were not groups of men carrying on a vigorous propaganda of denunciation of "vile aristocrats," "corrupt governments," "liberty crushing French wars," "heavy taxes," "iniquitous corn laws"—all on a frankly class war philosophy.* The immigrant Irish rebels were in "the troubles"—the advanced left wing of them, almost to a man, and this fact must have caused the

---

*See, for example, article on " A Tarbolton Reform Meeting in 1816," in *Kilmarnock Standard*, 16th March, 1912.

Government some concern since it had bribed the Roman Catholic Hierarchy during the United Scotsmen agitation, evidently with a view to keeping the influence of the church activity at work in preventing the Scots-Irish from identifying themselves with the Scottish rebels. The bribes were given in 1798—£600 down, a promised yearly allowance of £50 to the two R. C. Seminaries, as well as a sum sufficient to make up the salaries of the priests to £20 ; in addition each of the Vicars-apostolic were to get £100 a year and their coadjutors were to get £50 a year, and "The profoundest secrecy had to be maintained regarding this grant from the public funds and even the Roman Catholic laity were kept in ignorance."* But the bribes had been in vain. The Irish rebel was a rebel still.

Again the Habeas Corpus Act was suspended and the jails were filled. The first trial of the new batch of which we have details is that of Alexander M'Laren, a weaver, and Thomas Baird, a grocer and bookseller of Kilmarnock. M'Laren had made a speech at a meeting on the outskirts of Kilmarnock town and Baird had caused it to be published in a fourpenny pamphlet. The indictment gives part of M'Laren's speech :—

" We are ruled by men only solicitous for their own aggrandisement ; and they care no further for the great body of the people than as they are subservient to their accursed purposes. . . . Shall we, I say, whose forefathers defied the efforts of foreign tyranny to enslave our beloved country, meanly permit in our day without a murmur a base oligarchy to feed their filthy vermin on our vitals, and rule us as they will ? No, my countrymen ! Let us lay our petitions at the foot of the throne, where sits our august Prince, whose gracious nature will incline his ear to listen to the cries of the people, which he is bound to do by the laws of the country. But should he be so infatuated as to turn a deaf ear to their just petition, he has forfeited their allegiance. Yes, my fellow townsmen, in such a case, to hell with our allegiance."

M'Laren, in the course of his defence, declared that he had been working 15 hours daily for a weekly wage of 5s. ; but Lord Gillies, a Whig judge, despite the jury's recommendation to his clemency, sent both accused to prison for 6 months and ordered them to find a three years' security for good behaviour. In the same year (1817) the law officers endeavoured to have the Rev. Neil Douglas, one of the old Friends of the People Conventionists, now a dour, deaf, doited man, incarcerated for preaching in an Anderston Church about the licentiousness of the Regent. The case, however, broke down through the stupidity of the Government spies ; and two Glasgow weavers, Andrew M'Kinlay and John Campbell, were released after Campbell had exposed in open court the fact that the Advocate Depute and the Sheriff of Edinburgh had attempted to

---

*Meikle's *Scotland and the French Revolution*, p. 197 ; Bellesheim's *History of the Catholic Church in Scotland* (Hunter Blair's translation, iv., 256).

bribe him to give evidence against his friend M'Kinley. Had M'Kinley been convicted the authorities were prepared with a long list of Glasgow rebels ready for the dock on a similar charge, that of secretly pledging themselves to strive for "the elective franchise at the age of twenty-one, with free and equal representation to annual Parliaments." One William Edgar, and one John Keith of Glasgow, stood trial at the same time, but the records do not state what befel them.* James M'Ewan, M'Dowal Pate and John Connelton, other three illegal oath administrators in the Tradeston division of Glasgow, disappeared and were outlawed.

Meanwhile unemployment, particularly in the textile trade, was spreading, and the mobs were becoming desperate. Paisley, Dundee and Glasgow became veritable hotbeds of sedition, and Lord Cockburn says that he never knew the people to hate the Government so fiercely as they did in 1819. The intensity of this hatred was due not only to hunger and the corn laws, but to "the new and severe laws made for preventing popular meetings and punishing popular excesses," and by the reports of the savagery of the cavalry in its conflict with the mob at Manchester. The working class reformers, now called Radicals, to distinguish them from the philosophic Whigs, who had no thought of allying themselves with the emaciated weavers, or of clearing out the Tory aristocracy at the pike-end—the working class reformers began for the first time to have a regular press to focus their grievances. Cobbet's pamphlets, *Wooler's Gazette,* and *The Black Dwarf* had a wide-spread circulation, and in October, 1819, a rebel sheet, *The Spirit of the Union,* appeared in Glasgow. Only eleven issues were allowed to appear before Gilbert Macleod, the Editor, was arrested and the paper suppressed. It was a live, rebel sheet, and in its pages we get a glimpse of the real red-hot agitation which was being carried on. Great Reform demonstrations at Rutherglen, Ayr, Kilsyth and Paisley ; chairmen wearing the red cap of liberty during the proceedings ; 30,000 people present at an open-air demonstration at the Clayknowes, Glasgow ; Neilston musicians arrested for playing "Scots Wha Hae" at a meeting at Meikleriggs, without first securing permission from the authorities ; a great meeting at Airdrie, 6000 people present ; Government spies attempting to inveigle a Strathhaven blacksmith into the forging of 500 pikes ; but he "smoked" them and refused ; the parish minister of Newmilns refusing to baptise children who had been given reformers' names ; arrest of Glasgow newsvendors, charged with circulating seditious literature ; two thousand people attend a meeting at Broxbrae, Stirlingshire, to

---

*Peter Mackenzie, in his *Exposure of the Spy System* (1833), says that they were not proceeded against after the break-up of the Government's case over M'Kinley (p. 25).

denounce the Manchester massacres ; officials of the Airdrie "Union Society," Messrs. Rodger and Miller, arrested, and report of the great reception given them by their townspeople upon their release on bail ; denunciations of military outrages on the people, and accusations that they were deliberately stirring up the people to rebellion ; and then, the last issue on the eighth day of January, 1820, a brief announcement that the Editor lay in jail and that a newspaper would be started by friends ; its title would be *The Scottish Patriot*. Macleod was first charged with contempt of Court for his comments upon the trial of George Kinloch of Kinloch, a Forfarshire proprietor, who had made a seditious speech to a mob at Dundee. The "sedition" had lain in the fact that he had told the people to hold out for Annual Parliaments, Universal Suffrage, and Voting by Ballot. He himself had been anxious to face the charge (he rather fancied himself as an orator, and he had an idea that if he were given an opportunity of expounding his principles from the dock he would "convert" the Judge), but his Counsel knew it was Botany Bay for him, and urgently advised him to flee, leaving his bail money behind. This he reluctantly did, and lived as an outlaw in Paris until he was pardoned some seven years later; he was the first member for Dundee in the Reformed Parliament after 1832. For his comments upon the Kinloch case, Macleod had first to undergo four month's imprisonment ; and being really a dangerous man, a case against him for sedition was quickly furbished up, and before his first sentence had expired, he was hurried off to Botany Bay on a five years' sentence. His trial was a remarkable exhibition of the judicial savagery of the times, and of the extraordinary funk in which the ruling classes perpetually lived since the days of the French revolution. He was charged with publishing a "writing from an intense and contemptuous Gallowgate orator" in which appeared a statement that "the people's only prospect of relief lay in their correcting their own wrongs," and for declaring that the people should refuse to pay taxes, and that those who joined the Yeomanry, particularly in Lanarkshire, "should be publicly named and watched." The Lord Advocate excitedly asked the jury, "What should become of us all if he were not convicted," and the jury found the prisoner guilty, but added a recommendation to clemency in sentence—a recommendation which, though reinforced by a powerful speech from Jeffrey, prisoner's Whig Counsel, against transportation with its hulks, its distance, its dangers, its hopeless duration, its degradation and its desolation, found no kindly reception on the Bench. Five years' transportation was the sentence, Lord Pitmilly declaring that if he gave any other in such a desperate case "he could never lay his head upon his pillow in peace again." Poor Macleod died in exile before his term was completed.

Meanwhile, Lord Liverpool's Government, or at anyrate, the active members of that Government, Lords Sidmouth and Castlereagh, were busily engaged appointing spies and *agents provocateurs*, who should go about among the leaders of the militant section of the working class, encourage them in treasonable oaths and acts and generally provide victims for the scaffold. It was no concern of their Lordships that poor innocent weavers would be lured to destruction, that their wives would be made widows and their children fatherless. Their concern was class policy, statecraft, the convincing of the middle-classes that the flames of another "French Revolution" were ever ready to burst forth, and that all the property interests ought to abjure electoral reform and support in office and in power the landed gentry and their tools.* The charges against M'Kinley and others (see *ante*) had been instigated by Alexander Richmond, an ex-weaver who had been involved in the cotton spinners "conspiracy" of a few years before, and who had entered the service of Mr. Kirkman Finlay, M.P. for Glasgow,† and Lords Sidmouth and Castlereagh, not only as a Government spy, but as a deliberate instigator and fabricator of plots and conspiracies among the people. But Richmond was discovered ; the people *knew ;* and as he himself went about continually in fear of assassination, he was useless to the murderous ruffians who ran the administration of the country. There were, however, no lack of bribeable emissaries, and the louder they seem to have roared "Revolution" to the poor, the more likely they themselves seem to have been in the pay of the Government. Diligently did Alexander King, the spy weaver, and his associates organise little coteries of hungry weavers and urge them to the taking of treasonable oaths ; sedulously did they spread the information that a great rising was being planned in London, and that the King's hated ministers were to be murdered ; eagerly did they whisper that soon the signal would come for a rally ; and faithfully did they transmit to the police authorities the name of every honest leader and rebel spirit who heeded their lures. And then, when all was ready for the "Radical Rising," the treasonable placards were posted by Government agents, and the poor workmen dupes were rushed to their doom. How astonished must the middle class citizens of the

*The whole Machiavellian, scoundrel knavery of these *agents provocateurs* and their paymasters during the years 1816-1820 was unmasked in the *Narrative of the Conditions of the Manufacturing Population and the Proceedings of Government which led to the State Trials in Scotland*, etc., by Alexander Richmond (1824). Richmond himself was a spy, and, disappointed with his remuneration, published his exposure as a retaliation on his paymasters. See also Peter Mackenzie's *Exposure of the Spy System Pursued in Glasgow during the Years* 1816-1820 " (1833).

†Finlay later admitted he had paid three spies to stir up premature revolt.— *Glasgow Evening Post,* 28/9/33.

West of Scotland have been on Sunday, the second day of April, 1820, as they wended their way to church, and saw staring at them from every hoarding and gable-end the Call to Arms which had been posted during the night time by the Government spies !

"ADDRESS TO THE INHABITANTS OF GREAT BRITAIN AND IRELAND."

"Friends and Countrymen," ran the address with a wealth of floral adjective, "we have been reduced to take up arms for the redress of our common grievances."

"Our principles are few, and founded on the basis of our constitution. . . . Equality of rights (not of property) is the object for which we contend, and which we consider as the only security for our liberties and lives. . . . Liberty or death is our motto, and we have sworn to *return home* in triumph or return no more ! Soldiers, shall you . . . plunge your bayonets into the bosoms of fathers and brothers ? . . . Come forward, then, at once, and free your country and your king from the power of those that have held them too, too long in thraldom. . . We declare inviolable all public and private property. . . In the present state of affairs, and during the continuation of so momentous a struggle, we earnestly request of all to desist from their labour from and after this day, the 1st of April ; and attend wholly to the recovery of their rights, and consider it as the duty of every man not to recommence until he is in possession of those rights which distinguish the freeman from the slave, viz., that of giving consent to the laws by which he is to be governed. We, therefore, recommend to the proprietors of public works, and all others, to stop the one, and shut up the other, until order is restored, as we will be accountable for no damages which may be sustained, and which, after this public intimation, they can have no claim to. And we hereby give notice to all those who shall be found carrying arms against those who intend to regenerate their country, and restore its inhabitants their native dignity, we shall consider them as traitors to the country and enemies to their king, and treat them as such.—By order of the Committee of Organisation for forming a Provisional Government, Glasgow, April, 1 1820." Britons,—God—Justice—the wish of all good men, are with us. Join together and make it one good cause, and the nations of the earth shall hail the day when the standard of liberty shall be raised on its native soil."

For forty miles around Glasgow this placard was simultaneously exposed, even on the Church doors. In Glasgow we are told, great crowds stood on the streets all day, with "lowering expectation" on their faces. Nobody seemed to know what would happen. Perhaps the thought common to most was that the local bastilles should first be smashed. Had not the Habeas Corpus Act been long suspended, and were not hundreds of good and true Reformers already lying behind the bars, uncharged with any offence ?

Various accounts are to be had of the scenes which followed, the Whig writers minimising and the Tory writers exaggerating the "crisis," while honest Peter Mackenzie, the only Radical historian of the period who has come down to us, confines his somewhat polemical narrative to Glasgow. We shall therefore follow the register of events as they were supplied to the Duke of Hamilton by an anonymous writer whose concern seems chiefly to have been to impress his Grace with the widespread nature of the disturbances, and to furnish a plenitude of details not furnished elsewhere.* For months before there had been open drillings among the workmen, and at every blacksmith's shop the manufacture of pikes had gone on in undisguised feverishness. Then, suddenly, came the proclamation of the first of April, which, the writer admits, was openly denounced by the Radical leaders as an effort of "Government spies to trap the people." On the succeeding day (Monday) "almost all the labouring population abandoned their work," and by the afternoon the employers were so terrified that they discharged the few black-legs who had run the gauntlet of the strikers, and closed down their factories. "From Girvan to Stirling, 70 miles from east to west, and from Dumbarton to Lanark, 40 miles, all the manufacturing, mechanical and labouring population became, or were thrown, idle, and prepared for the most desperate designs." Paisley was thronged night and day from Monday to Thursday by huge, sullen, expectant crowds, waiting impatiently on the signal from England. Every blacksmith's and carpenter's shop was taken possession of by "strangers," and the manufacture of the munitions of war was carried on, files being hammered into pikes and bullets made in great quantities from lead stripped from house-roofs ; clegs (darts, lead pointed) to annoy cavalry, were issued to the older men ; pikes sold from 7d. to 1s. each ; and, "drilling in large bodies, at all hours, was open, extensive, and undisguised. Parties to the amount of many hundreds drilled during the day time in the Green of Glasgow, at Dalmarnock Ford, at the Point House at Tollcross, and many other places without interruption." Scouting parties, usually large in numbers, scoured the farmhouses searching for fire-arms, and "none durst oppose their projects," though in one affray at Foxbar, near Paisley, the leader of a Radical band was killed. The "respectable" families fled from Paisley in terror ; suburban families left their goods and chattels, and crushed into Glasgow for safety ; all country carriers were stopped, and "workmen openly and boldly declared to their masters that they would work no more till the Government of the country was changed."

It was a large scale, though spy-fomented strike for political freedom—a strike which the bulk of the participants expected would end in a bloody but successful revolution.

---

* "A Letter to His Grace the Duke of Hamilton and Brandon, detailing the Events of the Late Rebellion in the West of Scotland."—By " A British Subject " (John Smith & Son, Glasgow, 1820).

Still no news came from England that London had been captured ; and the Government troops were being swiftly moved to points of vantage, waiting on the Radical *coup d'etat.* Local eruptions were disregarded ; the Government was in no hurry ; the troops could bide their time until a Radical army of ill-armed, ill-disciplined rebel weavers had been gathered, and then, in one great carnage, would be taught a lesson that would serve to humiliate two or three generations of the discontented common folk. The Rifle Brigade, the 7th and 10th Hussars and the 80th Regiment, lay ready for service at Glasgow ; cavalry were massed at Hamilton, Airdrie, Stirling, and Kilsyth ; volunteers, sharpshooters and yeomanry were poured into Paisley, Falkirk, and Bathgate. The aristocrats were leaving nothing to chance. Meanwhile, the excitement in Glasgow was intense. Frenzied orators urged that the city should be set on fire ; on the Wednesday night threats were made that " there would be five hundred Percivals in Glasgow before the following dawn . . . they had groaned long enough under oppressions, and would submit to do so no more"; while some spun theories about the repudiation of the National Debt, others marked out the houses owned by "loyal " Volunteers, and promised the inmates an early burning when the signal should come ; armed bands of from four to six hundred people paraded the streets, cheering the French Revolution, and the leaders had considerable trouble on the Wednesday night in preventing a rash and ill-considered attempt to capture the barracks and the prisons. In Ayrshire, the people, especially at Galston, Newmilns, Sorn and Stewarton, were "seething with revolutionary madness." At the last named place, Orr, the cobbler, had proclaimed the new constitution with a drawn sword in his hand, and it was openly promised that "all would be equal. If they succeeded no person would have to pay any rent. All would dwell rent free. . . . Weavers were known to cut the webs from their looms, lock up their shops, and declare they would work no more." Nor was the rebellion confined to the towns. "Nearly all Renfrewshire," we are told, "the largest portion of Ayrshire, part of Dumbartonshire, and much of Stirlingshire, was ready to rise." Of the 40,000 weavers on the west coast "every one would join that (the Radical) side of the question " ; it was a class war "to degrade the high and exalt the low," or, as it was more accurately put by the *Edinburgh Review,* "a war of the rich against the poor—of the Government and the soldiery against the people."* At the Sandyhills near Cambuslang, great midnight meetings took place, and so great "was the turn-out that in one village, within a short distance of Glasgow, not a man was left, except an old man, a pensioner. In other villages every man was out." Young men who volunteered

---

Edinburgh Review, No. 64, p. 301.

for the Army of the Provisional Government were to be paid at the rate of 1s. per day from the outbreak of actual hostilities ; food supplies were organised ; but still no word came from England. Had the Provisional Government which had issued the placards, failed ?

Meanwhile the Government spies were active, and on the Wednesday morning they had succeeded in inducing a party of about eighty Glasgow men to set out upon a march upon the Carron iron works at Falkirk, where it was said an army from the English Provisional Government would shortly arrive, and assist the Glasgow men in seizing the Government cannon there. Eighty ill-armed men, some of them Castlereagh's spies, marched via Condorrat and Castlecary, straight into the arms of the 10th Hussars ! Among them was Andrew Hardie, a young weaver and ex-army sergeant ; at Condorrat they were joined by John Baird, the village smith ; with one excuse after another, the spies melted away ; and finally, the expedition, reduced to fifty in number, arrived at Bonnymuir.* What followed is well-known. How the troops dashed upon them, and how they crouched behind a dyke and fought desperately until almost every man of them was wounded and some were killed, and how nineteen weary and wounded men that night lay prisoners of war in Stirling Castle. That was the great battle of Bonnymuir, and in thanksgiving, Law and Order and Privilege rang its kirk bells, published special issues of its Court *Gazettes*, and offered *Laudes Deo* to Heaven. In Glasgow, for a time, the wildest stories were rife. French vessels had landed arms and money on the Ayrshire coast : the English rebel army had grown to 80,000 men : the Carron iron works had been captured, and the Government troops defeated ; but the truth soon leaked out, and the perfidy and the treachery of the spies who had urged the march upon Falkirk, becoming known, none durst trust his neighbour ; the wildest rebels were most suspect, and in this depression and suspicion the "revolution" fell to pieces in a single night.

Down in Lanarkshire, the Government emissaries had hocussed a detachment of Strathaven radicals into a premature march for the rendezvous at Cathkin Braes, near Rutherglen ; and how proudly they marched, these poor weavers and labourers, with their leading banner, "Strathaven, Liberty or Death ! " and how terrible must have been their disappointment as they lay all night in the cold and wet waiting, waiting, for the other battalions which never came ; in the morning, their spirit broken and knowing they had been duped and were now marked men, they wisely scattered for home.

---

*Hallowed for many a day afterwards in the popular ballad, "Dark Bonnymuir." See *Glasgow Herald*, 16/3/59, "The Story of Bonnymuir," by Peter Mackenzie.

In Paisley, blood had been shed, for the military had fired upon the mob ; and a riot took place in Greenock, where the jail was stormed and, despite magistrates, military, and volunteers, five Radical prisoners were set free, six men being killed and twelve wounded in the struggle. Still, beyond a local spluttering or two, all was over—meantime. The middle class had rallied to the aristocracy ; a "bag" of Reformers had been secured, and Sergeant Hullock was sent up from London to see that Jeffrey and the other Whig counsel who might defend them would be matched fully in legal subtlety, for Castlereagh wanted a "lesson on the scaffold " ; but worst of all, the workers as a class had ceased to believe in themselves ; the trail of treachery and spying led everywhere, and one's next door neighbour might be in police pay. The desperate men disappeared—no fewer than 72 "wanted " rebels flying from the Bridgeton district of Glasgow—but under bogus names they shot up again in other districts, with a fiercer revolutionary temper, with new secret oaths, and with terrible threats of assassination upon spies and informers.

Meanwhile, John Baird and Andrew Hardie, two of the spies' victims, were sentenced to be hanged, drawn and quartered—this barbarous proceeding being specially intended to impress the workers —and eighteen others, James Clelland, Thomas M'Culloch, Benjamin Moir, Allan Murchie, Alexander Lattimer, Alexander Johnstone, Andrew White, John M'Millan,* David Thomson, James Wright, Andrew Dawson, William Clarkson, Thomas Pike, Robert Gray, Alexander Hart, John Barr, William Smith, and Thomas M'Farlane, were transported for life. Twelve years later, during the general rejoicings following the King's assent to the Reform Bill, Andrew Hardie's poor old mother stuck up in her humble window a card bearing the words :

> " Britons, rejoice, Reform is won !
> But 'twas the cause
> Lost me my son."

Alas, the Reform that was won had left Andrew Hardie's class still outside the franchise !

Another victim of the dastard machinations of a conscienceless aristocracy was a poor old man, James Wilson, a hosier of Strathaven, who had been induced to march with the Strathaven rebels on that wild, mad night-march to the Cathkin braes. He had carried a banner with the words, "Scotland free or a desart ! Strathaven Union " inscribed upon it, and he was charged with, among other iniquities, *imagining the death of the king.* and one of the chief witnesses against him was Sheriff Aiton of Hamilton, who confessedly

---

*We trace M'Millan in Van Diemen's Land in 1835.—*Glasgow Evening Post*, 30/4/35.

had attempted to bribe men into forging pikes so that they should be liable for a charge of treason. And they hanged the old man on September, 1820, in the Jail Square of Glasgow, with thousands of cowed working men gaping at the murder, and lifting no hand in rescue ; and they buried him in the paupers' burying ground at the Cathedral as a last mean mark of contempt, but he did not lie there long, for in the night time his daughter and his niece tore up the clods and gathered the remains of the old martyr back to Strathaven again, within easy sound of the loom at which he had toiled for half a century.

During the succeeding ten years there was little political agitation among the working class, although "the old weaver orators" were occasionally on the stump. The spy system and the persecutions had broken or scattered the leaders, and widespread unemployment and poverty had destroyed any popular mass initiative for the franchise, while the Whig or rising Capitalist party contrived to gather to itself a propaganda blended of Catholic Emancipation, exposure of aristocrat sinecures, and lavish promises of franchise extension. The Whig case was overwhelming, and Sir Walter Scott himself admitted that reform could not be much longer delayed, though the gentry "are needy and desire advancement for their sons, and appointments and so on." No one seriously pretended to justify an electoral system wherein, according to Sir James Gibson Craig, the Sheriff in Bute, Mr. Bannatine, got the writ, named the day, and issued the precept for his own election ; at the meeting he was the only freeholder present, so he voted himself to the chair, read himself the oaths against bribery, appointed himself clerk of the meeting, proposed himself as candidate, and declared himself elected. If he had any sense of humor he must have capped the farce by proposing to himself a vote of thanks, and duly acknowledging the same amid his own loud cheers ! In August, 1830, the Revolution in France gave the Whig agitation a fillip. Demonstrations took place in Edinburgh and Glasgow. "Old Craig, the Radical," on Glasgow Green threatened revolution. John Neill, a Paisley weaver, moved amendments at Whig meetings, demanding cancellation of the National Debt ; town's meetings everywhere passed resolutions for political reform. In March, 1831, a Reform Bill was introduced. It was proposed to enfranchise £10 tenants in Burghs—"a safe class," said Lord Cockburn, the Whig leader—and £10 owners in Counties. Yet, in favour of this bogus reform the Whigs induced 100,000 people to assemble and march through the streets of Glasgow ! At Edinburgh the Tory Lord Provost was stoned, and when the House of Lords rejected the Bill working men carried black placards dedicated to the memory of Muir, Gerald and Palmer. At the Lanark hustings anti-reformers were stoned, and the military charged the crowd after the Riot Act had been read ; the Dumbartonshire Tory Candidate, Lord Graham, lay trembling below a bed while an angry mob searched for him ; at Ayr the successful Tory candidate, Colonel Blair, had to be escorted from the town by Dragoons ; at Jedburgh over 1000 Hawick weavers, described as "sad blackguards," gave Sir Walter Scott a rough time of it; the Trades of Glasgow called for the abolition of the House of Lords, and for the arming of the people ; stackyard fires broke out at Bo'ness and Montrose, and in Berwickshire ;* Lady Bute was stoned in her carriage on the streets of Rothesay at the instigation of Mr. Thom, the Whig owner of the Rothesay cotton mills (who extensively employed children of five years of age). In vain did the King by Proclamation order the Political Unions to dissolve ; they grew in strength and audacity, and, as transpired later, their Whig organisers were prepared, if need be, to foment rebellion.† In March, 1832, the Buccleugh family was hissed on the streets of Hawick : in May, dummy crowns were smashed on Glasgow Green, the factories were shut by placard order, and 120,000 people marched in procession carrying banners bearing the words : "Liberty or Death," "By the bones of our fathers we shall be free," "Better to die in a good cause than live by slavery," "He that hath not a sword let him sell his garment and buy one,"and similar injunctions. At Glasgow a permanent committee sat ; at Greenock and Falkirk strikes took place, bells were tolled, Callendar House was stoned ; at Dumfries there were riots, and an attempt to storm the jail ; and all over Scotland there was an organised refusal to pay taxes. And then came the "great" Whig Reform Bill of 1832 (still so described in our school history books !) enfranchising only £10 tenants and upwards in burghs, and £10 owners and £50 tenants with a 19 years' lease in counties, and carefully and deliberately leaving the working class outside, and indeed cancelling some fancy franchises as at Preston in England under which the workers had hitherto secured the rights of citizenship. The working class, which had provided the body of the agitation, had been betrayed by the capitalists to whom had been entrusted the leadership of the Whig party.‡ The Whigs sneered at the very claim of votes for "the dregs of the populace." On the report stage of the Bill, Jeffrey, the Whig Lord Advocate, proposed to make a £600 ownership of landed or heritable property a necessary qualification for a County M.P., and a £300 ownership a necessary qualification for a burghal representative.§ And scarcely

---

*Glasgow Courier, 5/1/32 and 3/4/32.

†Letter from Lord Melbourne's Secretary in 1832 to Colonel Napier.—*Scotsman*, 11/10/48.

‡Justin M'Carthy's *History of Our Own Times*, vol. i., p. 80.

§This proposal, said the Tory *Glasgow Courier* (28/6/32), " was introduced by the Whigs . . . . for the purpose of extinguishing their Radical stipendiaries."

had the Bill passed ere the Whig Government denounced the political unions as inconsistent with "good government," and expressed a wish that they would dissolve—a wish that was replied to in the industrial centres with a howl of indignation. The Whig leaders declared against the ballot and against shorter Parliaments, and Lord John Russell said the question of Parliamentary Reform had been settled, and that to push reform any farther would be a breach of faith ! A "votes for women " petition excited nothing but hilarity, and a frankly indecent discussion in Parliament.

The popular discontent thus engendered, and to which the Chartist movement fell heir, was at first organised by the Political Unions, who drew up " pledges " which they sought to impose upon all candidates for Parliament. Would the candidate, if elected, resign his seat if he found himself hostile to any measure desired by the majority of his constituents ? Was he in favour of free trade, burgh reform, abolition of Church patronage, the municipal franchise, work for the unemployed, abolition of the Corn Laws, vote by ballot, and limitation of hours of labour for children in factories ? And was he against slavery in the Colonies, and the farther alienation of Crown lands without wide advertisement ?* The Whigs mostly refused to answer to the satisfaction of the Unions, and their meetings were frequently interrupted and destroyed. At Edinburgh the *Trades Examiner* was started "for the working classes against all opposing parties."† An ex-soldier, A. J. Hamilton, appears to have been appointed as travelling organiser for the Unions. Cobbet toured Scotland, prophesying that the Whigs and Tories would "coalesce to prevent farther reforms," and in the Ayr Burghs something of a sensation was caused by the appearance of Dr. John Taylor, "a leveller," as prospective parliamentary candidate. A remarkable man was this Dr. Taylor ; he founded *The Ayrshire Reformer*, and later, *The Liberator ;*‡ he had spent his twenty-first birthday in a French prison, and after being bankrupted by Kennedy of Dunure as a result of a libel action, he challenged that gentleman to a duel, and for doing so was imprisoned for two months at Ayr ; in 1836 he was Chairman of the West of Scotland Radical Association, and he played a prominent part among the Scottish Physical Force Chartists. When he first appeared in 1833, the Whigs were congratulating themselves that the Political Unions had died away,§ oblivious apparently to the fact that a sterner Radical feeling was

*Glasgow *Saturday Evening Post*, 21/7/32.

†*Scottish Notes and Queries*, 2nd Series, vol. 7., p. 37.

‡A Radical Chartist journal, published in Glasgow, in which the Cotton Spinners' Union had invested £1000. Lord Cockburn said that Taylor was the Cotton Spinners' " champion," and the *Liberator* was " a blackguard newspaper."

§Lord Cockburn's *Journal*, vol. i., p. 49.

fermenting. The Paisley weavers were petitioning Parliament for the household suffrage and vote by ballot, and were raising money for monuments to Wilson, Hardie and Baird, the political martyrs of 1820 ; the *Glasgow Courier* was reporting Radical denunciations of Whig hypocrisy, and Abram Duncan and Peter Mackenzie were addressing the Political Unions and calling upon the Whig Government to resign.* The Government opposed voting by ballot and an enquiry into the pension list ; it opposed Sir John Maxwell of Polloc (the handloom weaver's champion) in his efforts at legislative redress for the distress and starvation of half a million weavers and their dependants. In November 1834, twenty thousand people paraded on Glasgow Green, and the "Liberty or Death" banners were again unfurled. At the beginning of 1835, Lord Cockburn was writing that " . . . everything, not excepting the monarchy, is in danger." A general election, resulting in another Whig victory, was remarkable chiefly for the Whig hot air thrown off at the hustings to cover Whig treachery. Thus :

> " Let us hope that the sun which we trust will shine ere long upon the ruins of Tory power and the consolidation of our national liberties may touch, with a reviving smile, the vine-covered hills and valleys of classic Italy, and may send a ray to the bleak and frozen north, that so the Po, the Danube, the Vistula, and the Neva may soon roll their glad waters amid the sounds of joy and triumph from freemen, rejoicing in the light and the happiness of well-ordered systems of social liberty. (Loud cheers)."†

But it was not the Whigs who won : it was the Tories with the Duke of Wellington at their head, who were defeated. Two hundred thousand people demonstrated on Glasgow Green—"the Loyal Irish Reformers and United Labourers with a flag costing £10"—to hear the oratory of Dan O'Connell and the Rev. Patrick Brewster of Paisley Abbey, and George Mills (son of the Provost) who polled as a Glasgow Radical candidate over 900 votes against the Whig Lord Bentinck's 1995. By December, 1836, two trades unions, the Masons and the United Iron-moulders, had declared for "political action," and Feargus O'Connor and Dr. Taylor, Alexander Campbell and John Fraser of Johnstone were founding branches of "the National Radical Association of Scotland " to fight both Whigs and Tories. There was no longer trust among any section of the workers

---

Courier, 18/4/33 and 26/5/33.

†*Glasgow Evening Post and Paisley and Renfrewshire Reformer*, 24/1/35. Dan. O'Connell told the Trades of Edinburgh that " Many an Irish mother, while she hugs her babe to her breast and sings it to repose with an Irish air, will mix the noble strain with " Auld Lang Syne " or " Scots wha ha'e wi' Wallace bled," and as the accents lull her babe to sleep, will raise a prayer to God to bless the generous people who stood by Ould Ireland in her days of need."—*Ibid*, 19/9/35.

in the Whigs. Lord John Russell, the Whig Premier, on being asked to arrange that a deputation of working men should be permitted to present a petition to the Queen, agreed, but insisted that the deputation should come in Court dress, whereat there was great laughter in the Whig clubs, and press headlines of "The Great Unwashed Nonplussed!" * In July the Whigs fought an election not on social or political questions, but on the right or otherwise of the Queen to select her own chamber women. The Whigs had refused political reforms, they had banished Dorsetshire labourers for combining to raise wages, they had refused to have weaver's wages fixed officially by a Trade Board, they had made an attempt to destroy the Factory Act. And the urban workers flocked to the Radical Associations, and, as at Kilmarnock, instituted boycotts of Whig and Tory shopkeepers.

The year 1838 saw the rise of the Chartist movement; we find demonstrations at Edinburgh where speakers declare there are two parties, and two parties only, "the rich oppressors and the poor oppressed"; John Fraser begins *The Edinburgh Monthly Democrat and Total Abstinence Advocate,*† which after four issues gives way to a weekly *The True Scotsman*, and speedily secures a larger circulation than the Whig *Scotsman ;* the *Ayrshire Examiner* was also Chartist; if Parliament refuses to hearken to the unenfranchised, it declared the people "will abstain from all liquor and tobacco and thus cripple Government revenue." On Monday, 21st May, an estimated crowd of 200,000 demonstrated on Glasgow Green, seventy trades unions marched in procession, all public works were stopped; the Strathaven detachment proudly bore a flag that had been carried at Drumclog; Moir, a Glasgow tea merchant, presided, and there was much insurrectionary talk and threats of "a solemn and sacred strike from every kind of labour." The Whig and Tory press became alarmed, and denounced the doctrines of "the division of property and the summary abolition of the public debt . . . now the language of thousands and probably the creed of millions." True, the six points of the Charter drawn up by the Working Men's Association in London were purely political—universal manhood suffrage, annual parliaments, vote by ballot, no property qualification for candidates, payment of members, and equal voting districts—but most of the propaganda was avowedly socialistic and economic.‡ A first principle of the Working Men's Association was that "the man who

---

*October 5th, 1837.

†The first number has a letter from the father of Andrew Carnegie.

‡For the Chartist movement in Scotland, see Morrison Davidson's *Annals of Toil*; "History of the Chartist Movement," by R. G. Gammage; Files of the *True Scotsman* newspaper(in Paisley Mechanic's Library), and Files of the *Chartist Circular*.

evades his share of useful toil diminishes the public stock of wealth, and throws his own burden upon his neighbours." The *True Scotsman* steadily denounced the Factory system and demanded an eight hours day; Chartist shops and Chartist churches were common institutions, and the theories of Robert Owen permeated every platform utterance. Addressing ten thousand people on Monkston Moor (Fifeshire), Bronterre O'Brien, one of the greatest of the Chartist orators, declared—and it is a fair sample of Chartist propaganda—

" If God sent the rich into the world with combs on their heads like fighting cocks, if He sent the poor into the world with humps on their backs like camels, then I would say it was predestinated that the rich should be born booted and spurred, ready to ride over the poor ; but when I see that God has made no distinction between rich and poor—when I see that all men are sent into this working world without silver spoons in their mouths or shirts on their backs, I am satisfied that all must labour in order to get themselves fed and clothed . . . According to God's law none except those who have not worked themselves or whose fathers and mothers have worked, should benefit by the result of labour. Unfortunately, those who have not worked themselves, whose ancestors never have worked, have all the good things, while those whose fathers and mothers have worked hard and who themselves have all their lives worked hard, endure all the privations and sufferings which can be inflicted in this world. . . . .You produce annually 450 millions of wealth, and the idlers take 4s. 6d. a pound of it. They take nearly one-fourth, though they are only one in two thousand of the people. Next come the profit-mongers—those who make their fortunes by grinding the poor and cheating the rich ; that class who buy cheap and sell dear, who spoil the wholesome articles you have made, and distribute them to others—they take 7s. 6d. a pound of the wealth which you produce. . . Thus 12s. is gone before you have a pick. They promise you a paradise hereafter. You pay 1s a pound to the clergy for that, on condition they preach to you to be content with your lot and to be pleased with what divine providence has done for you. . . . This 1s. is not taken from the 12s. That would leave you without merit. Then they take 2s. 6d. a pound for their military forces—to keep you down. This leaves 4s. 6d. . . . . By God's help this system shall be changed before the year's end."*

Demands were made that the Navy should transport emigrants without charge, and that "all writings and mouldy parchments regarding land property tenure—mere instruments for lawyer pillage—be made a bonfire of." The Chartist movement swept over Scotland like a flame ; every village had its organisation, orators went everywhere taking huge collections from great crowds ; in bothy loomshop, and smithy there was a ferment of discussion over the respective merits of the physical force and moral suasion doctrines which, right from its inception, split the Chartist movement in twain.

---

*_True Scotsman_, 22/6/39.

R

In Scotland, Dr. Taylor and John Duncan led the physical force section, while the Rev. Patrick Brewster of Paisley, John Fraser (editor of the *True Scotsman*), who had "done" four months in a dungeon after the disturbances in the West of Scotland in 1819, and the Rev. Abraham Duncan of Arbroath led the moral suasionists. The moral suasionists did not object to fighting in self defence, but they feared that an organised rebellion would simply mean disaster. It is difficult to gather which section had the sympathy of the bulk of the Chartists. At the frequent debates, the physical force leaders seem to have carried the audiences, but the moral suasionists had the press.* Among the other leaders of the Scottish movement were, Bailie Hugh Craig of Kilmarnock, Messrs. Moir and Purdie of Glasgow, Dr. M'Douall of Newton Stewart, James Dodds of Melrose, W. G. Burns, Alex. Halley, Patrick Mathew, W. S. V. Sankey, and J (?) O'Neill from Lanarkshire. Bailie Craig was put up as candidate for Ayrshire, and went to the poll, securing only 46 votes; but the general practice was to nominate a candidate at the hustings, where he was allowed to deliver his election address, usually of an hour's length, to the assembled crowd, and secure the moral triumph of having him elected by a huge majority on a show of hands; the Whig or Tory opponent of course demanded a poll vote by qualification, whereupon the Chartist candidate, having few qualified electors to support him, withdrew his nomination. Other favourite methods of Chartist propaganda were the organisation of sudden runs upon the Banks, the commercial boycott of opposing shopkeepers, and the chalking of their premises; they had choirs who sang the third to the eighth verses of the xciv. Psalm, and "Fall, Tyrants, Fall!" They got up monster petitions to Parliament "for," as they said, "the last time," and they were preparing a "Sacred month"—a great strike—to begin on 12th August, 1839, when the Whig Government swooped down upon their Birmingham convention, and arrested and imprisoned the leaders. A period of repression followed. At Perth, five hundred special constables were sworn in and a house to house search for pikes and fire-arms instituted; Dan O'Connell organised coal-porters to attack Chartist meetings; everywhere it was sought to stamp out the Chartist organisation by intimidation and violence; and a political agitation, designed as a counter attraction to Chartism, was opened by the new Liberal party. "Repeal the Corn Laws!" was vigorously denounced by the Chartist speakers as a new "ruse to sunder the working classes." A great Liberal demonstration at Dumfries was nullified by a "Mr. Thomas Johnston, writer," who insisted on moving a somewhat verbose amendment,

---

*The Chartist press, by the way, insisted strongly upon the political and social evils of alcohol, and a favourite song at Chartist meetings was Neil Gow's "Farewell to Whisky."

"That this meeting can only consider the present agitation as to the Corn Laws as the offspring of a heartless faction to create division among the people, and as an insult to the intelligent masters and a bitter mockery to the working-men. That, understanding there is a body denominated Charterists, in organisation the most perfect, in determination the most stern, and in number the mightiest that ever yet appeared in this country, have resolved with singleness of purpose, and devotedness of life and property, at once to strike at the root of all and every abuse by means of a House of Commons created by Universal Suffrage, which shall, in truth and very deed, carry into effect the wants and wishes of the people. This meeting deems the present agitation touching the Corn Laws to be injurious and therefore resolves to discountenance the same."

In his speech in support of his amendment, Johnston said "What do the Factory Lords say ? . . . ' As corn is dear, wages are high : so are our goods : thus we are met with competition and thus our profits are injured : therefore reduce the price of corn and we shall reduce the wages, and thus our own profits will not be injured.'" At Hawick, Dalkeith, Kilmarnock, Leslie, Kirriemuir and Kirkintilloch, the Chartists carried their amendments to Free Trade resolutions at Liberal gatherings. The imprisonment of some of the Chartist leaders had only intensified the enthusiasm of the rank and file Chartists, and as each leader came out of gaol, he toured the country as a martyr, attracting great concourses of excited and frenzied men. At Glasgow, 200,000 people welcomed Dr. M'Douall and Messrs. White and Collins, and even in the remote Highlands, Julian Harney, travelling on foot, flared up the discontent in the villages.

In vain the Liberal press pleaded that " the laws are equal and just and the franchise will not raise wages." At the elections in 1841 the Chartists put up their own nominees at the polls, though few of them did more than deliver a hustings oration. Andrew Wardrop, a stocking-frame maker, was nominated at Dumfries ; Lowrey, the eloquent working man tailor from Newcastle, went to the poll at Aberdeen and secured only 30 votes ; Thomasson, a teacher, was nominated at Paisley ; at Edinburgh, Colonel Peyronet Thompson and Lowrey, the Chartist candidates won, on a hand vote, but did not go to the poll ; at Glasgow, George Mills, the Chartist son of a Lord Provost, polled 355 votes, but required 2729 to win ; in the Ayr Burghs, "the Chartist mannikin, Jack —, treated the non-electors to a speech;"* for Clackmannanshire, Roxburghshire, Fifeshire and Perth there were hustings candidates. At Kelso a mob burned an effigy of the Duke of Roxburgh amid shouts of "Here go the last remains of Habbie Kerr." At the polling booths, voters of Chartist sympathies voted Tory when there was no

---

*Glasgow Herald.

Chartist candidate, and by doing so succeeded in ousting sufficient Whigs to smash Lord Melbourne's Whig Government.* A petition to Parliament was organised in 1842. It included a request for Home Rule for Ireland ; but in Parliament the Charter had only 51 sympathisers, and its most vehement opponent during the discussion on the petition was Macaulay, the historian, who sat for Edinburgh, and who, with his relations, seems to have participated in the sinecures and the political jobs of the period. In the public press for 1843 we find references to the "noxious sect" of Socialists, whose "spouters" could assemble on Glasgow Green crowds of 3000 of "the idle and the thoughtless, who are the only class who receive Socialist doctrines with laughter instead of disgust" ;† but the political Chartist movement seems to have been temporarily snowed under by the Free Trade agitation and by industrial troubles. By May 1844, however, Chartism was again to the fore, and a young man, Henry Vincent, polled 98 votes at a bye-election in the Kilmarnock Burghs. At the hustings he received thousands of votes, while his opponents only received five or six votes each. In 1845-6 Bronterre O'Brien was explaining Land Nationalisation to huge Chartist audiences, and the greatest orator of his day, Ernest Jones, threw himself passionately into the fray. There was a potato famine and hunger, and the Duke of Norfolk fanned the unrest by going about with a curry powder of his own device as a charm against starvation. Free Trade demonstrations at Edinburgh were broken up by Chartists who addressed the public as "fellow slaves" and demanded work and food for the unemployed. A Government threat to call out the Militia by ballot was promptly answered in Glasgow with placards bearing the words, "No vote, no musket," and by unanimously carried resolutions in the City Hall denouncing "war under any circumstances" and expressing a resolve "to resist militia service by every means, denying the right of the Government to call upon the unfranchised classes to fight the battles of the aristocracy, or any battle except that of their homes, families and labour, when these were assailed . . . Until the principles of the Peoples' Charter were carried into law and the working millions recognised in the constitution, they would refuse to fight for its maintenance." Funds were raised for "passive resisters". The General Election of 1847 took place amid great industrial distress, which the Chartists exploited at the hustings. At Greenock John M'Rae was nominated but did not go to a poll. At Dumfries Wardrop proposed the Returning Officer—an excuse for a long Chartist oration ; similar tactics were adopted by the Paisley Chartist leader, Robert Cochrane ; at Aberdeen two working men nominated James M'Pherson, who

---

*M'Carthy's *History*, vol. i., p. 89.

†*Glasgow Courier*, 5/9/43.

addressed the crowd and won on a hand vote, but did not go to a poll ; in Fifeshire a well-known Chartist called Gourlay proposed himself as an excuse for a propaganda address ; the Liberal candidate at Dundee, who was hostile to the Factory Act, was frank enough to inform the audience that he "did not care a straw for their hissing."* As the distress and unemployment grew, so did the Chartist move-ment. A great conference in Edinburgh decided to found a new paper, the *Weekly Express ;* Samuel Kydd, ex-shoemaker and Arbroath Chartist, drew vast audiences to his denunciations of landlordism ; half of the manufacturing population, says Lord Cock-burn, was always hungry and listening to Chartist orators; if the Chartists succeed "the higher orders of electors must everywhere be swamped by the lowest."† And then, while the middle and upper classes were setting up a howl of protest against an increase of the income tax, came the news of the Revolution and the Commune in France. Instantly there was insurrection in the large towns. At Edinburgh a mob smashed lamps and windows ere they were dis-persed by Dragoons. At Glasgow wild riots, known for long after-wards as the Bread Riots, followed on Chartist incitements in the City Hall. The unemployed had demanded work and a minimum wage of 2s. per day, but the Magistrates had offered soup tickets instead, and when this report reached a crowd on Glasgow Green, a speaker had declared that "if they would give him 300 men he would go up the town and bring every man an 8lb. loaf or two 4lb. loaves." The mob then tore down the railings at Monteith Row, and thus armed, proceeded to raid and sack shops and stores ; ironmongers' shops were raided for guns and pistols—in one shop at the foot of Candlcriggs they got 50 guns—shouting "Bread or Revolution," they controlled the north side of the Clyde. On the south side they seized all the bread and gun shops. "Men and women were seen running in all directions with cheeses, aprons full of meal, boots, shoes, etc."‡ By night time the authorities had collected sufficient cavalry, infantry and special constables to face the rioters, and thousands of special constables were being sworn in. The mob smashed all the lamps, and the streets were in darkness, but the cavalry made successive charges in the High Street and Saltmarket area, and 150 prisoners were secured. Next day the factories were "struck " ; in Bridgeton soldiers were attacked, two men were killed and several seriously wounded. Soldiers poured in from Edinburgh, and after the cavalry, headed by the Sheriff, had charged and scat-tered a mass gathering on Glasgow Green, a barricade had been

---

*Argus, 5/8/47. Robert Owen was a candidate for an English constituency, but polled only *one vote*.

†*Journal*, vol. ii., p. 217.

‡See press of the period, particularly the *Scotsman* for 26/2/48.

destroyed in the Gallowgate, and the two leaders, Smith and Crossan, arrested, the rioting was over. There is no evidence that the rioting was anything else than a spontaneous outbreak by hungry and enraged men, still less that the Chartists had anything to do with its direction. Crossan, it is true, was down in Lanarkshire as an emissary endeavouring to stir up the colliers to insurrection, and one John Daly is reported to have addressed a meeting in the Lyceum theatre, declaring that "prayers and petitions were the weapons of slaves and cowards, arms were the weapons used by the free and the brave. They could best help Ireland by keeping the army in Scotland," but there is no trace of premeditated and organised insurrection. A large proportion of the arrested men was Irish, and many were deported home. Upon the men brought to trial in Glasgow the sentences were savage; Crossan got 18 years; eight men, including Smith, got 10 years; two got 7 years; nine got 2 years; two (one of them a boy of 14 years) got 12 months' imprisonment.

At Kilmarnock, Ayr and Greenock there were "sympathetic" riots. At Edinburgh the Chartists and the Irish "fraternised," resolutions congratulating the Communards were passed, men sang the Marseillaise ; the Edinburgh delegates to the London Chartist convention reported that "the men of Edinburgh were ready for the stake, the dungeon or the field of battle." On the Calton Hill, John Grant of the *Weekly Express* denounced the "base, bloody and tyrannical Whig Government" which was passing a Crown and Government Security Bill against "open and advised speaking" whereby Chartist meetings of 50 people and over were rendered illegal. It was their duty to arm. Hugh Rankine, "upholsterer," preferred peace, "but if they were to have their rights only by force, then in the name of God let force be the order of the day." Another speaker, Hamilton (a tailor), urged the people to purchase muskets and pikes and to fraternise with the Army. One, Samuel Macdonald, said the people of Ireland were justified in resisting coercion "to the death," and Peter Duncan, described by the press as "a lad with a bonnet," lauded the late insurrection in Paris as a labourers' war and declared that the working man "had just as much right to have fine houses, fine carpets and fine coats as the rich man"—"extraordinary notions on the subject of property," comments the amazed *Scotsman*. A great demonstration was organised to synchronise with the presentation of the Chartist petition to Parliament. To that demonstration the Leith contingent came with a banner : "The Lion of Scotland has risen from his lair, beware Whigs, beware," dummy crowns were carried upside down and men wore the red cap of liberty. Thirty thousand people on the Meadows were told by Rankin that "the knowledge of chemistry had now entered the workshop of the artisan," and, by Hamilton, of how poverty could be abolished.

This meeting was scattered by the police acting under the powers of the new Crown and Government Security Act. At Aberdeen 5000 Chartists defied the police ; at Dundee, Dunfermline and in every large town there were meetings ; at Edinburgh the principles of Communism were publicly advocated by a "Mr. Brown"; several warrants were issued in Paisley, and four calico printers disappeared; seditious pamphlets were seized in Greenock ; the Yeomanry were under arms in Lanarkshire, and there was a slight "brush" with some riotous colliers at Holytown ; in Glasgow Chartist printers were arrested, and a secretly and suddenly arranged demonstration on the Green, of Lanarkshire colliers, and local factory operatives, three thousand strong, was scattered by a large force of police. Only one of the speakers, an old man of 78, Thomas Skerrington, who persisted in reciting passages from "The Black Book of British Aristocracy" after his auditors had fled, was arrested. Feargus O'Connor and Ernest Jones toured Scotland, both preaching physical force as the only remedy and the few Chartist moral suasionists who dared publicly to oppose physical force were, like young Shirron, the Aberdeen Chartist leader, roughly handled ; and Alexander Campbell, one of Owen's disciples, who dared to plead "for social emancipation before political power" was laughed down as a maniac. The Glasgow men were reported to be "able to keep all their soldiers to themselves" ; branches of a Chartist National Guard sprang up ; crowds, 100,000 strong, demonstrated on Glasgow Green despite the police ; the Aberdeen branch of the National Guard numbered 1000 and pledged itself "to support the Chartist National Assembly" should it declare itself a Parliament. But the Government struck while the National Guard was little more than bluff. Jones was sentenced to two years' solitary confinement ; others were transported : in Greenock Burrell and Neilson were arrested : in Glasgow James Smith was arrested, and in Edinburgh Grant and Rankin were tried for "Scots Treason," and given four months' imprisonment.* But it was not the Government or the police that withered "the Chartist year" of 1848. It was the new Liberal party, the Cobdens, the Brights and the Humes, who formed Peoples' Leagues and all sorts of counter attractions to the Chartist movement, most of them of course ostensibly formed "to obtain the equal and just representation of the whole people as set forth in the Peoples' Charter," but "with such alterations and amendments in its details as may appear necessary"†—a typical Liberal touch that !—the internal strife over physical force, the somewhat erratic leadership of Feargus O'Connor, the discovery of many bogus signatures (said by O'Connor

---

*Shaw's *Justiciary Cases*, 1848-1852, p. 17, *et seq.*

†*Scotsman*, 22/4/48, 29/4/48, 6/5/48, 27/5/48, 24/6/48. The *Scotsman* (then a Liberal organ) was in favour of " safe and gradual progress " only.

to be the work of Government spies) in the Chartist petition to Parliament, the tales of excesses in France, the association of the Chartists with the Irish revolutionists whose religion was used to frighten the tame working class in Presbyterian Scotland, the alleviation of the distress of the unemployed by charity doles, and the revival in trade—all these causes combined to destroy the threatened Chartist revolution. True, Bronterre O'Brien could secure audiences while he preached nationalisation of land, mines, fisheries, credit and markets, and the reservation of the privilege of paying the interest on the National debt to the rich; Feargus O'Connor, M.P., Sir Joshua Walmsley, M.P., and George Thompson, M.P., toured Scotland with a "constitutional" suffrage agitation, but the Liberal manufacturers would have none of it,* and they seemed particularly alarmed at Thompson's disclosures that of every 20s. spent by a poor man, 10s. of it went in tax to the Exchequer, whence Lord John Russell (the Liberal Premier) drew £5000 a year for himself, and had his brother, his father-in-law and other relatives all with their hands deep in the public purse : the Duke of Marlborough drew an hereditary pension of £4000 per annum from the Post Office, the Duke of Grafton £3400, the Duke of Schomberg £2900, the Hanoverian potentate £26,000, "the Prince" of Saxe-Coburg and Gotha £30,000, the Belgian King £15,000, and the Queen Dowager £100,000. This was not talk the working class should hear, and the Liberals declined to encourage it. But they subscribed to campaigns in sympathy with "the present struggle of Romans, Hungarians and Germans" against oppression, and the Liberal majority in the House of Commons heavily defeated a motion to extend the franchise and for the ballot and triennial Parliaments,† without any public outcry, so keenly interested were the British people in the sufferings of the Italian refugees at Malta.

On February, 28th, 1850, the Liberal Government again opposed an extension of the franchise to the working class, and again on 9th July, it opposed the reduction of the county franchise to £10, and when two days later Feargus O'Connor sought to move a Chartist resolution, the House of Commons was counted out. In the autumn we find traces of Ernest Jones, just released from prison, addressing Chartist meetings in Scotland. The year 1851 appears to have been given over to a spirited No-Popery agitation, though there was evidently sufficient radicalism in the Falkirk Burghs bye-election to hiss and defeat Loch, the Liberal candidate, on the ground of his family connection with the Sutherland clearances. On the other hand, Baird of Gartsherrie, the successful Tory candidate, who was against a national system of education, was highly recommended on

---

Glasgow Courier, 1/11/49.
†8/6/49.

the ground that he fed his workers in giving them work by day and by night, and that "Gartsherrie fires don't burn on Sundays." Nevertheless the Dragoons were called out to protect this benefactor of his constituents at Airdrie from a mob of misguided working men.* In 1851, Paisley, Edinburgh, Dundee and Glasgow sent delegates to the Chartist convention, and there was some propaganda kept going; but its vitality had been sapped, and the Congress of delegates held in Edinburgh in 1852 was curiously ineffective in face of a public opinion swinging towards the Liberal party, whose leader, Lord John Russell, had fathered a franchise "reform," whereby the urban suffrage was to be reduced to £5 and the county suffrage to be reduced to £20. In March 1852, however, when there was a danger of household suffrage and the ballot being carried, the Whigs and the Tories united and Lord John Russell declared that the ballot would endanger "the monarchy and the peerage." During the year 1853, the Liberal Government repeatedly announced that it was "considering" an extension of the franchise, and its chief organ in Scotland, the *North British Daily Mail*, was explaining that "under a £5 or a £1 suffrage, multitudes of people would be enfranchised who have no claim or fitness whatever in the sight of God or man to exercise the rights and privileges of citizens." On the other hand an agitation for Scots Home Rule made considerable headway, largely through the activities of Patrick Edward Dove.

In 1854 the Liberal Government, of which, by the way, Gladstone was a member, produced its long promised and well "considered" franchise reform bill, the expectation of which had been so largely instrumental in destroying Chartism. It was briefly explained by Lord John Russell thus : "It was most important that the influence of the middle classes should be preserved. He deprecated universal suffrage. All persons paying above £6 a year to have the right to vote, but they must have residence for 2½ years before being put upon the register, and should be upon the register 2 years and ten months before voting."† The county franchise was to be a £10 one. This ingenious measure died out in universal laughter.

At the general election of 1857 there was considerable heckling of candidates on the subject of the franchise, and one, Finlan, described as an "itinerant Chartist and Socialist agitator," gave some trouble to Liberal and Tory nominees in the West of Scotland, but the working class seems to have concentrated its attention chiefly on the dramatic contest in the Falkirk Burghs, where the Iron and Coal Liberal Capitalist Merry fought the Iron and Coal Tory Capi-

---

*One of Baird's gems at the hustings is thus reported :—" I will not vote for the Ballot, therefore, because it is not good for you, but I have no objection to it myself. (Disapprobation)."—*Courier* report, 13/7/52.

†*Courier*, 14/2/54.

talist Baird. In this contest Alexander Macdonald, the miners' leader, induced Merry to declare against Truck and for a general "Short Hours Bill." The Tories secured office and produced a Franchise Bill which in some respects was reactionary, for it sought to abolish the English 40s. freeholders, but its leading feature was a reduction of the county franchise to £10. The Liberals raised a clamour that the Bill did not go far enough, and Bright and Cobden headed a Manhood Franchise agitation in the country, which seems to have scared the Liberal capitalists and the ruck of the Liberal press. Manhood suffrage, these gentry feared, would inevitably lead to "the substitution of a republic for the monarchy, a division of the soil and the sponging out of the national debt," and Cobden had considerable difficulty in convincing them that Manhood Suffrage would not mean Socialism or State regulation of wages, but that under it the workers would be "conservative" and would "elect their chiefs from a higher class than their own."* In April, 1859, the Tory Franchise Bill was beaten in the House of Commons, and the Government resigned, though not before the House of Commons had carried a resolution in favour of the ballot by a majority of three.† Then the Liberals took office and produced an even more reactionary franchise measure than that lately fathered by the Tories ; but, reactionary as it was, they simply toyed with it, they "talked it to death,"‡ and finally, to everybody's relief, they withdrew its emasculated corpse from Parliament altogether. In 1861 the Liberal Government refused to touch the subject, and private members bills were handsomely beaten, Lord John Russell declaring that the middle classes, more than the aristocracy, feared political power being given to the working class.§ During the year there was a recrudescence of political radicalism in Scotland, many of the old Chartist orators appearing on the platforms, and the United Trades of Glasgow—35 Unions—organised meetings and canvassed signatures to Franchise Reform petitions. But neither of the two great political parties would move. Sadly the *Daily Mail* admitted that "It is true that the present ministry (Liberal, Lord Palmerston, Prime Minister) took office pledged to Parliamentary reform, and it is also true that that pledge is still unredeemed, and that no effort worth the name has been made to redeem it ; but the effort that was

---

*Cobden's letter in *Scotsman*, 25/1/58. One of John Bright's ingenuous arguments for Universal Suffrage was that it would occupy the workers' thoughts with something else than "contests with their employers."— *Ibid*, 15/11/60.

†The *Glasgow Herald* was swift to point out that this resolution meant nothing more than political stagecraft in front of a General Election.—15/4/59.

‡*Scotsman* (then Liberal), 7/6/60.

§*Daily Mail*, 14/3/61.

made was defeated by Parliament, by men who had always proclaimed themselves as Liberals."* And Disraeli frankly avowed
that the Tory party was hostile to a democratic franchise, though
he was not above secretly contracting with the Radicals that he
would bring in a £6 franchise measure if they would assist him in
office.† In April, 1864, a private members bill was opposed by the
Liberal Cabinet and defeated, and another privately sponsored
effort in the succeeding month to lower the burgh franchise to £6
was also defeated, Mr. W. E. Gladstone, though voting for the
Bill, declaring "that the present was not a period when it was advis-
able or justifiable." He was kind enough, however, to express his
conviction that it would be "the inclination of the working classes
to follow their superiors, to confide in them and to trust them.‡
The Trades Political Union promptly retorted that their stock of
trust was exhausted, and that they would oppose every politician
who would not definitely pledge himself to Manhood Suffrage and
the Ballot, no matter what political label he carried. The year
1865 saw an ingenious Franchise Bill moved, which would give, as
its mover was careful to explain, an additional 443,000 votes—three-
fourths of them to the "middle and upper class" and one-fourth
to the "lower class." This Bill was defeated, and the *Scotsman*
assured its readers that there was "no great occasion for dread
that the new Parliament will kill itself off in the flower of its youth
by zeal and haste in the work of Reform." The Government
(Liberal) agreed, and in December appointed a Commission of
Enquiry into the question of the Franchise. "A safe course,"§ said
the *Scotsman* approvingly, but one that seems to have fomented an
excited agitation and caused working men to declare that when they
got the vote they would use it to drive both Liberals and Tories from
Parliament. In March, 1866, Gladstone produced his great Reform
Bill on which he staked the existence of his Government. The
measure was greeted with a howl of disgust and disappointment
even from the Liberal press.‖ for it proposed only a burgh franchise
of £7, which "nobody has ever asked for," a county franchise of £14,
a franchise for lodgers in rooms rented at £10, and a franchise for
Savings Bank depositors who had £50 at their credit for at least two
years concurrently. In the last sixteen years, said Gladstone, five
administrations and seven Queen's speeches had promised political
reform, and now Liberal reform was an actuality—said Liberal
reform being such that the Liberal Lord Advocate could commend
it in the following terms :

---

*4/8/62.
†*Scotsman*, 27/6/63.
‡*N.B. Daily Mail*, 12/5/64.
§5/12/65.
‖*N.B. Daily Mail*, 13/3/66.

" Of those who will be admitted between £10 and £7, more will belong to the class of masters and shopmen than to the class of working-men. In Aberdeen 657 persons will obtain the vote who are not working-men, while only 229 working-men will be admitted ; but of 288 new voters in Ayr, only 36 will belong to the artisan class . . . only 38 additional working-class voters to the Haddington Burghs, 33 to Inverness, 26 to Montrose, with its large population, 27 to the Wick Burghs, and 15 to Wigton. . . .You are not in the slightest degree making a transfer of political power from one class to another. (Hear, hear !)."*

This was Liberal "reform." It was promptly beaten in the House of Commons, and the Liberals resigned office.

Again the Trades began marching in processions. On Glasgow Green 200,000 demonstrators were told by Ernest Jones that "the voice of the people was the voice of God ! " The old Chartist orators appeared again, re-inforced by men like Alexander Macdonald, the miners' champion from Lanarkshire. The new Tory Government promptly took advantage of the situation and "dished the Whigs " by introducing household suffrage for all males who paid poors rates in burghs, and for all tenants rented at over £14 in counties. The Bill for Scotland was passed in 1868 to the muttered disgust of the Scots Liberal press, which hinted that the Tory proposal erred "on the score of liberality."† The Radicals were in glee, set about preparing schemes of social reform, and the Working Men's Association proceeded to organise "a direct representation of labour interest by the return of working men to Parliament," raising an election fund for approved candidates and inviting the assistance and interest of Trades Unions and Councils, Co-operative Societies and other organisations of working men. When, however, the general election came in the autumn of 1868, Alexander Macdonald, the miners' leader, was the only purely labour candidate who entered the field. The seat selected was the Kilmarnock Burghs, and Macdonald drew great audiences. His programme was : triennial parliaments, disestablishment and disendowment of the Irish Church, compulsory education, enquiry into causes of pauperism and the working of the Poor Law, workmen's compensation, the legalisation of trade unions, conciliation courts for industrial disputes, and abolition of the law on arrestment of wages. The miners raised money for his election expenses by a voluntary levy of 1s. per head, but he refused to indulge in the ordinary electioneering bribery and corruption, and the mass of the workers were too ignorant to be able to withstand the free whisky and hard cash doled out by the capitalist organisations ; the far-seeing Liberals raised the cry of "Tory Gold " against him ; he denied being a Tory, but, as he said at Uddingston,

---

*N.B. *Daily Mail* report, 8/5/66.
†*Ibid,* 23/5/67.

"neither was he a Liberal in the ordinary sense of that term . . . . He remained content to be one of the friends of labour. His life had been dedicated to her, and he would not desert her sons. If he was returned to Parliament he would stand by her side and do his best to fight her battles." At Kilmarnock he declared that he stood as the champion of the class to which he belonged, but if his class wanted his services, his class must pay ; he would refuse to spend a shilling upon his election ; he would come among them regularly and give an account of his stewardship. But these sentiments were useless against the free whisky, and he withdrew his candidature. It was a depressing general election for the advanced spirits who had hoped for great things from a politically unchained democracy, and who based their visions on the Chartist demonstrations of twenty years before ; the facts were that the urban populations were densely ignorant and had been broken in *moral* by capitalism ; the political propaganda had been intermittent and, of recent years, organised by the Liberal Party—so much so that Labour critics of Merry the ironmaster (who was Liberal candidate for the Falkirk Burghs) on the ground of his treatment of his employees, required police protection from a whisky corrupted working class mob ; the Ballot Act was not in being, and bribery was open and unashamed. The Trades' Councils, however, heckled the candidates on industrial questions, and at Edinburgh stress was laid upon the necessity for railway nationalisation, compulsory and unsectarian education, and the proper inspection of ships going to sea.

Political agitation among the working class in Scotland seems to have been dead for the next three years, and only revived when the Ballot Bill was carried in 1872. During the passing of the Bill an attempt was made by the Labour Representation League to induce the Liberal Government to include a clause authorising payment of election expenses by the constituencies. Gladstone himself was favourable, but his party was hostile, and the Tories were more interested in securing vote by ballot in House of Commons divisions. An attempt at a Republican movement led by Sir Charles Dilke had some success in Scotland, but it was cleverly countered by a well-staged illness of the Prince of Wales, and by a united press, pulpit and platform thanksgiving for his recovery ; in one issue alone, the *Scotsman* devoted over 17 columns to the Thanksgiving. At the Miners' National Association Annual Congress held at Glasgow in May, 1872, the principle of direct labour representation in Parliament was carried unanimously ; and in 1873 the Glasgow Trades Council had great debates upon the question of the advisability of running Labour candidates ; at the first School Board election in 1873 the Glasgow Trades Council ran a leet composed of three worker representatives and a University Professor, upon a programme of

developing the national schools, absorbing the denominational institutions, and excluding denominational catechisms and formulae ; the candidates were handsomely beaten by the nominees of the Churches, James Barrowman, "the manager of the Wholesale Co-operative" being top workers' candidate, with 7463 votes. At Eastwood, at Dumbarton and elsewhere the Labour candidates were decisively beaten. All these manifestations of a disposition to vote as a class frightened the capitalists, and we find an employers' union formed, "a trade union of capitalists" to oppose the organised workers in their Parliamentary activities, and the *Glasgow Herald* frankly explained that "the extension of the burgh franchise made the working classes far more formidable than they ever were before."*
At the General Election of 1874 the Liberals under Mr. W. E. Gladstone made as their election war-cry the abolition of the Income Tax, and seemed greatly annoyed at persistent heckling on industrial questions. There were no Labour Candidates in Scotland, but M'Donald, the miners' leader, was returned for an English constituency, and after his election he declared at Wishaw that "Parties he would have nothing to do with . . . If the new Conservative Government brought in good measures he would support them ; if they brought in bad measures, the mighty will of the British people would soon hurl them from power and replace them again with the Liberals."†

In the year 1875 we find the oldest Trades Council in the kingdom, Glasgow, "warmly" supporting the proposal of direct labour representation in Parliament, and at the National Trades Union Congress an amendment to a resolution for labour representation secured only five votes ; but the Tory Government was securing a majority of 102 against giving the franchise to the agricultural labourer, and recked so little the Labour opinion in the country, that on the succeeding day it got the House of Commons to vote £142,000 to send the Prince of Wales on a trip to India.‡

For the succeeding few years political agitation seems to have been dormant in Scotland, though the miners can be traced passing resolutions for Labour representation ; such political interest as there was, manifested itself in the drama of the Irish Land campaigns, the Liberal press supporting Gladstone in his coercion policy and denouncing Parnell as "a political adventurer," while the Irish

---

*19/11/73. With equal frankness the same Journal had admitted (17/3/73) that there was no issue between the two orthodox political parties " except Gladstone or Disraeli—Liberal or Conservative—Whig or Tory . . . Neither wants or will concede the right of picketing to Trades Unionists. Neither cares a brass farthing about the female franchise."

†The Larkhall miners voted £100 to M'Donald's election expenses, Annbank voted £10, and the Maryhill men levied themselves 1s. per head.

‡9/7/75. *Glasgow Herald.*

retaliated by breaking up Liberal meetings.* In 1884 Gladstone introduced a Franchise Bill—carried after a struggle with the House of Lords—to give male tenants in counties the vote.† He thus "dished" the Tories by attaching the agricultural workers to the Liberal party, and setting them in antagonism to the Tory lairds, even as almost twenty years before Disraeli had "dished the Whigs" by enfranchising the workers in the towns and setting them in antagonism to the Whig capitalists. By the Act of 1884, some 200,000 new voters were added to the rolls in Scotland, and immediately Labour representation upon public boards became a question of prime importance. At Duirnish, crofter candidates were returned to the School Board ; in most large centres Working Men's Parliamentary Associations were formed ; speakers declared that hitherto "whatever party was in power, it was the privileged class who ruled" ;‡ a working man captured a seat on Govan School Board ; a Labour Representation Committee of Glasgow Trades Council asked 20,000 Trades Unionists to give 1s. each for Parliamentary candidatures ; at the General Election in 1885 Mr. M'Dougall polled 967 votes in Perth ; in Aberdeenshire West a "Radical Labourist" polled 1530 votes; in the Bridgeton division of Glasgow Mr. Forsyth of the Land Restoration League polled 978 votes; in Blackfriars (Glasgow) Mr Shaw Maxwell, a Socialist, polled 1156 votes; a crofter candidate in Sutherlandshire polled 1058 votes against the heir to the estate ; in Inverness-shire, in Argyllshire and in Caithnesshire crofters candidates were successful, Dr. G. B. Clark, one of the founders of the Social Democratic League, carrying Caithness with a majority of 892 votes.

In the following year, 1886, Gladstone's Government was defeated on Home Rule for Ireland, and the two most notable successes from a working class point of view were Mr. Cunninghame Graham's victory in N.W. Lanarkshire, and the victory of Angus Sutherland, a crofter's son, in Sutherlandshire. Both fought as Liberals, but with frankly "class war" programmes,§ and Graham became "the Miners' Justiceman" in Parliament.‖ Henry George had toured Scotland and had fired masses of men with his passion and his eloquence, and among those whom he most influenced was James Keir Hardie, the young leader of the Lanarkshire miners. In January, 1887, we find Hardie issuing a monthly magazine called the *Miner*, which, though specialising in mining questions, adopted an emphatic tone in its

---

*For example, *Weekly Mail*, 15/10/81 and 4/2/82.

†Gladstone refused to enfranchise women.—*Weekly Herald*, 14/6/84.

‡*The Exile*, 16/5/84.

§Sutherland's acceptance of a Government job at the Fishery Board was a great disappointment to the Labour movement of his day.

‖*The Miner*, 1888.

demand for direct labour representation in Parliament, and insisted that such representation should be independent of Liberal or Tory control. In March, 1888, Hardie was invited by the Larkhall miners to fight Mid Lanark ; he first offered himself as Labour candidate to the Mid Lanark Liberal Association, but on that body enquiring if he were prepared to abide by its decision in the selection of a suitable candidate, he promptly withdrew his request for their endorsement of his candidature. In the three-cornered contest that followed he received platform assistance from Dr. Clark, Mr. Cunninghame Graham and Mr. Conybeare ; he received letters of encouragement from Mr. Ramsay Macdonald, then secretary to the Scottish Home Rule Association, the Glasgow Trades Council, and the British Steel Smelters and the Associated Millmen ; and the National Labour Party contributed £400 towards his election expenses. Outside Larkhall he had no organisation, and *United Ireland* among the Irish workers and the *Weekly Mail* among the Scots workers were savagely bitter against him ; he polled, however, 617 votes. In the same year, 1888, Robert Smillie secured a seat as Labour representative on the Larkhall School Board, got an adult evening class started, and was himself the first student to enrol. In June the Scottish Parliamentary Labour Party was formed with a programme including adult suffrage, payment of M.P.'s, Home Rule, abolition of the House of Lords, Second Ballot, the "re-imposition of the old tax of 4s. per £1 upon the present value of land," taxation of land values, nationalisation of mining royalties without compensation, eight hours' day, State insurance against sickness, accident, death or old age, arbitration courts, minimum and weekly wage, direct veto on Liquor traffic, "no war to be entered into without the consent of the House of Commons," free education and power to feed necessitous children, Disestablishment, Nationalisation of railways and all other means of transit, Nationalisation of Banks and the issue of State money only, and a cumulative income tax beginning at £300 per annum. Mr. Cunninghame Graham was the first chairman of the new party. Its subsequent struggles and its supersession by a National Labour party, the history of the activities of the Independent Labour party, and an estimate of the part played by the Socialist League, the Social Democratic Federation and lesser Socialist organisations in stimulating and moulding the political energies of the working people of Scotland in the closing decade of the nineteenth, and in the first decade of the twentieth, century, would require a separate volume, and the difficulty of securing a proper historical perspective is obvious ; a polemical dust still clouds the vision of the observer, and all that is clear is a slow but steadily growing tendency to a working class political party—a party suffused, stimulated and inspired by an incessant Socialist propaganda.

CHAPTER X.

THE ANTI-COMBINATION LAWS.

"The Labour Question may be said to have come into public view simultane ously with the Repeal, between sixty and seventy years ago, of the Combination Laws, which had made it an offence for labouring men to unite for the purpose of procuring by joint action, through peaceful means, an augmentation of their wages. From this point progress began."—*W. E. Gladstone in " Weekly Star,"* 6/2/1892.

"Trade Unionists were a parcel of scoundrels who disturbed the peace of farm servants and other operatives, and who should be hanged.—*The Earl of Dunmore,* 1873.

IN the year 1426 the Scots Parliament granted powers to Magistrates in burghs to fix the wages of craftsmen ; in 1551 it empowered the Provosts and the Magistrates to fix craftsmen's fees and prices in burghs ; and in 1617 an Act of Parliament of James VI. authorised Justices of the Peace, sitting in Quarter Sessions, to determine the wages of non-burghal workmen, labourers and servants, to imprison such workers as might refuse to serve at the appointed hire, to farther punish them "at their discretion," and to compel the masters to pay the wages rates fixed.* There was no provision for imprisoning recalcitrant masters. The Act of 1617 was emphasised and repeated in the years 1665 and 1661, and that its provisions were at least occasionally used by the administrative authorities, we have already shewn in our citation from the records of the Burgh of Rutherglen. But by the beginning of the nineteenth century the Act had fallen into desuetude. The workmen would not set its machinery in motion, since the Magistrates and Justices who were to fix the wages were the employers ; and the employers, for their part, were in strenuous competition with each other, and relied upon great armies of hungry unemployed to keep the wages' rates low.

The workers' hope manifestly lay in the direction of Trade Unionism, and well-organised strikes; and the unions or combinations—particularly among the colliers—began to be a nuisance to the employers ; so, in the year 1800, Parliament prohibited all combinations for economic purposes. By Section IV. of the Act, any person could be punished for attending a meeting designed for the purpose of raising wages ; money could not be collected for strike purposes ; the local justices—usually the employers—were to try the offenders,

---

*c. 14.

and sometimes they heard witnesses, and sometimes they did not even trouble with such a formality ; sometimes they dispensed with the hearing of the accused person in his defence, and after hearing a foreman's complaint, consigned the rebellious or grumbling workman to prison without farther ado. Combinations among workmen were naturally driven underground amid a net work of secret passwords, signs and grips. Sabotage, arson, and vitriol throwing were substituted for the strike. On paper, of course, the employers could be compelled to pay wages' rates fixed by the Justices, and the Court of Session did, as a matter of fact, fix, in 1805, the rate of piece-work wages for the Edinburgh Printing Trade ;* but the historic failure of the cotton weavers to secure any effective minimum rate from the law courts discouraged any other trade from placing reliance upon the justiciary. After long and vexatious delays the Glasgow Justices, in 1812, actually scheduled a scale of wages for cotton operatives, but the employers appealed to the Court of Session on the ground that the action of the Justices was incompetent ; the Court of Session decided against the employers, whereupon these worthies simply refused to pay the fixed scale ; a great strike ensued, and the law, which had been defied with impunity by the employers, was brought down heavily upon the strikers, and penalties of from four to eighteen months' imprisonment were meted out to the strike leaders. Mostly, however, the Trade Unionism was subterranean, breaking out into violence and fire-raising, and it is a fact that the real inspiration behind the abrogation of the Combination Acts in 1824 was that such an abrogation would destroy the very necessity for Trade Unionism. Certainly, Francis Place, the reformer who manoeuvred the cancellation of the Combination Acts, thought so. He argued that "the combinations of the men are but defensive measures resorted to for the purpose of counteracting the offensive ones of their masters. . . . When every man knew that he could carry his labour to the highest bidder there would be less motive for those combinations. . . . Combinations will lose the matter which cements them into masses, and they will fall to pieces. All will be as orderly as even a Quaker could desire."† Place was the leading spirit in the triumvirate—Place, Hume, and M'Culloch of the *Scotsman*,—who practically smuggled through Parliament the resolutions abrogating the Combination Laws (six and a half foolscap pages in their titles alone), and the smuggling was done in the prosperous year of 1824, when the capitalist classes were too busy making profits to worry much about House of Commons' resolutions which passed "almost without the notice of members within, or newspapers without." But Place was wrong ; no sooner were the Combination

---

*Scottish Typographical Circular, June, 1858.
†*The Life of Francis Place*—Graham Wallas, p. 217.

Acts abolished than there arose a great development of Trade Unionism: unions grew up like mushrooms, and there were strikes everywhere. The affrighted capitalists got at the Vice-president of the Board of Trade, who, in 1825, introduced an amending measure to the House of Commons, declaring that unless the unions were suppressed "the Federal Republic of France would be revived in this country." His amending Act of 1825, however, exempted Combinations from criminal liability in agitations for raising wages, resisting reductions, or altering the hours of labour ; but it created new crimes of "molesting" and "obstructing," which, on being liberally interpreted, meant that it was extremely difficult to conduct a strike of any kind. Moreover, the evidence of only one witness was sufficient to send a Trade Unionist agitator to gaol for three months ;* and the laws relating to contracts between masters and servants were in themselves sufficiently class-biassed to be an effective masters' weapon against the Unions; the Combination Acts indeed were hardly required so long as, under the maze of master and servant contract legislation, Edinburgh mechanics who had no written contract of service—only a week's engagement—could be sent to prison for a month's hard labour for absenting themselves from their master's work without leave.† If a master broke a contract with a servant his was a civil offence ; if a servant broke a contract with a master, no matter how reasonable the excuse, his was a criminal offence, rendering him liable to three months' imprisonment. We find a poor collier at Edinburgh Sheriff Court explaining that he had left his work because there was no air in the pit and no exit but by the entrance shaft ; he had never signed nor agreed to any contract obliging him to give 14 days' notice of his intention to leave ; nevertheless he was fined £1 15s., and three guineas expenses‡—a special decision of illegal grace, inasmuch as the law allowed no fining, only imprisonment. A servant prosecuted by an employer could not give valid evidence on his own behalf ; he could be summarily arrested on a magistrate's warrant (and the magistrate was frequently the employer !), and from the magistrate's decision there was no appeal.

In the year 1863, Alexander Campbell, secretary to the Glasgow Trades Council, and who had been Robert Owen's chief disciple in Scotland, initiated an agitation for the repeal of these monstrous class-biassed contract iniquities. He shewed that in an average year there were no fewer than 10,339 cases of breach of contract before the Courts. In 1867 the grosser injustices were wiped out by the Master and Servant Act ; but what the master class gave with

---

*Glasgow Evening Post, 26/11/33.
†Ibid, 22/10/36.
‡Scotsman, 20/6/72.

the one hand it took away with the other; for in the same year, 1867, the Lord Chief Justice decided that the Trade Unions, while not being strictly illegal, were so far outwith the pale of law that they could not sue in the Courts and that any defaulting official who cared could embezzle their funds with impunity. In the year 1871, as a result of considerable working-class agitation, the Liberal Government of the day "legalised" Trade Unions and "protected" their funds, but at the same time contrived to pass a Criminal Law Amendment Act to codify and enforce all the stray law-court decisions that had been given against the Trade Unions, with the object of making strikes tantamount to criminal conspiracies; the strike itself in the abstract was lawful, but practically any act done in pursuance of a strike was unlawful and subject not to civil damages but to criminal penalties. Men got 12 months' imprisonment for preparing to "coerce" their employers by organising a strike; women were imprisoned for intimidating a blackleg by shouting "Bah" to him; peaceful picketting became "watching and besetting"—a heinous crime. Even the protection of Union funds was rendered nugatory by legal decision. Thus, the Sheriff at Greenock fined the officials of the Ropespinners' Union for "coercing" an employer by refusing to work with a blackleg.* The employers endeavoured to trap the secretary of the Edinburgh Tailors by sending blacklegs to his door soliciting money to enable them to return to England; had he paid, he had been guilty of "illegal conspiracy." On the other hand, the Master Builders could, without fear of legal proceedings, organise boycotts and black-lists and "discharge notes." Alexander Macdonald declared on Glasgow Green that if one non-unionist was sacked because ninety-nine unionists had struck work against his employment, the ninety-nine unionists were each liable to three months' imprisonment.†

Against all this there was great outcry and demand for "political action." A mass protest procession organised by Glasgow Trades Council took nearly two hours to pass a given spot. Edinburgh Trades Council gathered 60,000 Trade Unionists who promised to support only Parliamentary candidates pledged to the repeal of the "class criminal laws." But Mr. Gladstone and his Cabinet stubbornly refused to initiate any remedial legislation, and at the General Election in 1874, masses of working-class electors voted Tory, and the Liberals were swept from office. The new Tory Government at first temporised with the Trade Union demands; it appointed a Royal Commission of Enquiry on the "Labour Laws," the three most important members being judges. Labour as a whole refused to give evidence, but Andrew Boa, from Glasgow, latterly stated the

Glasgow Herald, 2/10/73.
†*Glasgow Herald*, 3/11/73.

case for the workers in the West of Scotland. The majority of the Commission reported, as was the general expectation, against the claims of the workers, though on some important points they recommended relaxations. The Government, however, was more alive to the situation than was its Commission, and the Tory Home Secretary introduced an Employers and Workmen Act, which, though still tainted with what the *Glasgow Herald* admitted to be "class legislation," legalised peaceful picketing, abolished the criminal conspiracy grievances, and recognised collective bargaining with all its necessary accompaniments. Thus, in 1876, after fifty years of struggle, the Combination Laws had disappeared. And not again until the famous Taff Vale decision in 1900, when the House of Lords decided that a Union collectively was liable for alleged illegalities of its officials and members, did the governing classes seek to use Parliament or the judicial bench for the destruction of Trade Unionism. The Taff Vale decision raised such a storm of indignation as made an effective Labour Party possible, and the Government, after an unsuccessful attempt at a shameless piece of legislative trickery was compelled by the Labour members of Parliament (assisted staunchly, be it said, by Sir Henry Campbell Bannerman, who refused to countenance the proposals of his law officers !) to pass the Trades Disputes Act which restored the Unions' position to what it was in pre-Taff Vale times, and which indeed in some respects strengthened it.

CHAPTER XI.

UNDER THE CAPITALIST HARROW.

The toad beneath the harrow knows
Exactly where each tooth point goes.
—*Rudyard Kipling.*

"Are not millions of starving people the necessary occasional sloughs of a very manufacturing nation ? "—*Lord Cockburn,* "*Journal*" (1831-1854).

"There were high and low, rich and poor, in this world, and we should be contented and happy in the situation in which we were placed. . . . The rich man depended upon the labourer for his wealth, and the poor man on him for employment, and thus there was a mutual dependence which it was highly essential to preserve."—*Duke of Newcastle* (1845).

IT is not true, as is commonly supposed, that the capitalist, as such, was unknown prior to the great mechanical inventions which from 1760 onwards transformed the basis of industry from the domestic circle to the factory. Human labour, as apart from human bodies, was, prior to 1760, bought and sold ; its price was its keep in a competitive market ; and the surplus values it created were taken by enterprising purchasers and hirers long before the days of the spinning jenny or the factory chimney. An Act of the old Scots Parliament in 1663, for example, conferred powers upon all manufacturing companies to seize vagabonds and set them to work "as they [the companies] shall think fit" for periods of seven years. Parishes so relieved of their unemployed were to pay the companies 2d. per vagabond *per diem* for the first year and 1d. *per diem* for the next three years ; and this bounty or subsidy was to be raised half from proprietors and half from tenants. In 1700 we find a pamphleteer distressed that so many poor people should be "forced to sell themselves as bound-servants to the plantations," and propounding a scheme whereby they should instead get employment at home with "no wages, but merely meat and cloath."* It is true that prior to the industrial revolution the manufacturer is never blamed for the existence of misery and poverty ; it is always the landlord. "If our nobility and gentry," says one writer, "would lower their prices of corns in time and not keep it up for a dearth," there would be less grinding of the faces of the poor.† After the famine of 1700 a Government Committee—packed, of course, in the landed interest—recommended the sinking of Irish grain at sea

---

*Anon. Edgh, 1700. Stirling Library Collection, vol. 20.
†*Ibid*, vol. 21.

in order to keep up prices in the West of Scotland ; and prices were indeed so raised that by 1748 land rent (except in the Highlands), cattle, sheep and fowls were double what they had been before the Union with England ; and most of the peasants in Scotland "have poverty wrote upon their very faces."* Yet, even so, prices were almost incredibly low ; meat sold at 3d. per lb. ; and in 1759 eggs in the north country could be purchased 7 for 1d. ; salmon was at 1d. per lb., and butter was 6d. to 8d. for 28 ounces.†

It is not until the beginning of the nineteenth century, when steam power and the aggregation of machines in factories were driving out the small cottage industrialist, and, aided by land clearances, were multiplying the population in the towns, that we usually date the capitalist system. But it is important to remember that the factory system and the capitalist system do not mean the same thing ; they are not coincident in time ; there was capitalist exploitation of the worker long before the advent of steam power, and even the weaver who owned his own loom and sold his web to agents was, though he owned his own tools, nothing but a wage slave ; he took "work" at the lowest competitive price consistent with a bare living for himself and his family !

No pen will ever paint even a dim picture of the horrors of the early years of the capitalist system in the factory towns. A plethora of labourers, cottars from the soil, handicraftsmen from the villages, driven to little, overcrowded, bleak and cheerless hovels, hastily erected around the factory walls ; compelled to sell their toil in foul and filthy working conditions, and for the barest pittances ; from dawn to sunset bullied and oppressed, the last ounce taken from their bodies by scarcely less oppressed overseers ; hunger, misery, dirt ; no sanitary or factory regulations ; no machinery fenced ; their children killed off like flies, and they themselves emaciated, consumptive, and without hope ; no Trade Union or Friendly Society benefits ; no co-operative societies ; no holidays at the seaside ; no part in citizenship ; the only relaxation being on the Sabbath, when a clergyman, voicing the desires of his chief paymaster in the raised pew, would urge submission to the present Hell as a qualification for the Paradise to come.

When the guilds were in dissolution ; and machine industry was in the earlier stages of supplanting the domestic workshop, the wages of skilled men rose. Masons, weavers and carpenters who made 6d. per day in 1750 could make 1s. or 1s. 2d. per day in 1790, and Gibson, in his *History of Glasgow*, assures us that the mechanic of that period lived very comfortably on 7s. per week ; but even the skilled men were soon to learn that capitalist "prosperity" was an

---

*Stirling Library Collection Pamphlets, vol. 33.
†*By-ways of History*—Colville, p. 49.

intermittent thing at the best for them ; that there were recurrent trade crises and panics, overproductions, slumps, market gluttings— all of them used to crush the worker back to the barest level of physical existence, consistent with his ability to stand at a machine, and indeed not always that.   The French revolutionary wars upset the markets, and there was great commercial panic, unemployment, and distress.   We find one commercialist, in 1793, frankly avowing that :

> "The late stagnation has been exceedingly useful to our trade, and if it does not go too far it will be attended with the most beneficial consequences to men of real capital. . . . The wages of our labourers had got to such a height that they . . . occasioned much idleness and dissipation, and much of the time of our workmen was consequently spent in ale-houses, where they became politicians and government-mongers, restless and discontented."*

These were the skilled men, not the labourers ; and generations had to pass away ere again they had surpluses to dissipate, though about their restlessness and discontent there was to be no question.

By the year 1808 the cost of living had risen 400 per cent. over what it had been in 1750, and although wages' rates were said to have increased during the same period by 500 per cent., they were not steady, employment was irregular, and the average wage earned over a year brought a man a very much lower standard of comfort than his father had enjoyed.   In the years 1810, 1816, 1819, 1825, and 1826, especially, was there acute trade depression, and the social consciousness of the upper classes did not run to much in the way of charity or relief works, so long as the weaker among the working-class died with a minimum of inconvenience to their masters. Here and there some braver spirit essayed theft, but with a penal code that had 25 different crimes—including theft by opening lock-fast places—punishable with death, there was no great encouragement to such a method of seeking sustenance.   One woman who steals two Bibles gets 7 years' transportation ; a man who steals 23s. in silver gets 14 years' transportation ; a Stirling woman gets 7 years' transportation for stealing a cotton gown and 'kerchief— poor woman ! she makes "no little lamentation on being removed from the bar ! "   A trooper in the Scots Greys, Somerville by name, writes a letter to the press dealing with the duties of soldiers during times of riot ; he is rewarded for his pains with 100 lashes.†   At Glasgow a family party of two elderly women and two young children go *en bloc* to gaol for 60 days for the theft of a piece of print from a shop counter ; a similar sentence is meted out to a Paisley boy for

Transactions Glasgow Archæological Socy., i., p. 78.
†*Courier*, 30/6/1832.

stealing a bottle of small beer.* Theft was the great crime ; a man guilty of culpable homicide got only half the sentence of the man who stole the 23s. in silver.

In the early thirties the competition of child labour and power loom was particularly severe upon the handloom weaver, driving down his earnings to 6s. 6d. per week ;† and how he, and the navvy who was drifting to the town from the country, managed to keep body and soul together we cannot now guess. The Church did a little for the "God-fearing poor," but the rich who alone were taxed —the poor's tax was then upon means and substance, not upon house rent, at the rate in Glasgow of 3s. to 5s. per £100 of income— saw to it that the relief was at a minimum. The Corn Laws, too, passed at the end of the Napoleonic wars to keep up farmers' profits and lairds' rents, added to the general misery of the times ; land rent in Scotland had risen four-fold between the years 1775 and 1815, and when the wars were over the lairds held out for big rents amid falling prices, and the Corn Laws had to be passed to enable the farmers to continue paying the lairds the rents to which they had become accustomed !

Paisley, at November, 1831, reported nearly 4000 unemployed ; everywhere there was hunger and poverty and compulsory abstinence. Everywhere, that is, among the working-class ; but among them was the abstinence confined, for, we read, at the laying of the foundation stone at the Jamaica bridge, Glasgow, there was a £500 banquet for the selected guests and one specially favoured individual, the Rev. Mr. M'Leod of Campsie, pocketed ten guineas for saying the prayer !

Every new development in machinery, every failure in the crops or the fishings, every fresh importation to the industrial districts, of famished Gaels or starving Irish, submerged another section of the workers ; thousands upon thousands wasted away and perished before the coming of the "Hungry Forties" of the Free Trade pamphleteers. They perished in the Hungry Thirties. In 1836 bread rose by 2d. per 4lb. loaf, the potato crop failed, coals rose 100 per cent., and the wages' rates fell concurrently. At the bleach-fields of Paisley the wages were admittedly less than the bare cost of food ; in other districts, as at Blantyre, the workers, by voluntary assessment out of their scanty and insufficient earnings, maintained the destitute, while the prosperous classes busied themselves in

---

*It can hardly have been from such derelicts as these that the douce magistrates of Glasgow made a personal profit on the sale of ale and porter ; nor surely was it from such as these that the gaolers of Nairn extracted 4d. per day as " keep " during the time of imprisonment.—*Municipal Corporations in Scotland*, Commissioners' Report, p. 64.

†*The Money Rate of Labour in Glasgow and the West of Scotland*—Strang.

transferring what miserable poor's rating there was from means and substance to rent.* Class oppression was rampant and manifest; there was still the Act of Parliament inflicting a £50 penalty upon anyone engaging in pony racing where the stakes were under £50; but let the stakes be over £50 and the racing was legal. There was the disabled army major with his annual pension of £200, and the disabled private with his pension of 9d. per day; there was the major's widow with a bounty of £250, and there was the widow of the private or the non-commissioned officer with no bounty at all!

During the decade 1831-1841, the population of Lanarkshire increased by over 37 per cent., mostly starving Highlanders or Irishmen, and all of them living precariously in squalor and dirt in ramshackle hovels; the death-rates there were never specially collected, and to-day, we can only surmise at the extent of the callously regarded massacre.

And so dawned the Hungry Forties!

In the eighth report of the Inspector of Prisons in Scotland, we are told that in 1842 "more than 200 persons in Glasgow were driven to crime by inability to find employment," and in addition there were 40 persons, mostly able-bodied, "voluntarily undergoing imprisonment in Glasgow in order to get food and shelter." The law not recognising such indulgence, these prisoners were discharged, only, however, to "qualify" promptly by the committal of a "crime," one young girl of 13 for an offence for which she was transported; she had overdone it! At Dundee and elsewhere the Chartists sought to prevent the sagging of wages by means of a general strike; they might as well have struck against the law of gravitation, since at every factory and workshop gate there struggled a mass of starvelings eager to be employed at *any* wages. At Greenock it was estimated three-fifths of the population were unemployed. At Glasgow and Paisley (where, in 1840, there was a series of commercial failures) thousands were unemployed. In 1842 the herring fishing failed, and there was depression everywhere from Lerwick to Dumfries, except, perhaps, among child labour, which, as at Kilsyth, was worked for 14 hours a day. Expert hosemakers in Shetland could only earn 3d. per day, and labourers in Glasgow, when employed, had to be content with 9s. to 12s. per week. The distress continued right through 1843—ten thousand unemployed in Paisley for over 12 months, cotton spinners in Glasgow sleeping in pig-styes, 711 parishes

---

*The Merchant Class in Glasgow in 1840 secured a special Act of Parliament to transfer half the burden to house rents over £7. Edinburgh secured the "privilege" much earlier; but as late as 1867 Greenock was still rated upon income.

in Scotland making no legal provision whatever for the poor.*
"Are not millions of starving people the necessary occasional sloughs
of a very manufacturing nation ? " cried the Whig Solicitor General
Cockburn, in despair.† The Poor Law Commissioners (1844) tell
us that during the early forties—as indeed always—food prices
varied greatly in the different districts, but one article of diet,
potatoes, seems to have been everywhere cheap. In the Highlands
we can find no parish in which potatoes exceed 2d. per stone, and in
the Lowlands nowhere were they dearer than 3d. per stone.

The Disruption in the Church of Scotland in 1843 was the prime
cause of the Poor Law of 1845. Prior to 1845 the infirm poor were
supposed to be relieved by the heritors and the kirk sessions, the kirk
sessions devoting part of their collections to the Poor's Fund. This
fund, being administered and disbursed by the Sessions as a Parish
Church charity, there was small chance of relief to any dissenter ;
such a system obviously operated against the new dissenting churches,
who stoutly demanded that poor's relief funds should be raised by
public rating and should be disbursed not by Parish Church sessions
but by popularly-elected Parish Councils.§ And the dissenters had
grievances enough to exploit ; they could point to an old man at
Inveravon, 80 years of age, who had been granted relief of 4¼d. per
day ; they could tell of an old woman in Glasgow who endeavoured
to commit suicide in despair at her failure to live upon her poor's
allowance of 3s. 6d. per month ; ‡ and they made capital out of the
declamations of the Rev. Patrick Brewster of Paisley, who declared
that the able-bodied poor were in law entitled to relief, but were
being cheated out of it by heritors' greed and judicial craft. His,
however, was a lone Established Church voice crying in the wilderness ; the barbarian ruling class of the period could hardly be induced to provide for the sick and infirm of body even when their
doctrine was beyond reproach ; and so, too, it was after 1845, when
the new Poor Law Act giving relief irrespective of theology was
passed as a result of the clamour of the dissenters, the able-bodied
were still outwith the pale, and could only qualify for relief by
first of all wasting away into the last stages of physical unfitness.
The heritors (landlords) met the new Act with their customary class
foresight and resolution ; they began to clear the aged workers and
all the potential poor out of their parishes. A Government Commissioner, Mr. Tremenheere, reports that "vast numbers of cottages
have been pulled down simply to prevent families gaining a settle

---

Glasgow Saturday Post, 21/10/43. As late as January, 1845, towns such as
    Campbeltown, Inveraray, Dingwall, Thurso, Perth, and Kirkcaldy were
    giving out licenses to beg.

†*Journal* (1831-1854), ii., p. 5.

§Called Parochial Boards.

‡*Argus*, 15/9/45.

ment who might have become chargeable to the poor rates."* Houses
being destroyed, young couples could not get married, and the result,
says Tremenheere, "is an amount of immorality and illegitimacy
which under different economical arrangements might probably be
altogether avoided." In the Highlands the Clearances were as
brutal as they had been 30 or 40 years before.† The *Times'* Special
Commissioner reported that the Glencalvie evictions were due to the
landlords' apprehensions about the new poor law—apprehensions
which were somewhat relieved by the learned judges of the Court of
Session, who decreed that not only were the able-bodied outwith the
right to relief, but their children and dependents also.‡ Dr. Chalmers' crotchet that "no violence should be done to the proprietary
feelings of the rich " was being observed to the letter.

In 1846 there was a serious potato blight, and wild riots in the
north against attempted exportation of potatoes to the high-priced
city markets. The Magistrates at Inverness were stoned in the
streets ; great destitution everywhere ; 300,000 people bordering
upon starvation ; meal, frantically gambled in, rose from 18s. to
30s. a boll, and could only be taken from the north under guard of
fixed bayonets ; at Macduff the mob barricaded the quay with
railway sleepers, and emptied the food ships ; an insurrection at
Aberdeen, flour lorries and mills plundered, special constables sworn
in, and 50 men and many women arrested ; at Granton the Sheriff
was compelled to release rioters whom he had seized ; soldiers
were rushed to Fraserburgh and Huntly to quell serious outbreaks ;
the Fort George garrison was moved to Caithness "with ten
pounders " ; at Avoch the people told a Riot Act reading Sheriff
that they might as well be shot as be starved ; ships of war policed
the Moray Firth ready to assist the civil authorities on the coast ;
and Edinburgh High Court was kept busy passing sentences of
deportation.   A Highland Relief Fund was hastily organised in the
cities to send back food to the dying peasants, but the fund appears
to have been systematically plundered, a leading grain contractor
in Glasgow, Alexander Bannatyne, being afterwards proved guilty
of mixing the relief meal he had been paid to send, with bran and
thirds ; his legal defence was that "everybody knew that merchants
in other trades were equally guilty of adulteration " ; he was sentenced not to deportation for ten years, like some of the hungry and
protesting peasants, but to 4 months' imprisonment and a fine of
£300.   The Relief Fund, too, appears largely to have been used by
the lairds to bring new land under cultivation and to form "many
miles of excellent roads," thus increasing the value of their estates.

*Fraser's Magazine, 1871, p. 646.
†Scotsman, 24/4/45. Times, quoted by Argus, 26/5/45 et seq.
‡Courier, 27/2/49.

One laird was reported to have told his starving tenantry to go and eat one another.* At Barra, the amiable Colonel Gordon refused to "recognise" the Poor Law, and the Government had to send a barrister north to assess him.†

But if in the Highlands the people were trying to exist upon a diet of boiled grass and nettles, the case was even worse in the city wynds. Within a circle of 12 miles of Glasgow, we are told, there were 10,000 paupers receiving on an average not more than 1s. 6d. per week.‡ Thousands of Irish immigrants, who had to be 5 years in the country before acquiring a residence for Poor Law purposes, were "dying of slow starvation . . . emaciated, squalid, and ragged." Thousands of "able-bodied" dined precariously at the soup-kitchens. Fever spread everywhere.§ Provisions in Glasgow rose by 50 per cent., but the new Parish Council—a body seemingly without bowels— refused to raise its rates of relief ; indeed, fresh applicants were more and more harshly disposed of, until the limit in cruelty was reached with a relief of 3s. monthly to a widow in the Gorbals with three children. In Aberdeen a cripple man with a wife and four children (one child likewise a cripple !) was "relieved" by 1s. 6d. per week ; he sought permission to appeal to the Court of Session and received the permission six months afterwards, when presumably he had no use for it, having starved himself to death in the interval. Learned Sheriffs decreed that women with families deserted by the husband and father were not entitled to relief : the women were "able-bodied ! "

The Parish Church clergy explained that the potato blight was God's punishment for the Disruption,‖ and the Government for a time affected to ignore the famine and busied itself with a Bill to permit the use of sugar and molasses in breweries and distilleries, and with the creation of courts for the recovery of small debts. But the Liberal press saw that the middle-class would soon be unable to collect any debts at all unless there was radical change ; the *Argus* called for the right of every man to subsistence from the soil, "either in work or alms, whether he be able-bodied or disabled," declaring it to be "high time that we should prevent revolution by making peacefully and legally the social changes which circumstances demand."a And finally the potato blight and its consequences drove

---

Aberdeen Herald, quoted by *Scotsman,* 2/12/48.

†*Argus,* 12/4/47.

§‡*Argus,* 18/2/47.

Small wonder ! In the Bridgegate cellars, with earthen floors several feet below the surface of the street, death was regularly busy. In one apartment 16 feet by 10 there were 25 people sleeping, and eight of them had fever.—*Argus,* 5/4/47.

‖*Argus,* 18/2/47.

a14/1/47.

Lord John Russell to declare at Edinburgh for full Free Trade. The fear of revolution swept Protection away.

The year 1848, "the Chartist year," was probably the worst the working-class ever experienced under capitalism. A Select Committee on Commercial Distress later reported that the specially hard times of that year were due to famine, shortage of cotton, and money crises, following upon a railway speculation mania and commercial recklessness. In 1848 we had the Glasgow Bread Riots—already described in another chapter—and hungry children sent to prison for stealing a turnip ; Edinburgh unemployed set to work at sixpence a day ; in Paisley alone three factors warning out 1000 families for non-payment of rent ;* Poor Law expenditure double what it was in 1844 ; starvation and hunger everywhere sweeping the working-class. Towards the end of the year food prices shewed a tendency to fall : meal, for example, went down a penny per peck in December ; and in 1849 trade revived and wages for a time rose in the midst of a good harvest.† But the capitalists speedily countered any permanent working-class betterment by encouraging a great immigration from Ireland. In one voyage alone the steamer "Thistle" from 'Derry carried 1900 human beings on her decks. Most of these hungry immigrants were absorbed in the Lanarkshire industrial hells, where they were utilised for the breaking of wage rates, but there was a steady overflow that scattered itself as far north as Dundee and as far south as Berwick. Thus the chief constable of Haddingtonshire reported in March, 1849, that he had knowledge of 1060 Irish in his area and half of them were vagrants living in beggary. When employment could not be secured, the alternative —theft—was not encouraged by the legal gentry at Edinburgh ; seven years' transportation was the punishment meted out to a poor woman for stealing a pair of boots ; ‡ a theft of 14s. was esteemed by Lord Cockburn to merit a penalty of fourteen years' transportation—on the basis evidently of a year for every shilling. "Unskilled" workers who found a master were fleeced wholesale and retail by all manner of ingenious trickeries, one enterprising clay-pipe manufacturer in Glasgow paying his workers not in money but in clay pipes "which they had to sell to a disadvantage," spending their Saturday evenings converting their pipes into cash.

By 1850, about one-fourth of the population of the industrial areas was Irish ;§ they constituted the bulk of "the reserve margin of labour " necessary to the keeping down of wages ; even in the rural districts, as we find the *Border Advertiser* complaining, they were working at 10d. a day and crushing Scotsmen out of a livelihood.

Scotsman, 29/4/48.
†Though half of the West Highland potato crop was rotten.
‡*Courier,* 10/11/49.
§Dr. Allison's *Observations on the Reclamation of Waste Lands,* 1850.

In 1851, except in handloom weaving, where wages fell lower than they had been since the century began, a trade "boom" absorbed the surplus labour, and wages rose again. Here and there the employers resisted the tide, the clay-pipe manufacturers, indeed, actually attempting to reduce wages by 20 per cent., and declaring they were justified in doing so by the low price of foodstuffs. But even the "unskilled" seized their opportunities. The Glasgow municipal scavengers struck against their nominal weekly wage of 11s., nominal because they had much broken time through frost and rain; and when there was rain the theory was that as the drains were flushed and the streets cleansed free there was no sense in paying scavengers wages.* The Edinburgh cab-drivers, with wages of 10s. weekly, had the temerity to ask for extra money for Sunday work, but were promptly told by their employers that they ought to be ashamed to ask for wages on the Lord's Day; a retort that the employers were not ashamed to pocket the hires for Sunday work was manifestly disrespectful and was resented by the employers, who brusquely intimated that they found employment for the cab-drivers, who should remember and be thankful.

To repress the upward surge of wages, the Law, the Police and the Armed Forces of the State were ruthlessly used. When the hired fishermen struck and prevented blacklegs going out at Helmsdale, naval assistance was supplied to the owners of the fishing fleet from the cruiser "Tartarus." An Alloa apprentice who, though not indentured, had given a verbal promise to serve for $3\frac{1}{2}$ years, was sent to prison for one month for attempting to emigrate before the $3\frac{1}{2}$ years had expired.† The Glasgow dockers, striking for an increase from 4d. to 6d. per hour on their intermittent employment, saw blacklegs poured in and afforded organised and effective police assistance. Naturally, these repressions stimulated what the Liberal press called "class hatred," and towards the end of 1853, when the boom in trade was disappearing, there was apprehension at the activities of "windbag agitators"—one of whom, Cooper by name, received special malediction from the ruling class for his activities among the unemployed. Socialist doctrines were being spread, particularly in the industrial districts in Lanarkshire, where, by the fever dens and the cinder heaps, the starvelings were told of the Bairds of Gartsherrie buying eight great landed estates at a total cost of £955,000 between the years 1850 and 1855.

The Crimean War of 1854 had "slackened" the cotton trade, and the cotton workers pawned their chattels and starved their bodies; the young men were advised to join the army, but "the great majority

---

*The *Glasgow Herald* unkindly described this form of efficiency in thrift as saving of "a cheese-paring or candle-end description" (30/11/52).
†*N.B. Daily Mail*, 10/5/53.

of the unemployed are weakly or partially worn out men, quite unfit for any strong physical exertion " ;* and upon the unemployed in Glasgow at mass meetings deciding to go in large gangs "begging from shopkeepers," the leaders were arrested. Worse and worse! wartime speculation drove up the price of food-stuffs ; wheat touched 80s. a bushel ; the unemployed (male) were set to break stones, but at pittances that could not feed them sufficiently to enable them to swing hammers ; the distress committees refused relief of any kind to unemployed women. Only in Dundee did the war bring "prosperity," and there the factory workers in 1855 secured wage increases.

About this period (1855) Alexander Macdonald, the great miners' leader, becomes prominent, taking part in all the working-class movements, and especially that against the Truck system ; under that mass robbery not only were miners and ironworkers compelled to go to their masters "stores" to buy their provisions, their clothing, whisky, and even Bibles, at ruinous prices ; but in the far Shetlands, in the quarries of Argyllshire, and indeed in monopoly areas all over the country, the poor workman was restricted to the purchaseing of his necessities of life, from his master, under pain of dismissal. These necessities were usually sold at a 20 per cent. profit by the store owner, and as none durst complain, the store keeper could make an extra illicit profit by adulteration and under-weighing. Drinking—particularly among workers' wives—was manifestly a thing to be encouraged, for that meant wages which were paid monthly were soon spent, and there was a long spell of "tick" until next pay day ; this "tick" had a value—1s. on the £1 or a penny on the shilling, and besides swelling the money bags of the "thrifty" employer it kept the workers continually on the rack of debt. In one year alone there were no fewer than 30,000 citations for small debts in Glasgow, and when such Unions as the slaters appealed for weekly wages instead of monthly, the employers sanctimoniously retorted that weekly wages, alas ! would mean more drunkenness.

The collier had everything trucked to him—except his coffin ; if he went on strike his children ceased to be educated, for the schoolmaster was trucked, supplied by the employer but paid by the worker, out of levies on his wages. Similarly the doctor was trucked. This iniquitous truck theft was the chief grievance of the middle fifties, and against it the workers waged unrelenting war.

In the early part of 1858 we find the unemployed at Edinburgh being offered "work" at sixpence per day ; if they refused and went begging they were given 30 days' imprisonment.† One Edinburgh employer who paid his workers 14s. 3d. for a week's toil was amazed that they should strike for 9d. extra and a Saturday half-holiday in

Courier, 5/12/54.
†*Scotsman*, 10/3/58.

addition. "Let us look to whom we bestow charity," he cried, "and not bestow it upon the indolent."* At Glasgow the Magistrates would do nothing for the unemployed, and sent the police to break up their gatherings. Workers driven crazy by poverty and misery were, so long as they survived, given a "special treatment" as pauper lunatics. In some districts, declared the London *Times*,

> "by day oppressed with fetters and manacles, by night lying naked, three or four in a bed of straw, without covering of any kind, rolling in filth and starved to desperation, the poor wretches who, in their helplessness, had passed into the hands of men whose only object was to keep them as cheaply as possible . . . led a life in comparison with which that of a well-fed pig in a sty seems a sort of paradisical existence."

The press of the late fifties and early sixties is simply one long catalogue of working-class misery. Journeymen bottle-blowers were sent to prison for "deserting the service" of their masters; Glasgow carters, with 16s. weekly, give eight months' notice of their intention to strike for an increase of 2s. : when the eight months expire they indulge in a procession with banners, and promptly their leaders are arrested ; the unemployed plead in vain for work or relief, and are urged by Alexander Campbell, the Owenite, to go in deputation about 1000 strong to the magistrates, but to interview the magistrates singly "so as not to take up too much of their time " ; the workless, organised for the purpose, filled selected Churches in Glasgow of a Sunday, doubtless to the disgust of the excluded Christians who owned the cushions in the seats ; at Paisley, we read the aged poor had to be content with a "parish " allowance of half-penny worth of meal per day.† The effects of the Civil War in the United States were felt all over industrial Scotland ; prices of the necessaries of life rose—the 4lb. loaf to 7½d., and potatoes to 7d. per peck. And by 1862 we find the leading Liberal newspaper in Scotland seriously warning the manufacturers and the Government that if they did not do their duty by the starving unemployed there would be "a probable destruction of property by mob violence."‡

The housing conditions were vile, almost beyond belief. At Hawick, in 1862, we read of 100 houses with two or more families to the single room ; at Edinburgh, one of the tenement warrens collapsed at night without anyone shoving it, and 22 persons were killed and many injured ; at Motherwell there were instances of 2 husbands, 2 wives and 3 children to a single room, and in one case there was an adult female lodger in addition ; the wynds of Glasgow were said to be the most unhealthy places in Europe. The census

---

* *Scotsman*, 25/3/58.
† *N.B. Daily Mail*, 28/11/61.
‡ *N.B. Daily Mail*, 15/7/62.

T

of 1861 gives us 226,723 families in Scotland living each in one room with one window (34 per cent. of all the families in Scotland), while no fewer than 7964 families lived in single rooms *minus* the window.

During this period, on what might be called the agitational side, there was little doing ; what organisation existed among the skilled men was being directed towards a nine-hour day, but the unskilled and unorganised were more interested in seeking relief during their periods of unemployment ; the employers were developing the "Black List" (*e.g.*, of revolting engineers) and the "sympathetic Lock-Out" (*e.g.*, among the miners). Property was sacred, not life. Theft was the most heinous of crimes—working-class theft, of course, for peculation on a big scale from the public, gambling in food-stuffs, rent-raisings, market riggings by the rich, these, when not openly commended as "good business," were privately excused. Turn to the Spring Circuit Court in Glasgow, 1864. Hugh Gray, for stealing a woollen lorry cover, gets 8 years' penal servitude ; Mary Love, for stealing 3 yards of drugget from a hedge, gets 6 years ; a man, Dogherty by name, gets 3 years for stealing a cloth cap from a shop door ; Jane Campbell steals 4½d. in copper, and gets 15 months ; but Alexander Still, for killing a man with a poker, gets off with six months !

The "Master and Servant Act" for 41 years had kept the wretches in order ; at a working-class demonstration in Glasgow, Alexander Campbell proves that its provisions were penal against the worker for breach of contract, but civil only against a defaulting employer.

> " Agricultural labourers even were subject to it, and he had no doubt a number of them would have recently seen that an agricultural labourer under this law had been sent to prison for refusing to obey his master by going to church on Sabbath day. The law indeed had not merely reference to absence from service, but also applied to the conduct of any workmen ; for if that conduct was not satisfactory either to his employer or his employer's agent or manager, they could proceed against him by complaint before a Justice of the Peace, and immediately obtain a warrant, a criminal warrant, to take him, even from his bench, coal pit, or any other place where he might be working, place him as a criminal in a police cell ; and without giving the workman a chance of engaging an agent to defend his case, bring him before a Justice of the Peace, and on evidence brought up by his employer against him, he was subject to be sent to prison for 60 days with hard labour."[*]

A St. Rollox potter, given 7 days' hard labour for leaving without giving his employers a month's notice, pleaded in vain that he had been engaged at 24s. per week, but had been set to a work whereat he could only earn an average of 6s. 1d. per week ; he had asked for

---

[*] *N.B. Daily Mail*, 29/12/64.

"good work" but it had been refused, and so he left without giving the month's notice. The judgment in this case roused the Trade Unionists to fury. The iron puddlers of England sent Glasgow Trades Council £150 to fight the iniquitous sentence ; the Glasgow iron moulders sent £50 ; money poured in from all sides, and the Court of Session quashed the conviction on appeal. In 1861 there were no fewer than 600 prosecutions of Scots workmen under the Act ; and the agitation against it so grew, that the Government was forced to appoint a Commission of Enquiry. Among the witnesses who gave evidence were George Newton (Glasgow Trades Council), Alexander Campbell (at that time editing *The Sentinel*), Alexander Macdonald (miners' president), and C. Steele (secretary, Scottish iron moulders). Newton said that workers were frequently dragged through the streets manacled. A case was retailed of a girl, too sick to go to her work one morning, being sent to gaol for 30 days amid thieves and prostitutes ; the Home Office had refused to interfere. A workman could not even be a witness in his own defence.* The report of the Committee, however, did not make for any alteration in the existing law beyond ensuring that Justices were to hear charges in the Criminal Courts and not in their own back parlours. Thus was an outraged working-class presumed to be pacified !

The Act of 1840, passed to prevent poor little boys and girls from being sent up sooty chimneys as brushers or cleaners by enterprising chimney sweeps, was only partially observed in the sixties. The poor victims still went up in climbing shirts, still had the skin stripped off their elbows and knees (and on the abrasions ulcers formed) ; still they were forced up burning flues, and beaten by their masters if they hesitated to be burned ; frequently, in descending, the climbing shirt crumbled up under the arms and the child stuck in the flue, and then another child would be sent to pull the victim down by the feet ; when another child was not available a rope was affixed to the victim's legs, and sometimes he or she was dragged down dead ; actually there were instances in which a chimney had to be broken up in order to extract the dead body of the youthful chimney sweep. In 1863 the Children's Employment Commissioners reported that boy-sweepers were on the increase because the fine of £5 levied upon the master who employed them was so "harsh" that magistrates were "indisposed to convict."

In the autumn of 1865 we find prices rising steadily ; butter and bacon" are only occasionally within reach of the vast mass of the people, while fresh butcher meat is seldom in their dwellings."† Butter was 1s. 2d. to 1s. 4d. per lb., bacon 8d. to 10d., boiling beef 8d. to 9d. The official explanation for these prices was that there

N.B. Daily Mail, 10/9/66 and 11/9/66.
†*Scotsman*, 12/9/65.

was a rinderpest among cattle ; but there was no rinderpest among house rents ; yet they too rose in an "unwarrantable manner," as a public meeting resolution in Glasgow had it.

In 1866 Scotland was in the throes of a commercial panic, the effects of which lasted to the end of the year 1869.   Terrible years these for the working-class—the House Proprietors and Factors Association in Glasgow driving up rents by from 10 to 25 per cent.; privies and middens converted into dwelling-houses ; 60,000 dwelling houses in Glasgow without water-closet accommodation ;   one-third of the people in single apartments ; the houses in the Broad Street district have "already cost the Barony Parish for relief to its inhabitants arising from its unhealthy character more than the value of the whole property " ;* wages everywhere falling, the Master Coopers of Glasgow frankly giving as their reason for reducing wages "that there were 40 men going idle " ; labourers' wages fell to 14s. weekly. Parliament, half-heartedly, sought to stem the economic disaster by passing an Act "to establish equitable Councils of Conciliation between masters and workmen."   Vain hope : it was as useless as the old and similar ideal Act of 1824 ; and when, in January, 1871, the puddlers of Lanarkshire got from an arbiter an increase of 6d. per day, the masters promptly stuck up fresh notices intimating a reduction.†   All over the country the employers strove hard during the improved trade conditions of the early seventies to keep their workers at the starvation level of 1869.   A large preserved provisions firm in Aberdeen, Moir & Sons, fixes the hours of toil for its employees from 6 a.m. to 6 p.m. "and also during such additional hours as might be required " ; two shillings weekly are to be deducted from each employee and retained by the firm as security for the employee's good behaviour ; if the worker breaks his engagement he is fined £2, and all his savings in the firm's hands are declared forfeit.   If he is disrespectful, unsteady, or intemperate he is similarly fined and mulcted !   But despite the efforts of the employers, wages rose, and the organised workers again concentrated their efforts upon the securing of a nine hours' working day, and against the monstrous robbery known as the Truck System.   At Neilson's Works, Mossend, "the lowest paid workers in Scotland " had their whisky trucked to them, and Mr. Neilson, being a J.P., saw to it that no other liquor license was granted for Holytown.‡ The Truck Act Commission, sitting at Edinburgh, got some remark-able evidence from Shetland.§   The Clerk of Supply at Lerwick declared that women shawl-knitters could make "at most " 4s. to

---

*N.B. Daily Mail, 19/1/70.

†*Glasgow Herald*, 14/1/71.

‡*N.B. Daily Mail*, 26/6/69.

§*Glasgow Herald*, 24/1/71.

6s. per week, but they seldom got paid in money. The stores through-out the island belonged to the great fish-curing companies; these companies dealt with their employee customers by barter, and pauperism due to that barter system was rife. The factor for Garth and Annsbrae, said girls had often to take their wages in fancy goods which they did not want—goods which the merchant employer could not dispose of otherwise. "The worsted of a shawl, selling about 30s., is worth from 2s. to 3s. The merchant nominally gives the worker 9s. for working it, and this in goods will be about 4s. Actually the merchant gets from 25s. to 26s. for the shawl." The success of the merchant

> "consists in being able to accumulate such an amount of bad debts about him as will thirl the whole of the families in his neighbourhood, and then he succeeds. . . . The crews for the boats are hired in December or January, and at the same time boys are engaged as beach boys. The boy is allowed to draw his coat to go to church with, and by the time the fishing is over the boy has overdrawn his account, and is thirled to be engaged for the next season, and he is thus thirled or trucked away until he is thirled into the grave. . . . Even the paupers were trucked by the Inspectors, who kept shops and served them with goods instead of with money."

But Commissions and evidence and agitation notwithstanding, the iniquity survived until the Act of 1896, and, indeed, in some out-of-the-stream places and behind specious subterfuge Truck still persists.

Despite Free Trade, the cost of living steadily rose in the sixties. In 1867 butter was dearer by 200 per cent. than in 1827; cheese had risen 150 per cent., the best boiling beef from 5d. for 22½oz. to 9d. for 16oz.; potatoes from 5d. for 2½ stones to 7d. or 8d. per stone; and even the loaf—the Free Trade loaf—was 7d. as against 5d. in 1827. Between 1846 and 1871 milk prices rose 50 per cent. and eggs had trebled in price; white fish had risen 200 per cent. and more; only tea and sugar had fallen. In 1871, due to a bad harvest, potatoes rose to 10d. per stone. In the succeeding year, 1872, there was again a bad harvest, but the great strikes which marked that year seem to have been directed—and successfully directed—not to the raising of wages but to the shortening of the hours of labour. Again, in 1873, there was a plethora of strikes, even the Glasgow tramcar guards striking against a 15 hour day; exactly how the strike ended is not recorded in the press of the period, but 10 years later the men were actually working 16 hours—from 7.30 a.m. to 11.30 p.m., and under, as the *Glasgow Weekly Mail* (1/12/83) said, "petty tyranny and worse than Egyptian slavery." Workers on the cars were regularly fined for petty offences; one driver, complimented officially for his carefulness, is mulcted £5 11s. 6d. in two years. A child falls off a car; the parent sues the Tramway

Company for damages ; in Court the case is heard and dismissed ; yet the Company surcharges the conductor 10s. 6d. for its lawyer's services ! Another case : a man starts in the morning, ill with diarrhoea ; relief is promised but none comes ; he hangs on to his car at work until 7 p.m. when he is compelled to go off, nearly dead ; he has a doctor's certificate, but the Company fines him £1 16s. 8d ; he has no right to indulge in diarrhoea in the Company's time ! Car workers were given no time off for food ; they had to consume their "pieces" while the cars were running, one hand on the "piece" and the other on the horse reins ; no overtime for Sundays ; no time off for a hair-cut ; no holidays ; no uniforms, and the miserable wages ran to little in the way of clothes ; so that drivers at work with rents and vacant spaces in the seats of their trousers was no uncommon sight on the streets of Glasgow.   On the other hand, it is interesting to read* that one of the promoters of the Glasgow Tramway Company received £60,000 for his trouble in promoting the venture !

In the winter of 1874 unemployment was widespread ; in 1875 there was a decided improvement, but in 1876 trade was again bad, due to "over-production," the Glasgow Trades Council is fighting the evils of "piece-work," and Alexander Macdonald is denouncing the legalised swindle of "common employment," whereby an employer was freed from obligation to give compensation to an injured workman so long as the workman was not working under the employer's *direct* instructions. If a manager was employed, then the employer was not responsible for injuries sustained by a workman ; both the manager and the workman were held to be in the "common employment" of the employer, and the employer was not liable to one servant for the mistakes and omissions of another.   Macdonald's Bill to ensure compensation for accident was brazenly described by a wrathful employer M.P. as encouraging "carelessness and idleness " ; and all the length the Government would go was to promise an "enquiry." It was indeed a period of great economic depression and savage legal repression of the common people.   In 1877 a strike of flint glass workers, which lasted for 33 weeks,† was met by the introduction of blackleg labour from England ; the strike officials induced the blacklegs to go home and paid their railway fares ; for this proceeding the strike leaders were sued by the employers and fined £50, whereat there was great indignation and gathering of subscriptions.‡

The trade depression, begun in 1876, lasted more or less acutely

---

Glasgow Herald, 18/5/75.

†The Alloa Glassworkers' Strike, 1878-79, lasted 56 weeks.—*Journal Stat. Socy.* 1880.

‡The High Court finally overturned this particular decision.

all through the years 1877 and 1878—Parliament being meanwhile industriously engaged upon the Contagious Diseases (Animals) Bill and the Russo-Turkish question—and a big Bank failure in the closing months of 1878 made matters worse ; thousands of Scottish families were destitute, soup kitchens were set going ; but in Glasgow destitution was dwarfed by the excitements aroused by the Working Men's Sabbath Protection Association in its campaign against the running of tramcars on Sundays. The Established Church Presbytery, in this agitation, stood at once manfully for principle and moderation in its application ; it saw necessity for the running of cars "immediately before and after divine service,"* but then only !

In the year 1879 there was still widespread unemployment and wage-breaking. At the Caledonian Locomotive Works, for example, wages rates fell by 20 per cent. between June, 1879, and September, 1879. Glasgow had 38,000 names on its Relief Roll, able-bodied unemployed were set to stone-breaking, oakum-teasing, and earth works ; there were deaths from sheer starvation ; but the Town Clerk, Sir James Marwick, gave it as his considered legal opinion that the Common Good Funds of the city were not available sources for donations to Relief Funds,† and the Government was busy with its Zulu and Afghan wars.

The year 1880 was marked by a piece of Liberal Government effrontery rare even in the annals of our ruling class. An Act—the Employers' Liability for Accidents Act—was passed with a flourish of trumpets ; but when the trump blowing was over Mr. Pearce, the Govan shipbuilder, and Mr Tennant, the great chemical manufacturer, hastened to reassure the affrighted employers. They said the Act was really so useless that there was hardly a conceivable accident for which they were liable ; no claim f contributory negligence could be proved ; the doctrine of common employment still a barrier to claims, the Liberal Attorney-General saying the country was not "ripe" for its abolition, and such abolition would enormously and unduly increase the responsibilities of the masters ; the masters could contract out of any liability by getting the workman to sign a voluntary surrender of his rights to compensation for accident as a preliminary condition of employment. The *Weekly Mail* (12/11/80) roundly declared that the Act did not give compensation, only "a right for action for compensation." And the action was usually lost !

Towards the end of the year 1880 wages were rising again, and had reached more than double what they were in 1840 ; but in the same period the price of meal was up 4d. per stone, potatoes up from 4¼d. to 6d. per stone, beef from 7d. to 1s. per lb., bacon from 6d. to

---

Weekly Citizen, 7/12/68.
†*Weekly Mail,* 12/11/79.

9d. per lb., pork from 6d. to 9d. per lb. ; bread had fallen by 1d. per 4lb. loaf to 8½d., but milk was up 4d. a gallon; salt butter had risen from 10½d. to 1s. 2d. per lb.; the rent of a room had risen from £4 4s. to £5 ; but tea was down from 5s. 4d. per lb. to 2s. per lb., brown sugar had fallen from 9d. to 2½d., and coals from 1s. 3d. to 8d. per cwt.

In Scotland the capitalists were on the horns of a dilemma. The developments in engineering and factory machinery necessitated a labouring class possessed of the rudiments of reading, writing and arithmetic ; on the other hand, as the far-seeing ones clearly saw, an educated working-class sooner or later made for radical changes in the economic and political structure of society. Education meant bigger immediate profits, but it was gambling with "revolution," and the more conservative and fearful chose to take no risks. Even the Glasgow School Board, we note, in 1881 protested by 9 votes to 2 against a Free Education Bill, one speaker saying his objection was based upon the fact that it would increase the number of children attending school !

In 1882 trade "boomed" again, and wages conditions generally improved ; but the potato crop in the West Highlands failed, and the resultant destitution speedily had its effect upon the industrial areas. In the Lews the famine was the worst since the black winter of 1849, and deaths from sheer starvation were continually being reported. Naturally the food scarcity caused the concentration of political attention upon the landlords and their practices, the chief Liberal organ, the *Glasgow Weekly Mail*, carefully differentiating between the idle aristocrats who "toil not neither do they spin " and "the frugal, hard-working capitalist." These frugal, hardworking ones we can trace throughout the columns of the same organ—frugal and hardworking by proxy, as, when Archibald Arrol, director of the Steel Company of Scotland (Blochairn), was indicted before the Sheriff for working a boy of 13 years from 6 a.m. on 6th February, 1883, to 5 p.m. on 7th February,"with some short intervals for meals and a rest of about three hours when the machine broke down." The legal limit in working hours for children at that period was 6½ per day, and here was a child toiling for 35 hours ! The boy had lost his fingers working at a saw—probably through sheer weariness—and the accident had drawn attention to the extraordinary overtime. The Sheriff, being a man skilled in equity, fined the frugal, hard working capitalist in the sum of 30s., and the parent of the now fingerless boy he fined 20s. The parent, it was true, had a wife and five children to maintain on a wage of 20s. weekly, but he ought not to have been so inconsiderate as to have a child who would lose his fingers in a saw. Besides, he might have damaged the saw with his fingers ! There were prosecutions for like offences against the Mossend Iron Company, the Dalziel Iron works, the Clydesdale Iron works and other frugal, hard-working groups of shareholders ; but during the year 1883, out of some 343 actions under the Employers' Liability Act, the law courts refused conviction and compensation, in all but 16 cases.* Truck still flourished openly at Summerlee as it flourished in Shetland, where the workers were paid in goods, no receipts being given, none having the temerity to solicit them.   At Foula the factor was a brother of the storekeeper, and "to the terror of prosecution for debt is added the fear of eviction . . . the people are kept in a state of terror."

By January 1884 wages were again being reduced all over the country ; trade was bad ; unemployment was severe, many men going idle for quite 12 months : in December of that year Glasgow had 11,687 unemployed males, Dundee 3000, and right from then to 1887 there were continual unemployed crises and agitations.†
In 1885 there were people dying of starvation on the streets of Glasgow ; the death-rate rose to 39 per 1000 living, as a city average, but in some working-class districts the death-rate was nearly 100 per 1000 living, and the *Weekly Mail* cried that "the state of affairs is too serious for exaggeration" ; Henry George discovered to his amazement that there were parishes in Scotland where "pauper relief" was at the rate of only 2s. per month, and that in Campbeltown, where a hunting dog cost two shillings a week to feed, a "pauper" got 9d. a week. By January, 1886, the unemployed were breaking stones at a weekly dole of 7s. ; the Government was sending a naval expedition to Skye to serve writs upon (among others) paupers, for the non-payment of Poor Rates ; on Glasgow Green, under Socialist auspices, 50,000 hungry men listened to the oratory of John Burns.

A century of commercialism and industrialism had passed, leaving the common people of Scotland physically broken and poverty-stricken, while merchant princes and industrial magnates had accumulated vast fortunes and lived in riotous splendour.

But the end was not yet !

---

*Proceedings of British Trade Union Congress, Aberdeen, Press, 13/9/84.
†*Contemporary Review*, 1887, p. 771.   Article by Bennet Burleigh, who advocated the Right to Work, an Eight Hours' Day, Reclamation of Waste Lands, the Feeding of Necessitous School Children.   The Caledonian Railway directors, on the other hand, proposed to *increase* the workers' hours from 10 to 12 per day.

CHAPTER XII.

THE GREAT MASSACRE.

" . . . . our streets are infested with miserable creatures, from whose faces almost everything human has been erased, whose very presence would put us to shame but for familiarity with the sight. Poor wretches! filthy in body, foul in speech, vile in spirit. Human vermin! Yes, but of our own manufacture, for every individual of this mass was once an innocent child."— *Cardinal Manning in " Nineteenth Century Magazine."*

"The English people never, by any plague, or famine, or war suffered such a deadly blow at its vitality as by the establishment of the factory system without the proper safeguards."—*Professor York Powell—Preface to Beard's " The Industrial Revolution."*

BEFORE the coming of steam-power and the industrial revolution, the recurrent wars, famines, and dearths produced a great army of migratory starvelings who maintained themselves in their itinerances upon the charity and generosity of the settled, though scarcely less-starved, peasantry. In 1723, for example, we are told that no fewer than 1000 mendicants—some of them from Ireland—attended the funeral of an Earl of Eglinton for a share of the charity-money—£30—distributed at the obsequies; and in the time of Fletcher of Saltoun it was estimated that no less than one-fifth of our total population was vagrant. Death, large-scale and dramatic, periodically thinned the ranks of these destitutes, but a famine or a war rapidly recruited them again. It was no uncommon occurrence for a pestilence to sweep a parish clear of its beggary, and for an "ill-harvest" to drive a fresh contingent of peasants to the aumous dish, so that the beggars were as numerous as before ; but with the growth of large towns at the beginning of the nineteenth century, and with factory and steam-power production, the sudden herding of the proletariat into the odd corners in the unclean and undrained towns, a capitalism unregulated either by law or by sentiment, and with long hours of ill-paid toil in death-traps, there began a massacre of human life beside which the casualties of the medieval battlefields and plagues were as farthing dips to the noon-day sun.

In the first 40 years of the nineteenth century some 350,000 "strangers" were "suddenly huddled" on the banks of the Clyde, where they suffered periodical decimation by typhus, and one writer[*] estimated a constant residue of 30,000 widows and orphans. In

---

[*]*Courier*, 13/7/44.

1775 the deaths in Glasgow from phthisis were one to every 267 inhabitants ; in 1853, one to every 158 inhabitants ; in 1854 one-third of all the deaths of persons in Glasgow over 5 years of age was due to phthisis. In 1819 (same city) there were 89 arrests for criminal offences ; in 1837 the number had risen to 3176 ; and in 1842 the number was 4189. The population of Lanarkshire doubled in the first 30 years of industrial capitalism, but crime grew six-fold. Dr. Allison notes after each commercial crisis and exceptional hungering of the people a special virulence in the typhus outbreak, and how the fury falls chiefly upon working-class fathers of families. Dr. Cowan, more discerning, earnestly advocates sanitary reform, since the typhus has a strange and uncanny lack of discrimination ; it does not abide in the working-class districts, but must needs spread even to the mansions of the rich.

In the five year period, 1825-1835, the Glasgow general death-rate was 1 in 41 ; in the period 1835-1840 it was 1 in 31 ;* and during these five years no fewer than 109,385 cases of "febrile and eruptive complaints" were registered in the city ; and 68,621 people took typhus, of whom 5844 died. While the Glasgow population rose by 33,031 in the decade 1831-1841, the number of houses only increased by 3551. Pawnshops taking 400 per cent. profits gaped at every corner ; in 1830 one house in every twelve, and in 1840 one house in every ten, was an alcohol shop.

Edinburgh, if anything, was worse. There, in 1763, could be found only one brothel and five prostitutes ; in 1783 the brothels had grown twenty-fold and the prostitutes a hundred-fold. "What would you have us do ?" cried the unfortunates in expostulation, "We cannot starve !" The Rev. Dr. Lee testified before the Commission on Religious Instruction that :—

> "He had never seen such misery as in his parish, where the people were often without furniture, without everything, two married couples often sharing one room. In a single day he had visited seven houses in which there was not a bed, in some of them not even a heap of straw. Old people of eighty years sleep on the board floor, nearly all slept in their day clothes. In one cellar room he found two families from a Scotch country district ; soon after their removal to the city two of the children had died, and a third was dying at the time of his visit. Each family had a filthy pile of straw lying in a corner ; the cellar sheltered, besides the two families, a donkey, and was, moreover, so dark that it was impossible to distinguish one person from another by day."

In the working-class districts of Edinburgh there were neither sewers nor drains ; refuse, garbage, and excrement were tossed from

---

*In London it was only 1 in 51.

the windows on to the narrow streets ; no privies were attached to the houses.*

A Government Commissioner † discovered rooms in the fetid wynds of Glasgow where from 15 to 20 persons slept—some clad, some naked, men and women indiscriminately, on beds of mouldy straw and rags. When a bread-winner fell idle from economic causes (and the steady streams of imported Irish destitutes always flooded the Labour "market") he got no parochial relief. In Glasgow, in 1841, there were 2000 families in unrelieved destitution, and "relieved" families without able-bodied fathers, who got the munificent sum of 1s. per family per week, starved to death with the "unrelieved," though doubtless at a mathematically slower rate.‡ The Superintendent of the Glasgow police, Captain Miller, described the condition of the poor as that of "squalid wretchedness, which is probably unequalled in any other town in the British dominions . . . . . thousands of miserable creatures. The houses in which they live are unfit even for sties."

From the evidence given to the Poor Law Commissioners § we get a terrible picture of the miseries of the thousands from whom the Capitalist system could make no profit. In Greenock aged "paupers" got 3s. 6d. monthly ; in some places Roman Catholics got nothing, and dissenters were discriminated against in the way of relief ; several Highland parishes donated 4s. per pauper yearly from the Kirk Session collections ; in Dundee the beggars "are supported chiefly by the lower classes" ; in the parish of Lochs they ate shellfish, and in scarce years had nothing but "grass cooked in milk" to eat ; the lodging-houses in the Tron parish of Edinburgh were so vile that "a policeman fainted on visiting one of them in consequence of the stench" ; at Kirkwall, one room 12 feet square contained 9 inhabitants, eight of them ill with fever. The general testimony was that the Irish immigrants were the most miserable (though Dr. Allison declared that there was a stratum of Scots below even the Irish), but more and ever more were poured into the industrial districts to keep the wage rate low; the fare from Belfast was 1s. 3d., from Derry 2s., and from Sligo 3s. 6d. We read of paupers committing suicide rather than enter the filthy lodgings provided by the Scone Kirk Session ; at Newhills "many became paupers owing to the lowering of wages" ; in the north, skin disease and dyspepsia became chronic. Town Councillor Wright of Edinburgh surveyed all this, and thought it had come to "a war betwixt poverty and property. . . . The idea in Edinburgh was that people should go

---

The Artisan, October, 1842.

†Mr. J. C. Symonds' *Arts and Artisan at Home and Abroad* (1839).

‡*Blackwood's Magazine*, 1841, p. 659 *et seq.*

§Three vols., 1844.

and take food in a peaceable manner ; that none should resist when apprehended ; but that they should let the police take them for stealing bread. They knew that it was not in the power of the Government to put the whole working classes in prison."

The failure of the potato crop in 1847 greatly intensified the degradation of the peasantry in the north. People in Brocadale and Barra died of starvation ; in Islay the oatmeal was poor in quality and the best of the barley was ordered off to the distilleries to pay for landlords' rent, while "5000 souls" were foodless ; the parish minister of Ulva reports families without food for two days— "many deaths here soon unless something done immediately." At Iona "most of the tenants have consumed their only cow" ; the minister at Tobermory feared "some will perish" and charitably fed even "two of the Frees" who "had no particle of food for their families."* These were the Hungry Forties, and typhus followed famine around the hovels and the rookeries, and cholera followed both.

The press began to preach "sanitation," the *Scotsman* pointing out that the rich catch diseases from "the ragged, the starved, and the degraded" ; when 60 per cent. of the population in a working-class part of Dunfermline took typhus, the disease did not stop there, as the alarmed capitalists observed, and there was general recognition that something more drastic was required than the special diet of "humiliation and prayer" which the Church had hurriedly organised. In Glasgow one preacher who announced that the cholera epidemic was God's reply to an attempt to push a Deceased Wife's Sister's Bill in Parliament, received scant consideration against Lord Ashley's detailed proofs that people with baths and wash-houses had in the main escaped.† The capitalist class, however, which had succeeded in transferring the old poor's rate levied on "means and substance," to a rental rate, half paid by owner and half by occupier, was chiefly concerned to keep the starving multitude in its place with not over-much sentimental humanitarian nonsense. Six half-famished navvies who stole a loaf and swallowed it dry between them were each sentenced to 30 days' imprisonment at Anderston Police Court, Glasgow ;‡ another man got 60 days for stealing a loaf ;§ another man got 7 years' transportation for stealing a gill measure ;‖ the

---

*Bogle pamphlets, vol. ii.—Glasgow Mitchell Library.

†Again, in 1853, the Presbytery of Edinburgh proposed a national fast as a remedy for cholera, but Lord Palmerston regarded the situation as too serious for nonsense of that kind, and recommended the clergy to turn their attention to slums and drains.

‡*Courier*, 22/2/49 ;

§*Ibid*, 21/4/49 ;

‖*Ibid*, 26/4/49.

Court of Session decided that the children of able-bodied poor were not entitled to relief.

Dr. Gavin, the reporter in Glasgow to the Board of Health, declared that the city workman had only an average life of 48 years 8 months, being 12½ years shorter than the life of the rural worker. Little wonder, he says, when

> "damp earthen, muddy floors, walls saturated with moisture . . . small closed windows admitting of no perflation of air, crowded apartments thatched roofs saturated like a sponge with water, an undrained soil and ash refuse cellars, within ten feet of inhabited rooms are the general characteristics."

The same writer assures us that in the rural districts swept by the cholera, conditions were no better. At Cramond, an agricultural village near Edinburgh, the house walls were of whinstone, the roofs of decayed thatch "covered with bright green fungoid vegetation"; the floors, a foot below the level of the adjacent soil, were of unhardened clay, often hollowed in some places and filled with water.[*]

The steady increase in typhus deaths in Glasgow—427 in 1860, 451 in 1861, and 516 in 1862—caused at last a real "sanitary panic among the upper class," and considerable publicity and attention began to be paid to the revelations of such reformers as the Rev. Dr. Begg. The Census Returns for 1861 shewed that one-third of the population of Scotland lived in single-roomed houses, and 7964 of these houses had no window. In Glasgow 100,000 people lived in one-room houses; of these one-room houses, 1253 housed 7 persons each, 596 had 8 persons, 229 had 9 persons, 84 had 10 persons, 30 had 11 persons, 11 had 12 persons, 5 had 13 persons, 3 had 14 persons, and 2 housed 15 persons. Edinburgh was as bad, 2000 dying annually from fever; but Greenock was worst of all. In Port Glasgow, declared Dr. Begg, a stable had been converted into a dwelling-house, and "during the whole summer that stable contained 83 persons besides a horse . . . a stream of dead bodies had been brought out about the time he was there . . . it would cost the community in the long run as much for coffins as it would have originally cost to have provided proper houses for the inhabitants."[†]

Chadwick, the sanitary reformer, declared that the Glasgow wynds were the worst he ever saw;[‡] in some of them off the High Street the apartments were 9 or 10 feet square and 7 or 8 feet high and housed two families in each; no ventilation—"not the slightest," no light. "Of course there was no drainage. . . . In Glasgow 50 per cent. of children born die under five years of age . . . also the highest proportion of still-born children in the kingdom; the ratio is one to

---

[*] *Courier*, 28/1/54.

[†] *N.B. Daily Mail*, 18/11/64.

[‡] Quoted from the *Builder* and *N.B. Daily Mail*, 3/2/62

every 12 births." In the year 1852 "the Roman Catholic children under five years of age constituted 45 per cent. of the whole deaths from small-pox throughout the city. . . . Thousands (of Irish) who fled from their miserable and starving homes in Munster and Connaught only arrived in Glasgow to find their graves. Of course the children were not long in following the parents. . . . The Glasgow closes, wynds, and vennels are about the most unhealthy places in Europe. The next worst in all probability are the closes of Edinburgh." In Glasgow "the liquid refuse of the chemical works, gas works, distilleries, manure manufactories, etc., is discharged into the common sewers." For those who escaped from the slums to the poorhouses, death was even more certain. In the Scots poorhouses in 1862 there were 7843 inmates, of whom 23 per cent. died. The wonder indeed is that so many survived in these middle-class bastilles ; their daily food allowance was valued at 3½d., and residence was regarded as "an efficient test of poverty " ; the sexes were separated ; "aged couples were ruthlessly parted " ; the only exercise allowed was "in narrow yards enclosed by high walls. . . . The diet is calculated to sustain life and no more, and so close is the calculation made that doubts will intrude whether it does not really fall short in the amount of nutriment necessary for health, and does not subject many of the inmates to slow death from gradual inanition."* Prison fare was twice the size of poorhouse fare, and no prison approached the poorhouses in mortality. But if the middle-class cared nothing for the bodies of the broken workers, it looked well after the souls, for systematic efforts were made to wean paupers who affected Roman Catholicism from their spiritual errors, and every facility was provided for proselytisation by emissaries of the Established Church. The Board of Supervision of the Poor in Scotland, when reporting that the physical condition of the children in Linlithgow poorhouse was "unsatisfactory," felt compelled to recommend "the introduction of more active and joyous games," and that the children should be taken out for exercise two or three times a week, a recommendation that speaks volumes. Govan poorhouse is described as being "as much a prison as the penitentiary. The inmates are all confined by bolts and bars and stone walls within the establishment and to the special part allotted to each." Aged couples are separated "just at the very time when the company and consolation of each other is most needed. View them now looking at each other through iron railings, forty feet apart, where they dare not speak to each other without infringing the rules of the institution " ; the allowance per head for food, clothing, lighting, bedding, fire, and cleaning was 4d. per day; the death-rate was high—100 between January and May 1867 ; the nurses were themselves

---

*Scotsman, 7/5/63.

inmates, and were paid no wages ; one nurse had 100 men to look after ; the management and control was, we need scarcely be told, in the hands of the rate-saving heritors and large ratepayers.*

Despite Chadwick's agitation, little sanitary improvement in the working-class districts of Glasgow was observed by the *Daily Mail's* special commissioner in 1869. His pen-pictures of the vile housing and sanitary conditions reveal an appalling state of affairs :—"Rags, scraps of blankets and old clothing, grey with dirt and crawling with vermin, are wound in frowzy coils round the limbs of little children and of grown-up men and women. . . . See the walls glittering with a moist film of condensed vapour and filth ; you can scrape it off ; a pasty mess." In the Garngad, vermin declared to be "as big as bum-bees." At 13 Middleton Place, a great rabbit warren, the beds were never empty and never free from typhus ; the infirmary van called, occasionally as often as six times in a day. Hovels with earthen floors earned rents of six shillings a month. In Oak-bank Street there were tenanted cellars that never enjoyed daylight. Commercial Court, Gallowgate, was packed with people at a density rate of 5000 to the acre. At St. Andrew's Lane there were no conveniences, and the human excreta was thrown over the windows, so that the window sills, the walls and the bottom of the court were "covered with human ordure." At Creilly's Crescent the children "are quite dwarfed and attenuated to mere skeletons, their crooked limbs and wasted bodies and little claw-like hands all combine to give them a weird appearance." The proprietor of Creilly's desirable mansions was a Sauchiehall Street banker who called personally for the rents, and was "very civil to those who pay promptly, but sharper than a serpent's tooth to unfortunates who may not be able at the moment to pay up." In 102 Main Street, Gorbals, were 46 houses, the tenants of which were all apparently liable to pay poor's rate, for we read of raids by Sheriff's officers for the poor's rate, "with expenses added." In one house the sole article of furniture, a chest valued at 4s. 10d., is seized ; in another case a woman complains that "they cam' an' took my pot aff the fire wi' a penny-worth o' liver in't for poor's rates."

During the last thirty years of the nineteenth century there were energetic efforts made to improve the insanitary conditions in which the working-class lived and died. The design was to wipe out contagious diseases, which had the inconsiderate habit of spreading to the habitations of the well-to-do. Cholera and typhus especially were marked out for attack, for they notoriously were no respecters of persons ; and in the closing years of the century, when the opinion spread that tuberculosis was contagious, the upper classes took alarm, and tuberculosis, too, was put upon the index. The result

---

*N.B. *Daily Mail*, 6/5/67.

has been a decline, due to increased and improved sanitation, in the adult death-rate. But infantile mortality among the poor, which is not easily, if at all, transmissible to the cradles of the rich, shews no decline.* In 1906, one child in every eight born died before it reached the age of twelve months—a massacre that might have appalled even King Herod—due chiefly to evil food, housing, and employment conditions. In 1903, the Royal Commission on Physical Training was told that 70 per cent. of the children attending four schools in Edinburgh were unsound or defective in some way. The adults, though saved from their fathers' chances of dramatic mass death by infectious and contagious disease, were more liable to the diseases of degeneration—cancer, heart disease, diabetes, Bright's disease, apoplexy, insanity, and general paralysis. The army recruiting standard has fallen from 5 feet 6 inches in 1845 to 5 feet 2 inches in 1897. In that latter year 22 per cent. of Scottish families lived in a one-roomed house, and in Glasgow 33 per cent. of the families were so "accommodated."†

The sanitarians had to struggle against great odds (even in contagious diseases) with the economic interests. In 1882, for example, we find the Duke of Argyll, who owned all the houses at Inveraray, warning out of his house the Medical Officer of Health, who had dared to report adversely upon the sanitary state of the burgh after an outbreak of small-pox ;‡ the middle-class ratepayers were always jealous of expensive sanitation, and reforms were only secured in spurts after some contagion had swept from the slums to the terraces. Malnutrition, underfeeding, chronic starvation, the intensification of toil—these things have left a physically enfeebled proletariat in the towns ; and Mr. Sidney Webb, in summing up the situation at the end of Queen Victoria's glorious reign, has come to the conclusion that there existed in 1897 "a greater sum, though a smaller proportion, of hopeless destitution than at any previous time."

---

*In 1855 125 per 1000 ; in 1915, 126 per 1000.
†In 1861 35% of Scottish family groups lived in a single room.
‡*Weekly Mail.* 6/5/82.

A DISEASE CHART UNDER CAPITALISM.

1775	1818	1825-1830	1831-1832	1836	1837
Glasgow—1 phthisis death to every 267 inhabitants.	Glasgow—First 8 months of year 32,000 people took typhus. Edinburgh, 6000 typhus cases.	Glasgow—Death-rate 1 in 41.	20,202 cases of cholera in Scotland and 10,650 deaths.	Glasgow — Typhus outbreak, 30,000 poor infected and 3300 died.	Edinburgh—10,000 typhus cases. Glasgow death-rate, 1 in 24.

1838-1839	1835-1840	1840	1842	1843	1847
Death-rate in Old Town of Edinburgh, 1 in 22.	Glasgow Death-rate, 1 in 31. 109,385 cases of fever registered, 5844 died of typhus.	Glasgow—One death in every 3.25 due to fever.	One-sixth of indigent population of Scotland took typhus.	Glasgow—12% of population took typhus. Of these, 32 per cent. died. Over two-thirds of the victims were unemployed poor.	Glasgow — General death-rate, 1 in 19. During February, out of 574 deaths, 201 were from typhus and 42 from phthisis. Potato famine and deaths from hunger in Highlands.

1848	1849	1852	1853	1854
Cholera outbreak in Scotland	80 deaths at Carnbroe, 110 cases at Kilwinning iron works.	Glasgow—2603 pauper funerals out of 10,675 deaths. 45% of smallpox deaths in Glasgow were R.C. children.	Glasgow—1 phthisis death to every 158 inhabitants; 151 cholera deaths; 4024 pauper burials. Dundee—Cholera epidemic. 337 Highland deportees put ashore at Queenstown suffering from fever and smallpox.	Glasgow—One-third of deaths over 5 years, due to phthisis. In first 10 days of year, 234 cholera deaths. Year's death-rate 37.2 per 1000; in reconstructed working-class parts of London, only 13 per 1000. Kirkintilloch—40 cholera deaths in 10 days. Rutherglen had no scavenger and heavy death-rate.

1856	1857	1858	1859
Glasgow mortality under 5 years—52.9%. Out of 4837 adult deaths, 1045 due to phthisis. Dundee—95 smallpox deaths in January and 70 in February. In Scotland 9077 deaths from phthisis.	Scotland—Phthisis death-rate 256 per 100,000 living; typhus death-rate, 110 per 100,000 living; bronchitis death-rate, 102 per 100,000 living. Death-rate in Greenock, 336 per 10,000 of population; Glasgow, 303; Paisley, 298; Per h, 283; Dundee, 247; Aberdeen, 218; Edinburgh, 213; Leith, 208. Glasgow—54% of total deaths among children under 5 years. Average town mortality in Scotland—23 per 1000. In Hawick 29 per 1000; in Hawick great congestion; Duke of Buccleugh held up feuing ground.	7264 phthisis deaths in Scotland. Greenock, 44% of deaths due to phthisis. Glasgow phthisis death-rate, 386 per 100,000 living. Infant mortality in Glasgow—53% of total deaths. General death-rate per 10,000 living—Glasgow, 301; Greenock, 287; Aberdeen, 204.	13.4% of death in 8 chief towns due to phthisis. In Greenock 54% of deaths were children under 5 years.

1860	1861	1862	1863
13.2% of deaths in 8 chief towns due to phthisis; in these towns 113 smallpox deaths. In towns death-rate 245 per 10,000; in rural districts, death-rate 153 per 10,000. Typhus deaths in Glasgow—427.	Glasgow typhus deaths, 451. Hawick; 100 houses with two or more families. Glasgow—Sheriff Allison says every year 6000 children under 5 years die; of these, 4000 under 1 year old.	Scotland—13% of deaths, phthisis; Greenock and Glasgow worst towns. Typhus deaths in Glasgow—516; 50% of Glasgow children born, die under 5 years of age, and there is 1 still-born child in every 12 (highest ratio in Britain).	Edinburgh—Death-rate in working-class districts double that in rich districts. In Main Street, Gorbals, Glasgow, 332 typhus cases.

1864	1865	1866	1868
Greenock—November, 25% of deaths due to typhus ; 126 out of every 1000 children under 5 ; four doctors died of it ; 93 per 10,000 of population died of phthisis. In 8 large towns phthisis caused 16.2 of the deaths. Glasgow—Feb.-Aug., 2000 typhus cases ; one-third of Glasgow houses had only one room.	Edinburgh—In 3 months Hyndford's Close had 38 fever cases, and Fountain's Close had 41. In every 10,000 of population, Greenock had 45 phthisis deaths, Glasgow 42, and Dundee 39.	Cholera outbreak.	12½% of mortality in eight large towns due to phthisis.

1873	1875	1877	1885
Dr. Russell, M.O.H., Glasgow, reports middle-class districts have death-rate of 23 per 1000 and working-class districts a death-rate of 41 per 1000 ; in the slum wards it was 45 per 1000 ; 32% of the houses have only one apartment.	Severe winter, and destitution ; death-rate in middle-class districts of Glasgow—24 per 1000, in the poor districts 68 per 1000. The *Glasgow Herald* was agitating for public libraries !	2000 prostitutes in Edinburgh.	Deaths from starvation in Glasgow, 39 ; in Edinburgh, 18.

CHAPTER XIII.

THE UNIONS.

I.—THE FACTORY WORKERS.

" The woollen manufacture is peculiarly favourable in promoting matrimony and consequently, population.   Children from five years of age may begin to be useful, and are even employed in different branches of it, which are singularly adapted to their infant state."—" *Essays in Trade, Commerce, Manufacture, and Fisheries of Scotland,*" *David Loch,* 1778.

" The lower orders—for God's sake quarrel not with the word lower, for they are as low as tyranny can tread then down. . . . You can have no conception of the waste of infants."—" *Blackwood's Magazine,*" *April,* 1833.

"When the Factory Act was first agitated for, some medical men asserted positively that so far from being pernicious, labour for 14 or 16 consecutive hours in a close stifling room was a sovereign specific for certain complaints of which scrofula was one.'—*Alexander Redgrave, Factory Inspector.—Address to International Philanthropic Congress,* 11/6/62.

" . . . if he saw any of that independent, uneasy disposition displayed amongst them [his workers] he should show them the gates."—*A Dundee Employer : N.B. Daily Mail.* 20/10/1862.

IT is commonly supposed that there was no factory system prior to the introduction of steam-power.   We have already shewn that such a supposition is untenable.   There were factories 150 years before Hargreaves and Arkwright and David Dale.   In 1648 the Town Council of Glasgow bought out James Bell's "work-loomes" ; * at an even earlier date—in 1610—the owners of a cloth factory at Ayr were "impressing" unwilling workers ; we have it upon record that William Flakefield, the ex-soldier who introduced the designs and inventions that created the linen boom in Glasgow after 1700, did not receive—neither he, nor his descendants—any reward, beyond being given in his penurious old age the post of Town Drummer at East Kilbride ; and we know that in 1704 pauper labour was used by the capitalists to reduce factory wages.   Indeed, it took from the middle of the eighteenth to well past the middle of the nineteenth century for the factory system and machinery to oust the home craftsman ; the process was slow, but it was steady, and it was accompanied by generations of physical and mental wreckage, by savage cruelties and murders, by intense suffering and misery.

---

*Medieval Scotland—Cochrane Patrick, p. 45

Captain Burt tells us that, about 1754, maids at spinning work got three half-crowns a year, a peck of oatmeal for a week's diet, and "happy she that can get the skimming of a pot to mix with her oatmeal for better commons." In addition she got every year one or two pairs of shoes.* This was at a time when beef and mutton sold for 1d. a pound, salmon for 1d. a pound, and hens, though lean, retailed at 2d. or 2½d. each.

About 1776 the male workers in the employment of Mr. Ballantyne, the wool manufacturer in Edinburgh, "could easily gain one shilling per day if they chose to exert themselves";† in Aberdeen about 1795 male workers in the linen factory could earn from 5s. to 12s. per week, women from 5s. to 6s., and boys from 1s. 3d. to 2s. 6d. In 1783, Richard Hargreaves had come to Scotland with his spinning machine, and two years later we find 12,000 Glasgow weavers protesting in vain against a Parliament, (many of whose members were financially interested in the East India Company,) imposing taxation favourable to the Company and hostile to the home-workers in linens and muslins. At this period there was, we are told, "a redundancy of hands," and the masters combined to reduce wages. The weavers retaliated with a Union, paraded on Glasgow Green, boycotted the most notorious sweaters among the masters, and smashed the looms operated by blacklegs. The ringleaders among the men were arrested, but were released by the mob ; soldiery appeared, but the infuriated workers charged the troops at the Drygate Bridge with bricks and stones. During the "battle" six men were killed and many wounded. Prosecutions followed, and the sentences varied from short imprisonment to whipping and banishment for seven years. The Weavers' Union was destroyed "and the operatives were obliged to submit to any terms the masters chose to impose."‡

In 1792, in the counties of Lanark, Ayr, Renfrew, and Dumbarton there were 30,000 weavers earning an average wage of 2s. per day ; 6000 women winders who each earned 8d. per day ; 12,000 tambourers and clippers at 9d. per day, and 2000 warpers, warehousemen, etc., at 2s. per day. In the cotton mills the average wage for all employees—men, women, and children—was 1s. per day ; calico printing wages averaged 2s. per day ; in 1798 the average wage of 5000 linen workers at Kirkcaldy was only £7 per annum. On the other hand, there were weaving families during the cotton boom who could earn £3 to £5 per week, and in 1795 there were weavers

---

*"Letters," i., 103.

†*Scotsman*, 7/5/68. In 1779 the stocking weavers appealed, unsuccessfully, to Parliament to fix their rate of wages.

‡*Scotsman*, 15/8/68 ; *Scots Magazine*, May, July, September, 1787, and July, 1788.

who could secure 3s. 6d. for weaving a lappet web ; half a century later the same web made by machinery was sold bleached at 3½d. per yard. From 1783 to 1799 David Dale, the father-in-law of Robert Owen, ran the mills at New Lanark, the best-conditioned and most humanely conducted of their kind ; yet even here there were 500 children who got no holidays, and who toiled six days a week for 13 hours a day, and were "educated " for two hours at the expiry of their thirteen hours' toil. These children were mostly orphans from Edinburgh, the parish authorities being glad to get rid of them, and no questions asked. For adult labour Dale had to depend upon starving unemployed, wrecked emigrants and evicted crofters, as the surrounding peasantry, so great was its aversion to factory work, could not be induced to "accept of house accommodation from Mr. Dale on the lowest possible terms."* When Robert Owen took over these mills in 1799 the child slaves were stunted in growth, their limbs deformed, and "sheer exhaustion made the night-school useless even for alphabet learning." Dale had secured a fortune from all this misery, but he was by no means the worst of his kind; in some mills, infants five years old toiled daily for stretches of 13 hours without food, and spent their Sundays in cleaning the machinery ; but Dale's theological convictions kept him from yielding to the temptation of exploiting infant misery on the Lord's day ! †

In 1808 the Scottish weavers joined the Lancashire weavers in petitioning Parliament to limit the number of apprentices and to fix a minimum wage ; but a Parliamentary Committee of Enquiry speedily reported that any such measures would be "injudicious." In Glasgow the Magistrates were invited to fix the rates of wages, as they were by the then existing law legally empowered to do, but they declined, and appeals to the Law Courts to have wages fixed were met with every possible legal subterfuge and delay. In 1811 the Scots weavers assured Parliament that their wages had fallen 75 per cent. during the previous 11 or 12 years.‡ Arbitration Boards were proposed, but the masters and agents declined to admit such "dangerous principles." In 1812 the cotton spinners of Glasgow again appealed to the Justices to fix their rate of wages under the old Elizabethan statute. The local legalists assured the Justices that the statute had lapsed, but Jeffrey, the counsel for the spinners, persisted, and finally the Justices agreed to act. The manufacturers

---

*Robert Owen—Frank Podmore, i., 72 ; also, *Adventures in Socialism*—Alex. Cullen.

†The Factory Commissioner Grainger actually discovered a child of two years old working in a Nottingham lace mill (1844).—Children's Employment Commission Report.

‡*Westminster Review*, July-October, 1833.

promptly appealed to the Court of Session, which upheld the decision of the Justices ; then the manufacturers disputed the relevancy of the Justices' action, and refused to lead evidence before them. After 10 months' wrangling the Court of Session itself fixed "moderate rates," but the manufacturers refused to pay, and 40,000 men struck work to enforce the Court of Session's award.   The strike lasted for six weeks, and was broken by the Government arresting all the men's leaders for their temerity in daring to strike to enforce a decision of the Court of Session ; and, upon the legal pretext that the said leaders had violated the Combination Laws of 1799 and 1800, sentences of eighteen months' imprisonment were distributed. Thus, says Lord Cockburn, was smashed the "most extensive and peaceable combination of workmen that had ever appeared in this part of the kingdom."* During the strike, Maurice Margarot, the only one of the political victims of 1794 who returned from transportation, was active among the workers.

Lord Cockburn, however, was mistaken in thinking that the Spinners' Union had been dissolved. It had begun in 1806 ; in 1810 we find the men of the West locked out until they signed a document dissociating themselves from the Union, but the signatures appear to have been given with "mental reservations," for the activities of the Union continued, as we have seen, in 1812. From 1816 to 1824 there were regular Union outbreaks and outrages— employers shot at, mills set on fire, blacklegs killed, mutilated, or burned with vitriol. The miserable wages simply drove the workers to desperate "remedies." In 1817, as we learn from evidence during the Baird and Maclaren trial, the wages of muslin weavers were 5s. 6d. per week of 14 hours a day ;† but the Cotton Spinners' Organisation was never wiped out, and from 1825 to 1835 it was continually organising and financing partial strikes all over the country with a view to the equalisation and the raising of wages. In the flax mills of Fifeshire and Forfarshire the conditions were terrible ; there, infants—"as soon as they can run about "—were working 16 hours a day ; and, says the Tory *Courier*, they are denied education, recreation, fresh air, and sleep ; their lungs are filled with metallic and vegetable dust, and "thus they grow up a miserable and squalid race, without morals and without comfort, and bring forth wretches like themselves to tread,without hope of amelioration, the same dreary path of social misery."‡   At Lanark, in 1832, the Duke of Hamilton broke up the local Weavers' Union by divid-

Memorials, p. 281.   See also Cunningham's *Growth of English Industry and Commerce*, iii., 736 ; *Reports (Artisans and Machinery)*, 1824, v., pp. 59-64, Richmond's Evidence.

†*State Trials*, vol. 33, pp. 1-145.

‡*Glasgow Courier*, 3/11/31, 10/11/31.

ing the Union funds among the non-unionists. His motive is clear—retaliation for the impudence of the Union in demanding an increased scale of prices—but the method by which he laid his hands upon the Union funds can only be conjectured. At this period the weavers of Sanquhar were so poorly paid by the Glasgow agents for whom they worked that the Duke of Buccleugh had to give them a bonus of ¼d. per ell to keep them living.†

In 1833 we read : "The whole manufacturing population is a mine—let a match be set in one department, the whole will blaze"; the women power-loom weavers are driven to form a Union ; harness weavers earn only from 6s. to 8s., plain weavers 4s. 8d. to 5s., and handloom weavers 3s. weekly ; strikers must give six weeks' notice of intention to desist from work ; children at the New Lanark mills earn 3d. a day ; calico printing apprentices at Kilbarchan are imprisoned for three months with hard labour "for acting under the influence of an association of apprentice printers" in adopting a ca' canny policy ; apprentices at Lennoxtown are given one month's hard labour for "intimidating" their foreman into joining a Union ; 100 guineas' rewards are offered for information that would lead to the conviction of men in Glasgow who assaulted blacklegs ; one boy is sentenced to sixty days' hard labour for intimidation ; another boy comes forward and confesses that he was the guilty person, but the J.P.'s refused to reconsider the sentence "in these turbulent times."

During the early part of 1834 the Master Calico Printers of the West, after careful and deliberate preparation, discharged thousands of their higher-waged employees and supplanted them by starving hand-loom weavers at a wage of seven or eight shillings. Riots ensued, and though most mills were guarded by soldiers and police, enraged operatives in the Strathblane and Vale of Leven districts invaded the mills and tore the blacklegs outside. The Government rushed military reinforcements into the disturbed areas, and hundreds of rioters were arrested and sentenced to anything from 14 days to 12 months hard labour. If no act of violence could be proved, a charge of "cruelty, tyranny and oppression" always secured a conviction ; the rebel spirits were cleared out of the calico printing districts, and the cowed starvelings who took their places—in the Vale of Leven, for example—have left behind a semi-serf tradition which paralyses to this day any local effort towards class freedom and human dignity. Yet the weavers, as a whole, were probably the most class conscious, as they were certainly the best read, of all sections of the workers, and their organisations really were strengthened by the drafting away of thousands of the less robust and more famine-stricken as blacklegs to the Calico districts. At Paisley we

---

† *Glasgow Courier*, 5/1/32

find those who were left passing purposeful, if rather quaintly-worded resolutions, such as :

> "That the weavers withdraw their labour from Mr. Archibald Yuill, the greatest enemy they have and the framer of the new table, never to receive him into the trade again in this world."

From the *Weavers' Journal* and the *Liberator*, the latter a cotton spinner's organ founded when the capitalist press had refused £30 to allow an advertisement to appear replying to allegations against the Union made by the masters, we get some idea of the agitations and struggles of the early thirties. The *Liberator* had distinct revolutionary tendencies. Had not the cotton spinners in the dark days of the Combination Laws been compelled to hold their executive meetings in secrecy in the Isle of Man ? and had the paper not had as editor such fiery spirits as Dr. John Taylor, the Chartist and Revolutionary, and John Tait, whose pen stabbed every tyranny ? The *Weavers' Journal* was more scientifically "class war"; it discussed such subjects as, "Do low wages make for liberty by rousing the people against oppression ?" Its leading articles discoursed upon "the monied monster" and upon the sinecurists and pensioners who were clothed in purple and fine linen and fared sumptuously every day.

> "God did not make this world for land-holders and capitalists; much less did He give them a charter for sacrificing the human race to their rapacity . . . The world, but for them, might be a paradise of virtue and happiness; they have made it a perfect pandemonium of crime and wretchedness—they have arrayed man against man, brother against brother—setting the nations of the earth to slaughter one another like so many fiends or beasts of prey."*

The years 1835 and 1836 saw much effigy-burning and striking and gaoling of agitators. For a brief spell an increase of 20 per cent. was secured in the East of Scotland; but the extraordinary depression in 1837 was seized upon by the masters to train starving weavers to cotton-spinning, and a great strike ensued in which the spinners were emphatically worsted, going back to work upon most miserable terms. The strike was followed by a notorious State trial of five members of the Spinners' Executive for illegal conspiracy and murder.† The illegal conspiracy alleged was the use of force "to raise or keep up wages," and the murder specifically charged was that of a blackleg, named John Smith, in Clyde Street, Anderston. The Crown produced witnesses who swore to a system of secret pass-

---

*The Weavers' Journal, March, 1837.

†Report of the Trial of Thomas Hunter, Peter Hacket, Richard M'Neil, James Gibb, and William M'Lean—By Archd. Swinton (Edin., 1838); Glasgow Courier and Argus Reports, January, 1838; Lord Cockburn's Journal, vol. i.

words, and secret funds to subsidise murder, arson, vitriol-throwing, and mutilation. Great excitement prevailed during the trial; 20,000 workers signed a petition to the House of Commons against what was regarded as a Government fabricated charge designed to destroy the strongest Trade Union in Scotland, and against the retention of the accused in gaol for five months before trial. Lord Cockburn reports that "four itinerant corrupters of the manufacturing population"—one of them the Rev. Joseph Stephen—"openly preached to the people of Glasgow the propriety of burning the mills of the cotton tyrants"; Feargus O'Connor, the Chartist, publicly contrasted "the five villains in scarlet" (the judges) with the "five respectable gentlemen in black" (the prisoners). Finally the jury acquitted the accused of complicity in murder and convicted them only upon some minor counts on the indictment, for which, however, the judges sentenced them to transportation to Botany Bay for 7 years—a brutal and an unjust sentence, as Alexander Campbell, the secretary of the Glasgow Trades, was prompt to proclaim—a brutal and an unjust sentence passed by the same judges who had sentenced in the same court a wealthy man's gamekeeper to nine months' imprisonment for the murder of a poacher !

All over the country tyranny grew bolder. In the Tillicoultry area every known unionist was sacked and their places filled at 10s. weekly, by hungry weavers from Milnathort, until knives, stones, and intimidation generally drove the blacklegs home in terror. At Douglas, in Lanarkshire, work had to be found for the unemployed at 1s. per day for married, and 10d. for unmarried men ; "individuals . . . . unconnected with the Union have had the preference." At Ayr no relief was given to those who "kept useless dogs or who belonged to any Trades Unions or similar combinations." In Pollokshaws 1000 weavers were idle ; in Paisley 15,000 hungry bellies were fed from the soup kitchens. The *Dundee Courier* reports : "Never before did we witness such real misery . . . no uncommon thing to see the merest infant in the arms of its mother snatching the roll from her hand with a greediness which betrayed the direst hunger and want." Fever spread everywhere ; evictions, especially in Paisley, were conducted upon a large scale ; at Kinross only one weaver in eight could find work ; Messrs. Houldsworth, at Airdrie, paid women for winding fine yarn, 5¼d. per day ; male linen workers at Kirkcaldy earned from 3s. to 9s. 3d. weekly ; the hecklers at Dundee worked in an atmosphere so thick with dust that they could not distinguish persons 30 yards off in the room, and wages were so low that the local *Courier* boasted that the Dundee fabrics "are driving the Germans out of the foreign markets"; at Dunfermline a mob, disguised with blackened faces, burned sweaters' looms and maltreated blacklegs. Little wonder, is it not, that

Chartist doctrines spread through the factory population like a prairie fire, and that, as a witness before the Assistant Handloom Weavers' Commission sorrowfully admitted, the tenets of Mr. Owen were gaining adherence and "some even stayed away from Church on principle ! "

In 1841 the average wage in the West of Scotland for female power-loom weavers was 7s., and for cotton spinners (male) 21s.—in both instances for a working week of 69 hours.* But these figures make no allowance for periods of unemployment, and what unemployment meant in those times is indicated by the fact that in November 1842 there were no fewer than 14,791 names on the charity list of the Paisley Relief Committee. At Cromarty old women at hemp-making could earn only 2d. per day ; women at Ullapool by sewing could make 20s. per annum ; at the hemp manufactory in Inverness, able-bodied men earned 8s. or 9s. per week, and women from 1s. 2d. to 3s. 6d. per week ; Dundee male weavers and Kirkcaldy female spinners each received 11s. fortnightly ; in Berwickshire there were weaving families whose total earnings were less than 3s. 6d. weekly ; women knitters at Lerwick earned not more than 1d. per day.† Agitators were brutally handled by the authorities. The Rev. John Duncan, John Pinney (mechanic), Hugh Ross (tailor), John Scott and Peter Bennet (flaxdressers) had taken part in a meeting held in Bell Street Hall, Dundee, to consider "the present state of wages." All five were arrested, and other four prominent participants who escaped arrest were outlawed ; the five arrested men were kept in jail for five months before being brought to trial upon a charge of a "wicked and feloniously assembling of multitudes of persons combined together for some illegal purpose to the great terror and alarm of the lieges." There had been processions at Forfar, but the Rev. John Duncan's chief crime appears to have been an incitement to "a general strike and advising men to go to the turnip and potato fields to take food." Lord Mackenzie, in delivering judgment, said "the charge of assembling in large numbers inferred a very serious crime. There was a dangerously illegal purpose in the charge pleaded to, viz., to compel men to give up work . . . by imposing and alarming displays of numbers . . . . The exhibition of a great number of men in a procession extending from Dundee all the way to Forfar was calculated to destroy the peace and security of the neighbourhood." All the prisoners except Duncan were sentenced to 4 months' hard labour, and Duncan, though found not guilty, was promptly re-arrested upon a new warrant. The law was capitalist law, and the Bench looked at the dock through masters' spectacles. "Are not millions of starving

---

*Dr. Strang, British Association, Economic Section, 8/8/56.
†Evidence before Poor Law Commission, 1844.

people the necessary occasional sloughs of a very manufacturing nation ? " asked Lord Cockburn, the leading Whig legal luminary, as he narrated how there had been 10,000 unemployed in Paisley for more than a year.*

Strikes in the year 1844 were easily beaten by the masters, though there was talk of arson, and the insurance companies were adjured to look to their policies ; at Brechin, James Gibson, a weaver, destroyed by fire Guthrie and Hood's factory. "He did not see why the world should be so ordered, why there should be such distinction of ranks " ; but unsympathetic judges saw, and sent him to study sociology at Botany Bay for 14 years !

In 1845 we find the dyers in the West striking against an average weekly wage of 10s. to 12s. ; at Dunfermline a mob of 2000 persons assembled at midnight by arrangement, smashed a factory building, and set the owner's house afire ; Andrew Kinloch, the first power-loom weaver in the world, whose mechanical inventions had been exploited by all the capitalists in the country, and was himself living in the direst poverty, had in this same year a public subscription raised to keep him out of the almshouse. A Dundee case raised in Parliament gives us a light on the factory conditions of the period. Six factory girls in the employment of Messrs. Baxter, their ages from 14 to 20, and their wages being 5s. 6d. per week, had the audacity to ask for an increase of a half-penny a day ; the request was refused ; after dinner they did not return to work ; by the rules of the mill they could have been fined time and half for under-time ; but next morning Mr. Baxter, instead of fining the girls, had them arrested and marched through the streets under police escort to a private office where was seated a magistrate, one of the Baxter family, and the overseer and the manager of the mill. The judicial Baxter there and then sentenced the girls to 10 days' hard labour ! †

In 1847 many mills were closed as a result of a financial panic following upon great speculation and gambling in railway stocks, and the period of unemployment appears to have been utilised for the installation of much new labour-saving machinery ; for in 1849, when a "boom " period again set in and the factories were humming twelve hours a day, we find the *Perth Courier* reporting that the new machinery had caused women's labour to fall to 2s. to 3s. per week, and in Glasgow the factory women could only earn 5s. to 8s. 6d. per fortnight.‡ The women in Glasgow struck two mills, but the federated owners promptly locked out all employees, and the women after a courageous fight of six weeks were hungered back on the old

---

*Journal, ii.

†*Argus* Report, 6/4/46. Baxter was a strong Free Trader, and had subscribed £600 to the Anti-Corn Law League.

‡*Glasgow Courie* , 26/4/89.

terms. During the struggle a man named Andrew Harley achieved some notoriety by advocating class action instead of craft action as the only means of meeting effectively class-conscious employers ; but his propaganda seems to have disappeared with the failure of the women's strike. There was some agitation over a Kilmarnock case, in which, when a big calico printing firm failed, the firm's creditors seized the workers' wages as part payment of their accounts; the creditors had the law on their side, and all the workers got was farther experience of the capitalist system.

In 1851 there was a general revolt and a widespread strike of calico printers, which was settled by compromise ; the calenderers and lappers struck for a ten hours' day and no overtime, and many of them spent the period of strike in prison for the crime of striking without due notice ; and a strike by cotton spinners against an insufficient wage of 17s. to 18s. per week. In each case the workers were beaten. Captain Kincaid, the Factory Inspector, whose fourteenth half-yearly report is almost ludicrous in its pro-capitalist bias, informed the Government that "Trade Unions are a great social evil . . . . Strikes for wages can never lead to any good, for though the masters may be made to listen to reason, they will never be found yielding to coercion." Still he admits that many women factory workers only earn 3s. weekly, and that there was a factory in Skye which only paid 14d. for every dozen pairs of stockings knitted. The philanthropist running this institution in Skye was an Aberdeen capitalist named Hogg. "Small though these wages be," comments the Factory Inspector with obvious unction, "they are of the greatest importance to the poor persons employed."

In the east and north-east of the country there was considerable depression in the year 1852, some of it at least a contrivance of the linen manufacturers of Forfarshire who put their factories on four days a week to create a scarcity and raise prices ; but in 1852 there ensued a "boom" and wages rose everywhere—the Paisley dyers up to 17s., the Dundee ropemakers up to 15s., the flaxdressers of Montrose by 25 per cent. ; Forfar bleachfield workers secured a reduction in working hours from 13 to 12 per day, and the weavers— hand and power loom—of Arbroath, after being "harangued by an Irishman," struck for "ninepence per bolt and no surrender." It was the agents and manufacturers who surrendered. The *Ayr Advertiser* reported that, despite the increasing supply of Irish labour, more increases in wages must be given if "check is not applied to the increasing emigration." The Crimean War, however, supplied the necessary corrective by interrupting supplies of flax, hemp, and jute, and wages again fell. The owners defied the provisions of the Factory Act requiring adequate fencing for their machinery and the half-yearly toll of accidents ranged from 220 to 658, but by no mischance did the factory inspectors ever initiate a prosecution. "Law," declared the *Scotsman* sarcastically, is "a sort of blasphemy against capital—the modern name of Mammon."* The factory inspector complacantly attributed the decline in the Hawick hosiery trade to the organised workers who had the audacity "to demand a voice in the adjustment of prices for work on the new power frame,"† but he failed to make any reference to the fact that the masters had sought to make the employees pay for the improved frames by reducing the rate of wages ! The year 1856 was "prosperous," and it had need to be, for muslin weavers had fallen to a wage of 14s. and pattern printers to 13s. 6d ;‡ but the "prosperity " was of short duration, for a great demand for money from the U.S.A. raised the rate of interest in Scotland to 10 per cent. ; many firms failed, and there were steady wage reductions and unemployments. Edinburgh factory needlewomen could make only 2d. an hour ; capmakers 6s. a week ; Alva pirn-winders 3s. a week; and many women workers possessed neither shoes nor stockings, but went to their toil barefoot. The county authorities made ready use of the police to intimidate any rebellious spirits. Capitalism ran riot. At Houldsworth's factory, Airdrie, the fines were so excessive that frequently the workers had no wages but were in debt to the employer. Sheriff Allison of Glasgow vigorously denounced the "vicious state of society" that was killing off the infants, so that were it not for immigration the factory populations would soon become extinct.§ The Medical Officer to the Privy Council pled for nursery rooms in the factories in order that mothers might now and again have access to their infants. When new fabrics were introduced the two most expert weavers were given the work, an official standing by, watch in hand, to time the processes, thus the price or wage was fixed generally at starvation point for the less expert weavers, and the frequent fines, short times, and unemployments kept the factory population in a state of chronic hunger and misery. In Glasgow alone during the American Civil War there were 15,000 unemployed factory workers who were for a brief period given relief work sweeping streets at 9d. a day, but were latterly left to starve ; the Government and the manufacturers were hostile to a policy of assisted emigration, being desirous of keeping a surplusage of "hands " at home in anticipation of a return to "prosperity " ; many of the wealthier manufacturers, however, did not subscribe a copper to the relief funds.‖ Labour-saving inventions, such as that of the Dun-

---

*2/5/55.

†Half-Yearly Report ending 31/10/59.

‡Dr. Strang, at British Association—*Herald*, 31/8/57.

§*N.B. Daily Mail*, 1/3/61.

‖*Scotsman*, 27/6/63.

fermline weaver, Charles Lawson, whereby one card, in a machine did the work previously done by eight cards, simply intensified the miseries of the operatives A half-century's improvements in linen weaving machinery, declared Mr. Brown of the *Dunfermline Press*, in 1863, had merely resulted in a two-thirds reduction in wages ; the increased product had gone entirely to the exploiters. The Glasgow magistrates "relieved the situation " by supplying tickets of admission to the poorshouse, where the cotton spinners could pick oakum twelve hours a day in return for a poorshouse diet, while their dependents outside were given a ticket for soup "to be obtained at the Night Asylum."[*] When trade improved we find the calenderers of Dundee slaving 60 hours a week " ; a dreary outline of life," says the Factory Inspector with singular insight, "for wages of 11s. to 16s. per week. Overtime forcibly shuts many a poor man's mouth in order to get the necessaries for a family." Overtime after 60 hours ! And the poor victims knew no better than that they must, at employers' instigation, "lobby" the House of Commons to keep calendering outside the Factory Acts ! The hand-frame hosiery workers at Hawick were also outside the Factory Acts, and their hours were fourteen daily and "longer towards the end of the week . . . the children must work as long as the men."[†] In 1864 the carpet weavers, stimulated thereto by their English brethren who had secured an increase conditional upon the Scots carpet factories falling into line, demanded and secured an increase on their wages, which had fallen as low as 13s. In 1868 the cotton spinners struck unsuccessfully against "speeding up "—*i.e.*, a reduction of workers at the spinning mules. The men offered to work at the rates paid in Lancashire, but the owners refused. The dyers at Stirling were earning 14s. a week ; the weavers at Alva were averaging 12s. to 14s. ; fishing-net weavers (male) at Musselburgh had a nominal 20s.; male floorcloth workers at Kirkcaldy 18s. to 23s. ; the tanners at Edinburgh 20s. Many who could scrape together the voyage money, emigrated ; those who could not were consoled (?) by press stories of "over production " as the cause of the recurrent waves of unemployment, but here and there, there were lone voices crying that the evil was not "overproduction " but "under-consumption," due to the inability of the masses to purchase anything beyond second-hands and cast-offs ; and the Factory Inspector reported that the employers were always struggling for cheap labour and that children were steadily supplanting adults in the factories ; during the period 1857-1862 adult male labour had decreased by 18 per cent., while child male labour had increased by 53 per cent., and child female labour by 78 per cent.[‡]

[*]*N.B. Daily Mail*, 19/11/64, and 26/11/64.
[†]*Scotsman*, 26/1/65.
[‡]*N.B. Daily Mail*, 25/8/69.

During the decade 1870-1880 there was in Scotland almost perpetual striking for reduction in factory hours and increase in factory wages,* Dundee alone during that period had 46 linen and jute strikes, one of which lasted twenty-four weeks, and resulted in the formation of the Union of Mill and Factory Workers. Perth had 14 dyeing and woollen strikes and Dumfries had 12 woollen strikes. At Newmilns the harness weavers in 1872 were working 12 hours daily for a weekly wage of 15s., less 1s. 6d. charges, and winders were only paid 4s. 6d. a week. In 1874 a reduction in Glasgow jute workers' wages was described as "the last straw ; our breakfast is taken away." During all that decade, with the exception of the boom period in 1874, the employers were triumphant, and the year 1880 saw the factory operatives, as their fathers had been before them, scrambling along miserably and wearily upon a level of bare subsistence.

So far, then, a general survey of the wages rate and hours of labour struggle in the factories ; there remains still to tell something of the sufferings of the hand-loom weavers crushed out in competition with machinery, something of the holocaust of child life, and something of the slow and grudging yield from Parliament of the legislation designed to curb and control the more murderous phases of factory exploitation.

II.—THE HAND-LOOM WEAVERS.

The evidence is overwhelming that before the introduction of the power-loom and the factory system the hand-loom weaver was a prosperous craftsman, as prosperity was then reckoned. The loom he worked at was usually his own property, and, assisted by members of his family, and perhaps by an apprentice, he could earn a decent, if not a luxurious, living. As late as 1797 he could make 27s. and more per week, † and that at a time when 7s. 6d. bought a stone of flour, 20 lbs. of oatmeal, one stone of malt, one joint of butcher's meat, one lb. of cross butter (18 oz. to the ℔) and left 4½d. over.‡ But with each successive weaving factory erected and with every improvement in the machinery in the new factories, and with the rapid growth of child labour at the new machinery, hand-loom weaving became less and ever less able to compete for work at a living wage to the weaver. The hand-loom weaver's wage fell steadily ; what was 30s. in 1806 was only 5s. 6d. in 1830, and what was 5s. 6d. in 1831 was only 4s. 4d. in 1838.||

---

*Apart from the boom year of 1874, when wages were " good."

†House of Commons Report   *Glasgow Evening Post*, 1/8/35.

‡*Chartist Circular*, 31/10/40.

||Hand-loom Weavers' Commission Report (1839), p. 11.

By 1832 the hand-loom weavers of Paisley were in a state of chronic starvation ; in " hundreds of cases " everything had been poinded by the house-lord for rent, even the beds were pawned ; women, when they could secure work at tambouring and veining, earned no more than 3d. or 4d. per day ; of one case in St. Mirren Street, Paisley, we read that "a poor, honest woman" who was living with her 4 children in a closet, had pawned her all, even her corsets and her shoes, and now lay down with her children, covered only with shavings, to die ; the house-lord took the shilling pawn ticket for her shoes, in payment of the rent of his closet.* The weavers of the West of Scotland petitioned Parliament in vain : they asked for a Wages Board to fix minimum rates, and to have them made enforceable by law, but the House of Commons refused even to grant an enquiry into the causes and the extent of the distress. In November, 1833, however, an enquiry was ordered, and evidence was taken. George Allan, representing the weavers of the West, says his average weekly wage working very hard for long hours is 5s. 10d., and he is a shilling better than many of his brethren. Though the loom is his own, he has to pay 1s. 4d. weekly for his loom stand ; he has to pay for wear and tear ; his net weekly income is less than 4s. 6d. Cheaper provisions would do no good,"our masters would take advantage of the cheapness" to reduce wages. Another witness complains that off their starvation pittances they must pay annual local taxation, 5s. police money, 3s. "for getting leave to walk upon our streets, which they call road money," and 3s. to the Hospital, the Scottish equivalent of the Poors Rate at that time. Parliament did nothing. But the weavers found champions in Sir John Maxwell of Polloc, and his son ; both attended weavers' demonstrations, and urged Trades Boards to fix minimum wages. At one gathering Sir John vigorously denounced "the current competitive traffic in the life blood of their fellow creatures " ; he said that in certain branches of weaving minimum wage boards had been established voluntarily by masters and weavers, and "had been productive of the best results " ; at this gathering resolutions were unanimously carried declaring (1) that "Labour is the source of all wealth," and (2) that "accumulated capital being the savings of the production of labour, therefore in proportion as it fell into the hands of the few it would to the same extent hurt the many." The Whig press was wroth, and presented Sir John Maxwell with leading articles hinting that if he and his class did not have a care Trade Boards might soon be applied to landlord's rents ! But Sir John was not intimidated. He introduced his Trades Boards Bill to Parliament, declaring that the weavers were not getting sufficient "to keep body and soul together." The President of the Board of Trade, in

*Courier, 7/1/32.

reply, said that Maxwell's proposal "was nothing more or less than a fixation of a minimum rate of wages, and being so, was a sufficient reason for his opposing it. . . . Fix a minimum rate of wages! Was it possible that any intelligent Government could ever sanction such an absurdity?"*   Maxwell was supported by Sir M. Shaw Stewart, and by Mr. Gillon (Falkirk Burghs), who pled for men who toiled 14 or 16 hours a day for wages not half sufficient to keep them; if this Bill was not passed Parliament was "a delusion upon the people." A delusion, then, it must have been, for Maxwell secured only 41 votes on a division, against the Government's 129. In 1836 he again introduced his Bill, but received only for his pains a threat from the Whigs that they would oppose his re-election; they advised him "to stick to politics and abolish the Corn Laws and the Irish Tithes." Had not Parliament "enquired?" Had it not appointed a Commission of Enquiry? And had not that Commission (which was a Whig one!) reported that the causes of distress among the hand-loom weavers was to be found in the Corn Laws and in Trade Unions—chiefly the latter? †

Down at Galashiels weavers, dyers, and dressers toiled for 10s. weekly, while women who sorted wool and yarn could earn only £11 6s. per annum; at Airdrie the parish minister reported: "Many of the weavers are feeble and small of stature"; they cannot get "even the necessaries of life," declared the parish minister of Hamilton; in the West many of them "never had meat," and the common diet was "pauper meal"; their children were "too poor to go to school"; for many years the bulk of the weaving fraternity lived in a perpetual state of soup kitchen. At Dumfries the weavers' committee testified that the net wages for the best weavers averaged no more than 4s. weekly; in Glasgow weavers who earned 5s. weekly had to work 14 hours a day to get it. At Perth they banded together, borrowed money, purchased beaming machines and endeavoured to secure direct contracts, but of the results of such a co-operative experiment we can to-day find no trace.‡

Attempts were made by enthusiastic souls to form the hand-loom weavers into Trades Unions, and we even read that the hand-loom weavers joined the General Federation of Unions, and offered to assist English masons and carpenters on strike; but they had sunk far, far below the level marked by Union fees and dues; they could buy nothing but two stones of meal with their wages, and when they bought that they had no money left for rent, fuel, light, clothing,

---

Evening Post Report, 1/8/35.

†Evidence and Report of the House of Commons Committee to enquire into the Petitions presented from Hand-loom Weavers. Not one-twentieth part of evidence published. See *Westminster Review*, July-October, 1841.

‡Similar schemes were inaugurated at Forfar.

or education.* And thus, said the *Chartist Circular* with no less truth than vehemence, they suffered "that the proud robber of the palace might be pampered ; that the mitred ruffian might be fed ; that the whip-bearing capitalist might have his coach ; and that the tax-gatherer might have his plunder."†

In the fifties machinery more and more displaced hand-loom weaving ; we read of over 1000 weavers at a Paisley soup kitchen ; when delegates from all Scotland met in 1851 to form "The Manufacturers' and Weavers' Protecting Society " (motto : "An injury to one is an injury to all "), wages had fallen to 4s. and 4s. 6d. per week. Free Trade had come, trade was brisk, but when the weavers asked for an increase of 1s. per 60 yards, the manufacturers and agents pointed "to the circumstance that the operative had now cheap bread," and refused an increase.‡ Emigration, assisted by the Government, was continuous, but there were always new strata of unemployed and semi-employed weavers being laid down by progressive developments in machinery to fill the miserable places of those who had emigrated. Occasionally there were booms, as at Perth, in 1856, when weavers could earn 15s. to 18s. weekly, but they were local and of short duration ; in 1857, at Hamilton, weavers received only 1s. 3d. a day.§ In 1864, when, as usual, the Parochial Boards were refusing relief because the unemployed weavers were "able-bodied," we find the *Daily Mail* declaring that they (the weavers) "do little better than wear out life in the best of times " ; now they are "starving of hunger and cold."‖ Gradually the hand-loom worker was crushed out altogether—in 1872 there were only 10,000 of him left in the counties of Lanark, Renfrew and Ayr ; the factory with its regular hours and its machine slavery had come to stay ; the loom shop, the clack of the shuttle and the famine-smitten but strong-minded race that had known no foreman or "gaffer " at its elbows, was scarcely more than a tradition and a memory.

III.—CHILD LABOUR IN THE FACTORIES.

In the early days of the factory system, child labour was universally employed ; it was cheap, could be got for bare food ; poorshouse (or hospitals as they were then called) governors were only too glad to be rid of the orphan brats whom the foreign wars and the home poverty had left parentless on their hands. Mr. Horner, the Factory Inspector, tells us that, in 1819, these poor orphan children

---

*Argus, 18/2/47.
†*Chartist Circular*, 31/10/40.
‡*Glasgow Herald*, 1/11/50.
§*Ibid*, 11/5/57.
‖*N.B. Daily Mail*, 15/11/64.

were "often sent one, two, or three hundred miles from their place of birth, separated for life from all relations." Gangs of them were put up with bankrupts' effects for sale to the highest bidder, "advertised publicly as part of the property"; one manufacturer contracted with a parish authority to take an idiot with every twenty sound children.* Some owners kept a private burying-ground where the bodies of the dead infants were unceremoniously buried. In 1831, in Scotland, infants were toiling in the flax mills for more than 14 hours daily, and the Fife and Forfarshire owners succeeded, by the use of their political influence, in keeping Scotland outside the Factory Act which restricted the hours of labour and prohibited night work for children.

Towards the end of the year 1832 we get some authentic details of child life in the factories from the evidence given before the House of Commons Committee on the Factories Labour Regulation Bill— evidence which, as the *Morning Chronicle* of the period declared, "makes a man almost loathe his species." Alex. Dean, an overlooker at Duntruin flax mill, four miles from Dundee, swore that :—

(1) Employees toiled 17 hours daily, exclusive of meal times. (2) Four or five orphans (supplied by " some poor institution " in Edinburgh) were all that were left out of sixteen ; there were always some deserting, and being brought back ; the children were kept at work in " a standing posture ; no leave was allowed for sitting ; " they were closely confined, " doors were all locked, both with check and turnkey ; they slept on the premises, which had iron-staunched windows and were guarded all night ; they had no chance of escaping till the morning, when he (the manager) released them for their next day's employment." It was always one of the sons that stayed at home and guarded them on Sunday ; he would not suffer them to go to church ; for the least fault they were severely chastised, " struck and abused."

" Where were the hands that did not sleep in the mill sent at night ? "

" The houses where the hands slept in were about 50 yards from the mill."

" What were they called ? "

" Bothies."

" In any of these bothies were the boys and girls mixed up indiscriminately at night ? "

" Yes ; I myself, with six boys, was in one apartment with oldish girls."

" What were the ages of those boys so locked up ? "

" From 14 to 16."

" And what were the ages of the females ? "

" From 12 to 14."

" And you state they were turned indiscriminately into the same bothy ? "

" Yes."

" And locked up there all night ? "

From other evidence we learn that at the same mill the children

---

Blackwood's Magazine, 1836, p. 114.

began work at 3 a.m., and finished at 10 p.m. ; that most of them
were employed at 6 or 7 years of age, and that two girls, driven
desperate, had escaped through the roof and had run away almost
naked. At Birdevy and Trollick mills, Dundee, the hours were
14 per day, exclusive of meals. At Maryfield mill (4½ miles from
Dundee) the hours were 16 per day ; here long standing had swollen
the girls' feet.

> " Does it occasion positive deformity sometimes ? " a witness was asked
> " Yes, very often ; the girls become knock-knee'd and bow-legg'd."
> " To a considerable extent ? "
> " Yes, to a great extent. I know one girl so bow-legg'd that you could put
> a chair between her legs."
> " Has it at all affected you ? "
> " Yes ; I am very much knock-knee'd."
> " Have you seen one of the witnesses in waiting, of the name of Openshaw,
> a boy ? "
> " Yes."
> " Is there anybody in your neighbourhood that you have witnessed
> as strikingly deformed as he is ? "
> " A great deal more so ; one man that is working now at a mill near
> Brechin, about 20 miles from Dundee, and who is about 30 years of age.
> This man does not stand, with his deformity, above 4 feet 6 inches high, and
> had he grown to his proper height I think he would have been about 5 feet
> 8 or 9 inches. He has been in mills since he was 5 years old, and he is re-
> duced to that state that he slides along on a stool to do his work—and though
> he is about 30 years of age, he can now do no more than a girl's work."

At Strathmartine Mill, near Dundee, the hours were nominally 15
per day, but the foremen's watches had been smashed by the proprietor and they had been "chastised for letting the hands know the
time of day." "No person," says the Tory *Glasgow Courier*, "will
have anything to do with any of the unfortunate wretches so reared,
for they are quite helpless. If the females when grown up are not
ugly they may find relief in prostitution. The flogging or strapping
is continual, and when it happens to the extreme, the overseer is
fined."

At Edwards' Mill (Dundee), an overseer was fined by a magistrate
for excessively punishing a child worker, but Mr. Edwards com-
pensated the overseer, discharged from his employment the witnesses
to the case, and declared that "he could do what he liked with his
own." Children had to be continually strapped to prevent them from
falling asleep.* In Glasgow children left their beds at 4 a.m. and
returned from the factory at 9 p.m.†

During this period the press, the pulpit, and the professional

---

Glasgow Courier Report, 12/1/1833.
†*Glasgow Evening Post*, 3/8/1833.

moralists were conducting an extensive agitation against negro slavery in the colonies !

There was no lack of special pleaders for the factory owners. Thus the Rev. John Campbell of Galashiels, in the *New Statistical Account*, tells us that the children could earn 3s. a week, and that their habits of industry acquired at an early age qualified them "for future service"; "there can be no training of the volatile minds of youth equal to that which is maintained at the factories." Even Dan. O'Connell told Lord Ashley (better known as Lord Shaftesbury) that his projects for limiting the infants' hours of labour were but "good-natured nonsense." The infantile death-rate must have been terrible. "The price which this country is paying for her manufacturing superiority is frightful," exclaimed the Tory *Courier* in 1838. Sheriff Watson of Aberdeen reported that the children of the working-class who went to the Industrial Schools were "dwarfish in body and mind . . . puny, pigmy, feeble, and deformed creatures."* In the forties and the fifties the practice of contracting out workhouse children to the manufacturers continued. We have seen a bond or indenture of date May, 1843, in which one of the girls in the Town's Hospital of Glasgow was contracted out to a Kirkintilloch manufacturer ; she, the girl, was bound for 5 years to "serve and obey" ; for every day she was off work during that time she was to serve two days free at the end of her 5 years' engagement, "which absent days shall be liquidated and proved by the master's word or oath if required . . . *in place of all other proof.*" Occasionally masters who maltreated these poor children were punished. John Hendry of Kirkintilloch was imprisoned in 1845 for brutality towards "three pauper apprentices from Edinburgh," he "having the habit of flogging them most un-mercifully, hanging them up by their wrists, and then inflicting cruel chastisement on their naked bodies, and with plunging them in a state of nudity into a well." But the general capitalist temper of the times may be gauged from the fact that the Whig Act of 1851 regulating magisterial punishment of young children allowed a sentence of 36 lashes.

In the first half of 1850 there were 323 accidents in Scots factories ; of these 183 were to children and young persons, but the Factory Inspector obligingly recorded that the accidents were due to "care-lessness on the part of the individuals themselves." One thing, however, stands to the credit of the Inspectorate, and that is its continued insistence that Parliament should compel at least rudi-mentary facilities for the education of the factory child. The owners in the fifties steadily protested against a law compelling them to release children under 13 years so many hours weekly for educa-

Glasgow Herald, 28/10/1850.

tion, and they devised many shifts to evade the law—shifts such as arranging supplies of education certificates by bogus schoolmasters. In 1856 less than one-third of Scots factory children could read or write ; and in 1861 there were alleged to be no fewer than 33,000 children in Glasgow of school age who were not at school ; "many are employed in dye-works and foundries ten or twelve hours daily at the age of eight or nine."* The much-boasted comparative excellence of the Scots educational system owes nothing to the manufacturing class.†

In 1859 the child serfs in West of Scotland bleachfields were being worked from 11 to 18 hours daily in stoves heated from 80 to 100 degrees ; at Pollokshaws children were occasionally worked "two and three days and nights consecutively " ; when the Bleachfields Bill of 1860 was before the House of Commons, Roebuck declared that these children led "the life of the damned ; the children's hands are often blistered and the skin torn off their feet, and yet they are thus obliged to work, the persons who overlook them being sometimes forced to keep them awake by beating on the table with large boards." In March, 1860, the number of hours worked in certain Scots Bleachfields were :—Monday 17½ ; Tuesday 16½ ; Wednesday 15½ ; Thursday 15½ ; Friday 15½ ; Saturday 7.‡ Lord Rosebery, speaking at the Social Science Congress in 1874, declared that "two or three years ago " there were some 30,000 children between the ages of 3½ and 17 carrying clay at the brickfields for 73 hours a week. The Convener of the Education Committee of the Glasgow School Board told the Factory Acts Commissioners in 1875 that the employers were defying the Education Acts ; Dr. Ebenezer Watson testified to the steady physical deterioration that was going on ; and Dr. Irvine declared that without continual recruitment from the country the town populations would soon die out. For three-quarters of a century the factory capitalists of Scotland exploited, maimed, and murdered the worker's child ; for it no sunlight, no childish games and laughter and joy ; it toiled and starved and died for a master's profit.

IV.—THE FACTORY ACTS.

The Health and Morals of Apprentices Act, 1802, is generally regarded as the first Factory Act, though in reality it was more of an extension of the English Poor Law regarding parish [pauper]

---

*N.B. Daily Mail, 21/10/1861.

†The second report of the Factory Commissioners for 1843, dealing with the North of England, shews that in 95 printworks only 8 have a school supported by the masters. Among the 8 we do not find the name of Richard Cobden, though he employed 244 children.

‡Scotsman, 22/3/60.

apprentices. The poor orphan children farmed out to the budding factory lords were being overworked and starved ; and Sir Samuel Romilly in his *Diary* declared that he knew instances in which these children were actually murdered by their masters in order to secure the premiums given by the Poor Law authorities with each fresh batch of children taken. The Act of 1802 sought to limit the exploitation of the children to 12 hours per day ; it stipulated for a certain rudimentary minimum in education ; that not more than two children should be sent to sleep in the one bed, and that they should be sent to church at least once a month. These restrictions made parish children less sought after by the masters, who thenceforth devoted their attention to "free" children—that is, to children of impoverished parents ; upon the labours of these "free" children there were no restrictions of any kind ; they could be withered up and destroyed twenty-four hours in the day.

Robert Owen strove in vain to induce the masters in the West of Scotland to join in demanding that the Government should limit the hours of labour in the textile factories. But, largely as the result of Owen's agitation, Sir Robert Peel consented to the appointment of a Committee of Investigation. The Committee sat for two sessions gravely inquiring whether it was injurious to a child to work 14 hours per day in a heated atmosphere filled with flying fibre dust ; and they took a great amount of suborned medical evidence on behalf of the manufacturers. Thus a Dr. Holmes was asked :

> " Suppose I were to ask you whether you thought it injurious to a child to be kept standing three and twenty hours out of the four and twenty, should you not think that it must be necessarily injurious to the health ? "

The Doctor replied :

> " If there were such an extravagant thing to take place and it should appear that the person was not injured by having stood three and twenty hours, I should then say it was not inconsistent with the health of the person so employed."

Another perjured medical witness, Dr. Wilson, thought it was not necessary for young children to have recreation. Still another testified that a child of six years, working twelve hours, so far from being fatigued, performed "the last hour's work with greater interest and spirit than any of the rest."

Robert Owen knew of children working in the cotton mills at three years of age, and Sir Robert Peel knew of children of seven who toiled 13 and 14 hours daily.

The Act of 1819 prohibited child labour in cotton mills and factories under 9 years of age, and children between 9 and 16 years could not work more than 12 hours a day. Scarcely, however, was the Act on the Statute Book ere it was amended backwards ; for example, time lost by water-power failure or other accident, it was decided, had to be made up. But the amending Act was really unnecessary, for the operation of the Act was left to the Justices of the Peace, and as these Justices were usually themselves manufacturers, the Act was all but a dead letter.

By the Act of 1825, J.P.'s who were owners of mills were prohibited from hearing complaints about violation of the Act of 1819. The Act of 1831 extended the twelve hours a day limit to workers under 18 years of age, and prohibited the night work of those under 21 years of age. The Bill as originally drafted applied to all textile industries, but the opposition of the Fife and Forfarshire flax spinners resulted in the measure being limited to cotton factories. In 1832 Sadler was proving that the factory child endured a slavery unknown to the felon, but all he could secure was another Commission of Enquiry, and packed with manufacturers' friends at that ! Nevertheless the evidence led was so damning that the Commissioners were compelled to report for farther "reform "; and when roving Commissioners were appointed by the Government they in turn reported wholesale evasions of such Acts as had been passed, despite the fact that "witnesses for the poor, generally from among the poor themselves, were racked, and tortured, and browbeat in the morning, after which the Commissioners dined with the rich oppressors."* The Commissioner in Scotland, Stuart, was anything but hostile to the masters, yet even he was compelled to protest to the Secretary of the Commission that "you have omitted all notice of the mass of evidence in Scotland unfavourable to your own views "; and when, in 1833, Lord Ashley (later, Lord Shaftesbury) did succeed in carrying farther legislation it was mutilated, twisted, and carved by the dominant manufacturing interest. The Act of 1833, nevertheless, established a factory inspectorate, stopped all night work by young persons under 18, limited their hours to 69 per week and provided that three years later (*i.e.*, in 1836) no child under 11 was to be employed more than nine hours a day. In 1836, and nine days after this particular clause became operative, the Government of the day moved and carried its repeal by 178 to 176 votes, Dan O'Connell being one of the majority ; he had always posed as a friend of the factory children, but it was significant that three days after his reactionary vote, he was presented with a purse of £700 by "millowners and others." But O'Connell's purchase money availed the millowners little, for the storm in the country was so great that the Government hastily withdrew its amending measure. Despite the Act of 1833, lace and silk factories still had privileges of child exploitation. At Aberdeen the master spinners seized the excuse of the

---

***Blackwood's Magazine*, 1836, p. 114 *et seq.* ; Hutchins and Harrison, *A History of Factory Legislation*.

Act to effect a reduction in wages ; and the part-time compulsory education of children between 9 and 11 led to the discharge of many children.* But the Government did not seriously enforce the Act ; and in 1835 Lord Shaftesbury was petitioned by 200 Sunday School teachers, who assured him of the uselessness of attempting to teach factory children owing to the children's "extreme weariness from over work " ; employers refused to fence their machinery, and even advanced journals † accepted the resultant accidents with resignation. "The frequency," they said, "of accidents by machinery in large factories should bestir the workers to form societies for the relief of their unfortunate and often destitute fellow-workmen in such circumstances."

A thriving trade seems to have been done in bogus birth and education certificates ; education fees were stopped out of children's wages ; the inspectors were hocussed and tricked ; the magistrates had small sympathy with interfering legislation, and imposed farcical penalties even when they could be induced to convict ; and the net result of it all was, as Lord Ashley assured the House of Commons in 1838, that the hours of labour for children in the factories had actually *increased* by four per day compared with 1817 ; the death-rate of factory workers under 20 years of age was as heavy as the death-rate of other workers under 40 years of age. Ashley introduced a new and stringent Bill, but the House of Commons walked out ere he had been on his feet two minutes. He was "counted out." Upon this episode the Tory *Courier* declared :

> " The subject is displeasing to Lord John Russell, who derives no small amount of support from the Radical mill-owners throughout the manufacturing districts of England and Scotland ; he was accordingly most anxious to evade the discussion . . . the factory children, not Lord Ashley, are the victims . . . the insult offered to humanity on the present occasion will be avenged by a widespread feeling of loathing and scorn."‡

In 1843, the year in which Tom Hood's "Song of the Shirt " was published, the Tory Government introduced a Factory Education Bill which was killed by the dissenting clergy, who objected to the Episcopal theology which was to be retailed under the Bill to the factory child. That, however, these worthies did not confine their opposition to the purely theological clauses is evident from the resolutions passed at a great protest meeting in Glasgow. Clergymen packed the meeting and resolved that the new bill was "illiberal,'

---

*Masters refused to " submit to the inconvenience."—Baines' *History of the Cotton Manufacture*, pp. 479-80.

†*The Glasgow Evening Post and Paisley and Renfrewshire Reformer*, 30/4/35. As late as 1855 we find in the Factory Inspector's Report that in Scotland only 108 out of 238 factory-owners had installed fencing for the machinery.

‡17/7/38.

inasmuch as it gave "fresh sanction and enlarged application to the principle of compulsory education "; and secondly, "by prohibiting the employment in factories of all children and young persons who are not able to present certificates of their having been instructed in schools under Government inspection, thereby tyrannically depriving employers of the liberty to receive, and workers of the liberty to give, the service which may be most convenient and desirable for both."*

The Government withdrew its Bill, but in the succeeding year, 1844, introduced a new Factory Act, restricting the hours of young persons and women to 12 per day, fixing holidays, providing for compensation for injuries, regulating factory hours by public clock (and not by the owners' easily-manipulated time-pieces), and making compulsory the fencing of machinery and the half-time system of education. Ashley moved an amendment limiting the hours of women and children to 10 per day. Not more than six per cent. of factory operatives, he said, were fit for work after 45 years of age owing to their "exhaustion from early labour; mothers were so long in the mills that they had to drug their children with laudanum." Despite a savage attack upon Ashley by John Bright, the amendment was carried by nine votes, but a subsequent strenuous whipping up by both parties secured an overturn of the decision, and Ashley was beaten. Even the Tory press thought Ashley was overdoing it, the *Courier* telling him that he had destroyed his Party, and Roebuck, who, after a visit to Glasgow in 1838, had said that "the sight of the Glasgow mill slaves at work froze his blood," turned now and declared that "the miseries of factory labour were exaggerated. It won't do to come to this House with exaggerated descriptions of misery, of want, and of suffering. I deny them all." Lord Ashley was accused of exciting "a servile war in the manufacturing districts ";† then the Government withdrew its Bill and introduced another, remarkable for its curious and intricate compromises. Again Ashley moved his ten hours' amendment, and again he was beaten.

In 1845 Ashley introduced a measure to safeguard the infants toiling in the calico print works, but the capitalists in Parliament succeeded in mutilating it so that it emerged as a measure giving powers to work children under 13 for sixteen hours a day. During 1846 the struggle for the ten hours' day continued : a Lace Factories Bill to prohibit all night working of children in the lace factories was beaten ; but in 1847 the reformers succeeded in carrying the Ten Hours Bill for women and young persons in the cotton factories, amid loud protests from the Liberals that this was simply the Tories

---

Scotch Reformers' Gazette, 20/5/43.

†The Liberal *Argus* denounced his "fanatical philanthropy."

paying them back for Free Trade, and counter gibes from the Tories that the Liberals had promised the workers a ten hours' day when Free Trade was secured, and now they were getting it. The employers, however, immediately set about defying the Act. The first step, as at Kirkcaldy, was to reduce wages ; the second to get a legal decision in favour of a relay system which kept the women and children hanging about the factory for 14 or 15 hours ; they only worked ten hours, but the relay system of women and children enabled the owners to keep the adult males upon whose labour there was no restriction employed for 14 or 15 hours. Both these steps naturally caused disgust among the workers, and many were induced to sign petitions to Parliament in favour of repealing the Act altogether ; but in such districts as Hawick the masters were compelled to resort to intimidation to get the workers to sign. The millowners of Britain, including 55 from Glasgow, petitioned Parliament to disregard "morbid public opinion," but in Scotland great counter petitions were organised by the more intelligent operatives to close up the leak-holes in the Act ; and in the year 1850 Parliament fixed a normal working day for women and children which prevented the relay system of evasion. For some time the masters kept in existence a more or less active Factory Law Amendment Association (which Dickens called "the Association for the Mangling of Operatives "), but the fight for the ten hours' day was over ; the cotton masters were beaten. Print works and bleachfields, however, were still exempt from the Act. The Factory Inspector, Tremenheere, reported that occasionally young girls of ten years of age might be found working in a bleachfield for 20 hours at a time in an atmosphere of 110 degrees ; attempt after attempt to bring in the bleachfields was frustrated until the Act of 1860, when bleach and dyeworks (except open-air bleaching) were brought within the factory regulations ; and in 1862 night work at open-air bleaching was prohibited. Even in that year, 1862, there were still almost 100,000 British children under one pretext or another outwith the protection of the Factory Acts. In Scotland a child under 13 in a print works might still be employed from 6 a.m. to 10 p.m. all the week. At the lace works there might not be (as was the case in 1842 when the Children Employment Commission sat) infants of two years of age employed in the manufacture of lace, but there still were children five years old working from 8 a.m. to 8 p.m. In 1864 six fresh trades were brought in, but the Government yielded to the bleachfield owners, and excluded finishers, hookers, and lappers in their employment, though the M.P. for Paisley, Ewing, declared that work was sometimes going on continuously in a Paisley Bleachfield for 30 hours.

The year 1867 saw Disraeli's Government place upon the Statute

Book the Factory Acts Extension Bill and the Hours of Labour Regulation Bill ; the former was a complicated measure with many concessions to powerful interests, and the latter covered workshops employing fewer than 50 persons. The joint effect was considerable, though fresh methods of evasion and indeed open defiance were resorted to by many owners. Thus, at the Johnstone factories in 1869 we read that women are still working 14 hours a day, and children of six years of age are being employed.* Speeding up the machinery and giving the workers more machinery to operate led to increased accidents, and a new agitation began not only to bring print, bleach and dye-works (hitherto under special Acts) completely under the ordinary Factory Acts, but to secure an all-round maximum fifty-one hour week and compensation for accidents.

The next Act, that of 1874, fixed the hours of factory women and children in most branches of industry at 56½ hours per week, but again print, bleach and dye-works were left out, one employer, Mr. Orr Ewing, M.P., from the Vale of Leven, asserting that a whole holiday to his employees once a fortnight "would lead to idle habits." The Hosiery Manufacture Wages Act of 1875 prohibited the hosiery employers from making deductions from the workers' wages to pay for the frames they were using. In 1877 a Bill was introduced authorising a weekly half-holiday, prohibiting factory work for children under 10 years, making it illegal to employ a girl under 16 in brickyards or salt manufacture, and prohibiting child labour altogether in metal grinding or dipping lucifer matches ; but the Consolidation Acts of 1878, while extending the classes of labour protected by law against the excesses of the factory exploiters, were weakened and marred as a result of a Women's Rights Agitation got up by some middle-class ladies who contended that farther restrictions upon female labour would end in the employers filling their factories with male workers. In 1887 the Truck Act of 1831 compelling masters to pay wages in cash and not in inferior or unsaleable or fictitiously valued goods—there are cases on record where Glasgow workers were paid in clay pipes !— was extended to cover all manual workers except domestic servants. In 1896 another amending Act was passed to stop the leak holes that had been discovered by ingenious masters ; employers were compelled to affix on their walls notice of the scale of deductions from wages that would ensue from bad workmanship, spoiled material, and so on, and arbitrary deductions on pay-days were no longer to be allowed.

**N.B. Daily Mail*, 2/4/69.

V.—THE BAKERS.

"It is sinful to . . . compel us to work from three in the morning till six, seven, and eight in the evening."—*Mr. Cuthbertson, Secretary, Operative Bakers' Association*, 1846.

From the early burghal times, when the "Lorde of the ovyn" had the charge for the use of his "ovyn" restricted by law, down to the second quarter of the nineteenth century, documentary references to the operative bakers are few and far between. In the thirties of last century we gather from the press that bakehouses were mostly underground and grievously unhealthy places; that the journeyman baker received bed and board and a small sum in money wages; and that his hours of toil might be anything up to eighteen out of the twenty-four. In the beginning of 1834 we are told that small local Unions of Bakers have federated, and that the Glasgow bakers are out on strike;* the immediate object of the strike we are not told, nor whether the men were successful, nor whether the masters executed their threat to supplant the rebels with unemployed weavers. In 1835 we find the Edinburgh bakers engaged in a public agitation to secure a regular twelve hours' day, from 5 a.m. to 5 p.m. in place of the current working day of an irregular 16 or 18 hours, and for the abolition of the bed and board method of payment, and the substitution of a full cash wage.† In 1845 the Edinburgh and Glasgow Unions federated into a "National Union"; and in 1846 public meetings to state their grievances were held. Journeymen bakers living on their masters' premises could not marry, and the consequence was that when a journeyman baker desired to marry, his friends scraped together a few pounds to set him up in business as a master baker. Competition in the baking trade was therefore "cut-throat," and the master bakers were advised in self-protection to cut off this incentive to competition by abolishing the bed and board system. "Let them pay regular wages and the journeymen will not so readily aspire to be masters!" About this period bakers' wages in Glasgow ran to 16s. or thereby per week.

Most masters accepted the demands for cash wages and a twelve hours' day; but at Leslie, in 1854, the journeymen were on strike to secure these "boons."‡ In 1857 the bakers of Greenock and Glasgow were on strike for a four shillings' increase on their sixteen shillings wage; blacklegs were introduced; the organised workers retaliated by boycotting the unfair shops; and a mass meeting of

---

Evening Post, 1/2/34 and 15/2/34.
†Pamphlets in Mr. J. Jeffrey Hunter's Collection.
‡*Glasgow Courier*, 29/7/54.

trades delegates in Glasgow asked the bakers to submit a plan shewing how the trades could unite "in setting on foot a co-operative baking establishment for the employment of those at present on strike."* This pressure seems to have been effective; but the masters gradually broke through the agreements they had signed to secure a cessation of the boycott; and Sheriff Steele of Glasgow obligingly gave a decision that a master was not bound to observe any stipulation given by him to employ only Trade Unionists; such a stipulation, he declared, was "*pactum illicitum* and contrary to public policy, as an undue restraint upon the liberty of trade "; he fined Trade Unionists who left their employment because the masters had violated their agreement by employing "scab-labour."†

Again, in 1859, the bakers of Glasgow and Greenock struck for a twelve hours' day and no start earlier than 5 a.m. The strike must have been successful, for at the "fifteenth annual soiree " of the Glasgow Operative Bakers, held in 1861, the claim was made that the days of slavery and forced celibacy in the bakers' barracks were over; and that the working day was now generally only one of 12 hours.‡ In 1862 the bakers of Edinburgh struck for a 10 hours' day and abolition of Sunday and night work; many masters, we are told, submitted. In 1863 the bakers of 23 towns were petitioning Parliament for exclusion of youths under 18 from night work§ and for inspection of bakehouses; and in the succeeding year they were voting money to assist the agitation against the Master and Servant Act. For some unexplainable reason the highest rate of bakers' wages in Scotland was to be found at Greenock; there the rate was 26s. 6d., while in Stranraer (the lowest rated town) it was 17s., and at Edinburgh, 22s., at which last mentioned place, however, the bakers had secured by the year 1872 a Court of Arbitration, and were hopeful of improvement.

In 1877, following upon the developments consequent upon the introduction of machinery into the bakehouses, the 12 hour day was broken, and the men driven back again to the irregular and unlimited hours. There were vigorous protests, of course, and a systematic attempt to crush out the blackleg shops, but all of no avail; and as late as 1884 the Glasgow bakers were striking against a working week of 80 hours (*plus* time on Sunday) and a wage rate of $3\frac{1}{2}$d. per hour.‖ Indeed, it was not until the year 1889 that the secretary

---

Herald, 22/4/57. The United Co-operative Baking Society, now the largest bakery in the world, was not formed until 1869.

†*Herald*, 30/11/57.

‡In 1861 the National Association of Bakers in Scotland had 18 branches and 1281 members.

§Under the Bakehouse Regulation Act young persons could be worked from 5 a.m. to 9 p.m.

‖*Weekly Herald*, 10/5/84.

Y

of the "Bakers' National Federal Union of Scotland" could assure the Trades Councils that after a long struggle and a thorough organisation of the workers in the industry, they had again secured a regular maximum working day of 12 hours in general operation all over Scotland.

VI.—THE COLLIERS.

" . . deadly physical oppression and systematic slavery of which I conscientiously believe no one unacquainted with such facts would credit the existence in the British dominions."—*Mr. Franks, Investigator, Children's Employment Commission Report* (1842)—" *Mines and Collieries,*" 26-28 p. 387,

"There must be rich and poor—there must be fortunate and unfortunate, for blessed purposes ; for if there were no poor there would be no sweet and holy charity."—*Mr. Baillie Cochrane of Cambusnethan, Colliery Landowner.—* "*N.B. Daily Mail,*" 27/10/1863.

" Trade Unions have been begun by the firebrands of demagogues who go among our working-men spreading distrust . . . and spreading disaffection between the employer and the employed, and fomenting this mischievous feeling by uniting them in a bond of union for unholy purposes."—*Sheriff Strathearn at Airdrie,* 1/3/59.

In previous sections we have described the state of the Scots collier in the old slavery days, and how and why he escaped from bondage in the last decade of the eighteenth century. Let us now envisage him as a "free" man empowered by law and compelled by hunger to sell his labour-power for a wage in money or in goods.

At the beginning of the "freedom" period the coalowners bought their labourers annually. The collier contracted to work for 12 months, to produce a fixed quantity of coal weekly for a fixed wage, but if the owner saw fit to lower his selling price, the collier must lower his wage in proportion ; "and if the whole of the coaliers shall at any time be idle without reasonable excuse" they must pay the owners' "rent of the coal for such time, or if one, or whatever number less than the whole of them, shall be idle, they must pay their proportion of the rent for such time." For giving " insulting language " they were fined 5s. for each offence ; every collier had to provide hi3 own "bearer "—usually wife or daughter—and if the collier was idle through the fault of the owner, he was given 1s. 8d. per day of " play wages."* Down to about 1817 it is difficult to arrive at any estimate of the rate of colliers' wages ; the rate seems to have varied greatly and the proportion paid in goods very high, but even allowing for the difference in money values, it seems to have been an improvement

---

History of Tranent—P. M'Neill, pp. 166-8.

upon the rate paid in 1612,* or even upon that paid in 1703.† But whatever was the rate, the colliers regarded it as insufficient, and, as we learn from the evidence given before the Parliamentary Commission of Enquiry into the Repeal of the Combination Acts, Trade Unions were formed and bitter strikes took place in the west country. At Bo'ness blacklegs were savagely maltreated. According to a Mr. Taylor, a coalmaster, the Ayrshire miners were organised into a Union in 1817 by a weaver named Fallhouse Wilson ; a strike ensued, but it was broken in a fortnight. In 1818 markets were high and wages low, and one coalmaster at least is said to have simultaneously taken 1s. off wages and raised prices by 2s. per wagon. At Govan, in 1821, a strike lasted for eleven weeks, but the men were beaten. In 1824 a strike lasted six months in the Edinburgh district, and blacklegs had their ears cut off. But in the same year a strong Union in Lanarkshire, Renfrewshire and Dumbartonshire raised wages from 3s. 6d. to 5s. per day.‡ In 1825 colliers' wages are said to have averaged 4s. per day of 8 to 10 hours.§ During the strikes of that period we find the first references to the importation of "strangers from Ireland" as strike-breakers, a practice which seems to have been one of the contributory causes of that intense anti-Irish feeling which has scarcely yet died away in many districts. It is noticeable, too, that, down at least to a legal decision in 1817, no one, owner or collier, believed that the Combination Acts applied to Scotland.

In 1826 and 1828 we read of great strikes among coal-miners; and in the former year the manager of the Govan colliery devised a sure specific against Trade Unionism by founding a "Friendly and Free Labour Society," which, as he said, "relieved the workmen from the pernicious effects of strikes." The method by which the new scheme was worked is not at all clear ; but when, in 1837, the miners of the west were striking against a reduction of 1s. per day, and the friendly and free colliers continued working, we read that the latter finally approached their employers and "desired permission to be idle so as not to bear the reproach from their fellow workmen." Permission was graciously granted for 13 weeks, after which period they, the free and friendly ones, dutifully went back to work at the same reduced rates against which the other miners had struck.‖ In 1832 there was an 18 weeks' strike in Lanarkshire, in which the

---

*5/6 per family.—Chambers' *Domestic Annals*, p. 217.

†For a woman coal-bearer £1 6/8 per annum, plus 3 pair of shoes, a shirt, and an ell of linen.—" The Barony of Lasswade," *Chambers' Journal*, August, 1912.

‡Assistant Hand-loom Weavers' Commission Report (1839), p. 16.

§*The Miner*, December, 1888.

‖Assistant Hand-loom Weavers' Commission Report (1839), p. 17.

men were beaten ; the employers armed their blacklegs, and one fierce encounter at Whiterigg is recorded, wherein the strikers, with their faces blacked for disguise, and armed with pistols and cutlasses, fought a pitched battle with the blacklegs, who lost 32 wounded. Many of the strikers were wounded, and one was killed.* In 1833 there are again strikes, the colliers boasting they will not starve "as long as God's barns are open " ; the press warned the farmers to look to their potato fields and boasted that the owners had accumulated stocks of coal, and that the men would speedily be starved into surrender. This latter prophecy was fulfilled. In 1834 there were many strikes. In 1836 the owners are said to have combined and raised the selling price by 100 per cent., and the men struck for and secured small increases.† Coal Consumers' Leagues had to be formed to protect the public against the coal owners.

The year 1837 saw a great colliers' strike in the West of Scotland, a strike that lasted for 17 weeks before the men were beaten ; they had endured misery and privation "without a murmur,"‡ says one writer ; from other sources we learn that during the strike there were 10,000 persons in sheer destitution at Hamilton, and that large numbers attended the Paisley Soup Kitchens. The owners brought in thousands of hungry weavers (whose nominal wages at the loom were 7s. 6d. to 8s. per week) to act as blacklegs, and saw to it that there was adequate military protection. The men returned to work at a wage of 4s. per day.

During the next two years there were no increases, though the owners were said to be making "fabulous profits."

In 1840 Mr. R. H. Franks, one of the investigators under the Commission of Enquiry into the question of the employment of children, had taken evidence in the East of Scotland that shocked and startled the non-mining public. Children of 11 years work from 5 a.m. to 5 p.m., "work all night on Fridays, and come hame at twelve in the day "—children carry one hundred-weight at a time, in water "coming up to the calves." "I have no liking for the work," says one little witness at Sheriffhall, Midlothian, "but faither makes me like it. . . . I am at night school, learning to read in the two-penny book. Jesus was God, and David wrote the Bible." One girl at Edmonstone Pit, Midlothian, began work at age 10, is now 17, and works twelve to fourteen hours a day ; her father gets 12s. every fortnight for her work at carrying coals. "Lassies hate the work," she says : " . . . it is ower sair for females." Another girl who can carry two hundred weight of coal on her back described how one day she was up to the neck in water. Another girl, Ellison

---

Glasgow Courier, 12/6/32.

†*Evening Post,* 3/12/36 and 10/12/36.

‡*History of the Rise and Progress of Coatbridge*—Millar.

Jack, of Loanhead Colliery, began at the age of 8 to work from 2 a.m.
till 1 p.m. or 2 p.m. in the afternoon. "I gang to bed at six to be
ready for work next morning . . . I have had the strap when I
didna do my bidding. I am very gled when my task is wrought as
it sair fatigues." Mr. Franks said this girl had to travel the height
(including the distance along the pit "road") of St. Paul's Cathedral
with 1 to 1½ cwt. on her back. "However incredible it may appear,
yet I have taken the evidence of fathers who have ruptured themselves from straining to lift coal on their children's backs." A
woman from East Linton tells of the effect of pit-work in producing
dead-born children and false births. "The work is only horse work
and ruins the women ; it crushes their haunches, bends their ankles,
and makes them old women at forty." The pit bottoms, says Mr.
Franks, are like "common sewers," slush and water, with an inclination of one in three, and along these common sewers the women,
half naked, crawl on hands and knees, harnessed "like horses" to
their bogie of coals ; little boys, aged four or five, sat all day in the
darkness at the trap-doors, cold and shivering, begging for a candle-
end for light. The contractors drive the girls, "for they do the work
cheap," says one girl. One Tranent boy of 10 years sits in the water
"at his work" and "seldom changes his clothes, as it is so late before
we get hame." Another boy works 13 hours, and when he falls
asleep "gets his licks." He "has some brothers and sisters : don't
know how many"; is sent to bed when he gets home, he is so
fatigued. David Neill of Tranent began work at six years of age at
4d. per shift and "6d. for long ones . . . Am very sick at times as
the work is hard and gets naething but bits o' bread." "Cannot
read, and does not know (now 9 years old) whether he lives in Tranent or not, but thinks he lives in Allan's Boons." Another boy at
Gladsmuir (Haddingtonshire), aged 10, whose father was "idle the
noo wi black spittle and bad breath," doesn't know the meaning of
the word "hours." Boys who run away "are caught." One girl
of 11 years says : "I gang with the women at five and come up with
the women at five at night ; work all night on Fridays, and come
away at twelve in the day." She carries a hundred-weight of coals.
Females at Arniston have been down the pits working to "the last
hour of pregnancy" ; they are prematurely "brought to the grave."

These and similar revelations shocked the House of Commons so
that Lord Ashley (later the Earl of Shaftesbury) succeeded in carrying *nem con* the second reading of his Bill to limit the starting age
of collier boys to 13 ; but the coalmasters quickly recovered and
succeeded in getting the starting age reduced to 10, and for boys
between 10 and 13 three days' work per week and 12 hours per day.
Ashley's Bill also entirely prohibited female labour underground ;
this part of the Bill was passed, and although the coalowners, in

1843, sought to have an amending measure carried, they were defeated by a majority of 114. The now-unemployed women vainly sought work in the pits, but in some places they were driven back with stones ; in Midlothian they disguised themselves as men to get work and a group of them were summoned to the law courts at Edinburgh, where they "displayed such ignorance on the most trifling things and made such ridiculous answers " that the grave and reverend Court was "convulsed with laughter." On promising not to repeat the offence they were dismissed.

In 1842 the Scots miners' wage was as low as 1s. 9d. per day* and strikes accompanied by wild rioting broke out in Ayrshire. Blacklegs in Ayr were fired at, many were assaulted, and one was killed. For this, three strikers were given 10 years' transportation. In Midlothian prisoners were forcibly taken from the police, and truck stores were raided. Finally the owners promised an increase of 1s. per day, and the men returned to work ; but the promise not being fulfilled the strikes broke out again in January 1843, and after three months of starvation and evictions the men returned to the pits like whipped dogs.

In 1843 we find a great British Miners' Conference being held in Glasgow. Roberts, the Chartist lawyer, warns the miners about a Bill then before Parliament to give powers to a single J.P. to imprison a "disobedient servant " for two months. A general strike of all British miners was proposed, but was beaten, largely by Scots votes. The Fifeshire delegates explained that they had only 300 men in the Union, and that the masters had great stocks of coal on hand. Three months later, however, there was a sudden and complete stoppage in Lanarkshire, with the colliers in the other parts of Scotland adopting the "wee darg " policy to keep the market empty. The men demanded 3s. 6d. for an eight hours' day, fortnightly wages, only 3 days' lying time, honest weighing of coals, and the abolition of the truck shops. After a prolonged strike the men were beaten. These continual repressions and starvations naturally thinned out the colliers, and no fresh labourers would engage in the mines if they could secure other employment. This colliery labour shortage drove up wages, and the year 1844 saw the colliers with 5s. a day and such a labour scarcity that at Newton the owners were bribing men from other owners and paying their debts to secure their services. As much as £80 down was paid for a skilled miner.† This scarcity of labour, however, was soon rectified by great importations of destitute Highlanders and Irish, and wages were driven down again to 3s. 6d. In 1845 we find the colliers complaining that

---

Weekly Mail, 6/9/79.
†Poor Law Commission (1844) Evidence, **vol. iii.**

after a pit accident, in which 17 men had been killed, the employers would not contribute a penny towards the funeral expenses.*

In July, 1845, the miners joined the new consolidated Union of Trades, for common industrial action. By the end of 1846 we read that wages have risen to 5s. again ; but again in 1847 the owners systematically organised immigration to the coal-fields, the firm of Merry-Cunninghame, for instance, importing some 70 destitute crofters from Tiree and setting them to work at 10s. per week. Only one week did they work ere they struck for an increase of 4s., which, being refused, they marched away, led by a piper, and the press complained of their "base ingratitude." Wages, however, were steadily driven down till they reached 2s. a day ; in Ayrshire strikes led to wholesale evictions, and we find the Cumnock men and their families camping out by the roadside ; the men of Muirkirk go about poaching in armed bands, and at Beith the Yeomanry have to be called out to prevent the pits from being destroyed.

All during the Chartist year of 1848 the Lanarkshire coalfield was in starvation. Fully three-fourths of the miners were now Irish, and the average wage was 2s. 6d. per day. Every now and again blacklegs were assaulted, and one (at Airdrie) was killed. By the, beginning of 1850 some semblance of organisation had been secured, and "extensive and well-organised" strikes of long duration took place for weekly pays and 4s. a day. The owners and their friends tried every trick. The anti-papal drum was beaten to drive the Scots and the Irish to antagonism, the press announced that the men in certain districts had surrendered, but was ruefully compelled to admit its "mistake" because the announcement was misleading to shipping firms ;† an Irvine striker was imprisoned by the Justices for having deserted the employment of his master";‡ and some hungry men at Legbrannock who attacked the local store were given six months' hard labour. Sheer starvation finally drove the colliers back at 3s. 6d. a day, but with a not unimportant victory, for they secured weekly pays. During the year it is officially recorded that on an average eight colliers in Scotland were killed monthly, and the Mining Inspector reported that for the year 1850-1 accidents in Scotland were nearly double what they were in England, despite the fact that the mines in Scotland were not so deep, and had, as a rule, more air shafts and less inflammable gas ; he explains, however, that in Scotland the owners supplied cheap cages—"simple platforms hung by the centre," and had no one appointed to look after the shafts or to give and receive signals to the surface ; many mines

---

*Argus, 31/3/45.

†Glasgow Herald, 22/7/50.

‡The High Court quashed the conviction on the ground that the trial had been held behind closed doors.

were worked "without any ventilating process whatsoever."* In the year 1851 the average wage of the collier in Scotland is stated to have been 2s. 6d. per day ;† but there were deductions for oil, pick-sharpening, etc., and this miserable pittance lasted until October, 1852, when it was increased by 6d. per day.   In 1852 the Scottish Miners' Association was formed, and Mr. Tremenheere, the Commissioner of Mines, waxes eloquent upon the woes of the employers in his annual report.‡   Something, he says, must be done to prevent "the spread of Socialism in the mining districts " ; there must be more elementary instruction as a preventative and longer and more frequent contact during susceptible years between the collier on the one side and the schoolmaster and the clergyman on the other. This would awaken "a deference for authority," and it would be unlikely "that those mischievous combinations which so obstruct capital and annually destroy so much of it . . . could long hold their ground." Restriction of output especially angers him. It is supported by the "phrases of Socialism " got from cheap translations of continental literature, from itinerant lecturers, and from Plato's "Republic," which is "much read " for its Socialism and Communism. He admits, however, that employers still evade the Truck Acts, that some truck shops make "thousands a year "; that £5 fines are useless ; and that the employers are hostile to a proposal that boys of 12 to 15 years should go to school for two days a week.

During the year 1853 wages rose, until about December they stood at 5s. per day ; but the huge profits taken at the compulsory truck shops kept the miners still in squalid misery and in feudal serfdom.§ Houldsworth of Coltness turned off the gas nightly at 10 p.m. to send his miners to bed.   Cholera swept through the rotten collier houses, taking its toll alike from Protestant and Catholic with an impartiality that must have amazed the more zealous sectaries who believed that low wages and general misery were caused either by King William of Orange or by the Pope of Rome. But the belief in the theological basis of low wages recovered itself. At Airdrie, in August, 1854, the pits were struck "until all the Roman Catholics should be expelled."

By March, 1856, the coal bings were well stacked and the Crimean War was dragging itself along ; there was over-production for a dull market and the coalmasters seized the opportunity to (a) reduce wages, and (b) attempt the imposition of new "slave rules " in the pits. The wages were low enough—nominally 5s. a day, but, as Alexander Macdonald shewed, what with a four-a-and-half-day

*Courier, 11/3/52.

†Scotsman, 20/1/68.

‡Courier, 28/8/52 and 31/8/52.

§Mr. J. Hill Burton's Report on Truck—Courier, 25/6/54.

working week, and swindling at the pit head weighing machines, and deductions for blasting powder and oil, in reality the miner had only 14s. a week clear. Moreover, miners were required to purchase their goods at the owners' store, and since "the baker who supplied these truck shops gave 2s. 9d. on the £1 worth of bread for the privilege and the shoemaker 3s. 6d. on the £1" to the coalowner, and since there were deductions for schoolmaster, doctor, and often blacksmith (and indeed sometimes the very clergyman was compulsorily trucked) the nominal 5s. a day represented sheer hunger and privation.* And now, although the selling price of coal was not lowered, the masters intimated a reduction to 4s. per day. As if this were not sufficient to infuriate already hungry men, an ingenious Glasgow lawyer had drawn up new pit rules for the masters, under which miners who failed to work "without intermission" for 10 to 12 hours in the confined and cramped workings were to be fined £2, or, if the Law Courts would oblige, sent to prison for 30 days. About 40,000 men in the West of Scotland struck work against these reductions and rules; they armed themselves with bludgeons to deal with blacklegs, and many were killed; they paraded with improvised bands of music soliciting subscriptions, until their masters' friends, the police authorities, seized the subscription sheets and imprisoned "mining beggars"; the Government Mines Inspector, Mr. Tremenheere, reported that the remedy for strikes was permanent mounted police, a suggestion in which he was anticipated by the mine-owners who had secured the calling out of the 1st Regiment of Militia at Hamilton, the supply of ball cartridge to the troops at Sanquhar, and the movement of police to threatened places.† Picketing was called intimidation, and those who indulged in it were fined 20s. or 20 days; at Wishaw alone 1200 families were evicted, though they were reported to have declared that "they were resolved to die rather than surrender." But at the end of three months' extraordinary hunger, and with their bairns slowly dying before their eyes, and seeing what market for coal there was supplied by East of Scotland colliers, and by Cumberland colliers (working for 3s. 6d. per day), the miners of the West crept back to work. The miners had pled for Government arbitration: their pleas had gone unheeded; they went back to the

---

*Courier, 6/5/1856.

†Here is one of the supplied paragraphs to the press of the period. It explains much: "Through the liberality of Messrs. Wilsons & Co., Summerlee; W. Baird & Co., Gartsherrie; and Mr. M'Kenzie, Dundyvan, suitable quarters have been provided for 200 of the militia, all of whom have for some time back been billeted on the inhabitants of Coatbridge."—Courier, 26/4/56. Liberality, no less! Another announced the introduction of American tunneling machines to displace the strikers unless they went back *instanter.*

4s. wages and the new pit rules which were designed to make the workers themselves responsible for accidents, and, as at Craigie Pit, Ayr, they were now "contracted" to increase their output from 60 cwts. to 71½ cwts. The anxiety of the masters to make the colliers responsible for "accidents" may be inferred from the fact that there was an annoying interest being taken by some middle-class humanitarians in the large number of badly-ventilated pits. The *Ayrshire Express* said that explosions were frequent and "something must be done"; Alexander Macdonald reported that in 2½ years in the burgh of Airdrie alone, no fewer than 310 miners had been killed. What the coalowners now did was to declare that the men themselves were responsible for any catastrophe that occurred.

By October, 1856, trouble had broken out again; the Hussars were at Carfin arresting the ringleaders in a riot; and the miners of Ayrshire were levying themselves 1s. to gather a strike fund, and were petitioning Parliament for an eight hours' day, an enquiry into ventilation, and the establishment of a just system of weighing coals at the pit-head.

The year 1857 was comparatively quiet; trade was depressed and the miners, on the advice of Alexander Macdonald, agreed to a farther reduction of 6d. per day. In 1858 it is doubtful if the Scots collier averaged a weekly wage of 10s.* In 1859 the nominal day's wage was driven up to 3s. 6d. again as a result of strikes in which the strike pay given by the Union was 6s. per week. Deputations appealed to the Lord Advocate for the removal of a host of grievances. Out of 529 pits there were only 42 in which the men did not allege swindling in the system of weighing—some owners demanded 28 cwt. to the ton and some even 30 cwts—the pitheadman was paid by and acted for the owner; 241 pits were not ventilated; pickets during a strike at Airdrie were sent to prison for 20 days for merely saying to black-legs "it was a shame for them to work."† When a miner was killed at his work, his dependents "went on the parish" and workmen's compensation was demanded to obviate "the scandal"; in the first half of the year 1859 alone, there were no fewer than 83 officially recorded pit accidents, and 90 deaths resulted; and the attitude of the owners was accurately stated by Wemyss, the coal owning M.P. for Fifeshire, when he said "he had a perfect right to keep his coal pits filled with black damp if he chose; he forced nobody to go into his pits and nobody was at liberty to constrain him to act otherwise than as he thought proper."‡

---

*The average wage is stated to have been 3/- per day (M'Intosh—*Hist. Civ. Scot.*, iv., 343, and *Weekly Scotsman*, January, 1868), but deductions must be made for light, sharpening tools, short time, colliery schoolmaster, etc.

†*Glasgow Herald*, 8/2/59.

‡*Ibid*, 15/8/59.

Of 1860 there is no wage change to record, the average of 3s. 6d. still ruled ; strikes in Lanarkshire for an increase of 6d. were beaten and a strike of the Oakley men in Fifeshire against a wage of 2s. 6d. had to be compromised. In 1860 the Fife County Miners' Association was formed. The report of the Western District Inspector of Coal Mines laconically states that most of the fire damp explosions "might have been averted.*

In January, 1861, the new Act for Regulation and Inspection of Mines came into force. Boys between 10 and 12 years of age could only be employed if in possession of education certificates ; notice of accident to be sent the authorities within 24 hours of the accident; wages were not to be paid in a public-house ; coals in future were to be well and truly weighed. The masters vainly endeavoured to induce the men to sign contracts binding them outside the Act, and, that having failed, their next recourse was to the law-courts, where the Sheriffs obligingly rendered the Act null and void. In the case, Harvie (collier) v. Farie (coalmaster) at Hamilton Sheriff Court we see how the trick was done.† Previous to the Act, if a collier sent up 4 cwts. of coal he was only paid for 2 cwts. at Mr. Fairie's pit. Now Mr. Farie declared that the men might have the coals re-weighed "as a matter of curiosity," but he would not allow a smaller weight than a 56lb. one at his pit head and he declined to alter his practice of under-payment. The judicious Sheriff (Bell by name) decided in Farie's favour, saying that "the Statute, while it provided that the material should be truly weighed, *did not enact that the men should be paid for what was so weighed.*" In other pits the rule was that hutches must contain 4 cwts, 1 quarter, and 9 ℔s. of coal ; if a hutch was one ounce short the whole was confiscated without payment by the owner ; ‡ on the other hand, nothing over the 4 cwts. 1 qr. and 9 ℔s. was paid for. Owners charged the men 1s 6d per week for house rent even if the houses were uninhabitable and the miners compelled to live elsewhere ; and frequently the owners made a profit of £18 or £21 a month by charging the miners more for the trucked doctor, schoolmaster and smith than the salaries they paid. The miners' housing was vile ; children at the Elgin Colliery, Dunfermline, were "nearly decimated " in 1861 by scarlatina. Wages averaged during the year nominally about 4s. per working day.

The year 1862 saw a miners' wage of 3s. per day driven up towards the end of the year to 3s. 6d. and 4s. as a result of sporadic strikes,

---

*At the Social Science Congress in 1860 it was stated that at age 20 the miners had an average sickness of 46% more than the general public ; at age 30, 70% ; at age 40, 78% ; at age 50, 76% ; at age 60, 53%.

†*N.B. Daily Mail*, 8/8/61.

‡*N.B. Daily Mail*, 13/2/61.

single pits being taken at a time, and these victories were secured despite an attempt by the masters to destroy the "single pit policy" by means of the "sympathetic lock-out" of the pits not being struck. In 1862 local friendly societies of miners were formed to give "greater permanency to the Union" by providing disablement and death payments. Macdonald shewed that during the years 1853 to 1860 there was an average of 80 deaths per annum from coal-mine accidents ;* if iron-stone pit figures were added, the average would be 106, the total number of widows and orphans being 7650 for the 8 years ; the number of miners "severely injured" for the same period was 2550.

The evidence is conflicting regarding nominal wage rates in 1863. An account some years later in the *Scotsman* puts the daily wage at 5s. 6d. ; but Alexander Macdonald declared it to be 4s. 6d., and so far as one can discover from the newspapers for 1863 it was only towards the end of the year that 4s. 6d. was reached. There were big strikes in the spring and the summer, both of which the men won. In 1863 the National Association of Miners was formed.

During most part of 1864 colliers' nominal wages averaged about 4s. per day despite a persistent policy of striking one pit at a time with the object of compelling the owners, one by one, to concede an extra sixpence. It was a time of prosperous prices for the owners, but they had large stocks of coal on hand, and it was not until August that they began to give the extra sixpence in wages. Towards the end of the year, the colliers, seeing the folly of over-production, commenced—led by the Fifeshire men—a policy of working five days a week, in the hope that restriction of output would put a strong wages increase lever in their hands.

In 1865 Alexander Macdonald toured the mining districts advocating an eight hours' day, greater inspection of mines, amendment of the Master and Servant Act, a share in the profits of coal for the miners, the abolition of the discharge note system, and the purchase by the miners of a pit "to be run on the co-operative principle." He also formed emigration societies, the men paying 6d. for their chance of the ballot. In one fortnight these societies paid the passages to America of no fewer than 100 miners. The cost of living rose steadily, and wages, despite partial strikes, fell by 6d. per day to 4s. again ; and the Govan district men complained that their wages were even 6d. per day below that figure. In Fife the newly-formed Lodge of Free Colliers was powerless to prevent reductions ; but the blacklegs at Halbeath had their houses wrecked. In the Falkirk area the owners offered to sell the colliers their "oil at market price and their powder at a reduction of 1s. 6d. per barrel" ; but this offer of diminished exploitation was refused as an unworthy substi-

---

*In 1862 the number was 111.

tute for a living wage. A miner at Tillicoultry, greatly daring, sued a coalowner for damages, as that gentleman had allowed black-damp to accumulate in his pit. The Sheriff decided that the miner had no title to sue.*

Sectional striking drove wages in 1866 up to 5s. and 5s. 6d. per day of twelve to fourteen hours, in every district except Midlothian, where for over a year an eight hours' day had been the rule ; and Macdonald set about an organised attempt to make an eight hours' day general. It was, said the *North British Daily Mail,* an "absurd project" of "interested professional agitators." The first fruits indeed were not promising. Twenty-seven Union Committeemen in Clackmannanshire were blacklisted, and every known Union man at Dalmellington was sacked, but great reductions in hours were secured, despite the introduction by the owners of large drafts of cheap blacklegs from Cornwall, and the Union organisations seem to have reached a high stage of efficiency. In the Lanarkshire area we find the colliers working short time in order to find work for locked-out iron-miners ;† but a year later (in 1867) a falling off in organisation enabled the employers to again reduce wages to 4s. and 3s. 6d. per day. Strikes were frequent, but they were doomed to failure so long, as at Wishaw, the miners struck one pit and left their employer to fulfil his contracts by working his other pits double-shift.‡ After a fire-damp explosion at Whifflet the poor miners were arrested and the pit manager and owner went free ; and the firm of Merry & Cunningham had the effrontery to seek avoidance of responsibility for compensation for accident by pleading that they had taken "reasonable care in the selection of their manager." In 1867, on the suggestion of several employers, a few local arbitration boards were formed, but they do not appear to have been very effective or to have lasted long. Early in 1868 an influx of labour to the coal pits from the shale and iron works where employment was scarce, caused farther wage reductions. Wages seem to have fluctuated considerably ; in one district we read of them being as low as 1s. 3d. per day : in many districts 2s. 6d ; and Alexander Macdonald told a demonstration at Uddingston that a collier had solemnly assured him of his intention to cut the throats of his children, as he could not feed them upon his wage pittance. Towards

---

*The Scotsman, 23/10/65.

†N.B. Daily Mail, 29/6/66.

‡Ibid, 22/7/67. In 1868 the same firm secured a House of Lords' decision in their favour abolishing accident compensation on the ground that " the miner received his wages not only for his work but also to compensate him for any risk he ran . . or any accident that might befall him." What meagre compensation was being paid to injured men, widows, and orphans now stopped. Wages at this time were 2/6 per day.—Scotsman, 9/6/68.

the end of the year, however, wages must have risen, for in 1873 Macdonald told a Select Committee of the House of Commons that during the year 1868 wages had averaged 3s. 6d. to 4s. per day for three days a week.* These starvation wages frequently compelled the miners to ask for part of their wages in advance of the regular pay day, which was fortnightly. "Advance" payments, popularly known as "sub," had interest charged against them at rates varying from 125 per cent. to 900 per cent. per annum.† The housing conditions at this time were reported as terrible, subsidence cracked hovels, earthen floors, no furniture in many cases, beyond a rudely constructed form, and rents at from 3s. 6d. to 5s. per month, according to the clemency of the owner of the death-trap. In 1869 wages rose to about 5s. per day, but full-time was seldom permitted, and the miners at Wishaw complained that after allowing for short time and for deductions their net wage was 13s. 6½d. per week. About this time we get some detailed revelations regarding the method of robbing the miner, known as the Truck system. The miner was compelled to purchase his goods from the coalowner's shop or store ; no other shop was allowed to open in the vicinity, and any thrifty housewife who sought to purchase her goods in some neighbouring town discovered that her husband or her son was promptly discharged from his employment. At Baillieston truck shop goods were 20 per cent. dearer than goods elsewhere ; at Chapelhall a truck shop manager died worth £10,000, which indicates something of the profits made, inasmuch as most part of that sum would be extra robbery on his own account after the coalowner had been satisfied ; complaints against the quality of the provisions were made in vain ; when a woman proved that a truck-shop manager had given her short weight in meal the account was squared by the sudden unemployment of her husband. Whisky was trucked, milk was trucked, and if the truck-store did not happen to have in stock any article demanded, a line was supplied to the collier entitling him to purchase in some neighbouring town at a price that yielded a comfortable commission to the coalowner. Thus very little cash kept a coal pit going.‡ Twenty pounds a month, we are told, kept a large works operating, the wages passing from the pay office to the truck store and from the truck store to the pay office, and sometimes the payment of wages was suspended until the first men who had been paid had purchased goods at the store and thus enabled the

---

*Glasgow Herald, 16/5/73.

†*Scotsman*, 20/1/68.

‡Money wages were given as seldom as possible. In one case that landed in the Law Courts it transpired that the Shotts Iron Company had paid a worker only 12/10 in cash during three years. Payments had been made in lines to the Company's store for groceries, etc.—*Glasgow Herald*, 3/3/59.

store manager to send up the cash to the wages office again.* During this year (1869) there seem to have been big secessions from the National Miners' Union ; this was greatly deplored at a Glasgow conference, where it was resolved that "District Unions are partial in their effects and no hope of general benefit can be entertained but through a national Union " ;† and to ensure stability to the Union it was proposed to provide compensation for accident from the Union funds. The new Mines Bill of the Liberal Government was a great disappointment ; it contained no clauses dealing with the education of miners' children, or with the Truck system, and it fixed the working hours of collier children over 12 years of age at not more than 12 hours a day ; children from 10 to 13 could be worked three days a week. The Home Secretary, Bruce, himself a mine-owner, refused to listen to the protests of the Miners' Unions ; he frankly refused to appoint a Committee of Enquiry into the question of Truck, saying that any farther restrictions could not be made "without interfering with trade," and that "the remedy was a moral one."‡

The Liberal *North British Daily Mail* declared that 1000 lives were annually "sacrificed in the coal mines," and the average miner was physically finished for work at 50 years of age, yet the Bill did nothing to improve pit ventilation. In the past the miners had paid a man "nominated by the employer to look after their safety. . . . The Law presumes this inspector will bring the master to book in the case of accidents." The new Bill provided for the appointment of a Board of Arbitration to settle disputes between the Government Inspector and the coalowner. That was all. No more inspectors were to be appointed, and already they were so few in number that they had no time to inspect ; all they could do was to record accidents after they had occurred. The Bill was a farce.§ Macdonald advocated "a national strike " if better inspection of mines was not ordered by Parliament ; he threatened the press with competition from a newspaper which should make public the grievances of the miners, and he succeeded in inducing the Home Secretary to agree to another "enquiry " into the Truck System.‖ During the year 1870 miners' wages are said to have averaged 4s. 1d. per day :a

---

*Investigations of *N.B. Daily Mail's* Special Commissioner, 12/6/69 *et seq.*

†The wages paid to Alexander Macdonald, the miners' leader, were 8/3 per day (11/- when in London), *plus* travelling expenses.

‡There had been three Truck enquiries shortly before—one in 1865, one in 1866, and one in 1867.

§*N.B. Daily Mail*, 24/2/70, 29/4/70, 30/6/70 ; *Glasgow Herald*, 10/2/71.

‖Among the facts elicited were that no Truck had existed in Clackmannanshire for 28 years, and that at the Duke of Buccleugh's lead mines at Wanlockhead *wages were still paid yearly.—Ibid*, 30/8/70.

a*Weekly Mail*, 23/1/86.

and their women folks earned, in Ayrshire at any rate, 1s. to 1s. 6d. a day in hoeing turnips or spreading manure for the farmers. There was the usual plethora of partial strikes, and the wives of Addiewell and Mossend earned some notoriety by stoning blacklegs. Attempts were made to form a Scottish Miners' Association.

Large demands for coal in Britain, due to the war between France and Prussia, drove wages in Scotland towards the end of the year 1871 up to 6s. per day ; but the hours of labour were considerably extended, and the Miners' Unions set on foot again an extensive agitation for an eight hours' day. There were proposals to demand an eight hours' day by legal enactment, which were, however, generally frowned upon by the miners' leaders, the accepted opinion being that "it was quite irregular to ask Parliament to interfere with adult labour." Alexander Macdonald complained that some pits had not been inspected for 15 years. During 1872 wages rose steadily until they reached 10s. for (in Fife and Clackmannan at anyrate) an eight hours day ; but the cost of living was high. A new Liberal Miners' Act caused trouble, for though it reduced the hours of labour for collier boys from 12 to 10 daily it increased Truck facilities, and among the new special rules was one (No. 55) laying upon miners themselves the obligation of examining, maintaining, and being responsible for the safety of their working-places. Macdonald urged a national strike against these rules, and widespread sectional strikes broke out at the end of 1872. During 1873 wages do not seem to have suffered any appreciable alteration,* and with the continued comparatively good wages there appears to have been a corresponding widening of ideas, some sort of conception that no permanent betterment could be secured by continual strikes and struggles for starvation wages that rose and fell with the higgling of a market. No longer, cries Macdonald, does the injured collier go on the parish ; the Union maintains him ; it looks after widows and orphans ; it projects schemes of old-age pensions ; it has subscribed £10,000 to purchase a co-operative colliery, and "through time we may have the whole of them " ; it was looking into sanitation ; † it demanded 12 months' lease of houses ; it "resolved " in favour of direct labour representation in Parliament ; and the capitalist press, gravely disturbed sought to still the new ferment by advocating profit-sharing after the masters had received 10 per cent. on their capital. But early in 1874 commercial depression, due to overproduction, became manifest, and wages began to fall; shilling

---

*The *N.B. Daily Mail* (10/10/74) estimated the average Scots colliers' wage in 1873 at 11/- ; the *Weekly Mail* (23/1/86), quoting the *London Times*, gives it as 9/6.

†At Benhar Miners' Rows in two months there were 136 fever cases. The ashpits were only 23 to 26 feet from the doors of the houses.—*Herald*, 25/3/73.

by shilling they fell until in some districts they reached only 3s. per day. There were strikes, of course, long-continued and bitter evictions by the thousand;* furniture, such as it was, stored in public halls ; at Woodhall men, women and children camping out ; but the men were beaten, and strike leaders, like Scott of Overtoun, compelled to emigrate. Macdonald had vainly endeavoured to prevent a strike and counselled submission, pointing out that the shipbuilding trades were on the point of striking and that the miners' wisest course would be to stay at work and assist the sh pbuilders on strike ; then when the shipbuilders had succeeded they in turn would assist the miners. His advice was unheeded, and he was hissed and booed by the miners for giving it. Proposals to fix wages on a sliding scale to be determined by the selling-price of coal, though agreed to by some employers, came to naught.

In 1875, as a result of investigations into miners' housing conditions by the *Glasgow Herald*,† we get graphic pen pictures of the terrible domestic conditions in the "Rows." In the Maryhill district of Glasgow there are open drains and two large ashpits in front of the colliers' houses: no chimney cans: roofs 6 or 7 feet from the floor. Of another row we are told there is no closet, and the only way to improve it is to sweep it away. At the Red Toon, owned by the Jordanhill Company, the "gables incline outward and probably would tumble down altogether but for rude insecure buttresses of timber, which a strong-limbed miner might kick away without greatly damaging his boots . . . holes in the roof . . . slope in floor like Renfield Street." At Knightswood the Summerlee Company have slung a chain across the road to prevent traders' vans coming to compete with their Store. "At Netherton there is a great stink . . . nursery for disease . . . houses below level of ground . . wall-paper peeling off . . . one house is an ox-stable. No sanitary inspector visits the place." At Blairdardie (Cunninghame's property) whooping-cough and eye disease is prevalent. At Calder (Dixon's property) "the rent of the houses which would be dear at any money is 3s. monthly " . . . windows are the size of "the crown of a man's hat " . . . houses so smoky that doors are wide open day and night. At Faskin (Baird's) houses are 3 and 4 feet below level of road. At Carfin the cooking water comes from one of Dixon's pits and is imperfectly filtered ; in summer it harbours "worms and wee creepers." At Jerviston Square (Simpson's) the houses are "most wretched "—stone floors, mouldy and damp walls, set-in- beds have stone bottoms. "Last summer smallpox and scarlet fever were prevalent." At Mossend (Mossend Iron Coy.'s property) houses

---

*Even the *Glasgow Herald* protested against the day-to-day tenure upon which miners held their houses.—11/3/74.

†January, February, and March, 1875.

"shockingly damp . . . . passing the hand across almost any part of the wall brought off a mixture of chalk and sand and water. In one of them, I even found damp in the ashpit under the fire." At Jawcraig, Slamannan, neither ashpits nor closets, nor drains, some floors are "simply soft clay . . . two piles of canvass cloth on the floors are wet through " . . . one women sees steam rising from her floor when the fire is lit. Rents here are 4s. to 6s. per month, and the owner, C. J. Alexander of Jawcraig, has intimated an increase. At Galston the miners' houses are so damp that "passing the hand across the wall brings off water and paint and lime." At Auchinairn rents are 6s. to 7s. per month for single apartments "with earthen floors broken and damp, small back windows and walls and ceilings from which the plaster has fallen in large pieces "; the beds are wet along the walls. At the Haggs, moisture falling from the roof is caught in bowls.   "The back room of one of the houses was cold enough and damp enough to give one toothache in ten minutes ; there are no ashpits and no water supply, so the miners must go for it to Castlecary "where a farmer gives water on condition that he shall receive a day's work from the recipients during the season." At Macmirrie (Lothians) some houses are so poor that the owner has not the impudence to charge more than 6d. per week in rent. At Forth (Carron Company) no attention is paid to sanitation. Fife and Clackmannan houses are on the average worse than those in Ayrshire. At Slamannan the houses "have almost no furniture, and ragged children run about with uncombed hair." At Easter Glentore typhoid is prevalent in the "dark and dismal holes "; the ground at the back is level with the roof, so that you may walk up the tiles and reconnoitre the interior down the chimney."

Wages during the year 1875 seem to have averaged about 4s. per day, and what that meant to the colliers is stated in a rather surprising leading article in the *Glasgow Herald*.* Four shillings a day for full time, says the *Herald*, is insufficient, "and full-time is from various causes hardly a possible thing. Let those who in parochial palaces practise on hundreds of paupers the art of cheap feeding make a study of such cases. For instance, 24s. a week divided by 7 and by 8 (7 days and 8 human beings) gives about 5d. per day per human being to keep up the supply of food and clothing." And 24s. is for full-time without deductions. But take half a day off per week—that is 2s. ; allow 1s. 6d. for house rent, and that would "shock the sanitary officer "; allow 1s. for coal, 9d. for trade deductions, 1s. 3d. for the education of the miners' children at school, and 2d. for taxes ; total deduction 6s. 8d.—thus reducing the

*3/2/76.

allowance for food and clothing to 3¾d. per head per day. "Need we wonder the men grumble ? "

In April, 1876, the colliers wages were 4s. 6d. a day for 4 days a week, and the masters had intimated a reduction of 10 per cent., and the Attorney General had the impudence to declare in Parliament that "they all knew mining was a dangerous employment and that it was well paid " ;* in December wages were "falling."

Sheer hunger abode with the Scots miners in 1877. Wages were 2s. 6d. to 3s. per day † for two and three days a week, and the Fife and Clackmannan miners were locked-out altogether for six months rather than submit to a 10 per cent. reduction, the lock-out occurring in the midst of a great shipbuilding strike and damped down iron furnaces, which diminished the demand for coal and rendered the struggle easier for the masters. Finally the men compromised on a partial reduction with a sliding scale ; sixpence per ton increase in the selling price of coal was to mean 4 per cent. increase on wages, sixpence decrease was to mean 4 per cent. reduction, and so on. But the trade depression continued, aggravated in 1878 by the City Bank failure, and wages fell to 2s. 6d. per day ; in most districts the Union went to pieces, and Macdonald and the other leaders were unheeded ; occasionally there were riots, as at Slamannan, where the houses of owners and managers were wrecked. In December a miners' conference asked Parliament to make enquiry into the causes of the trade depression which was causing them so much misery.

In the summer of 1879 some Lanarkshire miners were said to be working for 1s. a day ; ‡ and Macdonald, addressing 16,000 miners at Hamilton, declared that restriction of output or the "wee darg " in order to reduce coal stocks was the only way to secure a living wage. A vote of thanks to him was moved by James Keir Hardie, the young and newly-appointed secretary to the Lanarkshire miners. By October there was a revival in trade, and the *quid nuncs* in the capitalist press were busy proving that the long depression had resulted at least partially from the miners' eight hours' day and "wee darg " policies. And the Lanarkshire owners sprang a farther demand for a reduction of 1s. per day with the threat that if any one pit were "struck" the other owners would "finance it," and as punishment, enforce a reduction of another sixpence. The idea seems to have been to keep the miners "humble " and prevent them demanding increases. One owner defended himself in Hamilton Court from a charge of employing women at the pit-head after

---

Glasgow Herald, 25/5/76.

†These are M'Donald's figures. The *London Times* in 1886 stated that the wage had been 4/9 per day.

‡*Weekly Mail*, 21/6/79.

9 p.m. by saying he was paying the miners so small a wage "that the men could not support their wives upon it, and that therefore it was in the interest of both the miners and their wives that the masters were furnishing employment to the latter at fifteen pence a day as hutch-tippers on the pithead, increasing the payment to half a crown when the wives who had been working all day continued at their task till one in the morning." In another case, the "Hillington case," tried at Paisley, it was proved that the miners were being deliberately swindled at the pithead by 100 per cent.; the miner who made the complaint was sacked. The miner, says the *Weekly Mail*, in comment, "earning a pittance that confessedly will not keep him even in honest poverty is robbed of a portion of his small earnings . . . denied justice and badgered and bullied on all hands."*
And again :

> "Coal is dear, yet miners are starving . . . one's only wonder is that men are found willing to go down a pit, while there is an unoccupied ditch to die in above ground."†

For some reason, obscure to us now, Alexander Macdonald advised the men to temporarily accept the reduction in wages, whereat there was great disgust, and "some districts resolved against ever again taking the advice of Mr. Macdonald." By the spring of 1880 wages had been driven up to 4s a day, and in Ayrshire, under Keir Hardie's leadership, a strike was resorted to for another shilling; blacklegs were savagely maltreated—the trial of colliers' wives for intimidation was a common occurrence—but the Fife and Clackmannan men continued working full time and refused to restrict output to assist the strikers in the west. The Ayrshire strike collapsed, and the year ended in starvation.

In 1881 Alexander Macdonald died,‡ and Lanarkshire took "an idle day" out of respect to his memory. Wages in Scotland suffered little change during the year. In 1882 the masters offered an increase of 12½ per cent. if the men would abandon "restriction of output," but the Unions held out for an increase of 15 per cent.; in 1883 the men were agitating and working the "wee darg" for an increase of 6d., and a new note of anti-landlordism, probably the effect of Henry George's propaganda, begins to be noticeable. One speaker, M'Cowie of Cambuslang, says he works hard "producing a ton of dross for 4d., and the Duke of Hamilton, this idle spendthrift,

---

*8/11/79.

†6/12/79.

‡He was cradled in poverty, worked in the Lanarkshire pits at 8 years of age, hours so long that often he was three months without seeing daylight, except on Sundays. Then became a teacher, made money by speculation, and thereafter devoted his life to the raising of the *status* of his class.

gets 1s. 4d. for it." Cries of "Shoot the Landlords!"* Michael Davitt came to Lanarkshire advocating nationalisation of the coal mines, and his chairman estimated that the Duke of Hamilton took £114,486 in royalties during 1883, or £9 10s. 9d. from every working miner in the Hamilton coalfields.† During 1884 we find sliding scale proposals, four days a week policies, idle days, eight hours' day policies (which Fife and Clackmannan had kept for 14 years), all aiming at an increase of 15 per cent. The average wage during the year is stated to have been 4s. 1d. per day. In 1885 there are again resolutions to work only 8 hours a day, and, in Ayrshire, a struggle for 3s. a day. In 1886 the miners at Hogganfield have only 15s. for 6 days' work, and in Lanarkshire generally 2s. 6d. per day, and were charged interest at the rate of 250 per cent. per annum on all "sub," given before the fortnightly pay day. In 1886 the Scottish Miners' Federation was formed with James Keir Hardie as secretary.

In 1887 Keir Hardie founded a monthly Journal called *The Miner*, and in the September issue he proves that the net earning of the Lanarkshire miner are 11s. to 12s. per week.‡ At his instance, and as a result of his successful lobbying in the House of Commons, Parliament that year stopped the employment in the mines of boys under 12 years of age. In 1888 wages had risen to 3s. 6d. a day, Cunninghame Graham was introducing an Eight Hours Bill to Parliament, and Hardie had begun his Socialist propaganda.

VII.—THE AGRICULTURAL LABOURERS.

"In Ayrshire, stables, byres, cowsheds, dilapidated farm-houses, and dog kennels have been converted into labourers' cottages. Guano bags have in some cases been stretched across the rafters to prevent the mouldering thatch and rain from falling upon the beds and tables of the unfortunate occupants."— *Fourth Report of Royal Commission on the Employment of Children, Young Persons, and Women in Agriculture [Scotland]*, 1871.

"The bothies of Caithness are sinks of physical and moral filth and pollution. . . . In a Caithness bothy more or fewer well-grown lads and young unmarried men and women live together. . . . They pass the long winter evenings without any light except what comes from the peat fire—for neither lamp nor candle is allowed them by their masters. . . . all in the place where the lads undress and slept. The sleeping place of the females is generally some off closet or other place entering from the lads' apartment. . . . In some specially disgraceful instances the beds of both sexes are in the same apartment."— *Rev. Charles Thomson, Wick.*—"*Scotsman*," 23/10/1860.

I question whether it is possible to give any account that is worth

---

*Weekly Mail, 15/9/83.

†*Weekly Herald*, 20/9/84.

‡This seems to be confirmed by M'Intosh (*Hist. Civ. Scot.*, iv., 343), when he gives the average wage for 1887 as 2/6 per day.

the printing of the movements in agricultural wages for the past 150 years. The agricultural worker has always been paid partly in kind—in food and in housing, sometimes also in clothes and in fuel—and not only have these payments in kind varied from decade to decade in proportion and in value, but at the same periods they varied greatly in different districts, thus making averages very difficult to strike, and when struck, to all intents and purposes, valueless. What, however, is perfectly clear is that the agricultural workers as a class have always, generation by generation, fed better than the industrial workers as a class. The agricultural worker suffered famine in times of dearth (but then, so did the town worker); and he found rabbits and plover's eggs in the fields and trout in the burns, and wood for his fire when the town worker starved and froze; he had few mental excitements outside theology and sex : he toiled all the daylight hours that God sent ; in the "chaulmers" and the bothies and the clay biggins he spent the hours of darkness like a beast in a hole ; his old age frequently was an amalgam of charity dole and rheumatism ; but take it all in all, he fed better, lived longer, and lived healthier than did his brother in the city ; his powers of mental concentration were greater, and if he knew nothing of the playhouse he knew much of the Hillmen and the Book of Martyrs and the songs and satires of Burns ; and when the franchise came his way his traditional dissent stamped itself markedly on our national politics. Yet, while that is so, and although our disturbances during the crofting clearances were dramatic enough, we have nothing analagous to the long drawn out class war pictured for England in Hammond's "The Village Labourer." Indeed it is little over two and a half centuries ago since the Scots agricultural worker, as we know him, emerges at all. Dean Munro tells us of the labourers and the *adscriptae glebae*, and that "the others are gentlemen quhilikis labours not " ; we know that the serf faded into the bond labourer ; we know that land was sold *cum nativis et eorum sequelis* (with serfs and their followers or dependents) ; but we find it difficult to distinguish between early tenants, fermorers, cotters, and bondagers. By the year 1621 there must have been labourers who worked for wages as distinct from the "sma' men " farmers who tilled a patch themselves, paying rent in service or in kind to the laird ; for an Act of Parliament in 1621 describes the evils due to agricultural labourers who refuse to be hired unless at "great and extraordinary wages," or who engage themselves only from Martinmas to Whitsunday, and then cast themselves loose and masterless at the busy season of peat cutting ; henceforth no farm servant was to leave at Whitsunday unless he could prove himself engaged to some other master. Between 1576 and 1577, the "Register of the Privy Council" informs us that foodstuffs were cheap and

wages of "laubouraris and servandis " rose.* In 1660 one authority
states that the ploughman got £10 Scots (16s. 8d.) *plus* a pair of
shoes and stockings and food and lodging for a half year's work ; a
common labourer got ½ merk (6⅔d.) without meat, (sometimes 40
pennies with meat and drink) per day.† Another authority, however, puts farm servant's wages in 1665 at 25s.-30s. per annum—
women's wages were one third less—but there were considerable
extras—wood and peat, and land for pigs and geese.‡ Still another
authority affirms that prices and wages were stationary between
1640 and 1740.§ But perhaps this may have been due to the fact
that from 1656 onward the J.P.'s were empowered to fix the rate
of wages. During the eighteenth century, when threshing wages
were 1s. Scots (1d. sterling) per day, beef was 2d. Scots per ℔.,
mutton 1½d. Scots for 17½ ounces, and cheese 3d. or 4d. Scots for
24 ounces ; ‖ and Macintosh declares that in the early years of that
century the agricultural labourer's wage was 5d. per day in summer
and 6d. per day in winter.a The labourer could not go to labour
outside his parish at harvest time under a fine of 8s. per day ; if
he ran away when his master beat him, he was brought back, fined
20s., and judicially assured by the laird that his master had only
"beate him slenderly for his rogishness and stubornes."b

In 1737 outdoor workers at Ochtertyre got hog's feet and ears to
dinner when working at the lint, and pickled beef when at the corn ;
the shearers got an ox cut up into 20 pieces ; eggs (fresh at 2d. per
dozen) supplied the supper. The "servants at twal' hours got beer,
milk, porridge, oatcakes, kitchen fee puddings, and hagas, cows
draught and head, pigs and harrings, hog's head and feet, harrings
and pidgeons, oxpluck and puddings, the two joints of boyld lamb
that was in the broth."c In 1750 farm servants got £3 yearly, a
cow's pasture, 2 ells of harn, and as much hodden as make a jacket ;
female servants got 20s. yearly, 2 pairs of shoes, and the privilege
of sowing some lint ; in Fifeshire the labourer's wage was 5d. per day.

Whatever changes may have taken place in agriculture after the
rebellion in 1745, there was no immediate betterment of the farm
servants' position. In 1771 the day labourer could only earn 3s. 6d.
to 4s. weekly, and oatmeal was at 13d. and 14d. the peck ; and in
1774 the Aberdeenshire ploughmen's wages were only £1 8s. 8d.

*Vol. ii., O.S., p. 589.

†*Journal Stat. Socy.*, 1862, p. 425.   40 pennies Scots=3½d. sterling.

‡Macintosh—*Hist. Civ. Scot.*, iii., 290.

§Graham's *Social Life in Scotland*, p. 183.

‖*Records of the Baron Court of Stitchill.*

aHist. Civ. Scot., iv., 339.

bChambers' Journal, August, 1912.

cOchtertyre House Book—Scot. Hist. Socy., vol. 55.

yearly including board. But the following twenty years saw a great advance : the day labourer rose to 10½d. per day and the Aberdeenshire ploughman to £7 10s. yearly, again including board. The industrial revolution was enticing rural workers away to the industrial areas, thus creating a labour scarcity on the farms at a time when there was a vastly quickened demand for farm produce ; this labour scarcity, combined with the increased demand for produce, which led to so many agricultural improvements, enabled the farm servants to secure greatly increased wages and better treatment. The Fifeshire day-labourer whose daily wage in 1750 was only 5d. could earn 1s. 10d. in 1810, which sum was 6d. higher than the sum he could earn twenty-four years later, when the ruling classes had the economic situation again thoroughly under control. Cobbett, in his "Register" for 1832, in describing his visit to Scotland, says the unmarried bothy servants are hired by the year and endure "severe punishment" for misbehaviour or running away ; in many districts no servant could be feed or hired unless he could produce testimonials from his late employer and from the minister of his parish. Married servants had to find a woman's labour for 20 days at harvest —usually some female relative, but it developed into the sub-hiring and boarding of impoverished women, called "bondagers," and theirs was bondage indeed !—and Cobbett goes on to say that :

> "The labourer is wholly at the mercy of his master, who, if he will not keep him beyond the year, can totally ruin him by refusing him a character . . the man is a negro slave, worse off than the negro by many degrees . . . Six days' labour from daylight to dark. . . Almost the whole of the produce of these fine lands goes into the pockets of the lords ; the labourers are their slaves, and the farmers the slave-drivers."

It was not quite so bad as that, for there were always industrial employers who asked no questions if the man at the gate offered himself cheaply enough, but in the main Cobbett's picture seems to have been true. In Dumbartonshire we read of farm labourers sleeping under tarred paper roofs ; in Banffshire under turf roofs, and Cadell's "Story of the Forth" waxes lyrical upon the health-giving properties of the houses scooped out of solid blocks of peat "as a child hollows out the heart of a turnip to make a lantern." Wages had risen, but food prices had slowly followed, and their increased percentage almost balanced ; sheep walks were supplanting arable tillage, and there was a steady exodus from the south country, large numbers going to Canada, leaving their native land, as one clerical writer in the *Statistical Account* puts it, "without a tear, nay, with a shout of exultation." We get one case at the Haughs of Kinnaird, where a farmer prosecuted his ploughman for deserting his service. The defence was that the housing conditions were unbearable, and two medical men from Montrose testified that

the man's hovel was 13 feet in diameter,"without plaster to the walls
or ceiling to the roof. The floor is of mud, and damp, and below its
level is a pool of dity water, part of which is concealed by three or
four grey slates placed on it." The only furniture was a three-
foot form lying on its side, awaiting a missing leg ; and two small
barrels for holding meal. When the door was shut the only avenues
for light were holes in the roof and a hole at the foot of the door
large enough to admit a cat. The wise J.P. on the bench decided
that although the housing was "utterly unfit for men " the ploughman was bound to submit to it.* In some districts the men slept in
"chaulmers " or stable lofts, wholly devoid of sanitary convenience ;
in other districts the common bothies—common sometimes to male
and female workers, where sleeping was mixed—was the custom.
Against these sinks of bestiality, and the alarming illegitimacy
statistics, the Kirk fulminated regularly ; and the Rev. Dr. Begg of
Liberton carried on a persistent propaganda of public enlightenment.
" The villages," he cried, " have been swept away . . . for bachelor
colonies, the leading object being to raise the greatest amount of
rent to the landlord at the smallest possible outlay."† In 1858
the illegitimacy statistics shewed Aberdeenshire with 16.2 per cent.
of its total births, illegitimate, Banff 17.1 per cent., and Nairn 17.5
per cent. But the bothy system spread, for it was "economic " ;
it paid the farmers and the lairds.

In 1856 the Sheriff-Substitute in Peeblesshire decided that the
farmer had the right to refuse to allow a servant to go to a feeing
market ; it was for the farmer to say whether or not it was "suitable."‡ By this means a man could be tied to a master with no
prospect of escape. In vain Sir Andrew Agnew of Lochnaw endeavoured to secure a weekly half-holiday for farm labourers ; the
very idea was preposterous. Deserters from this slavery service
were hunted by the police ; in one case at Troqueer, in 1859, we find
a ploughman who was accused of desertion offering as his defence
that the salt beef and the salt pork given him to eat for a fortnight
was very bad ; the beef "was sometimes covered with maggots."
In 1860, we are told, farm servants in the South of Scotland got
coarse black bread, made from ground beans, to eat ; lads slept
without sheets in an empty stall or stable. When blankets were
supplied they were washed only once a year, and (to save soap)
with six months' old "sour wash from the chambermaid's pail."
The farm workers "are treated as brutes and they act as such."§
Female farm servants, declared Dr. Strachan of Dollar in 1860, toil

---

*Glasgow Herald, 8/7/57.

†Scotsman, 19/10/58. Cf Paisley case, Glasgow Courier, 4/6/33.

‡Courier, 1/3/56.

§Scotsman, 8/12/60 ; 22/12/60.

six days a week from 5 a.m. to 10 p.m., and their only recreation is going to church every alternate Sunday. As for the shearers— mostly Irish—they were supplied in gangs by contractors, and cases were not uncommon where the contractor disappeared and had omitted to pay the shearers their wages. In the vicinity of the larger towns during periods of industrial depression the farmers were occasionally favoured by the magistrates—as, for instance, at Dunfermline in 1858—with a supply of unemployed men and women and a bonus from the town funds of fourpence on every shilling of wages paid by the farmer !

In *Fraser's Magazine* for May, 1871, we get a lurid picture of the conditions of life "enjoyed" by the Scots agricultural labourer.* His housing conditions were "a scandal and a disgrace to any civilised community"; the one-roof hut was "divided into two apartments by a couple of box beds placed across the room; behind these the cow stood with her tail to the door. Forty per cent. of the houses in the shires of Berwick and Roxburgh have "only one or no window." In some of the single-room huts between Ailsa and Girvan "as many as ten or eleven persons are living. The damp, broken clay floors are covered with beds, the decaying thatch roof is pervious to rain." On the Queensberry estates similar conditions prevail : "the thatched roofs were in a state of mouldering decay, the mud floors were worn into holes, and the walls even in the month of June were saturated with moisture." We are told that "it is the labour of these miserably-housed hinds that has turned moor and bog into fertile cornfield and rich pasture, the produce of which is consumed by the owners, in the luxury of our own and foreign capitals." In Caithness men and women were herded into the same bothy. On the southern borders the bondager system was still rife ; by it the hind was required to find a female worker for his master, who only paid for the bondager's services as and when he required her, but the poor hind had to feed her all the year round. Sometimes we find mothers "working the bondage" to find the school fees for their children.

The opinion has already been expressed that any accurate survey or estimate of agricultural wages is impossible, owing to the varying proportions of these wages that were paid in kind ; but, roughly, it is true to say that wages rose steadily from 1837 onward, and by 1867 they had increased, around the industrial areas, by 100 per cent. ; costs of living, though rising steadily, do not appear to have risen *pari passu.* The chief wage movement periods appear to have been after the Irish Famine of the forties, the Crimean War period, and during the Franco-Prussian War (after which there was a slump). The abolition of the Corn Laws had little noticeable effect.

---

†See also *Cornhill Magazine* for 1864.

The House of Commons' return, issued May, 1861, shews agricultural labourers' wages running from 15s. in Dumbartonshire to 12s. in Argyllshire ; in 1862 the average wage is said to have been about 13s. 2d.* Women in 1870 got 1s. to 1s. 2d. per day without food ; but there were various fancy tricks by which they could be swindled out of their pittances. In 1849 we read of a Lanarkshire farm servant losing a half-year's wages for not coming back from church in time for the cow-milking ;† and in the *Independent Review* for 1905‡ a writer tells us that : "As the law at present stands, a farm servant may faithfully serve his employer until within a few weeks of the half-yearly "flittin' term." Then if a quarrel takes place, "the employee is dismissed without a farthing of his wages." One such case had got prominence "the other winter " in the South of Scotland; and the Sheriff, in deciding against the employee, said : "When a servant is summarily dismissed he loses all claim to any wages that may be due." This view was afterwards upheld by the Lord Advocate in his reply to a protest from the Secretary of the Ploughman and General Labourers' Federal Union.

Apart from a stray reference to an early ploughman's guild in the Lothians, we get no trace of organisation among the farm-workers until the year 1750 or thereabouts, when Ramsay of Ochtertyre writes of a certain "Windy " Shaw who organised the discontented ploughmen in the Carse of Stirling. "Windy " may have been the nickname given him for his oratorical powers. In 1834 some 600 ploughmen and agricultural labourers in the Carse of Gowrie formed a Union to secure a ten hours' day in summer and an eight hours' day in winter, all overtime to be paid at day labourers' rate ; they openly threatened stack-burning if Irish labourers were brought in as blacklegs. In 1845 an attempt to organise the ploughmen of East Lothian to refuse to bind themselves on feeing day unless they were relieved of the bondager system, was led by one Thomson of Tranent. The men broke away, and the "strike " failed, but the bondager system was afterwards quietly dropped by the farmers. In 1853 the women of Sanquhar threatened to stone any shearer who would shear for less than 2s. 6d. a day. About 1860 a Farm Servants' Union was formed at Dunbar ; that is all we know about it. In December, 1865, a Farm Servants' Protection Society was formed in Mid-Lothian, and a demonstration at Slateford was addressed by a Masons' Union official from Edinburgh. The programme of the Society or Union was 15s. a week, paid fortnightly, free house, coals driven, and one month's meat in harvest. The Mason's official strongly urged a "sick and funeral fund to keep the

---

Journal Stat. Socy., 1862, p. 425.

†*Courier*, 23/10/49.

‡Article by Wm. Diack on " The Scottish Farm Labourer," p. 315.

members from leaving." A month later the Union had spread all over the Lothians, Peeblesshire and Berwickshire. In July, 1866, it had branches in Perthshire, and a meeting of delegates was held in Perth. In 1867 the Falkirk district ploughmen were addressed by James Thomson, president of the Midlothian Society, and advised to hold out for £30 a year. In 1872 we find the Midlothian Union demanding 16s. weekly, the usual potatoes, free house and a month's food during harvest ; the wages were to be paid weekly, not every six months. And an organisation called The Fife and Kinross Labourers' Association, evidently composed of ploughmen, made itself prominent by its persistent and organised demand for increased wages, shorter hours, and fortnightly payments. The Midlothian Union certainly lasted for seven years ; what circumstances caused or attended its death no man to-day knows ; but it died, and Trade Unionism among farm workers lay dead until the beginning of the twentieth century, when the now vigorous Scottish Farm Servants' Union was born in Aberdeenshire.

VIII.—THE RAILWAYMEN.

An Engineer examined before the Select Committee on Railway Labourers in 1846 was asked if the patent fuse was not safer than the ordinary method of blasting, and answered, " Perhaps it is, but it is attended with much loss of time, and the difference is so very small *I would not recommend the loss of time or all the lives it would save.*"

" A day's work is twelve hours."—*N.B.R. Directors*—" *Scotsman,*" 25/1/72.

" At this period [1866-1871] railway employment may be well regarded as a system of white slavery."—" *Nineteenth Century Magazine,*" November, 1882.

Herbert Spencer has said that the story of the financial swindling in the promotion of our Railway Companies reads like to an Arabian Night's dream. Thousands of human gulls had their feathers plucked in each succeeding "railway mania," and such companies and combinations of shareholders as survived, struggled along endeavouring to make profits with a load of legal and "promotion" debt hanging round their necks. Naturally and inevitably they sweated and scourged the railway workers and labourers ; profits must be had somehow, and no considerations—human or divine— were allowed to block the way. From the first railway in 1812 (Kilmarnock to Troon), down through the "swindlers' golden age" in 1846, to the close of the nineteenth century, we get one long dismal record of sweating, underpayment, and overtoil ; we see the poor Irish immigrant and the dispossessed Highlander toiling frequently for less than a bare subsistence in the contractors' gangs ; we see signalmen at their responsible tasks for 15 hours a day and one day's holiday per annum ; we see porters compelled to eke out their pittances by petty larceny.

Strikes were frequent. In 1838 the Glasgow and Ayrshire railway labourers struck for a two-shilling rise on their wages of ten shillings, but "blacklegs" were plentiful, and the men were beaten.* In 1845 the navvies on the Edinburgh to Berwick line struck against the importation of famishing Irish, imported for the breaking of their wages.† And at Auchterarder a similarly caused strike of 400 men was crushed, although 60 men refused to work at a two-shilling wage reduction and went off to seek their fortunes elsewhere.‡ Theological feuds about Popery and Presbytery kept the labourers from forming a Union or making joint effort for betterment ; sometimes, as at Stonehaven, in 1848, they killed one another so that the true religion (and the contractor) might flourish. They were robbed, without distinction of religion, at the contractor's "Tommy-Shop"— for they generally got monthly pays, and truck flourished between times ; often they rioted when the contractor was over-bold in his robbery, but then the military interfered and the rioters went to gaol. Railway life was cheap, and every railway had its great annual death-roll—a matter of small moment, since charitable agencies like the Edinburgh Relief Committee could supply the Caledonian Railway Company with labourers at 1s. 3d. a day.§

In 1850 we read of a strike amongst N.B.R. firemen and drivers, the latter against a wage of 4s. per day and the former against a wage of 2s. 8d. per day.|| The men were beaten by blacklegs from the N.B.R. engineering shops. In 1853 the railway navvies in Aberdeenshire struck against their weekly wages of 12s., but they were starved back to work without an increase ; in 1856 we read that the navvies on the Ayr and Dalmellington line tore the clothes off a contractor who had not paid a penny in wages for five and a half weeks, and, rushing him to the bank in Ayr, compelled him to disgorge ; but in Ayr the troops were called out and several navvies were arrested.a In 1844 Gladstone had carried an Act giving the Government power to nationalise Irish railroads which yielded 10 per cent. profits on nominal capital, and in the sixties a curious agitation in favour of nationalisation arose in the capitalist prints. Thus the *Scotsmanb* opined that "to place the railways, like the roads, under State or Government management would not be a novelty, but a recurrence to a well-established principle and an immemorial practice " ; and

---

Courier, 28/7/38.

†*Argus*, 18/9/45.

‡1/12/45.

§*Scotsman*, 3/6/48.

||*Glasgow Herald*, 1/4/50.

a*Courier*, 15/5/56.

b15/2/65.

of all bodies in the world the Irish peers urged nationalisation.*
But the terms repeatedly proferred shocked even the *Scotsman*,†
and a capitalist House of Commons‡ turned down a Nationalisation
Bill by 241 votes to 56. As a rule, however, the railway interest
dominated the House of Commons ; motions to compel the adoption
of means of communication between passengers and guards, got
short shrift ; and the Companies in their accident statistics did not
even profess to include the figures of railway servants killed or
maimed.

By the year 1867 the railway workers had a Trade Union, the
Locomotive Engine Drivers and Firemen's Amalgamated Benefit
Society; the Caledonian workers, through it, secure wages increases,
and the N.B.R. drivers ask for a 10 hours' day, with time and quarter
for overtime and time and half for Sunday labour.   One Caledonian
driver at this time declares that he works 60 hours in two shifts ; §
the N.B.R. surfacemen have weekly wages of 14s., and the Caledonian
surfacemen weekly wages of 13s. ; N.B.R. cleaners have 16s. ;
stokers, 20s. ; guards, 18s. to 30s.

The years 1871-2 were years of great Union activity, and many
reforms were secured ; ‖ the A.S.R.S. came into being ; goods
guards had their hours of labour reduced from 84 to 60 ; drivers
were supplied with coats, and secured a ten hours' day, which "boon,"
however, was contemptuously withheld from the Caledonian porters
and pointsmen who, at Perth, toiled for 78 hours at a wage of 18s.
or $2\frac{3}{4}$d. per hour (while 4d. per hour was paid for street
sweeping !).

In 1872 the Companies were compelled to tabulate lists of accidents.
The first list shews 1145 killed and 3000 injured—more than half of
whom were employees.   In 1874 the railway servants killed or
injured totalled 3603 ; in 1875 the numbers were 4383 ; in 1879
the numbers were 4469 ; in 1880 the numbers were 5203 ; and in
all these lists it is alleged that not half of the injured were given.*a*
The doctrine of "common employment," which was conveniently
read into the law by judicial hacks of the capitalist class, forbade the
injured servant from receiving compensation, his injury not being
directly due to the negligence or fault of the Company, but to some
of the Company's servants who were in the same employment.

N.B. Daily Mail, 21/6/67.

†20/1/68.

‡29/4/74.

§*N.B. Daily Mail*, 2/4/67.

‖*Nineteenth Century Magazine*, November, 1882.   There was a week's strike
    of 1300 railwaymen in Glasgow in 1872.—*Journal Stat. Socy.*, 1880.

*a*Nineteenth Century Magazine, supra.

In 1873 the Caledonian goods firemen and brakesmen go on strike —the firemen against wages of 21s. and the brakesmen against wages of 17s., in both cases for 7 days a week. A mass meeting of the strikers at Motherwell was broken up by police searching for five railway servants from Carstairs who had dared "to leave their work to attend the meeting." As a result of the strike the men gained an increase of 2s. and a ten hours' day. In the *Glasgow Herald* * we find a report of a mass meeting at Perth. One driver alleged that "last week" he worked 90 hours in 5 days; a brakesman declares that his day's work averages 16 hours; a Perth driver declares that "last week" he worked one day 20 hours and another day 24 hours; another relates a case of 190 hours work in a fortnight; still another had been on his engine for 31 hours at a stretch. Naturally accidents were frequent. In one month (Sept. 1873) there were thirty-six. About this period considerable improvements were effected, but five years later the Companies tore up the agreements and set about increasing the hours of labour again. Groups of N.B.R. men are out on strike for four months and are supported by the other trades, but blacklegs are plentiful, and the men go back beaten. The Caledonian engineers, despite a strike, suffered a reduction of 7½ per cent. on wages, but retained the 51 hours' week. In 1881 we find the general manager of the N.B.R. announcing that there will be no betterment in working conditions until shareholders get 4 per cent. dividend, though some passenger drivers work 87 hours per week, and though crossing gate-keepers work 114 hours per week for 14s.† In January, 1883, the Caledonian workers to the number of 5000 refuse to submit to these slaveries any longer; they come out on strike. The N.B.R. and G. & S.W. directors hastily confer "concessions" upon their workers; but the Caley directors run their engines with blackleg female labour and declare that Bairds' and other coal-masters and iron-masters will lock out their workmen in sympathy with the Caledonian shareholders. Finally the manager conde-scends to discuss matters with the Union, and the men get promises of reform; they go back to work—all except the agitators, who are victimised—and they discover that they have got little beyond promises, and some actually suffer reduced wages.‡ In 1884 the Caledonian Company attempted to fix a working day of 12 hours upon locomotive drivers and brakesmen.§ For the next five years the A.S.R.S. set about perfecting its organisation in preparation for a struggle that was inevitable. On the one hand, wages were low, hours were long, and tyranny unashamed; on the other, the Com-

---

* 14/10/73.
† *Glasgow Weekly Mail*, 17/12/81.
‡ *Ibid*, 20-27 January, 1883.
§ *Glasgow Weekly Herald*, 24/5/84.

panies were obdurate, refused to recognise the Union, discharged agitators who ventured upon deputations, and treated memorials with disdain.* The movement was primarily for a ten hours' day, but finally resolved itself into a question of the recognition of the Union officials by the Directors. In the country districts the organisation was weak ; in the large towns it was strong. After prolonged and fruitless negotiations, the sudden strike was dramatically decided upon at a mass meeting in Glasgow, on the motion of "a man in the area." Amid loud cheering, an unknown speaker demanded a strike a week hence ; perhaps it was illegal, but railway servants had no time to study law ; if they were sent to jail, they would at least be sure of their hours. On 22nd December, 1890, the railwaymen of Scotland, variously estimated at "over half " and "under 9000," struck work.† In many districts the miners enthusiastically assisted in the punishment and deterrence of blacklegs ; for six weeks industry was paralysed ; again and again the Companies refused arbitration ; their attitude was that "the spirit of the men must be broken, and that whatever concessions might have to be made afterwards the men must be driven to surrender in order that the concessions might not appear to be the outcome of the strike. It was felt that, at all costs, the working-classes must not be allowed to 'taste' power."‡ Virtually this is what did happen. The men were beaten back, but the Companies recognised the Unions, and many reforms were secured ; for instance, a month after the strike, the G. and S.W. Company instituted a maximum working week of 60 hours. On the other hand, the number of men blacklisted and refused re-employment are given as : Caledonian, 300 ; N.B.R., 200 ; and G. & .SW., 30.

IX.—THE CARTERS.

There was certainly an organisation of carters in Scotland in the year 1861, for in that year the carters of Edinburgh engaged upon a sudden "paralysis strike," led by a man called Charles Cameron, the objects of the strike being to secure a wage of 18s. and payment for overtime. The carters of Glasgow promised financial assistance. In the Annual Report of the Glasgow Trades Council for 1873, it is stated that the average carter's wage is 24s. for a working week of 84 hours ; but at a public demonstration held in the same year the

---

Nineteenth Century Magazine, February, 1891. One memorial to N.B.R., sent in April, was not acknowledged until two weeks after strike began in December.

†See *Nineteenth Century Magazine*, February, 1891 ; *Economic Journal*, 1891. The daily Press and Professor Mavor's *The Scottish Railway Strike*.

‡*Economic Journal*, p. 204, 1891.

allegation was made that the railway carters worked from 14 to 16 hours per day, sometimes indeed 20 hours out of the 24 ; that there were no regular meal-hours ; and that wages ran from 20s. to 24s. In 1879 wages rates were from 22s. to 28s., and in 1880 from 18s. to 26s. Indeed, until recent years the carters seem continually to have bordered upon starvation levels and to have toiled for as many, if not more, hours per week than any other section of the working-class.

X.—THE SAILORMEN.

"The broad-clothed and button-holed moral carrion who swarm into the city every forenoon from Villadom to scheme the capture of the savings of industry and thrift by lying prospectuses and bogus companies, or to send gallant and daring—often too daring—men to death in their overloaded and unseaworthy ships."—"*Cattle Ships*," p. 107—*Samuel Plimsoll, M.P.*

"I ask, seriously and sadly, can anyone doubt but that if these brave men had been pigs or sheep the Legislature had long since been compelled by power-ful advocates to stop such losses ? Pigs and sheep are property, and property is well represente d in Parliament."—"*Our Seamen*," p. 87—*Samuel Plimsoll M.P.* (1872).

Traditionally the sailor has ever been easy prey to the harpy and the exploiter ; obviously it was difficult for him to combine with his fellows, and he suffered his wrongs far from the ken of the philan-thropist and the press.

As far back as 1457 we find Scots Acts of Parliament forbidding shipowners to sail unless they carried large stocks of their "awne gudis" or of goods committed to them. Thus even at that period the small man was frozen out and the wealthy monopolist encouraged. By 1632 there is evidently a difficulty in securing fishermen for the great Fishing Trust, and an Act is passed for the purpose of press-ganging "lazie and ydle people to worke" on the Trust boats ; and half a century later, in 1694, the members of the Merchants' House at Glasgow meet "to consider a tax of 8d. per pound on seamen's wages for the support of that class of poor"—thus bestowing the boon of compulsory thrift upon the "lazie and ydle people." A hundred years pass and we find the sailormen, during the political upheaval consequent upon the French Revolution, engaged in an organised and prolonged strike on the East Coast. At Leith and Aberdeen they unrigged the ships to prevent them going to sea, and at Aberdeen the dispute, evidently an economic one, had to be settled by the arbitration of the Provost, that gentleman apologising for his weakness in taking part in the arbitration proceedings, and pleading that no other course was open to him.* At Arbroath they

---

Scotland and the French Revolution—Meikle, p. 97.

seem to have had a pull of some kind, for there the Fraternity of Seamen were entitled to a vote in the election of bailies; but generally they were a class despised and apart, almost like the colliers; their wages were low—at Aberdeen in 1843 able-bodied seamen only received £2 per month—and their lives were cheap, so cheap that it cannot have been the loss of seamen's lives through ships being lost by deck-loading that induced Parliament in 1839 to prohibit the practice of deck-loading.* Shipowners had discovered that fortunes could be made by sending old leaky tubs to sea well-covered by insurance; if poor sailormen's lives were lost—well, that was no business of theirs; there was no employers' liability and there was no sentiment in profit-making. When sailors refused to sail on a coffin ship, they were "mutinous," and the Law Courts heavily punished them. To make matters worse, in 1862 the Government, by regulation and without the knowledge or consent of Parliament, as Samuel Plimsoll tells us, cancelled the Statute forbidding deck-loading, and immediately the loss of life at sea rose by 400 per cent. Naturally the seamen became more "mutinous" than ever. Prosecutions before the Justices of the Peace at Greenock became "very frequent," and as these Justices "in many cases" were shipowners, the full penalty allowed by law for the crime of refusing to sail in a coffin ship—ten weeks' hard labour—was always imposed. "Paisley Jail," the press of the period informs us, "has been largely manned of late with squads of sailors who have been sent from Gourock to undergo sentences for refusing to proceed to sea."† In one case, the men alleged that the ship was "utterly unseaworthy and unfit for the voyage" and had a large supply of gunpowder "not properly secured, whereby their lives were in danger"—allegations confirmed by the ship's carpenter, and surely proved by the Captain, when he admitted that his ship on her last voyage had accumulated 2½ inches of water per hour. Nevertheless the penalty for the "mutineers" was the regulation 10 weeks' hard labour.‡

In 1870 the Government projected a Merchant Shipping Act to deal with the coffin ships, but the *N.B. Daily Mail* announced that the shipowners objected; they objected to the clauses requiring certificated mates and the affixing of inscriptions certifying the maximum number of passengers; they declared that with the imposition of these and other clauses steamship navigation "could not be conducted any longer at a profit in this country."§ The Act as the shipowners in Parliament finally allowed it to pass, was

---

*This prohibition immediately reduced the annual loss of sailors at sea by three-fourths.—*Cattle Ships*, Samuel Plimsoll, p. 126.

†*N.B. Daily Mail*, 23/4/64.

‡*Ibid*, 22/1/64.

§*N.B. Daily Mail*, 12/1/70.

useless. It gave seamen the right to ask for a survey of a suspected ship, but they were compelled to find the expenses of the survey if the surveyor certified the ship as seaworthy ; * and seamen's wages did not run to such costly speculations.

By 1873 we find Samuel Plimsoll, the M.P. for Derby,† conducting a vigorous agitation on behalf of the seamen ; the Scottish Miners' and other Unions subscribed money, and Trades Councils distributed his literature and organised petitions to Parliament. The Board of Trade admitted that in the year 1868 "about half of the loss by wreck or casualty to vessels employed in the regular carrying trade is represented by the unseaworthy, overladen, or ill-found vessels of the collier class chiefly employed in the coasting trade." *More than 2000 coasting trade vessels had been lost during the preceding eighteen months in this coasting trade.* Week after week Plimsoll asked questions in Parliament : "Had seamen from the brigs ' Maggie ' and the ' Sir Robert Macdonell ' been imprisoned for refusing to sail ? Were these brigs now lying in the Firth of Forth condemned as ' leaky ' by a Board of Trade Surveyor ? " Official evasions only deepened public interest, and the agitation grew.

In 1874 Plimsoll's Bill to protect the seamen from their exploiters and—Plimsoll did not hesitate to use the word—murderers, was only beaten by 3 votes in the House of Commons. A Royal Commission reported against Plimsoll's proposal of a regular and compulsory Government survey of sea-going ships, on the ground—please note ! —that such a survey would destroy the shipowners' sense of responsibility.‡ What that sense of responsibility was may be gathered from the fact that out of the 294 ships surveyed between 1873 and 1874 no fewer than 281 were condemned. A shipowners' deputation, headed by Mr. Donald Currie, assured the Board of Trade that :

" while our seamen have enjoyed excellent treatment, losses at sea have resulted more from their neglect than from the negligence or cupidity of owners."

But this was too much even for the *Glasgow Herald*,§ which roundly declared that there was a class of shipowners who evaded all "human enactments" and "had no regard for the laws of God." The *Herald* denounced their "culpable recklessness, their unchecked greed and cruelty."

Our Seamen—Samuel Plimsoll, p. 73.

†Plimsoll was a Radical. As a boy he had been left with 5 children, younger than himself, dependent upon him. He never forgot his early struggles with poverty.

‡*N.B. Daily Mail*, 25/8/74. This, the leading Liberal journal in Scotland, considered that Mr. Plimsoll's agitation was well-meant, but that he ought not to worry respectable and responsible shipowners (24/12/74).

§4/2/75.

Plimsoll persisted with his Parliamentary questions. One boat had sailed from the Clyde for the Bay of Biscay with only 2 feet 1 inch shewing above the water. A Greenock Captain had been discharged for refusing to sail without means being first taken to prevent the cargo from shifting. The Board of Trade admitted that the ship had afterwards capsized and was lost.

Again, in 1875, a Government Merchant Shipping Bill came before Parliament, and the Glasgow *Herald* reports that the shipowners are "determined to eliminate from it everything which they consider to be dangerous to their interests." They seem to have set about their business successfully—perhaps too successfully, as events turned out. In July * Mr. Disraeli announced in the House of Commons that the Government would postpone the Bill to the next Session. Mr. Plimsoll sprang to his feet, pale with passion. The Government, he cried, are consigning

"some thousands of men to an untimely grave . . shipowners of murderous tendencies outside the House and who are amply represented inside the House (cries of Oh! and Order!) have frustrated and talked to death every effort to procure a remedy for the existing state of things (cries of 'Name!' 'Name!'). I will give names very soon. . . . The Secretary of Lloyds tells a friend of mine that he does not know of a single ship that has been broken up voluntarily by the owners, because she was worn, for 30 years. They gradually pass from hand to hand until they are bought up by some needy and reckless speculator, and then they are sent to sea with precious human lives (cheers) . . . continually every winter hundreds and hundreds of brave men are sent to death, and their wives made widows, and their children made fatherless, so that a few speculating scoundrels in whose hearts there is neither the fear nor the love of God, may reap unhallowed gains. (Loud cheers.) There are shipowners in this country that never built a ship, and never bought a new one. (Oh! oh!). They are simply what are called "ship knackers," and I recently heard an ex-Secretary of the Treasury describe one of the present members of this House—one of his own colleagues—as a ship knacker. (Cries of Order! and Name! Name!)."

The Speaker called him to order, but he went on to declare that he gave notice he would ask the President of the Board of Trade about four ships which were lost in 1874 with 87 lives,

"and as to the *Foundling* and the *Sydney Dacres*, abandoned at sea, either that year or early in the present—in all nearly 900 tons; and whether the owner, Edward Bates, is the Member for Plymouth, or some other person of the same name. (Cheers. Cries of Order! and great interruption)."

And then pointing to the Liberal Opposition Benches:

"I mean to ask some questions about members of this side of the House, too, for I am determined to unmask the villains who sent these people to death. (Great confusion, and then complete silence)."

*Press Reports, 23/7/75.

The Speaker asked him to withdraw the word "villains." He refused again and again. He shouted "scoundrels" at the Government benches, and to an expostulating friend he cried : "I will name them all ! You don't know these men as well as I do."

Disraeli, "speaking in low tones" and "with great reluctance," moved that Plimsoll be reprimanded, and the press hinted that he was "unwell," but the country seethed with excitement. Plimsoll eagerly seized his opportunity. He issued leaflets saying that while the postponed Government Bill had been "an atrocious sham" it could have been improved in the House of Commons. The Bill did nothing to repair or break up rotten ships, nothing to abolish deck cargoes, nothing to regulate grain cargoes in bulk ; Plimsoll laid upon the head of the Prime Minister and his fellows "the blood of all the men who shall perish next winter from preventible causes."

The Government bent before the storm ; it asked for more powers to stop unseaworthy ships ; it proceeded with its Bill, and it accepted amendments wholesale. The Liberals accused the Tories and the Tories accused the Liberals of frustrating legislation to save seamen from the greed of the shipowners ; the *Glasgow Herald* declared that "the heart is taken out of the shipowners' opposition," and the Government Bill passed its third reading on the fifth of August.

In the succeeding year, 1876, Plimsoll got a majority of 18 against the Government, and the shipowners combined for a reinstatement of the old law (illegally suspended by regulation) for the abolition of deck cargoes ; but the House of Lords allowed a three feet deck cargo amendment to be inserted.

By 1877 the question of seamen's lives *versus* shipowners' profits is in the forefront of working-class politics, and we find the Glasgow Trades Council asking M.P.'s if they were favourable to the fixing of a definite load line and not leaving it to the caprice of each individual shipowner : also if they were favourable to a Government survey of all vessels, to the abolition of deck-loading in winter, and to a breach of seamen's contract in British waters being regarded as a civil and not a criminal offence ?

But coffin ships still sailed the seas. In 1877 the ship *Glenafton* left Glasgow, and at the first port of call her sailors refused to proceed on the ground that she was unseaworthy ; the Board of Trade detained the ship, but the sailors were sent to gaol for hard labour.* In 1884 Joseph Chamberlain sought to get the Merchant Shipping Acts amended. Writing to a correspondent in Greenock, he says that the most violent opposition to his Bill comes from "shipowners on the Clyde and the North East Coast."† He declares that during the past 12 years 36,000 seamen have been lost—one in every six

---

Glasgow Herald, 10/3/77.
†*Weekly Herald*, 10/5/84 and 24/5/84.

employed, and when Captain Hatfield, M.P., opposed his Bill, he retorted that since 1873 Hatfield had owned 12 ships, eleven of which had been lost.   In 1887 the National Seamen's and Firemen's Union was formed, and during the period 1885-1894 various legal reforms were effected, but the close of the century still saw the seaman ill paid, ill-treated, and ill-protected against the hazards of the sea.

XI.—THE WOODWORKERS.

Lines of demarcation between the wood-working crafts are difficult to draw, and most part of the following notes upon the carpenters and the joiners might well have been included either in our section on the House-building, or in that on the Shipbuilding, trade; but as these reference notes stand they may be of some interest to the workers in wood generally.

As early as 1805 we find the cabinetmakers of Edinburgh bargaining collectively with their employers, but beyond learning that the carpenters, and possibly also the cabinetmakers, burned their books at the time the cotton spinners were prosecuted for conspiracy, we have no farther trace of the wood-working craft until 1833, when the cabinetmakers in the West of Scotland who refused to renounce their Union were discharged, some of them, as in Paisley, after serving 40 years in the same workshop.   In 1836 the joiners in Glasgow were locked out for a similar refusal, but after a five weeks' struggle the masters surrendered, though in the succeeding year they fought out a 12 weeks' strike and compelled the men to accept a reduction of 6s. weekly.   In 1840 cabinetmakers' wages ran to about 16s.; coopers, 18s.; sawyers, 23s.; and joiners, 20s.—all for a sixty-hour week.   In 1845 the sawyers in the west, assisted financially by other trades and by the sawyers in Ireland, struck successfully for an increase.   In that same year the joiners of Inverness could only earn 12s. weekly.   In 1850 we find five Glasgow joiners fined two guineas each for destroying the tools of, and throwing rats and stones at, blacklegs during a strike.   In 1853 joiners' wages were as low as 21s.; a year later a building boom drove them up to 24s.   In 1854 we find 1400 Glasgow joiners out on strike for a 57-hour week, and their declamations about "tyrannic capital" were answered by threats of the introduction of blacklegs from the provinces where wages were only 16s. to 20s.; the strikers, however, won, and the 57-hour week was secured.   At Dumfries, in 1857, there was a joiners' strike against a wage-rate of 18s. "for good men" only, and in Glasgow a strike against a threatened reduction to 22s. 6d. for 54 hours.   The joiners had prior to the year 1861 two Unions —one for the East and one for the West of Scotland; but in 1861 the two were fused into the Amalgamated Society of Carpenters and

Joiners, with almost 5000 members.* The year 1862 witnessed the
initiation of a nine-hours' day agitation among the Edinburgh
joiners. In 1864 the Glasgow carpenters were increased to 26s.,
but this lasted only for a month or two until a reduction of 1s. per
day was announced, the *North British Daily Mail* hailing the reduction as "a wise step, for the existing high rate of wages in the district may be the means of driving away work to other places where
labour is cheaper. If the operatives look to the proposal in this
light they are not likely to offer it any serious opposition."† The
year 1870 witnessed a prolonged joiners' struggle all over the country
for a nine-hours' day, and, in some districts, for increased wages also.
The nine-hours' day was won, but wages do not seem to have been
increased anywhere. Six years later the joiners in Glasgow were out
for 14 weeks, striking against an attempted reduction from 9d. to
8½d. per hour. For the former rate the men had a twelve months'
agreement, which the employers sought to break. In the end the
men retained their ninepence, but by 1879 their wages had again
been reduced to 6d. or 6½d. per hour ; in 1882 the week's wage stood
at 31s. 6d.

XII.—THE IRONWORKERS.

" We cam' na here to view your warks
    In hopes to be mair wise,
But only, lest we gang to hell,
    It may be nae surprise."
                                —*Burns.*

Though iron had been worked since the thirteenth century in
Scotland, it was not until 1760, when the Carron works began, that
the industry became of importance. Three years later, we are told,
there were 1200 workers employed by the Carron Company. About
1793 ironfounders' wages were 2s. per day ; then a generation passes
about which we can learn nothing of moment until in 1831 the
Associated Society of Ironmoulders of Scotland is formed, and
the "railway boom " causes a great demand for iron. In 1840 iron
moulders' wages are stated to have been 25s. per week.‡

In the press references to the industry, the general term "iron-
works " is frequently and confusedly used to cover either, or both,
iron-founding shops and iron-stone pits ; but the recurrent industrial
troubles at the iron-stone pits, due to the same miserable wages,
truck, and swindling, as already described in the notes upon the

---

*The Webbs, in their *History of Trade Unionism*, say the amalgamation took
    place in 1860, but James Watson, the Secretary of the Union, in 1869,
    declared it was not until in September, 1861.—*N.B. Daily Mail*, 10/9/69.
†4/7/64.
‡Chief Factory Inspector (Scotland)—*Weekly Mail*, 23/12/82.

coalminers' struggles, had no connection with the ironfounders, except when the pit strikes or locks-out by starving the foundries of raw material caused unemployment. Thus, while in 1857 we read that the employees of the Coltness Iron Company are compelled to sign away their claims to compensation for accident, and, if they live in the Company's houses, are forbidden to keep "lodgers, dogs, swine, poultry or firearms " or to hold meetings or attend meetings anywhere for any purpose, it is important to note that these rules and regulations refer to iron-miners, not to iron-moulders. Iron-moulding and steel-smelting were "skilled trades," were paid bigger wages; and were not subject to truck swindling. Still, they had their grievances. In 1846 we read that they are getting into a habit of striking at a moment's notice.* Though their wages rise 20 per cent. in the period 1850-3, they stand only at 28s. in 1855,† and the large number of apprentices threaten to reduce even that standard. In 1856 there was a prolonged spell of unemployment which ate into the Union funds ; and in 1861, at Hydepark, moulders' hours of work were apparently from 6 a.m. to 6 p.m. for 5s. 4d.‡ In 1862 the Associated Society of Iron and Steel Workers was formed. In 1863 and 1864 the puddlers secured an increase, but the masters sought to cut it off in 1865, and refused the men's request for arbitration, saying that arbitration was "erroneous in principle and could never lead to any beneficial result."§ In 1864 the newly-formed Union of Iron Puddlers struck at Coatbridge against non-union labour being employed, but as they had not given "legal warning " to strike, the Airdrie J.P.'s sentenced five of the ring-leaders to 30 days' hard labour ; and in the same year the Dundyvan men struck against a new monthly system of paying wages (instead of fortnightly as had been the case for the previous 40 years), whereby they were compelled to get "sub " at the truck store and be robbed of 20 per cent. of their wages through high prices. For puddlers, who had 8s. per day—although the nature of their employment engendered great thirst and costly beer-drinking—monthly wage payments were not so serious, but for the poor labourers who earned only 2s. a day it meant misery piled upon misery, destitution beyond description. Apprentice iron-moulders at Glasgow who absented themselves from work were given 30 days' hard labour. In 1865 there were wage reductions—puddlers by 6d. per ton and other workers by 5 per cent. ; but in the Edinburgh district, at least, the men were more concerned about getting their hours of labour reduced to 57 per week ; there the "iron trades " united against

---

Argus, 27/4/1846.

†Furnacemen had only 4/6 per day.

‡*Daily Mail*, 12/3/61.

§*Scotsman*, 10/4/65.

the masters when the latter reduced the meal hours as a counter-stroke to the Saturday afternoon half-holiday, which they had been compelled to concede, and "in one workshop the men were threatened with imprisonment should they persevere in asking the reduction of working hours."* In 1866 the demand was general for a shorter working week, and even during the wages reductions which took place in 1867 (10 per cent. to 25 per cent. in the malleable iron works and 2s. per week in the moulding shops) that demand was persisted in. At the beginning of 1868 moulders' wages ran from 26s. to 30s., and the employers evidently thought them over high, for they set about increasing the number of apprentices to 12 and even 15 for each journeyman,† and openly declared that the "obnoxious Union must be crushed." The hours of work were 60 per week. At Parkhead, the puddlers worked 12 hours for 8s. 6d. or 9s., but they had to pay assistants or "chaps" off that, so the wage for a full week's work was but 25s. to 28s. Yet the puddler seldom earned 25s. or 28s. ; during 1867 he had only 3 or 4 shifts per week.

In January, 1868, the Master Ironfounders determined to smash the Moulders' Union, and they locked out the Union men all over Scotland with the exception of a few country shops. After nine weeks' starvation the men went back beaten, making one condition only—that they were not required formally to renounce their Union. Upon all other questions the masters had triumphed—unlimited number of apprentices, employment of non-union men, the taking of apprentices above the age of 14 and piece-work (which last the men regarded as a wage-breaking trick). From 1868 to "the Iron Boom year" of 1872, apart from occasional wages trouble with the puddlers, which the Masters' Association threatened to meet with a lock-out of the iron workers generally, and apart from a steady grumbling from the moulders about their hours of labour, there is nothing of importance to record ; but in March, 1872, the moulders, as the result of a threat of a sudden strike in a rising market, got the 51 hours' week. They were, however, the only craft in the iron industry to secure the concession, and although they held it intact for a long time the anomaly of blowing one horn in a works at night for the moulders and a later one for the other workers, assisted the masters in the eighties and the early nineties to increase the moulders' working day to that worked by the other crafts. During the boom year of 1872, however, the moulders raised their wages considerably above the £1 to £1 8s. level, at which they had existed in 1871, and they also secured the restitution of most of their old Union restric-

---

Scotsman, 28/10/65.

†Previously only 3 apprentices had been allowed to each journeyman who had "served seven years to the trade."—Mr. Skimming, Secretary, Iron-moulders of Scotland—*Scotsman*, 12/3/68.

tions. In the next few years there is little of special interest to note. In 1874 puddlers' average earnings were but 5s. a day, and in 1877, largely owing to trouble in the shipyards, the whole iron trade conditions worsened, and a series of wage reductions began. By 1882 these reductions had been recovered, though at Kirkintilloch, after a 17 weeks' strike, the moulders went back still 5 per cent. under the old standard. In 1880 pattern makers' wages were 7d. per hour and dressers and moulders 6d. to 6½d. In 1882 moulders' wages are said to have averaged 31s.-34s. per week, while turners and fitters had 31s. 5d., and unskilled labourers 4d. to 4½d. per hour. In 1886 the British Steel Smelters' Association was formed ; and in 1889 a new society of ironmoulders, The Central Ironmoulders' Association, was created to look after the interests of piece-workers, men who had not served seven years to the trade, and some few men, who for various reasons were disinclined to pay the rather heavier Union fees demanded by the old Scottish Ironmoulders' Union.

XIII.—ENGINEERING AND SHIPBUILDING.

"The man who is able to exist by his toil is, after all, dependent upon what the merest breath of adversity may in a moment dispel. . . . Old age will come creeping on, and then with weakened intellect and diminished strength, the poorhouse is, in too many instances, the only refuge after a life of labour."— *Ritual Address to New Entrants, Amalgamated Society of Engineers.*

"The sole defence of the old Trade Unionism is its money-bag ; its only offensive weapon the cracked and crazy strike. Capitalism can afford to augh at both."—" *The Coming Force.*"—*Frank H. Rose*, p. 19.

"Small children are selected to go into the tubes to hold the end of the rivets, and in consequence of the great noise the drums of the children's ears get split and they become permanently deaf."—*Dr. Irvine, Glasgow—Evidence before Factory Act Commission, September*, 1875.

"While labour lives in hovels and starves in rags and capital lives in palaces and feasts in robes, speak no more of the castes of the tribes of India."—*James M'Neal, Secretary, Clyde Boilermakers and Shipbuilders*, 9/10/57.

The reader desirous of studying in detail the story of the formation and development of the Associated Society of Engineers, the Boilermakers and Iron Shipbuilders, the Associated Society of Blacksmiths, Carpenters and Joiners, Shipwrights, and other working class organisations whose chief field of activity is the shipbuilding industry, will find much material in Webb's "History of Trades Unionism."* Our purpose here is confined to a brief and broadly-limned relation of the greater class struggles in Scottish shipbuilding, taking the industry as a whole, from the thirties of last century, when

*For the Boilermakers see specially the *History of the United Society of Boilermakers and Iron and Steel Shipbuilders*—D. C. Cummings.

the old wooden sailing ships began rapidly to give place to steam-driven vessels.

In 1833 there were strikes of engineers on the Clyde and demands made for the apprenticeship system, without which the skilled craftsmen were continually at the mercy of the unskilled labour market. During these strikes blacklegs were very roughly treated. In 1845, the shipyard workers on the Clyde could be fined 1s. for talking during working hours, fined for injuring tools, using too much oil or waste ; and for every two hours absent from work "except in cases of sickness, of which previous notice must be given," they lost one-fourth of a day's wage.* In 1851 the A.S.E. was formed in England, and at the beginning of the succeeding year the masters faced a small strike by locking out all the A.S.E. men until they would sign a document repudiating the new Union. A bitter struggle ensued in England, and the men were at least nominally beaten, partly by the engineers on the Clyde who worked overtime, and by the Scots engineers who gravitated as blacklegs to the English work-shops. The increased earnings on the Clyde for this treachery to their English comrades did not long continue. The "boom" passed. In 1856 the apprentices at Dumbarton went on strike and rescued their leaders who had been arrested by the police ; Greenock ship-yard workers were imprisoned for 42 days for "absenting themselves from work without leave" ;† Barclay Curle's apprentices, for a similar offence, were given 3 months' hard labour. In the beginning of May, 1857, a strike broke out in the Clyde yards for a half-holiday on Saturday afternoons ; the struggle lasted for about six weeks, and latterly seems to have developed into a demand for increased wages instead of the shorter working week ; the men went back, trade by trade and yard by yard, on slightly better terms in some instances, but often on 10 per cent. to 20 per cent. lower wages. And immediately the strike was over we find Mr. Napier, the Clyde shipbuilder, boasting at a meeting of the British Association that he had found "half-starved nailmakers from St. Ninians, near Stirling, make passable rivetters in about a month" ;‡ and as they worked for 15s. per week, the conditions in the yards may be better imagined than described. Towards the beginning of winter there was commercial depression, which the masters utilised to still farther break wages and to increase the hours of labour. The *maximum* wages of carpenters was fixed at 24s., that of platers at 24s., that of rivetters at 20s., that of caulkers at 19s., and that of labourers at 13s.§ Short strikes took place, swelling the mobs who surrounded the soup

---

Glasgow Argus, 6/2/45.

†*Glasgow Courier*, 14/8/56.

‡*Glasgow Herald*, 7/9/1857 and 9/10/1857.

§*Ibid*, 14/12/57.

kitchens, but the men crept back glad to get work on the half-time shifts that the masters offered. From 1862—a boom year— conditions slowly began to improve, and by 1864 the engineers had secured a weekly wage of 27s. and (at Caird's yard) 28s. ; but by 1865 trade depression again ensued and the reductions re-commenced ; at Dumbarton, in spite of an unavailing strike against it, the carpenters and "furnacemen" suffered a reduction of 6s., rivetters and platers one of 5s., and blacksmiths one of 3s.* Work was brisk in 1866, and the men on the Clyde sought a reduction in hours of labour to 57 per week, a boon that had been secured in Aberdeen since 1863 and in Dundee since 1864; but the now Federated Masters replied with a lock-out of their 30,000 employees which lasted more or less from May to the end of August and caused widespread misery and suffering. The Liberal press carefully pointed out that the Poor's Rate could supply no relief for able-bodied people ; the Greenock shipwrights who had £2000 invested with the municipality were politely informed that they would not be allowed to withdraw the money without six months' notice ; and although the A.S.E. paid a strike benefit of 10s. per week to their members, they and the other Unions very foolishly were ungenerous towards the poor non-organised labourers who were locked-out with them ; true, they decided to support the labourers, but the support was insufficient—2s. 6d. per week—and upon that rock the Unions perished, for the labourers were the weak link and the weak link snapped because of hunger. Yard by yard and trade by trade the men went back, those who first broke away being savagely maltreated in the streets by the apprentices. In the succeeding year, 1867, there was prolonged stagnation on the Clyde ; some of the yards were completely closed, and large numbers of men were unemployed for 4 months. In 1868 the shipyard workers had secured a working week of 58 hours and wages ran as follows : Carpenters, 26s. 6d. ; smiths, 26s. ; fitters, 25s. ; engineers, 24s. ; rivetters, 19s. ; caulkers, 19s. ; strikers, 16s. ; chippers, 14s. 6d. ; drillers, 13s. 6d. ; and labourers, 14s. At Dundee the carpenters had only 20s. to 22s. ; the holders-on, 16s. ; smiths, 22s. to 23s. ; but the rivetters there had 23s. to 26s.† The ship's carpenters appear to have been the chief rebel element in the yards ; in 1868 they insisted upon supporting a strike at Greenock, and suffered a general lock-out in consequence ; in 1871 they again caused a general lock-out by refusing, as insufficient, a rise of 1s. 6d. upon their nominal wage of 25s. 8d , and after a fortnight's struggle secured a wage of 6d. per hour and time and half after 6 p.m. Late in 1871 the engineers in

---

Scotsman, 3/7/65.

†*Scotsman*, 24/2/68. The average wage of the A.S.E. member in Scotland at this period was 20/- to 28/- ; there were 3105 members and 33 branches.

England had succeeded in reducing their working hours to 54 per week, and the Clyde men followed upon the wave of that victory by demanding a 51 hour week which, after a short strike and arbitration, the masters agreed to upon the footing that until 1st November, 1872, fifty-four hours would be the week's work. When November came the masters sought to reduce wages *pro-rata*, but the other organised trades rallied to the support of the engineers and the masters surrendered. These conditions remained until November, 1874, when the masters, taking advantage of a spell of bad trade and unemployment, succeeded in reducing wages by from 5 per cent. to 15 per cent. ; a year later, in 1875, strikes took place, but the yards did not act in unison and the men were beaten, though the men at Dumbarton held out for 28 weeks. By 1877 starvation stalked the Clyde, many engineers working for but £1 a week ; there was "overproduction" followed by unemployment amid a period of rising prices of foodstuffs. In April the shipwrights demanded increased wages : the employers promptly retaliated by a general lock-out of all their workers and published broadcast their intention to introduce blacklegs from Holland. For 23 weeks the struggle lasted,* until finally the men went back upon a promise that the wages question would be submitted at a future date to Lord Moncrieff as Arbiter. In November that gentleman announced his award— that the state of trade did not warrant any increase upon the old rates. In 1878 the men were compelled to suffer a farther reduction of $7\frac{1}{2}$ per cent., and the 51-hour week was lost. It was a sad winter for thousands of working class families ; hammermen fully employed could only earn 15s. 11d., general labourers 17s., and red leaders 17s ; and at the beginning of February, 1879, no fewer than 37,904 persons were being stintedly relieved at charity soup kitchens and by oakum-picking and stone-breaking "gratuity employment" in the city of Glasgow alone.† By October, 1880, it is recorded, trade was again brisk and increased wages were being secured,‡ the shipwrights, the best paid workmen on the Clyde, reaching £1 9s. 3d. per week. In 1882 the engineers at Johnstone got their wages up to 29s. ; Clyde labourers reached 20s., and the smiths 31s. 6d. ; and the shipwrights made an attempt to secure 5s. 6d. per day, but failed after a strike of 11 weeks, through the importation of German blacklegs.§ By 1883, however, they had reached $7\frac{3}{4}$d. per hour ; ship fitters had secured as high as 10d. per hour, and labourers' wages varied from 4d. to 5d. per hour. In

---

*This lock-out cost the Boilermakers' Union funds a sum of over £30,000— *Fraser's Magazine*, 1879, p. 780.

†*Glasgow Weekly Mail.*

‡*Ibid*, 2/10/80.

§The English blacklegs were "got at" and induced to go home.

October of that year, bad trade again ensuing, a general reduction of 10 per cent. on all shipyard wages was agreed to without a strike ; and in January, 1884, there was another 10 per cent. reduction, and the hosts of men who had been unemployed for the past three months were recommended not to drink ! In April the Dundee shipyard workers struck in "the falling market" against a 10 per cent. reduction, but were easily beaten. In May another 10 per cent. reduction was announced on the Clyde. In June, 1500 men at Leith were on strike against a 10 per cent. reduction. By October, 1885, seven men out of every ten in the Clyde yards were idle, and by the end of the year 1886 piece-work rates in shipbuilding trades were lower than they had been for twenty years.†

XIV.—THE BUILDING TRADES.

"I have known some of the masons lie at their work all night and all they could make was 7/- or 8/- a week, working almost night and day."—*Masons' Delegate, "Scotsman," 16/12/65.*

Between the *status* of the stonemason under the Guild—to which we have already devoted some attention—and the *status* of the stonemason after the Industrial Revolution there is no wide gulf fixed. The "Cowan" who, not having served apprenticeship was refused admission to the Guild fraternity and was the object of insult and contumely, was succeeded by the starved and despised orraman mason. For the skilled craftsman the hours of labour were as long, and the grip upon the minimum decencies of life as insecure, under the one system as the other.

In the middle of the fifteenth century King James I. was compelled to import craftsmen from France and Flanders "for the Scottis were exercit in continewall wars frae the time of King Alexander the Third to thay dayis. Thus were all [native] craftsmen slane be the wars." In 1491 the Edinburgh masons began work in summer at 5 a.m., and with two hours off for food, toiled until 7 p.m., in winter they toiled during all hours of daylight. About 1500 they earned 9s. weekly (three shillings more than labourers !) and enjoyed two weeks' holidays at Christmas and nine other holidays during the year. By 1660 they earned double the wages of the labourers. In 1764 the Edinburgh masons went on strike against a wage rate of 1s. 1½d. per day in summer and 10d. in winter ; the strike was for an increase of 2d. per day, but the Lord Provost and Magistrates decreed that they must return to work upon the old terms ; "the journeymen were bound to work for the freeman master masons for such wages as the master should think reasonable, agreeable to use

---

† "Thirty Years of the Trade Union Movement."—Geo. N. Barnes, M.P., in *Co-operative Annual* (1914), p. 191.

and wont " ; at this period the hours of work in summer were from 6 a.m. to 6 p.m. By 1792 masons were said to be earning 2s. per day ; in 1825 during the Glasgow building "boom " they had soared to 27s. (summer) and 17s. (winter), but a year later the summer wages had again fallen to 17s., and by 1829 they were as low as 12s. weekly. A Union was inaugurated in Edinburgh, and the employers were given six months' notice that a demand would be made for a minimum of 18s. ; one by one the employers yielded, and the success put the Union upon its feet. During the thirties, say the Webbs, in their "History of Trade Unionism," the Stonemasons' Union was active and influential. First, "task " work was abolished ; then wages were fixed upon an hourly basis ; then (after a strike) a Saturday half-holiday was secured.* In 1831-1833, when the United Operative Masons of Scotland Society was formed, the men were demanding a sixty-hour week, and sheds to be erected at employers expense ; the death benefit of the Society was fixed at £1 sterling. In November a great strike broke out for 4d. an hour ; the employers refused to treat with the Unions, and made persistent efforts to introduce blacklegs ; the struggle lasted until February, 1834, and the strikers were assisted financially by the newly-born "General Trades Union "; in the end most employers recognised the Union and granted the wages' demand ; indeed, a month later, the employers in Paisley were compelled to offer a weekly wage of 18s. Wages rose during 1835, but in 1836 they fell again—bricklayers from 24s. to 14s. (after a strike raised to 18s.) ; the masons fell to 16s. ; but even during this period of acute depression the building trade workers collected large sums of money for relief among the famishing wage-serfs in the pottery districts in England. During 1837 the masons again secured 20s. ; in 1838 they had 22s., the increases being secured largely as a result of strikes and threats of strikes, undeterred in the slightest by Sheriff Allison's decision in Glasgow that the very intimation of a strike was a threat and as such was punishable by law.† In 1843 the Glasgow masons had 19s. weekly ; in 1845 the bricklayers were reduced, despite a strike, from 30s. to 24s. ; in 1847 the Edinburgh masons had 21s., and in 1848 the Glasgow men had 20s. and were striking for a 12½ per cent. advance. Between 1850 and 1852 labourers in the building trade had 12s. weekly ; in 1852 they had 16s. ; in 1853 they had 14s. Masons' wages in 1852 were 21s. for 60 hours, and joiners had the same rates.

The year 1853 witnessed a great masons' strike for an increase of 3s. 3d. weekly on 23s., and a Saturday half-holiday. In Glasgow alone 1700 masons were out and were financially assisted by other trades ; the plasterers gave £20 and lent £50, the hatters gave £30 ;

Scotsman, 16/12/65.

†United Operative Masons of Scotland *v.* Barr—*Evening Post*, 19/3/36.

on the intervention of the architects the employers gave way, conceding a 57-hours' week (off at 2 p.m. on Saturdays), 5d. per hour, and six months' notice from either side of any alteration ; these terms, though a considerable improvement, were still disgracefully low when account was taken of the irregular employment due to bad weather, etc. In 1853 the Scottish Painters' Society was formed in Glasgow ; the operative painters declared that the employers paid "a fair wage" for only four months in the year—the summer months —and then paid off a percentage of their employees, "telling them to look in next week, when they were informed that they might commence work again, but that the wages would be three or four shillings less than they had before." To destroy this practice was the prime purpose of the new Union, and the men succeeded in getting the employers to agree to engage by the year and to form an arbitration court to settle disputes. After four years, however, the Employers' Association, feeling itself strong enough, in a spasm of particularly bad trade, openly denounced the agreement and distributed gallons of "free ale" in the Edinburgh taverns in search of blacklegs. In 1856 the masons on the S.E. coast were striking for time and half on Saturday afternoons, but the men in the West had retained the shorter hours, and the Saturday afternoon clear. In that year the masons had 25s., joiners 24s., labourers 17s., and slaters 22s. ; but we read of special demands during a "boom" which followed upon a devastating storm ; Paisley bricklayers struck for a rise of 100 per cent. and slaters asked an increase of 11s.

In December, 1857, the building trades were compelled to suffer reductions ; and in 1859 the statement was made in Glasgow that after reckoning meal hours and time travelling to and from work, the employees were working 14 or 15 hours a day.* In the spring of 1861 began a prolonged struggle in Edinburgh for a nine-hours' day. The joiners, who were without funds, were soon beaten, but the masons, who were well organised and started with a strike fund of £7000, held out for three months and compelled the employers to yield. The struggle was a bitter one; the masters federated and induced the quarry masters, or some of them, to close their quarries, and by this means dry up the subscriptions which were pouring into Edinburgh ; the men, on the other hand, had financial support from most other organised trades, and they drafted their men away from the Edinburgh strike-roll to country jobs, whenever possible ; they also formed a Co-operative Building Society and took direct contracts ; we are told that the Society was very successful, and that the Rev. Dr. Begg laid the foundation stone of their first tenement amidst a great crowd composed of workers and their families on the same day that the Prince Consort laid the foundation stone of

Glasgow Herald, 7/9/59.

the General Post Office in Edinburgh.* By the end of 1863 they
had built or were building 117 houses and had 2300 shares taken up
in the Society. We can discover no reference to this interesting
experiment in "Industrial Unionism" in Mr. Maxwell's *History
of Co-operation in Scotland*, and the daily press of the period, while
it noted the speeches of "Mr. George Lorimer, builder," and Mr.
George Troup, who together led the Edinburgh strike and urged the
workers to "produce for themselves" and boycott all long-hour
grocers, tailors, shoemakers, publicans—"aye, any-hour publicans,"
is annoyingly silent about the later history of the experiment. All
we know of Lorimer is that he himself was a master builder and a
Chartist, and that at the successful conclusion of the strike, Robert
Lowry, the Chartist, was deputed to present him with a £60 watch
subscribed for by the workers of Edinburgh. Following upon the
nine-hours' day victory in Edinburgh, the men in Glasgow and
Dundee struck, and struck successfully ; soon in all the larger centres
the nine-hours' day was the rule. By 1870 the masons in 40 towns
had the nine-hours' day and sevenpence an hour, as against sixpence
an hour under the ten-hours' day system. In 1872 two hundred
Inverkip quarrymen left the village rather than submit to a ten
hours' day.

In 1864 the officials of the Glasgow branch of the Masons' Union
were sued for damages by a non-unionist for causing him to be dismissed because the Union men refused to work beside him. The
Sheriff awarded the non-unionist £12 and expenses.† In 1866 the
builders' labourers were striking against a sixty-hour week and
3s. 4d. per day, and the Glasgow masons struck work for 9 weeks
in a vain attempt to compel the employers to provide sheds in winter.
By 1877 the masons in the Glasgow area were receiving 9d. or 10d.
per hour, but in the year following, 1878, a year of many strikes and
great depression,‡ wages fell to 6d. per hour, and there was even
difficulty in securing employment at that. In 1878 the Kirkcaldy
masons were on strike for 36 weeks. At about 25s. wages remained,
and there was much emigration until the boom year of 1882, when
wages rose to 31s. 6d., bricklayers to 34s., labourers to 20s., and
painters, plasterers, and slaters to 31s. 6d. Even after the boom,
the Unions not only prevented the hour rate from falling, they
increased it. In 1883 joiners' wages were 7½d. per hour ; in 1888
they were 8d. ; in 1892, 8½d. ; in 1896, 9d. ; in 1897, 9½d. ; and in
1898, 10d. ; and the other building craft rates rose similarly. In
1905, however, the Glasgow joiners, after a 20 weeks' strike, were
driven down to 9½d., and in 1908 they were at 9d. per hour. That

---

N.B. Daily Mail, 20/11/61.

†*N.B. Daily Mail*, 15/3/64.

‡The year of the failure of the Glasgow City Bank.

is to say, the joiners, and the same may be said of the other building
crafts, were in 1908 where they were in 1896 so far as wage rate per
hour was concerned.   But the costs of living had increased, and
every winter, from October to February, there was great unemployment, which brought down the average craftsman's hour rate, taking
the whole year round, to about sixpence.   At the beginning of the
twentieth century building was a sweated industry and thousands
of skilled craftsmen were leaving it for other occupations.

XV.—THE TAILORS.

" For the last six years, eighty per cent. of the deaths among the journeymen
tailors of Paisley have been by consumption—almost every one of the victims
being young men."—*N.B. Daily Mail*, 28/2/1853.

" We have looked down through those trap windows into the damp dens
where he works, and as we shunned the breathing of the suffocating vapour
that rose from the gas, the damp cloth, and the confined air of the cellar,
stoving with the hot air of the crowded operatives . . . productive of as large
a proportion of disease as any of the filthiest dens in the *purlieus* of the city."—
Glasgow Herald, April, 1859.

The historic disaffection of the operative tailor is understandable.
His wages, even in the sixteenth century were fixed for him at
"12d. and his meitt" for a sixteen-hours' day "without leiff" ;*
even so late as the time of the Stuart rebellions he was being sentenced to two years' hard labour for refusing to work at his statutory
wage ; masters who paid him more were fined £5 and publicans who
had the audacity to "harbour" tailoring agitators lost their licenses.
In September, 1748, twenty-one Edinburgh tailors were prosecuted
by their masters for daring to strike, and were punished by imprisonment for 48 hours and thereafter until they had paid to their said
masters £6 6s. sterling as damages and expenses, and given a promise
that they would forswear all striking for the future.   It is nearly
a century before the Edinburgh tailors again appear as attempting
Trade Union activity.

At Aberdeen† we find the tailors on strike in 1768.   In 1720 their
wages had been fixed at 4d. per day and their hours from 7 a.m. to
9 p.m.   In 1734 their hours were increased—from 6 a.m. to 10 p.m.
and so continued for 30 years.   About 1764 their wages had risen
to 8d. per day, but the men demanded 10d. per day, the masters
retaliating with a "black list" of rebels to whom employment was
refused.   In 1797 the Aberdeen tailors struck and were prosecuted

The Incorporated Trades of Edinburgh—Colston, p. 117.   In 1656 itinerant
   tailors appear to have got 4d. per day, and their meat.—*Scotland and the
   Protectorate* (Firth), p. 408.

†The Merchant and Craft Gilds (of Aberdeen) Bain, p. 260-1.

for unlawful combination. Twelve of them were fined 10s. and given eight days in gaol and compelled to find sureties that they would return to their masters at the expiry of their sentences and serve them dutifully in the future for a wage of 7s. 6d. per week.* The leaders were impressed into the Army or the Navy, where, doubtless, they lustily fought Napoleon's levies for British freedoms and liberties !

On 12th March, 1824, "The Glasgow Union Journeymen Tailors Friendly Society" was formed "for mutual assistance and protection"; and in 1834 it amalgamated with other similar societies which were in being at Greenock and Paisley : and thereafter in all three towns a few daring spirits kept afoot the Union, and with it, an under-world of trouble for a living wage.

Tailors' wages are said to have been about 18s. per week in 1840† —and even at that figure it was the sixth worst paid occupation in Scotland—but the practice of hiring out work to middlemen sweaters had long driven the bulk of the trade far below starvation point, and into filthy, unregistered, non-inspected hovels where emaciated, diseased and dying men, women and children plied the needle. By 1850 two-thirds of the working tailors of Glasgow were in the employment of sweaters, and the middle classes, alarmed at the stories told by the "respectable master tailors" of the foul disease dens in which so many suits of clothes were made, openly associated themselves with the journeyman tailors in their anti-sweating campaign. Lord Provosts may have cared little or nothing at all about the low wages paid to working tailors, but they cared exceedingly lest they themselves should wear clothing manufactured in a fever den. The working tailors of Glasgow quickly grasped that fact, and led by one, Peter Henrietta, they made West End flesh creep. Henrietta told of a tailor sweat shop, 7 feet by 9 feet, wherein 3 men worked, of 3 women and 5 children in an adjoining small room, two of whom had their heads shaved (for fever)—and of how these tailors worked 18 hours a day and earned 6s. per week.‡ At Paisley twenty or thirty tailors worked in an underground cellar, described as a "dark and living grave" ;§ and an "agitator," called Donald M'Donald, kept going a perpetual stream of exposure about the underground, damp and dark workshops in Glasgow. Here and there trade was scared away from particular shops as a result of these exposures, but the conditions, owing to the introduction of machinery and a

---

The Tailoring Trade—Galton, p. lvi.

†Chief Factory Inspector at Paisley—*Weekly Mail*, 23/12/82.

‡*Glasgow Herald*, 31/5/50.

§ .*B. Daily Mail*, 28/2/53. When in 1853 Mrs. Harriet Beecher Stowe, the author of "Uncle Tom's Cabin," was in this country, a dress was made for her by girls who had to toil regularly for 16 hours daily.—*Ibid*, 19/5/53

plentiful supply of cheap labour, improved but little.   In 1865 tailors' wages in Edinburgh and Glasgow ran about 18s. for a working week of over 80 hours ; and a Scottish National Association of Operative Tailors was decided upon as a necessary preliminary to any betterment.*   William Cobb was the first secretary, and an elaborate organisation was speedily effected—so speedily, indeed, that by February, 1866, it called out on strike the tailors of Scotland for a 57 hours' week and a wages rate of 5d. per hour.   The struggle was a bitter one ; on the one side the masters imported German and Danish blacklegs, and on the other the organised trades rallied financially to the support of the strikers ; but by the middle of April the masters surrendered, agreed to discharge their blacklegs if they would not join the Union (entrance fee 10s.), fixed a fifty seven hour week for 12 months, with a minimum rate of 5d. per hour and time and half for overtime ;   disputes were to be settled by arbitration boards.   It was a remarkable victory, and the enthusiasm was so great that attempts by the masters to break the agreement during the great spell of unemployment in 1867 were unavailing.†   The arrest of the office-bearers of the London tailors in the same year (1867) for "conspiring to impoverish the master tailors"‡ still farther strengthened the Union in Scotland, and the ground gained in the battle of 1866 was never lost.   True, the tailors of Aberdeen were compelled to a strike of 57 weeks' duration (1875-6)—one of the longest strikes on record—to maintain their meagre standards, but even recurrent "introductions" of female and Jewish labour in the large towns never succeeded in breaking either the Union or the "living minimum" secured by the skilled tailor craftsmen in 1866.

*The Association may have been initiated in 1864.

†In Greenock the men started a Co-operative Tailoring department in 1867.

‡*N.B. Daily Mail*, 5/7/67.   This episode caused remarkable class-war demonstrations in Glasgow, with demands for labour representation in the House of Commons. the old Owenite, Alexander Campbell, being particularly prominent.

CHAPTER XIV.

THE COMMUNIST SEEDS OF SALVATION.

> " Fellow-workers might
> So work together for the common weal,
> To pour together in a common store
> Those sacred gains of labour which are life,
> As to become masters of themselves,
> Masters and lords of their own heritage,
> Of labour."
>
> —*Tennyson.*

I.—THE FRIENDLY ORDERS.

WITH technical improvements in transport and the opening up to the people of Britain of the great food-raising lands beyond the seas, the perils of both district and national famine have all but disappeared, unless in times of war. For half a century or so the working-class of Scotland has been delivered from the perils of natural famine. All its distresses have been class-created, artificial, and due to sectional privileges and monopolies, increasingly apparent and increasingly striven against ; and always in its warfare against class privilege and monopoly, as in its old-time struggles against natural famine, the weapons of the working-class have been communist or semi-communist. For centuries past (and it still is the custom) the farmers of a neighbourhood have assisted one another with free ploughing days and free harvestings and with the free loan of stock and implements. The Friendly Society in all its phases, from the mutual insurance of breadwinners against sickness and unemployment to the provision of decent burial ; the Co-operative Societies for the cheaper purveying of food-stuffs and clothes, growing into the Scottish Co-operative Wholesale Society with its ships, its factories, and its farms ; the steady municipal developments in the communal or collectivist supply of gas, water, trams, housing, and amusements—all spring from communal necessity and develop day by day before our eyes in the same communist direction.

The Friendly Society in Scotland we can trace for almost three centuries, and in the year 1883 there still existed, though with only two remaining members, the Old Wrights Society of Brechin, a society that had enjoyed a continuous existence since its formation in November 1625. In the same year of 1883 there was still extant the Linlithgow Fraternity of Dyers, founded in 1679 ; the Burgesses and Trades Poor Box of Anstruther-Easter, founded in 1701 ; the Journeyman Freemasons of Edinburgh, founded in 1707 ; the Dunfermline Ancient Society of Gardeners, founded in 1716 ; the Falkirk Gardeners' Society, founded in 1725 ; the Lesmahagow Masonic Society, founded in 1746 ; the Society of Weavers in Pollok-shaws, founded in 1749 ; the Old Kilpatrick Society, founded in 1756 ; the Journeymen Bakers' Society of Glasgow, founded in 1765 ; and the Journeymen Coopers' Society of Glasgow, founded in 1770.* The Printers' and Bookbinders' Society of Glasgow was founded in 1771 ; the Glasgow Water of Endrick Society in 1771 ; the Sailors' Society of Inverkeithing in 1775. There were other old mutual aid societies in Aberdeen and the Lothians ; and Bo'ness had two friendly societies, founded respectively in 1634 and 1659, which the Registrar reported as prospering still as late as 1862.

Some of these societies had a trade or craft basis, and some had mystic signs, passwords, and ceremonial rites at entry, but all were for the purpose of mutual aid among their members. And as we emerge into the period of industrial capitalism the societies manifestly become more and ever more centres where men meet to air common trade grievances and devise schemes for their removal, the friendly benefit subscriptions providing a strong incentive to class honesty, since black-legging meant expulsion and expulsion meant forfeiture of all subscriptions paid by the black-legger. Experience taught the early Trade Union pioneers that the surest bond among Trade Unionists was the friendly society benefit ; it gave the Union permanence and stability to have a sick, a disablement, an unemployment, or a death benefit fund. That being the case, the early Friendly Society lived precariously and in capitalist disfavour ; and there indeed seems to have been a period when official permission was required—and difficult to obtain—ere even a female benefit society could be formed. The wife of Fletcher, the advocate, discovered that. But then Fletcher was a reformer in 1793, and his wife was accused of guillotining hens in her backyard, so as to acquire skill against the time when aristocrat throats would be ripe for the knife ! And even as late as 1844 we find Dan O'Connell, the Irish Nationalist patriot (but intensely narrow in his anti-working-class prejudices), declaiming against the Rechabites as an illegal society.†

The Combination Laws and poverty, between them, shattered many of the Trade Friendly Societies against sickness, among the

---

*The Chief Registrar of Friendly Societies Report, 1883, puts the date at 1770, but the Webbs' *History of Trade Unionism* (p. 23) gives the date at 1752.

†*Glasgow Argus* 11/11/44.

weavers in the first half of the nineteenth century, but the funeral clubs guaranteeing the members freedom from a pauper's grave (that last and greatest horror to a working-class family) were almost everywhere kept going, though often at great sacrifice. Nevertheless, as "boom" periods came and the Unions rose again, they rose and strengthened around the friendly benefits. It might only be a few shillings to assist with funeral expenses, or as among the boot and shoemakers, "tramp money" to cover expenses when searching for work—there was an endless variety of disasters provided against —but around some such allurement the Unions grew. Then as they strengthened on the industrial side, the Union officials paid less and less attention to the friendly benefit, which more and more became catered for by capitalist companies and collecting friendly societies who sent canvassers and collectors round the houses for the premiums. These companies and societies had no trade or industrial basis ; they were *ad hoc* institutions, and some of them have netted enormous profits from the business—the well-known "Prudential" Company with a paid-up capital of only £8000 yielding annual profits to the few shareholders of about half a million annually. The collecting societies, though in theory mutual concerns, dividing profits among the members in the form of bonuses and what not, have in practice, most of them, been extravagantly and wastefully managed. Some of the Friendly Orders, with their passwords, signs, and grips—the Foresters, Shepherds, Gardeners, and Rechabites—still exist, but where not built around some common principle (*e.g.*, the Rechabites with abstinence from alcohol !) are in fair way to be supplanted by State or Capitalist insurance organisations.

II.—THE CO-OPERATIVE MOVEMENT.

"Each for All, and All for Each.—*Communist Motto.*

" . . . We perceive a hard struggle sustained by both the rural and industrial populations in order to re-introduce standing institutions of mutual aid and support."—*Kropotkin,* "*Mutual Aid,*" p. 283.

The rise of capitalist industrialism brought into being the co-operative movement in food distribution and production. The industrial capitalist gathered his workers around his factory or his mine, and opened a store where he sold food, clothes, etc., at ruinously high prices. The employee, who was usually paid his wages monthly, of course was compelled to get his goods from the master's store on credit, and for this credit the employer exacted a heavy interest over and above the high prices he charged for his goods. First, the employer withheld a man's wages for a month and then taxed him usuriously for the withholding of it. These stores in

Scotland were called Truck Stores, and against them the workers strove for three-quarters of a century, for so long as Truck existed the workman's co-operative store was impossible, and it was not until the Truck Abolition Acts cut at the roots of the vile system that the co-operative movement began to flourish.

There were, however, industries where for one reason or another the Truck system of robbery was not practised, and there co-operative trading began; there groups of penurious workers banded their coppers together to purchase in bulk the necessaries of life and retail these necessaries among themselves, thus escaping the rendition of profits to shopkeepers, or, as the economists of a later day would put it, escaping exploitation at the point of distribution. In this wise the weavers of Fenwick after, doubtless, careful discussion in their village parliament, bought and sold meal as far back as 1769, long before the days of the Rochdale pioneers, and when Robert Owen was in his cradle. A Govan victualling society was in existence in 1777, a Bridgeton victualling society in 1800, and there was one at Lennoxtown in 1812. Fenwick, says Maxwell in his "History of Co-operation in Scotland," was the first village in Scotland to enter the co-operative field.* The Lennoxtown Society, we are told, was paying dividends in proportion to purchases in 1812, but only when the purchases of the individual were less than his capital.† In 1817 we find Robert Owen, whose experiments at New Lanark mills pioneered our factory legislation and so many of our present-day educational theories, proposing the creation of villages of unity and mutual co-operation and employing as his secretary and propagandist lecturer, a remarkable man called Alexander Campbell, who really became the driving force behind most of the Reform movements in Scotland for the next half century. Owen was a Communist reformer who sought a new Moral World; to him the Co-operative Store at New Lanark was at best a palliative, which, while it saved the workers 25 per cent. in their expenditure, yielded him an annual profit of £700;‡ he was at no pains to disguise the fact that a system of "joint stock retailing" was no part of the "social system we contemplate";§ what he was after were big-scale experiments in the regeneration of human nature through Communism. Campbell, on the other hand, bent his energies and his propagandist talents chiefly to the propagation of the palliatives he believed capable of immediate realisation, and which he believed were in themselves the essential preliminaries to the fruition of

*pp. 46-47.

†*Memoirs of a Century : Centenary Record of Lennoxtown Friendly Victualling Society*—Flanagan.

‡Podmore's *Owen*, i., 86.

§*New Moral World*, iv., November. 1836.

Owen's schemes. He was undoubtedly a land nationaliser; he inaugurated a labour exchange bazaar in Glasgow where goods were exchanged at values based upon the labour time spent in their production, the cost of raw materials being also allowed for; labour currency notes to the value of 10s. and 20s. were used and were accepted as tender at the Co-operative Store. Campbell, too, was one of the founders of the Glasgow Trades Council, and acted as its secretary; for a time he was editor of the *Sentinel* newspaper; he wrote and lectured extensively, and he was the leading figure in the agitations against Truck and the Master and Servant Act. He claimed that away back in 1830 he had advocated Co-operation, with dividends upon purchases, to the people of Cambuslang, "and it was from him that the Rochdale friends took the idea up and wrought it out successfully."* He certainly had lectured in Rochdale on the subject, and the Rochdale pioneers consulted him when they were forming their famous Equitable Society in 1843-4.

The bigger regeneration, Owenite Colony, ventures, such as those of Abram Combes and Hamilton of Dalziel at Orbiston, near Bellshill, where £20,000 was sunk, and Queenwood and New Harmony, were all ghastly failures, and in them considerable sums of philanthropic money were lost, the colonists having too much of the Old Adam in them to live in oases of moral regeneration. These experiments served, however, at least one good purpose; they proved to Labour that Utopia could not be reared in a corner.

Distributive co-operation grew steadily, and by 1830 there were, says Mr. G. J. Holyoake, between 300 and 400 co-operative societies announced in the periodicals; but most of these ventures were unstable and impermanent, because they would not give credit and because they disbursed the profits weekly to their shareholders and not to the purchasers. Really it was not co-operation, but joint stock trading. In the long run, however, Campbell's influence told, and the societies began to distribute profits on the basis of purchases; co-operative distribution thereupon throve and prospered.

During the second quarter of last century we come across records of attempts at co-operative production societies, formed usually as the result of strikes or locks-out. Thus the Dundee and Lochee Weavers' Union, 1000 strong, resolved in 1834 to "make an attempt at manufacturing for themselves."† The A.S.E. and the Boilermakers during the "masters' strike" in 1852 seriously debated the erection of co-operative engineering works.‡ The trades' delegates in Glasgow during the bakers' strike of 1857 asked the bakers' delegates to submit a detailed plan for a co-operative bakery. An

---

*Campbell's Address to Social Science Congress, Glasgow, September, 1860.
†*Evening Post*, 14/6/34.
‡*Glasgow Courier*, 29/1/52.

Edinburgh co-operative building society was formed by the Masons' Union there during the strike of 1861, and, with borrowed money, a limited liability company was formed and tenements were erected. On at least two occasions the weavers of Forfar inaugurated a manufacturing society. Alexander Macdonald, the miners' leader, raised £10,000 for a co-operative coal mine.*   The coopers of Glasgow, out on strike in 1867, started a cooperage of their own, and got orders from the trade ;† this cooperage business lasted until May, 1879. In the year 1867 the Greenock tailors on strike started a co-operative tailoring business.

But on the whole productive co-operation was a failure until first the distributive societies were an assured success. Growing out of the needs of the distributive societies and having abundance of capital found for them and an assured and exclusive market, the productive societies made good. But so long as the distributive societies were weak, impermanent, isolated, unfederated, without the backing of a powerful Wholesale Society, at the mercy of local terrorisms, fluctuations in employment, truck, bothy systems, and what not, productive co-operation in the very nature of things could not succeed. We repeat that it was only when the distributive societies grew strong enough to form a Wholesale Society that productive co-operation may be said to have really commenced.

The Scottish Co-operative Wholesale Society was formed in 1868. Eight years later there were 264 distributive societies with a capital of £364,857 and sales of nearly two millions sterling. The Scottish Co-operative Ironworks had collapsed ; but all over the country productive societies were springing up—pavement manufacturing in Caithness, hosiery at Hawick, cotton weaving at Paisley and Dunfermline, tailoring at Dundee, wool spinning at Oakbank ; and there were at least two baking societies. These productive societies, of course, were simply wage-paying societies—better wages and healthier conditions than in private capitalist employment certainly, but still wage-paying—and only in so far as the productive workers were also shareholders reaping profits could they be said to differ in *status* from the workers in private capitalist employment.

By the year 1886 the distributive societies numbered 311, with a share and loan capital of $1\frac{1}{4}$ millions, and sales of almost 6 millions. In 1909 there was a share and loan capital of $9\frac{1}{2}$ millions, with sales of almost 23 millions.   In 1912 there was a membership of 430,598 (representing about one-third of the total population), a capital of $10\frac{3}{4}$ millions and sales of $25\frac{1}{2}$ millions, and on the productive side alone an annual wages bill of £826,014.   The productive factories run upon the most hygienic and best-equipped lines, the goods free

---

Scotsman, 23/11/65, and *Glasgow Herald*, 16/5/73.
†*N.B. Daily Mail*, 9/3/67.

from adulteration, the employees paid at the highest rates of wages, thousands upon thousands of working men and women trained as administrators on managerial boards and committees, a continuous educational propaganda upon the benefits of co-operation, at least a partial check upon the rapacity of trusts and other capitalist combinations, a guarantee to the worker against a food boycott, a buttress in his wage struggles, the bank of the common people, providing for the working-class a *status* and a security—who can estimate the value of all that upon the health, prosperity, education and social self-reliance of the working class ?

Attempts have repeatedly been made to line up the co-operative societies definitely and clearly with the political and industrial organisations of the workers, but only in recent years have these attempts had any measure of success. There was always the obvious danger of arresting the growth and development of the co-operative societies by the introduction of party politics, so long as the bulk of the working-class was scientifically split into Whig and Tory camps, and so long as the industrial workers were divided—half Trade Unionist and half unorganised. But with the rise of a unifying Labour Party and with the growth of Trade Unionism, so that many industries are now "blackleg " proof, there is no longer any reason why the worker—as worker, as co-operator, and as citizen— should act as if he were three separate individuals. There is, of course, no such thing as a political test in the co-operative movement, nor has there been since Chartist times, when the store at Hawick confined its membership to professing Chartists.*

In 1867 the Working Men's Association, with its headquarters in London, directly appealed to the Co-operative Societies to link themselves up with the Trades Unions for the purpose of securing direct representation of the working-class in Parliament, but the appeal was wholly without effect in Scotland. Six years later, at the first School Board election in Glasgow, Mr. James Barrowman, Manager of the Wholesale Co-operative Society, ran as a Labour candidate with co-operative backing ; he polled 7463 votes, but was unsuccessful. It is not, however, until very recent years that there has been any mass movement on the part of co-operators as such towards labour politics.

III.—THE SOCIALIST MOVEMENT.

" If all land and capital were owned by those who produce wealth, the wages of labour would be the whole of the wealth produced by labour, but as land and capital are owned by men who are not labourers, and as labour cannot be per-

*This, in 1839.

formed, without these, it follows that those who own land and capital are the masters of those who toil."—*Preamble to Rules of Ayrshire Miners' Union, drafted* (1884) *by James Keir Hardie.*

"The Common Good, as it stands, cannot therefore be held to be a legacy bequeathed by the care and prudent forethought of our forefathers, but rather it is the insignificant wreck of one of our noblest ancestral properties in Scotland."—*Sir James Bell, Lord Provost of Glasgow.*

The Socialist movement, the *conscious* Socialist movement, the deliberately planned effort to weave our national and civic life into a communist or semi-communist frame, the building of our economic relationships around a collectivist idea, is indeed barely one hundred years old. The horrors of the capitalist system at the beginning of the nineteenth century generated and nourished in the minds of men of goodwill a passionate desire for more equitable social conditions; and the machine, the factory, every development of collectivist production for the profit of one, stimulated, as they were bound in the nature of things to stimulate, an answering movement towards collectivist ownership, for the profit of all.

Yet though the conscious Socialist movement be but a century old, the labouring folk all down the ages have clung to communist practices and customs, partly the inheritance and instinct from the group and clan life of our forefathers and partly because these customs were their only barrier to poverty; and because without them social life was impossible.

In early times the land was cultivated on the "run-rig" principle. At the Gaelic feast of Nabachd (neighbourliness) men drew their rigs by lot, the produce of certain rigs were set apart for the poor, fines went to the Common Good fund for the purchase of fresh stock, bulls, tups, etc.; and as late as 1847, says Skene, there were still places in the Outer Hebrides where the land was tilled, sowed, and reaped in common, and the produce divided among the workers.[*] The run-rig tenants' houses were "warm, good, and comfortable"; the people worked with "friendly and wholesome rivalry, the enterprise of the one stimulating the zeal of the other." At Islay, in Pennant's time, the peasants ploughed, sowed, and reaped in common, and we are told that in "St. Kilda they distribute the fishing rocks among themselves by lot"; in Barra they "cast lots once a year for the several fishing grounds in the deep sea off their shores." Punishment fines went to the common fund, even when individual damage was done.[†]

The Guild (which we have elsewhere discussed) was probably in existence prior to the burgh, and undoubtedly in early times it carried something of its co-operative and communist principle into

---

[*]Skene—*Celtic Scotland*, vol. iii.
[†]"The Scotch Village Community."—John Rae, *Fortnightly Review*, 1885.

burghal life. And even as late as 1797, when the master bakers at Berwick-on-Tweed went on strike, refusing to bake bread at the controlled price fixed by the Assize of Bread, and refusing to sell meal, the Guild Council ordered an expenditure of £200 to break the strike. The £200 was spent in corn and the grinding of it ; thereafter it was sold to the citizens to enable them to bake their own bread.* At that time, too, Berwick-on-Tweed owned 4500 acres of land, provided bulls which were looked after by a municipal herd, kept municipal farriers, municipal mole-catchers and municipal salmon fishers, and owned collieries and quarries. In the towns of Scotland certainly there was a strong class antagonism aggravated through the frequent theft of common lands and property by the merchant class ; and when, at the beginning of the nineteenth century, political reform pamphlets began to appear in the burghs, it is noteworthy that references are quite numerous to the idea of equal distribution of property, said to be popular among the "lower orders." The heritors of Culross declared they would protect their properties against "all plunderers who may attempt to rob us upon principles of equality"; the common people, we are told, believed that if the political reformers succeeded there would be "an equal distribution of property."†

As late as 1800 there were great common properties extant ; many burghs, towns and villages owned lands and mosses; Forres engaged in municipal timber-growing ; Fortrose owned claypits ; Glasgow owned quarries and coalfields ; Hamilton owned a coal pit ; Irvine had mills, farms and a loom shop ; Kirkwall owned farms and a town hall ; Lanark a mill and an inn ; Lochmaben a farm ; Musselburgh had five mills, a brick and tile work, a quarry, a town hall, a steel yard and shares in a race stand ; North Berwick owned a bakehouse ; Paisley had an inn, house property, coal rees, a dyework, a foundry and a bowling green ; Peebles had a corn, flour and barley mill, a waulk mill with house and machinery, a farm and shares in an inn and in a gas company ; Earlsferry, a municipal golf course ; Perth, an oil mill, a sawmill, granaries, coal and wood yards ; Peterhead, a shipbuilding yard ; Wigton had ballrooms ; Pollokshaws had house property and an inn ; Dunfermline had farms and a coal mine ; Arbroath had an inn. Most towns, however, had been plundered bare, and we read of Coldstream that it did not even possess "rights in its street dung."

By the thirties of last century the old corrupt non-elected corporations had been displaced by elected councillors, who, though elected upon a franchise from which the working-class were excluded, nevertheless began to exhibit a responsiveness to public opinion, not

†*The Manor and the Borough*—S. and B. Webb, ii., 513.
*Scot.and and the French Revolution—Meikle, p. 99.

apparent in the doings of the old oligarchies, and which sometimes developed into a genuine democratic spirit of civic service. True, there is no connection between, say, the municipal gasworks at Greenock in 1833 and any socialist propaganda for the abolition of exploitation in public lighting. The new municipal ventures simply forced themselves upon the middle-class councils; public lighting of public streets became an obvious necessity when private gas companies ran an inefficient service at ruinously high cost; and a growingly active local administration of public health was manifest after every epidemic which, though it began in the slums, swept its way into the middle-class districts. Any socialist agitation there was had no place for municipal ownership; voluntary co-operation, "labour notes," class-war propaganda, repudiation of the national debt, but no municipalisation, no apparent conception of using the middle-class councils for the socialisation of property! The word "Socialism" has been traced back to 1827, and certainly by the thirties pure Socialist formulae appear in Scottish Labour resolutions and in articles in the *Weavers' Journal*, but, perhaps owing to the lack of the municipal franchise, there was no effort made by the working-class to encourage or extend municipal ownership.

South of the border, the failure of the Reform Act of 1832 to enfranchise the working-class produced a ferment of revolutionary thought with tags and catchwords which, almost a century later, are being re-issued as brand new and portentous discoveries in socialist propaganda and tactics. M. Beer assures us* that such terms as "general strike," "bourgeoisie," "proletariat," "class war," and "anti-politics" are as old as 1833. The very idea of a Soviet apparantly is not new, as we can find in the *Crisis* for 1834 a claim made that:

> "The only House of Commons is a house of trades, and that is only just beginning to be formed. We shall have a new set of boroughs when the Unions are organised; every trade shall be a borough, and every trade shall have a council of representatives to conduct its affairs."

William Benbow of the *Poor Man's Guardian* advocated the "social revolutionary general strike"; Robert Owen was all for antiparliamentary action; and the *Pioneer*, anticipating the economics of the *New Age* by almost three quarters of a century, cried that "social liberty must precede political liberty." This syndicalist phase in working-class agitation had its echoes in Scotland; but with the rise of the Chartist movement the phraseology of direct action disappears, and an effort is made to secure, in the words of Bronterre O'Brien, "the rule of the people in the State and the municipality." The reduction of the stamp duty upon newspapers from fourpence

History of British Socialism, i., p. 334.

to one penny, and the Municipal Reform Act, opened up new possibilities in propaganda and social change, and the Chartist movement bred both class-consciousness and communist orators, who did most effective work until they were either absorbed in, or submerged by, the Free Trade agitation of the later forties.

We find the *Glasgow Herald* in 1843 denouncing the "noxious sect" of Socialists who infested Glasgow Green. A lady in 1845 who, for the purposes of Socialist propaganda, took notes in a Glasgow church was fined £3 3s.—the prosecution and the fine indicating the uneasiness of the authorities. The "principles of communism" were openly advocated at many Chartist gatherings, and Feargus O'Connor promised that if the Chartists were successful "a new social system would supersede the present one." Bronterre O'Brien steadily advocated the nationalisation of the land. But the middle-class Anti-Corn Law Leaguers side-tracked the working-classes ; Cobden and Bright, had, so they said, a speedier remedy for famine and hunger ; free trade would cure the ills of the working people, and anyhow, Socialism was a far-off and dubious remedy for a very present and insistent emptiness of stomach. The Chartist organisation was split to fragments by the Free Traders, and the middle-classes fashioned a safe conduit for working-class politics in the organisation known as the Liberal party—a party so hostile to communist principles that its leader, Richard Cobden, in 1864, moved in the House of Commons that all Government factories and dockyards should be handed over to private contractors !

But the Socialist idea and propaganda never quite perished. Feargus O'Connor moved his Chartist resolution in the House of Commons in 1850, declaring that "Labour is the source of all wealth" ; in 1851 the advocates of land nationalisation could be heard at the street corners. Mr. Tremenheere, the Commissioner for Mines in Scotland, called in 1852 for something to be done to prevent "the spread of Socialism in the mining districts." In 1853 a "Mr. Cooper, a Socialist," was holding meetings in the West of Scotland and advocating "communism."* In 1857, James M'Neal, the Secretary for the Clyde Boilermakers and Shipbuilders, was writing to the press claiming that "the only pure and free labour that can exist is that system wherein the productions of labour are exchanged between producer and producer, and no party, in the shape of prince, lord, or master, to stand between the actual producers and exchangers, directly or indirectly, to claim the lion's share."† In Fifeshire, in 1858, the unemployed were addressed by a Mr. Coventry, a Socialist who pled for the "legal right to work or relief."

Not until the sixties is there evidence of a strong organised work-

---

*N.B. Daily Mail, 15/6/53.
†Glasgow Herald, 9/10/57.

ing-class push for the public ownership of any of the great monopolies. There was always a land nationalisation ferment on a small scale, but the first definite public ownership "plank" of the organised Unions was for the nationalisation of the railways. Away back in 1844 Mr. Gladstone had, by Act of Parliament, secured powers to nationalise the Irish railways; no farther steps had been taken; and in December, 1864, the *Economist* published an article on "The Forgotten Railway Act of 1844." In February, 1865, Gladstone refused to nationalise the Irish railways, but appointed a Royal Commission to enquire into "the economical facts connected with the railway system," whereat the subservient *Scotsman* (then Liberal) applauded, saying national ownership was but "a recurrence to a well-established principle and an immemorial practice."* Three years later the Irish railway directors, who were losing money, asked for nationalisation, but objection was taken by the Government's advisers to the high price demanded for the stock, and no deal took place. From that time onwards, however, railway nationalisation was in the forefront of the "demands" made at working-class political gatherings in Scotland.

Meanwhile, the municipalities, controlled by the wealthy middle-class, bitterly anti-socialist and filled with all the nostrums about competition being the life of trade and about the rights and virtues of private enterprise, were busily engaged socialising or municipalising service after service, without any apparent urge from the working-classes. Glasgow, for example, municipalised its water supply in 1855, its gas in 1869, and actually began municipal housing in 1871; and the real reason for these proceedings is not difficult to conjecture. The process began with the public ownership of streets; that in turn meant a public street cleansing department, a public sewage department, and a public street lighting department. Where private contractors cleansed the streets, the work was badly done; where private gas companies lit the streets by contract there arose all sorts of quarrels about the lights being turned off when the gas company directors expected (often erroneously) a moonlight night, and the lieges fell in the darkness into causey holes and puddles. Water could scarcely be left to private enterprise with money profits as the first consideration, and an adequate supply of pure water as the last, for the middle-class had to drink the water! Public health and "better housing for the poor" became more urgent municipal questions with every typhus, smallpox, and cholera epidemic that, starting in the slums and rookeries, invaded the mansions of the magistrates. Working class diseases could not be confined to the working class, which, though it lived in a "continuous condition of ill health,"* sent out its typhus revenges among the middle-class in periodic epidemics. And so, after 1869, when the death rate of Glasgow rose to 33.7 per 1000, we find a beginning made with a Municipal City Improvement Trust for the destruction of the housing death traps in the slummier areas of the city.† As between 1871 and 1911 the citizen of Glasgow had a double chance of life in the latter year, for by that time the death rate had fallen by half.

During the seventies traces of Socialist propaganda among the working class in Scotland are few. Andrew Boa, chairman of the Glasgow Trades Council, is reported now and again as reading papers on "Productive Co-operation"; small groups of un-named men at Aberdeen, Edinburgh and Dundee "held with the French communards"; but it is not until the middle eighties that the modern Socialist propaganda begins. Michael Davitt, in 1884, toured industrial Scotland preaching the nationalisation of the land with a burning eloquence unknown since Chartist times. And not only land but minerals also he demanded for the nation. Henry George came to Glasgow under the chairmanship of John Murdoch, and 2000 men joined the Land Restoration League at the conclusion of his meeting. Stuart Glennie and the Rev. Mr. M'Callum of Waternish stimulated land seizure movements in the far north-west; "No Rent" manifestoes flooded the Highlands, and a Liberal Government had to send the bluejackets to Skye to protect the factors' rents Some of these manifestoes lacked little in full-blooded incitement:

> "The enemy is the landlord, the agent, the capitalist, and the Parliament which makes and maintains inhuman and iniquitous laws. Cut down the telegraph wires and posts, carry away the wires and the instruments! Stop the mail-carts, destroy the letters, etc. . . . Burn the property of all obnoxious landlords, agents, etc. Set fire to the heather to destroy the game; disturb the deer; poison game dogs! The oppressed toilers of England and the millions of disinherited people are watching your actions. Their hearts are with you in your battle for right and liberty.
>
> "GOD SAVE THE PEOPLE!"

The Crofters' War followed these manifestoes, and a Crofters' Act temporarily cut across the peasants revolt and gave the lairds breathing space.

By the year 1888 James Keir Hardie was preaching "Christian Socialism" through Lanarkshire and Ayrshire, editing the *Miner*, and encouraging the formation of a Scottish Parliamentary Labour Party, with its curious mixture of Radical and Collectivist nostrums—Adult Suffrage, Triennial Parliaments, Payment of Members and Election Expenses, Home Rule all round, Abolition of the House of Lords "and all hereditary offices" (so the Throne was *camouflaged*);

Evolution of Public Health Administration in Glasgow—Dr. Russell.
†*Municipal Glasgow*, pp. 2 and 206.

Second Ballot, Nationalisation of Land and Minerals, an Eight Hours' Day, State Insurance as a substitute for the Poor Law, Arbitration Courts, a Minimum Wage, "Weekly Pays," Homestead Law, Factory Acts, Prohibition of the Liquor Traffic, No War without consent of House of Commons, Free Education and Feeding of School Children, Disestablishment, Abolition of Sinecures, Codification of Laws, State Ownership of Railways, Waterways and Tramways, National Banking and Issue of State Money only, and Cumulative Income Tax beginning at £300 per annum."* A propaganda literature poured steadily from the London printing presses up to Scotland ; William Morris, Morrison Davidson, The Fabians, the Social Democrats, Henry George, Annie Besant and Keir Hardie published pamphlets ; Cunninghame Graham, Tom Mann, Dr Clarke, John Burns, John Murdoch, H. H. Champion and others used the platform (the first public mention of Robert Smillie gives him as taking up the anti-socialist side in a public debate at Larkhall !), and five years later, in 1893, the Independent Labour Party was born.

But the Socialist movement in the last decade of the nineteenth century and subsequent years requires a separate chronicle ; we are too close to the figures on the stage to place them in proper perspective : too much involved in and too much influenced by the polemical distractions of our generation to estimate their proper historical values.

A recording of Socialist developments in our own time is not our present task ; here we have confined ourselves to a narrative which closes with the birth of the Modern Labour Movement.

Souvenirs of Scottish Labour, p. 4—David Lowe.

INDEX.

GLOSSARY

Act of Revocation,	Act cancelling previous legislation or decrees.
Act Recissory, (properly Rescissory)	Act cancelling previous legislation or decrees.
Adscriptitti,	Tied to the soil.
Anti-Erastian Clergy,	Those who denied the supremacy of the State over the Church.
Astricted,	Tied, as tenants compelled to go to a particular mill.
Birlaymen,	Assessors of damage.
Bonnach (Bonnage),	Bondage.
Burgage tenement,	House or land property in a burgh.
Burgh of Regality,	Royal Burgh.
Burlaw,	Popularly elected Court of Justice.
Casualties of Superiority,	Charge levied by Superior or owner upon happening of uncertain events, *e.g.*, coming of age of new heir.
Coitus cum diabolo,	Sexual relationships with the Devil.
Decreet arbitral,	Arbiters' decision or decree.
De novo,	From the beginning.
Distrain,	Levy by force.
Duplicands,	Double feu-duty.
Enach,	Satisfaction.
Escheit,	Forfeit.
Et seq.,	And following.
Fastern's Eve,	Eve of Lenten Fast.
Flyting,	Scolding.
Forestalling,	Intercepting and purchasing goods ere they reached the market. " Regrating " was the selling of such " cornered " goods at a profit.
Gowpen,	A double handful.
Ibid.,	The same.
Introitus,	Fine upon one entering in a tenancy.